In Search of Pinot Noir

Also by Benjamin Lewin

Wine Myths and Reality

What Price Bordeaux?

In Search of Pinot Noir

Benjamin Lewin MW

Vendange Press
Dover
2011

Copyright © 2011 by Benjamin Lewin

All rights reserved. Published in the United States
by Vendange Press.

Library of Congress Cataloging-in-Publication Data
Lewin, Benjamin
In Search of Pinot Noir / by
Benjamin Lewin
Includes bibliographical references and index.

ISBN 978-0-9837292-0-4

Library of Congress Control Number: 2011931690

Printed in China
1 2 3 4 5 6 7 8 9 10

Contents

Preface

Pinot Noir is one of the most elusive grapes in the world. Not physically scarce: it makes the list of the top ten planted black varieties. But the search to capture the essence of the grape is never-ending. Not for nothing has it been called "the heartbreak grape." André Tchelistcheff, the famous winemaker at Beaulieu Vineyards in Napa Valley in the post World War II years, is reputed to have said, "God made Cabernet Sauvignon whereas the Devil made Pinot Noir." After Josh Jensen, the founder of Calera Wines in California, told me, "I call Pinot Noir the 'especially grape,' because any general statement you can make about grapes is especially true of Pinot Noir," I found myself noticing how often I had written "especially for Pinot Noir" when I was describing some aspect of viticulture or red wine production. Pinot Noir is the ultimate terroir grape: its infinite nuances of expression in Burgundy have created what many regard as a unique reflection of terroir in the elegance and finesse of the variety. Its preeminence is long established: Saintsbury called it "the King of natural wines," in his *Notes on a Cellar Book* in 1920. Possibly only Riesling shows the same sensitivity to terroir.

Winemakers in cool climates (and some not so cool) all over the world have set out in search of the Holy Grail: to emulate the best Pinot Noir of Burgundy. Is it a case of "often imitated but never duplicated" or have they yet succeeded? Or have they instead discovered an unexpected flexibility in Pinot Noir, with a potential to make top-notch wines that do not necessarily resemble Burgundy, but which are excellent in their own right? To what extent does Pinot Noir share, after all, the ability of other varieties to make wines in different but equally interesting styles?

Our search starts, of course, in Burgundy. Then it focuses on other cool climates in France, passing through Sancerre and Alsace, before moving even farther north to Germany, where Pinot Noir production extends from Baden to the tiny region of the Ahr. We should not neglect enclaves for Pinot Noir production in Italy's Alto Adige and Switzerland's Graubunden. Then we cross the Atlantic to North America, viewing somewhat warmer climates, passing from Oregon in the north, through Russian River in northern California, to Santa Barbara farther south. Exhausting the possibilities here, we move to the southern hemisphere, to the contrast between Marlborough and Martinborough in the center of New Zealand with the extended region of Central Otago to the south, the wine-growing region closest to the South Pole. Not that we should ignore the cool climates in Australia, or indeed the southern tip of South Africa. But where does the search end: in one of the regions of the New World or back to Burgundy?

Ultimately we have to decide just what we expect of Pinot Noir. If only a Burgundian style will do, what exactly do we mean by that, given the differences between the Côte de Beaune and the Côte de Nuits, the southern and northern parts of Burgundy's Côte d'Or, not to mention the many differences between individual producers. Does the heart of Burgundy lie in the terroir? the climate? the clones? or centuries of experience? Even within Burgundy, isn't there enough stylistic variation at least to raise the question of whether terroir inevitably triumphs over vinification? So are the richer, more voluptuous, more alcoholic—in fact, more of everything—wines of the New World intrinsically different; or are they the logical extension of what Burgundy would become if its climate were better? They say that grapevines have to struggle in order to make great wine, but does Pinot Noir need to struggle more than most? Where is the soul of Pinot Noir?

Benjamin Lewin MW

Author's Note

This is a book about typicity and style, and regions and trends, so its focus is not on profiles of producers and detailed tasting notes. Certainly for Burgundy there are many profiles and notes available from highly knowledgeable commentators, not least Clive Coates in Europe and Allen Meadows (the Burghound) in the United States. So I have included profiles and tasting notes for Burgundy only in special cases, where adjacent terroirs are compared, or there are revealing contrasts of style depending on vineyard ownership. But the Pinot Noirs of other regions may be less well known, so in these cases each chapter concludes with profiles of leading producers and tasting notes that may be helpful in pointing readers to unfamiliar, but interesting wines. I am conscious in writing the tasting notes that individual palates differ greatly with regards to preferences for younger, more primary, fruits versus more developed, savory flavors, so the suggested window for drinking begins when I believe the tannins will become approachable, but ends with the start of tertiary development. Those who like older wines will be able to drink them well beyond the indicated range. Because the main purpose of the tasting notes is to indicate stylistic range, I have not emphasized ratings, but have given wines a mark from one to four stars as a rough guide. (One star is good, two stars very good, three stars excellent, four stars truly exceptional; and there are three wines that I felt compelled to award five stars.) References in the text to the tasting notes are indicated by a ϒ symbol.

Sources of photographs heading chapters

Chapter 1 A female Vitis vinifera silvestris is part of a population of wild grapevines at Ribera de Huelva river near Seville. Its leaves are brighter green than those of the tree. Photograph kindly provided by Rafael Ocete.

Chapter 2 The Hôtel Dieu in Beaune was a hospital funded by its vineyards in the Middle Ages. It is now the site of the annual Hospices de Beaune auction every November.

Chapter 3 The Chambertin grand cru marks some of best terroir for Pinot Noir. The sign was erected in 1952.

Chapter 4 Pinot Noir is planted on steep terraced hillsides in the Ahr valley of Germany, the world's most northern location for growing Pinot Noir.

Chapter 5 A view from the vineyards towards the surrounding hills in the Eola-Amity Hills of Willamette Valley.

Chapter 6 The Te Muna region of Martinborough is a river terrace close to the mountains.

Chapter 7 A cross marks the famous Romanée Conti vineyard in Burgundy.

1

The Ancient Pinot Family

MORE THAN 65 MILLION YEARS AGO, give or take a few million, the first grapevine developed somewhere in the landmass of the northern hemisphere.[1] This primitive Vitis was the ancestor of all modern grapevines.[2] A mere couple of million years ago, it diverged into two groups of grapevines.[3] Vitis vinifera and a handful of species developed in Eurasia, while a range of 50-60 other species of Vitis developed in North America, probably in niches that were isolated during the Ice Age.[4] Only Vitis vinifera is suitable for making wine.

During the Paleolithic era, perhaps 10,000 years ago,[5] the first wine was probably made from wild grapes.[6] The oldest actual signs of wine are in pottery from the Hajii Firuz Neolithic complex in the northern Zagros Mountains of Iran, dating from about 5400 B.C., that contains traces of tartaric acid, produced in this area only by grapes.[7] As man began to develop agriculture, the wild Vitis vinifera[8] became domesticated,[9] probably in Transcaucasia some time during the next millennium. The large number of wine grape varieties that we know today may all stem from this single domestication event.[10]

The start of viticulture and winemaking can be traced to the near East from about 4000 B.C. Indicating the production of wine from black grapes, anthocyanins (color compounds from the skins) have been found on artefacts from a cave complex in Armenia.[11] The artefacts included a basin that drained into a vat, which could have been a primitive arrangement for pressing grapes by stamping.[12] This was surrounded by storage jars. Pips appear to have come from domesticated grapes.[13]

Hieroglyphics record that viticulture and vinification were well established in ancient Egypt by 2700 B.C.[14] The Egyptians grew vines in walled vineyards, developed methods for training the grapevine on an overhead trellis, and may have used irrigation. In making wine, they may have added chopped up fruit (containing yeast) to initiate fermentation, and they developed methods for pressing the grapes. The entire wine production process, from viticulture to transport of the finished wine, was illustrated in tomb paintings. We know little about the grapes used to make wine, except that they are black in illustrations.

By the time of the Greeks and Romans, viticulture was a regular part of farming and trade. Grapevines, together with wheat and olives, were basic agricultural crops, and Vitis vinifera had now given rise to many different types of grapevines. Books on maintaining vineyards and making wine were published in both Greece and Rome, and winemaking became a significant economic activity.[15, 16]

In the first century C.E., Pliny devoted a good part of his writing to describing vines and wines, discussing in some detail the different grape varieties.[17] Already some attention was being paid to which varieties gave the best results in which locations. Wine was made from white as well as black grapes, and often was sweet. There seem to have been many varieties under cultivation, since Virgil said in 29 B.C. that they were "uncountable;"[18] a century later, Columella and Pliny distinguished about twenty of the most important varieties.[19] Unfortunately, none of the known names can be equated directly with modern varieties.[20]

Pinot Noir is generally thought to be one of the most ancient varieties of domesticated Vitis vinifera. Many of the cultivars (cultivated varieties) of grapes that are used to produce wine today are relatively recent, meaning that they have originated in the past thousand years or so. In fact, Pinot Noir is a parent of several of them. It has more similarities with wild grapevines than most cultivated varieties, and is one of a few modern grapevines whose origins might go back more or less directly to wild grapevines.[21]

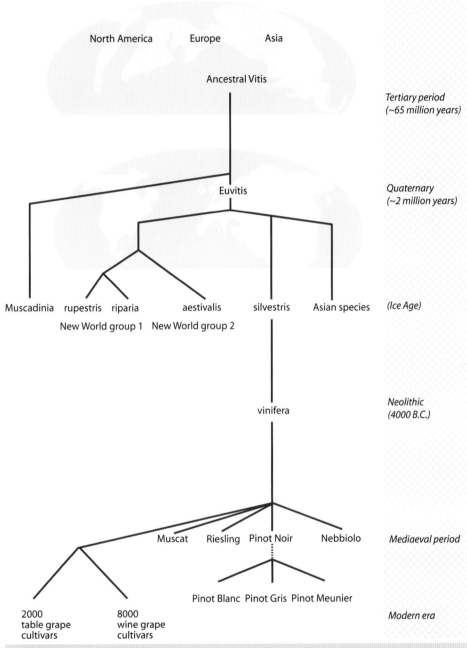

North America   Europe   Asia

Ancestral Vitis

Tertiary period
(~65 million years)

Euvitis

Quaternary
(~2 million years)

Muscadinia   rupestris riparia   aestivalis   silvestris   Asian species   *(Ice Age)*

New World group 1   New World group 2

vinifera

Neolithic
(4000 B.C.)

Muscat   Riesling   Pinot Noir   Nebbiolo   *Mediaeval period*

Pinot Blanc Pinot Gris Pinot Meunier

2000   8000   *Modern era*
table grape   wine grape
cultivars   cultivars

Vitis is indigenous to the northern hemisphere. It split into Euvitis and Muscadinia. The Euvitis divided into about 60 species, most in North America, but with Vitis vinifera in Europe. All Euvitis are interfertile, but they cannot breed with Muscadinia. The oldest known cultivars of Vitis vinifera can be traced back to the Middle Ages. The timing of the split between the varieties of Pinot is unknown.

Are any modern grape varieties the same as those cultivated in ancient times? Two of the descriptions of ancient cépages are suggestive of modern varieties. Pliny described one variety as Uva apiana (grape of the bees); this might have been Muscat, whose strong aroma makes the grapes especially attractive to bees.[22] Some people speculate that Pinot Noir could be a variety that Columella described: "The smallest and best of the three [Helvenacan varieties: grown in Gaul] is very readily recognized by its leaf, for it bears the roundest leaf of all of them; and it is praiseworthy because it endures drought best of all, because it bears cold if only it is free from rain, because in some regions its wine is racked off for long keeping."[23]

But the oldest unequivocal identification of modern varieties dates only from the thirteenth or fourteenth centuries. Pinot Noir is amongst them. A grape called Pinot, presumably Pinot Noir, was first mentioned in Burgundy in 1375, when Philip the Bold referred to "vin de pinot vermeil" (red Pinot wine).[24] Twenty years later, in an attempt to improve quality in Burgundy, he famously ordered Gamay to be uprooted and replaced by Pinot. (His success must have been quite limited, because a century later, in 1485, the authorities in Dijon complained to Charles VII about the increasing encroachment of Gamay.[25] This was a continuing story over the centuries.) So Pinot Noir is not only one of the oldest known cultivars, but was also marked right from the start as a high quality variety.

Trying to trace the history of grape varieties is confounded by the diversity of names for a single variety. The names Morillon and Noirien probably referred to the same variety, which may have been an earlier form of Pinot Noir.[26] Judging from tax records, two forms of Pinot were held in high esteem in the thirteenth century. "Vin formentel," made from the grape Fromenteau (an earlier name for Pinot Gris), was considered to be the best white wine, and was taxed at 12 sous per muid [456 liters]. "Vin moreillon," made presumably from Pinot Noir or its direct ancestor, was taxed at 9 sous. Ordinary red wine was taxed at 6 sous.[27]

In the sixteenth century, the variety was referred to as "Morillon appelée Pinot" (Morillon called Pinot).[28] The terms Noirien and Pinot continued to be used together until the nineteenth century.[29] All of this indicates that Pinot Noir was established by the thirteenth to fourteenth centuries. The historian Roger Dion suggested that Philip the Bold may have originated the use of "Pinot" to describe the variety, possibly because a better variant was selected at this time.[30] Outside Burgundy, Pinot Noir had yet other names.[31]

Pinot Noir is not only famous in its own right, but is the parent of several other important varieties. DNA fingerprinting shows that fifteen varieties found in France today are siblings resulting from a series of crosses between Pinot Noir and a grape called Gouais Blanc.[32] One of the most important of the progeny of these crosses is Chardonnay (which used to be erroneously regarded as a white variant of Pinot). Others are the white grape Aligoté, still grown in Burgundy, and Gamay, now largely grown only in the Beaujolais.

The common parentage for so many varieties implies that Pinot must have been growing in such close proximity to Gouais Blanc that chance cross-fertilization between them was relatively common. Where and when did this happen? Gouais Blanc is another name for the grape called Heunisch Weiss, which was widely distributed in central and eastern Europe. Known by the name Grobe, this variety was by far the dominant grape in the Hapsburg Empire in the early nineteenth century.[33] Gouais Blanc produces indifferent white wine. In fact, it was so poorly regarded that several attempts were made to ban its planting in the Middle Ages.[34] Gouais Blanc probably spread into France around the fourth century; by the Middle Ages it was one

The progeny of Pinot Noir - Gouais Blanc crosses are found all over northern France, with the bull's eye in Burgundy.

of the most widely grown grapes in northeastern France.[35] (There is no Gouais Blanc left in France today, and scarcely any in Europe at all.) The progeny of the Pinot-Gouais crosses are spread out over northern France, from Muscadet in the west to Alsace in the east, but the focus is in Burgundy, suggesting this was the point of origin. Pinot Noir was presumably an established grape in Burgundy before this happened. Gouais Blanc was probably the source for white Burgundy before either of its progeny came on the scene.

Wine has been produced in Burgundy since about 300 C.E., but the grape varieties are unknown for the first millennium, before Gouais Blanc and Pinot Noir were described. By the end of the fourteenth century, the battle for supremacy in black grapes had begun between planting Pinot Noir to make quality wine and Gamay to make ordinary wine. Some time later, Aligoté displaced Gouais Blanc for white wine, and subsequently Aligoté was in turn displaced by Chardonnay.

By the time Philip the Bold ordered Gamay to be replaced by Pinot Noir in 1395, Gamay must have become common. "This very bad and disloyal plant of Gamay has become very abundant.... and should be pulled out and destroyed," he said."[36] It's possible that his edict was prompted by protests from vignerons whose Pinot was threatened by increased plantings of Gamay, which was more productive, but of lower quality. (Concerned to reduce yields and to improve quality, Philip also ordered that fertilization of vineyards should stop.) Unfortunately, there are no good references to date the plantings of Gamay or any other of Pinot's progeny.[37]

As interest in wine grew, commentary on the region paid more attention to classifying vineyards than to discussing grape varieties,[38] but there was probably always a distinction between the varieties grown in the best vineyards to make fine wine and those grown elsewhere to make village wine. By the second half of the nineteenth century, the distinction for reds was between "Noirien" and "Pineau," used for fine wines, and "Jaboulet," "Melon Noir," and "Gamete," used for ordinary or village wines. It was only in 1896 that "Pinot" was adopted as the proper spelling for the principal black variety.[39] The best whites were made from "Chaudenay;" those made from "Melon Blanc," "Narbonne," "Chasselas" or "Gamete" were regarded as distinctly inferior.[40]

The Cistercian monks played a key role in spreading viticulture from Burgundy. The Cistercians take their name from Cîteaux Abbey (originally Cisteaux), just to the east of Nuits St. Georges, halfway between Dijon and Beaune in the heart of Burgundy. Cîteaux came to be a dominant influence in Burgundian viticulture during the Middle Ages, and was known internationally. Indeed, most of the places where Pinot is grown today in Europe can be traced back to monastic influences, most often Cistercian.

Founded in 1098, the Cistercians expanded greatly under the leadership of Bernard de Clairvaux in the first half of the twelfth century. Until 1120, Cîteaux was simply a single abbey, but by the time of Bernard's death in 1153 there were 341 daughter monasteries, subsequently growing to hundreds more all over Europe. The mandate for the Cistercians was to live a simple and self-sufficient life; self-sufficiency included the production of wine, so the Cistercians planted vineyards wherever they established monasteries.

The Cistercians were placed at the heart of developments in Burgundy by their ownership of Clos Vougeot. Its 50 hectares made it one of the largest individual vineyards, and at least until the eighteenth century, the Clos produced white as well as red wine, both being recognized as among the best produced in the area.[41] The wines also played a role in Church politics: in 1359, Jean de Bussières, the Abbé of Cîteaux, sent wines of Beaune and Chambertin to Pope Grégoire XI, who a few years later gave the Abbé his Cardinal's hat.

Were the monks the innovators of their time in viticulture and vinification? Well, they were certainly technically proficient in a variety of agricultural activities. They built granaries to hold grain, they constructed canals to bring water to the monastery, and their mastery of hydraulics extended to the cuverie at Clos Vougeot, where grapes were received and pressed.[42] They tried to relate the character of vineyard plots to the quality of the wine. Cîteaux was not the only abbey where wine production contributed to financial success, and many abbeys were technically sophisticated in vinification. At Clos Vougeot a few years ago, a visitor commented to me, "Imagine what wonderful wine we would make today if we had not lost the expertise of the monks because of the Revolution."

The Cistercians must have been the dominant force in Burgundian wine production during the period when Pinot Noir came to prominence, and Clos Vougeot would probably have been growing the best selections during this period. But there are no records indicating what attention they may have paid to cépages; the basic distinction is between red and white. This was common everywhere at the time. Writing about the vines in Champagne in 1718, the Abbé Godinot distinguished two types, "the high vines, which are four or five feet high, good producers with about 7-8 pièces of wine per arpent, and the low vines, which grow only to about three feet, and produce only about 2 pièces of wine per arpent,[43] but the wine is much more delicate."[44] It appears to have been Abbé Godinot who first introduced the concept of "finesse" as a characteristic of fine wine.[45]

How did Burgundy rank relative to other regions? There was a surprisingly wide variety of sources for supplying wine to Paris in the sixteenth century, when no individual region had emerged as consistently best. "Some

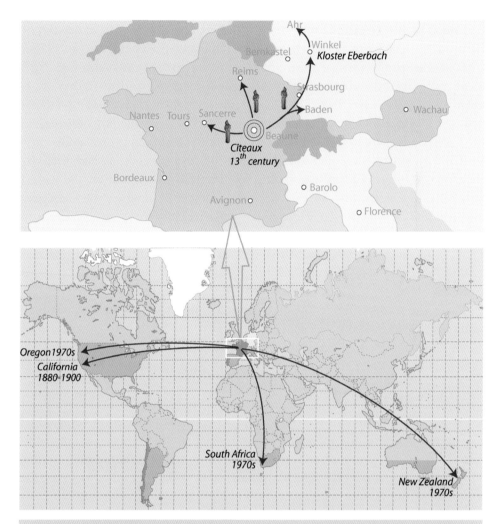

Pinot Noir probably originated in Burgundy by the thirteenth century. Cistercian monks spread it north in France and Germany by the fifteenth century. Most of the important migrations to the New World came directly from France, to California in the nineteenth century, and to Oregon, New Zealand, and South Africa in the twentieth century. Transport ranged from the casual or illegal to the official.

times the vins Français [from the Ile-de-France] are best, in some vintages Burgundy is the most expensive, other years the wines of Orléans are best, some years the wines of Anjou beat all the others," said an author in 1583.[46] Yet the most consistent serious challenger to Burgundy was the region of Champagne, a little farther north, which was producing still red wine in the Middle Ages, long before it became famous for its production of sparkling wine. The balance shifted to Burgundy during the mini ice age around the thirteenth and fourteenth centuries, when it became more difficult to ripen the black grapes in Champagne. But with better supply routes, sitting as it did

between Burgundy and the roads to Paris or to Flanders, Champagne continued to make sales through the fifteenth to sixteenth centuries.[47]

Even in the seventeenth century there was a "querelle des vins de Champagne et de Bourgogne," in which each region claimed superiority,
sometimes supported by rather spurious quasi-academic dissertations.[48] Both
claimed greater delicacy for their wines. Color was a big issue; "producers
have tried to make Champagne with the same red color as Burgundy, and
they have succeeded very well," said Abbé Godinot in 1718, although he
conceded that Champagne was not usually as good as Burgundy.[49] (The
desirable color was "clairet" rather than "rouge;" really dark red was considered to be a sign of vulgarity).[50] By the sixteenth century, the best wines in
the Champagne region were considered to come from the vicinity of Ay.[51]
Just to the north of Ay, the Montagne de Reims was devoted exclusively to
production of red wine from the sixteenth through the eighteenth centuries.[52]

Wines of Burgundy and Champagne had about the same penetration in
the Parisian market in the seventeenth century,[53] and their prices were not
very different.[54] There is no mention of cépages, but the directness of the
comparison leaves the impression that the wines of each region were considered somewhat similar. Probably the best wines were made from Pinot Noir.
It's often suggested that Burgundy's primacy was established when Dr.
Fagon, the court physician to Louis XIV, recommended in 1694 that his
patient should drink "le vin vieux de Bourgogne."[55] "Immediately the Court
drank Burgundy, and gave up Champagne,"[56] claims the BIVB.[*] By 1763,
proponents of Champagne were reduced to arguing that at least "one cannot
dispute that Champagne is the only wine in France to compete with Burgundy."[57] In any case, by the time of the French Revolution, Burgundy
(including the Beaujolais) had become the favored supplier to Paris.[58] Today,
of course, the Champagne region produces scarcely any dry red wine.

In reverse, Burgundy had a brief flirtation with sparkling wine, when
"champagnization" was introduced around 1822. The ambition was to rival
Champagne by making sparkling wine from the best Crus of Burgundy.
Sparkling wine made from "La Tâche" was claimed to rival the best of
Champagne, but the very idea of turning top Crus into sparkling wine attracted hostility and was soon abandoned.[59] Today, Crémant de Bourgogne, a
sparkling wine made by the Méthode Champenoise, is the fastest growing
segment of the Burgundy market, but it comes from inferior terroirs rather
than the best Crus.

The eastern edge of the Loire is about the same distance to the west of
Burgundy that Champagne is to its north. Pinot Noir appears to have been
grown here (most notably around Sancerre) since the Middle Ages, and it

_____

[*] The professional organization representing the producers in Burgundy.

seems plausible that it may have been monks who took it there. Folklore rates red wine of equal importance to white in the region in the period before phylloxera. "Pinaud" was mentioned as early as 1183 (although whether this was Pinot Noir is another matter),[60] and by the late nineteenth century "Pineau" was included on the list of quality black grapes.[61] There are stories that the monks at the Augustin Abbaye of Saint Satur (on the Loire river, adjacent to Sancerre) introduced Pinot Noir in the twelfth century. But this is no more than local legend; the monks may well have made red wine, but there is no knowing whether the variety was Pinot Noir.[62] All the same, Pinot Noir is one of the oldest established black varieties in the eastern Loire. (Just a little farther to the west, in the region of Tours, Gamay and Cabernet Franc are the predominant black grapes.) At the end of the nineteenth century, phylloxera greatly reduced the area of vineyards, and the subsequent replanting concentrated on white grapes.[63] Sauvignon Blanc took over the region until there was a revival of Pinot Noir after the 1950s. Today, Pinot's 900 hectares are almost a third of all production.

Alsace has had a more difficult history with red wine (indeed, for that matter, with all wine). The Rouge d'Ottrott is supposed to have originated in 1109 when Benedictine monks came from Burgundy to found the monastery of St. Leonard, near Strasbourg.[64] In Rouffach, at the southern end of the region, red wine fetched a higher price than white wine in the fifteenth century.[65] The monasteries appear to have produced a fair amount of red wine during the Middle Ages, but production declined sharply at the end of the sixteenth century.[66] Although white wine was predominant, the prestige of red wines was indicated by seventeenth century frauds in which white wines were colored with myrtle extract.[67] There is little evidence as to which grape varieties were grown, although Kleber (a German name for Pinot Noir) was grown at Wissembourg (close to the border with Germany) in the sixteenth century.[68] Over the following period, production concentrated more on grape varieties that were cheap and productive, and there was little quality wine, let alone Pinot Noir.[69] At Wissembourg, for example, Pinot disappeared until it was reintroduced in 1970.[70] So there is little tradition behind today's production of red wine. Pinot Noir is the only black grape now allowed in Alsace, and accounts for about 1,500 ha, which is 10% of all plantings.[71]

Curiously there is more direct evidence for the Cistercians' transport of black grapes to Germany than to other regions in France. The great monastery of Kloster Eberbach was founded on the banks of the Rhine by Bernard of Clairvaux in 1136; wine production from its vineyards became a major contributor to its economic success. Black grapes were grown well before Riesling was introduced to the area. The vines presumably came from Burgundy, but there is no direct evidence as to what varieties may have been planted.

It's altogether unknown what grape varieties were cultivated in Germany in the Middle Ages. Wines were described as Frankisch or Heunisch, the former being of higher quality, but it was not until the fifteenth century that the first individual varieties were distinguished.[72] The first clear reference to Riesling was in 1435, followed in 1470 by a reference to Klebrot, an early name for Pinot Noir, which became more commonly known as Spätburgunder (meaning "late Burgundy," a reference both to its time of ripening and origin).

Pinot Noir became common in the Rheingau, but it is not known when it first arrived. There's a popular story about grapes brought to the region by monks in the ninth century. Observing from his palace at Ingelheim that snow melted earlier on the other side of the river, Charlemagne is supposed to have ordered the monks to plant their grapevines on the opposite hill, in the vicinity of what is now the famous vineyard of Schloss Johannisberg. Some people think these vines could have been a variety of Pinot, since Pinot has since been found growing wild on an island nearby in the Rhine. One small problem with the story is that production at Schloss Johannisberg actually dates from somewhat later, around the twelfth century.[73]

A small amount of Pinot Noir is still grown in the Rheingau, and is also found all over Germany, from the really cool climate of the Mosel to the (relatively) warmer regions of the south. Curiously one of its most successful locations is in the most northern vineyards in Germany, in the protected microclimate of the Ahr valley. This is a relatively recent phenomenon, however, probably dating from the late seventeenth century.[74]

Pinot Noir was spread to Switzerland by war rather than by monks. Local legend holds that vines were brought from Burgundy to eastern Switzerland by the Duc de Rohan, when he led French troops who captured the Valtellina valley (just across the present border in Italy) in 1635 during the Thirty Years War. Whether these vines included Pinot Noir, we have no means of knowing. The monks of the period were cultivating a variety called Completer (still grown in the region). The origins of Pinot Noir are more prosaic in the Valais, the major region where it is presently grown in Switzerland, where it was introduced much later when the local authorities purchased 50,000 vines in 1848.[75]

Pinot Noir did not really spread successfully to the New World until the second half of the twentieth century. Enthusiasts brought many varieties of Vitis vinifera to the New World in the nineteenth century, but there were rarely any successes with the finicky Pinot Noir. During this period, grapevines could be freely transported, but of course today the unauthorized import of vines is illegal everywhere in the New World. To be imported legally, grapevines (and other crops) must pass through a lengthy quarantine process designed to prevent the entry of pests and diseases. It takes several years for imported material to be approved for release. In these circumstances, grapevines have made their way by various means, some legal and some more dubious, from Burgundy to the New World, with the result that the origins of the clones grown today are sometimes murky.

There are endless stories about "suitcase clones" being smuggled into the country by producers who were too impatient to sit out the quarantine period and who hid cuttings in their luggage or clothing. People stopped claiming that they had smuggled in cuttings from Romanée Conti only when the French authorities started to mutter that this might constitute a contravention of the producer's intellectual property rights.

One well-known case is the Abel clone of Pinot Noir, used by many premium wineries in New Zealand. The clones originated when cuttings, supposed to have originated at Domaine de la Romanée Conti, were confiscated by Malcolm Abel, then working as a Customs official at Auckland airport. (It's also known as the gumboot clone, because legend has it that it was hidden in a gumboot.) Realizing the potential importance of the material, Abel sent the cuttings to the state viticultural station, which used the material to generate virus-free, certified clones. In due course, Clive Paton planted the clone at Ata Rangi vineyard.

Some Pinot Noir was grown in California at the end of the nineteenth century, but the results were not encouraging,[76] probably because it was often planted in sites that were too warm.[77] Pinot Noir was reintroduced after Prohibition, and won some praise and awards during the 1940s to 1960s,[78] but it was still generally planted in relatively warm areas of Napa. It was not until the 1970s that Pinot Noir was planted in the cooler areas of Sonoma Valley and in Oregon. The first results in Oregon were somewhat mixed, because producers planted clones available from the University of California at Davis that ripened relatively late. The clones had been chosen for California in order to get a more extended growing season. The problem was that this required harvesting around the time of the autumn rains in Oregon, sometimes with disastrous results. In the early 1990s, the so-called Dijon clones were imported to Oregon, giving better results because they ripen up to two weeks earlier.

Clones are more important with Pinot Noir than with many other varieties. To be sure, every cultivar shows variation, but Pinot Noir mutates more frequently than most, throwing out a wider range of variants than the average.[79] "Pinot shows continuing variation in the vineyards—you see differences between the vines in a Pinot vineyard much more than you see with other varieties," says Boris Champy of Maison Louis Latour.[80] Established clones of Pinot Noir vary in their time of ripening, productivity, size of berries, and a host of other features that affect the quality of the wine directly or indirectly. (A clone, of course, is simply an extreme example of a subvariety, technically one that has been perpetuated from a single cell, or more practically from a small number of cells, to ensure homogeneity.)

Before the development of clones, when new grapevines were needed to replant a vineyard, vignerons in Burgundy would take cuttings from their existing vineyards. Many still believe in the value of this *selection massale*. It has the advantage, they hold, of relying upon genetic stock that has proven to be successful in their particular vineyards. And so long as cuttings are taken from a sufficient number of parent plants, it also perpetuates diversity. But for this to be effective, the parent material must be of high quality. It is impossible to break out of the circle if the vineyard was previously planted with a poor selection. Since Burgundy went through a protracted period in the 1970s-1980s when quantity was more important than quality, perpetuating those plants would be counter productive. On top of poor selection, many vineyards in Burgundy in the 1950s were infected with viruses that reduced production without increasing quality, pushing them into economic difficulties. Indeed, the initial impetus for developing clones in Burgundy and elsewhere was to eliminate diseased grapevines. Slowly the criteria changed towards developing clones that would give grapes of higher quality, and that were better adjusted to the environment.

No one knows exactly how many defined cultivars of Pinot Noir exist, but the number is thought to be at least several hundred.[81, 82] At the present, 43 clones of Pinot Noir are listed in the catalog of ENTAV,[83] the French organization that develops clones and guarantees they are free of viruses. But a handful of about six clones are widely used; in fact they are coming to

Fanleaf virus (shown by its effects on the leaf; left) is carried by nematodes, and causes poor fruit set; yield is reduced and the longevity of the grapevine is harmed. Leafroll virus (right) causes the leaves of black grape varieties to turn red in the autumn, very attractive, but damaging because the supply of nutrients is disrupted and the fruit does not mature properly. Photographs from William M. Brown Jr., Bugwood.org.

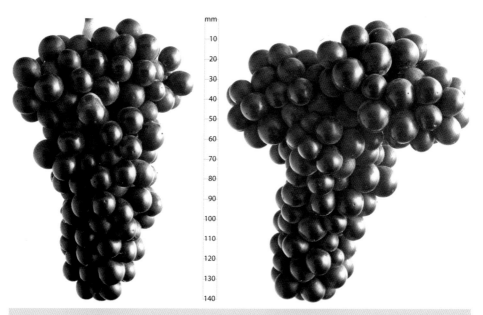

Dijon clone 115 (left) has smaller berries forming a smaller bunch than the Pommard clone from California (right). The Pommard clone has broader "shoulders."

dominate Pinot Noir plantings worldwide (for red wine; other, higher yielding, clones are used for sparkling wine).

Burgundy is the mother lode of clones. The Burgundians have the view that a thousand years of experience has perfected the match between Pinot Noir and the terroir. But which is the cart and which is the horse? "People say that the terroir of Burgundy is perfect for Pinot Noir," says Nigel Greening of Felton Road, where they make one of the best Pinot Noirs in New Zealand's South Island, "but it's actually the other way round. The grapes have been selected for the last thousand years to be perfect for Burgundy."[84] But is it axiomatic that the clones performing best in Burgundy will produce the best Pinot Noir elsewhere?

Today's dominant clones are called the Dijon clones, and originated in the vineyards of Domaine Ponsot in Morey St. Denis. The selection of clones at Ponsot goes back to the twenties. The M. Ponsot of the period (grandfather of Laurent Ponsot who runs the domain today) noticed when he was replanting the vineyards that many plants were sick. "Until then the general criteria for selecting for grafting was simply a strong branch—there was no other selection," says Laurent Ponsot.[85] His grandfather introduced the idea of selecting plants that were healthy and not too productive (his goal was to increase yields to 12 hl/ha!). He selected plants over two decades, for the shape of the grapes (bunched like a pine), tight clusters (not too open), resistance to diseases, and medium productivity, and in 1954 he replanted a large part of the Clos de la Roche with these selections, marking the selected plants with ribbons. When the government and winegrowers' association introduced the idea of selection to reduce illness in the sixties, the marked plants became the basis for the Dijon clones, which were selected by Raymond Bernard of the Dijon office of ONIVINS, a body governing wine production in France. (The clones have nothing to do with Dijon, but were given their name when they arrived in Oregon according to the return address on the package.) They are identified by numbers; the best known are 113, 114, 115, 667, 777 and (most recently) 828. Now 56 years old, the mother plants are still in the Clos de la Roche—Laurent could take you to them. (When Domaine Ponsot replant today, they use the clones.[86])

The clones differ in appearance and in the nature of their grapes. Some have more compact bunches, some have smaller berries, and the wines have differences in their aromatics and flavors. The general feeling is that no one of these clones by itself gives a really complete flavor spectrum, but that combinations make fine wine. But Allen Meadows, who writes the Burghound newsletter on Pinot Noir, believes the situation is worse than this. "The problem is…[the] …increasing, and troubling, emphasis of most new plantations to focus on just a few clones…115, 667, 777 and 828 dominate…these clones tend to taste more of themselves than reflect the site specific characteristics of where they're planted."[87] There's no doubt that plantings of these clones have been widespread in recent years, and in fact have elements of a brand about them—sometimes you even see "Dijon clones" on the labels of New World Pinot Noirs. It's hard to deny that this contributes to a loss of diversity (and potentially may make it more difficult to adjust to changing conditions in the future), but Nick Peay, of Peay Vineyards in Sonoma, believes that homogeneity may be caused more by late harvesting. "The true cause of the 'sameness' of so many of the Pinots…[is] …the late picking harvest decisions and the non-traditional vinification protocols… …When Pinot is picked overripe, the wines tend to taste the same regardless of clone or site."[88]

Clones are increasingly accepted, but there is still some suspicion about them, even in Burgundy. As the skeptics point out, they were developed in the 1970s, so they were based on selection for good performance during a cool period. They tend to ripen early, and in warmer conditions give high sugar levels and low acidity. Burgundians remain split between those who utilize the clones and those who continue to prefer selection massale. One difficulty for the traditionalists is that it is now illegal for a nursery to propagate diseased vines. Since some level of virus contamination is common, this makes it difficult to select vines for repopulating the vineyard: the vigneron has lost the ability to compromise by accepting vines that he thinks give good results in spite of a low level of virus contamination, unless he undertakes their propagation himself.

A Pinot Droit growing in upright mode. Note the characteristic thickness of the vertical shoots. Earlier in the season the bunches usually point up, but turn down after véraison.

The Dijon clones today may be moving towards world domination of new plantings, but there are still many old vineyards planted with other clones or unidentified selections. (A disincentive to replanting even when a vineyard is not giving top results is the period of several years before the new vines begin to give a usable crop.) Germany still has a high proportion of clones propagated by the Geisenheim research institute, which are known for their large berries and high yields. At the time when these were chosen, the main concern in Germany was to avoid the fungal problems caused by humidity in tight bunches. The clones first planted in Oregon were Pommard, based on a selection brought to California from Burgundy in 1951, and Wädenswil, brought to California in 1952 and named for its origin at the Swiss research institute.[89] These selections have the general property of ripening late, which was important for extending the growing period in California's warm climate, but they tend to be over productive and to have less character than the Dijon clones.

So does one size fit all? Jean Michel Menant, who has been selecting clones at the ATVB in Beaune, says, "We have tested the same clones in Bourgogne, villages, premier crus, and we see the same relative differences maintained. The terroir comes through each."[91] At this time he does not see any need to specialize clones for regions within Burgundy. All the same, some growers still like to replant their Volnay vineyards with vines from Volnay, their Beaune vineyards with vines from Beaune, and so on, following the belief that the vines adapt to very local conditions. This is at the far extreme from believing that clones originating exclusively from Clos de la Roche can populate the world. Of course, these clones are planted on different rootstocks in different places, which allows them to adapt to different soil conditions, and indeed allows for some control of productivity. And remember that Pinot Noir mutates rapidly, so the clones may change in situ.

Clones are under constant development, so the dominance of a few Dijon clones may be only transitory. Not everyone agrees that clones taken directly from Burgundy are the most appropriate for other locations, and indeed there are now some local selections available elsewhere, for example, from vines that have been grown in California for several decades.[92] But it's fair to

Protected under the blue netting, Frühburgunder has already changed color and is ripening in mid August, but the Spätburgunder on the left is still green and hard.[90]

The Pinot family has grapes of all colors. Pinot Noir is black, Pinot Gris has a light color, and Pinot Blanc has lost its color. (The grapes of Pinot Meunier have the same appearance as Pinot Noir.)

Pinot Noir

Pinot Noir and Pinot Blanc photographs kindly provided by the Institut für Rebenzchtung Geilweilerhof, Germany.

say that, although Pinot Noir is the most variable of cultivars, the dominance of the Dijon clones has reduced its diversity. And even if the recently developed clones are well adapted to present conditions, will they offer sufficient flexibility if conditions change?[93]

Concerned about the potential loss of diversity as clones are increasingly used for replanting, a group of fifty Burgundian producers has formed an association to create a library based on the oldest vines from their vineyards.[94] Criteria for quality include the size and shape of the leaf (which affects extent of vegetative growth) as well as the size and number of berries in a bunch, and the overall yield of the vine. "If there really is global warming, in 40 years we will have some vines that are good, even though they are too acid now. The high genetic diversity of Pinot Noir gives Burgundy an advantage in handling global warming," says Boris Champy.[95]

Pinot Noir has a major division between two strains known as Pinot Fin and Pinot Droit. Pinot Fin is the predominant strain, and is the origin of the various clones now distributed worldwide. Pinot Droit takes its name from its habit of growing more directly upright (indicated by "Droit") and is notably more productive. It gives distinctly lower quality wine, and a penchant for planting it during the 1970s was partly responsible for a decline in the quality of Burgundy during this period.[96]

One variant of Pinot Noir is distinguished solely by its early ripening. In France it's known as Pinot Noir Précoce, but in Germany it's described as a

separate variety, called Frühburgunder (early Burgundy) to distinguish it from Spätburgunder (late Burgundy), which corresponds to Pinot Noir per se. The effect on ripening is quite dramatic, with an advance of anywhere from two to four weeks.[97] The consequence is a smoother, softer wine, but to my mind with a simpler flavor profile that is rustic rather than delicate. If the only change is the control of ripening, it's a dramatic demonstration of the effect of the length of the growing season on the typicity of the variety.

Pinot Noir is the most famous member of the Pinot family, which has grape varieties ranging from black to white. In addition to Pinot Noir, the best-known varieties are Pinot Blanc, Pinot Gris, and Pinot Meunier. These differ in their skin color. Another variant, called Pinot Teinturier, actually has colored flesh, but it's not often used to make wine. Their genetic maps are all virtually indistinguishable, implying they all originate from the same ancestor.[98] Because Pinot Blanc, Pinot Gris, and Pinot Meunier have all lost features found in Pinot Noir, the original plant was most likely a Pinot Noir.

Pinot Blanc's lack of color is due to a mutation that prevents production of anthocyanin.[99] It might be more accurate to say Pinot Blancs, in the plural, because any time a mutation to prevent anthocyanin synthesis occurs in Pinot Noir, a new Pinot Blanc strain will be created. Most Pinot Blanc is probably quite ancient, and it appears to have been grown in Burgundy pretty much as long as Pinot Noir itself, but a new strain was found in Pierre Gouges's Clos des Porrets vineyard in Nuits St. Georges in 1936. Some 4,000

A mutation resembling Pinot Meunier shows in white leaves at the top of a shoot. The larger leaf (center) has a major sector with the mutation and a smaller sector without it. Meunier-like mutations have been observed on two vines in Louis Latour's 5 ha Chaillots vineyard in Corton.

vines were planted in the Perrières vineyard in 1947 (making a premier cru Nuits St. Georges), and then a larger vineyard was planted outside the Nuits St. Georges boundary in 1997 (making a Bourgogne Blanc).[100] The variety is sometimes called Pinot Gouges. It is a different wine altogether from Chardonnay. Pinot Gris has rather variable color, possibly the result of a mutation affecting only the cell layer that produces the skin.

Pinot Meunier differs from Pinot Noir in having leaves that are densely covered with fine hairs, whereas the leaves of Pinot Noir are smooth. The underside of the Meunier leaf has a white appearance, somewhat like dusting with flour, hence the description Meunier (French for miller). The difference between Pinot Noir and Pinot Meunier is due solely to a genetic change affecting only the outer layer of cells.[101] So far as we know, there is only one strain of Pinot Meunier, but similar mutations are occasionally observed in Pinot Noir.

The relationship between the Pinots is possible because grapevines are propagated vegetatively, by making cuttings, instead of being grown from seeds. When a plant is grown from a seed, all its cells have the same genetic constitution. But when it is propagated by cuttings, each cell layer can inherit the properties of the corresponding cell layer of the parental plant. So all Pinot Meuniers are descended from a single plant in which a somatic mutation changed the properties of just the outer cell layer.[102] In fact, if new plants are generated from the cells of this layer (the "true" Pinot Meunier?), they form dwarf grapevines of much reduced size but with increased fruit capacity. Because a large number of plants can be kept in a small area, these

The pixie grapevine is a dwarf generated from the outer cell layer of Pinot Meunier.

The internode length is one third that of a normal grapevine.

Photograph kindly provided by Joe Ogrodnick, Cornell University.

"pixie" grapevines may be useful for research purposes. If new plants are generated from other cell layers of Pinot Meunier, they are identical to Pinot Noir! So Pinot Meunier is a *chimera*, with all its cells exactly the same as Pinot Noir, except for the outer layer which is the same as the cells of the dwarf plants. In fact, all the Pinot varieties are chimeras, in which the genetic constitution of each layer is different, but in other cases the effects are not so dramatic.[103]

Pinot Noir has spread worldwide from its origins in Burgundy, but its distribution is far more restricted than its rival Cabernet Sauvignon from Bordeaux, or indeed than its white Burgundian counterpart, Chardonnay. Cabernet Sauvignon is an important quality variety in almost all major wine-producing countries, ranging from 7-20% of total plantings, but Pinot Noir rises above 1% of plantings in only a handful of countries. The only countries that have planted more Pinot Noir than Cabernet Sauvignon are the cool climates of Germany and New Zealand. While Pinot Noir is scarcely a niche variety, its restricted distribution attests to the difficulty of getting really good results.

France is still easily the world's leader in plantings of Pinot Noir, although more is planted for making sparkling wine in Champagne than for making

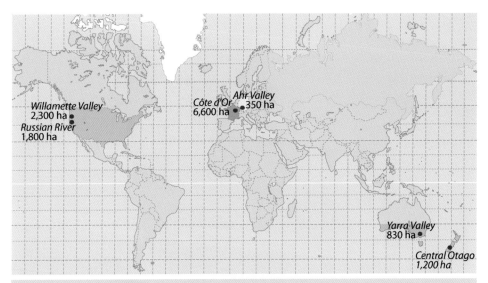

Top regions for producing Pinot Noir are cool (to the north in the northern hemisphere and to the south in the southern hemisphere) and rather small.[104]

Burgundy's famous dry red wine. Germany and the United States each have roughly the same total of plantings as Burgundy. Within Germany, most plantings are in the southernmost region of Baden; but the quality leader is the tiny region of the Ahr valley to the north. Oregon is the area most sharply focused on Pinot Noir in the United States; Central Otago and Martinborough are its counterparts in New Zealand. Pinot Noir is produced in smaller amounts in Australia's Yarra Valley and in South Africa, but it is not a major focus in the context of either country as a whole. In Switzerland, much Pinot Noir is not vinified as a varietal, but is blended with Gamay to produce a wine called Dôle.

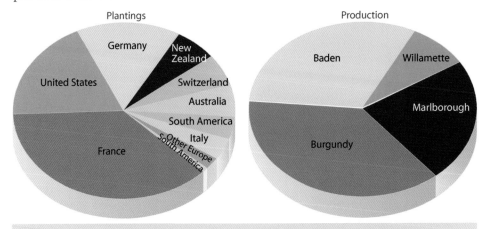

In plantings by countries (left) France has almost 30% of the world's Pinot Noir; the United States and Germany have another 30%.[105] *Production in the best-known regions (right) is concentrated on Burgundy, Baden, Willamette, and Marlborough.*[106]

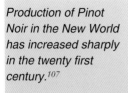

Production of Pinot Noir in the New World has increased sharply in the twenty first century.[107]

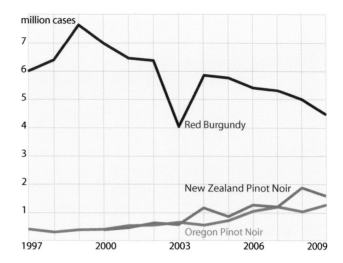

million cases

Red Burgundy

New Zealand Pinot Noir

Oregon Pinot Noir

1997   2000   2003   2006   2009

Pinot Noir is almost always produced on a small scale. The areas where quality can be achieved are quite restricted, and in each country the appellation that is best regarded for its Pinot production is small, often tiny. Burgundy's Côte d'Or has the largest contiguous area for plantations of Pinot Noir, but even that is less than 7,000 hectares. Compare this with the almost 30,000 hectares of Cabernet Sauvignon in Bordeaux.

The Côte d'Or produces about 3.2 million cases of Pinot Noir each year,[108] compared with about 11 million cases of red wine from the left bank of Bordeaux.[109] Burgundy remains the world's largest single producer of Pinot Noir, but production in Germany's Baden is now quite substantial. A difference is that a major proportion of red Burgundy is exported, but very little German Pinot Noir leaves the country. Production by New World countries has been increasing sharply, from almost insignificant levels in the late 1990s to about a quarter of Burgundy's production today in both New Zealand and Oregon. A significant amount of New Zealand's Pinot is exported to Europe and to America, but only a small proportion of Oregon's is available outside the United States.[110]

For a consumer in France, Pinot Noir is Burgundy; for a German consumer it is likely to be a Spätburgunder (the local name for the grape); and in the United States most likely Oregon or California. In terms of the styles that may be encountered by an average consumer (admittedly a mythical creature) outside of the country of production, Burgundy and New Zealand are the most common, giving very different impressions of Pinot Noir. As a (very) broad generalization, at the extremes we might regard Burgundy as representing European restraint and New Zealand as representing New World brashness. What is responsible for this difference? Is it natural differences in terroir or climate, or is it due more to choices in grape growing or winemaking?

Wine was very likely first made by accident, when grapes were collected, became crushed, and fermented spontaneously. Winemaking required the development of methods for pressing the grapes to release the juice, and finding containers to hold the wine. The nature of the container has a big effect on the character of the wine. In Roman times, amphorae were used, sealed with resin that affected the taste. During the Middle Ages wine was kept in animal skins: it had to be consumed quickly before it spoiled. Consumption within a few months of the vintage remained the rule until techniques were developed in the early eighteenth century to preserve wine while it was being matured in barrels and to stabilize it when it was bottled.[111]

What we now regard as the typical characteristics of modern wines began to develop from this period, and techniques for handling different grape varieties began to diverge. At this time, all wines were pale imitations of those produced today, especially red wines, where fermentation was much shorter, so the juice spent much less time in contact with the skins that give it its color. Grapes were picked earlier, at lower sugar levels, so the wines had only around 10% alcohol. The technique of chaptalization (named for Chaptal), in which sugar is added before fermentation to boost alcohol levels, was introduced in the early nineteenth century. During the nineteenth century, wine became more alcoholic, more deeply colored as fermentation periods were extended, and generally richer in response to popular taste.

Although the same trend is true for all grape varieties, the details differ with each cépage, and today Pinot Noir is handled differently from (say) Cabernet Sauvignon. Pinot Noir is a more delicate grape, with a thinner skin that has a lower content of anthocyanins (the pigments responsible for color) and tannins. This is why Pinot Noir is more lightly colored than Cabernet Sauvignon or Syrah, and why it is less tannic. The consensus is that Pinot Noir cannot take as much extraction as more deeply pigmented grapes, so during fermentation the skins that rise to the top of the vat are usually pushed back down into it (the process is called pigeage) by contrast with the pump-over used with Cabernet (when the juice is pumped up from the bottom of the vat and sprayed back over the top). For similar reasons, Pinot Noir tends to be less exposed to new oak during its maturation. Yet within this rather broad consensus, there are dramatic differences between Pinot Noirs made in different regions, and more subtle differences between wines from within each region. How do these differences relate to winemaking and to the modern fashion for "minimal intervention."

There's a theory that weather might be determined by a random effect such as when and where a butterfly flaps its wings. It's a poetic metaphor for saying that a tiny unimagined difference might have long term effects. Something of the sort also applies to winemaking, where a myriad of effects can change the results of fermentation.

Harvesting	Collect grapes Sorting and triage Cooling	
Prefermentation	Destemming Crushing Maceration	
Fermentation	Type of container Temperature Open *v.* closed top Indigenous *v.* cultured yeast Frequency of pigeage	
Pressing	Type of press Use of press wine	
Post fermentation	Time on skins Malolactic fermentation Cuves *v.* Barriques	
Ageing	New oak *v.* old oak Battonage Racking	
Bottling preparations	Fining Cold Stabilization Membrane filtration	

Wine making passes through a series of stages at which decisions, whether made knowingly or unknowingly, affect the nature of the wine.

The age of the vines, or any other factors that affect yield, influence the concentration of the must. The date chosen for harvest has a critical effect on the maturity of the grapes: will the criteria be to optimize the sugar/acid balance or to aim for "phenolic ripeness," which means picking later? And then once the grapes are in the basket, a series of critical decisions follow over the next days and weeks. Let's suppose the winemaker interferes as little as possible, so fermentation is accomplished by indigenous yeasts, and the time when malolactic fermentation occurs is decided by the bacteria. Even so, many decisions must be taken. You would be hard put to find a wine-maker in Burgundy who has never felt the need for chaptalization, and it's hard to argue that the level of alcohol does not affect the style.

Whether the grapes are put into the vat as whole bunches or as individual berries without their stems is a major factor in determining style. At one extreme is complete destemming—taking the berries completely off the stems. (One Bordeaux producer goes even further and takes off the pellicule where the stem joins the berry.) At the other extreme is whole cluster fermentation, where clusters of grapes are fermented whole and unbroken. Whole clusters add tannins and give more structure to the wine. But there is more to it than that.

The stems contain water (which reduces overall alcohol level), potassium (which lowers acidity), and also tannins, which are more bitter than those in the skins. These factors change the style of the wine more or less directly. And somewhat indirectly, including the stems makes for drainage paths through the must, changing maceration and fermentation temperature. The overall effect of destemming is a wine with more overt fruit and less tannic structure. Rather varied consequences for an apparently simple decision.

Wine styles in the 1970s changed not just in Burgundy, but worldwide, as the result of a move towards destemming. As a simplification, use of whole clusters remains more common in Burgundy than in the New World. Pro-ducers who use whole clusters are likely to include up to a half (the rest of the grapes being destemmed) depending on the character of the vintage. In a vintage where the berries have high tannins, whole clusters may be reduced or avoided, but in a vintage with more simple fruit character, more whole clusters may be included. "If you use too much whole cluster it will taste like a whole cluster wine and you lose terroir, but a touch lends a fine sense of texture," says winemaker Michael Martella of Thomas Fogarty Winery in California.[112]

The wheel may have come full circle here, because before the modern era, the grapes were pressed at an earlier stage, so there was less exposure to stems or skins during fermentation.[113] Destemming has always been a con-troversial issue. At Clos Vougeot in the 1830s, two thirds of the grapes were routinely destemmed, following what was presumably current thinking at the top level.[114] But generally during the nineteenth century in Burgundy, the "berries were thrown into the cuves and left to themselves," according to Camille Rodier, who went on to comment in 1920 that the advances resulting from electrification had made it possible to perform more or less complete destemming.[115] By the 1950s, the pros and cons were widely debated, advantages of destemming being the increase in alcohol and color, and reduction in excess tannin.[116] It's a measure of the change in a half century that these arguments could be reversed today; no one needs more alcohol now, and tannins are much better controlled during winemaking to avoid excess.

Today, grapes are handled much more gently; black grapes may even go into fermentation without having been crushed. (For white wine, grapes are pressed to release the juice before fermentation.) After fermentation has been completed, the wine is run off, and then the grapes are pressed. The wine released by pressing, the press wine, is coarser and may or may not be added to the free-run wine, depending on the nature of the vintage. (The recent development of very high quality vertical presses, in which the grapes can be pressed very gently without releasing harsh tannins from the pips, has improved the quality of press wine.)

Almost no one now leaves fermentation to occur without temperature control. It's just too risky. If harvest conditions are cool, the delay before fermentation starts may allow spoilage microorganisms to infect the must. If it is hot, temperatures may rise to a point at which the fruit is cooked and the wine is spoiled or fermentation becomes stuck. (Remember that fermentation is an exothermic reaction, one that generates heat, so as it proceeds, the must gets hotter.) Some producers believe in fermentation at relatively cool temperatures (for red wine this would be up to 28 °C) in order to retain the maximum of volatile aromas (which are lost progressively as the temperature increases); others prefer the increased level of extraction that occurs when the temperature is over 30 °C.

And what container will be used for fermentation? Producers all have their views on whether to use wood, stainless steel, or cement, although there really isn't evidence this has much effect. But if the container has an open top, up to 0.5% alcohol will be lost by evaporation during fermentation. If the top is closed, that alcohol will be retained. Whatever container is used, the skins will be pushed up by the release of carbon dioxide to form a "cap" on the top; to prevent it drying out, and to extract color and tannins, it is periodically immersed in the must. But what is periodic—daily or more or less often? When fermentation is finished, will the wine be run off immediately into new containers or will it macerate with the skins first for a while?

When the wine is run off, is it transferred into barrels or large cuves (well, for all top-flight wines it will be going into barrels), and will those barrels be new oak, one-year old oak, two-year old oak, or some combination. (Only the most inexpensive wines are bottled directly after fermentation; all others spend some period maturing first.) Anyone who lived through the craze for new oak of the 1980s-1990s knows that the type of oak has a huge effect on the wine. And it's not just the age of the oak, the way it is toasted affects how much flavor it transfers to the wine. (There's a popular misconception that more toast means more flavor, but actually the toast provides a protective layer against transfer of some flavors. Most producers use a medium level of toasting.) And once the wine is in the barrels, how often will it be transferred between barrels or stirred up. Every single one of these decisions has an effect; no one is right or wrong, there are good (and bad) wines made using every possible combination—but each has its own typicity.

Burgundy traditionally has been matured in barrels of 228 liters (just slightly different from the standard 225 liter barriques in Bordeaux). It's usually said that using new oak is a modern trend, but it was recommended by Camille Rodier in his book on Burgundy in 1920![117] However, it wasn't until the 1960s that producers generally could afford the expense of a significant proportion of new oak barrels. (A book on winemaking in Burgundy published at the end of the 1950s did not even mention new oak as a factor!)[118] As so often, Domaine de la Romanée Conti was in the vanguard, moving from around 20% in 1945 to almost 100% today. Even at DRC, the proportion most likely passed 50% only in the 1970s.[119] Most wines at higher levels today use some new oak, the custom now being that the proportion of new oak increases with the quality of the wine, on the grounds that greater fruit concentration can absorb more flavor from the oak without being overwhelmed. New oak has profound effects upon young wine, adding spices of cinnamon, cloves, and nutmeg, notes of vanillin, and sometimes even coconut. Wood tannins add to the structure provided by the grape tannins. The effect is much less pronounced when older barrels are used, and by the time the barrels are three years old, they are more or less neutral containers.

How far can we disentangle differences between Pinot Noirs from different countries as being due to intrinsic factors as opposed to fashions or traditions in winemaking? It is often warmer in the New World regions where Pinot Noir is grown; and the hazard of natural rainfall is replaced by the reliability of irrigation. This makes for growing conditions leading to riper grapes, so the wines tend to be richer and more alcoholic, a feature that is further emphasized by winemaking choices such as the extent of destemming. There is less vintage variation. Global warming has made conditions less marginal in Burgundy and other European locations for Pinot Noir, but it is fair to say that full ripeness is not easily achieved every year; much of the winemaker's work goes into compensating for vintage variation.

Making no prejudgment on the nature of these contrasting styles, still the infinite variation within each region is obvious. Every wine is different, whether due to the influence of the location where the grapes were grown or the producer who vinified it. Now it is time to look in more detail at whether and how location influences Pinot Noir in Burgundy, and whether we see the same relationship in other European locations and in the New World.

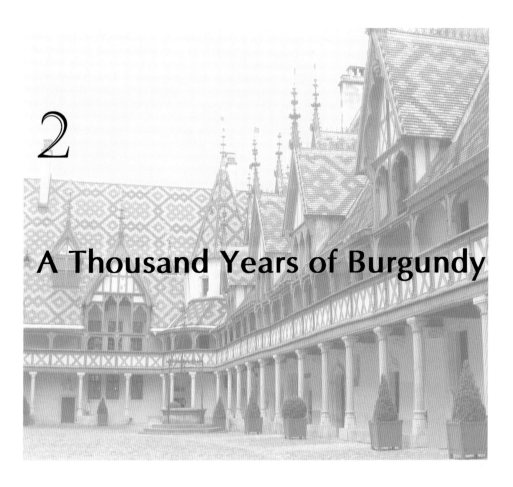

2

A Thousand Years of Burgundy

WINE WAS NOT YET BEING PRODUCED IN GAUL when Julius Caesar invaded in 58 B.C. After Roman culture was imposed, wine was imported from Rome.[1] Viticulture in France itself started on the Mediterranean coast, probably somewhere around Marseilles, by the Allobroges, a warrior tribe based at Vienne, who were allies of the Romans. Wine production spread steadily north, and by the first century C.E., the Allobroges were admired by the Romans for their skill in wine production. Their principal grape was a black variety known as Allobrogica, which resisted cold weather. They made a wine called "pomatum" (meaning pitch),[2] which took its name from the use of resin to seal the containers. In fact, the quality of the pitch or resin was regarded as influencing the quality of the wine.[3] The flavor was probably more like Greek Retsina than Burgundy as we know it today.

By the second century, negociants were dealing in wine from Lyon, and wine importing was a significant economic factor in the prosperity of the town.[4] At one time it was thought the negociants might have defended their

Archeological artefacts show that wine was being imported into Burgundy for several centuries before production started. An Etruscan wine vase of the sixth century B.C. (left) was part of the Treasure of Vix unearthed at Châtillon-sur-Seine, and a Roman wine jug of the third century C.E. (right), with an inscription referring to the famous wine of Falernus, was found at Lyon.[8]

established interests by delaying the local development of viticulture until the third century, perhaps until Emperor Probus issued his edict in favor of viticulture in 280 C.E.[5] But the fact that imported amphorae from the period 50-150 C.E. have traces of olive oil, but not wine, suggests that viticulture started earlier.[6]

Agricultural remnants suggest there was a vineyard in Gevrey Chambertin by the Roman era.[7] An archeological excavation when a housing estate was built in 2008 revealed a rectangular array of pits characteristic of Roman vineyards. Each pit probably contained two grapevines, planted in a system recommended by Pliny and Columella. The spacings within and between rows are multiples of the Roman foot (29.6 cm). Fragments of pottery found in the pits appear to date from the first century C.E. Certainly by the second or third century, the Côte d'Or appears to have been widely planted with vineyards.

Wine production had certainly become important by 312 C.E., when Emperor Constantin visited Autun. Still recovering from the devastation of recent wars, the inhabitants complained to the Emperor about economic conditions for wine production in the region.[9] "Even the famous Pagos Arebrignus [the area corresponding to the Côte d'Or], which is distinguished by its vineyards, is admired only by those who do not understand its true condition... The vines are exhausted... We lack the advantage of Aquitaine and other provinces which can find space for planting new vineyards, because we are caught between the rocks of the heights and the freezes of the plain."[10]

The speech referred to the difficulties caused by provinage, the traditional method of propagating vines by "layering," when shoots were stuck into the soil. "The roots, whose age we do not know any more, have formed a mass

An archeological excavation in Gevrey Chambertin revealed 316 rectangular pits (each 90-130 x 60 cm) aligned in 26 rows, which were interpreted as the remains of a vineyard from the first century C.E. (White marks are the site of older habitations predating the vineyard.)

Photo kindly provided by INRAP.

of thousands of interlaced folds, which prevent us from digging ditches." The implication is that the vineyards were already long established. And reference to the "famous" Pagos Arebrignus shows that the superiority of the Côte d'Or had already been recognized in an era when it was more usual to plant vineyards in sites offering better access to rivers for easy transport. Its difficult location may have pushed Burgundy to produce wines of higher quality, able to reach a price that would compensate for the high costs of transport.

The importance of viticulture was reinforced around 500 C.E., when a royal edict declared that anyone planting vines on fallow land would gain ownership of the land.[11] The entire region of today's Burgundy, from Chablis in the northwest corner, to the heart of the Côte d'Or between Dijon and Beaune, down to the south of Macon and the Beaujolais, was part of the Duchy of Burgundy.[12] With Dijon as their capital from the ninth to the fifteenth centuries, the Dukes of Burgundy ruled a region extending from Auxerre in the west to the Swiss border in the east, and to Lyon in the south.

Wine has been produced continuously in Burgundy since the vineyards were planted, but the thousand years until Philip the Bold's famous edict in favor of Pinot in 1395[13] is somewhat of a black hole for details about viticulture and vinification. Most of our information comes from the Church. In 587, Gontran, the ruler of Burgundy, gave a vast area "avec les vignes qui en font partie" (with the vines that are part of it) to the Abbaye de Saint-Bénigne.[14] In 630, the Duke gave vines at Vosne and Gevrey to the abbey at Bèze.[15] Charlemagne gifted a large area of vines extending from Aloxe to Pernand to the abbey at Saulieu in 775. This later became the area now known as Corton Charlemagne. Donations continued apace, increasing the importance of the monasteries.

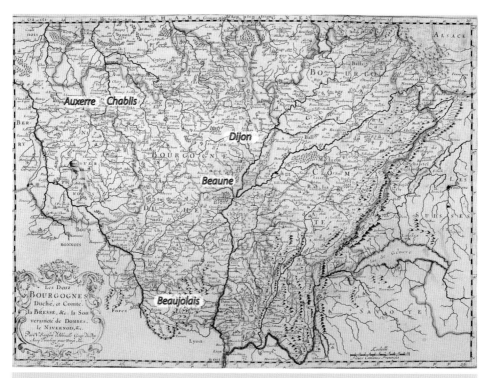

Nicolas Sanson's map of 1648 outlines the Duchy of Burgundy in green. The Duchy included all of the wine-producing regions of modern Burgundy.

By the next millennium, the Church had become the principal force carrying viticulture forward. Founded near Macon in 910, the Benedictine abbey of Cluny was a major influence, until it declined and was replaced by the Cistercian abbey of Cîteaux.[16] The monks kept busy, and the region from Auxerre to Beaune was described as "une mer de vignes" [a sea of vines] by 1248.[17] In today's Burgundy, the western region near Auxerre makes the white wines of Chablis, while red wines are made in the eastern part centered on Beaune.

By the thirteenth century, the wines of Beaune and Bourgogne[18] were known in Paris.[19] (Beaune referred to the region around today's Côte d'Or, Bourgogne to the region farther north around Auxerre;[20] it was only in 1416 that Charles VI declared that "vins de Bourgogne" should be used to describe both regions).[21] The vineyards around Beaune were regarded as one of the most important economic assets of the Duchy of Burgundy; and the wines were widely exported. In the fifteenth century, the Dukes of Burgundy proclaimed themselves "seigneurs des meilleurs vins de la Chrétienté" [owners of the best wines in Christendom].[22] There was a setback in the sixteenth century when Burgundy was absorbed into France, but by the seventeenth century, the wines of Burgundy were well integrated into the French econ-

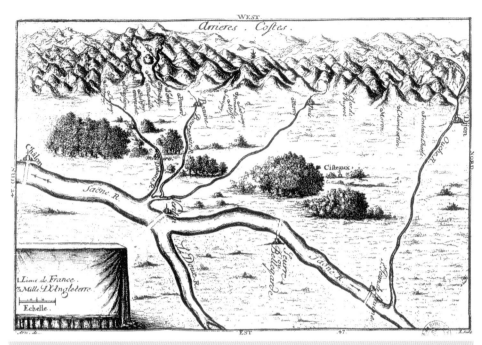

A book on Burgundy in 1726 included a map showing today's famous appellations of the Côte d'Or hugging the slopes well to the west (top) of the major rivers.[25]

omy.[23] By the eighteenth century, maps of the region showed a narrow strip of vineyards running south from Dijon, broadening out immediately to the north and south of Beaune. Burgundy's unique position was epitomized when the Prince de Condé was disappointed with the results of transplanting vines from Volnay to his estate at Chantilly. "Monseigneur," he was told, "you must also transplant the soil and the sun."[24] (The people who even today steal grapevine cuttings from the vineyards of Romanée Conti in the hope of replicating the magic might do well to remember this!)

Burgundy has been known for both white and red wine for at least a thousand years, but today the areas for growing black and white grapes have become somewhat segregated. Red wine predominates to the north of Beaune, although some areas (including Clos Vougeot) produced highly regarded white wine until the nineteenth century.[26] The most northern area now known for white wine is Corton Charlemagne, where the story goes that the wine takes its name from Charlemagne's wish to have white wine in order to avoid staining his beard with red wine. To the south of Beaune, Montrachet has long been established as the epitome of white wine. While the famous red wines have very likely always been made from Pinot Noir, there is no knowing what grape varieties went into Charlemagne's white wine, as there is scant information on the use of white grape varieties before the nineteenth century.

This retrospective painting by Albrecht Dürer shows Charlemagne with his beard going white. Does this date the origins of Corton Charlemagne from the second part of his reign, in the late eighth century?

The slope of the Côte d'Or falls off into a plain to the east. The distinction between the Côteaux (hillsides) and the surrounding plain goes back several hundred years. By the early nineteenth century, the best terroirs of the Côteaux were planted almost exclusively with Pinot (then known as Noirien or Pineau). Yet in spite of Philip the Bold's instructions several hundred years earlier, Gamay was still predominant elsewhere. Even along the Côte d'Or, Gamay occupied almost a third of plantings. In Nuits St. Georges, there was more Gamay than Pinot Noir in 1855, and Puligny Montrachet was largely planted with Gamay![27] In Burgundy as a whole, Gamay vastly outnumbered Pinot, occupying about 85% of all black grapevines.[28] "Gamay has invaded every area," said Dr. Lavalle in 1855.[29] It was far more productive, generating 60 hl/ha compared with Pinot's 20 hl/ha.[30] But Pinot Noir was the more valuable crop, generating two to three times more revenue per hectare than Gamay.[31]

The best wines were not necessarily made exclusively from Pinot Noir; they were often blends including Pinot Gris and Pinot Blanc (or Chardonnay),[32] until a fashion for more deeply colored wines developed in the late eighteenth century.[33] "We have abandoned the production of pale-colored wines to conform with the taste of foreigners. The fashion of the century is driving our methods," said the Abbé Tainturier of Clos Vougeot in 1763. "We have taken out of our vineyards the berries [of Pinot Gris] that gave our pale wine its quality."[34] The effect was especially pronounced in the area to the south of Beaune, where the wines had been prized for their delicacy. The trend towards darker, heavier wines intensified during the first part of the nineteenth century. Romanée Conti contained 20% of Pinot Gris and Pinot Blanc in the eighteenth century, which was reduced to 6% in the mid nineteenth century.[35] "Consumers believe that the wines should be strong and alc-

Cassini's map in the eighteenth century showed the vineyards of the Côte d'Or in the same locations as today.

oholic," complained a Parisian wine merchant in 1845.[36] He placed the blame on the influence of English importers. Anticipating concerns that have reverberated ever since, some commentators disapproved of the trend. "The

wines are more deeply colored and firmer; but is this at the expense of finesse and bouquet, and perhaps aging?" asked Dr. Lavalle in 1855.[37]

Things change slowly in Burgundy, and it took more than a century after
the move to more deeply colored wines for monovarietal Pinot Noir to
become the common red wine. "Growers who want to give their red wines
superior finesse and lightness keep at least an eighth of Pineau Blanc [sic] in
their plantings," was a countervailing view in 1846,[38] which remained common into the first half of the twentieth century. "Old vineyards have 1/5th to
1/20th Pinot Gris and Chardonnay; this blend gives great wines a certain
finesse," said an official report in 1929.[39] The reason for removing white
grapes was to make more deeply colored wines, but Pinot Gris was regarded
as increasing finesse without loss of color. As recently as 1949, Camille
Rodier commented that, "The finesse of wine made from Pinot Noir and
Pinot Gris is superior to that made from Pinot Noir alone."[40] Some growers
today still share the old view that complexity is increased by blending small
amounts of other varieties. Only a couple of years ago, one producer, whose
vineyards included a patch of old Pinot Gris (now illegal on the Côte d'Or)
told me that when the vines had to be replaced recently, he arranged with the
nursery to make a "mistake" and to send Pinot Gris instead of Pinot Noir.[41]

Cultivated largely to the south of Beaune, Chardonnay made the best
white wine. However, it was realized only in the twentieth century that Chardonnay is not the same as Pinot Blanc, which has also been grown in
Burgundy, so who knows what the top white wines were really made from?
"Pinot Blanc [also known as] Chardenay is largely cultivated only in the
villages of Puligny or Meursault," it was said in 1831.[42] Confining white
grapes to the south of Beaune was actually a fairly recent development, since
the famous Clos Vougeot was 60% Pinot Noir and 40% white grapes until
1820, when the white grapes were pulled out.[43]

The white grapes were partly included as a blend with Pinot Noir in the
red wine and partly used to make a white wine. Dom Denise, a Cistercian
monk, made an interesting comparison in 1779. "Montrachet is very delicate,
more graceful, and less alcoholic than the white wine of Clos Vougeot."[44]
Aligoté was clearly considered an also-ran by the nineteenth century, although better than Gamay Blanc or Melon (the grape variety now grown in
Muscadet).

The onslaught of phylloxera at the end of the nineteenth century devas-
tated Burgundy. After a spate of protests that the quality of the wines would
be reduced, producers became resigned to grafting all of their vines on to
roots of American species of Vitis. The combination of calcareous soils and
cool climate made it more difficult to find appropriate rootstocks than elsewhere in France,[45] but after grafting was approved in 1887, it rapidly became
the norm. There were few holdouts, but the Romanée Conti vineyard re-

mained planted on its own roots until 1945, when declining yields finally forced replanting on rootstocks.[46]

The Burgundians were especially concerned about the effects that grafting had on quality. The controversy raged for years before it was realized that both the vigor of the rootstock and the quality of the scion grafted on to it affect the result; perhaps there is no single answer. The comparison may have been biased when Pinots were chosen for grafting by selecting those with higher productivity,[47] exacerbating the general tendency of grafted vines to be more productive than those grown on their own roots. An indirect consequence of the transition was a great reduction in the planting density of grapevines, because the grafted vines were planted individually in neat rows, whereas the ungrafted vines had been propagated by layering shoots at random. This may also have increased yields.

Another result of phylloxera was the simplification of varieties associated with the transition to grafting, an effect seen all over France. Some of the ancillary varieties that had been grown in Burgundy were already disappearing by the end of the nineteenth century, although it could scarcely be said that the elimination of varieties such as Gouais Blanc was any great loss. After replanting, Burgundy focused almost exclusively on Pinot Noir and Chardonnay for top quality, with Gamay and Aligoté planted in lesser areas. The Côte d'Or was almost completely replanted, but growers in some of the lesser areas gave up production altogether.[48] Yet it took a surprisingly long time for the last effects of phylloxera to be eliminated entirely; even half a century later there were still significant plantings of hybrid varieties that had been introduced as a temporary measure.[49]

Laurent Ponsot of Domaine Ponsot in Morey St. Denis holds the iconoclastic view that Aligoté can make top quality wine. "Chardonnay needs a relatively thick soil while Aligoté grows very well on very poor soil and still extracts authenticity. So Aligoté used to be planted on top of the slopes and Chardonnay at the bottom," he explained to me. "There was Aligoté in Montrachet, Corton Charlemagne, Musigny Blanc—in Morey St Denis there were rows of white grapes, all Aligoté, in the grand cru vineyards. After phylloxera, Chardonnay was replanted because it gave a more productive crop more quickly. When Aligoté was replanted, it was planted at the bottom, actually in places that used to be planted to potatoes and other crops. Then to match the acidity they put cassis in [making kir]. The acidity is not intrinsic to the grape, it's coming from the locations where Aligoté has been planted."[50] Ponsot's vineyard in the Morey St. Denis premier cru, Mont St. Luisants, was planted with Aligoté in his grandfather and father's time, but they would never admit the wine was made from Aligoté. But when Laurent experimented by planting three grape varieties in the vineyard, the Aligoté made the best wine (the Chardonnay actually turned out to be rather acidic), and he now proves his point by regularly producing the Côte's only premier cru from Aligoté.[51] Another exception is at Domaine Henri Gouges, where Pierre Gouges makes an interesting white wine from the Pinot Blanc that his grandfather discovered as an adventitious mutation in the 1930s. But today the Côte d'Or is close to a monovarietal representation of Pinot Noir for reds and Chardonnay for whites.

Needless to say, they don't make Burgundy like they used to. In the Middle Ages, the wine, whether red or white, was intended to be consumed immediately; it would generally be considered past its peak by the time the next vintage arrived. Red wines were lightly extracted, with a color described as "oeil de perdrix" (the pale pink color of a partridge's eye); white wines sometimes had spices added.[52] Only occasionally was a vintage considered good enough for the wine to last beyond the year.

The style of Burgundy changed as Pinot Gris and Pinot Blanc disappeared from the blend, but perhaps more to the point, two extraneous factors helped the producers give the punters what they wanted. The first was the introduction of chaptalization, the addition of sugar, which is turned into alcohol during fermentation. Named for Chaptal, Napoleon's Minister of the Interior in 1801, the technique was used to increase alcoholic strength by two or three percent.[53] Chaptalization was not without controversy. Dr. Morelot, a well known contemporary critic on the wines of Burgundy, commented in 1831 that "one makes better wine, with a good taste; but this wine, I do not know if I am fooling myself, is no longer a true wine of Burgundy. Stronger, more alcoholic, and darker in color, it has lost its bouquet, and become more southern in style."[54] In 1845, a congress of vignerons in Dijon complained that chaptalization made it impossible to distinguish quality and origin, and called for it to be banned.[55] Nonetheless, by the 1850s chaptalization was widespread in France,[56] with Burgundy at the forefront.[57] Coupled with a longer period of maceration for the juice to extract color from the skins, this made the wines darker and more alcoholic.

The second influence was more sinister. Unable to make wines that were heavy enough to suit the popular taste, negociants took to blending in some darker, more alcoholic wine from the south. Warning against unscrupulous negociants in 1855, Dr. Lavalle told the story of a merchant who claimed the secret of his fortune was "always selling the wine of Burgundy without ever harvesting or buying any."[58] The area of Hermitage in the northern Rhône was a popular source, and "hermitager" became used as a verb to describe this practice of adulteration. (It was equally if not more used for the wines of Bordeaux; indeed, during the nineteenth century, Bordeaux shippers purchased vineyards in Hermitage in order to assure their supply, and as much as 80% of the production was shipped to Bordeaux.[59]) Right into the 1920s, growers in Châteauneuf-du-Pape were encouraged to produce Grenache because they got twice the price for selling it to "improve" Burgundy than they could get for Syrah or Mourvèdre.[60] Through the 1930s the majority of Burgundian producers may have resorted to including wines from the Rhône.[61] The misleading image of red Burgundy as a rich, heavy, red wine owes more to adulteration than to the nature of Pinot Noir, but persisted at least until the appellation contrôlée rules came into effect in 1936.

So several hundred years of Burgundian history offer little guidance as to the true nature of Pinot Noir. Red Burgundy of the Middle Ages probably more resembled a rosé of today. From the nineteenth century, alcohol levels owed something to the bags of sugar dumped in the vat; and until the mid twentieth century, a deceptive richness had some assistance from Grenache of the south. In the past twenty years, improvements in viticulture and vinification, coupled with warmer vintages, have restored a more natural degree of richness to the wine. (The limit for chaptalization was reduced from 2% to 1.5% in 2007.)

Burgundy's great reputation for Pinot Noir is concentrated sharply on the Côte d'Or. Burgundy as a whole makes more white wine, most of it from

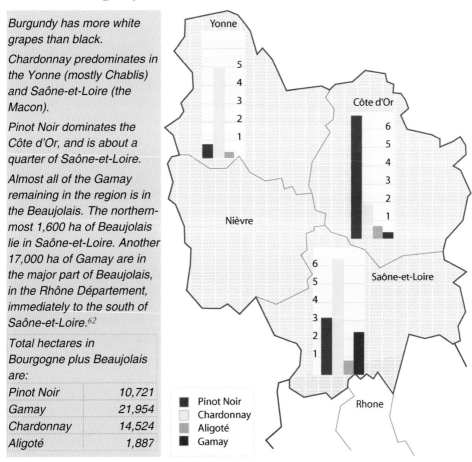

Burgundy has more white grapes than black.

Chardonnay predominates in the Yonne (mostly Chablis) and Saône-et-Loire (the Macon).

Pinot Noir dominates the Côte d'Or, and is about a quarter of Saône-et-Loire.

Almost all of the Gamay remaining in the region is in the Beaujolais. The northern-most 1,600 ha of Beaujolais lie in Saône-et-Loire. Another 17,000 ha of Gamay are in the major part of Beaujolais, in the Rhône Département, immediately to the south of Saône-et-Loire.[62]

Total hectares in Bourgogne plus Beaujolais are:

Pinot Noir	10,721
Gamay	21,954
Chardonnay	14,524
Aligoté	1,887

Pinot Noir
Chardonnay
Aligoté
Gamay

Chardonnay, with just a little Aligoté. (Whether the statistics showing that Aligoté is only about 10% of white plantings are true is another matter. One producer who purchased grapes in 2009 from Corton Charlemagne told me that a third of the grapes turned out to be Aligoté.[63] "Today there is quite a bit of Aligoté in Corton Charlemagne but the growers won't admit it," he said.[64]) But three quarters of the Côte d'Or is devoted to Pinot Noir (almost all the rest is Chardonnay). Less than 7,000 hectares in all, this small area provides the paradigm for Pinot Noir worldwide.

And what of the "infamous" Gamay? There is still a little left in Bourgogne, but most of it is in the small part of the Beaujolais that pokes up into the Saône-et-Loire Département. It is far outnumbered by the bulk of the Beaujolais, in the Département of the Rhône just to the south. The total production of Beaujolais is quite substantial compared to that of Bourgogne; in fact Beaujolais and Bourgogne produce about the same amount of red wine. But red Burgundy is basically Pinot Noir with one remaining exception. Generic Bourgogne Rouge can include Gamay (in a blend with Pinot Noir that is labeled Passetoutgrains, which loosely translated means "chuck in all the berries").[65]

Gamay in Burgundy proper has been in a major decline ever since phylloxera. When phylloxera hit the Côte d'Or in the 1880s, there were more than 30,000 hectares of vineyards, most devoted to Gamay. However, it is fair to say that already the best red wines were made (predominantly) from Pinot Noir, and the best white wines from Chardonnay. After vineyards had been replanted by grafting on to rootstocks of American vines, there were about 25,000 hectares. The area under cultivation then declined steadily, reaching a plateau only after the second world war. Most of the decline was due to abandonment of Gamay in the inferior areas.

Most of the Côte d'Or was planted with Gamay before phylloxera, but today there is little left in Burgundy. Pinot Noir also declined, and plantings revived only after 1945.[66]

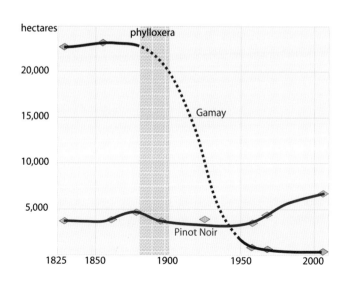

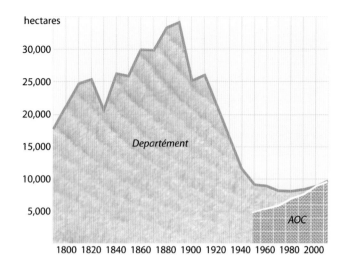

Vineyard area in the Côte d'Or Département peaked at the time of phylloxera. It has changed only plus or minus 10% since 1945. Since the AOC system was created, classified vineyards have increased steadily and now account for virtually all plantings.[68]

One aspect of the continuing battle between Pinot and Gamay was the establishment of the Hautes-Côtes (de Beaune and de Nuits). The appellation rules of 1919 restricted use of "Bourgogne" to wines produced from Pinot Noir or Chardonnay; Gamay could be included only in "Bourgogne Passetoutgrains." The producers on the Hautes-Côtes wanted to call their wine "Bourgogne" or "Bourgogne Hautes-Côtes," but the growers of the Côte d'Or objected, on the grounds that this was Gamay not Pinot. A court case in 1930 ruled in favor of the Côte d'Or, and subsequently a compromise was reached to call the wines Bourgogne des Côteaux Beaunois or Bourgogne des Côteaux Nuitons. Only in the 1960s, after replanting with Pinot Noir, was the Bourgogne Hautes-Côtes approved as an appellation.[67]

The clash between Pinot Noir and Gamay started by Philip the Bold in 1395 is still continuing six centuries later. Gamay may have been expelled to the south, but remains a current controversy. Growers in Burgundy have been concerned about a loophole permitting the labels Bourgogne Rouge and Bourgogne Blanc to be used for Beaujolais, allowing Bourgogne Rouge to be Gamay, and allowing the Beaujolais growers to use 200 hectares of recently planted Chardonnay to compete with the existing Bourgogne Blanc. "The BIVB [Bureau Interprofessionnel des Vins de Bourgogne] liner is heading straight for the iceberg of Beaujolais, risking drowning those who paid for the voyage," said a statement issued by the Syndicat de Bourgogne.[69] Resulting from this pressure, new rules issued in June 2010 prevent Beaujolais Blanc from being labeled as Bourgogne, and require red wine from the Beaujolais Crus (which can continue to be labeled as Bourgogne) to be described as Bourgogne Gamay if it has more than 85% Gamay.[70] It's ironic that the new rules reduce confusion about which varieties go into red Bourgogne, but they distinguish between Bourgogne Blanc and Beaujolais Blanc, although both are made from Chardonnay.

Negociants became established within the walls of the city of Beaune. The map dates from the early seventeenth century.

The Côte d'Or has now recovered about twenty per cent from its bottom in the 1970s, with around 10,000 hectares planted in the Département today. The most significant factor is not so much the total vineyard area, however, as the growth of the AOC. When the AOC system was introduced in the 1930s, about half of the vineyards were included; today virtually all vineyards in the Côte d'Or are part of the system.[71] Of course, the vineyards along the famous slope at the heart of the Côte d'Or have not changed; the vineyards that were lost after phylloxera, and the remaining ones that have been incorporated into the AOC over recent decades, are in the surrounding areas, sometimes pejoratively called the arrières-pays (back country).

Burgundy owes the nature of its wines today to the outcome of a clash between the growers and negociants in the 1930s. Merchants had handled the wine ever since growers started producing it, but in the eighteenth century a new breed appeared, the negociant-éleveurs, who took a much stronger hand in creating the style of the wine.[72] What were to become major negociants were established in the first decades of the century, including Bouchard Aîné and Maison Champy. Another wave of negociants followed after the Revolution, including Louis Latour, Bouchard Père, and Louis Jadot.

Beaune became the center of the wine trade. Most of the old negociants have their headquarters here. Although it's the names of the growers who bottle their own wines that grab attention today, the fact is that most Burgundy continues to be bottled by negociants. Many of the negociant names are recognizable from fifty years ago, unlike Bordeaux where there has been extensive turnover. A change over the past decade or so is that the negociants have been moving their headquarters out of the old town to more practical, purpose built, locations on the outskirts.

In the center of the old town of Beaune is the Hôtel Dieu, established as a hospital, the Hospices de Beaune, in the Middle Ages. The Hospices de Beaune is funded by wine produced from its own vineyards.[73] One of the highlights of the year in Beaune is a long weekend called Les Trois Glorieuses, at which a fancy dinner at Clos Vougeot is followed the next day by an auction of the latest vintage from the Hospices. The following day is La Paulée in Meursault, an extended luncheon where producers bring old bottles of wine to impress their friends.

A charity auction of wines made from vineyards owned by the Hospices de Beaune has been held annually at the end of November since 1859, as part of Les Trois Glorieuses The auction prices help to set the price for Burgundy for that year. The photograph shows the scene early in the twentieth century, when the auction was held in the courtyard of the Hôtel Dieu in Beaune. Today the auction is held in the modern covered marketplace opposite the Hotel Dieu.

The wine from the Hospices is sold to local negociants, who then take possession of the barrels and mature it in their own particular styles. Until 2005, only negociants could buy the wine, but then the auction was handed over to Christie's to manage, and opened up to private buyers.[75] The wine still must be matured locally, so a private buyer must contract with a nego-

Before the First World War, oxen were often used to transport the harvest.[74]

Even large negociants transported the harvest by horse in the early 1930s. This shows the harvest in Bouchard's Champinots vineyard in Beaune around 1930.

ciant to collect the barrel and mature the wine until it is bottled. At one time these wines were well regarded for their quality. Today the auction is more an occasion to kick off sales of the current vintage than a supply of top-flight wine. Sandwiched between the dinner at Clos Vougeot and La Paulée, it was never necessarily a sober affair, but the new approach of bringing in buyers from around the world has turned it into more of a media circus,[76] making prices more indicative of market buoyancy than the quality of the vintage.[77] "[The auction] has become decoupled from normal trading," says Anthony Hanson of Christie's.[78]

Conditions for wine production in Burgundy were fairly primitive until the second world war. Horses to work the vineyards became available only after the first world war. As Henri Jayer recalled, "The age of the horse in Burgundy is not an ancient practice in the way everyone romantically believes. In fact, [it] came about after World War I, after the army sold off literally tens of thousands of horses because they no longer had any use for them."[79] Tractors were introduced in the 1930s, but did not become common until the 1950s. In the period between the first and second world wars, only the largest negociants or cooperatives were able to modernize their presses; others still used old manual presses.[80] For the most part, the negociants retained control of production after the harvest.

Until the mid twentieth century, virtually all Burgundy was sold under the name of a negociant:[82] growers' names were virtually unknown to the public.[83] The different regions of Burgundy were already priced separately by negociants in the eighteenth century, but until the Appellation Contrôlée

Manual presses were still used by small producers into the 1930s.[81]

At the height of the dispute between negociants and growers, an advertisement for Maison Chauvenet in 1931 emphasized authenticity, origin, vintage, and quality —precisely the grounds of the dispute with the growers.

rules came into effect, the names were used as much to indicate style as to authenticate origin. "A wine with the characteristics of Pommard or Volnay would be named as Pommard or Volnay," says one historian of Burgundy.[84] Differences may also have been somewhat muddied by the common practice of blending with stronger wines brought in from the Rhône.

Conflicts between the negociants and growers developed between the first and second world wars. In 1919 the negociants proposed the principle of equivalence, in which the names of wines would be regarded as interchangeable within levels classified as tête, première, seconde, or troisième.[85] Quality and style were considered more important than origin.[86] Far from being ashamed of blending in wines from other regions, the negociants petitioned to be allowed to continue the practice with wines that were "judiciously chosen and blended."[87] Growers fought back by bringing court actions to restrict the use of appellation names. The conflict was emphasized by a public battle between Colette, the author, who was involved in promoting the wines of the negociant Chauvenet, and Gaston Roupnel, a leader of the growers, who went so far in the heat of battle as to say, "The majority of wines sold behind respectable labels are more often the product of the chemist's laboratory rather than the vintner's cellar."[88] The growers finally won when the Appellation Contrôlée came into effect in 1936.

Emphasizing the importance of origins strengthened the position of the growers. Domain bottling began in the 1920s when growers such as the Marquis d'Angerville, who led the growers' syndicate, began bypassing the negociants as the result of the dispute. Still a relatively small proportion until after the second world war, domain bottling began to increase in the 1960s and 1970s, becoming common with the most valuable wines: the premier and grand crus. Roughly 25% of premier and grand cru production was probably domain bottled in 1969, increasing to 45% by 1976.[89] Actually this was a mixed bag in terms of results: a fair amount of domain bottling was performed by mobile bottling plants, transported on the back of a truck, and quality was variable, to say the least.[90] By the 1970s, growers were installing equipment and gaining expertise. From the premier and grand crus, domain bottling has spread to become the norm for the communes today.

As this movement gathered force, some of the old negociants protected their positions by buying vineyards. Today the major houses mostly produce wines from their own vineyards as well as from grapes bought from outside growers. The largest houses (Bouchard Père, Patriarche, Louis Latour, Louis Jadot, Maison Faiveley, Joseph Drouhin, and Domaine de la Vougeraie) collectively own more than 400 hectares on the Côte d'Or.[91] More to the point, perhaps, they own around 15% of the premier and grand crus.

Today's producers vary enormously in size, from small family concerns producing a few thousand bottles a year, to large negociants producing millions of bottles. The generally small scale of production is indicated by the statistic that, even today, 80% of producers each vinify less than 5,000 cases per year.[93] The number of producers continues to fall, down from 13,000 in 1970 to 5,000 today.[94] There is the same tendency here as elsewhere for larger fish to gobble up smaller fish, although it is impeded by the small sizes

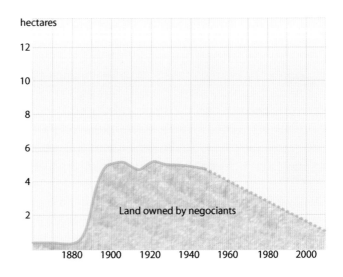

The rise and fall of the negociants is shown by how much they owned of Le Chambertin. During the first part of the twentieth century they owned a substantial part, but today most Chambertin is bottled by growers.[92]

Cuveries in Burgundy range from a tiny thirteenth century cave in the cellars of Michel Lafarge in Volnay (left) to the new winery that Jadot built in 1995 on the outskirts of Beaune and are presently expanding (facing right).

of the individual holdings. To assemble any sizeable vineyard area requires painstaking cultivation of many individual sellers who sometimes have only a few ares (hundredths of a hectare) each. Often only a few people in the village know there's an interest in selling. Sharply rising prices of land push inheritors to sell when estate taxes have to be paid, but simultaneously make it more difficult for small growers to expand their holdings. Jacques Seysses, who built the well-respected Domaine Dujac with a series of vineyard acquisitions since its inception in 1967, told me bluntly, "What I did then, I could not do today. You would need to be rich or brilliant at finding investors."[95] He adds that the whole economic situation has changed in Burgundy. "In the sixties, people were not wealthy. All except about six estates—headed by Rousseau, d'Angerville, Gouges—were selling their wines in bulk. In that period you would send your children off to some professional school [law or medicine, for example] not to work in the vineyard. But today [wine] has become profitable, there's a good living, young people come into it. It's a complete change." All the same, the population of wine producers is aging.[96]

While it's difficult to assemble domains piecemeal, some of the old-line negociants have been sold to outside buyers with deeper pockets. Louis Jadot was sold to its North American distributor, Kobrand, in 1985. Maison Bouchard Père & Fils was sold to Champagne house Joseph Henriot in 1995. Domain Leroy, at the top of the Burgundian hierarchy, has a silent partner in Japan. Within Burgundy, the fastest growing house has been Jean-Claude Boisset's Domaine de la Vougeraie, which has grown rapidly by acquiring

several failing domains, from l'Heritier Guyot to Pierre Ponelle. Separately from the vineyards that came with the various domains that were merged into Vougeraie, Boisset has bought several negociants, including Bouchard Aîné, Jaffelin, Ropiteau, and Mommesin, which continue to be run separately. Boisset's rapid rise has attracted some resentment. "Boisset is always there if you need him," one negociant who had got into trouble and was considering selling, told me ruefully.[97]

Becky Wassermann, who led the move to domain bottling in the 1970s by encouraging small growers to bottle themselves, says that even now, "Burgundy is not rich. People are finally fixing up their cellars, they have sorting tables, and the current generation have technical qualifications. But there's a contrast between public and private life. The international fame of a few has not necessarily trickled down into prosperity for the many."[98] The big issue in switching from selling your grapes or wine to a negociant to bottling it yourself was the element of risk. "When I started working in the mid 1970s," she told me, "there weren't people who bottled everywhere but there were enough so it wasn't unprecedented. The economics of bottling yourself meant you didn't get paid until much later, so vignerons felt it involved taking a risk. Grower bottling spread slowly as people saw the results of their neighbor's success."

Domain bottling greatly reinforced the importance of origins. Until the seventeenth century, few distinctions were drawn between wines of the region; at least so far as the consumer was concerned, they were all "vins de

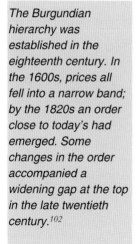

The Burgundian hierarchy was established in the eighteenth century. In the 1600s, prices all fell into a narrow band; by the 1820s an order close to today's had emerged. Some changes in the order accompanied a widening gap at the top in the late twentieth century.[102]

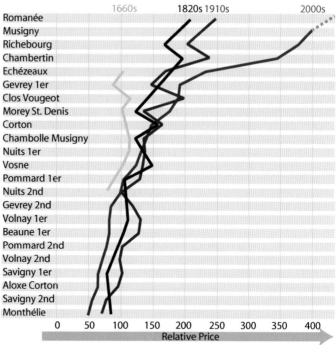

Beaune," in which price was determined by the reputation of the negociant.[99] The negociants certainly knew their Crus, however, and would put wine from the best Crus into the top blends.[100] Prices in the seventeenth century were remarkably flat: on the negociant market; wines from the top vineyards in the Côte de Nuits sold for under twice the price of those from the Arrières-Côtes or Pays bas (flat lands at the bottom), which were well outside the best areas.[101] Distinctions between regions became established in the eighteenth century.

The reputations of the wines were reflected in land prices. The clearest comparison comes from the sales of land seized during the French Revolution. At a sale of "biens nationaux" in January 1791, Les St. Georges was the most expensive at more than twice the price of "Vignes de Nuits" (presumably elsewhere in Nuits St. Georges). In second place came Les Chambertins (probably including parts of what today are Le Chambertin and Clos de Bèze). Volnay and Clos Vougeot were next, followed by Romanée St. Vivant and Richebourg.[103] The difference in the order compared to wine prices from the 1820s, only a quarter century later, most likely represents distortions of the auction process, but the important point is that clear distinctions between the values of different terroirs were evidently already well established (although the range was vastly narrower than today).

By the nineteenth century, there was a hierarchy of wine prices for appellations quite similar to today's, with a price range among the communes of the Côte d'Or strip of about 2.5 fold. Wines continued to be sold by negociants with little attention to individual producers, and prices were based on relatively broad areas roughly corresponding to today's villages. The price hierarchy for the regions was fairly stable.[104] By the end of the century, finer distinctions were being drawn, with Nuits, Gevrey, Volnay, Pommard, even Savigny, all split into 1er and 2nd classes. The price range widened to 3-4 fold between the top and bottom.

Recognition of the individual *climats* extended to a broader public during the eighteenth century,[105] and by the next century, the individual areas were defined in detail. The modern definition of individual parcels dates from the establishment of the cadastre (land register) between 1807 and 1830.[106] The boundaries between parcels, which became entrenched as definitions of terroirs, reflected current patterns of ownership. Lavalle's map of 1855 could virtually be substituted for today's map of the appellations. An official map, prepared for the exhibition in Paris of 1862, classified the vineyards into 1er cuvée, 2eme cru, and 3eme cru. This was to all intents and purposes the basis for the AOC classifications in 1935, corresponding to the grand cru, premier cru, and village AOCs.[107]

The reputations of the various appellations today closely follow those of a century ago. In the nineteenth century, Romanée and Chambertin were level

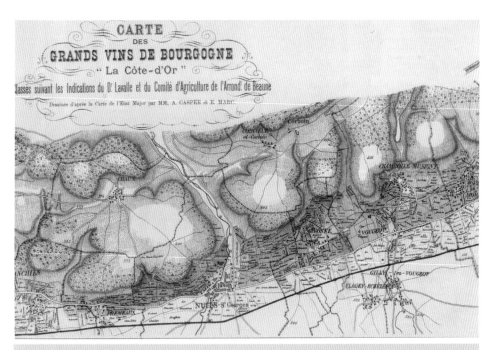

The official map of 1861 is scarcely different from today's AOC map. Vineyards were divided into three categories, indicated by the color as: premier – pink, deuxième – turquoise, troisième – green.

pegging at the top, with Richebourg close behind.[108] At the start of the twentieth century, Romanée was still at the top just ahead of Musigny, Chambertin, and Richebourg: the same four occupy the top positions today, although Romanée Conti is farther out in front, and Richebourg and Musigny have moved ahead of Chambertin. The biggest change is that the very top wines seem to have expanded their lead (much in the same way that the first growths of Bordeaux have expanded their lead over neighboring châteaux).[109] Another other major difference in the situation is that many individual producers have replaced negociants, so the grower's name has as much effect on price as the appellation.

The creation of the system of appellation contrôlée is usually presented as an attempt to ensure authenticity and to prevent fraud. But it owed just as much to the impetus to offer economic protection to an industry plagued by an excess of production over demand. The laws of 1905 and 1919 were intended to protect names of origin, but a side effect was that the system was taken over by inferior wines. By the 1930s, the volume of production had reached proportions that were called the "scandale des appellations d'origine." "The appellation no longer guarantees anything," said Joseph Capus, the moving spirit behind the AOC system.[110] (One wonders what Capus would have said about the enormous expansion of the AOC system in the past twenty years.[111]) One of his intentions in introducing the system was to distinguish fine wines from table wines and to restrict production of wines in the system by as much as half! A major part of the argument was that the means of production should be regulated as well as the origin. The overall effect this has on quality might be debated, but the most effective aspect with regards to production levels is undoubtedly the restriction on yields. This is a significant contribution to maintaining typicity.

Today the 10,000 hectares (25,000 acres) of the Côte d'Or are divided into

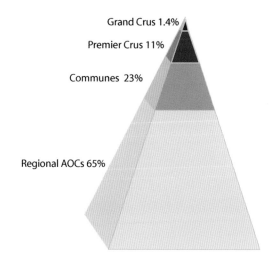

The Burgundy pyramid rises steeply from a base of regional wines to a tiny proportion of grand crus.

The top vineyards are concentrated in the Côte d'Or, which breaks down as:

AOC	hectares
grand cru	471
premier cru	1,412
village	1,939
hautes côtes	1,474
Bourgogne	4,335

Grand Crus 1.4%

Premier Crus 11%

Communes 23%

Regional AOCs 65%

27 communes, varying mostly from 100 to 300 ha. They include 375 premier crus and 32 grand crus, mostly less than 10 ha each.[112] The descriptions of land in the Côte d'Or are organized into a relatively steep pyramid, steadily narrowing from the base of two thirds of regional AOCs (such as Bourgogne) to 11% of premier crus and 1.4% of grand crus at the peak.

Before the French Revolution, most vineyards were owned by the Church or large landowners. The redistribution that followed their confiscation as "biens nationaux" triggered their subdivision. Today most premier and grand crus are split among multiple owners. Take Clos Vougeot, very large for a grand cru in Burgundy, whose 50 hectares are roughly equivalent to the average of a single Grand Cru Classé château in the Médoc. It is divided among roughly 80 growers; the largest has only 5.5 ha, and the smallest has only a few rows of vines.[113] Take Chambertin, where the largest proprietors have a couple of hectares, producing less than 10,000 bottles per year, and the holdings of the smallest proprietors are measured in ares (a hundredth of a hectare or 100 square meters), producing at most a few hundred bottles. Of course, each proprietor has other holdings, perhaps extending from generic Bourgogne in the vicinity of the village, some village AOC, and some parcels of separate premier or grand crus. But each wine has to be vinified and matured separately.

This seemingly uneconomic situation has two basic causes. The first is the highly detailed definition of terroir, intrinsic to Burgundy's form of organization. The question to be asked here, of course, is whether this genuinely represents detailed and interesting differences between vineyards, or whether it was invented as a way for the region to distinguish itself. The second cause is extrinsic, coming from French inheritance laws imposed by the Napoleonic code, which require that everything in an estate is divided equally among all the children. So a perfectly viable holding of a hectare in Burgundy may be subdivided into several uneconomic holdings of a few rows of vines each if the owner was unwise enough to have too many progeny.

The emphasis on family holdings in Burgundy means that each successive generation breaks up its already small holdings into multiple parts. Of course, sometimes holdings are united as the result of marriage, and the history is evident in the series of overlapping compound names for the producers in each village. Only the larger producers, who own vineyards across several villages, have adopted the model of the Bordeaux châteaux in turning their operations into corporations whose shares, rather than individual holdings, are distributed with an estate.[114] High inheritance taxes add to the difficulty of maintaining an estate, and contribute to the trend for domains in Burgundy or châteaux in Bordeaux to fall into the hands of larger organizations.

The diversity of ownership makes it difficult to get a bead on the supposed differences in style and quality between appellations. Suppose you want to define the difference between the adjacent communes Pauillac and St. Julien, in the Médoc. You have to account for 34 châteaux in Pauillac and 24 châteaux in St. Julien, each occupying around 35 ha, and producing on average 200,000 bottles per year. A fairly manageable situation. By contrast, if you want to compare the adjacent villages of Chambolle Musigny and Morey St. Denis on the Côte de Nuits, each less than 10% of the size of either of the communes in the Médoc, you have to identify wines from 58 growers in Chambolle and 29 growers in Morey, each producing a variety of bottlings from village wine, premier crus, and grand crus, with an average bottling of no more than a few thousand bottles at most. There might well be 500 different bottlings between the two villages. And the permutations multiply rapidly if you want to understand all the villages or the differences between the premier crus in a village.

Within the appellation hierarchy, the differences between village, premier cru, and grand cru wines are intricately connected with yields. This is one of the thorniest issues in wine production. There is a common belief that low yields are associated with higher quality. That is one of the reasons why production is prized from vieilles vignes (old vines): when they become sufficiently old, production decreases. The theory is that a vine puts a certain amount of energy into producing berries. At lower yields, the vine puts the same amount of energy into a smaller number of berries, which therefore have more concentrated juice, and correspondingly make better wine. There's no doubt that very high yields give wines with a dilute quality, but it's less clear just how much is gained at lower levels by continuing to reduce the yield.

Yield is usually measured as the amount of juice produced from a given area, expressed as hectoliters/hectare in Europe.* It might be more significant to look at the amount of juice or weight of berries produced by each vine, but that would be difficult to measure in practice. Yields are tightly regulated in Burgundy, as indeed everywhere in the AOC system in France. The principle is that as vineyards are classified at higher levels in the appellation hierarchy, they are restricted to producing lower yields. In Burgundy, the nominal limits for red wines are 55 hl/ha for generic or regional Bourgogne, 40 hl/ha for village wines and premier crus, and 35-37 hl/ha for grand crus. (Values are slightly higher for white wines.) Yield limits are the same for generic and regional Bourgogne—basically anything with "Bourgogne AOC" on the label can be up to 55 hl/ha. Curiously, village wines are not distinguished from premier crus, both coming in at 40 hl/ha for reds, although

---

* A hectoliter is about 11 cases of wine; a hectare is 2.47 acres. In the New World, yield is more often measured as tons of berries per acre. Very roughly 1 ton/acre is about 16 hl/ha (although the ratio is a bit different for red and white wines).

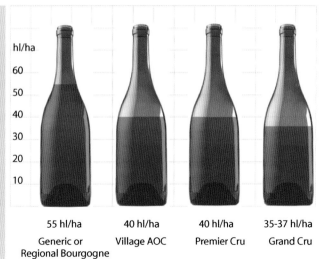

Yields decrease from Bourgogne AOC to village, premier cru, and grand cru.

The actual levels in 2008 were 52.5 hl/ha for generic Bourgogne, 54 for regional Bourgogne, 43 for village AOC and premier crus, and 34 for grand crus.

In a vineyard with 8,000 vines per hectare, a single vine would provide only 57% of a bottle of grand cru but 90% of a bottle of generic Burgundy.[116]

| 55 hl/ha | 40 hl/ha | 40 hl/ha | 35-37 hl/ha |
| Generic or Regional Bourgogne | Village AOC | Premier Cru | Grand Cru |

grand crus are lower, varying from 35 to 37 hl/ha. Yet for my money, the sharpest increase in quality level when I taste Burgundy is going from village wine to premier cru.

Is yield regulation somewhat of a self-fulfilling circle? After all, the point of better terroir is that it will produce better wines under the same conditions, so if you made wine at, say, 40 hl/ha in a village AOC, premier cru, and grand cru, shouldn't you see a steady increase in quality anyway? Well, yes and no. You would see such an increase, but the grand cru would not be as good as it would be if yields had been more restricted. Clive Coates, who knows as much as anyone about Burgundy, says flatly, "You simply cannot produce grand cru worthy of the name at 42 hl/ha, or premier cru at 48."[115] The practical issue is perhaps the reverse: the gain in quality of premier cru or village wine would not be great enough to justify the economic loss involved in bringing down the yields to the same limits as the grand cru.

The importance of yield is recognized everywhere quality wine is produced. Clones or rootstocks are selected for an appropriate level of vigor, pruning to control the number of shoots is de rigeur, "green harvest" to remove excess bunches is used controversially later in the season. (It's controversial because some people believe that late pruning causes the plant to compensate by increasing the size of the remaining berries.) Of course, it's one thing to reduce yields on the principle that this will improve quality, but it's another matter to ensure your yields fall exactly below the legal limit: a miscalculation in which the actual yield is too high means that berries can be used only up to the limit, so even if a village wine is made at the limit of 40 hl/ha, actual yield on the vine could have been greater, with the difference being lost on the sorting table, rather than reflected in the glass.

Yields on the Côte d'Or have increased steadily over the past fifty years.[118]

This is the average of village, premier cru, and grand crus in the Côte d'Or. It is higher for Burgundy as a whole, with a range up to 60 hl/ha in the past decade.[119]

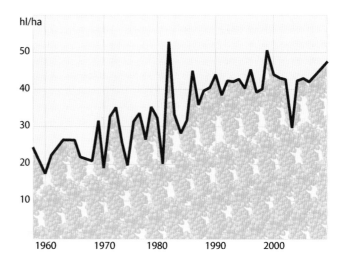

What effect does yield have on the typicity of Pinot Noir? Are the effects more pronounced than with other varieties, such as Cabernet Sauvignon? Certainly there's a view that Cabernet does not need such low yields. "It's not that you don't produce fine wines with 20-25 hl/ha, but it's not necessary, at least in Bordeaux... A low yield in a well-maintained vineyard with homogenous production of 40 or 45 hl/ha with old vines is perfect," says Jean-Michel Cazes of Château Lynch Bages in Bordeaux.[117] Cabernet Sauvignon may retain its character better over a wider range of yields, whereas Pinot Noir tends to lose its typicity at high yields. This raises the question of what has happened to typicity in Burgundy with the general increase in yields that has occurred over the past fifty years.

When yields were around 20 hl/ha in the first half of the twentieth century, the low levels were partly due to a series of poor vintages, and no doubt also due to a large proportion of diseased vines that were under-producing; the steady increase to around 40 hl/ha represents better management of vines in better condition. Improvements in viticulture have narrowed the range between poor and good vintages, with yields swinging from 20 hl/ha to 35 hl/ha in the 1970s, but showing more consistency since 1990.[120] But if yield continues to increase, will it reach a point at which typicity is lost?

It's a loaded question because the reality of yields in Burgundy as a whole is somewhat distant from the myth of tight regulation to ensure quality. Originally the limits applied to labeling rather than production.[121] In the infamous "cascade" system, if you actually produced 60 hl/ha in a grand cru, you could label wine as the grand cru until you reached the 35 hl/ha limit. The rest of the production could still be sold, but had to be labeled according to the limits for lower-level appellations. You might label the next 5 hl/ha as village wine, to bring you to a village limit of 40 hl/ha, the next 10 hl/ha as Bourgogne AOC to bring you to the limit of 50 hl/ha for the region, and then the rest would have to be sold outside the AOC. So there could be a whole range of bottles, labeled from Vin de Table to Grand Cru Burgundy, but all containing exactly the same wine.

The authorities came to their senses in 1974 and changed the rules so that the limits actually applied to production: in a grand cru with a limit of 35 hl/ha, you could only produce that much. But in case that was too onerous, they increased the limits. The normal yield limit, which is quoted as indicating the quality of the particular AOC, is called the rendement de base (base yield). But the limit could be increased in any particular year by (nominally) up to 20%. This is the PLC (plafond limite de classification). In theory, this is intended to allow a response to the particular conditions of the year, for example, allowing an increase in good years that produce high yields. However, this is a rule honored more in the breach than the observance. INAO set the PLC at 20% (and occasionally even higher) irrespective of vintage conditions. In effect, grand crus are habitually allowed to produce at levels that would be appropriate for premier crus, premier crus are allowed to produce at limits that would be appropriate for village wine, village wines have limits more appropriate for the region, and as for the region—well let's say we are approaching the point at which you ask about loss of typicity.

Only once in an entire decade was the actual yield in Burgundy remotely close to the rendement de base. That was 2003, when the excessively hot vintage conditions caused the vines effectively to shut down. In most years, production was slightly above even the maximum 120% level. From 1998-2000, the excess was closer to 30%. And there can be no excuse that the high yields relate to vintage conditions; there is absolutely no correlation between the permitted increase and the quality of the vintage.[122]

The system changed again in 2004 by introducing the notion of variation around an average based on a decade for the Côte d'Or. The rendement de base has been replaced by the RMD (rendement moyen décennal), a ten year average. Yields can be varied up or down by 3 hl/ha each year, provided that the rolling ten year average is within the limit. The RMD levels are around 35-37 hl/ha for the grand crus, 40-45 hl/ha for premier crus and village wines, and 55 hl/ha for regional wine, so the system is starting off on the high side.[123] Whether it will stem the seemingly inexorable rise in yields remains to be seen.

One of the big issues in making red wine is always the size of the berries. As they become larger, the ratio of skin area to volume of juice decreases, so extraction of color and tannins is reduced. As vintage variation demonstrates, local conditions obviously have a big effect, but the starting point in setting the basic characteristics is with the choice of plants. A major emphasis in selecting plants—whether as clones or by selection massale—is for low yields with relatively small berries. This gives more concentrated juice and a better

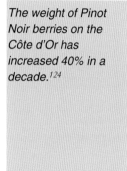

The weight of Pinot Noir berries on the Côte d'Or has increased 40% in a decade.[124]

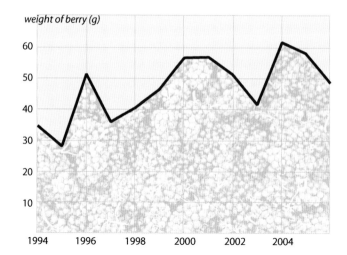

ratio of skin to juice. One of the laments about the use of Pinot Droit in the sixties and seventies is how its large berries led to less concentrated wines. Yet in spite of this history, over the past decade the size of the berry has been steadily increasing. Whatever the cause, changing the skin to juice ratio is likely to affect the style of the wine.

When Pinot Noir became established in Burgundy, it was not quite at the northern limits for successful cultivation. The boundary was really defined by Champagne, where red wine was successfully produced until the seventeenth century. Of course, once the craze for bubbles took off, there was no need to force the limits, and Champagne relinquished the crown for dry wines to Burgundy. During the nineteenth and twentieth centuries, good vintages were sporadic in Burgundy. If conditions were not quite marginal, they were certainly not reliable. Over the sixty years between the great 1945 and 2005 vintages, Clive Coates rates only 22 vintages as "very good" or better.[125] That is a fairly typical opinion; in the preceding century, roughly one vintage in three was judged to reach an acceptable standard.[126] And for every vintage that was excellent, there was one that was terrible.

It rains a lot in Burgundy. In fact, I remember so many rainy days driving up and down the N74 that it's hard to believe total rainfall is only around the 700 mm per year that the grapevine needs. The rainfall is distributed throughout the year, usually heaviest in May and June, but sometimes can be a problem around harvest time. In terms of its destructive potential, how-ever, hail can be even worse. If hail occurs during the growing season, berries are irretrievably damaged to the point where just a few of them can give the wine a sour, rotten taste that makes it undrinkable. (This ruined the 1983 vintage, when many wines developed a taste of rot within a few years.) After a series of severe thunderstorms in 1900 and 1901, vignerons were so des-perate that giant cannons shooting up into the sky became widely used to try

The "canon grêlifuge" for dispersing hail was invented about 1770 in Burgundy and used in wine-producing regions. It works on the principle of firing an explosive charge of acetylene to generate a shockwave that is supposed to disrupt the hail. This photograph from Chambolle Musigny dates from 1902; Clos Vougeot can be seen in the background. Hail cannons are still manufactured today, but remain of rather doubtful efficiency.

to disperse hail on the Côte d'Or.[127] They were not terribly effective, and even today there is no really good method for avoiding hail; the one relieving feature is that it is usually quite localized. The other precipitation problem, frost, has been less common in recent years as global warming has taken hold.

Climate change is not a new issue in Burgundy. In 1855, Lavalle asked whether the climate had changed on the Côte d'Or since Roman times.[128] He concluded there had not been much change, at least not since the fourteenth century when the harvests may have been a few days earlier on average.[129] But in the past two decades, global warming has come to the Côte d'Or as to everywhere else. Since the 1980s, the average temperature during the growing season (April-September) has risen by 1 °C, more than the average historic difference between Burgundy and Bordeaux, well to the south. This means the average in Burgundy today is higher than the average was in Bordeaux in the 1970s! In fact, if you look at the average temperature during the *best* vintages of the 1960s-1970s, it was around 16.25 °C in Burgundy and 16.75 °C in Bordeaux. The strength of the warming trend is indicated by the fact that both regions have now risen to *averages* above these levels. To be sure,

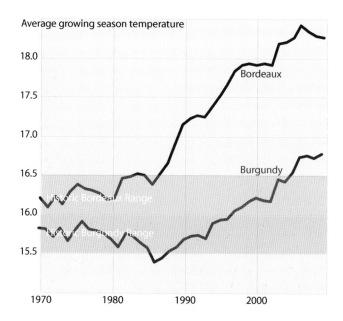

Temperatures have increased steadily in Burgundy since the 1980s. The average temperature in Burgundy during the growing season is now above the average for Bordeaux in the 1970s. (Average temperatures in Bordeaux today are above those of the Rhône in the 1970s.)[130]

other factors, such as the timing of rainfall, mean that not all vintages now are good: but the proportion of good vintages is increasing. Certainly no one has suggested that Burgundy should grow Cabernet Sauvignon instead of Pinot Noir, but you have to ask what effect these steadily increasing temperatures are having on the typicity of Pinot Noir.

Global warming is an issue everywhere wine is produced, and the effects on growth of grapevines in Burgundy have been quite dramatic. The common trend is that the whole season is advanced and shortened: bud break (when the first new shoots begin to push out of the stems) is earlier, and harvests have become increasingly earlier. In France as a whole over the past 50 years, bud break has advanced by 5 days, and harvest has advanced by 17 days.[131] In Burgundy, the average for harvest dates in the past 50 years is earlier than at any time since 1370;[132] and the recent regression in harvest dates shows increasingly early spikes. In the exceptionally hot year of 2003, vignerons who had taken their traditional summer break in August—nothing much usually happens in the vineyard then—had to rush back to Burgundy and organize pickers for the earliest harvest on record (August 23). They started even earlier in the Beaujolais, on August 15.

(Many Burgundies of 2003 were somewhat overcooked. I used to hold tastings in which I would compare 2003 red Burgundy with Châteauneuf-du-Pape to see whether people could tell the difference blind; it was not always obvious. The unusually hot conditions also meant that differences in the appellation hierarchy did not always follow the usual relationship. Some climatologists believe that the extreme conditions of 2003 might become the average by 2050, in which case a rethinking of the appellations, not to mention whether Pinot Noir is the most appropriate choice of grape variety, might be necessary.)

The regression in harvest dates would be even greater if it were not for a competing trend: grapes are being harvested at a later stage of ripeness. This worldwide trend reflects the replacement of sugar level as the main criterion for harvest by the new idea of "phenolic ripeness." This somewhat imprecise concept means waiting until the tannins are more mature (mostly judged by tasting the grapes), rather than harvesting as soon as an acceptable sugar level is reached.[133] Later harvesting means higher sugar levels, which translate into higher alcohol levels in the wine.[134]

The trend is exacerbated when the growing season is shorter, because in these circumstances the gap widens between sugar accumulation and achieving phenolic ripeness. The heart of the problem is a discordance between sugar production and phenolic development; sugar levels respond more strongly to temperature than phenolic development.[136] The warmer (and shorter) the growing season, the faster sugar accumulates relative to phenols; so if a particular level of phenolic ripeness is the criterion for harvest, warmer conditions will give more sugar and therefore higher alcohol.[137] Seeking phenolic ripeness has previously been more of a factor in driving the trend to higher alcohol levels in warmer regions, where the growing season is generally shorter, but the effects of global warming are now making it more of an issue for cool climate varieties also.

Pinot Noir is not a variety that carries high alcohol very well—the delicacy of the fruit flavors is easily overwhelmed. This was not a problem in the historically cool conditions of Burgundy, where for more than a century it was the norm to chaptalize the must in order to bring sugar up to an acceptable level (typically around 12.5% alcohol). With Pinot Noir grown today in somewhat warmer conditions, both in Burgundy and elsewhere, and with improvements in viticulture giving better growth, the pendulum has swung to

Harvest dates have become steadily earlier in Burgundy since 1945.[135]

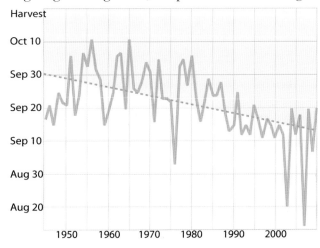

the opposite extreme; now it can be a struggle to keep alcohol levels below 14%.

What does all this do to the nature of the wine? Shorter growing seasons, with harvests prolonged as late as possible, lead to richer, more extracted, more alcoholic wines. The major factor is the effort to harvest all the grapes at "optimum" maturity. No one could quarrel with the idea that the grapes should be mature—who wants to drink green, stalky wines?—but doesn't harvesting *all* the grapes at the same stage of maturity lead to a certain lack of variety in the wine? Have we ignored something that the monks knew very well over two centuries ago? In 1763, the Abbé Tainturier of Clos Vougeot explained the advantages of blending from their various terroirs: "We need [grapes that are] cooked, roasted, and green; even this last is necessary; it improves in the cuve by fermenting with the others; it is this that brings liveliness to the wine."[138] Dom Denise punched the point home in 1779. "To make good wine in Burgundy, it is necessary to assemble together very mature berries with berries that are almost mature. Extremely mature berries give wines that are sweet and syrupy. Excess maturity is only slightly less damaging than lack of maturity."[139] Has the need for flavor variety in creating complexity been forgotten today in the stampede to harvest grapes at riper and riper levels?

Burgundy has resisted change better than other regions. Whereas the wines of Bordeaux today resemble those of Napa Valley more than they resemble Bordeaux of the 1960s or 1970s, the wines of Burgundy have retained more of their traditional characteristics. Of course, this is relative; in absolute terms, Burgundy also has changed to richer wines, more extracted with higher alcohol and less acidity, but the concept of phenolic ripeness has had less extreme effects on Pinot Noir than on Cabernet Sauvignon. Bordeaux has made a transition from flavors tinged by herbaceousness to flavors hinting of blackcurrant jam; Burgundy has shifted from one end of its vintage range to the other, but still gives the same impression of earthy strawberries or cherries. On the other hand, a herbaceous touch can be delicious on Cabernet Sauvignon, but is rarely attractive on Pinot Noir. All the same, the lack of any objective criterion for phenolic ripeness makes me wonder how far the pendulum should swing, and whether those last few days of extra ripeness really produce additional flavors that offset the gain in alcohol and the loss of acidity.

The forerunner for the modern style of vinification was Henri Jayer. Becoming a vigneron by accident when he was asked to look after the Camuzet vineyards during the second world war, he introduced new vinification methods at the end of the 1970s. Actually, destemming was not new to Burgundy, but it became a routine only as the result of Jayer's advocacy. Destemming diminishes herbaceousness, increases the fruitiness of the wine, and reduces overt impression of tannins. "Rarely ripe, the stems bring only astringent tannins. Destemming gives deeper tannins that respect the fruits. This does not harm aging," Henri Jayer said of destemming.[140] He followed total destemming by delaying the start of fermentation for a week by lowering the temperature to around 15 °C. (There's always a delay before indigenous yeast start fermentation, usually about three days, but it's prolonged by the low temperature.) "I noticed that in cold seasons, when fermentation was slow to start, the wines were fruitier. Furthermore, their color was brighter. Applying this technique to warm vintages by controlling temperature, the wines become fruity, complex, and well balanced... The berries should macerate for four to six days before starting fermentation. Contrary to some opinions, there is no need for high sulfur." If this does not sound familiar yet, it certainly will by the time we reach the New World, where destemming and cold soak are virtually de rigueur. Jayer enjoyed cult status for his wines, especially the Cros Parantoux of Vosne Romanée. You might say he was the first producer (Burgundian or otherwise) to produce Pinot Noir in what has since become the modern style. Yet he remained a traditionalist who was skeptical of excessive manipulation. "Oenologues with modern techniques produce a type of wine that is well made but without personality and with an uncertain future," he said.[141]

Hundreds of years of winemaking in Burgundy have created some degree of consensus on how to treat Pinot Noir—for example, pigeage, in which the cap is pushed down into the must, is traditional rather than pump-over, when the must is sprayed back on top—but even so, although superficial descriptions of winemaking may not vary much, there are significant differences. And fashion plays its role. In the 1980s, the oenologist Guy Accad proposed the use of extended cold maceration, in which the grapes are kept in contact with juice at low temperature for a prolonged period before fermentation is allowed to start. Essentially this prolongs Jayer's cold soak up to ten days by keeping the temperature down to 4 °C and using doses of sulfur to block fermentation. One consequence is that cultured yeast have to be added to start fermentation (because the sulfur kills the indigenous yeast). Accad's technique generates more deeply colored wines—attractive in some markets—and was highly controversial, with some critics believing it destroyed typicity, while practitioners argued that it was (finally) bringing Burgundy into the modern era. Most of the trends, including long periods of cold soak and heavy use of new oak, have come and gone.

Pinot Noir has a relatively narrowly defined range for maintaining typicity. Whereas Cabernet Sauvignon can make a recognizably Cabernet-ish wine over a wide range of yields and extraction, Pinot Noir loses character at the extremes, becoming what the Australians pejoratively call "dry red wine" at high yields, and losing delicacy and subtlety at excessively high extraction.

With Pinot Noir more than any other grape, the great need is for balance between ripeness of phenols, level of alcohol, and acidity.

Burgundy today is better than it has ever been. There are far fewer really poor vintages, and the technical quality of wines at all levels from Bourgogne to grand cru has increased. But that's not to say it is universally good. There are still producers living on their laurels, taking advantage of the appellation name without making a corresponding effort. This makes the producer's name a much bigger factor in setting price than the fabled terroir. But it's almost always true that any individual producer's grand cru will be better than his premier cru, which will be better than his village wine, and it's time to investigate just what effect terroir has on the wine.

3

The Quintessential Terroir Grape

"WE DO NOT MAKE PINOT NOIR, WE MAKE BURGUNDY." Such was the response from Burgundian producers when I said I was writing a book on Pinot Noir. When I asked about the typicity of Pinot Noir, I was gently rebuked. "In Burgundy we don't believe in typicity of Pinot Noir, we believe in typicity of place. Pinot Noir is a translator, it translates what is in the soil. It's an interpreter so the appellation takes over the variety," says Olivier Masmondet of Maison Jadot. "Pinot Noir is the cépage transparent par excellence," says Jean Lupatelli of Maison Bouchard Aîné. Aubert de Villaine of Domaine de le Romanée Conti was forthright. "The typicity of Pinot Noir first is to be Burgundian."[1]

No one expresses more clearly the view of Burgundy's primacy in Pinot Noir than Aubert. "There is a marriage here in Burgundy between a vine that has not much taste in itself, and that has been chosen for that, and which

The Côte d'Or consists of the Côte de Nuits (from Nuits St. Georges to the north) and the Côte de Beaune (from Aloxe Corton to the south).[2]

Gevrey Chambertin, Morey St. Denis, Chambolle Musigny, Vougeot, Vosne Romanée, and Nuits St. Georges are the great communes in the Côte de Nuits, all devoted to red wine.

In the Côte de Beaune, Aloxe Corton and Beaune produce more red than white, Pommard and Volnay are exclusively red, while Meursault, Puligny Montrachet, and Chassagne Montrachet are white.

The AOCs of the Hautes Côtes and Côtes de Nuits and Beaune lie on either side of the line of communes.

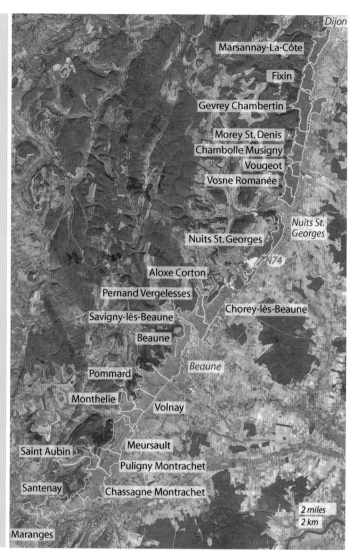

reflects the place it comes from. We had the recognition of terroir, that the wines of each place are different, and that one place makes a better wine than another. For this we need a translator [an interpreter] that expresses the specificity of the place, and Pinot Noir is the grape that does this," he says.

Terroir is a controversial concept in the world of wine, and nowhere is the issue more precisely framed than in Burgundy. Local legend holds that the Cistercian monks tasted the soil to try to understand the differences between their terroirs. (If they did, this would have left them more puzzled than enlightened, since there is no evidence that components of the soil directly relate to flavors in wine.)

Every plot of land is classified in a hierarchy ranging from generic Bourgogne, through the broad appellations of the Côtes de Nuits and Côtes de

Beaune, to the famous communes and their premier and grand crus. Classification reaches its apotheosis in the vineyards of the Côte d'Or, that narrow strip of land extending from Dijon to just south of Beaune. Less than 30 miles long and a mile wide, its 10,000 hectares are divided into some 500 different appellations. There is a world of difference between a red Burgundy from a regional appellation, coming from vineyards to one side or the other of the fabled strip, and wine from the premier or grand crus at the heart of the slope. But it's a much sharper question how and why character changes between vineyards at the very highest levels. Does variation in the terroirs of the premier and grand crus really produce distinctive characters in each of their wines? And are such differences equally clear for village wines made from larger areas, such as the "masculine" Vosne Romanée and the "feminine" Chambolle Musigny? Would the vineyards of the Côte d'Or display characteristics of terroir for any grape variety or do they reflect a unique match between terroir and Pinot Noir?

"Côte d'Or" is translated literally as "slope of gold," but for all its fame, the exact derivation is unknown. Until the eighteenth century, the vineyards were simply known as La Côte or La Bonne Côte. When France was divided into Départements after the Revolution, a parliamentary deputy from Dijon suggested that the Département should be named after the vineyards as the Côte d'Or.[3] It is unclear whether this was based on an abbreviation for Côte d'Orient, meaning a slope facing east,[4] or could be taken as an ironic reference to the fame of the vineyards. Whatever its origins, this was the beginning of a folkloric movement that has served Burgundy well.

The Côte d'Or is a narrow escarpment running roughly south to north, with hills sharply defining its western boundary. All the great names of Burgundy are here, with a group of appellations devoted to red wine in the northern half, the Côte de Nuits, and both red and white wine produced in the southern half, the Côte de Beaune. (Until the nineteenth century, the part to the north of Chambolle Musigny was distinguished as the Côte de Dijon.) Along the Côte d'Or much is made of the intricate variations in terroir, but the common feature giving the region its general character is its gentle slope and the south-east exposure. The N74 (Route Nationale 74) is the famous dividing line, recently renamed the D974 in a fit of mad French bureaucracy. Entirely unaware of the bureaucrats' lack of romance, the locals still call the quality line the N74.

To the east the land is much flatter. The Côte de Nuits is quite narrow; at some points, the band of vineyards is only a couple of hundred meters deep; even at its widest it is not much more than a kilometer. The Côte de Beaune sprawls out more widely around Beaune. North of Beaune, there's a less constricted feeling if you go out to Savigny-lès-Beaune or Chorey-lès-Beaune, the satellite regions to the west and east of the Côte d'Or. South of Beaune the land opens out more to the west, and the slope of the Côte d'Or can be much broader. Keep going south, and after a break of woods and pastures, you come to the Côte Chalonnaise.

Burgundy is the land of faults; a myriad of small faults cause the underlying geological structure to change rapidly. But the major defining geological feature is the Saône fault, the large fault running along the side of the Côte d'Or.[5] The N74 pretty much marks the line. To the north of Nuits St. Georges, the Saône fault is just to the east of the road, and to the south it is just to the west. The road crosses back over the fault around Beaune. To the west of the fault the terroir is based on variations of limestone, ranging from white limestone at the top of the slope to crinoidal (ochre-colored) limestone at the bottom. There is also some marl (a mixture of clay and shale). Chardonnay tends to be planted on the soils that are richer in marl, Pinot Noir on the most active limestone. To the east of the fault, the soils are deeper and richer, having filled in to some depth when the fault collapsed, and the water table is higher (increasing fertility of the vines).

Two geographical axes impact the wine. Going up the N74 from the Côte de Beaune in the southern part to the Côte de Nuits in the northern half, the wines become firmer, less earthy, perhaps even a touch more austere, although each commune is different. And going across the slope from the N74 at the bottom to the woods at the top, the highest quality is found in the middle. Position on the slope is the main determinant of level in the classification hierarchy, with the upper middle considered to produce the best wine. Vineyards at the very top and bottom of the slope are classified for village wines (those on the other side of the N74 are classified only as regional). The premier and grand crus occupy the center of the slope (with the grand crus for red wine concentrated towards the north).

The effect of the slope is due to a mixture of having the most consistent drainage together with the best exposure to the sun. The climate in Burgundy historically has been marginal for ripening Pinot Noir. The key to quality in a marginal climate is always which sites ripen best. When the relationships between the village vineyards, premier crus, and grand crus were defined,

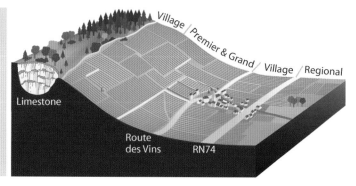

The best terroir lies in the middle of the slope along the Côte d'Or.

The grand crus have an elevation of 250-300 m.

Illustration from École des Vins de Bourgogne / L. Groffier.

those in mid-slope had an advantage and became the premier and grand crus. Will this remain true if global warming continues? So far, the rising tide has lifted all boats, but there may come a point when the relationship changes.

One view of terroir, held especially in the New World, is that it's mostly a matter of drainage. The water supply is a major determinant of whether the vine puts its energy into vegetative growth or into ripening berries. A situation in which the vine has deep roots makes for a more even supply of water, and a reduction in the supply after véraison encourages ripening. The combination of aspect and drainage can explain much of the superiority of the middle of the slope compared to the top or bottom. But can ripening alone explain the detailed classification? How are we to account for the differences between villages: why is Volnay more refined than Pommard, why is Chambolle Musigny more delicate, Nuits St. Georges sturdier, Vosne Romanée so precise, Gevrey Chambertin tighter? Is this due to physical or chemical properties of the soil—or are traditions of winemaking in each village a contributory factor? Is there any better way to seek the typicity of Pinot Noir than to travel up the N74 searching out the wines of each commune?

To the south of Beaune, red and white wines are about equally represented. Today the communes Chassagne Montrachet and Puligny

The greatest white wines in Burgundy come from the slope above the village of Chassagne Montrachet, with Le Montrachet sandwiched in mid slope between Bâtard Montrachet and Chevalier Montrachet. Montrachet became the form of the name in 1473, preceded by Mont Rachet, Mont Raschat, and Mont Rachaz.[6]

Montrachet are almost exclusively white, with the great grand crus centered on Le Montrachet at their intersection. Thinking about the infinitely subtle matches of terroir and cépage in Burgundy, you will no doubt ask what is special about this land. The short answer is that no one really knows. The marl and limestone mix is well suited to Chardonnay, and certainly there are differences between the vineyards. Going up the slope, the soil changes from 20% clay and 80% pebbles at the bottom to 50% clay and 50% pebbles at the top,[7] but the key features are probably the aspect and drainage.

More to the point, however, is the fact that Puligny and Chassagne's reputation for white wines is relatively recent. In the eighteenth century, red wine from the Morgeots vineyard in Chassagne Montrachet sold for twice the price of the white Le Montrachet.[8] Even as recently as 1939, when his vineyard Les Blanchots Dessus in Chassagne Montrachet was classified as premier cru, vigneron Jules Morey said, "Why bother? It's only white wine," when it was suggested that he should appeal for promotion to grand cru status.[9] In the mid nineteenth century, most of Puligny Montrachet was

The Clos des Mouches at the southern boundary of the Beaune appellation is one of the few premier crus where both red and white wines are produced. However, there is now a trend to replant with Chardonnay, although Drouhin, who own more than half of the 25 hectares in the cru, continue to grow equal proportions of Pinot Noir and Chardonnay. Chanson, who own 4.5 ha, also have both varieties. The terroir varies from rockier soil at the top to limestone and marl in the center, but is not related to the relative locations of the grape varieties. Photograph kindly provided by Maison Drouhin.

planted with Gamay; the best parts were divided between Pinot Noir and Chardonnay, with the reds and whites having roughly equal reputations, although admittedly today's grand crus were already acknowledged as nonpareil for white wine.[10] Chassagne Montrachet was almost exclusively devoted to red wine.[11] The third of today's white wine communes, Meursault, was divided about equally between red and white.[12] So does today's concentration on white wine in these communes owe more to fashion than to matching cépages to terroir?

Fashions certainly swing one way and then the other. We might look at premier cru Clos des Mouches in Beaune, which grows both Pinot Noir and Chardonnay. One knowledgeable commentator stated confidently at an MW seminar that the white grapes are planted on a streak of limestone running through the vineyard. But when I asked Philippe Drouhin, in charge of Joseph Drouhin's famous vineyard in the Clos des Mouches, about this, he was puzzled. Drouhin is maintaining its traditional balance between red and white in the vineyard, he told me, but he fears they may soon be the only producer left for red Clos des Mouches, as most producers are replanting with Chardonnay, which is cheaper to handle and produces more. "The reds and whites are more or less planted in alternating bands, there really isn't any distinction according to the terroir. It is more a commercial matter in response to market demand," he said.[13]

White wine is also prominent in the most northern commune of the Côte de Beaune, where a single grand cru (although with several individually named *climats*) occupies the hill of Corton. The largest grand cru in Burgundy, it occupies 160 ha altogether. Proportions devoted to red and white production have changed dramatically. Most of the white is called Corton Charlemagne, but in addition there is some Corton Blanc produced elsewhere in the grand cru. Most of the area of Corton Charlemagne is on the end of the hill facing southwest. Emperor Charlemagne owned vineyards on

The hill of Corton has vineyards all up the slope, with the Forêt de Corton at the summit giving an impression of a topknot. Parallel with the N74, Le Corton lies at the top of the slope to the right. Corton Charlemagne occupies the south-facing slope as the hill turns around at the left.

the hill, but whether or not he had anything to do with the development of white wine at the time, by the early nineteenth century it was known more for red Corton.[14] At mid century, white wine was being made from a 16 ha area described as Le Charlemagne on the upper slopes,[15] but most white grapevines had been replaced by black.[16] The focus on red wine production changed to white during the twentieth century, and today some 72 ha are classified for the white Corton Charlemagne.[17]

The hill is based on a substratum of limestone, but there is a difference in the topsoil going up the slope, from more iron and pebbles lower down (thought to be better suited to Pinot Noir) to higher clay content at the top. Going round the hill towards Pernand Vergelesses, there is more flint in the soil, giving more austerity to the white wine (and creating difficulties for black grapes in ripening.) But here as elsewhere, market forces push growers to replant with Chardonnay when vineyards come up for renewal.[18]

Volnay and Pommard are the southernmost regions for the top red wines, but although they are adjacent, the communes have different styles. Volnay is the epitome of elegance, with precisely delineated red fruit flavors that at their best have a remarkable crystalline quality. Pommard has softer, more lush fruits, often considered to be a touch rustic. Just to the north of these communes, Beaune itself is somewhere between in styles, but much harder to pin down because it is so large and the quality is so disparate. What is responsible for the difference between the elegance of Volnay and the opulence of Pommard?

Volnay is one of the smaller communes; perhaps that is why there is more consistency to style and quality. Volnay sits on a limestone base, with some variety in the types of limestone, but the base is generally light in color and relatively crumbly. The best wines come from the southern end, where the top premier crus of Caillerets, Taillepieds, and Clos des Chênes are located. At the northern boundary, Volnay joins Pommard, where the limestone-based soils have more clay. Pommard has more "active limestone,"[19] which interacts with the clay. This is stated to give the wines of Pommard their sturdier character. There's also more iron in Pommard, due to ferrous oxide in the soil. Volnay has finer tannins compared to Pommard. Benjamin Leroux of Comte Armand says that the differences in extraction are quite evident when you make the wine. "With Volnay the tannins are extracted slowly and tend to come at the end of fermentation. You don't have to look for extraction in Pommard, it is there straight away, because the tannins come at the beginning."[20]

It's really a mistake to think that because red Burgundy is based on one grape, no *assemblage* is involved. Blending is not as complicated as, for example, in Bordeaux, where the proportion of each variety may change significantly according to the vintage, but there is so much variation in the

Clos des Epeneaux is a monopole owned by Comte Armand, at the junction of Grands and Petits Epenots. It is surrounded by a wall built when both Epenots had only a single owner, soon after the French Revolution.

Burgundian terroir that even plots close to one another may give quite distinct wines. As most growers do not have large contiguous plots, even when a wine comes from a single appellation, it may involve blending from areas within the appellation that have different characteristics. When the appellation is (relatively) large, and the plots are distant, the wines may be quite distinct before they are blended.

The Clos des Epeneaux in Pommard is a good example. Within the walled area of only 5 ha, there is significant variation in the soil. The topsoil is deeper right at the top of the Clos and at the bottom, with 60-80 cms resting on fragmented rocks. In the middle, the topsoil is shallower with only 20 cms of depth, sitting on a horizontal stones and a compact bedrock. A tasting of barrel samples from the 2009 vintage with Benjamin Leroux at Comte Armand showed its complexity in the form of differences from wines coming from different parts of the Clos and from vines of different ages.

From a plot just below the top, the wine from 25 year old vines gives an immediate sensation of ripe, rich, red fruits with some sturdy support. From another plot with the same geology but with 55 year old vines, there is more concentration, black fruits showing as much as red, dense on the palate, with ripe and supple tannins. There is a touch of extra everything. From younger vines on a lower part of the Clos, the wine is softer, less powerful, more elegant, more resembling Volnay. And then from fifty year old vines on the lower terroir, there is more obvious fruit and greater depth, a more precise edge, more minerality and tautness. And an assemblage somehow brings the fruits out more clearly on the palate and you see the extra complexity that comes from the combination. "Terroir is not only a function of geology, it is the mix of vineyards," says Benjamin Leroux.

Immediately to the north of Pommard lies Beaune, quite different in character. The large overall size of the Beaune appellation, the large number of premier crus, and the fact that they represent three quarters of its surface, makes for what might kindly be described as variability in quality. (Personally I would demote several of the premier crus, and judging from the low prices they fetch, the market agrees with me.[21]) The effects of terroir are made clear by the very different characteristics of two of the top premier crus, Clos des Mouches and Grèves, almost at opposite extremes of the appellation of Beaune. At the southern point of Beaune, at the boundary with Pommard, the Clos des Mouches tends to be calcareous, with significant variation in the depth of the soil. Terraces face from east to southeast and are relatively breezy. Two kilometers to the north, Grèves is more east facing, with a steep slope; the soil is clay and limestone, shallow with lots of stones and there is often a water deficit. (Grèves is local dialect, equivalent to Graves in Bordeaux, meaning stony.) There is lots of iron in the soil. Drouhin's vineyards in the two crus are tended in the same manner and the wines are made in exactly the same way, but the differences in soil and exposure create two very different wines, Clos des Mouches lighter with more aromatics and finesse, Grèves sturdier with firmer tannins and structure. As a side by side tasting through the vintages shows, the difference remains reliable through both warm and cool vintages and over time (Y page 104). The stylistic difference goes beyond effects of ripeness per se into the character of the wine.

Moving through Beaune and Corton, both red and white wine are produced at levels varying from village through premier cru to the grand cru of Corton (this last being rather a mixed bag where the reds are concerned). The east-facing slopes looking down on the N74 are the best locations in Corton for Pinot Noir, but quality is variable, and the wines can lack generosity. Coming down into the premier crus and village wines of Aloxe Corton, perhaps the wine tends to be a bit sturdier than that of Beaune, but personally I do not think it has the same interest as wines from the Côte de Nuits.

Extending from Premeaux to Fixin, the Côte de Nuits is devoted to reds. The exclusive focus of the Côte de Nuits on Pinot Noir is a relatively recent phenomenon (which means a century or so in the context of Burgundy). In the early nineteenth century, white wines from Clos Vougeot and Le Chambertin were regarded on a par with Le Montrachet.[22] Today there is not much white wine left. De Vogüé makes a famous Musigny Blanc; Domaine de la Vougeraie make a white premier cru from the Clos Blanc de Vougeot; there is also a little white Morey St. Denis, among which Ponsot's Mont St. Luisants (Aligoté rather than Chardonnay) stands out; and Gouges makes some Pinot Blanc from Nuits St. Georges Les Perrières. But with a few exceptions, the Côte de Nuits is Pinot Noir country.

The Côte de Nuits has a line of premier and grand crus along the middle of the slope.

Gevrey Chambertin

Morey St. Denis

Chambolle Musigny

Flagey Echézeaux

Grand Cru

Premier Cru

Vosne Romanee

Vougeot

Village AOC

Nuits St. Georges

Premeaux

1 mile

1 km

The emphasis on nuances of terroir sharpens on the Côte de Nuits. In the major communes (Nuits St. Georges, Vosne Romanée, Flagey-Echézeaux/Vougeot, Chambolle Musigny, Morey St. Denis, and Gevrey Chambertin), there are 125 premier crus and 23 grand crus.[23] The grand crus start with La Tâche in Vosne Romanée and go all the way up to the stretch of Chambertin and Clos de Bèze. (Corton is the only grand cru for red wine south of Vosne Romanée.) If you are looking for the ultimate expression of Pinot Noir in Burgundy, this is where you will find it; and this is the place to try to define that indefinable quality that lifts a wine from premier to grand cru.

The arrières-pays (the backwoods) are omnipresent all along the Côte de Nuits. At the narrow stretch at the southern tip of Premeaux, they loom over the monopole of the Clos de la Maréchale, where the vineyards are only a couple of hundred meters wide. Here is an interesting opportunity to look directly at the influence of the winemaker. The Clos de la Maréchale has belonged to Domaine Mugnier since 1902, but for 53 years from 1950 was cultivated under a "fermage" contract by Faiveley. A common type of arrangement in Burgundy, fermage is a long term contract in which the land is rented to a farmer, who takes all responsibility for its maintenance and production. When the contract came to an end in 2003, the vineyard reverted to Mugnier.

So up to 2003, the wines were made by Faiveley; for subsequent vintages, they have been made from the same vines by Mugnier. When Frédéric Mugnier took over the Clos de la Maréchale, he changed the method of pruning and the way of working the soil. And he changed some of the plantings to introduce white grapes. He was encouraged by tasting some white wines made in the Clos in the 1930s-1940s, which he thought were so remarkable it was worth reintroducing. The soil in the most northern part has less iron and is lighter in color. Pinot Noir did not do very well there and Frédéric thinks it is better suited to Chardonnay. He field-grafted Chardonnay in order to keep the old roots, and has made a white Clos de la Maréchale from it since 2005. In addition, he has introduced a second wine, called the Clos des Fourches, after the name the vineyard had until the late nineteenth century. The wine is made on the basis of a selection, representing up to a third of production from those cuvées that don't fit the profile of Clos de la Maréchale itself. It's intended to be lighter and pleasant to drink more or less immediately, and is labeled as an AOC Nuits St. Georges.

So Mugnier's Clos de la Maréchale is made from a slightly reduced terroir compared to Faiveley's, but the change in style goes beyond that. Faiveley's Clos de la Maréchale always had that slightly four-square quality that is often found in Nuits St. Georges; Mugnier's has something of the same elegance that characterizes Chambolle Musigny. This is perhaps a comparison of extremes between Faiveley's forceful, not to say aggressive, style, and Mugnier's delicacy. It is hardly surprising that such different approaches to winemaking should produce very different results (Ⓣ page 106). Yet the terroir shows through with the wines from either Mugnier or Faiveley. Faiveley's Clos de la Maréchale was always softer compared, for example, to their

The Clos de la Maréchale in Premeaux, just south of Nuits St. Georges, is one of the narrowest points in the Côte d'Or, only a couple of hundred meters wide. Consisting of 9.76 ha, it is the largest monopole on the Côte d'Or. The average age of the vines in 2010 was about 46 years. The vineyard was under contract to Maison Faiveley until November 1, 2003, when it reverted to Domaine Mugnier.

Gevrey Chambertin. Mugnier's Clos de la Maréchale is always sturdier compared to his Chambolle Musigny. It's somewhat as though the whole spectrum has been shifted from one producer to the other, but the relative place of Clos de la Maréchale within that spectrum remains the same.

When you compare Mugnier's Clos de la Maréchale with his Chambolle Musigny, immediately you see a common style. The wines are fine and elegant, with an underlying opulence. All Mugnier wines, from village to grand cru, are made in the same way, using 15-20% new oak. "I don't have a very romantic idea of winemaking," says Frédéric Mugnier. "It's not a creative process. The creation is done by nature. I'm just in charge of providing the proper environment for the grapes to transform themselves into wine."[24] Until he regained Clos de la Maréchale, he had made wine only in Chambolle Musigny, where his other vineyards are located. "Some people say it's a Nuits St. Georges made in a Chambolle Musigny style," says Frédéric ruefully.[25] But while Mugnier's Clos de la Maréchale shows a similar style to his Chambolle Musigny, the Chambolle is yet more elegant, with more precise fruits and sharply delineated flavors. Mugnier's Clos de la Maréchale is certainly in a lighter style than many Nuits St. Georges (where there is perhaps a tendency to high extraction), but the tannins are more obvious than in his Chambolle

The appellation of Nuits St. Georges is divided into three parts. Premeaux is at the southern tip (at the beginning of the Côte de Nuits). The rest of the appellation is divided into two parts by the town itself, the largest between Beaune and Dijon. There are 37 premier crus, forming a band along the middle of the slope, except at the very narrow southern end where they fill the whole width. The premier crus occupy 143 ha; the village AOC has another 175 ha.

Vosne Romanée

Damodes
Boudots
Au Cras
La Richemone
Murgers
Chaignots
Vignerondes
Bousselots
Araillas

N74

Nuits St. Georges

Rue de Chaux
Le Procès
Pruliers

Roncière

Poirets
Perrières

Cailles

Les St. Georges

Didiers

Forêts

Corvées

Argillères
Premaux
Clos Arlot
Clos de la
Maréchale

Nuits St. Georges AOC

Premier Cru

500m

Musigny, and the finish is drier. The difference in tannic structure is more evident than any difference in the fruits; here is the reflection of terroir. The Chambolle Musigny usually has less concentration than the Clos de la Maréchale, but then of course we are comparing a village wine (albeit a very fine one) with a premier cru.

The Clos des Fourches is less sophisticated and less complex than Clos de la Maréchale. Does it actually express the true typicity of Nuits St Georges better than the more elegant Clos de la Maréchale? Does Mugnier's Clos de la Maréchale owe as much to selection as to terroir? You would certainly pick out Mugnier's Clos de la Maréchale and Chambolle Musigny in a blind tasting as coming from the same hand, but you would be unlikely to identify Faiveley's Clos de la Maréchale as coming from the same vineyard. And there's the rub: if vines in the Clos de la Maréchale can give Nuits St. Georges style for Faiveley and Chambolle style for Mugnier, what price terroir?

Nuits St. Georges has something of a split personality. Starting with the Clos de la Maréchale monopole, the southern part of Premeaux gives lighter wines than the more northern parts of Nuits St. Georges. Together with Clos de la Maréchale, another monopole, Clos Arlot, stands out at the southern end. Immediately to the north of Premeaux comes the main sweep of premier crus and village wines, starting with Les St. Georges, the best premier cru in Nuits St. Georges, sometimes mentioned as a possible candidate for promotion. (When the grand crus were defined, Pierre Gouges refused to have Les St. Georges considered, on the grounds that this would "create inequalities."[26]) The mixture of clay and limestone along this stretch makes this the best part of Nuits St. Georges. The wines can be rich and structured, but even here they rarely achieve the finesse and silkiness of, say, Vosne Romanée. Perhaps there is too much clay in the soil.

The two major parts of the commune are separated by the gentrified village of Nuits St. Georges itself—quite changed over the past decade from a shabby town to one with an extensive pedestrian precinct where parking is restricted to the outskirts. The rest of the appellation lies to the north of the town, with the best premier cru in this part, Les Boudots, adjacent to Vosne Romanée. Clive Coates reports that a series of tastings failed to reveal any palpable connection between the styles of the wines and a geological survey of the wide variety of soil types.[27] Indeed, the size and variability makes it difficult to draw a clear bead on Nuits St. Georges. It's sometimes said that the most common feature is a certain four-square quality, a lack of the refinement, breed, and tightness that you see farther north.

Immediately to the north of Nuits St. Georges, Vosne Romanée is the epitome of refinement. To understand the basis for the difference between the—let's say robust rather than rustic—reputation of Nuits St. Georges and the aristocratic refinement of Vosne Romanée, I turned to producers who make wines from both appellations. Immediately I met an interesting response from Jean-Nicholas Méo of Domaine Méo-Camuzet. "The case you would like to discuss isn't necessarily the most typical, because our Vosne is well structured and our Nuits St. Georges is more feminine, the inverse therefore of the reputation of each village."[28] Indeed, a comparison of Méo-Camuzet's village wines showed the Nuits St Georges, which comes from a parcel right at the junction of Nuits St. Georges and Vosne Romanée, to be round, soft, and supple, while the Vosne Romanée, which largely comes from a cooler location up the hill, had good structure with something of the solidity of Nuits St. Georges (ϒ page 109). The contrast between two premier crus, Boudots from Nuits St. Georges and Chaumes from Vosne Romanée, which touch at their corners, was even more striking. The Boudots showed elegant, precise fruits, while the Chaumes was firmer and more structured. This may not be a completely fair comparison, because unusually some whole clusters were used in the Chaumes in this vintage—but this is at the least a provocative demonstration of the effects of winemaking decisions on apparent characteristics of terroir.

A new generation of enthusiastic winemakers are steadily changing the view of Nuits St. Georges. "The reputation of Nuits St. Georges for rusticity is largely undeserved," says Jean-Nicolas Méo,[29] although he admits that perhaps the classification is a little too generous with some of the premier crus, which still give traditional robustness. A revealing comment about traditional attitudes came from a visit to Domaine Arnoux-Lachaux, which as Domaine Robert Arnoux used to make robust Nuits St. Georges and powerful Vosne Romanée. Today run by son-in-law Pascal Lachaux, the aim is to produce elegant wines. Tasting his 2009 premier cru Clos des Corvées Pagets from Nuits St. Georges, Pascal Lachaux commented, "This is not typical Nuits St. Georges, it is too elegant."[30] Admittedly, this wine comes from a patch of lighter soil in the area of Premeaux. Together these tastings forcefully made the case that each lieu-dit gives distinctive results (as influenced by the winemaker), but the old generalizations of village character don't necessarily apply.

The vineyards of Vosne Romanée are at the heart of the Côte de Nuits. "There are no ordinary wines in Vosne," said a French historian dryly in the eighteenth century.[31] And indeed this is the location of the most fabled wine of all, Romanée Conti, a monopole of the Domaine de la Romanée Conti. Standing at the top of the slope of grand crus overlooking the town of Vosne Romanée, Aubert de Villaine of DRC pointed out to me the locations of the grand crus. Just below us, stretching down to the cross at the bottom is La Tâche. To its left, presently being replanted, is La Grand Rue. Beyond, also in the middle of the slope, with the same exposition but slightly less incline, is Romanée Conti itself. Beyond is Richebourg. Romanée Conti, Aubert de

Romanée Conti lies at the heart of the great slope of grand crus overlooking the village of Vosne Romanée. La Tâche is immediately above the village, Romanée Conti is farther north east, Richebourg is above Romanée Conti, and Romanée St. Vivant is below it. All around the grand crus are premier crus.

Villaine explains, has the most homogeneous terroir of all, whereas La Tâche has five or six different soil types going up the slope, with slightly more variation in its exposition. At the edge of Richebourg, part of the vineyard has lain fallow for two years and it will not be replanted for another three. The vines had not been of good enough quality, and in spite of all efforts it had not been possible to include the wine in Richebourg. Beyond the holdings of DRC, in the distance to the east were more premier and grand crus, and then, in the far distance, Musigny. Above us was Les Champs Perdrix. Quite a panorama of grand crus, with Romanée Conti right at the heart of them.

By general acclamation, Vosne Romanée is the best village on the Côte. It's usually considered together with Flagey-Echézeaux, because with the exception of the grand crus Echézeaux and Grands Echézeaux, the wines of Flagey-Echézeaux are labeled as Vosne Romanée premier crus. The questionable case of Echézeaux accounts for more than half of the 75 ha of grand crus, but there is no doubt about the quality of the rest. Four of them are monopoles, most famously Romanée Conti and La Tâche owned by the Domaine de la Romanée Conti, the others being La Romanée (owned by Liger-Belair)[32] and La Grande Rue (owned by François Lamarche, and having the unusual distinction of being promoted from premier to grand cru in 1992)[33]. So here, without the complication of multiple ownership, you get a clear view of each grand cru through the vintages. The other grand crus all have many producers. Richebourg is widely acknowledged to be the best cru after the monopoles, Romanée St. Vivant to be the most delicate and elegant, with Grands Echézeaux in third place. The reputations of Richebourg and Romanée St. Vivant are not hurt by the fact that their largest proprietors are

The village of Vosne Romanée is at the center of the Côte de Nuits. Seen from the heights to the west (in the foreground), the village lies between the premier and grand crus, and the N74 and the plain to the east (in the background).

the Domaine de la Romanée Conti and Domaine Leroy (generally acknowledged to be the best producers in Burgundy).

To the north lie Chambolle Musigny and Morey St. Denis, the lightest wines on the Côte de Nuits. Chambolle Musigny is often said to produce the most elegant wines, with a delicate floral edge: they are sometimes described as feminine. At its southern end is the great grand cru Le Musigny, just on the west side of Clos Vougeot. At its north end, Bonnes Mares runs into the group of grand crus in Morey St. Denis, where Clos de la Roche usually has the edge over Clos St. Denis. Les Amoureuses, the best premier cru in Chambolle, is often judged to be of grand cru quality; often more expensive than most grand crus, it would very likely be promoted in the unlikely event of a reclassification.[34]

Only a couple of miles apart as the crow flies, Vosne Romanée and Chambolle Musigny are poles apart in terms of style, and a tasting at Louis Jadot to compare two of their premier crus made a forceful point about the effect of climate on style (Ⴒ page 110). At the center of Vosne Romanée, adjacent to the grand crus Richebourg and Romanée St. Vivant, Les Suchots showed the typical firm but silky structure of the appellation from the barrel samples of 2009 to the 1996 vintage. Les Baudes, a premier cru in Chambolle Musigny, was lighter in each vintage, showing more elegance and less power, a typical feminine contrast to the more masculine Suchots (although Les Baudes is one of the firmer wines in Chambolle). Certainly rising temperatures lift all fruits, and the differences were less obvious in warmer vintages, such as 2005, than in cooler vintages, such as 2006. But when we got back to the unusually hot vintage of 2003, the tables turned. Here the tannins in Les Suchots seemed more four-square, bringing a touch of rusticity to the wine. Les Baudes showed greater opulence than usual, but retained its silky mineral quality. Whereas in other vintages I had placed the Suchots equal or ahead of the Baudes, in 2003 it clearly seemed to offer a lesser experience. Since the worst projections for global warming suggest that the conditions of 2003 may be typical by 2050, does this suggest a potential realignment of the relationships between appellations?

So why are the wines of Chambolle Musigny noted for their fragrance and delicacy? The story is that the soils are marked by a high proportion of active limestone (which decreases acidity in the soil) and a low proportion of clay. The generally light and pebbly soils make for lightness in the wine. Yet commenting on this long-established quality in 1831, Dr Morelot remarked, "The finesse does not come only from the excellence of the soils...but from the inclusion of a certain amount of white grapes."[35] If the style was in fact created by the negociants of the nineteenth century, to what extent has it been perpetuated by traditions of winemaking?

The coherence of each appellation is diminished by the small size of today's average vineyard holding, which divides production among many individual producers. Now an integral feature of Burgundian production, this situation arose from the seizure of the large holdings of the Church and major landowners after the French Revolution. Napoleonic law for estate inheritance subsequently forced redistribution of the land with every generation. The consequences of this "morcelization" are nowhere better illustrated than in the history of Clos Vougeot, the famous grand cru at one time belonging to the Abbaye de Cîteaux.

The Abbaye de Cîteaux had its origins in 1098, when dissatisfied by the lack of rigeur at the Benedictine monastery near Chablis, Robert de Molesmes left with a group of twenty monks to found a new abbey at Saint-Nicolas-lès-Cîteaux, a few kilometers to the east of Nuits St. Georges. The region was already quite extensively planted with vineyards, and by Christmas of that year, the new monastery acquired its first vines, in the form of the gift of a vineyard at Meursault, from the Duke of Burgundy.[36] Over the following centuries, the monks received more gifts of vineyards and other lands. Their holdings extended from Meursault in the south to Chenôve, close to Dijon, and were supplemented by purchases and exchanges.[37]

Initially the monks produced wine solely for their own consumption, but by 1160-1180 they had started to produce wine commercially.[38] Viticulture became an important part of their activities. There were ups and downs over the centuries, and at times the Cistercians had to sell vineyards to meet their obligations; in the sixteenth century they sold their holdings in Pommard, and in the seventeenth century their domain at Aloxe-Corton.[39] Nonetheless, at the time of the French Revolution, when the assets of the monasteries were confiscated as "biens nationaux," the Abbaye de Cîteaux was still a huge landholder on the Côte d'Or.[40] The Abbaye held 10,000 hectares of land altogether;[41] its vineyards were included in the 1,361 ha of vines that were seized in the Revolution (almost 10% of the total vineyards of the Department of the Côte d'Or!), with Clos Vougeot as the jewel in the crown.

The acquisition that led to the creation of Clos Vougeot was a gift of 9 ha in 1109.[42] Over the next two centuries more land was donated or purchased, some as existing vineyards, some as raw terrain that the monks planted with

The château at Clos Vougeot stands at the northwest corner of the clos. Part dates from the middle ages, but it is no longer used to make wine. It is now the headquarters of the Confrérie des Chevaliers du Tastevin, which in spite of its medieval robes was formed in 1934 as part of the folkloric movement to promote Burgundy.

vines. By the early thirteenth century there were references to a "clausum" or "clos,"[43] and the wall was built to enclose an area of 50 ha by 1336.[44] It's not known how the exact contour of the Clos was decided, since the monks owned other adjacent vineyards that were not included. Certainly it was not on the basis of homogeneity of terroir, since the Clos is in fact extremely variable in its constitution.

A substantial cellar was built in the Clos towards the end of the twelfth century.[45] The splendid château that now stands in the center of the Clos mostly dates from a reconstruction and expansion in the eighteenth century.[46] Following their seizure in the French Revolution, the château and the Clos were sold together with the nearby Seigneurie of Gilly at a sale in Dijon in 1791.[47] By 1818, Clos Vougeot had passed to the ownership of Jules Ouvrard in what was widely recognized to be a money laundering operation.[48] Ouvrard and his successors hung on to Clos Vougeot until 1889, a full century after the Revolution, when the vineyards were divided between fifteen vignerons and negociants.[49] The "morcelization" of the Clos had started. Today there are around eighty individual proprietors. The château itself was purchased in 1946 by the Confrérie des Chevaliers du Tastevin, an organization formed in the 1930s to promote Burgundy. Members of the Confrérie hold rather splendid dinners in the château each month.

One wonders what politics were involved in making the whole of Clos Vougeot a grand cru. The monks were well aware of the differences among *climats* within the Clos, especially with regards to where the vines ripened best. (A current map of the Clos recognizes 16 different *climats* by name, although their identities are not usually allowed on the label.[50] This is virtually a repetition of the sixteenth century map.) But the main determinant of quality is simply position on the slope. By 1816, it was recognized by commentators that "vines in the highest part give a fine and delicate wine; the lower parts, especially those close to the road, give much inferior wine."[51] (Dr. Morelot reported in his book of 1831 that the monks used to make three cuvées. The best, from the top, was not sold but was kept as the reserve of the abbey; with some hyperbole, Dr. Morelot said it was reserved for crowned heads and princes.[52] The second, from the middle, was almost as good and was sold at high price. The third, from the bottom, was somewhat cheaper.[53]) In fact, Clos Vougeot extends across the Saône fault, so it is only the terroir in the upper half that has the characteristic limestone base of the Côte d'Or; the terroir at the lower part is more like the land that usually lies on the other side of the N74. Indeed, when the official map was prepared in 1861, a proposal to divide Clos Vougeot into two parts, "tête de cuvée" for the best and "première cuvée" for the rest, was defeated by the proprietor.[54] So the Clos remained unified on the maps, and in due course became the biggest discrepancy in the AOC.

*Maps show three eras
of Clos Vougeot.
Initially it was a single
entity, although lieu-
dits were recognized
within it (and from time
to time some of them
were rented out by the
Abbaye). It survived
the French Revolution
intact, but in 1889 was
divided into plots
(following the old lieu-
dits) that were sold off
separately. Further
division followed, until
today it has about a
hundred recognized
plots divided among
almost as many
proprietors.*

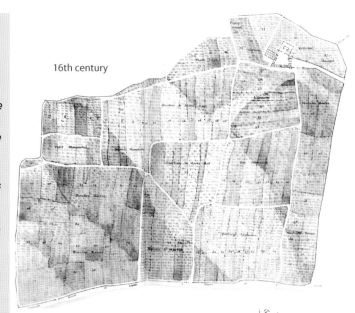

16th century

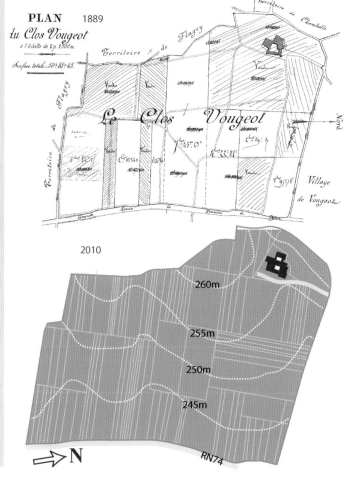

PLAN   1889
du Clos Vougeot

2010

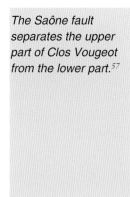

The Saône fault separates the upper part of Clos Vougeot from the lower part.[57]

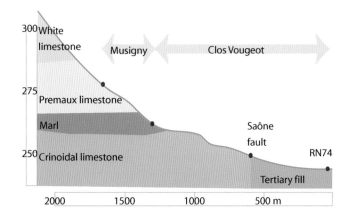

A few growers have more than one plot in the Clos, so tasting barrel samples before the assemblage allows you to see the differences directly. Although there is a consensus that the middle is best, this is not an infallible guide given the variations in style and quality between producers. Yet other factors can also come into play. Drouhin has two plots, and as Stephen Skelton MW remarks, "The lower plot is planted with the slope—north-south—whereas the upper plot is planted east-west because the plot is very narrow in the north-south direction. Even though they are in all other aspects the same, this difference in row orientation accounts for the different style of the individual wines—an argument that the soil and the site (terroir?) is not perhaps as important as the viticulture!"[55]

Immediately adjacent to Clos Vougeot, Echézeaux is the next largest grand cru, with more than 36 ha. It is similarly variable and may have even less claim to be treated as a single area of grand cru quality. Echézeaux is a relatively modern concept, going back to the first definition of grand crus in 1925, when a lawsuit was brought to prevent the use of Echézeaux to describe wines that did not come from the climat Echézeaux du Dessus (an area of only 3.5 ha). The loss of the lawsuit allowed Echézeaux to be used for a much wider area, and the grand cru was finally defined as including eleven *climats* in the vicinity.[56]

Basically the court recognized prior abuse of the geographical description as a precedent for the future![58] In previous classifications, several of the *climats* had been placed one level lower. Many people believe that much of this area does not live up to grand cru status. It's an indication of Echézeaux's reputation that it used to be sold as Vosne Romanée premier cru.[59] (There is, however, no question about the grand cru status of Grands Echézeaux, a much smaller area of 9 ha, which lies between Echézeaux and Clos Vougeot. The original distinction between Grands Echézeaux and Echézeaux may have been no more than that very long rows ran continuously, and those at the far end were known as Grands Echézeaux.)

The central part of the Côte de Nuits, stretching from Vosne Romanée to Vougeot, has the top grand crus of Romanée Conti, La Tâche, Richebourg, and Romanée St Vivant, as well as the most questionable grand crus, Clos Vougeot and Echézeaux.

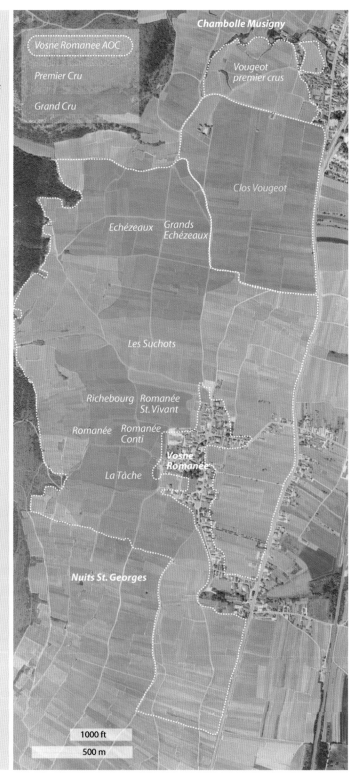

Chambolle Musigny

Vosne Romanée AOC

Premier Cru

Grand Cru

Vougeot premier crus

Clos Vougeot

Echézeaux   Grands Echézeaux

Les Suchots

Richebourg   Romanée St. Vivant

Romanée   Romanée Conti

Vosne Romanée

La Tâche

Nuits St. Georges

1000 ft

500 m

Clos Vougeot and Echézeaux together total 86 ha, almost a fifth of the 471 total hectares of grand crus on the Côte d'Or. Couple this with the 160 ha of Corton, a rather sprawling grand cru with a variety of *climats* of varying quality,[60] and this is not a very impressive start to viewing classification as a guide to the quality of terroir. Excluding these large areas, it's fair to say, however, that the rest of the grand crus, varying in size from under 1 ha to almost 20 ha, consistently produce the very finest Burgundy (with the addition of a couple of under-classified premier crus).

Returning to the nineteenth century, when most wines were bottled under fairly general geographical descriptions, the main determinant of typicity was as much the negociant as the place.[61] The formation of the Appellation Contrôlée in 1935 was the decisive moment in establishing the primacy of place rather than marque. Yet the argument as to whether winemaker style triumphs over terroir persists to this day. Indeed, one of the common criticisms of the large negociants is that their house style tends to be more noticeable in the wines than the nuances of place. Refuting the argument, Olivier Masmondet of Maison Jadot says, "The style of the house does show past terroir, but this is just as true of small producers as the large negociants." It's just that when a producer only has a few wines, the differences between them may be more evident than the similarities. Indeed, you could find half a dozen "minimalist" producers in, say, Chambolle Musigny, all claiming to allow the grapes to speak clearly in the wine, and yet every one of their village wines will be different. The key thing is not so much whether styles are distinct from producer to producer as to whether their wines show relative differences reflecting each individual terroir.

As the largest commune on the Côte d'Or, and with vineyards extending from village level (and including as a rarity some on the "wrong" side of the N74) to premier and grand crus, Gevrey Chambertin offers fruitful ground for investigating terroir. (Some of the vineyards to the east of the N74 included in the original appellation in 1936 were removed in 1964 as the result of action from the vignerons of Gevrey Chambertin who felt they were not of sufficient quality.[62]) Among the vineyards presently included to the east of the N74, the Clos de la Justice is an exception that is sometimes felt to offer wines above the usual village level.

Vineyards in the village appellation extend from the N74 up to the premier and grand crus, which fall into two stretches. To the south of Gevrey Chambertin, running almost uninterrupted from the town to the boundary with Morey St. Denis, is the lineup of grand crus. The grand crus run continuously along the upper edge of the slope, with Chambertin and Clos de Bèze at their center. Just below them on the slope is a second line of vineyards, with Charmes, Griotte, and Chapelle Chambertin immediately below Chambertin and Clos de Bèze, giving way to premier crus to the north. Then

The northernmost part of the Côte de Nuits stretches from Chambolle Musigny to Gevrey Chambertin.

Chambolle Musigny produces the most elegant wines and has grand crus at both ends of the appellation, with the southernmost Le Musigny adjacent to Clos Vougeot, and the northernmost Bonnes Mares adjacent to the grand crus of Morey St. Denis.

Gevrey Chambertin, which is harder-edged, has a set of grand crus in a contiguous group to the south of the town, with the greatest of all, Chambertin and Clos de Bèze, at the center. A group of premier crus lies to the west of the town. It is the only appellation of the Côte d'Or to have extensive vineyards on the eastern side of the N74.

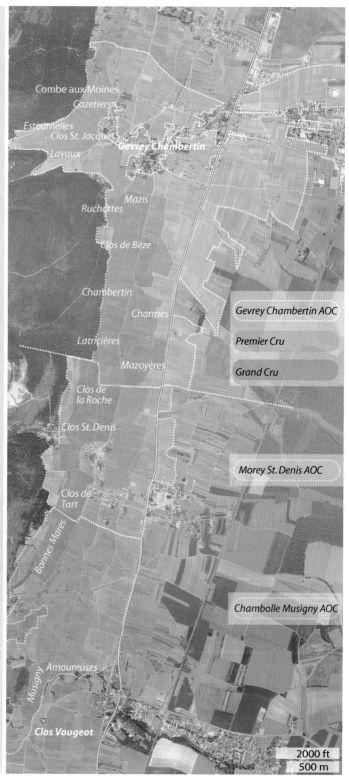

Gevrey Chambertin AOC

Premier Cru

Grand Cru

Morey St. Denis AOC

Chambolle Musigny AOC

Combe aux Moines
Gazetiers
Estournelles
Clos St. Jacques
Gevrey Chambertin
Lavaux
Mazis
Ruchottes
Clos de Bèze
Chambertin
Charmes
Latricières
Mazoyères
Clos de la Roche
Clos St. Denis
Clos de Tart
Bonnes Mares
Musigny
Amoureuses
Clos Vougeot

2000 ft
500 m

beyond the town itself, running around the edge of the hill to the west, is a sweep of premier crus, including Lavaux St. Jacques, Estournelles St. Jacques, and Clos St. Jacques, with Les Cazetiers and Combe aux Moines to their north.

Although immediately adjacent, Les Cazetiers and Combe aux Moines are distinctively different. Combe aux Moines has a cooler exposure because it faces more to the north than Cazetiers, which faces more east. This difference is accentuated by the fact that Cazetiers extends farther down the slope and so has slightly lower average elevation. Also this means that at the bottom of the slope the soil is a bit deeper (and may be a fraction darker in color than Combe aux Moines). Ripening is slightly slower in Combe aux Moines, which harvests two days later than Cazetiers, but the difference in the berries is not in the sugar levels, it is in the maturity of the skins. As a side by side comparison of Faiveley's Cazetiers and Combe aux Moines made clear, a difference in the wines is consistent over decades (and survives changes in winemaking style). The comparison is compelling because the vineyard plots, about 2 ha in Les Cazetiers and 1 ha in Combe aux Moines, are contiguous; "The tractor doesn't stop," says Jérôme Flous of Maison Faiveley. The vines are about the same average age, and they are tended, and the two wines are vinified, in exactly the same way. The difference is due essentially to sunlight exposure; phenolic ripeness doesn't quite catch up in Combe aux Moines. Yet the impression is not simply that Cazetiers is a riper wine than Combe aux Moines; Cazetiers always has a finer impression, Combe aux Moines a more four-square impression. Cazetiers offers a sense of savory minerality whereas Combe aux Moines offers more direct fruits, so the difference is as much in the spectrum of aromas and flavors as in their intensity or overt ripeness (⏵ page 111).

Clos St. Jacques, the top premier cru of Gevrey Chambertin, provides an unusually clear demonstration of the impact that producers make on terroir. Most people think that it really should be rated as a grand cru, and indeed, its price is usually at the level of the grand crus.[63] Its rating as a premier cru is a historical hazard of local politics. Dr. Lavalle rated it below only Chambertin and Clos de Bèze in 1855,[64] but at the time of classification in 1935, its owner, the Comte de Moucheron, refused to comply with the procedure and insulted the tribunal.[65] As a result, it became a premier cru, although it has a good slope with perfect southeast exposure. Clos St. Jacques was a monopole until the Moucheron family sold it in 1956 at auction, where the present five owners, Armand Rousseau, Louis Jadot, Domaine Fourrier, Domaine Bruno Clair, and Domaine Esmonin, purchased it. Unusually for Burgundy, instead of being subdivided higgledy-piggledy, each owner has a strip running from top to bottom of the Clos. There's quite a bit of variation in soil from top to bottom, but not much running from side to side, so each owner has the advantage of the same diverse soils that lend complexity. Since their plots are exactly parallel, it's reasonable to associate differences in the wines with differences in viticulture or vinification.

Tasting the wines of all five producers together, it is immediately obvious that each is different (Y page 117). The producers' distinctive styles are most evident in the youngest vintage; as the wines develop with time, the relative differences seem less evident from year to year. No one in the blind tasting could reliably identify all the individual producers in each year, so to that extent producer style does not simply over-ride vintage and terroir. But clearly there is no uniform expression of the terroir of Clos St. Jacques. Yet if you could compare the Clos St. Jacques of each producer with other premier or grand cru vineyards from the same producer, the same relative differences between vineyards would very likely emerge in each case. Terroir is relative rather than absolute.

Differences in the ages of the vines and viticulture do not seem to be significant (although Fourrier's vines are the oldest, dating back almost a century). The main significant difference in vinification is Sylvie Esmonin's use of whole clusters. She also uses 100% new oak, compared with 60% for

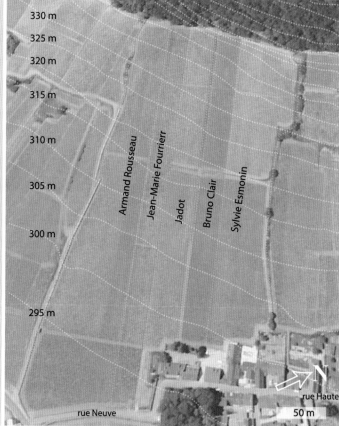

The 6.7 ha of Clos St. Jacques are divided among five owners. Each owner has a parallel strip running from top to bottom. Armand Rousseau is the largest owner with one third of the Clos.[66]

Clos St. Jacques runs right up to the woods. To the left of the wall are Estournelles and Lavaux St. Jacques, which are less protected because they are more exposed to the breeze from the Combe Lavaux as the vineyards curve around to the west.

Rousseau (but with almost complete destemming), 50% for Bruno Clair, 33% for Jadot, and less than 20% for Fourrier. Perhaps resulting from this, generally the sense of structure comes through most obviously on the wines from Clair and Esmonin, especially when young. Jadot shows their usual sweet, ripe fruits with support from firm tannins. Fourrier usually has the most precisely defined fruits. Rousseau's breadth and profundity usually make it the wine you would be most likely to recommend for promotion to Grand Cru status. Rousseau and Fourrier often vie for simply being the most drinkable.

At the very top of the hierarchy, only the grand crus of Gevrey Chambertin, notably Le Chambertin itself and Clos de Bèze, challenge those of Vosne Romanée for leadership. Chambertin and Clos de Bèze have historically been set apart from all the other crus of Gevrey Chambertin, but the distinction between them has not always been clear. The name of Chambertin became better known to the point at which few wines were labeled as Clos de Bèze during the eighteenth or nineteenth centuries; almost all were simply described as Chambertin.[67] (Chambertin is supposed to have been Napoleon's favorite wine.) When the crus were defined for the appellation contrôlée

Chambertin and Clos de Bèze are intimately connected. Wine made in Clos de Bèze can also be labeled as Chambertin. Chambertin has been known by its present name since 1276, deriving from Champs de Bertin (the fields of Bertin, an early proprietor). Clos de Bèze takes its name from the Abbaye de Bèze, which was given the vineyard by the Duke of Burgundy in 630.

system in 1930, a committee was formed to defend Chambertin's position against encroachment from other potential grand crus. Ultimately it was decided that only crus touching the stretch from Chambertin to Clos de Bèze were allowed to append Chambertin to the vineyard name.[68] (This set a precedent that was followed a few years later when Montrachet was classified.[69]) Clos de Bèze itself could be sold under its own name, as Chambertin, or as Chambertin – Clos de Bèze. A claim for Clos St. Jacques to be allowed to call itself Côte St. Jacques Chambertin was rejected. The basis for these decisions lay in local history and politics rather than tasting the wines. Historical use of descriptions was more important than geology.[70]

Until the start of the twentieth century, the reputation of Le Chambertin was more or less level pegging with Romanée Conti. One reason why Romanée Conti and La Tâche are now far ahead may be their status as monopoles; under the aegis of the Domaine de la Romanée Conti, their quality has been consistently at the top. Divided among many growers, by contrast, Chambertin's quality is far more variable. And no proprietor single-handed can define its quality and character. This is bound to diffuse reputation. Le Chambertin makes a fascinating contrast with the adjacent Clos de Bèze. Usually Le Chambertin has the edge when aficionados argue about their relative merits, although there are some who give the candle to Clos de Bèze on the grounds that it can be bottled as Chambertin, where Chambertin can only be bottled under its own name. This, however, is a mere historical accident and has no real implication about the wines. (But it can complicate efforts to understand differences between these grand crus by tasting the wines, because some wines labeled as Chambertin may come from plots in Clos de Bèze.)

Pinning down the distinctions between these vineyards, lying along the same slope with little superficial difference between them, is an exercise to question the reality of terroir. When I tramped over the vineyards with Françoise Vannier-Petit, a geologist who is making a study of the terroir of Gevrey Chambertin, she explained to me that the general geology, slope, and elevation are similar between Chambertin and Clos de Bèze. The upper slope of both vineyards, running along the edge of the woods, is a white limestone band about 50 m wide. Down the slope, this changes to crinoidal limestone, with an ochre color that you can see in the walls of the old quarry constructed from local stones at the junction of Chambertin and Clos de Bèze.

Quarries were common in the Côte d'Or until the mid nineteenth century. This plot at the junction of Chambertin, Clos de Bèze, and Griotte Chambertin lies in the site of an old quarry; it is part of the Clos de Bèze appellation, which extends above it in the background. The walls are made from the local ochre-colored limestone that dominates the terroir of Chambertin and Clos de Bèze.

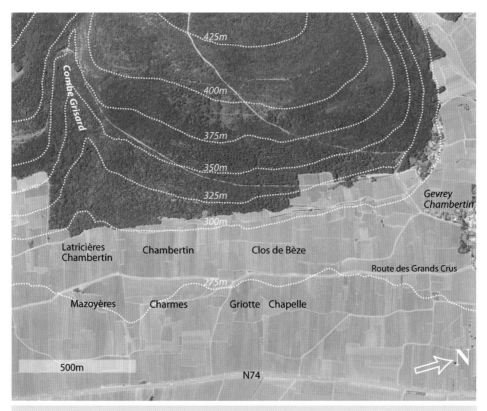

Le Chambertin is exposed to winds from the Combe Grisard, a valley running west-east between two folds of the forest, but Clos de Bèze is more protected.

The one difference in the soils between Chambertin and Clos de Bèze is that the center of Clos de Bèze is occupied by a layer of marl (a mixture of limestone and shale), rich in soft oyster shells that degrade easily. If you were defining appellations solely by geology, you might have one running along the top of the slope parallel with the woods, another in the middle of the Clos de Bèze, and a third occupying everything else down to the bottom.

In terms of climate, there is a slight difference between Chambertin and Clos de Bèze, because Chambertin is more exposed to the small valley that divides Gevrey Chambertin from Chambolle Musigny. Cold winds slide across the upper part, the Combe Grisard, and may make Le Chambertin cooler than Clos de Bèze, which is more protected. No one has actually measured any physical difference, but a telling measure is that Eric Rousseau says that Domaine Rousseau always harvest their Clos de Bèze earlier than their Chambertin; the difference may be a day or more, and varies with the year.[71] A specific difference in exposure, but one that distinguishes the top of the slope in both appellations from the lower slope, is that the vines at the very top tend to be shaded by woods, so they get a little less sunshine.

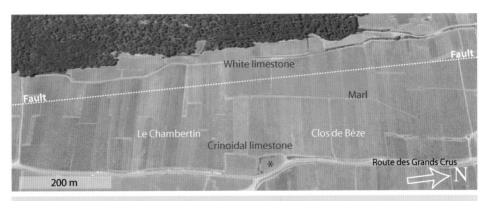

The terroirs of Chambertin and Clos de Bèze are similar except for some marl in the middle of Clos de Bèze. Above (to the west) of the fault line, there is white limestone. Below it the limestone is crinoidal. The position of the old quarry is marked by an asterisk.

So how do these factors play out in the wines? Is there really a consistent difference between Chambertin and Clos de Bèze? The comparison is complicated by the fact that few growers have both, so direct comparisons can be made only in a handful of cases. Both grand crus are broken up into many small parcels, Chambertin more so than Clos de Bèze. There are 53 different parcels in the 12.9 ha of Chambertin, and 32 different parcels in the 15.4 ha of Clos de Bèze. Armand Rousseau, the largest proprietor in Le Chambertin also has some Clos de Bèze. Pierre Damoy, the largest owner in Clos de Bèze, has four separate parcels in all parts of Clos de Bèze; he has a single parcel in Chambertin that touches his southernmost parcel in Clos de Bèze.

Damoy has such a large area of Clos de Bèze that he sells off most of his grapes. He keeps the berries from two parcels, one at the north end and the other at the extreme south next to Chambertin, and the assemblage is done before fermentation. Sometimes he produces a Vieilles Vignes cuvée, which comes from old vines in all the parcels. Rousseau has representative plots all over Le Chambertin, and two much smaller plots close to the northern and southern extremes of Clos de Bèze. All the grapes from Chambertin are assembled together for fermentation. If there's indeed a general difference between the two appellations, the wines from Damoy and Rousseau are where it will be found, so I tasted them over a series of vintages to see what differences I could detect (Ⓣ page 113).

The conventional wisdom is that, perhaps owing to its very slightly cooler location, Le Chambertin has more evident structure when young. Charles Rousseau used to say that, "Le Chambertin is masculine. It lacks a little finesse in its youth, but then rounds up. Clos de Bèze is more complex, classy, delicate."[72] Pierre Damoy says that, "Clos de Bèze is more flowery, Le Chambertin is more reserved."[73] These views were certainly borne out by the most recent vintages, when from both Pierre Damoy and Armand Rousseau,

the Clos de Bèze seemed a little fuller, richer, and more refined. The difference was most marked in 2005 where the great vintage really brought out the
extra richness of Close de Bèze. Going back in time, the relationship slowly
reverses. Somewhere beyond ten years of age, Chambertin seems to pull
ahead in sheer elegance. By twenty years, with the 1990 vintage, Rousseau's
Chambertin showed an ethereal elegance that Clos de Bèze could not equal.

Comparing vintages, you get the impression that Chambertin has the advantage in the riper vintages, when its fruits take on a delicious ripeness, but
that in cooler vintages the best balance is obtained by Clos de Bèze. Yet
every vintage is distinct: in both Jadot and Rousseau's wines in the 1996
vintage, the hard acidity of the vintage was more clearly evident in the Clos
de Bèze. What was crystal clear from the tasting was that for each producer
the Chambertin and Clos de Bèze were quite distinct wines in each vintage.
What is less clear is whether this is really an attribute of each appellation or
due more to the individual plots owned by the producer. Pierre Damoy says
that it's like night and day if you compare the berries from his adjacent plots
in Clos de Bèze and Chambertin.[74] I suspect that you might see just as much
variation in the wines if they were made separately from the two plots at the
extremes of Clos de Bèze. Indeed, I am inclined to the view that there is a
continuum of differences all along the stretch of the two appellations, and
that the differences you will see in the wines depend on the individual micro-
plots. Yes, terroir and climate are crucial determinants, but no, they are not
tightly defined by an arbitrary line between the two appellations.

People who are intimately acquainted with Chambertin and Clos de Bèze
are sometimes a bit dismissive of the other grand crus of Gevrey Chambertin. Personally, I think this is somewhat snobbish: there are some terrific
wines from the other Chambertins. Just below Chambertin and Clos de Bèze,
a little lower on the slope, are Griotte Chambertin and Chapelle Chambertin,
another interesting pair with terroir differences that are not obvious. Laurent
Ponsot has plots in both vineyards, planted around twenty years ago with the
same selection of clones. The plots are about 300 m apart, and there is little
superficial difference between them; Griotte has a slightly steeper slope with
a little more variation in the depth of the topsoil. The vineyards are usually
harvested one day apart. Whether the vintage has been warm or cool, the
difference between them has been consistent from year to year. Chapelle is
always more concentrated, with deeper color and more backbone. Over two
decades' span, with very different vintages, to me the fruits always seem
better rounded and the tannins more supple in the Chapelle Chambertin
(𝖸 page 116). Laurent says that when you empty out the vats after fermentation, there's more impression of kirsch from the Griotte and redcurrants
from the Chapelle. The cause of the difference between the wines is not at all
obvious, but as they are treated identically and matured only in old oak, what

else can it represent but a difference in the fruits resulting from some barely perceptible change in terroir?

Comparisons between appellations are complicated by the fact that each producer is different, with changes in viticulture and vinification overlaid on differences between the terroirs. And comparisons between producers are complicated by the fact that no two terroirs are identical: given the rapidity with which the ground changes in Burgundy—"Everything is chaotic here, it changes every 20 m," says Benjamin Leroux of Comte Armand in Pommard—even comparisons between wines made by different producers from plots within the same appellation may owe some of their differences to terroir. But the wines of the Hospices de Beaune offer an unusual opportunity to see how much difference the élevage—the maturation of the wine after fermentation has finished—can influence its final style.

The auction at the Hospices de Beaune in November each year is at the very heart of Burgundy. Some 45 different cuvées coming from vineyards all along the Côte d'Or, many from premier or grand crus, are auctioned in barrique. For a hundred and fifty years, the prices have set the general market level for the vintage. But here is an irony. Burgundy functions on terroir, but almost all the cuvées represent blends across terroirs. Selling them under the names of historical personages from Beaune, the Hospices effectively has replaced terroir with brands. While some of them represent the amalgamation of parcels that would be too small to vinify separately—there are ten cuvées of Beaune premier cru in this category—others could be vinified under the name of the individual terroir. Take the cuvées of Corton grand crus: the Cuvée Baronne Du Baÿ comes from 0.84 ha of Clos du Roi and is labeled with the appellation, but the cuvée Charlotte Dumay is a blend from 1.69 ha of Corton Rénardes and 0.97 ha of Corton Bressandes. Does the Hospices believe more in brands or in terroir?

The vines are cultivated, and the wine is made, by the Hospices. Wine from a few parcels is actually kept back from the auction and matured and bottled by the Hospices, but everything else is sold at the auction to negociants (who buy either on their own accounts or for clients). After the auction, barrels are transferred to the purchasers, and are then matured by the individual negociants, who "bring up" the wine until it is bottled. As the wine is sold in individual barriques, it is common for one cuvée to be dispersed among several negociants, so here is an opportunity to see what difference the élevage can make.

For some years the vineyards of the Hospices were not tended as carefully as they might have been, and the winemaking was less than perfect, but the appointment of a new régisseur has led to improvements.[75] All the same, I have never been much impressed with the wines made directly by the Hospices, which tend to my mind to have a somewhat disjointed quality. Is this due to winemaking or élevage? Are those vinified by negociants better? Things are not quite so simple as they seem, because the Hospices uses three different coopers, so a purchaser who has tasted a sample from one barrique may end up owning a barrique coming from a different cooper or forest.[76] And all the barriques are new, so the wine spends at least the first four months of its life, before the barrel is transferred to its purchaser, in the new wood. At that point, the éleveur can make his own decision on whether old or new oak best suits the wine.

Charlotte Dumay is one of the larger cuvées, with around 24-32 barriques depending on the size of the vintage. It is usually sold in lots of 3-4 barrels. Some lots are sold to private buyers and so do not appear on the commercial market, but I was able to find several that had been brought up by different negociants from the 2005 vintage. I tasted these wines to see whether terroir would come through the variations in élevage, and how much difference each producer had made. The wines had been vinified by the Hospices itself, Michel Picard (a producer in Meursault, who often buys at the Hospices), Charles Thomas (part of the large negociant Moillard), and Louis Jadot (the respected major grower and negociant, who undertook the élevage for a buyer in the United States).

None of the Hospices de Beaune Cortons for 2005 reached the heights of grand cru complexity. Far and away the best was Jadot's Charlotte Dumay, a well made wine where Jadot preserved all of the fruit there was to preserve and balanced it nicely with a judicious use of oak. (But the wine shows less generosity than Jadot's own wines.) By comparison, all of the others lost some concentration in the élevage, a striking demonstration of the adage that quality can't be gained and can only be lost once the grapes have been harvested. Except for the Jadot, all tasted like negociant's wines in the old sense. I would definitely not pay a premium for the Hospices de Beaune label.

It's a common view in Burgundy that village wines, premier crus, and grand crus should be treated differently. Usually yields are lower as you ascend the hierarchy, so the wines are more concentrated. As a result, it's often felt that the higher the level of the wine, the more it will benefit from new oak. This complicates the comparison of terroir, of course, since more new oak brings more tannins to the wine. ("If you want to see terroir, you need to taste from barriques of old oak," says Benjamin Leroux of Comte Armand.) But some producers believe in treating all their wines in the same way. Jean-Marie Fourrier of Domaine Fourrier uses 20% new oak for all his cuvées, and says that anyway the new oak is more to renew the barrels than to add flavor. Frédéric Mugnier of Domaine Jacques-Frédéric Mugnier similarly uses 15-20% new oak for all his wines. "It took me years to realize that the best way to vinify the different terroirs was to make all the wines exactly the same," says Frédéric. And Laurent Ponsot of Domaine Ponsot goes to the extreme of using only old oak for all of his wines. "The new way of winemaking, especially the use of new oak, hides the terroir," he says. His barrels age from five to fifty years and are used to provide a neutral medium for élevage, no more and no less. None of these producers objected when I asked if they would describe themselves as minimalists, although Jean-Marie Fourrier prefers "biologist," Frédéric Mugnier suggested "essentialist," and Laurent Ponsot described himself as lazy, preferring to have Nature do the work.[77] Does terroir shine through their wines more clearly? I would say that at the least, their wines show purity of fruit, which is the prerequisite for displaying terroir.

At the other extreme is the use of "200% new oak" introduced by Dominique Laurent, a former pastry chef turned negociant. His technique consists of maturing the wine in new oak, and then racking it into barrels of more new oak, although he is reported to have backed off a bit as he has become more satisfied with his supply of barrels. He refused to discuss his approach, saying only, "Like any good French artisan, I have no wish let alone need to discuss Pinot Noir... My experiences and research are secret from a commercial perspective and not to be published, do you understand my position? It should be sufficient for your book to give an umpteenth comment from a more or less well judged tasting. Every time I return to the subject it's a can of worms...I have no wish to discuss a subject which has given me so much stupid criticism."[78]

I thought the most acid test of the effects of 200% oak might be include Laurent's Clos St. Jacques with the Esmonin Clos St. Jacques, as part of the tasting to see winemaking effects in Clos St. Jacques (page 117). Since Dominique Laurent obtains his grapes for Clos St. Jacques from Sylvie Esmonin, this is a direct comparison, all the more so since the Esmonin style is to use 100% new oak and whole clusters. Laurent's unique oak regime doesn't necessarily play out in the same way in every vintage. In 2002, the sheer purity and concentration of fruits shines through the obvious use of new oak; the Laurent wine was a standout. Yet in 1999, the new oak is still obtruding by pushing the fruits into the background; the fruits showed more clearly on Esmonin's wine. In 2002, Laurent's wine is not only richer and better rounded now, but it promises to last longer, whereas in 1999 there is a question as to whether and when it will come around.

Every producer has his characteristic style, but sometimes a transition occurs with a change in generations. When Erwan Faiveley took over from his father François in 2004, there was a drastic change, with a whole new winemaking team taking over. "For a long time Faiveley was famous for vins de garde for long aging, but we thought it should be possible to produce wines for aging that would be more drinkable young," says Technical Director Jérôme Flous.[79] A series of changes in winemaking basically involves gentler handling of the fruit so there is less extraction of harsh tannins, fermentation now typically lasts two weeks rather than four weeks, and the supply of barriques has been changed. Asked about the drastic nature of the change, Jérôme says it's more a reversion to the original style. Prior to 1993 the wines were not so hard, and then, perhaps to compete with Bordeaux and to appeal to American critics, Faiveley turned to a much more extracted style with more concentration. Now they are going back more to where they were. Wines will be more enjoyable young, but will they age as well? "Un vice deviens une virtue," says Jérôme Flous, taking the position that in an era when it was not possible to get ripeness and to make approachable wines, the idea of requiring aging was turned into a marketing tool. It became an excuse. "If you want to make a wine that will be beautiful for a long time, it needs to be beautiful at the beginning," he says. "It's impossible to become a good graduate if you aren't a good student."

Of course, there is more to Burgundy than the slope of the Côte de Beaune and Cote de Nuits, which amounts to about 4,000 ha. There is as much again in the surrounding areas of the Hautes Côtes de Beaune and Hautes Côtes de Nuits, not to mention the areas to the south in the Côte Chalonnaise and Mâcon.[80] But outside of the Côte d'Or, conditions are less favorable, especially for Pinot Noir; essentially the wines are similar in style but lighter, partly because aspect tends to be less favorable, partly because

The terroir of the Hauts Côtes de Nuits is different from the Côte d'Or. This view overlooks Arcenant, about 5 miles to the west of Nuits St. Georges, but separated from it by the spine of hills. Vineyards do not all have the favorable south-east exposure of the Côte d'Or and are located at various elevations and exposures on a series of hills.

there is less protection from the west wind, so ripening takes longer and is less reliable. Also, it is cooler because the vineyards are at higher elevation. The best wines approach the lighter wines of the satellite regions around Beaune. They can be good value for wines to be drunk fairly soon, but are not of much assistance in our search for the typicity of Pinot Noir.

The appellation hierarchy of the Côte d'Or conforms well overall with the potential quality of wine from each vineyard. Certainly there are some large exceptions, with Clos Vougeot, Echézeaux, and Corton often unworthy of grand cru status; and Clos St. Jacques, Les Amoureuses, and perhaps Les St. Georges, worthy of promotion from premier to grand cru. Some of the premier crus, especially those in Beaune, should be demoted. But even aside from the variability imposed by the diversity of producers, the appellations are bound to be approximations. The boundaries originated in nineteenth century patterns of land ownership rather than geological mapping of the terroir, and were further complicated by a variety of political considerations as and when the assignments were finalized (mostly tagging lesser areas on to better areas). In fact, it's amazing they have come out as well as they have.

Wines from premier and grand crus are usually labeled as such; economics (and the small plot sizes) argue against declassifying any barrels. But sometimes selection or declassification is used to maintain vineyard specificity. If a producer declassifies part of his production of a premier cru to village level, is he maintaining the quality conforming to his image of the site, or is he reducing an expression of terroir that would be purer if left intact? When a new world producer selects only the best barrels for a bottling of a single vineyard site, is he capturing the best of the terroir or the best of vinification?

Pairwise comparisons between specific premier or grand crus should convince any skeptic of terroir that consistent differences between wines from different plots are sustained over many vintages and through many producer styles. The differences extend beyond features such as ripeness of the fruits per se, which might be explained by physical features such as water or heat accumulation, or hours of sunshine exposure: they speak to the very character of the wine, the nature of its fruits, the texture of the tannins, the balance between elegance and rusticity. We know this is not due to any simple chemical features of the soil. There remain some profound features that still defy explanation for the relationship between grapevine development and the character of the site, encompassing the chemical and physical features of the ground together with its climatic exposure. The nature of this interplay may elude us, but that does not make the phenomenon any less real.

Perhaps counter-intuitively, it is less difficult to understand differences between closely located individual sites than between villages. Grapes exposed to wind, for example, develop thicker skins, so even a small difference in exposure may lead to more tannin in the wine from the windy spot. But the villages are relatively large compared to the scale on which the soil changes. Yes, there is more iron in Pommard than in Volnay, there is more active limestone in Chambolle Musigny, but there can be as much difference between wines from the ends of a village as between one village and the next. The more *calcaire* villages, such as Volnay and Chambolle Musigny, tend to make more elegant wines than the more *argile* villages, such as Pommard and Gevrey Chambertin, but I do wonder whether some part of village character is an unconscious conformity to a perceived style. Viticulture and vinification have changed enormously in the past century, but through all these changes Chambolle Musigny retains femininity compared to the masculinity of Nuits St. Georges. Has terroir expressed itself by surviving unchanged through all these changes, or have winemakers perpetuated a tradition? Will the increased pace of climate change bring all this into question? Sites that ripened best in the nineteenth or twentieth centuries may ripen too fast in the twenty first; sites that have been too cool in the past may reach perfection in the coming decades. But one thing is sure: there will continue to be differences.

Perhaps interference with winemaking is less evident in Burgundy than many areas—certainly there is less use of some of the new technologies, such as machines to remove water and concentrate the must—and the increased proportion of good vintages has helped to avoid the need to interfere in recent years. Yet even if the wine speaks more clearly and directly of the grape than elsewhere, still it speaks as much of the producer as the terroir. The producer's name remains the most important determinant of quality. But even allowing for the range of styles from minimalist to interventionist producers, and from terroirs ranging from Volnay to Gevrey Chambertin, Burgundy has a relatively restricted range of styles, with common features such as good balancing acidity and moderate alcohol (albeit higher than it used to be). Burgundy is not a region for extremes of style. To investigate just how far climate can stretch style with Pinot Noir, it is necessary to turn to more marginal climates in Europe, mostly farther north but also in the south of France. And then in the New World, we return to the question of whether Pinot Noir more reflects the natural conditions of terroir and climate or the hand of the winemaker in viticulture and vinification.

Tastings of Beaune Premier Crus

Joseph Drouhin

Joseph Drouhin started as a negociant in Beaune in 1880. When his son Maurice took over in 1918, he began the move to becoming a negociant-grower by buying vineyards in Beaune's Clos des Mouches and in Clos Vougeot. Today one of the larger negociant-growers, Drouhin remains located in its old cellars in the center of Beaune, some dating back to the twelfth or thirteenth centuries. The firm is presently run by four siblings of the fourth generation. Drouhin has also invested in Oregon, where it produces both

Pinot Noir and Chardonnay in Willamette Valley (see Chapter 5). Although Clos des Mouches was the first vineyard to be purchased when the estate was established, it took a decade for Maurice Drouhin to assemble all of the (41) parcels. Drouhin have 14 ha altogether of the total 25 ha in the appellation. Roughly half are planted with Pinot Noir and half with Chardonnay. Drouhin's parcel in the 33 ha Beaune Grèves premier cru is a contiguous single hectare. The Clos des Mouches and Grèves vineyards are planted with the same selection of clones and are tended in the same way. Spontaneous fermentation occurs in open top fermenters, and punch down or pump over is used as seems appropriate. Oak is handled lightly, almost always using less than 30% new wood. The Drouhin style is elegant. Differences between the two wines were consistent through a series of vintages; wines were tasted at Drouhin in Beaune in November 2010, except as otherwise noted.

Beaune, Clos des Mouches, 2006
Medium ruby-garnet color. Touches of earthy strawberries on an attractive nose. Lovely soft fruits on the palate, elegant balance with just a touch of minerality. Very fine, silky tannic structure. This shows the typical elegance of the appellation. *** Drink 2011-2022.

Beaune Grèves 2006
Medium ruby-garnet but a little rosier in hue than the Clos des Mouches. More closed on the nose but a sense of ripeness from red and black cherry fruits. Smooth on the palate, with firm tannins and structure, a spectrum of ripe red and black fruits, altogether firmer and sturdier than the Clos des Mouches. *** Drink 2012-2021.

Beaune, Clos des Mouches, 2005
Attractive nose of spicy red fruits, cherries tinged with strawberries. Lively red cherry fruits on the palate, somewhat primary and not at all developed yet. Fine tannins on the finish reinforce the light, precise, elegant style. Very youthful now, will benefit from another couple of years, and then slowly will mature to an elegant softness. (February 2011) *** Drink 2013-2021.

Beaune Grèves 2005
Less forthcoming on the nose than the Clos des Mouches, showing a mix of black and red cherries. Sturdier on the palate, with a nice depth to the black cherry fruits, but a slightly more four-square impression to the fruits, supported by tannins that are less fine, and showing a touch more astringency on the finish. (February 2011) ** Drink 2012-2019.

Beaune, Clos des Mouches, 2002
Classic nose of red fruits mingling with savory aromas indicating the start of development. Elegant impression on the palate, perfect balance between the developing red fruits with the supporting acidity and refined tannins. A touch of black tea shows on the finish with a suspicion of chocolate coating. Refined and harmonious as it ends its first decade; delicious now but should continue to improve and intensify for the next five years or so. A great success for the vintage. ***(*) (May 2011) Drink now-2016.

Beaune Grèves 2002
Fruits just a fraction more forward on the nose than on the Clos des Mouches, making a slightly spicy and more rustic impression. Sturdy red fruits make a fuller impression on the palate, with less overt development—just a savory tingle in the background—and overall showing more weight but less elegance. In fact, this vintage is unusually refined for Grèves, but still doesn't match the special harmony of the Clos des Mouches. (May 2011) *** Drink now-2015.

Beaune, Clos des Mouches, 2000
The lighter, cool vintage brought out the differences between Clos des Mouches and Grèves. Rosy-garnet color. Immediate whiff of developed aromas on the nose, a touch of sous bois and gunflint with hints of strawberries. Soft and elegant on the palate, the fruits now lightening up a little, and showing just a touch of development. A nice result for this more rapidly maturing vintage. ** Drink now-2018.

Beaune Grèves, 2000
Deeper color than the Clos des Mouches and more garnet in hue. More austere nose gives spicy black fruit impressions, perfume of violets, and smoke. The sense of austerity follows to the palate, where the fruits have the same density but do not have such rounded aromatics as the Clos des Mouches, and the structure is more evident with firm tannins. ** Drink now-2018.

Beaune, Clos des Mouches, 1993
Lightening color but still quite rosy hue. Some development shows as a touch of sous bois on the nose, with faint perfume underlying the sense of minerality. As always, this is a little more aromatic, and shows more finesse than the Grèves. The touch of sous bois continues on the palate of developed red fruits, more strawberry than cherry, with a touch of creaminess on the finish. *** Drink now-2014.

Beaune Grèves, 1993
Lightening color, more garnet than the Clos des Mouches. More depth to the nose but a touch of austerity on the perfume that develops in the glass. Fruits initially are more black cherries than strawberries on the palate, but they emerge slowly in the glass and become more red. Those firm supporting tannins are evident. Sturdier but less interesting than Clos des Mouches as it ages. ** Drink now-2012.

Tastings of Clos de la Maréchale

Jacques-Frédéric Mugnier

In the early nineteenth century the Mugniers developed a successful business in liqueurs in Dijon. In 1863 they purchased the Château de Chambolle Musigny, an imposing château in Chambolle Musigny at the foot of the mountain, and they acquired the vineyards that form the basis of the domain. All the vineyards were in Chambolle Musigny until their last purchase, the Clos de la Maréchale in Nuits St. Georges, in 1902. The vineyard was leased to Faiveley and reverted to Mugnier only in 2004; now it is their largest single vineyard. The vineyards are not formally organic, but there is no use of fertilizers, herbicides, or pesticides. Use of new oak is light, at 20% for all cuvées. All the wines are red, except for the white Clos de la Maréchale. Frédéric says that the 2005 was the first white wine he had made and he had to learn everything; having started by taking advice from his neighbors, he is now adjusting the style to his own taste. (My impression is that the style has become more precisely delineated as he has slowly brought to the white wine the elegance of his red wines.) Since Mugnier took over the Clos de la Maréchale in 2004, three wines have been produced: the (red) Clos de la Maréchale itself, the second wine, Clos des Fourches (produced by selection of cuves), and the white Clos de la Maréchale. Until 2003, a single wine from the Clos de la Maréchale was produced exclusively by Faiveley, which during the period after 1993 was producing wines in a highly extracted style (see Faiveley profile, page 111). The Faiveley wines in this tasting showed a tendency to density without concentration. Wines were tasted in March 2011.

Clos de la Maréchale Blanc, 2008
Fruity nose with a faint impression of oak showing more as a texture than aroma. Some notes of gunflint emerge later in the glass. A very clean linear impression on the palate, a lovely blend of mineral citrus fruits with a faintly plumper edge of peaches and cream. There are some suggestions of oak on the finish, which also shows a touch of heat. There is a faint touch of the hardness you sometimes find in whites from the Côte de Nuits, but it dissipates in the glass. This is the leanest and the most precise of the three vintages. In a blind tasting, most people would think about Puligny Montrachet. But drink it while it stays fresh. *** Drink now-2014.

Clos de la Maréchale Blanc, 2006
Initially redolent with vanillin on the nose on top of some buttery citrus notes, but calms down after a while. The palate is more subtle than the nose, with good citric fruits softened by those buttery touches on the finish. This vintage is less graceful than the 2008, and less full and ripe than the 2005. It becomes softer in the glass but never achieves the presence on the palate of either the 2008 or 2005. * Drink now-2013.

Clos de la Maréchale Blanc, 2005
This wine is a conundrum. Initially it shows more oak than either of the more recent vintages of 2008 and 2006, with strong smoke and some gunflint notes reminiscent of Puligny. You expect a steely, mineral-driven palate. But then it shows the sweetest and ripest fruits of the recent vintages, a reflection of the year, becoming soft on the finish although still initially retaining that mineral impression. In the glass it becomes softer and richer, and the vanillin comes out full force, threatening to develop into a blowsy old age. The initial delicious impression is lost. ** Drink now-2013.

Clos de la Maréchale, Jacques-Frédéric Mugnier, 2009 (barrel sample)
Even in the barrel sample, the nose reflects the house style; you see those chocolaty elegant red fruits with an impression of opulence. The underlying structure of Nuits St. Georges shows through, precise here yet with firm but supple tannins supporting red cherry fruits, then some tea-like tannins on the finish. Tannins are more obvious here than in the Chambolle Musignys, and the finish is drier. The difference in the tannic structure is more evident than any difference in the fruits. (November 2010) *** Drink 2015-2022.

Clos des Fourches, Jacques-Frédéric Mugnier, 2008
Soft, black fruit nose showing mostly as cherries. The palate fits the profile of ready to drink, with quite elegant but light fruits, showing more as red cherries, balanced acidity cutting the softness of the finish, still some tannic support, but certainly a wine to drink in the immediate future. All the same, it would show better by waiting a year. There is a touch of heat on the finish. ** Drink 2012-2016.

Clos de la Maréchale, Jacques-Frédéric Mugnier, 2008
Less showing on the nose, more restrained, a slightly stern impression biased towards red fruits. Sweet more rounded fruits on the palate showing as black cherries, generally elegant in style but darker and more concentrated than the Clos des Fourches. There are firm tannins in the background, but because the fruits are deeper and rounder, the wine will be ready to drink as soon as the Clos des Fourches, and it should have the structure to age for longer. This resembles Chambolle Musigny in its style much more clearly than does the Clos des Fourches. *** Drink 2012-2019.

Clos des Fourches, Jacques-Frédéric Mugnier, 2007
A restrained impression of red fruits on the nose with a faintly herbal quality. Sweet, ripe, soft red and black cherry fruits on the palate, some soft tannins in the background, but an impression that there isn't much stuffing or backbone, making this a wine for the shorter term. This is ready to start drinking now, with a similar flavor and aroma profile, but much less structure than Clos de la Maréchale. ** Drink now-2015.

Clos de la Maréchale, Jacques-Frédéric Mugnier, 2007
Similar ruby-garnet color to the Clos des Fourches but a touch darker. More an impression of softer, rounder, black fruits on the nose. In this vintage there is more similarity between the palates of the two labels than in 2008, but the Clos de la Maréchale is just a touch deeper on everything, showing more rounded fruits, with a fine tannic structure bringing elegance. A very fine impression of precisely delineated black fruits on the palate. Soft and furry tannins show on the finish, and the wine will benefit from another's year aging. ***(*) Drink 2012-2017.

Clos des Fourches, Jacques-Frédéric Mugnier, 2006
Medium ruby color with appearance more youthful than the 2007. A well rounded black fruit impression on the nose, which follows to sweet fruits on the palate, black and nicely rounded, with some firm tannins showing, perhaps very slightly rustic, but lending support to the fruits. Overall the flavor variety seems simpler compared to the Clos de la Maréchale. In this vintage. the difference with the Clos de la Maréchale is not so much in the lightness and approachability, but in a more rustic as opposed to elegant style. ** Drink now-2016.

Clos de la Maréchale, Jacques-Frédéric Mugnier, 2006
More depth to the nose than the Clos des Fourches, with a chocolate coating to the deep black cherry and plum fruits. The flavor profile is similar to the Clos des Fourches, following on from the nose, very harmonious and elegant. The tannins here are finer grained, giving the finish a silkier, more elegant impression. The greater finesse to the structure will support a longer aging, but there is less difference than in the younger vintages. ***(*) Drink-2018.

Chambolle Musigny, Jacques-Frédéric Mugnier, 2006
Just a touch more ruby and youthful in appearance than the Nuits St. Georges. More restrained on the nose with an impression of precise, linear black fruits in an elegant style. This impres-

sion is confirmed on the palate, where the sheer elegance of the style carries all before it. Fruits of black plums and cherries are finely delineated, with an impression of greater finesse than the Clos de la Maréchale, a clear demonstration of the differences in terroir. The finish is fine-grained and silky. Overall concentration is a little less than the Clos de la Maréchale, and the wine will not age quite as long. Right now I find the Chambolle the most complete wine, but that difference may reverse three years from now. *** Drink now-2017.

Clos de la Maréchale, Jacques-Frédéric Mugnier, 2005
Just a faint touch of development showing in orange hints on the rim. The nose much resembles the 2006, but is a touch lighter in intensity, with black cherry and plum fruits fading into a subtle chocolate coating. A very fine palate, with black cherries followed by soft tannins providing gentle support on the finish, overall a most harmonious impression. The character really comes out clearly here, reflecting the riper vintage. *** Drink now-2017.

Clos des Fourches, Jacques-Frédéric Mugnier, 2004
Restrained on the nose, slight impression of red fruits. Nicely rounded red fruits on the palate give a slightly four-square impression, with the tannins seeming just a little rustic. But the overall impression on the palate is really delicious, the wine is à point, although I would not keep it too much longer. ** Drink now-2014.

Clos de la Maréchale, Jacques-Frédéric Mugnier, 2004
A touch of chocolate on a subtle nose of black fruits. A faint herbal suspicion is all that remains of the green impression that this vintage made when it was first released. Very fine now on the palate, with black cherry fruits, hints of raspberries, and that touch of chocolate coming back on the finish, where the tannins are firm. Dryness on the finish attests to the underlying tannic structure. There is however less complexity than found in either the 2005 or 2006. *** Drink now-2016.

Chambolle Musigny, Jacques-Frédéric Mugnier, 2004
More developed nose than either of the Nuits St Georges with the first tertiary aromas just beginning to show. A very fine impression on the palate, showing the same relative difference with the Clos de la Maréchale as the 2006 vintage, just a touch less concentrated in the fruits, but a little lighter and more refined on the tannins, with notes of black tea on the finish, giving that classically elegant fine impression of Chambolle Musigny. *** Drink now-2015.

Clos de la Maréchale, Faiveley, 2003
Deep garnet color. The nose is not very forthcoming or developed at first, but shows some touches of chocolates with a suggestion of dark fruits, developing into more attractive spices. Very dense on the palate, but the tannins are rather four-square, and the dryness is carrying the palate rather than the fruits. This manages to avoid the cooked fruits of many wines from 2003, but the impression is hard rather than ripe. There's an impression of Côte de Nuits rather than Côte de Beaune but the real typicity of Nuits St Georges is not showing through. From now it will survive rather than develop. * Drink now-2012.

Clos de la Maréchale, Faiveley, 2002
Medium garnet color. There are some hints of savory notes on a rather restrained nose. Here there are clean black fruits, supported by firm tannins, but there is still a great deal of dryness on the finish, making the wine rather unapproachable. The ripeness of the year has not really come through to this wine. ** Drink now-2013.

Clos de la Maréchale, Faiveley, 2001
Medium garnet color. Restrained nose, slightly smoky, faint savory impressions of dark fruits. This seems a little thin on the palate, the fruits are over-extracted, and the tannins are taking over, the fruit aromatics are dumb. This was not a great year, and this wine is perhaps a fair expression of what happens with a relatively extracted style in a poor vintage. * Drink now-2012.

Clos de la Maréchale, Faiveley, 2000
Lightening garnet color. Quite different nose from all the younger vintages, some spices and herbal notes fading into black cherries and chocolates, then reverting to medicinal notes. The palate shows a more delicate profile than the younger vintages, better fruit aromatics, with a better balance of fruits to tannins, which are less rustic than other vintages, but there is still more tannin than the fruit can really bear. ** Drink now-2013.

Clos de la Maréchale, Faiveley, 1999
Medium garnet color shows some development. Restrained nose shows cereal and savory aromas, with some floral perfumed notes developing in the glass. This is the best balanced

wine of the Faiveley vertical, with ripe fruits showing as a mixture of cherries and strawberries, with a slightly mineral edge. Here the tannins are tamed and much better integrated than in the other vintages, showing support for the fruits without such an overt presence. There is some dryness on the sweet finish, but it is cut by some floral aromatics, and the wine has reached a good point of development, although it is unlikely to develop much further. *** Drink now-2016.

Clos de la Maréchale, Faiveley, 1995
Medium garnet color. Slightly medicinal nose. This wine is on the verge of coming around, with fruits approaching a savory spectrum, showing some aromatic complexity on the palate of developing red fruits, but the tannins remain on the rustic side, and there's bit of a challenge as to whether the fruits will outlast the tannins, as the finish is still rather dry. ** Drink now-2015.

Tastings of Nuits St. Georges and Vosne Romanée

Domaine Méo-Camuzet

This is an old domain, with holdings in Clos Vougeot (purchased by Etienne Camuzet in the 1920s in conjunction with the purchase of the château itself), Vosne Romanée, and Nuits St. Georges. Most of the estate vineyards are premier or grand crus. Production today is divided between the grapes of the domain (60%) and purchased grapes. Usually everything is destemmed and pumping over is used during fermentation. Grand crus are vinified in 100% new oak, premier crus in 60%, the village wine in 50%. The petit vins—Marsannay or Bourgogne—get 0-10%. The domain's present high reputation dates from a revival since 1988; before then the vineyards were leased out and the wines generally sold to negociants. Wines were tasted at Méo-Camuzet in May 2011.

Nuits St. Georges, 2009
This comes from a parcel in the lieu dit Au Bas de Combe, at the corner of Nuits St. Georges and Vosne Romanée. Immediately to its north is Nuits St. Georges Boudots; immediately to the east is Vosne Romanée Chaumes. The vines are fifty years old and give only 30 hl/ha. Redcurrants and red cherry fruits come up on the nose. The first impression is the fruitiness, with a slight tarriness following. There is a soft impression on the palate, not quite silky but very supple, which is typical of this parcel. The roundness of the vintage comes through, with a supple structure, but the softness goes beyond the vintage. *** Drink 2012-2017.

Vosne Romanée, 2009
This wine comes from a blend from two separate parcels. Three quarters is in a location up the slope (relatively cool because of breezes from a gap in the hills, so giving good acidity), the other quarter comes from the center of the village. The vines are over 30 years old on average. Typically the harvest is a week later than for the Nuits St. Georges village wine. The wine is typically firmer than average and ages slowly. A mix of black and red fruits shows on the nose with stern overtones and some faint hints of chocolate and mocha. The palate is rich and chocolaty and there are furry tannins on the finish. The black cherry fruits with hints of blackcurrants show good structure, with something of the solidity of Nuits St. Georges. *** Drink 2012-2018.

Vosne Romanée , Les Chaumes, 2009
Black fruit nose is quite restrained and makes an austere impression. Restrained black fruits are quite sturdy on the palate with chocolaty tannins on the finish. This is partly due to the unusual inclusion of 10-13% whole clusters in this vintage. The main impression you get at the present is really the firmness of the structure and the need for aging, which will be rewarded. *** Drink 2013-2022.

Nuits St. Georges, Les Boudots, 2009
There's a touch more intensity of black fruits on the nose here than on the adjacent Vosne Romanée Chaumes. Black cherries are accompanied by hints of blackcurrants. This is fine, elegant, and silky on the palate, with precision of fruits and purity of line. Elegant tannins show on the fine grained structure, with a light chocolate edge. Far from the robust impression of Nuits St. Georges as an appellation, more like a Vosne Romanée. ***(*) Drink 2012-2021.

Tastings of Les Suchots and Les Baudes

Louis Jadot

Maison Louis Jadot is one of the most important negociant-growers in Burgundy, with a total of 160 ha in the Côte d'Or, more than half of which are premier or grand crus. They produce more than a hundred different wines. They have also expanded significantly to the south, buying some top producers in the Beaujolais and Pouilly Fuissé. The firm originated as a negociant in 1859, and was run by the Jadot family until it was purchased by their American importer, Kobrand, in 1985. Their old cuverie in the center of Beaune was replaced by a modern cuverie on the outskirts in 1995, which was expanded further in 2010. Most (60%) of their production in the Côte d'Or is from their own vineyards, the rest from purchased grapes (on rare occasions they buy finished wine; sometimes they will exchange wine with a small grower in order to get a barrel of some specific appellation.) They work with more than 200 growers on the Côte d'Or, usually with 5 year contracts. Many growers bottle some of the production themselves and sell some grapes to Jadot. Jacques Lardière has been in charge of Jadot's winemaking since 1970 and believes in minimal intervention. "The impression that you can determine quality by controlling winemaking is crazy, you need to have the confidence to work with Nature and allow the terroir to express itself. It is man who makes the mistakes," he says. The two vineyards in this tasting represent the breadth of Jadot's reach. Les Baudes in Chambolle Musigny is part of Domaine Gagey, owned by André Gagey who is in charge of Jadot, and is managed together with Jadot's own vineyards. Les Suchots is owned by an independent grower who has a long term contract with Jadot. Bedrock and topsoil in the two vineyards are actually quite similar, although Les Baudes has more active limestone. The vines are about 38 years old in Les Baudes and may be slightly younger in Les Suchots. The wines are made in the same way. Wines were tasted at Louis Jadot in November 2010 except as noted.

Chambolle Musigny, Les Baudes, 2009 (barrel sample)
An impression of apples on the nose. Soft, opulent and chocolaty, some mocha and nuts. Soft and well rounded on the palate, with supple tannins, but acidity a touch lower than usual (a mark of the vintage). *** Drink 2013-2018.

Vosne Romanée, Les Suchots, 2009 (barrel sample)
Apples with cinnamon spice on the nose. Silky and chocolaty on the palate, long opulent black cherries supported by ripe, round tannins. Low acidity not so obvious here. *** Drink 2013-2019.

Chambolle Musigny, Les Baudes, 2008
Light nose with some red cherry fruits. Sweet ripe red cherry fruits again on the palate, supported by light and supple tannins. Good balance, soft style, the typical femininity of Chambolle. ** Drink 2012-2019.

Vosne Romanée, Les Suchots, 2008
A little more weight to the nose than the Baudes and a suspicion of earthiness. Following on to the palate are more black fruits, slightly higher acidity, and a firmer, meatier, tannic structure. ** Drink 2013-2020.

Chambolle Musigny, Les Baudes, 2007
Medium garnet color. Light red cherry fruits with a faintly savory edge on the nose. The palate follows the nose, smooth and elegant in the feminine style of Chambolle. Tannins show a light supporting structure. * Drink 2012-2017.

Vosne Romanée, Les Suchots, 2007
Medium garnet, a touch darker than the Baudes. More force here to the nose—Jacques Lardière describes it as meatier—with savory notes and hints of fresh-cut mushrooms. Fruits as much black as red on the palate, smooth, weightier and more opulent than Les Baudes. Firm tannins give a sense of underlying structure. ** Drink 2012-2018.

Chambolle Musigny, Les Baudes, 2006
Medium ruby-garnet color. Red fruit nose with some savory mineral notes. Taut, elegant fruits on the palate, with fine tannins in the background. Acidity more evident, reflecting the vintage. ** Drink 2012-2018.

Vosne Romanée, Les Suchots, 2006
Medium ruby garnet color. Black fruit nose with hints of cereal. Soft, round, opulent fruits, good body with a sense of fat and glycerin on the finish, supported by firm but supple tannins. *** Drink 2012-2020.

Chambolle Musigny, Les Baudes, 2005
A slight mineral touch to the nose, fruits tending to red cherries. Soft, nicely rounded fruits on the palate. Smoother than 2006, reflecting the vintage, the fruits are riper and rounder. But they are still taut and elegant, showing the finesse of Chambolle. Acidity is more noticeable than in the Vosne Romanée (or is allowed to show more clearly by lower fruit concentration) and lifts the fruits on the finish. ** Drink now-2016.

Vosne Romanée, Les Suchots, 2005
Red and black cherry fruits show on the nose, leading to beautifully rounded fruits on the palate, supported by balanced acidity. The black and red cherries are supported by soft and supple tannins, with that sense of silky power you find in Vosne Romanée. A soft, slightly glyceriny finish is very attractive, although possibly a sign that longevity will be limited. A complete wine, everything in harmony at the present. *** Drink now-2018.

Chambolle Musigny, Les Baudes, 2003
Quite dark ruby color. Silky nose of mineral red fruits with some smoky notes. Smooth and silky on the palate with more weight than usual (not a surprise in this vintage) but still retaining freshness. Not likely to be very long lived but retains the usual elegance. A good result for the vintage, and—a harbinger of things to come with global warming?—much more appealing than the Suchots. *** Drink now-2016.

Vosne Romanée, Les Suchots, 2003
Dark color. Restrained nose with some bitter black cherry fruits. Faintly aromatic black fruits on the palate, opulent and silky with a touch of liquorice on the finish, coated by chocolaty tannins. A touch nutty on the finish. Tannins seem more four-square than usual, giving an impression of rusticity. ** Drink now-2015.

Chambolle Musigny, Les Baudes, 2002
A slightly more garnet hue than the Suchots suggests a little more development. Restrained nose shows earthy strawberries and a touch of minerality with just a hint of acidity, softening to a gentle earthiness in the glass. Elegant mineral fruits on the palate form a delicate filigree, supported by balanced acidity. Generally a tighter impression than the Suchots, although a slight impression of acidity gives a lift to the strawberry fruits on the finish. (January 2011) **(*) Drink now-2016.

Vosne Romanée, Les Suchots, 2002
More depth to the fruits than on the Baudes, with black cherry notes joining the red cherries and strawberries on both nose and palate. The fruits are slightly deeper, slightly more rounded, and it is fair to describe this not so much as a difference in quality, but the difference between masculine and feminine styles, although you have the impression of an extra layer here, making the wine seem more complete. This is a very fine result with the silky power you expect of Vosne Romanée projecting good longevity. (January 2011) *** Drink now-2017.

Tastings of Gevrey Chambertin Premier Crus

Maison Faiveley

Dating from 1825, Maison Faiveley is one of the major domains in Burgundy, and now has about 60 ha of vineyards on the Côte d'Or, almost half in premier and grand crus. Based in Nuits St. Georges, they have always focused on red wines, but recently have been expanding into the Côte de Beaune and into white wines. The style has always been sturdy, but became more extracted and harder in 1993. When Erwan Faiveley took over from his father François in 2004, he started to soften the style, so a Faiveley vertical over the past two decades is also an exercise in seeing the effects of transitions in styles on expression of terroir, with the old style before 1993, the heavily extracted style until 2006, and since then a more forward fruity style. It's not so much the total amount of tannin that is different as the nature of the tannins; they were harder when Faiveley was striving for extraction, and to some extent this narrows the difference between terroirs by hiding the subtleties of the fruits. Yet the difference between Les Cazetiers and Combe aux Moines persists through the winemaking changes, although it narrows a bit with age. Style may trump terroir insofar as the winemaker sets the general nature of the wine, but the relative difference between the two terroirs remains consistent. Wines were tasted at Faiveley in November 2010.

Combe aux Moines, 2009 (barrel sample)
A black fruit nose shows hints of chocolaty aromatics. Rounded red fruits with black hints and supple tannins display the typical richness of the vintage. Quite approachable, good acidity for the vintage, touch of heat on the finish. To say this was fuller but coarser than the Cazetiers would be to over-simplify, but it certainly gives a more rustic impression. ** Drink 2012-2019.

Les Cazetiers, 2009 (barrel sample)
A faint touch of minerality to the nose, with underlying earthy red fruits. A more savory impression than the Combe aux Moines. More finesse on the palate, altogether finer, with a sense of minerality overshadowing strawberry fruits that intensify in the glass. *** Drink 2013-2020.

Combe aux Moines, 2008
The red fruits hide behind some mineral notes on the nose. Fruits are sweet and ripe on the palate, with medium concentration and balancing acidity. The lighter style reflects the vintage, tannins are evidenced by the dry finish, which is a touch hard. This is a little more direct, a little less refined than the Cazetiers. ** Drink 2102-2018.

Les Cazetiers, 2008
In this vintage, the noses of Cazetiers and Combe aux Moines are more similar, but there is a more piercing sense of minerality in Cazetiers. Following on the palate are those smoky, flinty notes, with elegant red fruits supported by good acidity and fine-grained tannins. ** Drink 2012-2018.

Combe aux Moines, 2007
Mix of earthy red strawberry fruits and mineral notes on the nose. Nicely rounded fruits on the palate, earthy strawberries with a touch of anise. The greater overt emphasis on fruit serves this lighter vintage well to show medium concentration with a nicely supple finish. ** Drink 2011-2017.

Les Cazetiers, 2007
A similar minerality on the nose to the Combe aux Moines, but the fruits are less direct, more savory. Refined red fruits show on the palate with a flinty, mineral edge. Earthy strawberries strike the dominant note here, supported by fine tannins, light but certainly sufficient for the fruits. This is a medium term wine, but has turned out much better than expected at bottling, when the level of acidity seemed too low (some carbon dioxide was retained to compensate). ** Drink 2011-2016.

Combe aux Moines, 2002
Earthy strawberries, a touch of sous bois developing on the nose. Red fruits on the palate, softening but still with a hard edge from the tannins in the extracted Faiveley style of the period. The more four-square quality of Combe aux Moines shows through. The tannins are a bit obtrusive and it's unclear whether and when it will really all come together. ** Drink now-2018.

Les Cazetiers, 2002
Earthy mineral strawberry fruits with some sous bois on the nose. Refined, elegant fruits on the palate. There's still a hard edge on the tannins, but the contrast with the fruits is not so obvious here as in the Combe aux Moines. This is a better integrated wine, with more finesse and femininity. *** Drink now-2020.

Combe aux Moines, 1999
Developed garnet color. Restrained nose shows some development with traces of sous bois. Soft developed red fruits on the palate have an underlying mineral edge. Perhaps this is presently a touch more developed than the Cazetiers, but even so, the more four-square, direct quality of the fruits is apparent. *** Drink now-2019.

Les Cazetiers, 1999
Developed garnet color. Fugitive mineral red fruits on nose with a touch of sous bois. Refined fruits on the palate convey a sense of finesse, developing nicely with faintly savory overtones. You might place this just a touch behind the Combe aux Moines in the pace of development, but it is more refined and better balanced. *** Drink now-2019.

Tastings of Volnay Santenots

Faiveley took over production of the Matrot-Wittersheim domain in 2007, so a vertical is an interesting comparison of wine made before and after the handover. (Vintages prior to 2007 were actually made by Matrot-Wittersheim but existing stock is labeled as Maison Faiveley). The Santenots plot is actually just over the boundary into Meursault. Its red soil is not a terroir to give finesse, but the wine is rich and concentrated. The vines represent a clone planted in 1967. The character of the vineyard comes through both winemaking experiences. Wines were tasted at Faiveley in November 2010.

Volnay Santenots 2009 (barrel sample)
Fruity nose shows black and red cherry fruits. Elegant fruits on the palate develop some notes of earthy strawberries in the glass, a little like the 2003, but with a distinct tannic edge. At this stage it seems somewhat straightforward. ** Drink 2015-2012.

Volnay Santenots, 2008
Restrained nose shows some briary fruits. Restrained and stern on the palate, an iron backbone, dry on the finish. Concentrated but really tight at the moment. A touch of mineral strawberries develops in the glass, reminiscent of the 2002. The concentration defies the vintage. ** Drink 2015-2020.

Volnay Santenots, 2007
Some softening on the nose now apparent, showing red fruits of strawberries and cherries. Medium fruit concentration, soft on the palate, dry finish. ** Drink 2014-2020.

Volnay Santenots, 2003
Medium ruby garnet color. Attractive nose of earthy strawberries with notes of sous bois. Sweet ripe fruits of developing strawberries with a faint edge of sous bois. Very well balanced for 2003. Some tannins still dry the finish but quite supple. ** Drink now-2015.

Volnay Santenots, 2002
Medium garnet color still shows some rosy hues. A more mineral nose here with a touch of smoke. Smooth on the palate, with elegant fruits, that mineral edge coming through as flinty strawberries, good supporting acidity. ** Drink now-2014.

Volnay Santenots, 2001
Restrained nose with a fugitive whiff of over-ripe fruits (!) following to a touch of mushrooms. Medium density fruits on the palate but a dry edge as tannins begin to outlast the fruits. * Drink now-2013.

Tastings of Chambertin and Clos de Bèze

Armand Rousseau

Armand Rousseau is the doyen of Chambertin, widely acknowledged to set the standard with his premier and grand crus. The domain is the largest single owner of Le Chambertin and has a substantial parcel in Clos de Bèze, as well as holdings in three other grand crus and three premier crus in Gevrey Chambertin. The eponymous Armand Rousseau was involved in the drive to domain bottling in the 1930s; today his grandson Eric is in charge of the domain. As is evident from the generally soft style, there is at least 90% destemming. (In 2009, whole clusters were increased to 15-20%.) Vinification is the same for all wines; the only difference is in the use of new oak. Both Chambertin and Clos de Bèze have their élevage in 100% new oak; Clos St. Jacques is 60-70%. "I am completely against over extraction of color and material. I prefer Pinot Noir with elegance. If you go too far, you eliminate the effects of terroir," says Eric Rousseau.

Pierre Damoy

The Damoy domain has substantial holdings in three important grand crus, Chambertin, Clos de Bèze, and Chapelle Chambertin, but was a significant under achiever until Pierre Damoy took over in the 1990s. He is the largest owner in Clos de Bèze, but sells most of the grapes. The Clos de Bèze is made from an assemblage (of the berries) from the northernmost and southernmost parcels. The vines in the northern parcel are younger; the southern parcel, and the parcel in Chambertin, were mostly planted in 1973-1974. Pierre Damoy harvests late, "I like ripe berries," and uses 100% new oak for the top cuvées. Sometimes there has been a separate Vieilles Vignes cuvée from a small part of Clos de Bèze. There may also be a Reserve bottling (just two barrels), which is not usually commercialized.

Jadot own a plot in Clos de Bèze but purchase the grapes for their Chambertin. All wines were tasted in May 2011.

Le Chambertin, Pierre Damoy, 2010 (barrel sample)
The nose is just a little sturdier than the Clos de Bèze. The deep black fruits are more reserved and a touch of chocolate comes out. The fruits are a fraction less well rounded, showing as black cherries. The overall impression isn't quite so tight and refined as the Clos de Bèze; the wine seems a bit sturdier with less precision. *** Drink 2016-2023.

Clos de Bèze, Pierre Damoy, 2010 (barrel sample)
Fruits on the nose show as black cherries with faint overtones of blackcurrants, giving a very refined impression. Rounded black fruits follow on the palate, mostly black cherries again. Firm, fine, elegant tannins: very tight at this moment. *** Drink 2015-2022.

Le Chambertin, Pierre Damoy, 2006
Some gamey notes on the nose lead into a mélange of red and black fruits, which slowly come to the fore. A lighter red fruit impression on the palate than Clos de Bèze, mid density fruits, tannins not making much impression. The style is quite light for a grand cru, elegant and sweet on the finish, but with a touch of tannin that needs to soften. *** Drink 2012-2018.

Clos de Bèze, Pierre Damoy, 2006
Gamey but slightly nutty on the nose with an impression more of red fruits than black. Sweet ripe refined red fruit palate; similar to Le Chambertin, the fruits are only mid density and the tannins are quite soft in the background, becoming tea-like on the finish. A touch more aromatic, a fraction lighter and sweeter than Le Chambertin. *** Drink 2012-2018.

Le Chambertin, Pierre Damoy 2005
A savory impression to the nose hides the mix of red and black fruits. Sweet ripe, dense fruits are more black than red on the palate, tannins refined but firm, just showing on the finish, still a very faint touch of bitterness. A touch less powerful and fractionally more aromatic than Clos de Bèze, and not so harmonious, really requiring another year for the tannins to recede into the background. ***(*) Drink 2012-2020.

Clos de Bèze, Pierre Damoy, 2005
Faintly gamey bouquet on the nose overlays black fruits. Sweet ripe black fruits come out on the palate, some faintly nutty overtones, sweet and dense, tannins firm but at first in the background, slowly bringing some dryness and a faint touch of bitterness to the finish. Just a touch more powerful, better rounded, and complete all round than Le Chambertin. The harmonious quality of the fruits makes this already drinkable but there will be a more complete integration of tannins within the year. **** Drink 2012-2022.

Le Chambertin, Pierre Damoy, 2004
Restrained nose, faintly gamey and savory, with a slight tea-like impression. Precise fruits, as much red as black, but the tannins not so refined as in the Clos de Bèze. Some of the linearity of the vintage still remains with a slightly angular edge on the finish. **(*) Drink now-2015.

Clos de Bèze, Pierre Damoy, 2004
Just a touch more developed in appearance than the Chambertin. Black tea dominates the nose and gives a slight herbal impression. Precise, well delineated black fruits, yet well

rounded, supported by refined tannins in the background with a faint sense of black tea on the finish. **(*) Drink now-2016.

Le Chambertin, Armand Rousseau, 2004
The medium garnet color is just a touch more developed in appearance than the Clos de Bèze. Restrained nose, a little gamey, with some savory fruit aromas. Sweet ripe fruits on the palate, in the red spectrum, not as sweet as Clos de Bèze, but in the same style. **(*) Drink now-2016.

Clos de Bèze, Armand Rousseau, 2004
Medium garnet color. Medium intensity gamey nose with some smoke and black tea aromas. Sweet ripe fruits on the palate more in the red than black spectrum, a touch of earthy strawberries and raspberries, tea-like tannins quite pushed into the background. *** Drink now-2017.

Le Chambertin, Armand Rousseau, 2002
Some generosity is evident on the nose, a very faintly buttery touch to the strawberry fruits. Sweet, ripe, round fruits show on the palate, slightly nutty on the finish; the nicely developing fruits subsume the tannins. There's some bottle variation here, because six months ago the wine seemed more closed, but with more potential for long term development, but this bottle seems to be closer to its peak, with less potential for extended longevity. ***(*) Drink now-2018.

Clos de Bèze, Armand Rousseau, 2002
Medium garnet with some darker hues than the Chambertin. Muted nose with a whiff of earthy strawberries and a mineral edge. Sweet ripe red fruits on the palate with a mineral character, a faint touch of tea to tannins just noticeable on the finish, then the minerality coming back with a touch of chocolate and nuts. The structure is more evident here than on the Chambertin. Less obviously enjoyable now but probably longer lived. **** Drink now-2019.

Le Chambertin, Armand Rousseau, 2000
Complex nose of spicy red and black cherries, with some touches of tobacco. Black fruit palate with spices and tobacco notes, good supporting acidity and integrated tannins. A top result for the vintage, refined and elegant, showing the breed of the Grand Cru in a way that even the Clos de Bèze does not achieve in this vintage. (October 2010) ***(*) Drink now-2016.

Clos de Bèze, Armand Rousseau, 2000
Initially a spicy, chocolaty, red fruit nose, opening out to some vanilla and black fruits. Fruits of red cherries with hints of strawberries on the palate, solid rather than elegant, even a bit four-square, a touch nutty on the finish. In this vintage, the contrast with Le Chambertin, which is more elegant and refined, is quite pronounced. *** Drink now- 2015.

Le Chambertin, Armand Rousseau, 1999
Smoky gunflint notes on the nose. Sweet ripe red fruits showing as soft nutty strawberries: a great increase in complexity over 2002. Long layers of flavor on the palate, a mineral overlay to the strawberries, the soft ripe tannins are way in the background yet the texture to the fruits shows the presence of a supportive underlying structure. This is deliciously at its peak. **** Drink now-2017.

Clos de Bèze, Armand Rousseau, 1999
A similar nose to Le Chambertin but somewhat more restrained. Similar sweet ripe red fruits on the palate, the strawberries show as a little more mineral, a slight tea-like note to the tannins on the finish, more evident sense of structure. Here the structure restrains the overt quality of the fruits, so the fruits display more delicacy, less overt fruitiness, and it will really come to its peak only in another three or four years. **** Drink now-2021.

Le Chambertin, Louis Jadot 1996
Slight gamey nose clears to reveal sweet, ripe red and black fruits. Very characteristic of Jadot at the top end: firm, ripe tannins with a faintly sturdy impression support the sweet ripe black fruits. Dense, ripe and rich, the intensity is evident. **** Drink now-2022.

Clos de Bèze, Louis Jadot, 1996
A fugitive whiff of gunflint clearing to show a mixture of sweet ripe red and black fruits. Again sturdy tannins support intense black fruits, the strong acidity of the vintage is more evident in this wine than in Le Chambertin. *** Drink now-2020.

Le Chambertin, Armand Rousseau, 1996
Restrained nose with sweet ripe red fruits and a touch of nuttiness. Sweet ripe fruits more in the red than black spectrum, much less acid and mineral than the Clos de Bèze, the fruits more approachable. Some nutty notes develop on the finish. Here the acidity is just restrained enough for the fruits to come through, showing a difference between Chambertin and the more backward Clos de Bèze. ***(*) Drink now-2020.

Clos de Bèze, Armand Rousseau, 1996
A slightly mineral touch to the red fruit nose. The minerality intensifies in the glass, the acidity of the vintage is still quite pressing, the ripe fruits are a little suppressed by the minerality and acidity and this wine is not ready yet. There's no doubt about the quality and the intensity but is there some doubt whether the tannins will resolve in time to let the fruits dominate? Wait three years and try again. *** Drink 2014-2022.

Le Chambertin, Armand Rousseau, 1993
Mineral nose with some perfumed notes of violets. Beautiful developed palate, just short of savory, slightly tea-like and herbal on the finish, complex layers of flavor. The perfume carries over to a subtle palate, developed fruits integrating perfectly with background acidity and tannins, a very long perfumed finish. ***(*) Drink now-2020.

Clos de Bèze, Armand Rousseau, 1993
Mineral nose but quite fragrant, with a suspicion of perfume, a fugitive whiff of gunflint. Tea like, slightly herbal and savory, a nicely developing palate, with a very long finish. Just a touch more minerality and structure here than the Chambertin, where the fruits stand out a little more obviously. ***(*) Drink now-2020.

Le Chambertin, Armand Rousseau, 1990
The wine of the tasting. Restrained nose with very faint tertiary notes and tea-like aromas. The ripest and sweetest fruits of the flight, still the most evidently fruity, with savory, herbal, tea like notes forming an overlay on the fruits. Very complex layers of flavor, some remnants of the original red primary fruits just evident, a sweet/sour/savory kick to the finish—this has it all. The direct sweetness of the fruits speaks directly to Le Chambertin (and to the warm vintage). ***** Drink now-2021.

Clos de Bèze, Armand Rousseau, Rousseau
Medium garnet. Some tertiary notes developing on the nose and some tea-like aromas. The tea-like notes intensify on the palate, the fruits are quite developed. There's a delicious savory to fruit balance on the palate, a very subtle balance, a long finish with a herbal suspicion giving a very slight leanness to the wine. The contrast with the Chambertin is the most dramatic of any vintage in the tasting, and much beyond any expectations of slight terroir differences. But there may be some significant bottle variation: a bottle tasted six months earlier was more developed, mineral, and sturdier, and rated a point higher. ***(*) Drink now-2020.

Tastings of Griotte and Chapelle Chambertin

Domaine Ponsot

William Ponsot established the domain in 1870 with the vineyards that are still at its heart: the premier cru Monts Luisants and the grand cru Clos de La Roche in Morey St. Denis. Jean-Marie Ponsot came into the domain in 1942 and took it over in 1957; expanding the domain by marriage, and becoming mayor of Morey St. Denis, he gave the impression of a local notable who knew which cupboards had skeletons. Laurent Ponsot, who took over in 1981, expanded the domain further with arrangements to manage vineyards in premier and grand crus extending north into Gevrey Chambertin and south into Chambolle Musigny. The new winery is an impressive building extending several storeys underground. Laurent Ponsot marches to the beat of his own drum. Vinification is "non-interventionist," in vineyard and cellar, but without commitment to any named regime, such as organic. Laurent harvests late in order to get maximum ripeness: usually he is the last to harvest in the village. He uses no new oak, regarding it as a fashion that panders to some critics, the wines are not filtered, and there is minimum use of sulfur. In Monts Luisants, he has the only premier cru vineyard that is planted with Aligoté. Ponsot's vineyard in Clos de la Roche was the origin for the now-famous Dijon clones. Chapelle Chambertin came from his mother's father; Griotte is farmed under a métayage agreement. Wines were tasted at Domaine Ponsot in November 2010 except as noted.

Griotte Chambertin, 2009 (barrel sample)
The nose offers some tea-leaf impressions, with faintly spicy fruits. Elegant black cherry fruits on the palate show some light aromatics. The fruits certainly shine through, supported by balanced acidity and fine grained tannins with slightly chocolaty notes. You scarcely notice the very high alcohol (14%). *** Drink 2013-2025.

Chapelle Chambertin, 2009 (barrel sample)
A touch more intensity on the nose, with red and black cherry fruit notes predominating. Slightly rounder fruits on the palate, just a touch more weight than the Griotte, the tannins a little more supple, more chocolate and mocha. There's a general impression of more complexity and fullness. **** Drink 2013-2027.

Griotte Chambertin, 2004
Medium garnet color. Lightly spicy red fruit nose with a faint smokiness and notes of chocolate. You see the tannins of 2004 here, but they subside in the glass against the elegant fruits, although the finish remains quite dry. The wine opens out in the glass to reveal chocolate-coated black fruits, supported by balanced acidity. A good result for the year. ** Drink 2013-2020.

Chapelle Chambertin, 2004
Medium garnet color but a touch darker and more ruby than the Griotte. Again there is more evident fruit concentration on the nose, showing as black cherries with a faint chocolate edge. The fruits are more rounded on the palate, more weight and layers, a soft impression with more supple tannins less evident overall. *** Drink 2012-2020.

Griotte Chambertin, 1998
Nose is quite restrained but shows some spicy red fruits with a touch of cinnamon and hints of minerality. There are red cherry fruits on the palate; reflecting the vintage, they are not so concentrated as usual. The tannins are fine but dry on the finish. ** Drink now-2018.

Chapelle Chambertin, 1998
Very restrained nose gives quite a mineral impression. A touch more weight to the fruits, fractionally better rounded, but there is less evident difference between Chapelle and Griotte in this vintage. There is more sense of texture, and some chocolate on the finish. Overall a slightly softer and less mineral impression. ** Drink now-2018.

Griotte Chambertin, 1993
Only slightly developed on the nose, with a subdued savory quality. Fruits are a little sweeter and less savory on the palate than the nose would suggest, but there is a certain lack of presence. The palate gives the impression that the fruits are beginning to dry out with a touch of dilution showing, allowing a faint bitterness to overtake the finish. The overall impression is not exactly rustic, but this seems a less refined, and certainly less complete, wine than the Chapelle, and has probably reached its natural lifespan. (March 2011) ** Drink now.

Chapelle Chambertin, 1993
More to the nose than the Griotte Chambertin, with a savory, steely impression ending in a touch of gunflint. Well rounded savory fruits dominate the palate, with that touch of gunflint turning faintly to bitterness on the finish. But the fruits are nicely concentrated on the palate, and slowly more savory elements develop in the glass, even a herbal touch of tea. Nicely balanced now, this probably will not improve any further, but it gives the impression of a more complete wine than the Griotte. (March 2011) *** Drink now.

Tasting of Clos St. Jacques

Each producer's typical style shows most clearly in the youngest vintage. Fourrier shows his quintessential elegance and precision, Rousseau his generosity, depth, and profundity, Jadot that sturdy structure, Bruno Clair a rather tight structure fighting with the fruits, and Esmonin a deep structure holding in the fruits. In older vintages, terroir begins to assert itself, and there was at least one exception every year to the expected producer styles. The wines showing the most typical "Gevrey" character, meaning a certain tightness of tannic structure, are those of Esmonin and Bruno Clair, where new oak usage is high (coupled in Esmonin's case with exclusive use of whole clusters). Yet the Esmonin style has lightened, as can be seen by comparing 2005 and 1999. Clair's structure was most obvious in 2005 and 1999, but muted in 2002. The Jadot wines are also well structured, but appeared less generous than usual in this tasting. Fourrier's vintages varied between the 2005 and 1999 that seemed as soft as Rousseau, and 2006 and 2002, which showed his usual precise, elegant style. Rousseau was almost always the favorite of the flight, typically earthy and almost nutty in the older vintages, but quite closed in the youngest. Wines were tasted in March 2011 and May 2011.

Jean-Marie Fourrier, 2006
Primary red fruits show on the nose with tarry overtones, but overall there is a fruity impression. Youthful sweet fruits on the palate with that finely delineated edge so typical of Fourrier. The palate is dominated by the breed of the appellation and the purity of the fruits achieved by Fourrier's style. Refined, precise tannins on the finish require another two or three years to resolve, when the purity of the fruits will shine through. **** Drink 2014-2021.

Louis Jadot, 2006
Black fruit nose with some primary cherries and blackcurrants, subsiding in the glass to show some herbal notes of tobacco. Sweet ripe black fruits on the palate, tending to cherries, very much Jadot's style, becoming a little nutty in the glass. Firm, sturdy tannins on the finish require three or four years to resolve, when the wine will become warm and generous. *** Drink 2014-2020.

Armand Rousseau, 2006
Tarry black fruit nose is quite stern and brooding at first, clearing in the glass to become nutty and earthy in Rousseau's typical style. Sweet ripe fruits, the most complex of the vintage, already showing a delicious depth and generosity, with just a suspicion of a buttery piquancy on the finish. In another couple of years this will become the most generous Clos St. Jacques of the vintage, and it is the wine that at this stage already shows the typicity of Pinot Noir the most clearly. **** Drink 2013-2020.

Bruno Clair, 2006
Stern fruits on the nose with just a kick of sweet ripe blackcurrants and cherries coming in at the end. A nice precision of black fruits shows on the palate, still quite tight, the tannins just a touch hard at this stage, but in another two or three years the wine will develop in a refined style. *** Drink 2014-2020.

Sylvie Esmonin, 2006
Stern nose with a medicinal almost herbaceous impression followed by some notes of tobacco and almost a gamey impression. The palate shows the extensive use of new oak, quite smoky, the wood tannins are distinctly drying on the finish, the earthy smoke is strong on the aftertaste. There's a long finish. There's good fruit concentration here but it is hidden by the new oak, although it should come around in time. *** Drink 2015-2021.

Jean-Marie Fourrier, 2005
Some cereal and nutty notes on a nose showing red cherry and strawberry fruits. Soft on the palate with a nutty impression to the finish. Good fruit density, with the structure showing through, although the nuttiness seems to be taking over a bit. Surprisingly soft for Fourrier, who usually shows a more sharply delineated style. ***(*) Drink 2012-2020.

Louis Jadot, 2005
Some notes of tobacco add to mineral strawberries on the nose. The first impression of the palate is the crisp acidity. Relatively light fruits show more as red cherries than strawberries. The wine becomes slightly aromatic as it develops in the glass. The fruits are not as rounded and generous as Jadot's usual style, and the wine is not quite ready yet. There is a touch of heat on the finish. *** Drink 2012-2018.

Armand Rousseau, 2005
This is the most closed on the nose of the vintage, with just a faint suggestion of minerality and earthiness, and less obvious fruits. Tight black fruits show as cherries on the palate, elegant and precise, supported by taut tannins. The most elegant of the vintage, this is somewhat tighter than usual for Rousseau. **** Drink 2014-2021.

Bruno Clair, 2005
Some minerality on the stern black fruit nose. Crisp acidity with mid weight black fruits on the palate. A touch of bitterness comes through to the finish, making this the wine that most shows that hard edge characteristic of Gevrey Chambertin. ** Drink 2013-2018.

Sylvie Esmonin, 2005
Just a touch of black fruits on the nose as well as mineral and earthy red fruits of cherries and strawberries, conveying a sense of structure. Some meaty spices develop in the glass. Soft black fruits on the palate show as cherries with a slightly nutty finish. Elegant and attractive, this is the most generous Clos St. Jacques of the vintage, with a touch of structure showing through the fruits, and some black tea emerging on the finish. ***(*) Drink 2014-2020.

Jean-Marie Fourrier, 2002
Rather subdued on the nose with a faint touch of mineral strawberries, and a slowly emerging herbal impression. Medium weight density fruits on the palate with nicely balanced acidity, and fine tannins turning to tea on the finish. Fruits are precisely delineated in Fourrier's typical style. The taut tannins make this the most finely structured Clos St. Jacques of the vintage, and it vies with Esmonin for the most elegant. *** Drink now-2018.

Louis Jadot, 2002
Medium ruby color. Somewhat stern on the nose, a rather tight impression of black fruits. Sturdy black fruits on the palate, just a touch four-square. There's the usual strong structure of Jadot, which should give a fine balance when the fruits are allowed to come through. The wine may aspire to generosity rather than to elegance. *** Drink 2012-2017.

Armand Rousseau, 2002
Lighter color than most in this vintage. Slightly nutty and earthy red fruit nose. Crisp acidity leads into generous red fruits with nutty overtones. Taut tannins on the finish contribute to an elegant, yet soft, style, although this wine has not softened as much as you usually find with Rousseau. Structure still shows through, promising good longevity for the lovely, broad red fruits. **** Drink now-2019.

Bruno Clair, 2002
Cereal notes on the nose with a faint impression of mineral strawberries. Crisp acidity leads into mineral red fruits on the palate with a faintly nutty finish showing a touch of heat. This is the softest and most gentle Clos St. Jacques of the vintage. *** Drink now-2018.

Sylvie Esmonin, 2002
More nutty than fruity on the nose, but with red cherry fruits slowly emerging in the glass. Elegant red fruit palate shows a touch of tea and almost tobacco on the finish. This shows the most overt sense of structure in the vintage, with a herbal and tobacco note to the finish presumably resulting from the use of whole clusters. The fruits are fine and elegant, with a lovely sense of precision, making this overall the most elegant Clos St. Jacques of the vintage. ***(*) Drink 2012-2019.

Dominique Laurent, 2002
Stern impression of black fruits on the nose, developing into a herbal impression in the glass. Good depth of fruits and concentration with a refined precise impression of black fruits tending to cherries. There is a very faint impression of extra precision over the Esmonin Clos St. Jacques, and the fruits seem just a touch richer. Laurent's belief in 200% new oak shows as an extra smokiness on the finish. ***(*) Drink 2013-2021.

Jean-Marie Fourrier, 1999
This has the most to offer on the nose for any Clos St. Jacques of the vintage, with nutty, broad, red fruits. It is certainly the most ready to drink, with an impression of strawberries broadening out into other red fruits, leading into a lingering nutty red fruit finish with some earthiness. *** Drink now-2017.

Louis Jadot, 1999
Tight nose gives an impression of mineral red and black fruits. Fruits are more black on the palate, also still quite tight, but a lovely sense of structure coming through, with refined tannins on the finish and chocolate coating developing in the glass. This is finely balanced between fruits for drinking now and the subtle underlying structure for longevity, and is developing in Jadot's characteristic style. *** Drink now-2019.

Armand Rousseau, 1999
Restrained nose with faintly nutty, tight black fruits, following on to a palate with precisely delineated black fruits, with overtones of black tea and spice on the finish. The most precise Clos St. Jacques of the vintage, this displays an extremely elegant and refined style with potential to age gracefully for a decade or more. **** Drink now-2021.

Bruno Clair, 1999
Herbal and spicy impressions on the nose. Refined black fruits on the palate are quite tight and still need more time. Fruits tend to blackberries. The typical hardness of the tannins of Gevrey shows through at first, although the overall impression is quite refined. Slowly the fruits develop more generosity in the glass and become more precisely delineated. *** Drink 2013-2019.

Sylvie Esmonin, 1999
A rather tight impression on the nose with a faint touch of black tea. The tightness follows through to the palate, with a touch of the typical hardness of Gevrey Chambertin. The fruits still need some time to come out. This is the most evidently structured Clos St. Jacques of the vintage, but when it resolves, it should have a beautiful balance integrated for longevity. *** Drink 2013-2020.

Dominique Laurent, 1999
Stern black fruit nose with slightly herbal impression, which continues through to the black fruit palate. Tending to black cherries, the fruits are still rather reserved. The oak hasn't really resolved completely enough yet to let the fruits show through (unlike the 2002 vintage where it has enhanced the fruits). There's good purity and concentration of fruits, but how long will it take until they can shine through the oak? *** Drink 2013-2020.

Tasting of Hospices de Beaune Cortons

Charlotte Dumay is a blend from 1.69 ha of Corton Rénardes and 0.97 ha of Corton Bressandes. Dr. Peste comes from four different sources within Corton. There is also a Corton Clos du Roy and a Corton Vergennes. The latter two, named for the *climats*, sell at higher prices. Dr Peste is usually more expensive than Charlotte Dumay. But these relationships are not closely reflected in the quality of bottled wine, which owes far more to the éleveur.

Charlotte Dumay, Hospices de Beaune, 2005
Red fruit nose with slightly nutty and herbal overtones. Slightly flat on the palate, red fruits are rather subdued, a bit lacking in aromatic complexity, especially on the nose. Rather dry on the finish, needs another year or so, but the basic concentration isn't there. * Drink 2012-2016.

Charlotte Dumay, Louis Jadot, 2005
Restrained black fruit nose, slightly smoky, with mineral overtones. Black fruit palate with some mineral overtones, tannins still firm and tight. Needs another couple of years for the tannins to soften, when this will become pleasant and soft, but it won't reach the heights to which Corton should aspire. ** Drink 2013-2019.

Charlotte Dumay, Michel Picard, 2005
Slightly flat nose, almost sour. Becomes a little perfumed and more interesting in the glass. Following to the palate the black fruits seem rather flat and lacking in flavor variety. Tannins still a bit tight on the average length finish. Needs another year or so, but no better than average, and disappointing for the vintage. * Drink 2013-2018.

Charlotte Dumay, Charles Thomas, 2005
Restrained black fruit nose, with hints of earthy black cherries poking through. Black fruits follow on the palate, just a hint of aromatics, but a bit lacking in flavor variety and complexity. Already becoming a little softer, nuttier, and earthy on the palate, should hold well for three or four years. Decent but not great: should do better in this vintage. *(*) Drink now-2018.

Dr. Peste, Maison Champy, 2005
Slightly nutty earthy black fruit nose. Black fruits on the palate, but a certain flatness on the finish. A slight touch of soapiness and sour acidity on the finish. Overall it's just a bit too lacking in flavor variety and complexity. * Drink 2012-2017.

Dr Peste, Pierre-Yves Colin-Morey, 2005
Attractive nutty red fruit nose with earthy overtones. Palate tends to red fruits as much as black, with firm tannins drying the finish. Quite a nice wine in the making, as soon as the tannins resolve just a little bit, will be soft and gentle, if not showing great complexity. *(*) Drink 2012-2017.

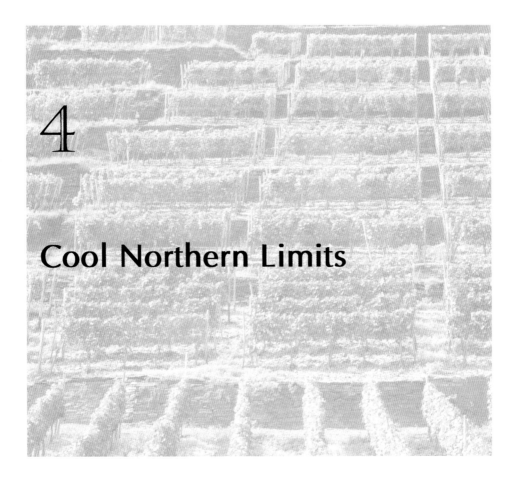

Cool Northern Limits

Pinot Noir is *the* black grape for cool climates. It is the predominant grape grown in the wine-producing regions closest to the north pole (Germany's Ahr Valley) and to the south pole (New Zealand's Central Otago). Those precisely delineated, yet generous, red fruits of Pinot grown at its preferred temperatures all too rapidly become jammy and diffuse in warmer climates. Whether Burgundy offers the perfect climate might be questioned; after all, Pinot Noir ripened sufficiently well to give really good vintages only about two or three times each decade through the twentieth century. Yet Pinot Noir has not spread south from Burgundy, but rather has gone north into even more marginal climates, where the cool temperatures generally confine production to white wine.

Elsewhere in France, Pinot is mostly grown around an arc to the north of Burgundy. Just to the west, and only a few miles farther north, Sancerre has grown Pinot Noir since the Middle Ages. Almost directly to the north of Burgundy, about a third of the Champagne district is planted with Pinot

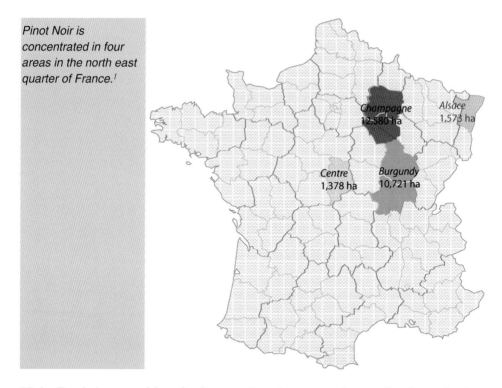

Pinot Noir is concentrated in four areas in the north east quarter of France.[1]

Champagne 12,580 ha

Alsace 1,573 ha

Centre 1,378 ha

Burgundy 10,721 ha

Noir. But it is several hundred years since it was used to make dry red wine; almost all of it is used for sparkling wine, so there is less demand to reach full ripeness. (A little dry red wine is made in Bouzy, but it's not really very interesting.) A little farther north yet, in the north eastern corner of France, Alsace focuses on Riesling and other cool climate white grapes, but produces a small amount of Pinot Noir.

Burgundy does not have the largest plantings of Pinot Noir in France. There is more Pinot Noir planted in the Champagne area. Together with the fact that a significant part of the production of Pinot Noir in Alsace or Sancerre goes into rosé wines, it's a moot point whether more Pinot Noir in France is used to make dry red wine than sparkling or rosé.

Other regions in Europe that produce interesting Pinot Noir are to the north and east of Burgundy. More or less directly east are the wine-producing regions of Switzerland and Italy. Crossing the northern border from France into Germany, Pinot Noir is grown in increasing amounts in the southernmost region of Baden (due east of Alsace) and in the Pfalz (to the immediate north). The surprise is that the highest concentration of Pinot Noir plantings in Germany is found in its northernmost wine-producing region, the Ahr (just south of Cologne), where a steep valley creates a protected microclimate. Which brings to mind the fact that a little Pinot Noir is grown in England, like the Ahr outside the nominal limits for wine grape cultivation, but more successfully for sparkling than for dry wine.

Climates for Pinot Noir lie in a narrow range of latitudes at the cool limits for winemaking.[2]

Temperatures are shown as the average over a growing season extending from April through September in the northern hemisphere, October through March in the southern hemisphere.

Sunshine hours give the total for each day from sunrise to sunset during the growing season.

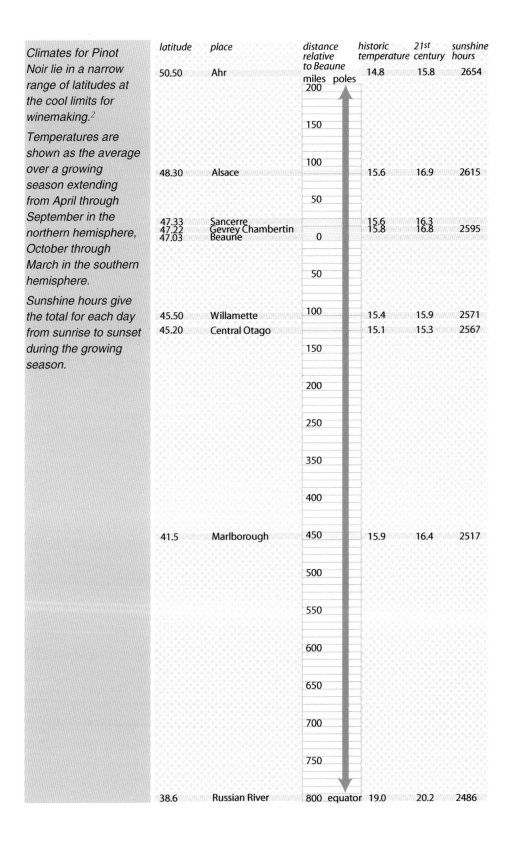

latitude	place	distance relative to Beaune miles poles	historic temperature	21st century	sunshine hours
50.50	Ahr	200	14.8	15.8	2654
		150			
		100			
48.30	Alsace		15.6	16.9	2615
		50			
47.33	Sancerre		15.6	16.3	
47.22	Gevrey Chambertin		15.8	16.8	2595
47.03	Beaune	0			
		50			
45.50	Willamette	100	15.4	15.9	2571
45.20	Central Otago		15.1	15.3	2567
		150			
		200			
		250			
		350			
		400			
41.5	Marlborough	450	15.9	16.4	2517
		500			
		550			
		600			
		650			
		700			
		750			
38.6	Russian River	800 equator	19.0	20.2	2486

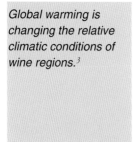

Global warming is changing the relative climatic conditions of wine regions.[3]

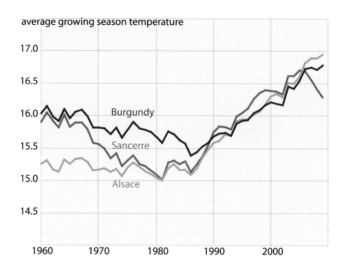

The question indeed is how these cool northern climates, historically even cooler than Burgundy, reflect the typicity of Pinot Noir. One critical factor is the temperature during the growing season; this is scarcely the only determinant of a region's suitability for a particular variety, but it's a good enough starting point. From this perspective, the average temperature during the growing season for the *best* vintages in Burgundy over the past two decades has been 16.4 °C. Over this period, the average temperature overall has increased from 15.8 °C to 16.8°C, essentially moving from the bottom to the top of the range for quality vintages. That's partly why good vintages are more frequent today.

Prior to 1990, the average in Sancerre or Alsace was 15.6 °C, just below the average of 15.8 °C in Burgundy. But since then the relationship has changed. All regions have become warmer, but Sancerre and Alsace have closed the gap, and in some years have even been warmer than Burgundy. The averages in Sancerre and Alsace today are warmer than Burgundy prior to 1990 (just as Burgundy itself today has about the same average temperature as Bordeaux in the 1960s). Even the far northern outpost of the Ahr now reaches temperatures close to Burgundy's historical average. (The other major climatic factor that differs significantly between the regions is rainfall. And the cooler temperatures of regions nearer the poles are compensated to a small degree by more hours of sunshine.) So other things being equal, should we expect these regions to become pretenders to the throne?

In spite of the ancient origins of red wine production in Sancerre, it is only recently that its Pinot Noirs have really achieved interest. Production focused on white wine following the replanting after phylloxera, and as recently as 1947 the Directeur des Services Agricoles du Cher wrote that, "Red wines and some rosés are also produced from Pinot and Gamay [in Quincy, Reuilly and Côteaux du Cher], but as in Sancerre, these wines have

The hilltop town of Sancerre dominates the appellation contrôlée vineyards, which form a semi circle to its west. This view was taken from the direction of Bué, to the southwest of Sancerre. The fault separating the calcareous from the silex terroirs lies in the fold of the hills close to Sancerre.

no future."[4] Indeed, when the Sancerre AOC was created in 1936, only white wine was allowed. It was only in 1959 that red wine, made from Pinot Noir, was added. Before the AOC was created, it was common to mix a little Gamay into the red wine, but today it is one hundred per cent Pinot Noir.

There were only a hundred hectares of Pinot Noir in the region (roughly 10% of the plantings of Sauvignon Blanc) when the Sancerre AOC was established. At the end of the following decade, Pinot Noir had almost doubled. Today there are almost 900 hectares of Pinot Noir, relative to 3,000 hectares of Sauvignon Blanc.[5] Percentage wise, it's probably gone up here more rapidly than anywhere else in France. What has happened to the quality over this period?

The red Sancerre I remember from twenty or thirty years ago was somewhat of a poor man's Burgundy, relatively light in color, somewhat in the same flavor spectrum with notes of earthy strawberries, but usually not very concentrated, and sometimes with the acidity overwhelming the fruits. More red than rosé, certainly, but not completely convincing. Things have changed, and today there are some fine red Sancerres made by the top producers.

When you visit vignerons known for their Pinot Noirs in Sancerre, it seems more like visiting in Burgundy. There is talk of terroir and of vintages, there is discussion of how much new oak is used, and there is emphasis on the need to preserve the fruit and delicacy of Pinot Noir. The wines may take time to mature: those of recent vintages tend still to be too young, while those of older vintages have developed interesting tertiary aromas and flavors. Above all is that sense of the cépage, of the need to seek the typicity of Pinot Noir. Yields at the top producers are kept low, around the same level as premier crus in Burgundy.

There is the same morcelization of terroirs, with most individual vineyard plots being quite small. The major difference here is that, although vignerons are conscious of the nuanced differences between their plots and will vinify them separately, at the end of the day, there will be an assemblage of a single cuvée, because there is not the same emphasis in the market on terroir. When you taste barrel samples, the differences between wines from different terroirs, especially calcareous versus siliceous, are quite clear, but this is rarely represented in the bottled wine. "Peut-être un jour... Perhaps one day it will be possible to have different cuvées for each terroir," muses Gilles Crochet, of Domaine Lucien Crochet, commenting ruefully that the top wines are sold (and consumed) too young. "Red Sancerre is still not known very well outside of France. People do not really understand the aging potential of Sancerre rouge," he says (⍦ page 173).[6]

The Sancerre AOC forms a semicircle to the west of Sancerre, with the old town at the center. The vineyards are planted on a series of hills radiating through an arc of communes. The AOC vineyards are all on the hills and slopes, and stop where the land becomes flat at the bottom. A geological fault running north to south separates terroir based on limestone to the west from siliceous terroirs to the east. The type of limestone base becomes more recent in geological age as you climb up the hills. Running along the summits of the hills, the soil is Portlandian at the very top (although the overall percentage in Sancerre is rather small), Kimmeridgian in the middle, and then Oxfordian at the bottom. The sizes of the stones decrease going down the slope, from large jagged stones in the Portlandian soil at the top, to pebbles in the middle, and small pebbles, known locally as griottes (French for cherries) at the bottom. You can see the differences clearly when the land is dry, with the summits showing brown due to the Portlandian soil; the Kimmeridgian center, which is the most calcareous, showing white—it is known locally as terre blanche; and then the in-between color of the Oxfordian soil, which has more clay. Most of the Pinot is planted on Kimmeridgian soil.

The extension of the AOC to red wine was a great spur to the production of Pinot Noir. At Domaine Lucien Crochet, Gilles Crochet told me that his grandfather planted some small plots of Pinot Noir with vines selected at Gevrey Chambertin, and made a small amount of Pinot, but his father put in the first major plantings in 1964. At Alphonse Mellot, Pinot Noir was intro-

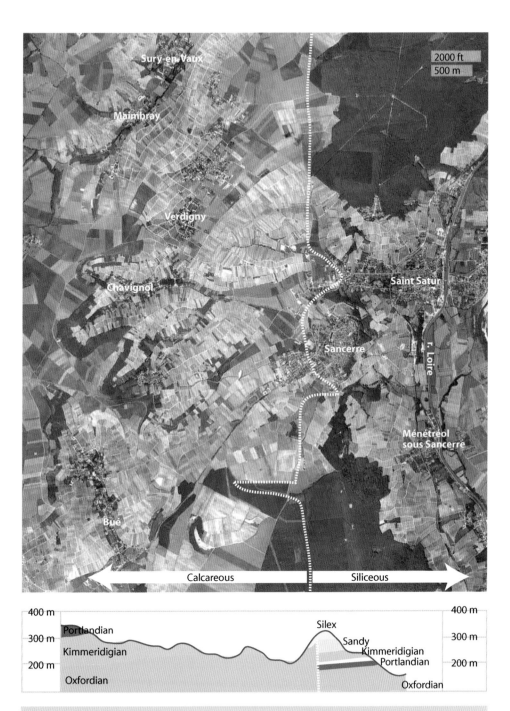

The Sancerre AOC vineyards are mostly to the west of the geological fault (dotted white line) that separates calcareous soils from the siliceous soils on the eastern side (map at top). A cross section through a line running from Chavignol to Sancerre (bottom) shows that Portlandian soils are found on the hilltops, Kimmeridgian soils on the slopes, and Oxfordian soils at the bottom. The structure is different to the east of the fault line.

duced as an enthusiasm of the younger generation. The domain was producing only white wines, but Alphonse Jr. persuaded his father to add red wines. Alphonse Sr. made and makes white wine, but now expresses frank admiration for the reds that his son produces (⅄ page 177).

"In Sancerre you can find all styles of Pinot. There is no single image that characterizes Sancerre red," says Jean-Marie Bourgeois (⅄ page 176).[7] Indeed, Sancerre reds vary from wines that have the traditional lightness to those with significantly more extraction in the modern style. "The image of red Sancerre is the clairet," says Pascal Reverdy, "but it's really not true any more."[8] In much the same way as a century earlier in Burgundy, there's some discussion of whether this represents loss of the traditional typicity. "Today in some wines I find it difficult to see the identity of Sancerre, they taste more like Oregon, they can be good wines but lack the identity," says Jean-Marie Bourgeois. Jean-Marie should know, since Domaine Henri Bourgeois, which has turned the village of Chavignol into a theme town with its new purpose-built winery (called by other vignerons half affectionately and half pejoratively "the American winery"), has expanded into the New World. Their Clos Henri in Marlborough is roughly the same size as Henri Bourgeois itself, and the wine is quite light and European in style.

Burgundy remains the major influence on Pinot Noir production in Sancerre; many producers have close contacts there. They do not necessarily aim to emulate the style directly. "It's not possible to make Burgundy here. We don't have the same terroir or climate. We are closer to the sea so the climate is less Continental, there are differences in rainfall—in 2004 the rain stopped at Sancerre and did not reach Burgundy. It's not a frontier but it's different. Even if you practiced exactly the same vinification it's not possible to make the same wine," says Gilles Crochet.[9] Yet it is with Burgundy that comparisons are drawn in describing the wines. "Our wines are more like Volnay or Chambolle Musigny, they are never masculine," says Vincent Pinard.[10]

This is all fair description, but to my mind there has been a definite increase in intensity in Sancerre red over the past ten or twenty years. The characteristic of the red Sancerre remains its tight quality, with mineral overtones. This tightness is not so much a quality of the cépage as the demonstration of the cool climate conditions. It comes through in the whites as well as the other red varieties, most notably Cabernet Franc, grown farther to the west. There is more minerality and less fat in the Pinot Noir compared to Burgundy.

A vertical tasting at Domaine Vacheron forcefully made the point that Sancerre can age beautifully, generally along the same lines as Burgundy, although perhaps after the first decade on a more rapid time scale (⅄ page 175). But in 2010, wines back to 1990 and 1989 were still vibrant; perhaps the Sancerre reds of the early 1990s were more like red Burgundies from the mid 1980s, but they showed a similar tertiary development with underpinnings of *sous bois* (that delicious savory element described in French as aromas of the undergrowth). So, yes, the best Sancerre reds do age well, following the Burgundian pattern, although twenty years may be a reasonable limit on longevity for most tastes.

When I visited producers in Sancerre, there was much discussion about terroir, mostly about the effects of the different limestone soils, but a common comment was, "Ah, you should visit the Vacherons, they grow some Pinot Noir on silex, it is quite different." Indeed, half of the Vacherons' vineyards are on silex, half are on calcareous soils. The Pinot is mostly on calcareous plots but there is some on silex, which gives a tauter quality to the wines, accentuating the sense of minerality. Most of the Vacheron's Pinots represent an assemblage of terroirs, but their top cuvée, the Belle Dame, comes exclusively from a southwest-facing vineyard on silex soils. Its refined quality makes you think of Volnay.

Most top producers make more than one Pinot Noir, but the distinction is more usually based on selection of cuvées or the age of the vines rather than the terroir. Lucien Crochet, Vincent Pinard, and Henri Bourgeois all produce multiple cuvées of Pinot Noir where the top wine comes from Vieilles Vignes rather than a specific terroir. A vertical of Pinard's top Charlouise cuvée showed an elegance and precision reminiscent of Volnay through a variety of vintages (Ỵ page 174). The top wines from these producers all fetch good prices, running into the range of premier cru Burgundy, but production is fairly small and the market is not ready to pay the further premium that would be required to segregate the bottlings by vineyards. Alphonse Mellot is unusual in having taken the leap to a series of cuvées coming specifically from different vineyards, ranging from calcareous to silex soils (Ỵ page 177). Each cuvée is distinct, with the calcareous more rounded and the siliceous tauter, extending to an old vines calcareous cuvée that could easily come from a top site in the Côte de Nuits. Development is held back by lack of interest in Sancerre's terroirs. "The problem with Sancerre is that there are no Crus," says the younger Alphonse Mellot. He would like to see a classification system introducing premier and grand crus.

So what is the future for red Sancerre? The wines are steadily improving, and although direct comparisons may be invidious, I think it is fair to say that the gap with Burgundy has been closing. There's no direct attempt to compete with Burgundy, but that is where I find the closest stylistic comparisons in tasting the wines, although Sancerre, especially when concentrated, can be quite perfumed. In good vintages, there are some very fine red wines, with unmistakable Pinot Noir character, and with good aging potential. (Sancerre shows a similar range of vintage variation to Burgundy.) Yet it has to be said that these remain exceptional demonstrations; there is still a large amount of red Sancerre that is perfectly good wine, but more resembles Beaujolais than Beaune, and it can be hard to get Pinot typicity from it. But among the better wines, there is something of the same stylistic range of variation from the lighter, earthier fruits you get in the Côte de Beaune to the firmer fruits of the Côte de Nuits, more reflecting winemaking style than terroir, although accentuated if you compare wines from calcareous and siliceous terroirs. The wines from siliceous terroirs share a characteristic tautness with wines of the Ahr or Mosel, but are generally tighter on the finish.

How does value for money compare with other regions? Up to the mid range, there are some good values, with prices less inflated than other regions. At the very top, prices venture into the territory of Burgundy's premier crus, and here you have to ask if the market is ready to pay the same premium in Sancerre for the nuances of terroir. It's a great shame that, for the most part, you have to taste barrel samples to understand the complexity of the effects of terroir on Pinot Noir in Sancerre.

The largest plantings of Pinot Noir outside of France are in Germany, where the two ultimate terroir grapes, Pinot Noir and Riesling, are often grown in intimate proximity. Wine has been made in the southern part of Germany since Roman times, when apparently most was red.[11] In the early nineteenth century, Cochem (on the upper Mosel) was claimed to produce "chiefly red wine from the Klebrot vine."[12] Klebrot, Klävner, and Clevner are all old names for Pinot Noir, which is more usually known as Spätburgunder in Germany, acknowledging its origins in Burgundy. (The name literally means "late Burgundy," referring to the time of ripening.) Red wine production, and possibly production of Pinot Noir, has long been established in Germany, originating mostly likely with vines brought from Burgundy to the great monastery at Kloster Eberbach. But by the twentieth century production was focused on white wine everywhere except in the Ahr. Red wine was mostly produced from rustic varieties, and kept sweet to hide its deficiencies.

A recent move to quality has been led by increased plantings of Pinot Noir, and in the past two decades, Germany has become the most important producer of Pinot Noir after France. With almost 12,000 hectares now planted, there is more Pinot Noir grown in Germany than in Burgundy.[13] The rapid expansion of Pinot Noir has not been without problems. One of the issues raised by growing black grapes in a northern climate is the need for a prolonged growing season in order to reach ripeness. Unlike Burgundy, where harvesting was traditionally always one hundred days after flowering (usually some time in September), the harvest in Germany usually does not occur until October.

Keeping the grapes on the vine increases susceptibility to the problems caused by humidity, especially the occurrence of mildew and rot. Anxiety

The growth of Pinot Noir plantings in Germany has been exponential until a recent leveling off. It is grown in almost all regions.[15]

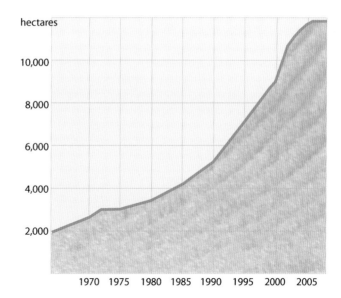

about humidity problems led to planting clones that resist humidity better than the old Burgundian Pinot Noirs; known as Geisenheim clones after their origin at the Geisenheim Institute, these clones also produced yields that were rather too high for quality wine. They were widely planted through the seventies and eighties, but as Alexander Stodden of Weingut Jean Stodden says, "The Geisenheim clones gave sugar but not taste."[14] The original Geisenheim plants are now quite old, but even so, require a lot of attention in order to keep yields down to a level that gives quality. Since the nineties, producers have been planting the new Dijon clones from Burgundy, with lower production levels being the main criterion, giving much better results. And, of course, like everywhere else, selection of berries has become paramount. This has particularly pronounced effects on late harvests, because today berries with botrytis are eliminated, whereas thirty years ago some would probably have been included.

Not surprisingly, the bulk of Pinot Noir production (more than half) is in the most southern wine-producing region, Baden, but less obviously, some of the highest quality Pinot Noirs come from the tiny valley of the Ahr in the north. Terroirs vary widely. In the southern regions, soils are often limestone; they vary in type but are broadly similar to the Burgundian terroir. But there are also volcanic or sandstone soils, each giving Pinot Noir of somewhat different character. And to the north of a line connecting the Mosel to the Rheingau, soils are mostly based on slate. The differences play out in Pinot Noir in much the same way as for Riesling, with richer, rounder wines coming from limestone, and tighter, more mineral wines coming from slate.

Especially with the recent run of warm vintages, ripening Pinot Noir has not been a problem anywhere from Baden to the Ahr. You might think of

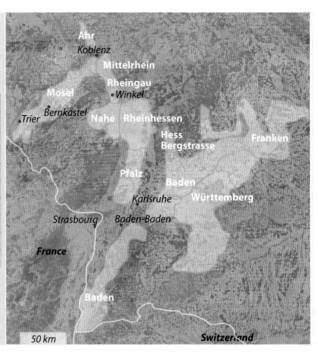

Most wine-producing regions in Germany have some Pinot Noir, but plantings are concentrated in the south.

Region	Ha	
Baden	5.855	37%
Pfalz	1.585	7%
Rheinhes-	1.342	5%
Württemberg	1.278	11%
Rheingau	380	12%
Mosel	359	4%
Ahr	342	61%
Franken	254	4%
Nahe	248	6%

Hectares are total plantings of Pinot Noir; percent is proportion of total vineyards in region.[16]

Pinot Noir production in Germany as challenged by cool conditions, given that it's quite a bit north of Burgundy, but actually a common refrain among producers, from south to north, is that they need to pick before the grapes become over-ripe. Even so, sugar levels tend to be rather high by the time of harvest, as producers usually reckon that physiological ripeness does not occur until potential alcohol reaches 13-13.5%. But even when ripeness is achieved at lower sugar levels, there is a tendency to chaptalize to bring the alcohol level up to 13.5%. There's a general view in Germany that red wine requires at least 13% alcohol to have sufficient richness. So producers will routinely chaptalize if levels are lower. Many producers told me they believe they make a better wine by harvesting earlier and chaptalizing, than by allowing sugar levels to increase to a point at which grapes might become over-ripe.[*] But personally I believe they might make more elegant wines if they left Nature alone and simply produced wines with slightly lower alcohol levels.

So is there any common defining quality for Pinot Noir in Germany? "You cannot say we have a German Pinot Noir," said Paul Fürst of Weingut Rudolph Fürst, when I asked him about this. Hansjörg Rebholz, of Oekonomierat Rebholz in the Pfalz, reinforced this view by telling me, "There is

---

[*] Sugar levels are measured in Germany on the Oechsle scale, basically a reflection of the density of juice in the grape, which corresponds to sugar content. An Oechsle of 91.9 corresponds to 12.5% potential alcohol, 95.6 equals 13%, and 99.5 is 13.5%. Producers generally quote a limit around 98-100 Oechsle (13.3-13.6% alcohol) for harvesting.

no distinctive style for Pinot Noir in each region, it's more a matter of individual producer styles."[17] Yet German red wine production has traditionally emphasized overt fruitiness, and if I were to define a single characteristic that I see in the Pinot Noirs, it would be a tendency to a touch of glycerin giving a superficial opulence on the finish.[18] When young the wines tend to have more obvious fruit than (say) Burgundy, taking the form more of red or black cherries than strawberries. The effect is more pronounced in the south, where a superficial richness or opulence hides the precision of fruits you see in the more mineral wines from the north.

Quality has increased enormously in the past decade. Most producers of Pinot Noir make an "estate wine," assembled from a variety of plots and carrying a broad regional description, a village wine from local holdings, and a top wine, labeled as Grosses Gewächs if they are a member of the VDP, from single vineyards.* Usually the estate wines are matured in large old oak foudres, and are generally intended to satisfy the craving of the German consumer to drink wines of the most recent vintage, offering rather simple, straightforward fruits. "On January 1 they want the new wine and not the old wine," says Phillip Kuhn of Weingut Kuhn in the Pfalz.[19] Clients wait for the next vintage to be bottled. Some producers bottle before Beaujolais Nouveau, he says ruefully. Several producers actually call their entry level wine "Tradition," implying that it honors the old German style of fruity wines for immediate consumption.

The village wines are usually matured in a mix of large casks and a few barriques of old oak, and will benefit from a little aging, while barriques of new French oak are commonly employed for the grand crus, which can show real Pinot Noir typicity in developing interesting aromas and flavors as they age. With some rare exceptions, German Pinot Noirs tend to follow a similar, but more rapid, aging pattern to Burgundy, and are sooner to reach what I think of as the turning point, when the fruit-dominated spectrum begins to be replaced by more savory aromas and flavors. Whereas a top Burgundy might take ten or more years to reach the delicious point of sous bois, a German Pinot Noir or Sancerre red might achieve it in five. The balance is different. Burgundy develops tertiary aromas at a later point, when the fruits have begun to recede, but more rapid development in Germany means that the tertiary notes mingle with fruits that are still overt rather than replacing them.

---

* Grosses Gewächs are defined as individual vineyards capable of producing top quality and are intended to be the equivalent of Grand Crus. Indeed, many producers now use the term Grand Cru rather than Grosses Gewächs in conversation. In each region, the use of Grosses Gewächs is restricted to the top varieties.

And terroir plays out on the styles of this most transparent grape variety as effectively as anywhere. In the north, the Ahr Valley, Mosel, and Rheingau grow Pinot Noir on slate-based soils. "If you believe what the books say, it's not possible to make red wine in the Ahr valley because we don't have chalk, we have slate," says Alexander Stodden.[21] Indeed, the Ahr Valley defies all the mantras about wine production. The northernmost region for wine production in the world, not only is it above the nominal 50° latitude where wine grapes can be cultivated, but the majority of plantings are black.[22] There's a myth that Pinot Noir production is possible due only to the unique protected microclimate; but although the steep walls of the valley provide an unexpectedly warm environment, it's not unique. Average temperatures and rainfall are the same as the Mosel, where Pinot Noir is produced only by a handful of producers. The difference is due to a historical accident: local legend has it that black grapes were established in the Ahr because its rulers in the fourteenth century preferred red wine. This may be exaggerated, since one historian states that red wine production started only at the end of the seventeenth century, and become predominant by the eighteenth,[23] but whatever the cause, the Ahr has been red for at least a couple of hundred years, whereas the Mosel established a tradition for Riesling. Originally production in the Ahr focused on rosé, then the wines became a light red color; they were described approvingly by Saintsbury in his Notes on a Cellar Book in 1920 as "red hock."[24] But they were sweet, and production of dry red wine is a phenomenon of the past twenty years.

The geography of the Ahr Valley is dramatic. The Ahr itself is a small river with twists and turns on an east-west axis. Rising up on its northern side are extremely steep terraces covered in vines. All of the terroir is based on slate, but it changes significantly along the valley. At the eastern end at Bad

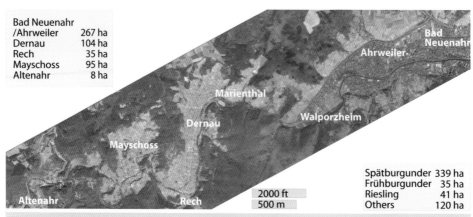

Bad Neuenahr /Ahrweiler	267 ha
Dernau	104 ha
Rech	35 ha
Mayschoss	95 ha
Altenahr	8 ha

Spätburgunder	339 ha
Frühburgunder	35 ha
Riesling	41 ha
Others	120 ha

2000 ft
500 m

The wine-producing areas of the Ahr valley form a narrow band only 15 miles long from Bad Neuenahr to Altenahr.[20]

Vineyards in the Ahr valley are steeply terraced.

Neuenahr, the valley opens out, and the soils are richer and the slopes not so steep. Going west, the valley becomes a fraction tighter at Ahrweiler, and then narrows around Walporzheim, where the vineyards are compressed into slate-covered, south-facing terraces rising up steeply from the Ahr river. Terroir is clearly reflected in the wines. Just as slate produces Rieslings of extraordinary tension, so it is reflected by a taut, mineral quality in Pinot Noir. Producers in the Ahr display varying styles, but a common feature is that the wines are more rounded and softer from the eastern end, becoming progressively more mineral moving along to the west. The unique quality that I find in Pinot Noir from slate soils is tautness: an extremely precise delineation of fruits and a palpable sense of tension in the wine. Only the siliceous soils of eastern Sancerre produce a comparable texture.

The Ahr practices small scale production with a vengeance. Total volume is only around 500,000 cases per year. Individual vineyard holdings are tiny, often only a few rows of vines. So many of them are below the level of economic wine production, that most growers send their grapes to one of the two cooperatives, which together account for about half of all production.[25] The high quality Pinot Noirs on which the reputation of the Ahr depends actually represent a vanishingly small proportion of production, and come from (literally) a handful of producers. Three top producers in the Ahr show varying styles, with J. J. Adeneuer the softest, Meyer-Näkel the most precise, and Jean Stodden the most powerful.

Adeneuer produces only red wine—"we have been producing Pinot Noir for five hundred years," says Marc Adeneuer—and his aim is to produce Pinot Noir typifying the region. This means less tannin in a more overtly fruity style (Ⴗ page 179). Mayer-Näkel has a well deserved reputation for the elegance and precision of its Pinot Noirs (Ⴗ page 180). When I asked Meike Näkel how she would describe her wines, she said, "Very special. You do not often find Pinot Noir grown on slate, which gives the wine a layer of minerality. The stony thing is the first to come out; and then the tannic structure is different from Pinot grown on calcareous soils, it's always a little finer, these are elegant not big wines. The slate gives the wine a certain sweetness."[26] At Weingut Jean Stodden, Alexander Stodden is a minimalist. "I'm not a winemaker, I'm a wine watcher," he says. He looks for clean fruit, good balance with tannins and acidity; he thinks soft wines do not have enough character. The Stodden wines are more forceful than most Burgundies; his general style follows the German liking for overt fruit, but there is no mistaking their absolute quality (Ⴗ page 182). Tasting the wines of these producers makes it completely clear that conventional wisdom is wrong: not only can you grow Pinot Noir on slate, but the wines clearly reflect the terroir, showing increased tautness and minerality with the concentration of the slate, casting another light on the typicity of Pinot Noir.

In searching for typicity, it's perhaps worth mentioning Frühburgunder at this point. As the name suggests ("Frühburgunder" means early Burgundy, compared with "Spätburgunder," which means late Burgundy), this is an early-ripening variant of Pinot Noir. Elsewhere it is known as Pinot Noir Précoce, but with the German love of classification, it is distinguished as a

Vineyard holdings are tiny parcels in the Ahr. Six separate holdings can be seen in fewer than fifty short rows in this vineyard above the old monastery at Marienthal in the Ahr.

Frühburgunder at Ahrweiler has to be protected from birds with blue netting in August. The Spätburgunder on either side has not yet reached véraison and is not vulnerable. In fact, you could probably estimate how much Frühburgunder is grown in the Ahr by counting the area of blue netting in late August.

separate variety. Indeed tastings for any producer who grows both varieties usually show Frühburgunder to be quite distinct from the Spätburgunder. The Ahr was almost the last holdout of the variety. It's always been grown here, but practical difficulties led to a decline to only about 15 hectares in the 1960s. Since then there has been a revival of interest, and today there are 250 hectares in Germany.

The distinguishing feature of Frühburgunder is that it ripens quite a bit earlier than Spätburgunder, anywhere from two to four weeks. It's difficult to handle in the vineyard because it blossoms very early, and the crop can be lost to frost. It ripens at the end of August or early September, just at a point when wasps and birds are around to spoil the crop. The berries are rather small and give high fruit extract with relatively little tannin. The resulting wine usually has much simpler, more direct, fruit flavors than Spätburgunder, rustic and crowd-pleasing without any of the delicacy or complexity of Pinot Noir (Y page 196). I think the Germans have a point in calling it a separate variety.

The Mosel has similar terroir and climate to the Ahr, but production of red wine is vanishingly small.[27] In fact, it was illegal to plant Pinot Noir in the Mosel until the ban was lifted in 1985. There are a handful of generic wines, but very few producers make single vineyard Pinot Noirs. Markus Molitor is a pioneer who started producing Pinot Noir in 1987, but has as yet attracted few followers. His single vineyard Pinot Noirs from Brauneberg (the Mandelgraben and Klostergarten vineyards) and the Graacher Himmelreich are very fine, showing a progression of increasing minerality. Graacher Himmelreich has the classic gray slate, which forces the grapevine roots to delve deep into the earth, and might be the world's steepest vineyard of Pinot Noir.

Covered in gray slate, the Graach Himmelreich vineyard rises up vertiginously from the Mosel. The top of the vineyard is about 150 m above the river. Just at véraison in late August, the Pinot Noir needs to be protected with blue netting. (At this time, it is sweeter than the Riesling and therefore is most attractive to birds.)

Molitor freely admits that there was a learning curve as they acquired expertise to handle red wine, especially in the use of oak, but the wines I tasted from the first decade of this century were certainly refined and elegant. Molitor's model is Burgundy, and I would say the closest comparison is with Beaune, although the wines display that taut, lean minerality characteristic of slate (Ⲧ page 183). Yet the wines may not have been a commercial success, since Molitor is not extending his plantings of Pinot Noir.

Cistercian monks may well have planted the first Pinot Noir in Germany at Kloster Eberbach in the twelfth century. Following the principles of the original domain at Clos Vougeot, they extended their vineyard holdings all around the Rheingau. After the dissolution of the monasteries, the vineyards became the property of the state-owned Domäne Assmanshausen, whose top wine comes from the single vineyard Assmanshausen Höllenberg, which has a special soil with a violet-colored variation of gray slate. Diurnal variation is higher in Assmanshausen because the temperature falls off more at night, and the top wine, called Mauerwein, comes from a plot at the edge of the vineyard, protected by the surrounding wall. Vintages back to the 1950s

The Cistercian monastery at Kloster Eberbach is probably where red wine production started in Germany.

demonstrate the potential of the vineyard, with the characteristic minerality of slate, although they are not as taut as the wines of the Mosel or Ahr. Today's vintages are good, rather than great, and to my mind too rarely achieve the heights of which they would be capable if the dead hand of the state were lifted (⍦ page 184).

South of a line from the Mosel to the Rheingau, terroirs vary widely, including sandstone, volcanic, and limestone. At the eastern extreme in Franken, where Sylvaner reigns supreme, and Riesling is planted only in the stoniest locations, Weingut Rudolf Fürst has been a pioneer with Pinot Noir. Vineyards are at 100 m elevation in the protected environment of a river valley, on sandstone terroir. Fürst's aim is for freshness rather than sweetness in the grapes or strong tannins. "Sandstone gives wines that are light in the mouth, fresh rather than smooth. The wine should dance in the mouth," says Paul Fürst. His wines are light and elegant (⍦ page 186).

The large plain of the Rheinhessen, extending from the Rhine river, is known more for bulk production from low-grade varieties than for quality, but some producers stand out for quality Riesling, and a few of them also produce some Pinot Noir, although there is no one who regards himself as a red wine specialist. The landscape of Rheinhessen merges imperceptibly into the Pfalz, which has the most plantings of Pinot Noir after the Baden region. "Pinot Noir is a traditional variety in the Pfalz," says Volker Knipser of Weingut Knipser. But it disappeared and Portugieser was grown instead. By the twenties, there was not much Pinot left. And although there is a tradition of red wine production, there was really no quality red wine until recently. Knipser pioneered the reintroduction of Pinot Noir in 1983, and together with Phillip Kuhn, has made the village of Laumersheim a center for quality production of Pinot Noir. Terroirs vary from limestone to sandy, but Pinot Noir is most successful on the limestone. Phillip Kuhn is impressed by Burgundy, but not by its lightest wines; he prefers Côte de Nuits to Côte de Beaune. His wines display a style somewhere between the Côte de Nuits and the fruity German tradition, and age quite slowly (Ⓣ page 187). I felt the Kuhn wines were generally around two years behind the Ahr in development. His is a rich style, richer than Burgundy perhaps. But judgment should wait because the vines are all still young, and we need to see what will happen as they age.

Some of the most elegant wines of the Pfalz come from Oekonomierat Rebholz where Hansjörg Rebholz says his aim is to make Pinot Noir in a Burgundian style with the potential for aging. "For me Pinot Noir is the red brother of Riesling which can show minerality and elegance," he says.[28] A geological fault in the vicinity results in a variety of soil types; Riesling is largely planted on the red slate, and Pinot Noir is planted on the Muschelkalk terrain, a fossil-rich limestone. The wines are smooth and elegant, with a certain fatness on the finish, and as you move up the quality scale, the fat integrates better and the red fruits change more to black (Ⓣ page 188). Rebholz wines age more slowly than most in the Pfalz, and Hansjörg attributes this to the Muschelkalk soil, but I think his skill as a winemaker has something to do with it. I was astounded by a 1979, tasted blind, which I would have placed in the late eighties, and which is still delicious (albeit a little past its peak).

Friedrich Becker in Schweigen, at the southern tip of the Pfalz, is one of the most fascinating producers in the region, because most of his vineyards are across the border in France! A century ago, cross ownership was quite common; today it is an anomaly that permits German wine to be made in France. Of the vineyards in Schweigen classified as Grosses Gewächs in the German system, 70% are actually in France. Walking around the vineyards, you encounter in juxtaposition plots that are part of the Sankt Paul or Kamenberg Grosses Gewächs and those that are cultivated for AOC Alsace. The terroir is limestone, the difference between the two top vineyards being that Sankt Paul has a thinner topsoil than Kamenberg.

Many of the vineyards are located around the old monastery of Wissembourg that dominated the region from the eleventh century. Today only one of its four original towers is still standing. Around it is a mix of vineyards and forest land, but the vineyards around the monastery are not necessarily in the same relative locations as originally; over the past three centuries, the monastery's original vineyards often became uncultivated and reverted to forest,

Only one tower remains of the monastery at Wissembourg that dominated vineyards in the eleventh century. Today vineyards of Pinot Noir (foreground) together with some uncultivated land (background) surround the tower. Some of the vineyards produce wine for the German village of Schweigen, others for the Alsace AOC.

and when new vineyards were replanted more recently, it wasn't necessarily in the same locations. The Becker family actually owns the remaining tower, and Fritz Becker would like to get permission to make wine there; then there could be Sankt Paul from the surrounding vineyards under both the German and the French AOC systems.

Pinot Noir was being grown here in the sixteenth century, but by the twentieth century there was no longer any red wine. Fritz Becker's father planted the first Pinot Noir in 1967; "everyone thought he was crazy to try to produce red German wine here," Fritz remembers.[29] The wines were thought to be too sour (remember that most German wine was sweet at the time). Local criticism extended to refusing a certificate for the best wines (because they had been aged in barriques), so even to this day Becker's top wines are produced as Tafelwein (table wine). They have a rich dense structure (page 190), entirely different from wines made from adjacent vineyards in the Alsace AOC.

Original vineyards consist of individual rows following the contours of the hills (left at Oberegen), while others have been extensively reconstructed with terraces (right at Ihringen Winklerberg).

With German and French vineyards intermingled, this is the perfect occasion to compare German with Alsatian Pinot Noir. Almost all the French growers send their grapes to the local cooperative at Cleebourg, so to see the difference between the French and German approaches, I tasted the wines at the coop. Perhaps it's unfair to compare the cooperative's wines with a top producer, but it's certainly fair to say that the coop's wines are much closer to what the monks probably drank. In fact, they are perfectly serviceable, well-made wines for quaffing; but nothing to compare with Becker's wines, which meet his objective of "the iron fist in the velvet glove," as he describes it. His ideal is Musigny.

Just to the south of the Pfalz, Baden is the heartland of German red wine production, with more than half the planted area of Pinot Noir. Vineyards lie between Alsace to the west and the Black Forest to the east. Pinot Noir really is a tradition here, but quality is somewhat held back by the tiny size of most vineyard parcels. Many are uneconomic, and the largest producer in the area is the cooperative in Achkarrer, which takes the grapes from the individual growers. But three top growers produce wines each in their own distinctive style, yet also reflecting the terroirs of their individual vineyards, and demonstrating the potential of the region. Weingut Dr. Heger in Ihringen, reputedly the warmest spot in Germany, started as a hobby for Dr. Max Heger in 1935. Weingut Bernhard Huber in Malterdingen became independent only in 1987, but previously there were five generations of expertise with wine. Weingut Salwey is the most recent, founded in 1950.

Terroir here varies widely; in fact, one problem is that the official vineyard descriptions do not distinguish between the flat land in the valley (which gives somewhat inferior grapes) and the steep slopes on the hills (which are much superior). As a practical matter, producers use only the vines on the hillsides for their Grosses Gewächs wines, but the rule is unwritten. The lie

of the land is stunning. Vineyards were originally cramped into the hills, often with single rows running along the contours. After the reorganization of vineyards that followed the 1971 reclassification, many were reconstructed by building terraces. Local producers feel this was a mistake that reduced the total vineyard area significantly, changed the quality of the terroir, and increased vintage variation.

At Ihringen, the aim for Weingut Dr. Heger is "direction Burgundy," says winemaker Markus Mleinek, "with long-lasting Pinot, cherry fruits when young, strawberry when older." The main issue is not to let the Pinot Noir get too hot and become too jammy; it's actually planted in the cooler sites. The first Pinot Noir vineyards were established in 1954, when selections from Clos Vougeot were planted on their own roots in the Ihringen Winklerberg vineyard. Winklerberg's dramatic terraces are more exposed than the other top vineyard, Achkarrer Schlossberg, which is in a protected canyon. The volcanic soils of these vineyards produce a sort of half way house between the taut minerality of slate and the greater opulence of limestone, veering more to the former in Schlossberg and the latter in Winklerberg (⯆ page 191).

Bernhard Huber's vineyards at Malterdingen are on limestone terroirs. The old tradition of Pinot Noir here is indicated by the fact that Malterdingen was actually a synonym for Spätburgunder in the Middle Ages. Close to the Black Forest, there is strong diurnal variation from the cool night breezes, but vineyards are hot during the day; vineyard workers call their warmest vineyard, Wildenstein, which is part of Malterdinger Bienenberg, "the oven." Until 2004 what are now their Grosses Gewächs were assembled into a single "Huber Reserve." The wines were always vinified separately, and with 2004 they started to be bottled separately to represent the individual vineyards, a sign of the increasing interest in vineyard variations for Pinot

Noir. Once again there are interesting differences depending on the topsoil and the elevation of the vineyards (Υ page 193).

Brimming with enthusiasm, Konrad Salwey, who now makes the wines at Weingut Salwey, simply says "local," when asked about his stylistic aims. Some of the most intense Pinot Noirs of the region come from here, and the style is his own, but in it you can see both German and Burgundian traditions. The vineyards are mostly on limestone, but the Kaiserstuhl vineyard is an exception that is volcanic. Most plantings are the Freiburg clones (thought to have come from Burgundy and to have been established in Freiburg about 150 years ago), which ripen just a bit later, but they require strong pruning to keep yields down. Konrad does not want too intense a tannic structure, but for the wines to become smooth with age. One of his main concerns is to dispel the impression that German Pinot Noirs do not age; he feels his are perfect after about six years. They offer a terrific example of what you might call the new German Pinot Noir, where you see reflections of terroir through the hand of the producer (Υ page 194).

So given Germany's variety of terroirs, is there an exquisite matching of variety to vineyard? Well, yes and no. The best sites are reserved for the best varieties. In most cases this means that exceptional vineyards are planted with Riesling; sometimes they are planted with Pinot Noir. But there is no distinction between terroirs that should be planted with Riesling and those that should be planted with Pinot Noir. The best vineyards—usually those on the slopes with stonier soils—are simply viewed as better for all varieties. Whether Riesling or Pinot is planted on a particular top site is more a commercial question of which variety the producer wanted to have available at the time when the site needed to be replanted. This brings us back to the question of whether terroir is simply a matter of ripening; the best sites have exposure and soil conditions producing more reliable ripening, whether it's Riesling or Pinot Noir that's planted there. The comparison between the Ahr and Mosel is a forceful demonstration that historical accident may be the main determinant of which variety is planted.

It is striking that most German Pinot Noir is sold in Germany—relatively little is exported. This is not because it is cheap: the top wines sell at the same price range as good village Burgundy or premier crus. In fact, less than 5% of the Pinot Noir drunk in Germany comes from Burgundy; and exports from Burgundy to Germany have been falling steadily, as production of Spätburgunder has increased.[30] (Some producers are now simply labeling it as Pinot Noir.) The German consumer views the typicity of Pinot Noir in a German light.

Production of Pinot Noir in Germany has many similarities with Burgundy. Variety of terroir is reflected in the wine; in fact, compared to Burgundy's variations on a theme of limestone, Germany offers Pinot Noirs from limestone, sandstone, volcanic soils, and slate. The tradition of vineyard mapping has carried over directly from Riesling to Pinot Noir, and the Grosses Gewächs define a series of single vineyard "Grand Crus" comparable in range and complexity to Burgundy's premier crus. Going from north to south, you see the same change from a steely minerality to a more opulent, more rounded style in Pinot Noir that is already familiar from Riesling. Terroir variation is overlayed by each producer's individual style—or each producer's style is overlaid by terroir, it all depends on how you look at it—but just as in Burgundy, the producer is the most important determinant of quality. There is no single definition of style for Spätburgunder, but that recognizable yet indefinable quality that speaks of Pinot Noir shines through the top wines: a mixture of red cherry and strawberry fruits sometimes mixed with a hint of black cherries, good supporting acidity and a relatively light tannic backbone, an earthy or mineral impression to a silky or velvety finish. So Burgundy does not have a stranglehold on typicity; but now it is time to return to France.

"The problem is that Alsace faces the wrong way," said Markus Mleinek, when I asked him why he thought the Pinot Noirs of Alsace were less interesting than those of Baden.[31] Was he speaking literally or metaphorically?

Local legend claims that the region around St. Hippolyte and Rodern, near the town of Ohrschwiller, has long been established for red wine and Pinot Noir. The great castle of Haut Konigsberg looms over the vineyards.

Limited by the Vosges mountains, the Alsatian vineyards tend to face east, although some have warm southern exposure. And the focus is really on white wine, with few producers having expertise or making more than token efforts with reds. But the major factor influencing wine growing in Alsace from the nineteenth century through the first half of the twentieth was more the state of war between France and Germany than any intrinsic consideration of terroir or cépages. Whether under French or German occupation, the focus became directed to cheap wines—what the French call *vins de comptoir*—rather than to quality. In the period following the second world war, there were almost no plantings of quality varieties, and among them the amount of Pinot Noir was vanishingly small.[32]

The vineyards of Alsace nestle under the Vosges mountains. The Pfalz of Germany is to the north, and Baden is to the east.[33]

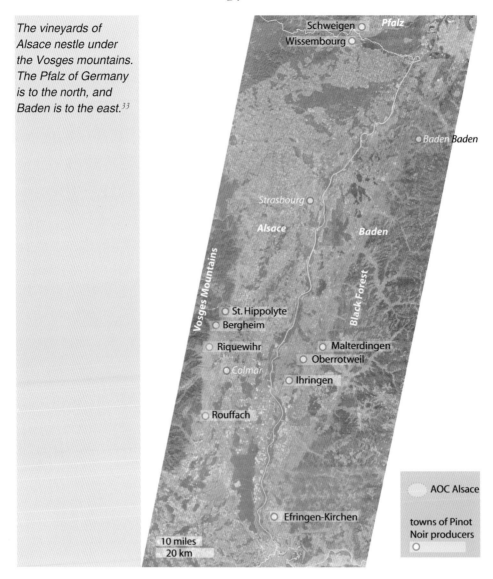

Bad weather often stops on the Vosges mountains immediately to the west of the Alsatian vineyards.

The coolest climate in France for making dry wine, Alsace has concentrated on white grape varieties that can ripen in its cool summers. The protective effect of the Vosges mountains means that this is the driest region in France for winemaking, sometimes with barely enough rainfall for the annual cycle of the grapevine. The major consequence of the recent run of warmer vintages has been an increase in the proportion of white wines with some residual sugar rather than any additional focus on reds.

Alsace has always used its cool climates to excuse the lack of intensity in its Pinot Noirs. Indeed, this has been regarded as part of the typicity, with reports that wines achieving real intensity have sometimes been refused the right to the AOC label. Looking across at Baden makes this excuse seem pretty feeble. Certainly it is now warm enough to make Pinot Noir in Alsace; Olivier Humbrecht, one of the most respected winemakers in Alsace, who makes a little from time to time, notes, "I would almost say that if Pinot Noir is produced the right way, it is almost too hot now in Alsace for this grape."[34]

Pinot Noir is the only black variety authorized in the Alsace AOC, which extends over the Départements of the Bas-Rhin (including vineyards from south of Strasbourg to just north of Colmar) and the Haut-Rhin (immediately to the south). Today virtually all vineyards in the region are part of the AOC, with almost a quarter of total production devoted to sparkling wine; the rest is a mix of dry and sweet wine, somewhat depending on the vintage.[35] Plantings of Pinot Noir have increased more rapidly than any other quality variety since the 1970s.[36] They have doubled since 1982, perhaps not coincidentally as vintages have become steadily warmer. But Alsace makes much less red wine than might be suggested by the area of grapes. There are 1,500 ha of Pinot Noir, but of the production of almost 1.2 million cases, 40% is Crémant (sparkling wine), and another 50% is rosé, leaving only 120,000 cases of red wine.[37] There may be only around 200 ha of Pinot Noir vineyards devoted exclusively to production of red wine, which is one reason why it is so difficult to find interesting examples. There is no producer for whom Pinot Noir is anything more than an insignificant part of total production.

Even the appearance of "rouge" on the label is not a guarantee of really red wine, since a fair proportion of the reds aren't much darker, or more flavorful, than the rosés. One reason is that production limits allowed by the AOC are much too high, the highest in France for dry wine, in the case of Pinot Noir 60 hl/ha.[38] Indeed, when asked why Alsatian Pinot Noir isn't better, Etienne Hugel, of the major negociant-grower Hugel, says, "One word: overcropping. When you are in a white wine region that has a reputation for overcropping, and you start to make red wine, applying the same methods does not work." Another factor contributing to lack of interest in quality Pinot Noir may be collateral damage from the grand cru system, which limits use of the name of a grand cru to four white varieties.[39] Since naming a grand cru on the label fetches a premium, the exclusion of Pinot Noir is a disincentive to plant it in some of the best sites. On the other hand, the grand crus were defined with different criteria in mind, and Olivier Humbrecht points out that much of Alsace's terroir is sandstone or granite, not optimally suited for Pinot Noir, and adds that, "Pinot Noir is perhaps today the most popular wine in Alsace and therefore is planted everywhere and without the care this grape requires (lower yields, higher density)."[40]

Although there was red wine in Alsace several centuries ago, for most producers it has been a new venture to produce high quality Pinot Noir. For Hugel, it was somewhat of a hit and miss experience at the beginning. They had been compelled to take Pinot Noir from their growers in order to obtain more desirable varieties, but they sold the grapes off in bulk. When they decided to make their first vintage in 1977, Johnny Hugel, the winemaker at the time, said "If you force me to make Pinot Noir, I'll make vinegar."[41] So his brother made the wine, but it was not very successful and was sold off. The next year, Hugel started to make Pinot Noir in earnest, with better equipment, but the move to top quality really started in the early 1980s. In 1985, a half hectare of twenty year old vines in Pflostig came up for sale. The Hugel family refused to purchase it, so the next generation took a decision, and brothers Etienne and Marc with their cousin Jean-Philippe (the three nephews) bought it. Johnny Hugel wanted them to uproot it and replant with a white variety. As Etienne Hugel recollects, "During numerous visits to top growers in Côte d'Or, I and my brother just fell in love with this most fascinating grape. [Making Pinot Noir] was a way for the 'youngsters' to show the family what they had learned."[42] Pflostig is the most Burgundian site in Alsace, with chalky soil at the surface. Later they acquired another hectare in the vicinity (now called La Bourgogne) and replanted it with Pinot Noir.

Etienne is enthusiastic about the potential for Pinot Noir in Alsace today. "With the climate change, we probably now have the same climate in Alsace that Burgundy had twenty years ago," he says, adding that Pinot needs slow ripening to achieve intensity of flavor, and Alsace has an advantage that you can usually afford to wait to pick, whereas elsewhere they are forced to pick earlier. "If there is one grape that doesn't stand compromise, it is Pinot Noir." Their top Pinot Noir, the Jubilee bottling, has been an estate wine since 1985, initially including only the first vineyard, later made from both vineyards. But in line with Hugel's general philosophy (they do not use the grand cru system) it is not identified as coming from any specific site (⍑ page 196).

The restriction of grand crus to specified white varieties, and a ban on using local place names, means that single vineyard Pinot Noirs are rarely identified as such in Alsace. It's somewhat of an alphabet country, with René Muré's "V" coming from the Vorbourg grand cru, André Ostertag's "E"

Hugel planted a different clone of Pinot Noir every four rows at the La Bourgogne vineyard in order to emphasis diversity. The vines with leaves turning red in the autumn are a Pinot Teinturier, where the juice is also colored red.

Pinot Noir is planted in cooler spots in Alsace. René Muré's vineyard in the Grand Cru Vorbourg is in an exposed location at the top of the hill overlooking the town of Rouffach.

coming from Epfig, and following the trend, "W" standing simply for Do-maine Weinbach's top Pinot Noir (it comes from vineyards in the Altenbourg lieu-dit and the Schlossberg grand cru). But all of these wines come from vineyards with a particularity for Pinot Noir.

René Muré have two Pinot Noir vineyards in the Vorbourg grand cru. "V" comes from an east-facing vineyard overlooking the town of Rouffach, where the soil is limestone and clay with a little loess, and the wine is light and elegant. At the southern tip of the grand cru, in Clos St. Landelin, the soil is a red clay with calcareous stones, and the exposed vineyard gets con-tinuous wind, an important feature in avoiding buildup of humidity with problems of botrytis (always a concern with Pinot Noir in Alsace). Even allowing that the vines in Clos St. Landelin are older, still you see an immedi-ate difference, with more concentration and presence (⏀ page 198). "Clos St. Landelin, c'est le paradis for Pinot Noir," says René Muré. In somewhat the same way as the difference in regimes for premier crus and village wines in Burgundy, the sturdier Clos St. Landelin spends longer in barrique and uses more new oak. "We don't want to copy Burgundy, the thing is to find our own style, but it's true that for balance and style we are not looking at other wines in Alsace, we are looking at Burgundy," says Véronique Muré.[43] The

Murés are concerned about climate change, because although Pinot Noir is the earliest variety they pick, it does not reach ripeness until sugar levels are at 13-13.5% potential alcohol. So next to the Pinot Noir vineyard in Clos St. Landelin they have planted a small experimental plot of Syrah, just enough to make one barrique, to see whether it will reach maturity at lower sugar levels.

"We are not really specialists in Pinot Noir," said Catherine Faller doubtfully when I said I would like to discuss red wine production. Domaine Weinbach started producing Pinot Noir forty years ago, when Robert Faller planted it in response to market demand; people who came to buy white wine asked for a red, and he became tired of referring them to other producers.[44] But the trigger to start producing a serious Pinot Noir came with the hot vintage of 2003, which was such a perfect year for the Pinot Noir that they decided to introduce the "W" bottling. The style of the house—refinement and elegance—comes through as clearly to the Pinot Noir as it does to Domaine Weinbach's much better known Rieslings (⊤ page 200). "There's no in-between for Pinot Noir, it's either good or it's terrible. Pinot Noir cannot cope with mediocrity," says Catherine Faller.

André Ostertag believes that the big jump in Alsace was when people realized they could not treat Pinot Noir in the same way as Riesling. "Pinot Noir is starting to be important in Alsace because people are beginning to realize it can be good here. The biggest quality jump is that previously people have made red wine in the same way as white, they didn't distinguish between Pinot Noir and Riesling," André says. "It's not a winemaking revolution, it's a viticultural revolution," he continues, referring to the need to get away from overcropping and poor vineyard management.[45] His father planted the vineyard that is now used to produce the Fronholz single vineyard wine, and he planted some further vineyards to make the village "E" wine (⊤ page 199). He would like to produce more Pinot Noir, but has been unable to find suitable soils. He comments sadly that Riesling is more profitable. "To make great Pinot Noir you incur the same costs as Burgundy, but we don't get the same prices," he says ruefully. Indeed, most producers think that making Pinot Noir involves some financial sacrifice, because yields need to be kept below about 40 hl/ha, whereas they believe they can make good Riesling at much higher yields.

Jean-Michel Deiss, who is acknowledged to make one of the best Pinot Noirs in Alsace, marches to the beat of a different drum. "Cépage is a non-sense, it is a modern concept," he said at the start of our interview, not a very promising start to a discussion about Pinot Noir in Alsace. "It's impossible to make a great wine from a single cépage," he concludes.[46] Perhaps trying to provoke, "You could make red wine from a white cépage because the color is not important, it's the tannins," he added. Well known for his belief that Alsace has taken the wrong path in emphasizing individual varieties, but rather should express place by making wine from a diversity of varieties planted in each vineyard, he extends the concept in a more limited way to Pinot Noir. The rouge de Burlenberg comes from several calcareous plots, which Deiss says have always been planted to Pint Noir. The rouge de St. Hippolyte is a village wine intended for relatively rapid consumption. Both are largely Pinot Noir, but contain small amounts of other varieties, planted in the vineyard in juxtaposition with the Pinot Noir—all the other Pinots (Blanc, Gris, Meunier) and also some Chardonnay (Ⲧ page 201).

So what is the future for red wine in Alsace? Does the failure to take advantage of warmer temperatures reflect economic conditions in which it is simply more advantageous to grow Riesling? It's probably true there are only a relatively small number of terroirs where Pinot Noir will really produce excellent results, and no one is going to replace Riesling or Gewürztraminer at the risk of financial sacrifice. Perhaps Burgundy is simply too close for Alsace to produce Pinot Noir that is competitive—but a similar closeness has not stopped producers in Sancerre. The potential is made clear by comparison with the Pfalz or Baden. Possibly the window for producing fine Pinot Noir in Alsace will close if the climate continues to become warmer and there's no incentive to identify those exceptional microclimates that suit it best. There is a similar situation in Italy's Alto Adige, where the key to making fine Pinot Noir is to identify those relatively cool spots with appropriate exposure and elevation. But there isn't the same competition with other successful varieties.

Pinot Nero, as Pinot Noir is known in Italy, is an extremely minor player among black varieties. There is little more than 3,000 ha in the whole country, half of it in Lombardy, but virtually all the Pinot Noir of any interest comes from the Alto Adige. Just south of the Alps, the northernmost area for growing wine in Italy, Alto Adige consists of three valleys forming a "Y" with the town of Bolzano at the center. There is a little Pinot Noir in the Valle d'Aosta, the valley to the northwest, where the wines give an impression of tautness, and not much to the northeast. Most of the 350 ha devoted to Pinot Noir are part of the major concentration of vineyards in the valley on either side of the river Adige to the south of Bolzano. The Strada del Vino runs down the western side of the valley and passes through most of the vineyards. The Pinot Noirs of Oltradige, the northern part from Appiano to Lake Caldaro, convey a softer impression than those from the southern part or from the well known Mazon plateau on the east side of the valley.

Wine is as controversial an issue in Alto Adige as politics. The political issue is the playoff of the German heritage, going back to when the South Tyrol was part of Austria,[47] against its more recent incorporation into Italy. Alto Adige may nominally be part of Italy, but German remains the most

Most of the vineyards of Alto Adige lie in the valley to the south of Bolzano. Vineyards push up against the mountains on the western and eastern sides; the valley floor has various crops, concentrating especially on apple orchards. Pinot Noir tends to be grown in the northern half of the valley, on the west side between Appiano and Termeno, on the east side on the Mazon plateau.

commonly spoken language. The winemaking tradition comes from Germany, with winemakers tending to get their qualifications from Geisenheim.

The tradition of making red wine is actually quite long established. When Alto Adige was part of Austria it was one of the few places where black grapes were successful, but most production was of the local grape Schiava, grown on pergolas for high yields. The move to quality started in the 1960s, but focused on white wine, and success with Pinot Noir (or other quality black varieties) is really a feature of the past two or three decades.

Alto Adige is a relatively narrow valley on a north-south axis, with steep mountainous terrain rising up on either side. The valley floor is planted to a variety of agricultural crops, of which apples are the most important; Alto Adige is one of the biggest providers of apples for Europe. Vineyards are located on the hillsides, most on the western side of the valley so they face east. Although there are some terraced vineyards on inclines, most of the vines are planted on small, flat plateaus, nestled into the hills, often not easily visible from below. The soils on the valley floor are alluvial, but on the hillsides there is wide variety, with terroir changing rapidly. Soils include porphyry (purple-colored volcanic rock), decomposed limestone, and gravel. Given the rapidity with which the underlying soil types change, elevation and aspect are more important determinants of where to plant individual varieties.

There are more apple orchards than vineyards in Alto Adige. In between Manincor's vineyards in the foreground and those running down to Lake Caldaro in the background are apple orchards under the protective netting.

Many vineyards of Alto Adige are on plateaus hidden in the folds of the mountain slopes. Alois Lageder's Appalonia vineyard at Appiano is at an elevation of 500 m overlooking Bolzano.

Sometimes apple orchards are interspersed with the vineyards; as apples are a more profitable crop, there can be resistance to replacing them with vines even in locations that would be appropriate for vineyards. Apples are certainly more important to the local economy, with about 8,000 farmers and 20,000 hectares,[48] compared to the 5,500 growers who cultivate 5,000 hectares of vineyards.[49] Most of the orchards are on the valley floor, whereas the vineyards are at elevations from 200 to 1000 meters.[50] Potential vineyard area is fully planted, and there is some concern about lack of diversity. "We have too much monoculture here—with apples on the valley floor and vines on the slopes—and my big project for the next twenty years is thinking how to break this, which other plants we could grow," says Alois Lageder, one of the most influential wine producers, who is often regarded as a leader in the region.[51]

Most (70%) of the wine is made by cooperatives, buying grapes from growers whose average vineyard holdings are less than a hectare. Even though the cooperatives have an unusually good reputation, still this does not necessarily develop maximum potential from the region. Production as a whole is about equally divided between white and red, and there remains a substantial amount of production from traditional varieties, such as Schiava and Lagrein (which account for most of the red production) in rather rustic styles.[52] Most producers have a wide diversity of varieties—ten or more is common—and production of quality varieties, including Pinot Noir, is usually only a small part of production.

Pinot Noir was not introduced until the mid nineteenth century; more recently, other international varieties, including Cabernet Sauvignon, Merlot, and Syrah, have been planted.[53] As this roll call suggests, Alto Adige is not a particularly cool climate. Its capital, Bolzano, is in a basin where three river valleys converge, protected by the surrounding mountains. Sometimes this is the hottest spot in Italy. So far as Pinot Noir is concerned, summer temperatures are higher than Burgundy,[54] so Pinot Noir is usually planted in the cooler vineyards, where it is one of the first varieties to be picked. You might say that Alto Adige is cool climate for Pinot Noir by choice rather than necessity. The wine certainly gives an impression of cool climate production, reflecting the elevation of the Pinot Noir vineyards (usually over 300 meters) and their exposure to cooling breezes. Plantings of Pinot Noir are on the increase, up about 50% since 1996.[55]

A single DOC covers the whole region.[56] Combined with a wide diversity of varieties, this makes it difficult to establish a distinct identity. "What Alto Adige is missing is a leader. Actually we have leader varieties—Lagrein and Schiava—but they have no impact," says Martin Hofstätter, who has established his Barthenau estate as Alto Adige's leading Pinot Noir. "5,000 ha is too small to compete on the world market; the only way to do it is with specialties. For years I have been fighting for regional distinctions," he says.[57] Small individual holdings make it more difficult to produce single vineyard wines, but all the leading producers' top Pinot Noirs do in fact represent special sites.[58] There are no top cuvées based on barrel selections.

Making Pinot Noir with typicity in Alto Adige requires a change of focus. The tradition here is for light, fruity wines to drink immediately, so it's a new idea to make wines with some longevity. The top Pinots are made following Burgundian principles, but alcohol is a little higher, acidity is a little lower, and for the most part longevity is under a decade. A fair number of wines now achieve a decent village standard in a lighter style; in terms of a comparison with France, they are more like Sancerre reds than Burgundy. But the top wines show elegance and persistence in a distinctive style.

One source of improvement in Pinot Noir has been the switch to Burgundian clones. German influence through the 1970s-1980s led to planting high-yielding clones with large berries. Since the 1990s, quality producers have been planting various Dijon clones. It's a fine calculation whether it's best to pull out the old clones, which may have difficulty fully ripening but which do at least finally have lower yields resulting from age. Different producers have made different decisions, and it's fair to say that the full quality of the replanted vineyards probably will not show for another decade.

One of the best terroirs for Pinot Noir is the Mazon plateau, a west-facing area of 70 ha at 400 m elevation on the east side of the valley. Cooling breezes from the south help to keep the grapes dry, avoiding problems with humidity. Soils vary from limestone and clay to gravel or thin topsoil on rock. This is the location of Hofstätter's Barthenau estate. At the heart of the estate are vineyards planted in 1942 and 1962, where the old vines are still pruned in a pergola. Pinot Noir has been vinified as a separate variety since 1959 (before then it was blended with Schiava). (The estate is named after Ludwig Ritter Barth von Barthenau who brought Pinot Noir to Alto Adige from Burgundy and planted it around Mazon in the late nineteenth century.) This is probably the longest-lived Pinot Noir of Alto Adige. "Barthenau is like a diesel engine, it starts very slowly but runs for ever," says Martin Hofstätter. The wine begins to get into its stride around ten years of age, and I have found twenty year old wine still to be vibrant and lively (Ⓣ page 202). A second wine, the Mazon Riserva, comes from younger vines on the estate.

On the other side of the valley, Alois Lageder has two Pinot Noir vineyards near St. Michele, close to Bolzano. He regards Pinot Noir, together with Pinot Blanc, as the most difficult variety to grow. "The problem has always been the susceptibility to rot (caused by the relatively tight bunches) but the more homogeneous features of the new clones have changed the situation completely," he says. The Krafuss vineyard is on a plateau at 500 m,

The pergola system where vines are pruned along an overhead canopy has mostly been replaced in Alto Adige, but in order to keep the old vines Hofstätter still has a Pinot Noir vineyard that was planted in 1942 in a pergola.

replanted at 6,000 vines per hectare in 1991 when Dijon clones replaced the old Freiburg clones. A vertical tasting showed interesting reflections of vintage conditions, with the oldest vintage (from 1998 when the vines were still quite young) showing well (ᵀ page 203). Appalonia is a new vineyard, just a little farther north, with the first year of production still maturing in bottle, and it will be some time before the vines become old enough for its potential to show fully. But it's a move towards discovering the expression of Pinot Noir in different terroirs. Alois regards Pinot Noir as a work in progress. "Of course we try to produce our own style, but the comparison is Burgundy. The aim is an elegant style. The combination between acidity and sugar has to be achieved," he says.[59]

Near Lake Caldaro, some producers have had problems with Pinot Noir because of humidity, but Manincor produce two bottlings from the Mason vineyard just north of the lake. Soils are stony, partly calcareous, with good drainage. The Mason di Mason bottling is from a plot of old vines, dating from 1959. The Mason bottling comes from the rest of the vineyard. The wine is elegant, with minimal wood influence, usually spending a year in barrel, but sometimes maturing in larger tonneaux (ᵀ page 205). "We don't want to have the taste of oak," says Count Michael Goëss-Enzenberg. "Our intention is to produce fine and elegant but never too concentrated wines."[60]

Indeed, the craze for new oak never seems to have infected Alto Adige. In terms of oak, the wines have a fairly light influence comparable to the level in village wines from Burgundy. None of these are weighty wines; the tendency is towards restrained red cherry fruits. The best wines have their own individual styles, but there is no single common identifying feature, perhaps because the vineyards are so disparate. The wines can be fairly tight when young, and a tasting of recent vintages from thirty producers showed a tendency for the light fruits to let some tannic bitterness show.[61] As more single vineyard bottlings emerge, it will be interesting to see how terroir plays out in Alto Adige; the verdict is not in yet. Getting top quality Pinot Noir here is still a challenge.

North across the Alps, less than a hundred miles to the west, is Graubunden, the easternmost canton in Switzerland. There's actually quite a fair bit of Pinot Noir in Switzerland; it's about a quarter of all vineyard plantings, the largest concentration being in the Valais (farther to the west).[62] But by far the most interesting Pinot Noir in Switzerland comes from Graubunden, where the focus is heavily (80%) on red wine, and Pinot Noir is 95% of the reds.[63]

Although the Pinot Noir amounts only to 325 ha, producing just over two hundred thousand cases annually, this is the driving force for quality red wine production in Switzerland. You don't in fact see "Graubunden" on the label, because the village name is used to describe the wine, the most important villages being Fläsch, Maienfeld, Jenins, and Malans. In German style, the wine is labeled in the form Fläscher or Malanser, meaning from Fläsch or from Malans. With the vineyards divided among roughly 75 producers, production is quite small scale.[64] A producer with 3 hectares describes himself as medium size, and views 5-6 hectares as indicating a major winery. There is unlikely to be much expansion here, because there is little unplanted land that would satisfy the requirements of the AOC for exposure and elevation.

The wine villages lie at the edge of a plateau at an elevation around 500 m, with the vineyards located close to the mountains. Average growing temperatures are just a little cooler than Burgundy, making for a long growing season in which the harvest here usually starts more or less as it is finishing in Burgundy. Proximity to the mountains ensures strong diurnal variation. Around Fläsch the soils are varied, but farther south they are mostly schist. The

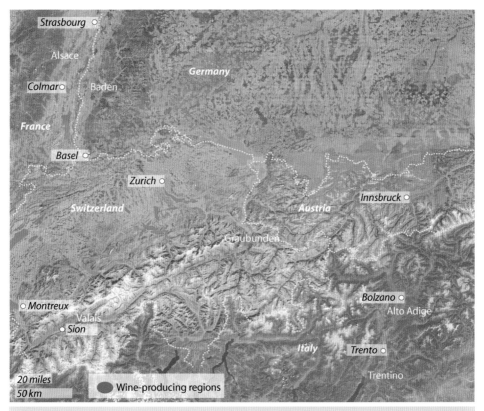

Pinot Noir is grown in the mountains of Switzerland and Italy. The vineyards of the Valais run along the Rhône river valley from Sion; the Graubunden vineyards are nestled into a plateau around the town of Chur. The vineyards of Trentino extend south from Trento, and those of the Alto Adige are centered on Bolzano. More or less on a line with Beaujolais, the vineyards are well to the south of Alsace and Baden, but at higher elevations.

The major wine-producing villages of Graubunden lie between the river and the Alps. Vineyards are on a plateau between the villages and on the slopes at the base of the mountains. Other crops are closer to the river.

general pattern of development here is the same as other areas where wine production used to be peripheral. Wine was made in a light, fruity style for immediate consumption; it is only more recently that producers began to think about more serious wines with ageworthiness. Mundane Swiss clones were replaced with clones from Burgundy, yields were reduced, and the usual Swiss emphasis on quantity rather than quality was reversed. Partly as a function of scale, partly because the quality phenomenon is so recent, the emphasis at top producers is more on producing one really high quality wine than looking to express terroir in single vineyard bottlings. As Thomas Studach says dryly when asked about individual vineyards, "First we should have a hundred years of experience with Burgundian clones."[65]

As elsewhere in Switzerland, most of the wine is sold within the country, but international attention has been drawn to the region by Daniel and Marta Gantenbein, who are widely recognized as making Switzerland's top Pinot Noir. The oldest vines date from the creation of the winery in 1982, and today more than 90% of the 5 ha of Pinot Noir (there are 6 ha of vineyards altogether) are planted with 8-9 clones brought directly from Burgundy. Each of 19 parcels is vinified separately. Daniel Gantenbein believes that at present

Vineyards lie between the town of Fläsch and the foot of the Alps. (This view looks north along the road into Fläsch and corresponds to the vineyards just above the Fläsch at the left in the previous figure.)

the most complex wine is made by an assemblage from all the parcels, but hopes that as the vines gets older he will understand the terroir by individual tastings and will be able to produce individual bottlings of interest. He is a great Burgundy enthusiast, with an impressive selection of choice bottles from Burgundy in his cellar. "Our ideal for Pinot Noir is Burgundy, that's not in question," he says. "We aim for a wine that is well rounded in the mouth, with good extract but not too massive. We like best the complexity, softness, and refinement of Vosne Romanée."[66] Usually his wines are very fruity for the first couple of years, he says, and then they close up for a bit before opening out again. When you taste a vertical here, you feel you could easily be in Burgundy, although the resemblance is perhaps more with Beaune than the ideal of Vosne Romanée. The oldest vintage I have had, almost fifteen years old, might have been difficult to distinguish from, say, a twenty year old Burgundy (☂ page 206).

A couple of villages away in Malans, Georg Fromm makes a series of Pinot Noirs. His Klassisch bottling falls into the tradition of fruity and easy to drink, the barrique bottling shows more serious stuff, and there is a single vineyard wine, Schöpfiwingert, from a small plot of only 0.7 ha that used to be owned by the local monastery before it came into the Fromm family about 300 years ago. "We don't compare ourselves with Burgundy, of course, but the Pinots have a really good terroir here," he says. "I have worked for almost forty years with Pinot Noir, and in the last ten years I have found where I want to go," he adds,[67] saying that there has been a real emphasis on quality, and increasing interest in single vineyard wines, in the past decade. He sees the wines as developing somewhat more rapidly than Burgundy (⟊ page 207).

There is some way to go before Graubunden finds an identity that is clear to the outside world. Of course, with the wines selling easily in Switzerland at prices that are roughly comparable with good village wines from Burgundy, there is little pressure. It will remain difficult to define exactly how this region expresses the typicity of Pinot Noir until producers develop more understanding of terroir, and there are more examples to compare of bottlings from different terroirs. This should be achievable, since although the area is very small, it is so heavily committed to Pinot Noir; after all, there is almost as Pinot Noir in Graubunden as in the Alto Adige.

On the same latitude as the Beaujolais but some two hundred miles to the east lies a relatively unknown outpost of Pinot Noir. The vineyards of the Valais in Switzerland run along a thirty mile stretch of the Rhône river before it turns north to the eastern end of Lake Geneva. About one third of Switzerland's Pinot Noir is in the Valais.[68] Most of the vineyards are on the north side of the river and have a southeastern exposure, roughly similar to that of the Côte d'Or.[69] But there the similarity ends. The best known red wine of the Valais is a blend of Pinot Noir and Gamay, called Dôle; the blend has to contain at least 85% of these two varieties, of which Pinot Noir must be a majority. The other 15% can come from any other (black) varieties authorized in the Valais. Wine with the same blend, but that does not meet the standard for Dôle (for example, the alcohol level is too low), can be called Goron, the name of a virtually extinct old black variety of the region. So Dôle is one of the rare cases where Pinot Noir is blended; its closest similarity would be with the (somewhat disdained) Bourgogne Passetoutgrains, another blend of Pinot Noir and Gamay.[70]

Wine production in the Valais could be almost as old as Burgundy. It's possible that viticulture spread through what was then Gaul from Burgundy, to the Moselle and Rhine, and into the valley of the Valais, possibly around the second century C.E.[71] There is as always a long gap between the archeological evidence for wine consumption or production and the written evidence for existence of vines and vineyards, which in this case dates from 1052, when the Bishop of Sion gave some vineyards to his clergy.[72] The first mention of specific cépages came in 1313 as references to "Neyrun, Humagny, and Regy or Reyse."[73] The identify of Neyrun is unknown (it may have simply meant Noir, or black), but Humagny and Rèze are black and white grapes, respectively, that are still cultivated in the region. By the sixteenth century, the major cépages were Muscat, the ubiquitous Gouais Blanc, Savignan Blanc, and Gross Bourgogne. In spite of its name, this latter did not necessarily have anything to do with Burgundy and is effectively a lost grape variety.

So when did Pinot Noir and Gamay come on to the scene? A variety called Malvoisie, which may have been Pinot Gris, first appeared in 1698, but Pinot Noir was not introduced until the Conseil d' État bought 50,000 vines of "Cortaillod rouge," being none other than Pinot Noir, in 1848.[74] But it does not appear to have become really prominent until everything changed with phylloxera, which arrived relatively late in the Valais, so the vineyards were reconstituted quite slowly between the 1920s and the 1950s.[75] By the 1930s, Dôle had become a name for the quality red wine of the region, largely, but not necessarily exclusively, made from Pinot Noir. The addition of Gamay increased during the 1930s, and by the start of the next decade "Dôle" was protected as the name for a Pinot Noir-dominated blend with Gamay from the Valais.[76]

Dôle is the world's largest production of Pinot Noir as a blended dry wine, around four times the volume of Burgundy's Passetoutgrains.[77] To what extent do these wines represent Pinot Noir and how do they compare? Passetoutgrains must contain at least one third Pinot Noir; Dôle typically contains two thirds Pinot Noir and one third Gamay.[78]

The blend of Pinot Noir and Gamay is not a marriage made in heaven. Although generic Bourgogne AOC Pinot Noirs are rather light and lack any real stuffing, still they can show a nice clean flavor profile. In the best examples you can see the purity of Pinot Noir coming through even at this level. Blended with Gamay, the profile is somehow flattened, the flavors are muddier, and you have more of a simple generic red wine for quaffing. Pinot usually has a light, refreshing acidity that lifts the fruit profile, whereas Gamay seems heavier and less interesting. Comparing Bourgogne Pinot Noir with Bourgogne Passetoutgrains from the same producer, I did not find any case where I preferred the blend. (Of course, I don't know the exact quality of the Pinot that went into the blends, but it isn't obvious that it's been improved by blending with Gamay. It might make better wine to work on the quality of Pinot than to blend it with Gamay.) The Pinots from the Valais have a heavier, muddier quality than the generic Bourgognes—they lack that lift of refreshing acidity. Perhaps they are slightly over extracted, at any rate they give a slightly clumsy impression of being over-chaptalized. It can be difficult to find typicity. There tends to be a medicinal aftertaste, and one advantage of the blend with Gamay is that the heavier fruits compensate for the medicinal overtones. Here in pairwise comparisons I could see some point to the blend—although once again I think a better result would be obtained by working for a lighter touch with Pinot Noir rather than blending.

So is there any advantage to blending with Pinot Noir? The usual rationale for blending is to complement the flavor profile of each grape. The austerity and structure of Cabernet Sauvignon, in Bordeaux for example, are complemented by the fleshiness of Merlot. And of course both are considered to be quality grapes, although different in character. But Pinot Noir can offer good variety of aromas and flavors across the palate. And Gamay is scarcely considered to be at the same quality level. So is it surprising that the blend of Pinot and Gamay shows more the coarseness and character of Gamay than the refinement of Pinot Noir? The original rationale for blending might well have been to balance Pinot that was too light and acid with Gamay that would just have been too heavy by itself. But is this still true in the era of global warming? Could the Pinot make a good wine by itself? Personally, I am inclined to the view that Pinot simply does not benefit from blending—but, of course, if it were vinified alone, what would they do with the Gamay?

Red wine obtains a major part of its character by extraction from the skin. The nature of Pinot Noir, and indeed of all red wine, has changed significantly over the past two centuries as cuvaisons[79] have become longer and more material has been extracted. This factor is much reduced for rosé or sparkling wines, where skin contact is minimal or absent, making it more difficult to see directly the origins of the grape.

Quite a lot of Pinot Noir goes into rosé or sparkling wine. Neither shows the typicity of the grape variety with as much clarity as a dry red wine.[80] But some fine, elegant rosés are made from Pinot Noir, especially in Sancerre, where top producers use direct pressing of grapes especially grown for the purpose.[81] (A certain amount of rosé is made inadvertently, especially in Alsace where traditionally some of the red wines have been so light as to be confused with rosé.) And even in Burgundy, some Pinot Noir is used for the Crémant, a sparkling wine made by the same methods as Champagne.[82] Crémant's position as the fastest growing market segment in Burgundy[83] puts it in a good position to mop up any excess production.[84]

The "secret" of Champagne is blending. There are few single vineyard bottlings, most Champagne is blended from a mixture of cépages (including some or all of Pinot Noir, Pinot Meunier, and Chardonnay), and almost all is blended across vintages. So this is not the obvious place to look for typicity of Pinot Noir. Yet more Pinot Noir is used to produce Champagne than dry red Burgundy, and most of the world's plantings of Pinot Meunier are in the Champagne region. What does Pinot Noir bring to Champagne, and why is its close sibling Pinot Meunier the most disdained grape in Champagne (most Champagne houses stress their reliance on Pinot Noir and Chardonnay; their expressions of enthusiasm for Pinot Meunier are rather muted, to say the least).

Long before sparkling wine was invented, the Champagne region produced still wines, both red and white. By the end of the eighteenth century, an *échelle des crus* had been established to set relative prices for each village on the basis of quality. For black grapes, the villages in the Montagne de Reims, and those around Ay, were at the top of the scale.[85] Most likely the grapes were Pinot Noir. White wine production was concentrated between Ay and Epernay, and commanded a premium. Historically, the wines of Ay had been considered better than those of the Montagne de Reims, where black grapes, although widely grown, had had a problem ripening.[86] After the climate turned cooler, and the Champagne region could no longer compete with Burgundy as a supplier of red wine, the situation was rescued by the invention of sparkling wine.

Grape varieties were originally chosen for producing dry wine, and when the transition to sparkling wine occurred, Fromenteau (as Pinot Gris is known in the region) may have been the dominant variety, together with Pinot Noir. It's unclear when Chardonnay was introduced. Of course, there was major replanting after phylloxera, concentrating on today's three varieties

Bollinger's Vieilles Vignes Françaises comes from very small, enclosed vineyards of Pinot Noir planted on its own roots. One vineyard is just behind the Bollinger maison; Clos St. Jacques is just opposite, where some of the vines are planted individually in the old system of "en foule." The entire production for 2010 was only five barrels (the sixth small barrel, on top, is used for topping up).

in the northern areas, but with a focus on Gamay in the Aube to the south. Gamay began to be removed after 1919, became nominally illegal in 1927, but did not finally disappear from Champagne until 1945. Through the 1950s and 1960s, Pinot Meunier was the dominant variety, constituting almost half of all plantings.[87] Pinot Noir became the most important variety by the twenty first century. The proportion of Pinot Meunier has declined in the past two decades, but this is because its total area has remained static, while plantings of Pinot Noir and Chardonnay have increased.

As the northernmost winemaking region in France, Champagne has been a marginal location for growing Pinot Noir. Yet the elaboration of Champagne requires that the grapes are used only to make a base wine, low in alcohol and high in acidity, and (in the case of Pinot Noir or Pinot Meunier) lacking color, which is turned into Champagne by a second fermentation and some adjustments including addition of sugar. The base wine would not be judged ripe by the criteria of dry winemaking regions; indeed, if it achieved the level of ripeness typical farther south, it would not make very good Champagne—it would be too rich and heavy. In addition to Champagne blended from two or from all three of the varieties, a small amount is made

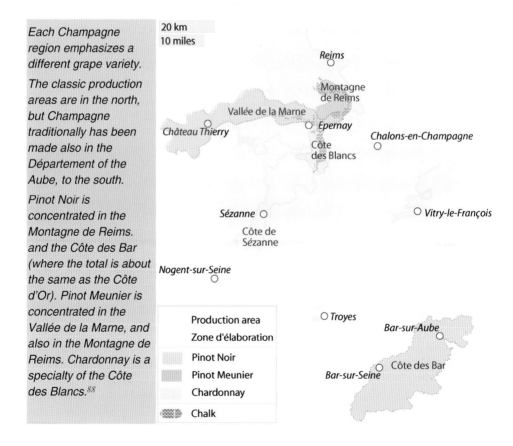

Each Champagne region emphasizes a different grape variety.

The classic production areas are in the north, but Champagne traditionally has been made also in the Département of the Aube, to the south.

Pinot Noir is concentrated in the Montagne de Reims. and the Côte des Bar (where the total is about the same as the Côte d'Or). Pinot Meunier is concentrated in the Vallée de la Marne, and also in the Montagne de Reims. Chardonnay is a specialty of the Côte des Blancs.[88]

20 km
10 miles

Reims

Montagne de Reims

Vallée de la Marne

Château Thierry   Epernay   Chalons-en-Champagne

Côte des Blancs

Sézanne   Vitry-le-François

Côte de Sézanne

Nogent-sur-Seine

Troyes

Bar-sur-Aube

Production area
Zone d'élaboration

Pinot Noir
Pinot Meunier   Côte des Bar
Chardonnay   Bar-sur-Seine
Chalk

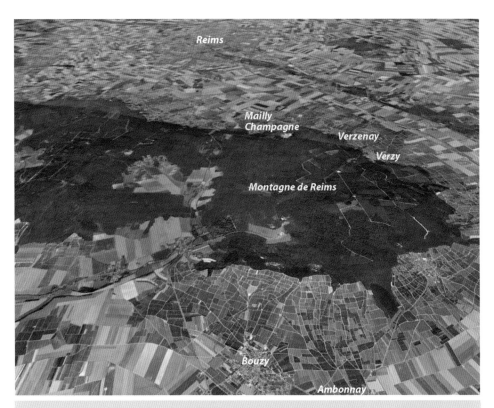

The Montagne de Reims is a forested area between Reims and Epernay (off to the bottom left). Many of the most famous Champagne villages are clustered around the mountain. Bouzy was well known for red wine; Ambonnay is famous for Pinot Noir. Vineyards run close up to the Montagne; farther away are areas for other agricultural crops.

exclusively from Chardonnay (Blanc de Blancs) or from Pinot Noir (Blanc de Noirs)[89]. Pinot Noir is much in demand for its contribution to the assemblage, and not very much is available for Blanc de Noirs, which is correspondingly rare. The best Pinot Noir comes from the Montagne de Reims, and very little Blanc de Noirs is produced in the other regions.[90]

The distribution of grape varieties is influenced by both soil and climate. The subsoil in the region is predominantly limestone. The most pronounced outcrops of chalk are found in the Montagne de Reims and the Côte des Blancs, with a small stretch also running along the river in the Vallée de la Marne. Down in the Côte des Bar the soils are more marl, a calcareous clay. Pinot Noir and Chardonnay are concentrated on the chalk outcrops. Pinot Meunier is grown elsewhere, partly *faute de mieux,* but also because of the frost issue. Because Pinot Meunier flowers a week after Pinot Noir, it is less susceptible to being caught by a spring frost, so it tends to be planted in the areas that are most susceptible to frost, especially at the bottom of the valley.[91] It does best on the local soil type called sparnacien, a mixture of clay and chalk. But is Pinot Meunier still necessary in the era of global warming?

Pinot Meunier is generally disdained as a grape outside the Champagne area. It is rarely used to make dry wine, but one is produced from a vineyard in Carneros at Domaine Chandon, Moët & Chandon's outpost in Napa Valley. It's interesting to compare it side by side with Pinot Noir. The impression is similar but less refined. It is muted on the nose, reasonably smooth on the palate, with red fruit flavors, and a touch of bitterness coming out on the finish with some earthy strawberries. You might very well take it for a rather rustic version of Pinot Noir; the flavors tend to be muddier than the purity of line you see in Pinot Noir (Ŧ page 209).

But how much typicity comes out in Champagne, after you have added yeast and sugar to produce a second fermentation in the bottle, not to mention adding extra sweetness in the form of the *dosage* at bottling? You can tell the difference between Blanc de Noirs, which tends to be a little richer, and Blanc de Blancs, which tends to be a little more acid, but the overwhelming impression of each is the bubbles, rather than the fruits characteristic of Pinot Noir or Chardonnay. There are few opportunities to directly compare the properties of Pinot Noir and Pinot Meunier in bottled Champagne, but in 1999 Benoît Tarlant started to make a Blanc de Noirs from his La Vigne d'Or vineyard of Pinot Meunier. "This was pushing the limits when I did it," he says, "but now there are several others."[92] I tasted La Vigne d'Or side by side with a Blanc de Noir produced more conventionally from Pinot Noir. Both were from the 2003 vintage; neither had yet been released, and "recently disgorged" took on a whole new meaning when Benoît disgorged the wines by knocking off the crown cap. A gush of disgorgement, and the wines were ready to taste. Both showed a citrus and stone fruit spectrum, nicely rounded and full bodied as you might expect from the vintage, but the purity of line was more evident in the Pinot Noir, compared to a less precise, if not quite rustic, impression from the Pinot Meunier (Ŧ page 209).

Pinot Meunier is somewhat disdained even in Champagne, but the opinion is not universal. The polarity is evident from the very different attitudes of two top houses. Bollinger pride themselves on using the least Pinot Meunier of any major house: less than 15% in nonvintage, and none in vintage, because it ages too fast. There is no Pinot Meunier in the reserve wines (the wines that are stored for several years and used in the assemblage to strengthen and ensure consistency in the nonvintage Champagne). This is a fairly typical, if more extreme, example of the view that Pinot Meunier has too simple a fruit flavor spectrum and does not age well. Most houses are extremely discreet about how much of it they use. With a quite different view, Krug is the one major house openly admitting that Pinot Meunier is widely used in their cuvées; and no one could say that Krug does not age well! The core of Krug's policy is to look at individual parcels rather than cépages. "The character of each parcel surpasses the nature of the cépages or terroir," says winemaker Julie Cavil, adding, "We never refer to variety in the tasting room at assemblage. You cannot say there is a specific proportion of a variety, we never speak of varieties, this is a nonsense."[93] Krug uses Pinot Meunier in its reserve wines as well as in current releases, its one concession to the general view being that reserve wines of Pinot Meunier are not kept so long.

Even Pinot Noir needs to be treated carefully in making Champagne. "My own opinion is that Pinot Noir can become heavy, and requires very careful vinification... In terms of viticulture, Pinot Noir is the most demanding cépage. It requires chalky terroirs to conserve its finesse. Chardonnay succeeds in slightly cooler conditions, and Pinot Meunier is generally more rustic," says Charles Philipponnat of Champagne Philipponnat.[94] Yields in Champagne are so high—roughly the equivalent of 89 hl/ha—that it actually seems a little surprising that much difference can be detected between varieties; after all, conventional wisdom is that you don't see much typicity in dry wines above yields of 50-60 hl/ha, and here the wines have gone through the further changes of a second fermentation. This doesn't lend a great deal of support to characterizing the typicity of Pinot Noir, but perhaps it's fair to say in summary that it tends to bring purity of fruit with a refined, elegant, impression.

The conventional view (or perhaps more accurately one might say the Burgundian view, which has been successfully propagated along with the grapevines) is that Pinot Noir is strictly a cool climate grape and that it is enormously reflective of terroir. Stephen Skelton MW has a slightly different take. "Pinot Noir is a very versatile animal. It shows a high degree of adaptability to environment, and reflects winemaking more than the terroir," he told me.[95] The way to investigate this, perhaps, is to look at the results of making Pinot Noir at the margins, both hot and cold, and in the winemaking conditions of both Europe and the New World, to see just how adaptable Pinot Noir is, and just what are its limits. With a span from Burgundy to Germany now considered mainstream in Europe, and Oregon and New Zealand regarded as definitive for the New World, I wanted to push the boundaries. So I took a look at Pinot Noir from England, which is just about as cool as possible, and from the Languedoc, which is just about as warm a location as can be found. The question in my mind was whether I would find genuinely interesting wines, in a range of styles reflecting location or winemaking, or whether it would be as Dr. Johnson described the dog walking on hind legs: "It is not done well; but you are surprised to find it done at all." How far can you stretch the elasticity of typicity before deciding that the wine is not Pinot any more?

Pushing well beyond the nominal margins for winemaking, wine is made in England well to the north of the 50° latitude. Wine was supposedly made in England under the Romans (although there may have been somewhat less than commonly supposed), but certainly by the time of the Domesday Book in 1086, there were 42 vineyards in the southern part of England.[98] During the Middle Ages, wine production was slowly abandoned.[99] A handful of vineyards run by enthusiasts survived until the first world war, but modern wine production in Britain dates from a revival in the 1950s. Today there are about a hundred and fifty vineyards spread all over Britain (although concentrated in the south of England), with more than a thousand hectares in production.[100] Roughly 40% is classified as quality wine, but only quarter of that is red or rosé.[101] Increased emphasis on sparkling wine has led to a great growth in the trio of Pinot Noir, Pinot Meunier, and Chardonnay, which now represent almost half of Britain's vineyards, with Pinot Noir in the lead as the most planted variety with 250 ha.[102] English wine expert Stephen Skelton thinks it could increase further over the next decade to more than half the total plantings.[103]

There is some skepticism about wine production in England generally and about red wine in particular. Asked for a bottle of English Pinot Noir, the manager at one of London's grandest stores told me, "We have some very nice white wines, some of the sparkling wines are lovely, but—although there may be some out there—I've never had a good red wine."[104] The climate is just too marginal—too cool and too wet—for Pinot Noir (and most other

"Just one word: plastics."[96] Beyond all limits, Pinot Noir and Chardonnay are grown in polytunnels at Worthenbury Wines in North Wales to make both sparkling and still wines. Plastic protects the grapevines against the inclement weather, and is used even farther north in Scotland and Scandinavia.[97] What price terroir?

black grapes) to ripen reliably enough to make good red wine. "Sparkling wines here can be world class, but with still wines we are still struggling," Stephen Skelton says, admitting that making good red wine reliably is a lost cause at the moment.

Will global warming change this by making marginal regions, such as England, attractive for winemaking?[105] The terroir in southern England is often claimed to be similarly chalky to Champagne;[106] could a small temperature shift make this an attractive area for producing high quality sparkling wine? A team from leading champagne house Louis Roederer was spotted in England in 2007 hedging their bets by investigating the purchase of vineyards.[107] However, a significant difference in terroirs is that most of the chalk outbreaks in southern England are in locations that are too elevated and too exposed for vineyards. "My mantra is that in the U.K. you need shelter, shelter, shelter," says Stephen Skelton.

Most English sparkling wine is produced from the three classic grape varieties of Champagne (often planted in the proportions of 40% Pinot Noir, 40% Chardonnay, 20% Pinot Meunier). With relatively low alcohol and crisp acidity, you might feel that the closest classic parallel for English sparkling wine is the Champagne of a few decades ago. Yet by the same measure, one might ask: if England becomes climatically appropriate for Champagne production to be successful, won't this mean that the climate in Champagne is too warm for the wine to maintain its traditional delicacy? Some feel that already the style of Champagne is becoming heavier than it used to be.[108] Increased concentration due to greater ripeness is partly offset by the increasing yields, for which Champagne has been much criticized.[109] So what is the future for Champagne? How long can it continue to offer the world's best expression of Pinot Noir as a sparkling wine?

And now for the opposite extreme. One of the warmer climates where Pinot Noir is made is the Languedoc—the large region in southern France stretching from Nîmes (just to the south of Châteauneuf-du-Pape) to the Spanish border. Production is devoted mostly to typical warm climate grape varieties, such as Grenache or Syrah, and Pinot Noir is a vanishingly small proportion, only about 3% of total production, but that's still more than 10% of the production of Burgundy. One insight into the typicity of this wine is suggested by the fraud that came to light when export figures revealed that between 2005 and 2008, the Aude region of the Languedoc supposedly sold 1.3 million cases of Pinot Noir to the United States each year. That's almost three times the Languedoc's total production of Pinot Noir of about 500,000 cases each year! Winemakers and cooperatives sold the wine (which was actually made from inferior varieties) to the negociant firm Ducasse in Carcassonne, which sold it to the huge producer Sieur d'Arques. Sieur d'Arques then sold the wine to Gallo, for their Red Bicyclette brand. This was a profitable scam, because Pinot Noir sells for about twice the price of other black grapes.[110] The defense was déjà vu all over again: "There is no prejudice. Not a single American consumer complained," said the lawyer for Sieur d'Arques. Others defended themselves by arguing that they delivered a wine that had "Pinot Noir characteristics." Indeed, this doesn't say much for the ability of those farther along the chain to distinguish Pinot Noir from generic red wine! At a minimum it suggests that Pinot Noir from the Languedoc is not easily distinguished from other, supposedly inferior, grape varieties that are grown there. Gallo claim that the only vintage to have been affected was 2006, so I tasted several recent vintages to see whether I could detect a difference.

The wine gives a generally southern impression, warm and a little nutty, very soft on the palate, with interdenominational red fruit flavors; with little tannin or backbone, it seems more like Grenache than Pinot Noir. In fact, it usually contains 15% Grenache, and I suspect most tasters would identify this as the most likely grape in a blind tasting. Characteristic of a major brand, there is little vintage variation; in fact, it would be difficult to place a series of vintages in the right order. This is a reliable wine for quaffing that remains consistent through the years, but there's little Pinot character in evidence; and in all honesty you can see why no one spotted the substitution. I'm just left a bit puzzled as to what were the "Pinot Noir characteristics" that were being matched.

Pinot Noir's main limiting factor is climate: it needs conditions that are not too warm. But success in many different niches in Europe both confirms and refutes conventional wisdom. Although variations of limestone give infinity nuanced results, Pinot is by no means restricted to it. The ability of a variety of terroirs—limestone, sandstone, slate, siliceous, volcanic—to give Pinots of interest demonstrates that the variety truly is a nonpareil interpreter of terroir. So is our view of Pinot Noir too much biased by its origins on the limestone terroirs of Burgundy?

The monks at Clos Vougeot were at the forefront of developments when Pinot Noir became recognized as the predominant grape of Burgundy. Very likely they took the grape to the Kloster Eberbach and established it in the Rheingau. Stories that the monks took Pinot Noir elsewhere cannot be verified, but are plausible given that the Church was the driving force for spreading the grapevine through the Middle Ages. But suppose for a moment that Cistercian history had been a little different. If the movement had focused on Kloster Eberbach rather than Clos Vougeot, would our historical impression of the typicity of Pinot Noir be dominated by its characteristics when grown on slate? Would we then regard limestone-based Pinots as really a little too well rounded? History is written by the victors in wine as in war.

Producers and Tastings in Sancerre

Most wines tasted were from the recent vintages, 2008 and 2007. "2008 was a top vintage here, the best since 96," Clément Pinard told me. Indeed, 2008 vintage wines generally tended to be lush and opulent, although always with the backbone of good acidity. 2007 was a much more difficult vintage, some vignerons despairing during August, but then rescued by a warm, dry spell through September. The wines are lighter, and acidity shows more clearly. Other recent vintages follow Burgundy, 2006 fairly tight with good acidity showing, 2005 with generous fruits, 2004 somewhat tight, and 2003 tending to too much extraction. Of the most recent vintages, 2009 is ripe (with high alcohol) and 2010 had a cool autumn (optimists compare it with 2002 or 2005).

Domaine Lucien Crochet

The Crochet winery is an all-modern facility with sparkling new equipment, in Bué to the north of Sancerre. There are about 38 ha in the domain, 29 ha planted to Sauvignon Blanc and 9 ha planted with Pinot Noir. The vineyards are mostly in the vicinity of Bué, and the Pinot Noir is planted on Kimmeridgian terroirs. Driving through his vineyards, Gilles Crochet points to nuances in the changes in terroir in much the same way that a vigneron might in Burgundy. The older vineyards tend to be planted at 5,600 vines/ha, but with replanting there is a move towards increasing the density to 8,800 vines/ha, although as Gilles Crochet says, "The more vines, the more work." Harvesting is by hand, grapes are taken in small containers to the winery, where they are examined on a sorting table, and Pinot Noir has been vinified in stainless steel since 2003, with pigeage. It's necessary to chaptalize about 3 out of 5 years. The Croix du Roy Sancerre bottling is a play on the name of the famous Clos du Roy, one of the best terroirs in Sancerre. The Cuvée Prestige is made from old vines only in the best years. Most wines were tasted at the domain in June 2010, some later in the year.

Sancerre, La Croix du Roy, 2008
Youthful medium density ruby-garnet color. Fresh red fruit nose of raspberries and strawberries with faintly tarry overtones. Slightly earthy and mineral overtones on a palate of lovely red fruits, supported by nicely balanced acidity. A light touch with the winemaking is evident, very much a wine for food. You could easily be mistaken into thinking you were in Beaune. ** Drink 2011-2016.

Sancerre, La Croix du Roy, 2007
Medium rosy color with some garnet hues. Faint notes of fresh cut mushrooms, but generally fresh red fruits with a mineral edge and a faint sense of chocolate on the finish. Overall a slightly mineral impression. * Drink 2011-2014.

Sancerre, Cuvée Prestige, 2005
Quite dark ruby-purple color is undeveloped. Faintly stern nose, quite tarry. Powerful on the palate, more resembling Côte de Nuits than Côte de Beaune, giving a highly extracted impression. Powerful rather than elegant, almost to the point of obscuring the black cherry fruits. Firm tannins give a solid structure. Closed and tight right now, too young to drink; the question is whether there is too much extraction for Pinot Noir and whether the fruits will outlive the tannins. ** Drink 2014-2020.

Sancerre, 2005
Dark color. Black fruit nose with slightly tarry aromas. A vin de garde with lots of force and concentration, a sense of some underlying power. ** Drink now-2015.

Sancerre, Cuvée Prestige, 2003
Very dark ruby/garnet color, a little dusky at rim. Quite tarry on the nose although retaining freshness. Concentrated fruits of black cherries just coming out with support from firm tannins. Fruits just a bit firmer and more obvious than the 2005 vintage. A slight touch of chocolate to the finish. ** Drink now-2015.

Domaine Vincent Pinard

Pinard produces about 30% Pinot Noir and 70% Sauvignon Blanc. The chalkiest soils are planted with Sauvignon Blanc; the Pinot is planted on chalky-clay soils. Pinard's vineyards fall into 40 different blocks in Bué, with about 10 separate parcels of Pinot Noir. Pinard regularly makes two cuvées and adds a third in top vintages. The first two are distinguished by the age of the vines: the first cuvée is from the youngest vines (30 years old), matured in barrels but not using new oak. The second is the cuvée Charlouise (named for his grandfather Charles and grandmother Louise), made from 45-year-old vines, and using up to 70% new oak. In exceptional years he makes a Vendanges Entières using whole bunches with no destemming. All wines are made with gentle pumping over during fermentation. There has been no chaptalization in the past ten years. Each wine comes from a different set of parcels. They are planted at 10,000/ha and yields are progressively 35, 30, 25 hl/ha for the three cuvées. Production is about 9,000 bottles of the domain wine, 6,000 Charlouise, and 1-2,000 of Vendanges Entières. Wines were tasted at the domain in June 2010.

Sancerre, rosé, 2009
There is a small production of this rosé, only 2,000 bottles, made by direct pressing. It shows a pale salmon color with a lovely fresh nose. Some hints of apple accompany the light red fruits on the palate. Nice finish. Excellent quality. ** Drink now-2012.

Sancerre, 2008
This wine is a medium garnet color with a rosy glow. Faintly spicy red fruit nose. Silky, fine-grained tannins dominate the finish, following from elegant and precise fruits, with a mixture of red and black fruit impressions on the palate. Good supporting acidity with a tinge of minerality to the finish. ** Drink now-2014.

Sancerre, Charlouise, 2008
Medium rosy/garnet color. Restrained nose offers impression of black fruits and minerality. Refined, precise fruits on the palate are backed up by silky tannins and good supporting acidity. Elegant style. Put this into a blind tasting and people might be fooled into thinking about Volnay. ** Drink 2012-2016.

Sancerre, Vendanges Entières, 2008
Conditions were so good in this vintage that a substantial proportion of whole clusters was used for this wine. The restrained nose offers an impression of black fruits with a hint of minerality. Tannins are silky but some hardness still grips the finish, showing the quality of the structural support. Good acidity and freshness, a nice spicy touch to the well rounded fruits on the finish, lovely concentration. A very fine result. *** Drink 2013-2018.

Sancerre, Charlouise, 2007
Medium garnet color. Spicy nose shows some cloves and other new oak aromas. (New oak was 50% this year.) Elegant style with nicely rounded fruits, minerality on the finish, quite silky—again a somewhat Volnay-like impression to the purity of the fruits in spite of the difficult year. ** Drink now-2016.

Sancerre, Charlouise, 2006
Medium ruby color still with some purple hues. Quite stern on the nose, almost tarry. Tight on the palate, quite closed at this stage, partly reflecting youth, partly the vintage. Faint touch of chocolate develops to accompany the tight tannins on the finish. ** Drink now-2015.

Sancerre, 2005
Medium garnet color. Faintly tarry nose hides the red and black fruits. Nicely rounded on the palate, with very nice fruit concentration in an elegant style, supported by silky tannins. More resembles Côte de Nuits than Côte de Beaune, true of many top red Sancerres in this vintage. Still needs another year but should open out. ** Drink 2011-2016.

Sancerre, Charlouise, 2004
Medium garnet color, red fruit nose, very faintly spicy, showing a delicate, fine-grained structure with a hint of minerality. Fine tannins are well integrated. Although there is a little heat on the finish, the 13.2% alcohol is completely natural. A top result for the vintage. *** Drink now-2015.

Domaine Vacheron

Domaine Vacheron is run by two cousins, Jean-Dominique and Jean-Laurent. Half of their vineyards are on silex, half are on calcareous soils. There are 11 ha of Pinot altogether, mostly on calcareous plots but there are some on silex. (Other vignerons admire the distinctive quality of their wines from the silex soils). The domain wine is based on an assemblage from all the terroirs, but the Belle Dame cuvée comes from a vineyard with southwest exposure on the silex terroir. They do not chaptalize. In addition to the red they make a rosé, by direct pressing rather than by saignée. The domain wine usually has yields around 38-48 hl/ha, the Belle Dame has around 28-35 hl/ha. Belle Dame is grown on a cordon (which does well in conditions of low productivity), as opposed to the other vineyards, which are trained on the traditional Guyot. The wine spends one year in barrique with up to 30% new oak, and then spends a year in an oak cuve. Belle Dame has a very refined character; when you taste the wine, you think you could be in Volnay. Annual production is around 8,000 bottles. The style changed in 2008 when the Vacherons decided to look for more elegant tannins, to give greater emphasis to the fruits. The emphasis has always been on making a vin de garde, but they say ruefully that the consequence is that people here do not always understand Domaine Vacheron. Their philosophy is that "le vin, c'est une histoire de vigneron." Notes come from a splendid vertical tasting at the domain in June 2010, which provided an impressive demonstration of the aging potential of red Sancerre.

Sancerre, 2008
Youthful purple hue. Slightly tarry nose with black cherry fruits breaking through. Good acidity, perhaps just a bit to the fore right now, supports nicely concentrated black fruits on the palate, very much in the sturdy house style. If I were told this came from a village in Burgundy, I would have some difficulty placing the village, but I would not dispute the quality level. ** Drink 2012-2017.

Sancerre, Belle Dame, 2007
Medium garnet color. Nicely rounded fruits, strong supporting acidity, with quite a mineral edge on the finish. Refined but firm tannins. Still a touch hard on the finish, needs another year or so. A good result for the vintage. ** Drink 2012-2016.

Sancerre, Belle Dame, 2006
Medium garnet color with rosy hue. Restrained nose. Smooth and round on the palate, but a slightly hard edge still shows. Still very tight but the dry finish shows the presence of refined tannins that will give structure for good aging. ** Drink now-2015.

Sancerre, Belle Dame, 2004
Slightly spicy and faintly nutty nose. Round fruits show on the palate with firm tannins and a distinct mineral edge to the medium length finish. Decent structure and quite dry on the finish. Not as generous as some other vintages but still very good. * Drink now-2015.

Sancerre, 1990
Two bottles showed rather different stages of development. Both a light, mature garnet color, but the first quite raisiny on the nose, showing clear notes of oxidation. Probably a problem with the cork, because the second, although developed, was not oxidized, with the nose showing minerality and flintiness, with some smoke. On the palate, developed red fruits showed smokiness and a touch of sous bois. Tannins resolved. Nice balance, showing the capacity of red Sancerre to age in the same style as old Burgundy (albeit on a more rapid time scale). *** Drink up.

Sancerre, 1989
Light garnet color shows some development. Smoky mineral nose has some notes of gunflint, not as overtly tertiary as the 1990. Sweet ripe fruits on the palate are less developed and more

rounded than 1990. At a gorgeous stage of development, just balanced between the sweet, ripe red fruits and the developing sous bois. Tannins resolved, fruits supported by fresh acidity, overall an elegant impression. Some disagreement as to whether 1989 or 1990 was the better wine at this point. *** Drink now-2013.

Sancerre, Belle Dame, 1988
This was the first vintage when malolactic fermentation was performed in barrel. The wine has a developed nose, with some tertiary notes of barnyard mingling with smoke and gunflint. Smooth on the palate, nicely developed, but not as much as the nose would suggest. Medium density fruits are supported by good acidity and show some lovely sous bois notes on the finish with notes of smoky strawberries. Very fine tannins and the supporting acidity give good freshness. Lovely balance between developed fruits and smoke and gunflint on the finish. A very fine demonstration of the ageability of red Sancerre. *** Drink now-2012.

Sancerre, 1985
Paling garnet color shows age. Developed tertiary notes on the nose, a faint touch of oxidation showing. Lovely well-rounded light red fruits. A little less overt minerality than 1990, but the same general flavor spectrum of developed red fruits with savory undertones. A little dilution is beginning to show. ** Drink up.

Sancerre, Fûts nouveau, 1985
This wine was an experiment using all new oak. It shows more concentration than the regular bottling, with better-rounded fruits, and has retained better freshness. Layers of flavor and depth to the developing red fruits with a lovely smoky, mineral finish. Not commercially available, but **.

Sancerre, 1977
Light garnet color. A faint note of fresh cut mushrooms on the nose, which shows developed tertiary aromas with some notes of smoke and minerality. Now becoming a little vegetal, showing especially on the finish. * Drink up.

Domaine Henri Bourgeois

Bourgeois is a sizeable operation, perhaps the largest in Sancerre. Their several buildings, including a brand new modern winery, occupy much of the village of Chavignol. The domain has expanded steadily from its 2 ha in 1950 to about 65 ha of vineyards today, spreading out from Chavignol. (They have also established Clos Henri in Marlborough, New Zealand, which is roughly equivalent in size.) Jean-Marie Bourgeois feels that, "It's not the winemaker who makes the wine, it's the vigneron. A vigneron should not love wine, he should love the vines. Contact with the land is essential." In the vineyards, they stopped using pesticides 30 years ago and they "travailler le produit le moins possible." The new winery is a gravity-fed operation that makes wine with minimal perturbation. In 1962 they started to vinify separate cuvées of Pinot Noir. There are two bottlings, Les Baronnes and Les Bonnes Bouches, which are matured in a mixture of new and old oak. The top cuvée, La Bourgeoise, comes from Vieilles Vignes (over 50 years old), which give a lower yield (36 hl/ha, compared with the 45 hl/ha of the other bottlings). The principal difference between the cuvées is the age of the vines, although La Bourgeoise does have more silex terroir. The wines are made in a light style reflecting the traditional typicity of Sancerre and were tasted at the domain in June 2010.

Sancerre, Les Baronnes, 2007
Limpid ruby color with garnet hues. Light red fruit nose with touch of minerality. Following through to the palate, light red fruits in a mineral context. * Drink now-2014.

Sancerre, La Bourgeoise, 2006
Medium ruby to garnet color. A touch of smoky strawberry fruits on the nose. Lovely elegant red fruits on the palate, strawberries turning mineral with a touch of gunflint, balanced acidity, an impression of austerity with some structure suggesting there will be some longevity. ** Drink now-2015.

Sancerre, Les Bonnes Bouches, 2006
Some minerality on the nose. Nicely rounded red fruits on the palate, with refined light tannins, and a mineral touch on the finish. * Drink now-2014.

Sancerre, La Bourgeoise, 2005
A whiff of fresh cut mushrooms on the nose. Nicely rounded, medium weight red fruits are supported on the palate by supple tannins, but the dry finish indicates good structural support, with balanced acidity. Not quite yet at peak, should hold five years or so. ** Drink 2011-2016.

Sancerre, La Bourgeoise, 2003
Slightly dark color, medium garnet still with some ruby hues. First signs of development showing on the nose, just a suspicion of tertiary aromas adding to the notes of strawberry jam. Good depth, nicely rounded red fruits, still fresh, just a touch of smoky minerality on the finish. At its peak now and should hold for five years. Did not succumb to the heat of 2003. ** Drink now-2016.

Sancerre, 1997
Garnet color with broadening orange rim. Becoming tertiary on the nose. Still shows sweet ripe fruits, with a slightly austere finish, just a touch short, but very good for vintage. * Drink up.

Sancerre, 1990
Medium garnet color with orange hue. Tertiary notes on nose, some sous bois developing. Nicely rounded red ripe fruits on palate, tannins seem resolved, acidity showing as just a touch low to support further longevity. * Drink up.

Sancerre, 1983
Garnet with some pronounced orange hues. Developed red fruits show tertiary aromas on the nose, with a fugitive touch of gunflint. Developed red fruits show on the palate, just a bit short and austere on the finish, with some loss of fruit concentration beginning to show. But very good for age and vintage. * Drink up.

Domaine Alphonse Mellot

Alphonse Mellot occupies a rabbit warren of medieval caves right under the town center of Sancerre, some dating from the 15th century. They now have 13 ha of Pinot Noir planted in Sancerre, mostly in quite small individual parcels, and a separate block of 6 ha (Les Pénitents) outside the Sancerre AOC in the Vin de Pays des Côteaux Charitois. The Sancerre vineyards have been biodynamic since 1989, and Les Pénitents since 2005. Each of the five separate cuvées of Pinot Noir is based on separate parcels. Les Pénitents is on south-facing calcareous soil, with vines 12-16 years old, usually giving about 27 hl/ha. La Demoiselle comes from a 1 ha vineyard on silex soil on the eastern part of the appellation, where the vines ripen more slowly. La Moussière comes from a 5 ha plot of vines up to 45 years old on Kimmeridgian soil, and En Grand Champs is a 1 ha parcel at the top of La Moussière with 62 year old vines. The top wine is Generation XIX (named for 19 generations of Mellots), which comes from old vines in the Le Paradis parcel, planted at high density and giving an average yield only about 21 hl/ha. Yields in the other vineyards are generally in the range 25-30 hl/ha, not more than 36 hl/ha. They never chaptalize. In 1993 there was a jump in quality after they reduced yields and introduced sorting tables. All the wines use several days of cold maceration before fermentation starts. The wines from the old vines, En Grand Champs and Generation XIX, are neither fined nor filtered. "The spicy quality with notes of fruit is the Sancerre typicity," the Mellots say of their wines. A tasting of recent vintages in August 2010 revealed the same fascinating interplay of vintage and terroir that you see in Burgundy. Generally the 2008 vintage showed the youthful opulence of this top year, and the differences of terroir came through more clearly in the lighter, more restrained, 2007s. Notes are in order from young vines on siliceous terroir to older vines on calcareous soil.

Les Pénitents, 2008

Youthful ruby color. Restrained nose of red fruits with some intimations of black cherries. Denser fruits than the 2007, more an impression of black fruits on the palate, very workmanlike well made wine, if not showing the complexity of the Sancerre AOCs. There's a faint suggestion of a mineral edge. The wine needs another year to integrate. * Drink 2011-2015.

Les Penitents, 2007

Red fruit nose, more raspberries and redcurrants than strawberries. Quite taut, light red fruits on the palate with just a hint of strawberries, a soft and smoky impression overall, with just the faintest impression of gunflint. Very expressive of the terroir. * Drink 2011-2014.

La Demoiselle, 2008

Nose just beginning to show aromatics, blackcurrant fruits, and some floral and perfumed notes of roses. Some notes of wood spices develop in the glass. Very attractive and intriguing, promises to develop interesting complexity. Youthfulness shows in the slightly tarry edge to the fruits. Smooth on the palate and more black than red, a nicely spicy quality, with those notes of blackcurrants coming back on a long finish. Some time is needed to let the tannins integrate. ** Drink 2012-2016.

La Demoiselle, 2007

Some aromatic notes of black cherries on the nose, with a fugitive whiff of violets. Terroir shines through here in the taut quality of the red fruits on the palate, nicely balanced acidity, and an average to long finish. The step up from Les Pénitents is evident. ** Drink now-2014.

La Moussière, 2009

Very youthful appearance, medium purple color. Fairly direct red fruits on the nose, leading to nicely rounded red fruits on the palate in a straightforward style with faintly buttery notes on the finish. Smooth on the palate, with soft, ripe tannins. Not a great deal of stuffing, but lovely short-tem drinking. ** Drink 2012-2015.

La Moussière, 2008

Dusky purple color. Very restrained nose, just a faint impression of black fruits. Smooth fruits on the palate are more black than red (the difference with Les Pénitents reflecting the smoothness of calcareous versus the tautness of siliceous terroir). Medium weight fruits on the palate, balanced acidity, tannic support just still showing, a wine to enjoy in the next couple of years as the tannins resolve. ** Drink 2011-2016.

En Grand Champs, 2008

Deep dusky purple suggests a good level of extraction. Mélange of red and black fruits on the nose with a slightly perfumed note. Still a faint buttery touch of vanillin. Soft, smooth, opulent on the palate, with a faintly nutty edge to a long finish. Tannic support shows as an edge on the long finish of ripe black fruits. Very fine indeed, with the concentration of the old vines showing clearly. An elegance and lightness of touch reminds me of Chambolle Musigny. *** Drink 2012-2018.

En Grand Champs, 2007

Medium dusky purple to garnet hue. Slightly vegetal note on the nose at first, slowly developing more as a note of tobacco. More acidity showing on the palate here, supporting medium weight red fruits, presently quite restrained on the palate. Needs to come out of its shell. ** Drink now-2014.

Generation XIX, 2008

Deep dusky purple color. More of a black fruit nose here, quite spicy, with some of the tarry overtones of youth. Real density of extract reflecting the low yield of the old vines and the opulence of the vintage. Lovely rich mouthfeel, touch of blackcurrants to the fruits on the palate, faintly perfumed, long finish with the ripe tannins subsumed by the fruits, some layers of flavor already showing and promising to develop as a classic. This is a vin de garde. You might well be in a top commune of the Côte de Nuits here. *** Drink 2012-2018.

Generation XIX, 2007

Medium to deep ruby/garnet color. A slightly piquant red fruit nose follows through to the palate, the piquancy not a problem but adding complexity. Reflecting the vintage, a much lighter impression than the 2008. Taut fruits more red than black, supported by balanced acidity and fine tannins. ** Drink 2011-2016.

Producers and Tastings in the Ahr Valley

Wines were tasted from current vintages back to 2004, the point at which most producers' wines begin to show some tertiary development. Those from the western part of the valley, which is narrow and where the slate-covered vineyards rise up in steep terraces, are generally tauter than those from the eastern end at Bad Neuenahr-Ahrweiler, where the valley broadens out and the soils are heavier. 2009 promises to be another ripe, lush year; 2008 produced leaner, more classic wines; 2007 was another ripe year, producing lush wines; 2006 was a little difficult; 2005 had a dry summer, producing ripe wines that tend to age faster than 2004, which was a classic year.

Weingut J. J. Adeneuer

Describing itself as a "rotweingut," Adeneuer produces only red wine from its 13 hectares, which are divided into a variety of parcels varying from 0.1 to 1.5 hectares. Pinot Noir, which Marc Adeneuer says his family have been producing for five hundred years, is 90% of production; Frühburgunder, introduced about twenty years ago, is another 7%. Wines vary from the basic range, intended for consumption soon after release, to the estate wine labeled No. 1, and the single vineyard wines. Grosses Gewächs wines are produced from the two top vineyards. Ahrweiler Rosenthal has heavier soil, and makes a more rounded wine; Walporzheim Gärkammer has more slate, and produces a tauter wine, with perhaps slightly longer aging potential. Marc says his aim is "to produce a typical wine for the region, which means a fruitier style with less obvious tannins." There is no chaptalization, so the typical alcohol levels of 13.5-14% represent the ripeness of the fruits. Wines were tasted in August 2010 at Adeneuer.

Ahr, Spätburgunder No. 1, 2008
This is the higher level of Adeneuer's two estate Pinot Noirs that are matured in barriques (in this case using a mixture of new and 2-year oak). Already showing a medium garnet color, it is slightly spicy on the nose, with a mélange of red and black fruits. Quite smooth on the palate, where the earthy red fruits show mineral overtones. Nice mildly spicy, earthy, finish. * Drink now-2013.

Ahrweiler Rosenthal, Spätburgunder, Grosses Gewächs, 2008
Youthful, rather primary, strawberry fruit nose, verging on buttery. More mineral impression on palate, taut red fruits, but then softness showing on the finish. Good fruit concentration in a medium weight style, elegant finish with refined tannins. ** Drink 2012-2017.

Walporzheimer Gärkammer, Spätburgunder, Grosses Gewächs, 2008
Taut fruits with mineral impression on nose. Well rounded fruits on palate, a little more fat showing than the Rosenthal, but then the minerality comes back to cut the finish. Balanced acidity and fine grained tannins support the fruits, leading to an elegant finish with a little more power than the Rosenthal. ** Drink 2012-2018.

Ahrweiler Rosenthal, Spätburgunder, Grosses Gewächs, 2007
Slightly earthy, spicy, strawberry fruits on the nose. Restrained and taut on the palate, smooth red fruits with faintly nutty overtones and a suspicion of vanillin, supported by fine-grained tannins with a silky finish. The clay in the soil makes this little more rounded than the Gärkammer. A touch of heat shows from the high alcohol (14%). ** Drink 2011-2015.

Walporzheimer Gärkammer, Spätburgunder, Grosses Gewächs, 2007
Slightly spicy mineral edge to the nose. More red fruits than black on the palate. The tautness of the slate soil comes through clearly on the palate of spicy red fruits, with faintly nutty overtones showing on the finish. Silky tannins lend good structural support. Tighter than the Rosenthal. ** Drink 2012-2017.

Ahr, Spätburgunder "R", 2006
This wine was a special bottling from the best barrels from the Gärkammer vineyard. The restrained nose gives a slightly spicy, slightly mineral impression. It is smooth and taut on the

palate, with restrained youthfulness, spicy, mineral fruits showing on the finish with mineral overtones. The fruits are supported by firm, silky tannins. A very fine effort, which still really needs a little more time. *** Drink 2011-2016.

Ahr, Spätburgunder No. 1, 2004
A good demonstration of aging potential, Adeneuer's top estate wine is nicely ready to drink at six years of age. There is a slightly smoky, slightly earthy edge to the nose. Earthy red strawberry fruits show on the palate, still with some tight tannins giving a little bite to the finish, with its characteristic nuttiness. This carries its high alcohol (14.5%) well. ** Drink now-2015.

Weingut Meyer Näkel

The Meyer-Näkel winery originated in 1950 with 1.5 hectares used to produce wine for the Meyer-Näkel's restaurant. After Werner Näkel took over the winery in 1982, he built it up slowly to its present 15 hectares, which consist of 50 individual parcels stretching over a 15 kilometer length of the Ahr Valley. 75% is Spätburgunder and 12% is Frühburgunder. The top vineyards are Sonnenberg, in Neuenahr where the soils are relatively rich, Krauterberg in Walporzheim, and Pfarrwingert in Meyer-Näkel's home town of Dernau, where the vineyards are steep and covered in slate. For the basic wines, grapes are usually picked when acidity is dropping and then chaptalized. The top wines usually reach a natural ripeness around 13.4% alcohol and are not chaptalized; they are matured in 70% new French oak. "We do not want to make international wine, we want to show as much as possible of the natural quality of the wine that comes from Pinot Noir grown on slate. We would not want to hide it with enological technology," says Meike Näkel, who trained in Baden and Burgundy. Indeed, the Meyer-Näkel wines are among the finest and most elegant in the Ahr, with that unique tautness of slate shining through according to the vineyard. Wines were tasted in August 2010 at Meyer Näkel, except as noted individually.

Ahr, Spätburgunder, 2009
This is the entry level wine, produced in the traditional German style (which means using quick fermentation to bring out the fruit), and intended for rapid consumption. There is a slightly tarry nose with light red fruits, and some spicy and buttery overtones showing on the palate. The tannic structure is more pronounced this year than usual, giving a slight bitterness on the finish. It's a serviceable wine, showing its geographical origins in the lightness of touch. * Drink now-2013.

Blauschiefer, Spätburgunder, 2008
Blauschiefer means "blue slate" and this wine comes from the steepest and stoniest parcels around Dernau. It spends one year in 2-4 year old barriques. It now shows a medium garnet color, and has a taut, mineral quality to the nose, with some underlying hints of raspberries, and smooth, elegant, taut red fruits on the palate. There is a good balance of acid to fruits, very fine tannins offer some potential for aging, and some interesting herbal spices come out on the finish. This should soften gently over the next few years. ** Drink 2011-2016.

Ahr, Spätburgunder "S", 2008
This wine comes from parcels around Dernau. It is matured in 50% new oak for 14 months. It shows a light to medium garnet color, with a spicy, herbal nose, a whiff of red fruits, and definitely conveys a sense of terroir. Relatively soft on the palate, but still with the sense of tension that characterizes the Meyer Näkel slate-based wines. A soft elegance on the palate is sustained by taut tannins and opulent fruits in beautiful balance. *** Drink 2011-2018.

Neuenahr Sonnenberg, Spätburgunder, Grosses Gewächs, 2008
Coming from Neuenahr, where the terrain is not so steep, and there is more loess on the topsoil, this wine usually is relatively charming and forward. Restrained on the nose, it offers a whiff of red fruits and a faint impression of the 70% new oak used in maturation. Smoothness on the palate is the first impression, with some earthy strawberry fruits, slightly spicy, and fine tannins with slightly nutty overtones on the mineral finish. Just a touch of heat shows from high alcohol. *** Drink 2013-2018.

Walporzheimer Krauterberg, Spätburgunder, Grosses Gewächs, 2008
The vineyard is located between Neuenahr and Dernau, just at the point where the valley becomes narrower. The style is between the richer quality of Neuenahr Sonnenberg to the east and the leaner quality of Dernauer Pfarrwingert to the west. The red fruit nose gives a mineral impression. On the palate there is a taut impression, but with smooth, well rounded, underlying red fruits coming back to cut the mineral edge on the finish. ** Drink 2012-2017.

Dernauer Pfarrwingert, Spätburgunder, Grosses Gewächs, 2008
This comes from the home vineyard, located on the hill directly above the village of Dernau. The vineyard is extremely steep with a very high content of slate on the surface and powdered slate in the soil. The wine shows a restrained, taut nose, with hints of minerality, extending almost to a touch of gunflint, mingled with strawberry fruits. Fine and elegant on the palate, it displays mineral red fruits, supported by balanced acidity and fine, taut, tannins on a long finish. *** Drink 2012-2017.

Dernauer Pfarrwingert, Spätburgunder, Grosses Gewächs, 2007
Slightly earthy, slightly tart nose, some intimations of strawberries. Good acidity on the palate, earthy, smoky strawberries dominating the light to medium weight fruits, with some light, tea-like, refined tannins on the finish. Typical European style Pinot Noir, although there is some perceptible heat on the finish from the high alcohol. Flavor spectrum is a little obvious at the moment, but no doubt in due course will develop some complexity (September, 2009) ** Drink now-2015.

Dernauer Pfarrwingert, Spätburgunder, Grosses Gewächs, 2006
Earthy nose with some faint smokiness and suggestions of strawberries. Crisp palate with elegant fruits. Quite a smoky bite of earthy strawberries with some faintly angular, tea-like tannins on the finish. Good balance but needs another two years for the tannins to soften. This vintage is developing slowly and seems significantly more backward than the 2007. (September, 2009) ** Drink 2011-2017.

Dernauer Pfarrwingert, Spätburgunder, Grosses Gewächs, 2005
Appearance holding up well with medium ruby-garnet color. First development beginning to show on the nose, where the characteristic mineral red fruits are overlaid by the first tertiary aromas, with a very faint air of sous bois. Nice weight to the fruits on the palate, taut but smooth; the palate is less developed than the nose but there is a lovely sweetness to the ripe fruits on the faintly nutty long finish. Just coming up to that delicious turning point where savory overtake fruity aromas and flavors. *** Drink now-2017.

Dernauer Pfarrwingert, Spätburgunder, Grosses Gewächs, 2004
Light garnet color. Earthiness is the first impression on the nose, accompanied by a faint smokiness. A faint tartness on the palate and a suggestion of faintly jam-like strawberries. Acidity is a little to the fore, reinforcing the touch of gunflint on the smokiness, and making the strawberries on the finish just a fraction tart to cut the barely perceptible touch of butter. (September, 2009) ** Drink now-2014.

Dernauer Pfarrwingert, Spätburgunder, Auslese trocken, 2003
This would be a great wine if it weren't so brutally extracted as the result of the heat of the vintage. You see immediately from color, nose, and palate that it's just past the turning point from fruity to savory. The nose offers a delicious blend of tertiary aromas and black fruits. A little less developed, the palate shows intense fruits with some bitterness on the finish. Pushed by the whopping alcohol of 14.5%, the bitterness clouds the finish. The usual elegance of Meyer-Näkel is there underneath, but you just can't completely beat the vintage. (September 2010) * Drink now-2013.

Ahr, Spätburgunder "S", 2001
Color not very developed: still more ruby than garnet. Slightly tarry notes with the fruits buried somewhere underneath. A touch of alcohol shows on the nose. Dry and slightly spicy on the palate, the bitterness on the finish is beginning to outrun the fruits. ** Drink up.

Dernauer Pfarrwingert, Spätburgunder, Auslese trocken, 1999
Auslese trocken was the description for this wine before it became labeled as Grosses Gewächs. At eleven years of age, this vintage is fully mature. The garnet color with its orange rim shows some development. The nose is quite tertiary with a fair amount of sous bois and a fugitive whiff of oxidation. Lovely balance on the palate, ripe fruits, now just very slightly past its peak, so time to drink up as we see the limits of longevity. ***.

Weingut Jean Stodden

From 56 tiny parcels, the largest being only 0.35 ha, Alexander Stodden uses his 6.5 hectares to produce some of the most intense wines in the Ahr. 90% of his vineyards are planted to red wine, most of it Pinot Noir. The range of wines extends from the entry level Ahr to single vineyard Grosses Gewächs. The lower level wines are made in an old fashioned style, meaning that they spend 10-12 months in large foudres, as his grandfather might have used. The top wines spend 16-18 months in barriques. (They must celebrate Christmas twice in the barrel, Alexander says.) The Grosses Gewächs use close to 100% new French oak; they are bottled unfined and unfiltered. The top three vineyards extend from the relatively richer soils of Sonnenberg in Neuenahr, through the Rosenthal vineyard in Ahrweiler, to the stony slate of Herrenberg in Rech. The wines offer textbook examples of differences between the individual vineyard terroirs and the 2007 and 2008 vintages. Describing his style, Alexander says that winemaking is adjusted each vintage according to taste—"all winemaking is done with glass in hand." His aim is to produce wine that makes people think about the Ahr when they want a Pinot Noir. Wines were tasted in August 2010 at Jean Stodden or at the VDP tasting in Wiesbaden.

Neuenahr Sonnenberg, Spätburgunder, Grosses Gewächs, 2008
Rich red fruit impression on nose, more cherries than strawberries, followed by some mineral notes. Well rounded rich red fruits on the palate follow the nose. A richer, softer, impression than you usually get in the Ahr, reflecting the heavier soils in the Bad Neuenahr area. Very good with potential for developing into a soft, earthy wine. *** Drink 2012-2019.

Ahrweiler Rosenthal, Spätburgunder, Grosses Gewächs, 2008
Restrained nose, faint impression of mineral red fruits. More tautness shows on the palate compared with the Sonnenberg. Ripe red fruits in restrained, tight, elegant style, supported by balanced acidity and refined tannins, and giving overall a mineral impression. *** Drink 2013-2019.

Recher Herrenberg, Spätburgunder, Grosses Gewächs, 2008
Restrained nose with a faint impression of red fruits. Ripeness of fruits strikes you immediately on the palate, rich, well rounded, supported by ripe tannins, cut by a mineral edge. The most powerful of Stodden's single vineyard wines each year, this should age well, developing layers of complexity in time. *** Drink 2013-2020.

Ahr, Spätburgunder "JS", 2007
The grapes for this cuvée come from Bad Neuenahr and Dernau. A tarry light red fruit nose. Smooth on the palate with light, well rounded red cherry fruits showing a slight bitterness on the finish. * Drink 2011-2015.

Neuenahr Sonnenberg, Spätburgunder, Grosses Gewächs, 2007
A hint of mint on the nose, then some faintly perfumed red fruits with very faint hints of black-currants. Smooth, opulent impression on the palate with faintly buttery notes on the finish. The softness of the red fruits reflects the relatively heavier soils of the Neuenahr area. The richest of the three single vineyard wines. ** Drink 2011-2016.

Ahrweiler Rosenthal, Spätburgunder, Grosses Gewächs, 2007
This vineyard was planted with a clone selected in Stodden's vineyards. The wine has a taut impression on the nose, with red fruits showing hints of wood spices. Nicely rounded, slightly spicy red fruits on the palate are supported by fine-grained tannins giving a long finish. ** Drink 2011-2016.

Recher Herrenberg, Spätburgunder, Grosses Gewächs, 2007
Taut nose with faintly mineral red fruits showing some wood spices. Slightly spicy red fruit on the palate, you can see the tension coming from the slate soils. Concentrated fruits (yields were only 30 hl/ha) are supported by a very finely grained tannic structure, elegant and taut on the finish. The very high alcohol of 14.5% is surprisingly well integrated and scarcely noticeable. ** Drink now-2016.

Ahr, Spätburgunder Alte Reben, 2007
"Alte Reben" indicates really old vines, planted in the 1920s-1930s on their own roots, on the same slope as the Grosses Gewächs Recher Herrenberg. (This was the material that was propagated to replant the Ahrweiler Rosenthal vineyard.) There's a slightly herbal, spicy impression on the nose, lovely concentration of red fruits on the palate (yields were only 18 hl/ha), ripe tannins supporting the finish, and a good sense of terroir in the wine. This top result would be a credit to Pinot Noir anywhere. **** Drink 2012-2020.

Mayschosser Monchberg, Spätburgunder, 2007
Produced in tiny amounts, this wine is available only at the annual VDP Nahe/Ahr auction. Intense is the word for this wine, but the style remains elegant. Striking mineral red fruits dominate the nose. Concentrated red fruits are smooth but taut on the palate, supported by a filigree of tannins, leading to a long finish. Layers of flavor promise great development for at least the next decade. **** Drink 2011-2017.

Recher Herrenberg, Spätburgunder, Grosses Gewächs, 2006
The slate of the vineyard is represented in the wine by the clean, pure lines of the fruit, elegant with a dominant minerality. Evidently ripe and sweet, the fruits have a faint touch of earthy strawberries showing more on the palate than the nose. The red fruits come through with great purity, supported by fine grained tannins on the finish. The wine opens and softens in the glass, but retains its purity of line, a harbinger of future development. Very fine indeed. **** Drink 2011-2020.

Producers and Tastings in Mosel and Rheingau

Weingut Markus Molitor (Bernkastel)

Markus Molitor took over this estate in 1984, when he was twenty and the vineyards amounted only to 3 ha, and has increased it to its present 42 ha. Acquisitions are confined to steep vineyards (defined as having slopes of 30-65%). The oldest vines are more than 120 years old; 55% of the vines are ungrafted. Plantings are almost exclusively devoted to Riesling (94%) although there is 2% Pinot Blanc as well as the 4% Pinot Noir for which Molitor is a pioneer in the Mosel. There is one basic Pinot Noir and three single vineyard wines. Following the old German principle of detailed classification, the single vineyard Pinots are given one, two, or three stars to indicate ascending quality; assignment is by taste, although of course it correlates with ripeness. The Brauneberger Mandelgraben is usually one star. Klostergarten (where the soil is similar to Mandelgraben, but the vineyard is a little more south facing and therefore warmer) offers an opportunity to compare two star and three star (the latter usually in tiny quantities, coming from the better parcels, and amounting in all to less than 1,200 bottles in an average year). Graacher Himmelreich, the steepest and stoniest vineyard, and their largest (1 ha), harvests a week earlier than the Brauneberg vineyards, and usually is three star. Molitor would compare his wines more with Burgundy than with other regions of Germany. Wines were tasted at Markus Molitor in August 2010.

Brauneberger Mandelgraben, Spätburgunder (*), 2007
Showing Molitor's typically light, elegant style, this wine was tasted a few weeks before bottling. Faintly spicy red fruit nose leading to medium density, youthful red fruits of cherries and strawberries. Clean pure fruit lines. Good acid balance but a slightly acerbic touch from the fine tannins on the finish. ** Drink 2012-2017.

Brauneberger Klostergarten, Spätburgunder (**), 2007
A little spiciness shows on the nose but the fruits are somewhat obscured at the moment. They show as a little more intense and better rounded on the palate than Mandelgraben, with a slight glyceriny softness on the finish, and hints of spices. The tannins are quite ripe and silky. A fine, elegant style. ** Drink 2012-2018.

Brauneberger Klostergarten, Spätburgunder (***), 2007
Going up to the three star, there is more intensity all round than the two star. The color is a little darker and more purple in hue. The nose is somewhat closed at present, offering a youthful impression of spiciness, which continues to the red fruits on the palate. The softness of the two star turns to silkiness in the three star, with supple tannins supporting the more concentrated fruits. Slightly longer, the finish also shows a little more spice. *** Drink 2012-2018.

Brauneberger Mandelgraben, Spätburgunder (*), 2006
Slightly spicy and mineral notes show on the nose, with the spiciness following through to the palate. Age here has produced a faint sense of dilution of the mid palate, with the light fruits and lean style letting a little alcohol show on the finish, although the fruits become sweeter and more persistent in the glass. The closest parallel in Burgundy would be a village wine from around Beaune. ** Drink now-2013.

Graacher Himmelreich, Spätburgunder (***), 2006
A little nutty on the nose with underlying red fruits. An elegant style shows on the palate, with strawberry fruits that are surprisingly soft and supple, but with good supporting acidity and quite soft tannins. *** Drink 2011-2016.

Brauneberger Klostergarten, Spätburgunder (***), 2005
Relatively closed on the nose but some earthy strawberries slowly emerge in Burgundian style. Soft but with lean lines on the palate; earthy almost nutty strawberries are supported by balanced acidity, with refined tannins providing supporting structure on a dry finish. *** Drink now-2016.

Brauneberger Klostergarten, Spätburgunder (**), 2004
Not much development in its medium garnet appearance. First signs of development show on the nose as some tertiary aromas and a hint of sous bois overlaying the generally mineral impression. Tertiary impressions are less evident on the palate, where well rounded fruits are evident. Earthy and mineral undertones fade into a slight nuttiness, with the very long finish showing an impressive minerality. **** Drink now-2015.

Graacher Himmelreich, Spätburgunder (***), 2004
As always, the Graacher Himmelreich displays the leanest and most refined lines of Molitor's Pinot Noirs, showing beautifully as the wine now achieves some maturity. A little age is evident in the medium intensity garnet appearance, and tertiary notes have begun to appear on the nose. Right now this wine is at a beautiful balancing point in its development. This is very much a food wine, with those slightly savory notes of development just cutting the ripe red fruits that dominate the palate. The tannins are slowly resolving to reveal a lovely long finish. **** Drink now-2015.

Domäne Assmanshausen (Kloster Eberbach)

Whether or not the fable is true that the monks at Kloster Eberbach introduced Pinot Noir to Germany, there has certainly been long experience in making wine here. Not content to cultivate vines solely in the immediate vicinity of the monastery, the monks acquired vineyards in neighboring villages to their west. With the dissolution of the monasteries, these vineyards became the property of the state, and are still described as the Hessische Staatsweingut. Much of the wine is sold in the shop at Kloster Eberbach. Although the winery is now (finally) run as an independent operation, some of the effects of control by the state still linger. The 20 ha in Assmanshausen today are planted mostly with Pinot Noir, some with Frühburgunder. The 22 ha in Rudesheim include 3 ha of Pinot Noir. There are another 15 ha in the rest of the Rheingau, used to produce the entry level wine. With almost 40 ha of Spätburgunder altogether, this is the largest producer of Pinot Noir in the Rheingau, perhaps in Germany. The trends in German wine production are writ large in the history of the estate. Until the 1970s, all the wines were sweet. The oldest Pinot Noir vineyard was planted in 1970 with Geisenheim clones. More recently, higher quality clones have been planted. Yields have been coming down, but vary widely, from a high in 2008 at an average 62 hl/ha to a low in 2009 at an average 32 hl/ha. My impression of the wines was that a more even control of yield, and an average reduction of 10-20%, would produce significant improvement, bringing more of the wines up to the levels usually achieved only by the special bottlings. Wines were tasted at Domäne Assmanshausen in August 2010 except where otherwise noted.

Assmannshäuser Höllenberg, Spätburgunder Spätlese trocken, 2009
Slightly austere nose, somewhat restrained with a herbal touch. Austerity follows through to the palate where red fruits are subdued by some fine tannins. Still needs another year. * Drink 2011-2014.

Assmannshäuser Höllenberg, Spätburgunder Spätlese trocken, 2008
Matured in a classic large foudre, this wine shows a soft nose with faintly buttery red fruits. The softness carries over to the palate, where strawberry fruits show some intimations of jam. Not a great deal of backbone. * Drink now-2013.

Assmannshäuser Höllenberg, Spätburgunder Aus dem Cabinetkeller, 2008
Aus dem Cabinetkeller is Assmannshausen's description for wine at the Auslese trocken level. The herbal nose is quite enticing, with hints of sage and fresh-cut mushrooms. The palate offers balanced red fruits with some earthy strawberries, with soft supporting tannins showing on the finish. ** Drink now-2014.

Assmannshäuser Höllenberg, Spätburgunder Aus dem Cabinetkeller, Mauerwein, 2008
Mauerwein is the wall at the base of the vineyard. Holding the heat, it results in greater ripeness in the parcels close by. Usually there is just one barrique. Restrained nose with some hints of freshness. Red fruits on the palate offer a faint impression of earthy strawberries, but seem less concentrated then the older vintages. * Drink now-2013.

Assmannshäuser Höllenberg, Spätburgunder Spätlese trocken, Goldkapsel, 2007
The product of a single barrique of new oak, the wine shows a slightly astringent red fruit nose. Good acidity supports the red berry fruits on the palate; tannins are integrating nicely on the finish. * Drink now-2014.

Assmannshäuser Höllenberg, Spätburgunder Aus dem Cabinetkeller, 2007
A faintly savory herbal note marks the nose. Nice red strawberry fruits on the palate are slightly jammy, although cut by an edge of minerality. ** Drink now-2014.

Assmannshäuser Höllenberg, Spätburgunder Aus dem Cabinetkeller, 2006
Light strawberry jam nose. The palate follows the nose with a light jammy fruit impression. There is good supporting acidity but not much tannic support. * Drink now-2013.

Assmannshäuser Höllenberg, Spätburgunder Spätlese trocken, 2006
Medium ruby-garnet color. Slightly austere red fruit nose. The austerity follows through to the red fruit palate, but there's a rush of ripe red fruits on the finish to balance the slightly stern tannins. A little heat shows on the finish. * Drink now-2014.

Assmannshäuser Höllenberg, Spätburgunder Spätlese trocken, Goldkapsel, 2005
Typically just one barrique of this wine makes the grade for the Goldkapsel labeling. Nose of red berry fruits with some earthy strawberries. Nicely concentrated red cherry and strawberry fruits on the palate with a faint buttery touch on the finish, where some fine tannins are evident. A softer, more rounded impression than the regular bottling. ** Drink now-2015.

Assmannshäuser Höllenberg, Spätburgunder Aus dem Cabinetkeller, Mauerwein, 2005
Faint notes of savory development on the nose suggest that this wine is developing more rapidly than the 2004 vintage. Ripe fruits of red and black cherries on the palate have a faintly nutty impression and a nice chocolate coating to the finish. There's more bottle variation than usual because of a problem with corks in this vintage. * Drink now-2012.

Assmannshäuser Höllenberg, Spätburgunder Aus dem Cabinetkeller, Mauerwein, 2004
Slightly stern red fruit nose. Quite deep fruits on the palate of red and black cherries, good balancing acidity, and ripe, firm, supporting tannins. A good result that well expresses the vintage. ** Drink now-2014.

Assmannshäuser Höllenberg, Spätburgunder Aus dem Cabinetkeller, 2003
Medium ruby-garnet color. Quite fresh red fruit nose, with deep, spicy red fruits following on the palate. Almost brooding, with an opulent impression on the finish, with rich fruits matched by ripe tannins. Very high alcohol (14.5%) does not obtrude. A very good result for this hot year when so many wines were cooked. ** Drink now-2014.

Assmannshäuser Höllenberg, Spätburgunder Spätlese trocken (***), 2001
Medium garnet color doesn't show a lot of development, and the nose has tarry fruits. Fruits are drying out on the palate, but still have a nice ripe touch on the finish, although the age is

showing here. As the fruits lighten up, a slightly bitter rasp comes on to the finish, suggesting that this vintage produced a bit too much tannin for the fruits. * Drink up.

Assmannshäuser Höllenberg, Spätburgunder Spätlese trocken, 1999
Restrained nose develops some touches of oxidation, indicating the wine is close to its limit of longevity. Color is light and more developed than 2000 or 2001. Nice sweet ripe fruits on the palate are only just beginning to show the first touches of dilution, but overall a nice balance. A little alcohol is evident. * Drink up.

Assmannshäuser Höllenberg, Spätburgunder Spätlese trocken, 1989
Classic Pinot nose of earthy strawberries with faint aromatic overtones and suggestions of wood smoke. Good balance on the palate, quite earthy, some wood smoke and gunflint, tannins resolving but still providing some taut support. Long tight finish, the smoke and gunflint coming across to give a slightly austere impression. (September, 2009) ** Drink now-2014.

Assmannshäuser Höllenberg, Spätburgunder Spätlese trocken, 1959
Just a little more garnet than the younger vintages, but otherwise not showing much age in its appearance. Faintly tertiary intimations on the nose, with a faint sense of very ripe fruits over-laying the smoky, earthy strawberries. Tertiary notes on the palate are quite subtle, smoky, minty, earthy, strawberries giving a faint buttery impression to the long, taut, finish with a sweet, ripe impression. Enticing notes of spices develop in the glass. This could easily be compared with a Burgundy of the same vintage. (September, 2009) *** Drink now-2016.

Producer and Tasting in Franken

Weingut Rudolph Fürst

Rudolf Fürst is well out of the mainstream in Franken. This is mostly a white wine region given over to Sylvaner, but with Riesling grown in the best sites. Extending over a long east-west axis, it has the most heterogeneous soils in Germany. The Fürst vine-yards are at 100 meters elevation in the protected environment of a small river valley. Paul Fürst took over the vineyard in 1979, and has increased it from 2.5 ha to 20 ha, with a large holding of 15 ha in the Centgrafenberg, a steep south-facing slope where the soil is red sandstone, with loam topsoils of varying thickness. The vineyard is fo-cused on the Pinot family, with 40% Pinot Noir, 7% Frühburgunder, and 15% Pinot Blanc. Paul's aim is to emphasize the capacity of the terroir to produce light, elegant wines. In the mid eighties he introduced Burgundian vinification methods. "Especially over the past ten years," he says, "the aim has been for freshness rather than sweetness in the grapes or strong tannins." The current vintage was tasted at the VDP in Wies-baden in August, 2010, the older wines in September, 2009.

Klingenberger Schlossberg, Grosses Gewächs, 2008
Light earthy strawberries on the nose, with herbal overtones. The aromas follow through to the fruits on the palate, red with fresh, herbal overtones. Fine tannins recede into the background on the finish. The most complex of the three Fürst wines at the VDP tasting. ** Drink 2011-2016.

Bürgstadter Centgrafenberg, Grosses Gewächs, 2008
Restrained nose. Light earthy strawberry fruits on palate, more direct and less herbal than the Schlossberg, quite light tannins on the finish. * Drink 2011-2015.

Bürgstadter Hunsrück, Grosses Gewächs, 2008
Light red fruit nose with faint mineral overtones. Nicely balanced, light, well rounded fruits on palate, cut by a faintly herbal, mineral touch to the finish. * Drink 2012-2015.

Bürgstadter Centgrafenberg, Franken, Grosses Gewächs, 2007
Slightly sour impression on the nose with sharpish red fruits. Palate also seems a little sharp. Gunflint on the palate, some light strawberry fruits, leading into a medium length finish. * Drink 2011-2016.

Bürgstadter Centgrafenberg, Franken, Grosses Gewächs, 2005
Slightly acid impression on the nose, hints of gunflint and earthy strawberries intensifying in the glass. Light fruits of earthy strawberries showing on the palate, balancing acidity, slightly angular tannins on the finish. * Drink now-2013.

Bürgstadter Centgrafenberg, Franken, Grosses Gewächs, 2003
Slight impression of gunflint on the nose. Fruits just a touch sharp on the palate, strawberries tinged with gunflint. A faint retronasal impression of butter on the finish. This is a very good result considering the hot conditions of the year, with good freshness retained in the wine. * Drink now-2014.

Bürgstadter Centgrafenberg, Franken, Grosses Gewächs, 1997
Faintly mineral on the nose, perhaps a slight tertiary impression. Balanced acidity supports fresh earthy strawberries on the palate with a nice touch of richness and a faintly buttery impression on the finish. * Drink now-2014.

Producers and Tastings in the Pfalz

Weingut Phillip Kuhn (Laumersheim)

Phillip Kuhn is at the forefront of the drive to produce quality Pinot Noir in the region. Half of his 23 ha are red, including 6 ha of Pinot Noir and 1 ha of Frühburgunder. His basic wine is labeled "tradition" meaning it uses the old German clones, is matured in old (4-6 year) barrels, and is easy to drink. He likes his wines to have a certain weight, Côte de Nuits rather than Côte de Beaune, but "It's not possible to take Burgundy as a model, you have to make your own," he says. When he decided to plant Pinot Noir it was well out of the mainstream. Phillip planted his first Pinot Noir in his best site at Laumersheim to replace a Huxelrebe vineyard in 1988. Only Geisenheim clones were available then, but since the mid nineties he has been planting Dijon clones. He ferments in stainless steel but plans to test wooden fermenters next year. Chaptalization is rare; the last year it was necessary was 2000. Usually the wines naturally reach 13-14% alcohol. Some years he saignées to produce a rosé. The Grosses Gewächs are matured for 16-18 months in French oak, with 50-60% new oak. His best vineyards are Kirschgarten (literally cherry garden), which is an amphitheater that protects the vines against the wind, giving more obvious ripeness and richness than Steinbuckel, where the soil is similar but the elevation is higher, and the wines have more obvious structure. His top wine used to be called Mergelwes, which was the old name for the best vineyard in Kirschgarten, but (together with Weingut Knipser) he lost the fight to keep the name, and they had to abandon it after 2005. Kuhn produces vins de garde that age quite slowly. Wines were tasted at Philip Kuhn in August 2010.

Pfalz, Spätburgunder Tradition, 2008
Bottled three weeks before tasting, this still has a medium purple color, with more of a black fruit nose than red, and some slightly aromatic overtones. The palate makes a fruity impression. Using German clones, this is a well made wine at the basic level. * Drink now-2013.

Laumersheimer Kirschgarten, Spätburgunder, Grosses Gewächs, 2007
Dusky medium to deep ruby color with some purple hues. A black cherry nose has some tarry notes from new oak. Smooth, rich, and full on the palate; good supporting acidity and ripe tannins give an elegant impression to the black cherry fruits. The dense fruits match the tannins and hide the structure, so you could drink this now, but it really needs a couple of years. A little heat shows on the finish, which has a glycerin quality cut by the acidity and tannins. Very fine. *** Drink 2012-2016.

Laumersheimer Steinbuckel, Spätburgunder, Grosses Gewächs, 2007
Medium to deep dusky purple color. Some spice shows on a red and black fruit nose, with a slightly savory edge, less evidently ripe than the Kirschgarten. The palate shows an elegant,

smooth style, with ripe, silky tannins, and black cherry notes coming back on the finish. *** Drink 2013-2017.

Laumersheimer Steinbuckel, Spätburgunder, Grosses Gewächs, 2006
Medium garnet color. Some savory notes are beginning to appear on the nose to add to the black cherry fruits. Mineral and herbal elements cut the fruits on the palate, a slightly leaner style reflecting the vintage. The finish is quite glyceriny, with some fine, firm tannins. *** Drink 2012-2016.

Laumersheimer Kirschgarten Mergelweg, Spätburgunder, Grosses Gewächs, 2005
Medium to deep garnet color. First tertiary notes showing here, with a touch of gunflint on the nose. The richness of the vineyard shows clearly in the ripe, black fruits, dense and glyceriny on the finish, cut by some bitter black cherries. Still fairly closed, the firmness of the tannins shows on the finish, the wine still needs more time. *** Drink 2012-2019.

Mergelweg, Spätburgunder, 2004
Still a dark color, more ruby than garnet in hue. A mixture of savory herbal notes and black fruits on the nose. Fruits are less obvious than the younger vintages. A slightly herbal note on the palate shows as a faint grassiness now; it was more inclined to asparagus when the wine was younger. The leaner style reflects the vintage, with the tannins now integrating. ** Drink now-2016.

Mergelweg, Spätburgunder, 2002
Medium garnet color. Tertiary notes show on the savory nose, with slightly pungent hints of gunflint and sous bois. Mature tannins have integrated perfectly on the palate, which still shows those rich, black cherry fruits clearly on the long finish. There is a lovely harmonious balance, and the wine is presently at that delicious turning point between fruity and savory. A very fine result indeed. **** Drink now-2014.

Weingut Oekonomierat Rebholz (Siebeldingen)

Hansjörg Rebholz says his aim is to make Pinot Noir in a Burgundian style with potential for aging rather than for fast drinking. He looks for elegance and pure minerality in the finish. Most of his 19 ha are located around Siebeldingen, with 3.5 ha devoted to Pinot Noir. Usually most of the Pinot is produced as dry red wine, but there is also a rosé, a dry Blanc de Noirs, and a rather good sparkling wine, whose proportion is increased in poor vintages, perhaps explaining the more consistent quality of his dry reds across vintages. Hansjörg's grandfather planted Pinot Noir in the 1940s, but the oldest Pinot Noir vines presently date from 1964; most of the Pinot Noir vines are about 20 years old. Hansjörg worries about the increasing dominance of the 777 Dijon clone and tries to ensure clonal variety in his vineyards. The vineyards have been organic since 2005 and now are biodynamic. Winemaking is natural, and there is no chaptalization or filtration. The basic quality wine is intended to sell straight after bottling, usually starting in November. The next level (the Vom Muschelkalk cuvée) is matured for one year and then sold a year later. The top wine comes from the Im Sonnenschein vineyard in Siebeldingen, and spends two years in a mixture of French and German oak, including 50% new barriques, and then spends three years in bottle before it is released. The style is elegant. Even the basic wine here, although called "Tradition," has a refined, elegant style far removed from the real German tradition. There's a steady increase in concentration and smoothness going up to the Vom Muschelkalk bottling and then to the Grosses Gewächs. Wines were tasted at Rebholz in August 2010.

Sekt, Blanc de Noirs, 2005
Fresh nose with some stone fruits. Notes of apples on the palate, nice dry finish with low dosage letting the fruits speak. Fine acid structure. *** Drink now-2012.

Pfalz, Blanc de Noirs, 2009
Rebholz makes an unusual Blanc de Noirs, essentially a dry white wine, from Pinot Noir, as well as the sparkling version. Made by whole cluster pressing, it has a light citric nose, with some stone fruits showing. Citrus is more emphasized on the palate, with an elegant finish. ** Drink now-2012.

Pfalz, Spätburgunder rosé, 2009
This is made by 24 hours of skin contact before pressing. The nose is restrained, there is citrus on the palate, a little more presence than the dry Blanc de Noirs, but generally a similar fruit spectrum of citrus tinged with stone fruits. ** Drink now-2012.

Pfalz, Spätburgunder Tradition, 2008
This is the entry level red wine. The nose of light red fruits shows some buttery raspberries and strawberries. The direct red fruits are notably smooth and elegant on the palate for a "basic" wine. Just a touch of glycerin shows on the finish. * Drink now-2013.

Pfalz, Spätburgunder Vom Muschelkalk, 2008
The name of this mid-level cuvée reflects the fossilized limestone soils of the vineyards. This vintage presently appears a youthful ruby color. The nose is mostly red fruits, cherries and strawberries, with some hints of black cherries. Smooth red and black cherry fruits dominate the palate, with a faint herbal, nutty touch on the finish. There are smooth, ripe, fine tannins on the finish. ** Drink now-2014.

Im Sonnenschein, Spätburgunder, Grosses Gewächs, 2008 (barrel sample)
The wine shows a medium ruby color. More black cherry fruits on the nose compared to the vom Muschelkalk. More presence on the palate, sweet ripe fruits focusing on black cherries, a long finish with some persistent nutty and herbal notes. The ripe, smooth tannins are barely obvious. *** Drink 2013-2018.

Pfalz, Spätburgunder Tradition, 2007
Medium ruby color with just a touch of garnet. Less obvious fruit on the nose than in the 2008. Spicy red and black fruits on the palate with some herbal/nutty overtones, supported by good acidity. A smooth black cherry finish shows ripe tannins. ** Drink now-2013.

Pfalz, Spätburgunder Vom Muschelkalk, 2007
Medium ruby color with a rosy rim, not much evidence of development. Aromas more intense on the nose than in the Tradition bottling, with herbal notes and a touch of cedar and tobacco. Smooth black cherry fruits are supported on the palate by firm, ripe tannins and balanced acidity. The medium to long finish has just a touch of tannic youthfulness, which will soften over a year or so to a fine, elegant style. ** Drink now-2015.

Im Sonnenschein, Spätburgunder, Grosses Gewächs, 2007
Medium to deep ruby color has no obvious development. Cereal overtones to the nose disappear to reveal black cherry fruits. Precisely delineated black cherry fruits are very fine on the palate, with soft ripe tannins subsumed by the fruits on the finish. Refined and elegant style makes you think of the Côte de Nuits. *** Drink now-2020.

Im Sonnenschein, Spätburgunder, Grosses Gewächs, 2005
Medium ruby garnet color. A touch of tertiary development just shows on the nose, obscuring herbal red fruits. Red fruits on the palate are on the verge of development, you can still see the rich, ripe fruits of youth, but there's the first faint touch of sous bois, and then a delicious finish with soft tannins. *** Drink 2012-2016.

Im Sonnenschein, Spätburgunder, Grosses Gewächs, 2004
As often true in Germany, this wine of the 2004 vintage is maturing more slowly than its counterpart from 2005. The herbal red fruit nose gives over to slightly spicy medium weight red cherry fruits with nicely delineated flavors on the palate. The refined elegant finish shows support from smooth, ripe tannins. Very clean, pure lines give an almost mineral impression. **** Drink now-2020.

Im Sonnenschein, Spätburgunder, Grosses Gewächs, 2002
Medium garnet color but still quite youthful appearance with some rosy hues. Restrained nose releases only some faint red fruits and hint of nuts. Good acidity supports a red fruit palate of cherries and strawberries, cut by a faintly bitter note on the slightly nutty finish. A barely perceptible hint of sous bois shows the very first signs of tertiary development. Plenty of fruit on the palate but the tannins still seem rather dry on the finish. *** Drink now-2015.

Im Sonnenschein, Spätburgunder, 1997
Medium garnet color shows a little age. A touch of gunflint on the nose, then some tertiary aromas develop in the glass. Soft red fruits on the palate, a touch of drying tannins on the finish. This is just at the cusp of tertiary development. At its peak now for those who like developed wines. **** Drink now-2017.

Im Sonnenschein, Spätburgunder, 1979
Age shows in the broad orange rim on the medium garnet color. The tertiary nose has savory notes of mushrooms and sous bois but is scarcely oxidized. Some raisined notes show faintly on the palate of well developed savory fruits. There is a delicious tertiary finish. The fruits have naturally started to dry out, but there is still a kick of sweet ripe fruits giving liveliness to the finish. Even though it's past its peak, it clearly demonstrates the potential for aging; in a blind tasting you would probably place it a decade younger. **** Drink up.

Weingut Friedrich Becker

The Becker winery is located at the southern tip of the Pfalz, within a stone's throw of the border with Alsace; in fact, most of the vineyards are actually in France. The dominant climatic influences are the Vosges mountains to the west and the Black Forest range to the east. The terroir is a limestone plateau and slopes, with a clay and loam topsoil. There is some sandstone. Almost all of Becker's limestone terroir is planted with Pinot Noir; elsewhere he has the usual Alsatian varieties. One exception is the Herrschaftswingert bottling, which comes from an 0.3 ha vineyard with sandstone terroir that was a recent purchase. Becker has about 18.5 ha, with some 60% planted to Pinot Noir; 2 ha are Grosses Gewächs. His best two vineyards are Sankt Paul and Kamenberg, which are separated by only 500 meters. Sankt Paul has very little topsoil and is planted with 20 year old vines, one third French and two thirds German clones. Kamenberg has heavier, deeper topsoil with loam and a mix of older German clones, Swiss, and French clones, average 43 years age. Before the war, Pinot Noir was common here, but then it disappeared. When Becker's father planted the first post-war Pinot Noir in 1967, the wines were criticized. Responding ironically to the view that the wines were too sour, Becker used as his label an illustration of Aesop's fable about the hungry fox who disdained grapes as sour because she was unable to reach them. Pioneering efforts continued with the first use of barriques to mature Pinot Noir in the mid eighties. Becker likes to harvest around 12% potential alcohol and chaptalize slightly at the end of fermentation. The top wines now are matured almost completely in new oak. Today Fritz Becker says that his aim is to see elegance and freshness in the fruit. He does not want to copy Burgundy—"an imitation is never as good," he says—but Musigny is his model. Becker was refused a certificate for his top Pinot Noirs as lacking typicity in the late eighties. So the best wines were bottled as table wines, as they continue to be today, although this will have to change when the category is abolished by the EU. Wines were tasted at Friedrich Becker in August 2010.

Pfalz, Spätburgunder, Cuvée R, 2008
This entry level wine was matured in foudres of old oak. It has a medium ruby color and restrained nose. The palate shows bright red cherry fruits with good supporting acidity and a touch of strawberries and raspberries coming out on the finish. Well made for an entry level wine. * Drink now-2013.

Pfalz, Spätburgunder, "B", 2008
A slightly deeper ruby color than the entry level wine. The black cherry fruit nose has just a hint of blackcurrants. There's more presence on the palate, tending to black cherry fruits, with a hint of bitter cherries on a long finish of smooth, well rounded fruits, with just a touch of glycerin. ** Drink now-2015.

Pfalz, Spätburgunder Kalgestein, 2008
This comes from the Grosses Gewächs vineyard but does not carry the name because the vines are only 28 years old; the Grand Cru description is reserved for the 43 year old vines. Instead it is described as Kalgestein, meaning limestone plateau. The wine shows a medium to deep ruby color. There is more of a black fruit nose here. Then red cherry fruits show a good presence on the palate with some hints of blackcurrants, good supporting acidity, a smooth opulence to the ripe tannins, and a suspicion of nuts on the finish. This is already very accessible, but will develop well with further time. ** Drink now-2018.

Schweigener Kammerberg, Spätburgunder, Grosses Gewächs, 2008
Medium ruby color with some purple hues; darker than the Sankt Paul. Restrained nose is more spicy than herbal. Spicy, quite concentrated fruits on the palate tend more to black cherries, rich with deep layers of flavor. An opulent impression on the finish is supported by smooth, ripe, firm tannins with just a touch of youthful bitterness. Something of the style of the Côte de Nuits here, with some time needed for the tannins to integrate. *** Drink 2013-2020.

Sonnenberger Sankt Paul, Spätburgunder, Grosses Gewächs, 2008
Light ruby garnet color. Restrained nose shows taut herbal and mineral overtones. Lighter on the palate than the Kammerberg, with medium density sweet, ripe, elegant red fruits of cherries and mineral strawberries. The palate is quite fresh, and the supporting tannins are firm and silky, evident only by a little dryness on the finish. ** Drink 2012-2017.

Tafelwein Spätburgunder, Reserve, 2008
The "Reserve" is a selection of the top barrels, which in this vintage came from Sankt Paul. The nose is rather restrained. But the palate opens out with smooth, concentrated, black cherry fruits supported by balancing acidity and opulent tannins. Although the fruit concentration and freshness make it accessible to drink now, it will develop enormously over the next few years. **** Drink 2012-2020.

Tafelwein Pinot Noir, 2008
Becker's top wine comes from a special parcel in the Sankt Paul vineyard, and simply carries the description "Pinot Noir Tafelwein." The restrained black fruit nose has hints of spices. Concentrated, ripe black cherry fruits dominate the palate. The intensity of the brooding fruits obscures the structure, but as it ages the wine will develop layers of complexity. This is a very fine effort indeed, quite putting to shame most production in the region, so you can see why it might be refused a certificate for being "atypical"! **** Drink 2012-2020.

Pfalz, Spätburgunder Herrschaftswingert, 2007
Red fruit nose with suspicion of nuts. The sandstone terroir definitely gives lighter wine than the limestone. Smooth sweet fruits of red berries, showing as slightly earthy raspberries and strawberries, with a persistent nutty sweetness on the finish. ** Drink now-2016.

Sankt Paul, Spätburgunder, Grosses Gewächs, 2006
Quite buttery nose leads into rather direct strawberries. The fruits are more red and black cherries on the palate, but still with buttery overtones, a little too much for my taste. A little monotonic in flavor spectrum right now, may develop more variety with time, but I suspect the fruit will flag as it ages. * Drink now-2016.

Producers and Tastings in Baden

Weingut Dr. Heger

Wine production here started in 1935 as a hobby for Dr. Max Heger, a country doctor in Ihringen. The original holdings around Ihringen form the foundation of today's Weingut Dr. Heger. Other vineyards, acquired since 1986, form Weinhaus Heger, which produces more basic wines. Dr. Heger aims for a Burgundian style. The main issue is not to let the Pinot Noir get too hot and become jammy; it's actually planted in their cooler sites. Winemaker Markus Mleinek considers that the wines reach a suitable maturity for drinking after five or six years. The Pinot Noir vineyards are well established. In 1954 selections from Clos Vougeot were planted on their own roots in the Ihringen Winklerberg vineyard, which has a thin layer of loess on volcanic soil sculpted into dramatic terraces on a steep hillside. The other top vineyard, Achkarrer Schlossberg, was planted on rootstocks in 1964, so the vines are a little younger. Overlooking the village of Achkarrer, the vineyards are on the slopes of a canyon with protective hills on either side, so the climate is hotter, with less diurnal variation. Markus says the wines have become more concentrated since 1997 as the result of improvements in vinification. Current wines were tasted at Dr. Heger in August, 2010; wines prior to vintage 2004 in September, 2009.

Achkarrer Schlossberg, Spätburgunder, Grosses Gewächs, 2008
Medium ruby color, a little darker than the Winklerberg. The nose starts off with a surprising array of developed aromas, with savory aromas cutting the red and black cherry fruits. Smooth round fruits, more black than red on the palate, with an impression of elegant opulence, and warm nutty overtones on the smooth finish, which shows ripe tannins supporting the concentrated fruits. A touch softer than the Winklerberg. *** Drink 2012-2018.

Ihringer Winklerberg, Spätburgunder, Grosses Gewächs, 2008
Light to medium brilliant ruby color. Restrained, faintly spicy red fruit nose with hints of strawberries; a tight impression. Lighter red fruits on the palate than for the Achkarrer Schlossberg, elegant, fine, precise, with hints of earthiness, fine tannins supporting the medium weight fruits, and a faint touch of glycerin softening the finish. ** Drink 2012-2017.

Ihringer Winklerberg "Häusleboden", Spätburgunder, Grosses Gewächs, 2008
Light to medium ruby color. Slightly earthy strawberry fruits on the nose, elegant red fruits on the palate, with fine tannins giving some structure to the finish. Just a hair's breadth more intense than the Winklerberg. ** Drink 2012-2017.

Ihringen, Pinot Noir Mimus, 2007
The Mimus bottling takes its name from Joachim Heger's father's nickname. The grapes come from a variety of parcels in the Winklerberg vineyard, with vines aged from 8-22 years, but it is labeled only as Ihringen in order to avoid confusion with the Ihringen Winklerberg Grosses Gewächs bottling. Sweet ripe fruits on the palate have a touch of strawberries with a light elegant finish, somewhat in the style of Savigny-lès-Beaune. ** Drink now-2014.

Achkarrer Schlossberg, Spätburgunder, Grosses Gewächs, 2007
Restrained nose with just a faint impression of red fruits. Soft, less acidic on the palate than the Winklerberg, fruits a little more rounded giving a less mineral impression, more approachable with silky tannins on the finish. ** Drink now-2014.

Ihringer Winklerberg, Spätburgunder, Grosses Gewächs, 2007
Faintly aromatic red fruit nose leads to fine red fruits on the palate, with precise, elegant, mineral strawberries, supported by finely grained tannins. There is a touch of heat and bitterness on the finish. * Drink 2011-2016.

Achkarrer Schlossberg, Spätburgunder, 2005
Earthy strawberries but quite a fresh impression on nose and palate. This was harvested earlier than previous vintages, in a move to preserve freshness, and you can see immediately the effects on the palate, which is lighter. Slightly nutty impression on the finish, and a faint bitterness to the light tannins. ** Drink now-2015.

Ihringer Winklerberg, Spätburgunder, 2004
Right at the start of tertiary development, with the first faint savory notes just beginning to develop on the nose. Development is less evident on the palate, with some sweet, ripe strawberry fruits, and a mineral touch to the finish, coated with some faint chocolaty tannins. Another year to the turning point when a savory fruit spectrum will overtake the fruits. **** Drink now-2015.

Ihringer Winklerberg, Spätburgunder, 2001
Quite tertiary on the nose, still with some suggestions of earthy strawberries. Smooth on the palate, earthy strawberries with notes of gunflint, persisting with some buttery notes on the finish. ** Drink now-2015.

Achkarrer Schlossberg, Spätburgunder (***), 2000
Brilliant ruby color, not much sign of age in its appearance. A curious dichotomy presents itself on the nose. Warm nutty aromas suggest a warm climate, but then the fruits come through with precise delineation and purity of line. This is to ignore the slight touch of oxidation that has developed with age. The palate shows a wonderful purity of red and black cherry fruits, with refined silky structure and texture showing on the finish. Then there is an odd reversal in which the oxidized notes recede and spices come out on the palate. * Drink up.

Ihringer Winklerberg, Spätburgunder, 1999
Some spices of cinnamon and cloves on the nose. Smooth on the palate, spices and just a hint of eucalyptus showing on the finish, otherwise quite Burgundian. Well integrated and balanced, just a faint touch of warmth on the finish. ** Drink now-2015.

Ihringer Winklerberg, Spätburgunder, 1993
Restrained nose with faint suggestion of gunflint. Acidity just breaking out on the finish; quite stern strawberries supported by vaguely angular tannins, quite taut fruits. * Drink now-2014.

Weingut Bernhard Huber

The Huber winery is 23 years old, but there have been five generations of expertise, originally with bulk wine, until one generation ago when Bernhard's father founded the cooperative. The winery became independent in 1987. Huber's 26.5 ha consist of extremely broken up holdings; the largest vineyard plot is only 40 ares (4000 m²). Pinot Noir is the most important grape, representing 70% of plantings. Basic wine starts in stainless steel then spends 6 months in 3-year old barriques. The Malterdingen (village wine) spends 1 year in 3-year old oak. Grosses Gewächs stay in barriques for 18 months, with all new oak for the reserve and about 50% for the Alte Reben (old vines). Burgundy is the benchmark, but they look for expression of their own character, reflecting the limestone terroir; good fresh acidity is a running theme at Huber. The top wines were assembled into a single "Huber Reserve" until 2004, when they were bottled separately to represent the individual vineyards. The soil in Bienenberg is shallow and stony, Sommerhalde has some loam on the top soil, with 50 m higher elevation, and is nearer to the Black Forest so there is more diurnal variation. Heckling Schloss is a very steep vineyard which they bought about 15 years ago and replanted at 13,000 vines/hectare. This is their warmest vineyard, together with Wildenstein (a special parcel within the Bienenberg vineyard). Wines were tasted at Huber in August, 2010, except where otherwise noted.

Pfalz, Spätburgunder, 2008
Light, slightly dusky, rosy-purple color. Restrained on the nose. Light red fruits on the palate are a little tarry, with a slightly hot finish, but a creditable entry level wine. * Drink now-2012.

Malterdingen, Baden Spätburgunder, 2008
The village wine comes from 12-20 year old vines. Concentration was increased by a saignée (used to make rosé or sparkling wine). There's a light to medium dusky purple appearance. The nose is slightly tarry. Good acidity, almost a prickle, shows with the red cherry and strawberry fruits on the palate, without a great increase in quality over the basic entry level wine. * Drink now-2013.

Malterdinger Bienenberg, Spätburgunder, Grosses Gewächs, 2008
Faintly spicy red fruit nose, following through to the palate where well-rounded, dark red fruits have spicy overtones. Firm, fine tannins give a slight bitterness to the finish, which displays a touch of heat. Quite fine structure, needs some time. ** Drink 2013-2018.

Bombacher Sommerhalde, Spätburgunder, Grosses Gewächs, 2008
A touch darker than the other 2008s. Slightly spicy red fruit nose. Spiciness comes through to the red and black cherry fruits on the palate, firm ripe tannins give good structure to the finish. This may be the richest and longest lived of the 2008 vintage. ** Drink 2013-2019.

Hecklingener Schlossberg, Spätburgunder, Grosses Gewächs, 2008
Restrained nose with impression of red fruits, livelier on the palate than the Malterdinger Bienenberg with slightly higher acidity, red cherry and hints of strawberry fruits. Overall there are lighter tannins than the Malterdinger Bienenberg, but the fruits are not quite so intense. ** Drink 2012-2017.

Malterdinger Bienenberg, Spätburgunder, 2007
The vines in this vineyard are 22-40 years old. The wine has a light red fruit nose. There's more fruit intensity on the palate than you might expect from the nose, with earthy overtones, but still fairly bright and fresh in the house style. There's a slight tarriness and touch of heat on the finish. ** Drink now-2015.

Bombacher Sommerhalde, Spätburgunder, 2007
More to the nose than on the Bienenberg, with some interest in the form of earthy strawberries with a faintly buttery note. The fruits are more rounded on the palate, there's a little more concentration than the Bienenberg, and a nice smooth finish with refined tannins. ** Drink now-2016.

Hecklingener Schlossberg, Spätburgunder, 2007
A little spice showing on a red fruit nose with just a suggestion of strawberries. The spiciness comes through to the palate, where elegant red fruits are supported by refined tannins and

fresh acidity. Overall a smooth, elegant impression, a little more refined than the Sommerhalde, but does it justify the extra price? ** Drink now-2016.

Bienenberg Wildenstein, Spätburgunder, 2007
Quite spicy on the nose, showing red fruits with just a hint of black. More concentration than the regular single vineyard bottling shows immediately on the palate, some spiciness, with firm tannic support more evident here than in the other wines. At the moment the tannins are just a touch noticeable, but with a little time they will integrate beautifully with the ripe, elegant fruits. *** Drink now-2013.

Hecklingener Schlossberg, Spätburgunder, 2006
At first some earthy strawberries on the nose, then some rancid butter notes. Quite full on the palate, showing smoky strawberries, with hints of butter coming back on the finish which is a little bitter and also shows notes of gunflint. (September, 2009) * Drink 2011-2015.

Hecklingener Schlossberg, Spätburgunder, 2005
Restrained nose gives a faint impression of strawberries and gunflint. Smooth on the palate with earthy, smoky strawberries, still a little bitterness showing on the finish. Seems youthful. (September, 2009) ** Drink 2011-2015.

Baden, Spätburgunder Reserve, 2002
Light to medium garnet color, some orange evident on broadening rim. Some mineral notes on the palate, just at a turning point with the first savory aromas appearing. Lovely balance on the palate, poised between fruity and savory flavors, red fruits cut by an earthy minerality. Fine tannins are resolving to reveal an elegant finish. Drink in the next two or three years before the fruits start to dry out. *** Drink now-2013.

Baden, Spätburgunder Reserve, 2001
Distinct tertiary aromas mark the nose—seems more than a year older than the 2002—but the palate shows sweet ripe fruits with earthy, nutty notes. This is just past the turning point from fruity to savory. Overall impression is a little rounder on the palate but not quite so fine as the 2002 vintage. ** Drink now-2015.

Baden, Spätburgunder Reserve, 1990
This was the first vintage of the Reserve, when the vines were 36 years old. It now has a mature appearance with a medium garnet color, some brown hues revealing age, and a wide orange rim. It is fairly restrained on the nose considering the age, with a sense of sweet ripe fruits. The fruits are becoming more dilute on the palate, with reduced intensity although still evidently ripe and sweet; the wine is surviving well, but declining gracefully into dilution rather than developing further. ** Drink now-2015.

Weingut Salwey

Salwey is quite a young winery, founded in 1950 by Konrad Salwey's grandfather. Wine became the main focus after 1964 when his father started buying farms in the vicinity and planting vineyards. They were able to acquire more vineyards as the result of a sale following the bankruptcy of a local producer. Today's 23 ha are spread over more than 200 parcels, many on the steep terraces around the village of Oberrotweil. About 40% of Salwey's production is Pinot Noir, three quarters red and one quarter rosé. Most of the terroirs are limestone, but the Pinot Noirs from Kaiserstuhl and the Eichberg and Kirchberg vineyards come from volcanic soils. The vines today are all 20-30 years old, except for Henckberg which is only 10 years old. The aim of representing local style extends to buying the local oak harvest—Konrad buys all of it in Kaiserstuhl, which amounts to about 14 barrels—matures it, and has it sent to Burgundy where they make the barrels (the rest come from French oak). Konrad's general aim is to be completely natural in wine production and to reflect vintage variation, producing smooth wines that age well. In terms of aging Konrad thinks the 2004/2005s are perfect now. His wines from volcanic terroirs perfectly express a halfway house between the slate of the north and the limestone of the south. Wines were tasted at Salwey in August 2010.

Baden, Spätburgunder, 2008
The regional wine comes from limestone terroirs and is a brilliant ruby color. The red fruit nose is slightly musty. Nicely rounded red cherry fruits show on the palate with some hints of black cherries. Light tannins support the finish. Smooth and pleasant, for immediate consumption. * Drink now-2013.

Oberrotweiler Käsleberg, Spätburgunder, 2008
Coming from vineyards in the vicinity of the winery, this is an expression of limestone terroir. The nose is slightly musty, but gives over to smooth red and black cherry fruits on the palate, with balancing acidity. Ripe, soft tannins are not very noticeable. There is a slight glyceriny touch to the finish. ** Drink now-2014.

Kaiserstuhl, Spätburgunder "RS", 2008
The description "RS" means "Reserve Salwey" and is a signal to consumers not to drink this wine straight away. Nose of red and black fruits is slightly herbal. Refreshing acidity supports the black fruits on the palate, giving a more precise impression compared to the greater opulence of the previous vintage. ** Drink now-2016.

Glottertaler Eichberg, Spätburgunder, Grosses Gewächs, 2008
Fruity, aromatic nose of spicy red and black cherries. Balanced acidity supports smooth black cherry fruits on the palate. The fruits are a little more intense, and more precisely delineated, than the Oberrotweil Kirchberg, a function of the Gneiss-based terroir. Tannins are smooth and ripe on the finish. *** Drink 2012-2017.

Oberrotweiler Kirchberg, Spätburgunder, Grosses Gewächs, 2008
Medium to deep ruby color. An almost minty herbal nose promises future development of complexity. Some faintly aromatic, spicy black fruit aromas develop in the glass. The palate shows a mix of red and black cherries, balanced acidity, very fine, elegant fruits on the palate, and a very fine-grained tannic structure. The fruit precision reflects the volcanic origin of the stony terroir, but the tightness may also owe something to the whole cluster pressing. *** Drink 2012-2016.

Kaiserstuhl, Spätburgunder, "RS", 2007
The brilliant medium density ruby color shows little sign of any age. Some savory aromas develop on the nose in the glass. The palate shows lovely black cherry fruits, smooth and opulent with balancing acidity, somewhat a German version of the Côte de Nuits. There's a faintly aromatic black fruit impression on the finish, which is very fine. ** Drink now-2016.

Glottertaler Eichberg, Spätburgunder, Grosses Gewächs, 2005
Medium garnet color with some orange showing at rim. Savory notes are just beginning to show on the nose. Also just evident on the palate, the first touch of sous bois, as the underlying red fruits begin to turn savory. There's nice balancing acidity, and a very faint bitterness just shows on the finish. This is now at a delicious turning point from fruity to savory. *** Drink now-2014.

Oberrotweiler Kirchberg, Spätburgunder, Spätlese trocken, 2004
This was the last vintage to be described as Spätlese trocken, before Salwey switched to Grosses Gewächs. In this sterner vintage, they destemmed completely to keep the wine light. The wine appears a little older than the 2005, with a slightly broader orange rim on the garnet core. The nose is savory, with an almost pungent impression of gunflint. Delicious on the palate, absolutely at the turning point from fruity to savory, with a lovely piquancy to the savory red fruits and a very long finish. A perfect demonstration of Pinot Noir caught in the act of aging. **** Drink now-2014.

Oberrotweiler Kirchberg, Spätburgunder, Spätlese trocken, 2003
This vintage used 100% stems in order to keep freshness and to maintain the concentration of tannins. Even so the wine developed a whopping 14.5% alcohol, but the approach was successful in avoiding overcooked fruits and producing a wine which, although powerful rather than elegant, is maturing well. It's still a very dark color with some black hues. A stern nose has black fruits with a faint hint of cooked fruits. The black fruits on the palate are intense and concentrated with aromatic hints of blackcurrants. This huge wine is developing very slowly. For people who like big Pinot Noirs this is superb, maintaining freshness with intense fruits and some kirsch on the finish. Those who like more conventional Pinots should stick to the 2004 and 2005. *** Drink now-2014.

Frühburgunder Tastings

Neuenahr Sonnenberg, 2009, J. J. Adenauer
Slightly nutty, earthy, strawberry fruit nose. Smooth strawberry fruits on the palate, rather light and direct, less stuffing than the Pinot Noirs, with nutty notes returning on the finish. Light and agreeable for immediate consumption. * Drink now.

Dernauer Hardtberg, Grosses Gewächs, 2008, Weingut Kreuzberg
The very model of a modern Frühburgunder, with a pure strawberry nose, following through to slightly piquant strawberry fruits on the palate A lovely refreshing summer drink, but not much apparent typicity of Pinot Noir. * Drink now.

Dernauer Pfarrwingert, Grosses Gewächs, 2008, Meyer-Näkel
Restrained nose with hints of strawberries. Fruity palate, cherries and strawberries, some light tannins showing on finish: more like Pinot Noir than most Frühburgunders. * Drink 2011-2014.

Recher Herrenberg, 2008, Jean Stodden
Faintly nutty nose with a slight perfume and hint of blackcurrants. Smooth red fruits on the palate, an impression of opulence supported by ripe tannins, but doesn't quite have the concentration of Pinot Noir, although very good for Frühburgunder. ** Drink now-2013.

Pfalz, 2007, Phillip Kuhn
This comes from the top-rated Kirschgarten vineyard, but this is no longer allowed to be stated on the label. It is relatively serious for a Frühburgunder. There is gunflint on the nose with fruits more red than black; and then sweet ripe fruits, more black cherries than red, on the palate. Somewhat softer, with less evident tannins and concentration than the Spätburgunder, with the Frühburgunder heritage revealed by a slightly buttery, crowd-pleasing finish. * Drink now-2013.

Rheinhessen, 2008, Wagner Stempel
Surprisingly stern on the nose, some amorphous red fruits showing through. Smooth fruits on the palate, smoother than the Spätburgunder, a crowd-pleasing glyceriny opulence on the finish without much tannin. Drink now-2013.

Rheinhessen, 2007, Wagner Stempel
Light red cherry fruits on the nose. Fruits on the palate are a little more sophisticated than the 2008, with some light tannins showing on the finish. A bit softer, a little more glycerin, than Pinot Noir. Drink now-2012.

Laumersheimer Kirschgarten, 2004, Phillip Kuhn
A rare example of a Frühburgunder that can age shows more potential to this grape than is usually apparent. The savory herbal nose is followed by smooth fruits on the palate with quite a good structure. ** Drink now-2012.

Producers and Tastings in Alsace

A string of warm vintages has been almost uninterrupted. Of course, vintage ratings for Alsace usually take account of whether conditions were suitable for late harvest wines, which can be the opposite of producing great red wine. For Pinot Noir, the harvest was late and cool in 2010, yields were low, and the wines have good acidity; 2009 was almost too hot, but harvest conditions were very good; 2008 was classic, giving wines with both good fruit and acidity; 2007 was cold but rescued by an Indian summer; 2006 started late and then was spoiled by rain in September; 2005 was splendidly fruity; 2004 offered mixed conditions; 2003 was of course the year of the canicule (heat wave), as brutal in Alsace as elsewhere; a rainy start to 2002 was followed by dry hot conditions, Pinot Noirs tending to show high yields; and 2001 was harvested in an Indian summer, giving good, if not great, reds.

Maison Hugel & Fils

Maison Hugel dates from the seventeenth century and today is run by brothers Marc and Etienne. The winery occupies a rabbit warren of buildings in the heart of the old town of Riquewihr. Hugel is one of the larger negociant-growers, owning 38 ha of vineyards and purchasing grapes from some 300 growers who cultivate another 100 ha. There are five lines of wines. The house style is dry, so Classic, Tradition, and Jubilee are always fermented completely dry. Only the late harvest wines, Vendange Tardive and SGN, are made in sweet styles. Hugel produces all of the Alsatian varieties. Pinot Noir is a tiny part of their overall production, with the entry level Classic including purchased grapes (although they have been moving towards estate grapes in recent years), and the single source Jubilee coming from their two vineyards at Pflostig. They have been producing Pinot Noir since 1978, and the Jubilee (initially called the Reserve) has been an estate wine since 1985. Hugel are well known for their rejection of the grand cru system, so their wines do not carry geographical indications of origin other than Alsace. Etienne Hugel thinks they were the first to make Pinot Noir in Alsace following the Burgundian model. Jubilee is harvested under 40 hl/ha, never chaptalized, and usually has 12.5% alcohol. Wines were tasted at Maison Hugel in October 2010.

Pinot Noir, Jubilee, 2007
Brilliant ruby color, nose of earthy strawberries with quite bright fruits, turning to more herbal tones in the glass. Soft, ripe, red cherry fruits on the palate, with some light tannins showing on a tight, youthful, finish. There is a touch of heat on the finish. ** Drink 2013-2019.

Pinot Noir, Jubilee, 2005
Herbal red fruit nose. Tight red cherry fruits on the palate, with good supporting acidity emphasizing a mineral edge. Medium density fruits on the palate, light, tight tannins on the finish, somewhat reminiscent of Beaune. ** Drink 2012-2019.

Pinot Noir, Les Neveux, 2003
This wine comes from the oldest parcel of Pinot at Hugel, planted in 1966 at Pflostig. The name refers to the group of three nephews who purchased the vineyard for Hugel against the advice of the older generation. The vines give yields only around 30 hl/ha. This lot is usually the heart of the Jubilee bottling, but was bottled separately in 1990 and 2003. Deep color. Closed on the nose; some intimations of black cherries. Well balanced on the palate; the high alcohol is not really noticeable. Aging slowly, black dense cherry fruits are deep and long, fruits are ripe but not over-ripe. Supple tannins are quite sturdy. No tertiary development yet. Some complexity very slowly begins to show in the glass, a promising sign for the future. *** Drink now-2020.

Pinot Noir, Jubilee, 2001
This is an extraordinary result for Alsace, a Pinot Noir that more resembles Burgundy than the usual light, almost rosé, product often found here. The relatively deep color and precise black cherries of the nose are reminiscent of the Côte de Nuits. The low yield shows in the well concentrated and nicely delineated fruits. The fruits are developing slowly, and there seems to be good life ahead. This is quite Burgundian in quality and style, with a slight minerality that is more northern than southern; it would not be at all difficult to mistake this for Burgundy in a blind tasting. *** Drink 2010-2015.

Pinot Noir, Jubilee, 1999
Restrained nose with faintly herbal, savory notes. With this vintage came the first softening on the palate in a vertical tasting. Tight mineral red cherry fruits supported by balanced acidity. Earthy red fruits with some taut tannins on the finish, nicely integrated and evident only by their drying effect, which is cut by a touch of glycerin. ** Drink now-2016.

Pinot Noir, Jubilee, 1992
Restrained red fruit nose. softening red fruits with hints of black cherries on the palate. Tannins are quite drying on the finish. Acidity is just a touch lower than usual. Developing slowly with some herbal notes beginning to show on the finish. ** Drink now-2015.

Pinot Noir, Jubilee, 1990
Some development showing on the nose in the form of savory aromas with some tertiary notes and a slight suggestion of gunflint. Some sous bois develops in the glass. Less developed on

the palate than the nose, with sweet ripe red and black cherry fruits, almost at the turning point from fruity to savory, with some layers of flavor developing in the glass. Tannins nicely integrated, with a faintly nutty and herbal finish. *** Drink now-2015.

Pinot Noir, Jubilee, 1983
Slightly piquant and quite raisined on the nose. This development is not so noticeable on the palate, where black cherry fruits dominate. Tannins still dry the finish. Flavor profile becomes a little flat in the glass. * Drink now-2013.

Domaine René Muré

René Muré have been producing wine since the seventeenth century. Today they have 22 ha of their own vineyards and buy grapes from growers under long term contract for another 26 ha. The winery is just south of Rouffach, overlooked by the grand cru Vorbourg, which includes the Clos St. Landelin which is a lieu-dit at the southern tip. Their wines are divided into those under the René Muré label and those under the Clos St. Landelin label, which include the grand crus around Rouffach. Pinot Noir is about 10% of production, and has increased in proportion with the recent run of warm vintages. There is a Pinot Noir under the René Muré label, and two single vineyard bottlings under Clos St. Landelin, the "V" from Vorbourg and the eponymous Clos St. Landelin. Véronique Muré says that when they bought Clos St Landelin in 1935, there was already some Pinot Noir, but not in the best locations, so her grandfather and father planted new vineyards. Today some of the vines date from the 1970s, the rest being ten to twenty years old. The Pinot Noir is at the very top of the hill, with southern exposure, and the soil of red clay with calcareous stones gives a weightier wine than the "V" coming from the nearby vineyard in Vorbourg. The Vorbourg vineyard has clay, limestone, and a little loess, and faces southeast overlooking Rouffach itself. It has been partially replanted recently, and extended into an adjacent area that used to be planted with Gewürztraminer. Yields for the estate wines are 30-35 hl/ha for Pinot Noir, compared with 35-40 hl/ha for Riesling. The production regime is a little sterner for the Clos St. Landelin, which uses 10-20% whole clusters and spends 15 months in new oak; "V" is completely destemmed and spends one year in oak half of which is new. Véronique thinks V is ready to drink after 6-8 years, Clos St Landelin after 8-10. Wines were tasted at René Muré in October 2010.

Pinot Noir "V", 2009 (barrel sample)
The difference between barrel samples of "V" and Clos St. Landelin in this vintage is less than the difference you usually see in the bottled wines. At this stage, the wine is still a medium to deep purple color with a restrained black fruit nose. Nicely rounded spicy black fruits on the palate, good structure, and supple tannins are promising for future development. *** Drink 2013-2018.

Pinot Noir, Clos St. Landelin, 2009 (barrel sample)
The wine is a medium to deep, but still brilliant, purple color. Some light spices on a black fruit nose. Good concentration for the black fruits on the palate, more weight and concentration than the "V" with rich, supple tannins that are already integrating with the fruits. This is a fat wine with good structural support. *** Drink 2014-2020.

Pinot Noir "V", 2008
The lighter of René Muré's two single vineyard Pinot Noirs comes from a plot in the Grand Cru Vorbourg, but the name of the Grand Cru cannot be included on the label for a Pinot Noir, so it is labeled as "V." The wine is a light to medium ruby color with some garnet hues. There is an elegant nose of earthy strawberry fruits, leading to a fine red fruit palate. Fruits show as a mix of red cherries and strawberries, but a little lacking in concentration on the mid palate. There is good supporting acidity and light tannic support, more like Côte de Beaune than Côte de Nuits, with a touch of minerality on the finish. ** Drink 2011-2017.

Pinot Noir, Clos St. Landelin, 2008

Clos St. Landelin is at the southern peak of Grand Cru Vorbourg. René Muré's Pinot Noir vines are older here, and the site has better exposure than the plot used to make the "V" bottling from Vorbourg. Extra concentration shows with the appearance just a touch darker than the "V" bottling. There are intimations of herbs and spices on more of a black fruit nose, and a faint impression of nuts. Well rounded fruits have some weight on the palate, with hints of black cherries as well as red, good structure supporting the mid weight fruits, and slightly austere notes coming on the finish from the supple tannins. The overall impression is smooth on the palate, but the wine is a bit shy at the moment. ** Drink now-2010.

Pinot Noir, Clos St. Landelin, 2005

Medium ruby with some garnet hues developing. Some herbal spicy notes on the nose. Smooth with well rounded fruits on the palate, only just beginning to come out of its closed phase. Soft black fruits, with acidity just a fraction below balanced, allowing a touch of glycerin to show on the finish. There may be a touch too much tannin for the fruits. ** Drink now-2020.

Domaine Ostertag

This domain was created by André's father in 1966, who abruptly handed over the winemaking to André in 1980 when he was 20. There's more freedom to innovate here than in a domain bound by a long history. The domain now has 14 ha, André essentially works it alone, and all the wines are made from his own grapes. He regards this as crucial because the major part of quality comes from the work in the vineyards. There are three series of wines: the basic series are AOC Alsace, there are some grand crus, and then there are the Vendange Tardive or SGNs. Except for the latter and for the Gewürztraminer, all the wines are dry. His Pinot Blanc is matured in barrique and (unusually for Alsace) goes through malolactic fermentation. In fact, the grand crus are sometimes refused the agrément on grounds of lack of typicity, and a compromise has been reached in which the name of the grand cru is put on the back label rather than stated on the front. About 7-8% of production is Pinot Noir, with a village wine coming from a vineyard that André planted twenty years ago, and the single vineyard wine, Fronholz, coming from a vineyard his father planted forty years ago. André would like to plant more Pinot Noir but so far hasn't found the right soils. There is 100% destemming to make the wine as soft as possible, and délestage (a procedure in which the must is racked off and pumped back) is used rather than pigeage. The village wine uses one third oak and is bottled in July. The Fronholz has 100% barriques including one third new and is bottled in September after 11 months in oak. Wines were tasted at Domaine Ostertag in October 2010.

Pinot Noir "E," 2009

"E" stands for Epfig, which is the source of the grapes, but it's no longer legal to use the name on the label. The fresh red fruit nose has some intimations of blackcurrants. Light, elegant, fruits on the palate are more black than red. Light tannins on the finish. Quite stylish for a wine intended for current drinking. * Drink 2011-2015.

Pinot Noir Fronholz, 2008

This is the single vineyard wine Some faint herbal notes on a nose of red cherry and strawberry fruits, becoming quite spicy in the glass. Fruits are more black cherries on the palate, precisely delineated, very fine and elegant, supported by a sense of tension, with fine-grained tannins and a spicy finish. ** Drink 2012-2018.

Pinot Noir Fronholz, 1988

Medium garnet color with broad orange rim. Quite developed on the nose, savory, tertiary, with some sous bois aromas. Not quite so developed on the palate; the red fruits are still soft and sweet before the tertiary notes come through. Tannins are resolving, but there is a just a touch of bitterness. Still vibrant and lively. *** Drink now-2018.

Domaine Weinbach

Is it always like a French farce at Domaine Weinbach? Doors open and close, Madame Faller departs and one of her daughters arrives, then she leaves and her sister takes over. A baby is crying in the background. On my first visit, there was a general air of incipient chaos, too many events all happening simultaneously. Confusion is built in, perhaps, since the domain is shown on the label as "Domaine Weinbach," but the wall surrounding the Clos de Capucines at the heart of the vineyard says "Domaine Faller" on one side and "Le Weinbach" on the other. (Weinbach is actually the name of the lieu dit). The official address is in the town of Kaysersberg, but if you ask in the town for Domaine Weinbach, they scratch their heads, and then refer you to Domaine Faller, just outside the town and in fact with an entrance in the neighboring town of Kintzenheim. The wines of various grapes varieties mostly also bear the description "Cuvée Sainte Catherine". But the wines! There is absolutely no quarrelling with the quality and precisely delineated flavors of all the varieties they produce—where else do you find such elegant Muscat or refined Gewürztraminer, let along the granular Pinot Gris and the steely Rieslings. On a recent visit to investigate Pinot Noir, things were calmer. It was during harvest and a group of pickers were singing in the kitchen. Catherine Faller produced a vertical back to the first year of their top "W" Pinot Noir, which comes from vineyards in the lieu-dit Altenbourg and the grand cru Schlossberg. Pinot Noir is only 4% of production, and Catherine says this is enough, but it's a pity; the hallmark elegance and refinement come through clearly, and the wines show an unusual potential for aging. Alsace could do with more Pinot Noirs like this. Wines were tasted at Domaine Weinbach in October 2010.

Pinot Noir "W," 2008
Purple color (this was bottled only three weeks ago). Restrained nose with intimations of black fruits and spices. Ripe black fruit palate in restrained style, tight tannins evidenced by dry finish. Good acidity gives freshness. Showing its youth now, needs at least three years. ** Drink 2014-2020.

Pinot Noir "W," 2006
Medium ruby color. Herbal and spicy nose of black fruits. Well rounded, soft fruits on the palate are supported by supple tannins, now nicely integrating, with a faintly nutty touch on the finish. The palate emphasizes red fruits. The fine structure should support maturation to a soft elegance. *** Drink 2012-2018.

Pinot Noir "W," 2005
A little garnet creeping into the ruby color. The very first savory notes are showing on the nose of red and black cherry fruits. Smooth on the palate, elegant, refined, with the black fruits just beginning to soften a little. A touch of opulence from glycerin cuts the supple tannins on the finish. *** Drink 2011-2017.

Pinot Noir "W," 2004
Herbal savory notes on a red fruit nose. Now just beginning to show its potential, with mineral red fruits supported by good acidity, a nice touch of earthiness on the finish, tannins integrating nicely and only evident by the dry finish. The overall impression is an elegant filigree of fruits, with a very fine texture on the palate. There is a good sense of the potential for elegant aging. *** Drink 2016.

Pinot Noir "W," 2003
Soft black cherry fruit nose, a touch of anise developing in the glass, following to ripe, rich black cherry fruits on the palate with intimations of blackcurrants. Soft, almost opulent, but remaining quite fresh. If the leaner 2004 was like the Côte de Beaune, this is more like the Côte de Nuits. Fine-grained, silky tannins support a smooth, long finish. This is a top result for such a hot vintage and puts many Burgundies quite to shame. Here you get a sense of a possible alternative future for Alsace if global warming makes conditions like those of 2003 more common in the next twenty years. *** Drink now-2015.

Marcel Deiss

My discussion with Jean-Marcel Deiss had a surreal air. I found him doing the pigeage, physically immersed in a cuve of Pinot Noir, in the old way. I had to perch on top of a ladder leaning against the vat to talk with the disembodied head of Jean-Marcel as he wallowed in the must. Jean-Michael has the air of a fanatic. He expresses strong views on viticulture and terroir, on the relationship between cépages and the land. But he is a fanatic for making wine true to what he sees as the ancient tradition of Alsace: from more than one variety rather than from a single cépage. He is quick to point out that he does not produce his wines by assemblage, the mixing of wines made from different varieties, but as a single wine produced from grapes of different varieties that are inter-mingled (complanté) in the vineyard. Indeed, floating in the must of the Pinot Noir you could see several bunches of white grapes. He makes two Pinot Noirs. Coming from granite terroir, in a terrain that Deiss claims has traditionally produced red wine, the St. Hippolyte is intended for relatively rapid consumption. Spread among several parcels of calcareous soil in the Burlenberg vineyard, Deiss has 2 ha of Pinot Noir, which makes a longer lived wine of some intensity. Wines were tasted at Marcel Deiss in October 2010 except as otherwise noted.

Rouge, St. Hippolyte, 2008
St. Hippolyte is one of the Alsatian vineyards that has long been associated with the production of red wine. Lighter than Burlenberg, the wine comes from a small vineyard, less than half a hectare, with granite soil, but I suspect the lighter style owes more to the use of stainless steel instead of oak rather then to the difference in terroir. The nose is light and floral. There is a touch of perfume on the elegant, refined palate, with floral notes adding to the taut red fruits on the finish. Comparing St. Hippolyte with Burlenberg is somewhat a comparison between beauty and the beast, elegance versus power. ** Drink 2011-2016.

Pinot Noir, Burlenberg, 2004
The Burlenberg Pinot Noir comes from several parcels that together total 2 ha. The vineyard has been planted with Pinot Noir as long as anyone can remember, but in Deiss's usual style, there are small amounts of other varieties interspersed with the Pinot Noir. The soil is calcare-ous, but solidified by heat; in fact, Burlenberg means the roasted colline. The label on the bottle says "Alsace Premier Cru," a classification that does not yet exist, although some vignerons have been campaigning for it. The deep black cherry nose has overtones of chocolate. The concentrated black fruits have real depth of flavor, supported by good acidity and robust, chocolaty tannins, with some notes of tobacco on the finish, which however is a fraction hot. In a tasting, the sturdy underlying structure might well lead you to place this somewhere on the Côte de Nuits to the north of Vosne Romanée. *** Drink 2012-2020.

Pinot Noir, Burlenberg, 2003
You might expect the very hot vintage of 2003 would bring Alsace Pinot Noir somewhere into the Burgundian realm for an average year, but this wine shows the same cooked, over-ripe fruits as many Burgundies. Two years ago the high alcohol was a little tiring, and the wine certainly gave the impression of warm rather than cool climate, but the acidity was sufficiently refreshing to carry it through; now it does not seem to be aging well. Some chocolate on the nose with raisiny overtones gives an impression of over-ripe and slightly oxidized fruits. The palate shows dense cooked fruits, slightly raisiny, not at all like the usual Pinot Noir from Alsace. There seems to be too much extract, too much color, for the delicacy of Pinot Noir, and the alcohol is punishingly high. * Drink up.

Pinot Noir, Burlenberg, 2002
Red fruit nose shows strawberries and some faintly acid hints of minerality. The acidity is just a touch pressing on the palate of direct red fruits, with just a very faint acrid touch to the finish. Tight tannins bring some tea-like notes. The style resembles a lesser area of Burgundy from a cooler year. The overall impression comes up just a touch short on flavor and interest. (May 2011) ** Drink now-2014.

Producers and Tastings in Alto Adige

There has been a run of good vintages since 2001, with less variation than in previous years. There has been the same reversal here as elsewhere from three good vintages per decade to three poor vintages per decade. This is especially true for Pinot Noir where variation is usually greater than for other grape varieties. 2009 was a hot vintage; 2008 was cool and wet, so the wines lack concentration; 2007 was a hot vintage, perhaps too hot for top results with Pinot Noir; 2006 was a classic vintage for the region; 2005 and 2004 were cooler, after the heat wave of 2003; 2002 was cool but rescued by an Indian summer; 2001 was cool and rainy; 2000 was hot (but not as hot as 2003).

Josef Hofstätter

Hofstätter is one of the few producers who specialize in a small number of varieties. The bulk of production is split between Pinot Noir (from the Barthenau estate on the east side of the valley) and Gewürztraminer (from the Kolbenhof estate at Termeno on the west side). His three Pinot Noirs are an estate wine, the Riserva Mazon (matured for 12-14 months in three to five year old oak), and the Barthenau (from the oldest vines at Mazon, now matured for 12-14 months in an equal mix of new and one year old oak; from 1987 to 1995 the oak was all new, but now Hofstätter has backed off). The main concern in harvesting is to maintain acidity, which usually brings in the grapes around 13-13.5% potential alcohol. Martin Hofstätter thinks that recent vintages, 2007 through 2009, have had higher, more vibrant, acidity than previously. "Of course the aim is to go as close as possible to Burgundy, and I would love to be like Chambolle Musigny," says Martin. "But Barthenau has its own distinct character. It is a great compliment when people open up a bottle and say 'that's Barthenau'." A vertical tasting showed the style running through the vintages, with appropriate variation, and still lively after two decades. Wines were tasted at the Barthenau estate in October 2010.

Barthenau, 2008
Medium ruby color with a garnet/orange hue at the rim. Restrained nose with cool red and black fruit aromas, a fugitive whiff of stewed apples sweeping across the nose. More black than red cherries on the palate, smooth with a faint touch of black aromatics. Smooth, fine-grained tannins contribute to the elegant finish. *** Drink 2013-2020.

Mazon Riserva, 2007
Bright ruby with garnet hues. Light red fruit nose. Nice bright red cherry fruits on the palate, somewhat direct and straightforward, a tincture of tannins on the finish, but a vibrant wine, virtually ready to drink already. ** Drink now-2014.

Barthenau, 2007
A slightly austere nose with cherry fruits breaking through a mineral edge with a faintly herbal quality. Elegant cherry fruits are smooth on the palate, with some refined tannins drying an attractive, nutty finish. Needs another year for the tannins to integrate more completely, but should become soft and elegant. ** Drink 2012-2020.

Barthenau, 2006
Light to medium brilliant rosy color with some garnet hues. Earthy red fruit nose is characteristic of the variety, following through to earthy red strawberries on the palate. There is quite a touch of bitterness on the finish, but this should soften in the next couple of years. This presents as a cool climate Pinot, somewhat reminiscent of the traditional style in Sancerre or perhaps Savigny-lès-Beaune. ** Drink 2011-2016.

Barthenau, 1997
Medium garnet color with orange rim. The nose is enticing and the palate is developing beautifully. Savory aromas are followed by tertiary aromas, notes of tobacco and herbs, and some sous bois. Less overtly developed on palate than on nose, at first you see red fruits of cherries

and strawberries, then the tertiary notes begin to come through, and slowly the wine shows that delicious balance of the turning point from fruity to savory. Martin Hofstätter says that it's begun to develop its tertiary quality just in the last twelve months. It is now really harmonious. *** Drink now-2016.

Barthenau, 1993
This was Martin Hofstätter's first vintage. The wine is a medium garnet color with some orange hues. There is a herbal, almost minty quality on the nose, turning more to tobacco in the glass, but leaving an austere impression. Ripe fruits on the palate have only a slight tertiary touch. The nose remains more interesting than the palate, whose development seems to be a bit arrested, something that seems to happen sometimes in hot vintages in Alto Adige. ** Drink now-2016.

Barthenau, 1989
Developed garnet color with a broad orange rim. Quite developed on the nose, tertiary with pronounced notes of sous bois. Lovely balance on the palate, with mineral savory fruits, the minerality becoming more distinct in the glass. Good supporting acidity brings out the fruits; underlying tannic structure should ensure longevity. A vibrant wine still with a long time to go. *** Drink now-2019.

Alois Lageder

Alois Lageder is one of the movers and shakers in Alto Adige wine production, having built up an estate of 50 ha, which accounts for a third of production; the rest is from grapes purchased from almost one hundred farmers, making him one of the largest individual producers. His vineyards stretch from Magré to Bolzano, with more than half in the immediate vicinity of the village of Magré, which although not exactly a Lageder theme village, nonetheless has his vast modern winery as its principal feature. Alois Lageder took over the estate in 1974, and started to modernize the vineyards and winery. The home estate has been biodynamic since 2004, but converting the individual farmers is more difficult. Three quarters of production is white; Pinot Noir is 5%, and planted in the coolest spots. Cabernet Sauvignon and Petit Verdot are planted in the warmest spots. "What we are all trying to do now is to concentrate on specific vineyards," Alois Lageder says. Krafuss has been his most important Pinot Noir vineyard, and the wine is matured in oak for 13-14 months with up to 30% new oak depending on the year. Lageder is conscious that the vines are still not really old (the vineyard was planted in 1991), and that it will be even longer before the vines at the newly planted Appalonia vineyard reach a sufficient age to judge the wine. Yet a vertical tasting of Krafuss showed good results with even the oldest wines, when the vines were still young. Wines were tasted at Lageder in October 2010.

Appalonia, 2009
Medium dusky ruby with a faint garnet hue. Light black fruit nose with hints of cherries and blackcurrants, opening out to more aromatic black fruit notes. Light and elegant with balanced acidity, but with some hints of black jam at this youthful stage, cut by light tannins with a faintly austere impression. Very fine with some potential for long term development in a soft style. ** Drink 2014-2020.

Krafuss, 2009
Medium density dusky purple hue. Black fruit nose of cherries and blackcurrants, intensifying as the wine opens in the glass. Blackcurrants more evident on the palate than black cherries, with an aromatic uplift developing in the glass. Tannic presence evidenced by the dry finish, with nice persistent aromatics. More concentration than Appalonia, reflecting the older age of the vines. *** Drink 2014-2020.

Krafuss, 2008
Restrained savory-herbal red fruit nose with hints of tarragon, reverting in the glass more to earthy strawberries. Light red fruit impression on the palate, quite tight at the moment, more cherries than strawberries, becoming slightly aromatic and nutty in the glass. Seems a little

lacking in concentration on the mid palate, a reflection perhaps of the relatively cool season (which was rescued by an Indian summer.) ** Drink 2013-2018.

Krafuss, 2007
Initially an intensely savory nose, with hints of gunflint, then earthy red strawberries emerge. Earthy red fruits show on the palate, with the savory notes of the nose showing here as a mineral edge. The wine seems to be developing more rapidly than average, with savory impressions already as strong as fruit impressions, a result of the hot vintage. The medium length finish is slightly nutty. ** Drink 2012-2017.

Krafuss, 2006
Restrained nose of mineral red fruits, a fugitive whiff of strawberries, then savory sensations with a herbal touch of tarragon. Developing nicely on the palate with a mélange of mineral red strawberry fruits and the first tertiary notes of sous bois, with more overtly fruity notes slowly coming out in the glass to match the initial savory impression. Now at a delicious turning point. Elegant and refined, on its way to a classic soft development in the style of Beaune. The growing season had average temperatures, and this vintage reflects the normal pace of development for this wine. ** Drink now-2016.

Krafuss, 2005
Restrained nose with some faint savory impressions. On the palate the acidity is more pro-nounced than usual (reaching a more Burgundian level at first, but then the impression softens in the glass), balancing the red fruits on the palate. Tannins are integrated but still show in the dryness of the finish, which slowly becomes earthier in the glass. ** Drink now-2015.

Krafuss, 2004
Medium garnet color is a touch darker than the 2005. Restrained nose with a first impression of jammy strawberry fruits, followed by savory overtones that take over in the glass. Elegant, refreshing red fruits on the palate are more cherries than strawberries, with tannins integrated on a medium length, dry finish. This was a cool vintage in which the wine has now achieved a lovely mineral/fruit balance, and is at a delicious turning point. *** Drink now-2015.

Krafuss, 2003
Still quite a ruby, rosy hue to the garnet color, whose depth reflects the heat of the vintage. Restrained nose with impression more of black fruits than red, but then a surprising yet refresh-ing note of apples comes through. Quite full on the palate, fruits more black than red, following the nose, still some tannins drying a slightly nutty finish, with black cherries emerging. In spite of the extreme heat of the vintage (and the resulting high alcohol in the wines), this wine has avoided cooked fruit aromas and flavors and retained freshness. ** Drink now-2013.

Krafuss, 2002
Medium garnet color. Restrained savory nose, with a mineral impression of red cherry and strawberry fruits, more savory aromas developing in the glass, and a faint tertiary whiff. Good acidity supports the developing red fruits, just at the point of showing a mélange of fruity and savory influences at a delicious turning point. Overall the impression is quite mineral, with the tight red fruits on the verge of softening. A nice reflection of the vintage conditions, when a cool summer was rescued by an Indian summer. *** Drink now-2014.

Krafuss, 2001
Medium garnet color with some ruby hues. Herbal, savory, restrained nose, a touch of tarragon coming out. Mineral red cherry fruits on the palate, tannins integrating, but leaving a faint bitter note, with persistent, earthy, mineral notes on the finish. Here you can see the cool and rainy conditions of the vintage. *** Drink now-2013.

Krafuss, 2000
Medium garnet with some orange hues. Ripe fruit nose, even a faint impression of over-ripeness coming through to the palate, with a persistent nutty finish, reflecting a very hot year (although not as extreme as 2003). *** Drink now-2014.

Krafuss, 1998
Medium garnet color. Savory, herbal nose, with some faintly earthy, strawberry fruits, and hints of minerality developing. Soft red fruits on the palate are balanced by a mineral edge, some layers of flavor beginning to develop, with a long mineral finish; earthy red fruits show retrona-sally. Layers of flavor are beginning to develop. This was a very good result for a cool, difficult vintage (and of course the vines were quite young at this point). ** Drink now-2012.

Tenuta Manincor

The Manincor estate dates back to 1608 (the name means heart in hand). It is the largest estate in Alto Adige to make wine exclusively from its own grapes. Michael Goëss-Enzenberg took over in 1991. Since then he has replanted 48 out of 50 ha and converted the estate to biodynamic viticulture; it was certified by Demeter in 2005. He is a fervent believer in biodynamics, using preparations such as nettle or chamomile tea in homeopathic amounts according to climatic conditions, in addition to the usual range of preparations. Underneath and to the side of the old mansion is a modern, three story, energy-efficient winery, constructed on gravity feed principles. "The more we avoid pumping and filtering the more we can see the natural quality," says Goëss-Enzenberg. Wine making is as natural and local as possible; barrels are made from oak grown on the estate. Manincor produce a wide range of varieties; in addition to Pinot Noir, their other international wines are the Sophie Chardonnay, and the Cassiano blend of Merlot and Cabernet Franc (which also includes small amounts of Petit Verdot, Syrah, and Tempranillo). The winery is close to Lake Caldaro, and the Mason vineyard of Pinot Noir is just to its north. The Mason bottling comes from the whole vineyard, except for a small plot of 0.8 ha of vines dating from 1959 that is used for the Mason di Mason bottling. The extra concentration of Mason di Mason (yields around 30 hl/ha) is evident when compared directly with Mason (yields around 45 hl/ha). Wines were tasted at Manincor in October 2010.

Mason, 2008
Light ruby with garnet hues. Slightly alcoholic red cherry fruit nose. Pleasant red fruits on the nose, light strawberry impression, faint suspicion of butter, generally soft. * Drink 2010-2013.

Mason di Mason, 2008
Light ruby with garnet hues. Restrained nose, faint impression of red cherry fruits. Soft red fruits on the palate, supple tannins, overall a soft impression of light fruits in an elegant style. ** Drink 2010-2013.

Mason di Mason, 2007
Closed and rather austere on the nose, more black fruits than red, but not very forthcoming. Tight on the palate, black fruits again, at first an impression of lack of concentration, but then picking up in the glass as the fruits soften. Definitely a food wine. ** Drink 2012-2017.

Mason, 2004
Light but elegant red cherry fruit nose, with some mineral strawberries and a hint of tobacco. Sweet ripe cherry fruits on the palate with a strawberry influence, nicely balanced by supple tannins. An elegant style with a refined finish, slowly turning soft, but relatively short lived. "This is the ideal moment to drink it," says owner Michael Goëss-Enzenberg. *** Drink now-2014.

Mason di Mason, 2001
Medium garnet color with some orange hues. Savory herbal nose with some impressions of gunflint. Lovely balance on palate, just on the cusp of turning from fruity to savory, tannins still just detectable with a faint touch of bitterness and the impression of gunflint returning on the finish. *** Drink-2014.

Tenuta Stroblhof

The winery and a hotel form a complex on a small plateau above the town of St. Michele. The estate dates from the sixteenth century (there's been a hotel here for 160 years, but the modern facility dates from 1997). Underneath the old buildings is a modern winery built in 2003 (with a very snazzy tasting room). The elevation is around 500 m, and 3 ha of Pinot Noir and Pinot Blanc surround the winery. There is another hectare of vineyards around Lake Caldaro. Terroirs are a mixture of calcareous with porphyry (volcanic) rocks, but the cold wind from the mountains is the most important influence here. Pinot Noirs are all Dijon clones. The Pigeno bottling, named for the village, is the estate wine. The Reserve comes from old vines—older than 35 years—with yields around 40-45 hl/ha. Wines were tasted at Stroblhof in October 2010.

Pigeno, 2008
Slightly savory red fruit nose with faint impression of gunflint. Soft red fruits on palate, but still a little bitterness showing from the tannins that will resolve in the next year. * Drink now-2013.

Riserva, 2007
Restrained nose. Nice palate of soft red fruits, in the strawberry spectrum, balanced acidity, some light tannins showing on the finish. * Drink 2011-2014.

Pigeno, 2005
Slight development shows on the red and black fruit nose with a faint mineral edge. Bitter red cherry fruits show on the palate, mid density, quite bright; the fruits remain sweet and ripe but some bitterness obtrudes on the finish, although softening in the glass. * Drink now-2014.

Riserva, 2005
Slightly tarry nose of red and black fruits with some nutty overtones opening out in the glass. Altogether much denser than the Pigeno. Sweet ripe fruits fill the palate supported by a tannic backbone with just a trace of bitterness. An initial slight impression of earthiness and minerality accentuates in the glass, a harbinger of future development. ** Drink now-2014.

Riserva, 2000
Medium to deep garnet color. Savory red fruit nose, not really tertiary but certainly distinctly savory, with herbal overtones, some tarragon, and a touch of tobacco developing in the glass. Development is less obvious on the palate, where sweet, ripe, red fruits are earthy and soft, but show a touch of bitterness through an impression of glycerin on the finish. ** Drink now-2015.

Producers and Tastings in Graubunden

Daniel and Marta Gantenbein Winery

The Gantenbein winery is famous in the vicinity and abroad for its post-modern construction. The original winery was extended in 2007 with a building constructed by new robotic techniques for working with bricks. It has a textured appearance like a living, breathing, object. It's not that large from the outside, but you don't see the half of it, because it extends well underground. Most of the vineyards are around the winery, but there are two hectares on the slopes behind the town of Fläsch. The Gantenbein's emphasis is on meticulous work in the vineyard, to the extent that berries are selected entirely in the field, and there is no need for a sorting table. The must comes in at about 10 °C and goes into a cold room to macerate at 4 °C for 10 days. A layer of carbon dioxide is used to block oxidation. Then the temperature is brought up to allow fermentation, which usually starts naturally. Vinification is quite intensive, with several pigeages per day during fermentation at 30-32 °C. The wine is siphoned off and matures for 13-14 months exclusively in new oak. Within the winery, wine is moved either by gravity feed or by physically moving the cuves; there is no pumping, filtration, or fining. Wines were tasted at Gantenbein in October 2010.

Pinot Noir, 2008
Lovely, spicy, red and black cherry fruit nose with some aromatics slowly releasing in the glass. Elegant and refined on the palate, somewhat reminiscent to my mind of Chambolle Musigny, with nicely balanced red and black cherry fruits supported by good acidity and refined tannins. The overall impression is very classy. *** Drink 2012-2020.

Pinot Noir, 2007
By 2007 most of the vineyard was planted with Burgundian clones, and the wine shows the extra concentration this produced. There is somewhat of a spicy, smoky, new wood nose at the moment. Nice spicy red fruits show as mineral red cherries on the palate with some notes of strawberries, well rounded on the finish. This vintage now displays a taut, elegant, quality, and should mature well. *** Drink 2012-2020.

Pinot Noir, 2004
This was an average year, says Daniel Gantenbein, so the wine is a good representation of his style. An initial impression that the wine has scarcely developed is partly deceptive, because the fruits become sweeter, and the tannins recede, as the wine slowly opens in the glass, with the fruits developing layers of flavor. It remains youthful on the nose, with faintly aromatic red fruits. Sweet, ripe, red fruits show on the palate. The wine is beginning to soften a little, with supple tannins supporting the earthy strawberry fruits. The overall impression is quite Burgundian, more like Côte de Beaune than Côte de Nuits, with earthy notes coming back on the finish and strengthening in the glass. ***Drink now-2018.

Pinot Noir, 2001
This was a great year in Graubunden, says Daniel Gantenbein, drawing a parallel with Burgundy 2001, which he feels was much better than was recognized by the press. The wine is a medium garnet color with a spicy nose, austere but opening out on the palate to show mineral, earthy red fruits, more cherries than strawberries. Fruits are presently quite tight and there is a mineral finish. ** Drink now-2015.

Pinot Noir, 1996
Medium to deep garnet color appears quite developed. Tertiary red fruit aromas, savory with quite pronounced sous bois and a touch of gunflint, follow on the nose. Beautiful development on the palate; savory flavors have certainly taken over from fruits, but you can still see ripe fruits supported by integrated tannins. This was a difficult year due to problems with rain, and this wine largely reflects the Swiss clones that were planted at the time, but it is still vibrant with time to go, and shows better than many Burgundies of the same vintage, which have never quite come around. **** Drink now-2016.

Pinot Noir, Beerenauslese, 2000
We were just tasting the Vin de Paille Pinot Noir that Daniel Gantenbein had poured for the finale of our tasting, when he had a short discussion with Marta and said, "We have just had a better idea for the finale." This was a Beerenauslese that had been produced in the unusual conditions of the 2000 vintage. Just before harvest there were two days of rain, resulting in botrytis. So the Gantenbeins went through the vineyard removing all the botrytized berries in order to make their Pinot Noir, but then they took advantage of the situation and fermented the berries with noble rot separately to make a splendid Beerenauslese. The wine shows an apricot color with a lovely botrytized nose, following through to light, elegant, fresh apricot and plum fruits on the palate. Wonderful fruit concentration, but with refreshing acidity. **** Drink now-2030.

Pinot Noir, Vin de Paille, 1999
This unusual wine was made by collecting mature berries one by one, air-drying, and then fermenting very slowly before maturing in barrique for 18 months. Only one barrique was produced. The selected berries were of course very mature, but this was not a late harvest. The result is quite delicious. The wine shows a sweet, slightly raisined nose, giving up spicy red and black fruits. Sweet, raisined flavors are nicely balanced on the palate by good acidity, so the wine remains refreshing. There is lots of character here, you can still detect the red strawberry fruits coming through to show a complex, long finish. *** Drink now-2025.

Georg Fromm Winery

The fourth generation to run the estate, Georg Fromm has 4.5 ha, two thirds devoted to Pinot Noir. In addition to his three ranges of Pinot Noir, Burgundian influence also extends to an elegant Chardonnay. His vinification is natural, with grapes picked when they are cool in the morning, allowed to wait a week in the cool before fermentation starts spontaneously, and then fermented for three weeks at 30 °C. He also has experience of other styles since he founded the Fromm Winery in Marlborough, New Zealand, where he made Pinot Noir on a larger scale, until recently selling the winery. But his winery in Graubunden is an average size for a family estate, and can be run without permanent employees. Defining his style, he says that, "Fruit should be there, of course, but not emphasized, by comparison with sandpaper it should go to the finer grades, with more silkiness but with backbone. Tannins should show at the entrance with backbone but be silky. The wine should not be too extracted." Wines were tasted with Georg Fromm in October 2010.

Pinot Noir Klassisch, 2009
The "village wine" was fermented in tank, transferred to 3,000 liter wooden cuves after fermentation, and then finished off by two months in barriques. It is a medium ruby color with a very fruity, forward nose, more raspberries than strawberries. Quite pure fruits, fresh, but a touch of jamminess showing on the finish. The fruits are really upfront: not much stuffing here, but a nice wine for summer drinking, fulfilling the intention that it should be fruity and fresh. * Drink now-2012.

Pinot Noir Barrique, 2008
The nature of this premium wine is indicated by its label, which says "George Fromm" in large letters, with the village description "Malanser" underneath in much smaller type. The restrained nose offers just a suspicion of black fruits. The palate of red cherries and plums is quite taut, with fine-grained tannins supporting the finish. This is a wine for the immediate future. ** Drink 2011-2016.

Pinot Noir Schöpfiwingert, 2008
This single vineyard wine is fermented in wood and then run off into barrels. Usually about 30% whole clusters are included but in this year everything was destemmed. Some restrained black fruit aromatics lead into a nose of black cherries and plums. The ripe palate of sweet black fruits is tight and elegant, acidity just below balanced, refined tannins are evident by the dryness of the finish. Certainly needs another couple of years. ** Drink 2012-2019.

Pinot Noir Barrique, 2007
The wine makes a cooler impression than 2008. A very faint touch of savory development accompanies the bright red fruits on the nose. Still quite austere on the palate, light red cherry fruits supported by balanced acidity, with a refined tannic presence on the finish. * Drink 2012-2018.

Pinot Noir Barrique, 2006
Quite tarry on the nose, obscuring the red cherry fruits. But the palate opens out to show soft strawberry fruits, with an impression of minerality cut by a touch of glycerin on the finish. Supple tannins are now resolving, lending support to the fruits. This should mature to an elegant softness. ** Drink now-2017.

Pinot Noir Barrique, 2005
Red cherry and strawberry fruits dominate the nose with some notes of sous bois emerging in the glass. The palate is at a delicious turning point from fruity to savory with those classic underpinnings of sous bois for the sweet, ripe fruits. Supple tannins are nicely integrated but still dry the finish. The wine is vibrant and lively. One indication of the potential for significant longevity is that the tertiary notes recede a little after opening, so the wine seems more youthful. *** Drink now-2016.

Pinot Noir Schöpfiwingert, 2004
Some maturity is evident from the garnet color. The nose is beginning to show savory aromas, which intensify and then turn to sous bois in the glass. There is a lovely balance on the palate, with savory red fruits showing overtones of sous bois on the finish. The cool vintage produced a restrained style in the wine, which showcases the depth and layers of flavor in the developing fruits. *** Drink now-2015.

Pinot Noir Schöpfiwingert, 2003
Medium to deep garnet color with broadening orange rim. Fairly restrained on the nose with some savory notes developing. Rich, deep red fruits on the palate, a touch of glycerin, evidently a warm vintage wine, but still retaining freshness. Developing quite nicely and slowly, although the flavor variety seems less than 2004 or 2005. A very respectable result for this rather hot vintage. ** Drink now-2014.

Thomas Studach

With 3 ha, Thomas Studach sees himself as a small producer. He has 70% Pinot Noir, 15% Chardonnay, and 10% Completer, spread through five vineyards, the smallest of which is only a few ares (hundredths of a hectare). Vinification follows classic lines, with fermentation temperature up to 30°. "I am very traditional, I am not a friend of cold fermentation and hocus pocus," he says. He used to use 70-80% new oak, now he has backed off a bit, more towards 60%. Two thirds is French oak, one third is Swiss oak. He thinks 5 years age is the right age to start drinking the wines, and they should then drink well for another five years. Wines were tasted at Thomas Studach in October 2010.

Pinot Noir, 2008
Spicy black fruit nose. Sweet black fruits on the palate, just below balanced acidity, the spices coming back on the finish. Youthful, needs a little time to develop and for the tannins to soften. * Drink 2011-2016.

Pinot Noir, 2007
A little tarry on the nose, impression more of black than red fruits. Presently stern on the palate, with rather direct black cherry fruits, a bit monotonic in flavor at the moment, sturdy supporting tannins. Some spiciness begins to emerge slowly in the glass, the wine becomes smoother and more elegant, and there is a developing sense of longevity. Too young now, it needs at least three years. ** Drink 2013-2019.

Pinot Noir, 2005
Restrained black fruit nose. The sweet ripe black fruits on the palate are quite refined, showing hints of aromatics on a spicy finish. Fruits are well rounded with a touch of glycerin showing on the palate. There is just a touch of heat on the finish, but the wine carries its high alcohol well. * Drink now-2015.

Pinot Noir, 2001
Quite stern black cherry fruits on the nose with hints of blackcurrants. Good supporting acidity on the palate but the youthful flavor spectrum is a bit monotonic and structural support isn't very obvious. This is partly explained by the fact that this vintage was produced largely from Swiss clones, whereas today the vineyards are mostly planted with Dijon clones. * Drink now-2016.

Pinot Meunier *v.* Pinot Noir

Champagne, Le Vigne d'Or, Champagne Tarlant, 2003
Benoît Tarlant produces this Blanc de Noirs exclusively from fifty year old vines of Pinot Meunier in the Pierre de Bellevue vineyard in the village of Oeuilly in the Marne valley. Immediately disgorged, it shows a slightly nutty nose, very faintly toasty overtones, nicely rounded but fresh fruits, quite full as one might expect from the vintage. Citric fruits of lemon and grapefruit on the palate, but just a little rustic in the overall flavor spectrum compared with Tarlant's Blanc de Noirs from Pinot Noir.

Champagne, (Blanc de Noirs), Champagne Tarlant, 2003
This is a new bottling of a Blanc de Noirs (made conventionally from Pinot Noir) coming from the Mocque Tonneau vineyard only in the best years. The vineyard has calcareous soil with a very steep slope in the village of Celles-les-Condé (famous in the middle ages for its dry red wine). Not yet on the market, the wine is identified at Tarlant by the internal code WW, with its final name yet to be decided. It shows a refined, fresh nose. Ripeness shows on the palate, with well rounded citrus and stone fruits. Purity of line shows through, with good delineation of flavors, quite taut and long—a very classy thoroughbred. This was disgorged one minute after the Vigne d'Or and tasted at Tarlant in October 2010.

Champagne, Les Vignes de Vrigny, Egly Ouriet, nonvintage
This champagne is made exclusively from Pinot Meunier coming from premier cru vineyards. The fruits on the nose are warm and well rounded, leading into a relatively soft, full bodied palate. The impression of the weight of Pinot is enhanced by slightly lower acidity. The wine is a tad heavier than the Brut Tradition and shows a touch of the rusticity associated with Pinot Meunier by comparison with the greater elegance of the Brut Tradition. There is also more impression of toast and brioche here, but that may reflect earlier disgorgement relative to the Brut Tradition.

Champagne, Brut Tradition, Champagne Egly Ouriet, nonvintage
The Brut Tradition is a mix of 70% Pinot Noir and 30% Chardonnay coming from grand cru vineyards. The nose is light and elegant with a nice suggestion of freshness. The wine is

refined and elegant on the palate, with a light dosage. A faint hint of toast and brioche add some complexity, but with its recent disgorgement (one year before tasting) the main impression is freshness. The flavor spectrum is classic, with clean, precise impressions on nose and palate, and greater purity of line than the Vignes de Vrigny. Both wines were tasted in November 2010.

Yarra Valley, Blanc de Noirs, Domain Chandon, 2007
Just about to be released, the restrained nose makes a faint citrus impression. There's a nice citric balance with soft dosage in the background, just a faint touch of red fruits, all showing the combination of refinement and weight expected of Pinot Noir.

Yarra Valley, Pinot Meunier Blanc de Noirs, Domain Chandon, 2004
Made exclusively from Pinot Meunier, this offers more of a red fruit impression than the Pinot Noir Blanc de Noirs, with some chocolate and nutty overtones on the nose. Some toast and brioche is just beginning to show on a broad palate, enhancing a sense of rusticity. Even allowing for the age difference with the Pinot Noir from 2007, the lesser precision of flavors is evident. Both wines were tasted at Domaine Chandon in March 2011.

Pinot Meunier, Carneros, Domaine Chandon Winery, 2007
The dominant grape of Champagne is rarely vinified as a still wine varietal. The impression is quite like its close relative Pinot Noir, but somewhat rustic. This is muted on the nose, reasonably smooth on the palate, with red fruit flavors, and a touch of bitterness coming out on the finish with some earthy strawberries.

Pinot Noir, Carneros, Domaine Chandon Winery, 2007
Rather muted on the nose, a faint impression of strawberries. Nice clean palate shows some elegant classic strawberries with just a touch of earthiness coming out on the finish. Carries the high alcohol well; elegant for Carneros. Both wines tasted at Domaine Chandon in February 2010.

5

The North America Migration

A historical view might say that viticulture in Oregon had its roots in the famous Columbus Day storm of 1962. This was a windstorm of unprecedented power that swept through the state on October 12. Aside from the damage to populated areas—undamaged homes were the exception in Willamette Valley—it decimated the fruit and nut orchards that were a major agricultural activity in Oregon at the time. Many of the orchards never recovered; economics did not favor replanting, and for years after the storm, the landscape was still littered with uprooted fruit trees.[1] Purchases of distressed orchards formed the basis for many of the early vineyards in Oregon. Potential vineyards were cleared of the remnants of the fruit trees—most often former plum orchards—and planted with vines. The plum industry was dying anyway—much of it was devoted to the production and sale of prunes rather than fresh plums—but the Columbus Day storm gave a powerful impetus to its demise. Growth of viticulture was gradual through the 1970s, but has been exponential since the 1980s.

Damage from the Columbus Day storm in 1962 in Monmouth, just south of the wine growing regions in Willamette Valley. One and two hundred year old trees were commonly uprooted.

Photograph from National Weather Service Portland

Although Oregon produces a smaller total volume of Pinot Noir than California, it is the leader for cool climate production in North America. Of course, Pinot Noir has a much longer history of production in California, going back to nineteenth century attempts to emulate French wines. Yet "Burgundy" historically had no connection with Pinot Noir in the United States. In the nineteenth century, lower quality California wines were labeled "Burgundy" for heavier reds and "Claret" for lighter reds. A century later, Gallo's Hearty Burgundy was based on Petite Sirah (Durif) and Zinfandel. Perhaps the concept of Burgundy owed more to the old style of wines thickened by additions from the Rhône; and indeed, to be fair to the American producers, Burgundy and Claret were used as generic descriptions of wine styles in Britain up to the 1970s when the United Kingdom joined the European Union. In Burgundy itself, prior to the AOC rules coming into effect, "Nuits St. Georges" and "Volnay" were used as much to describe heavier and lighter styles as to identify wines coming from those specific communes. In any case, it's only since the 1970s that there have really been attempts to make varietal Pinot Noir in North America that might bear some relationship with the authentic wines of Burgundy. Struggling with richer soils and warmer climates, the style of Pinot Noir from California is interestingly different; but the cooler climates of Oregon may offer a more direct challenge to Burgundy.

Virtually all the important wineries in Oregon are in Willamette Valley, just to the southwest of Portland. "Valley" has a somewhat broader significance for Willamette compared with other wine-producing areas, since the valley is about forty miles wide. Located in the western part of the valley, the vineyards extend for about forty miles from Portland to Salem. To the west of the valley, the Coastal Range of mountains blocks moisture from the Pacific, while the Cascade Mountains block the Continental climate from the east.

Willamette Valley is the umbrella AVA for the entire area, and can be used to describe wine from anywhere in the valley. But under the system of American Viticultural Areas (AVAs), Willamette has six individual sub-AVAs, and wines coming from any one of those areas can be labeled with

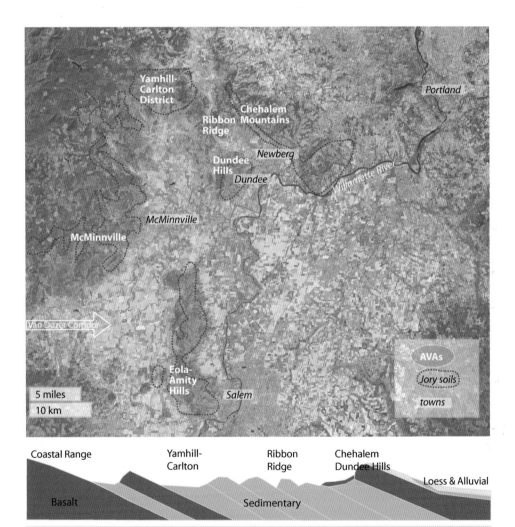

Willamette Valley has six individual AVAs within it (top). A cross section (below) running on a diagonal from SW (McMinnville) to NE (Portland) shows that the major soil types alternate between basalt and sedimentary. The famous basalt Jory soils represent close to half of the AVA areas.

Red Jory soils predominate in Dundee Hills and Eola-Amity Hills. They consist of a red-brown clay with a volcanic substratum.

the individual name. Sub AVA labeling is now the norm for the top wines, especially those from single vineyards, although it's common to leave Willamette Valley on the label for better identification. After all, the pioneer winemakers can remember when most consumers had no idea that Oregon even produced wine. On his early sales trips, David Lett of Eyrie Vineyards used to tell people, "The wine comes from Oregon, you know, it's the second one down on the left along the Pacific Coast."[2]

Blends between different AVAs can be labeled only as Willamette, but the name must also be used for wines from all vineyards outside the sub-AVAs. Winemaker Ben Casteel at Bethel Heights Vineyard says the argument against the Willamette AVA is that it is too encompassing, because the valley floor is really not suitable for making wine. It is too fertile and also too liable to frost, so most vineyards are on the slopes. Casteel would have liked to see a Willamette Hillsides generic appellation for those quality wines from the hills that don't fall in the present AVAs.[3]

The important terroir distinction in Willamette is between sedimentary and volcanic soil types: this is a better guide to wine style than the AVA, since the two soil types correlate only loosely with the AVAs. Most AVAs have a mixture of both types. The sedimentary soils are up to 50 million years old. About 15 million years ago, basaltic lava erupted from eastern Washington and Oregon; sheets flowed towards the sea, covering the northern half of Willamette Valley. Then the floor of the Pacific slid under western Oregon, pushing up the Cascade mountains. About 5 million years ago the boundary between tectonic plates shifted, moving the Cascades farther east, and pushing up the sedimentary crust to create the Coastal Range mountains. The crowning glory came during the Ice Age, when Lake Missoula repeatedly flooded Willamette Valley, creating a thick layer of silt on the valley floor. The result is that the valley itself is highly fertile, suitable for many agricultural crops but not for grapevines, and the surrounding hills have a mixture of the remaining basaltic soils, interrupted where sedimentary soils were pushed up. The topsoils on the basalt are reddish brown, known as Jory soils, and are quite acidic.[4] The topsoils on the sedimentary base (either sandstone or siltstone) are dark brown, less acid,[5] and are called the Willakenzie series.

The most important climatic distinction is between Yamhill-Carlton, Dundee Hills, and Chehalem mountains to the north, and McMinnville and Eola-Amity Hills to the south, because the van Duzer corridor, a gap in the Coastal Range of mountains, allows breezes from the Pacific to cool the two southern AVAs. This has as much effect as the soil differences, which are fairly heterogeneous in each region. Within the sub AVAs, vineyards must usually be above 200 feet elevation (70 m). Elevations can go up to 250 m or even higher, which has a large effect on development of the grapes, together with the angle to the sun.

Wine was made in Oregon in the nineteenth century, but as much from fruits as from grapes. All production ceased during Prohibition. Richard Sommer planted the first Vitis vinifera after Prohibition in 1961, at Roseburg in the Umpqua Valley in the southern part of the state.[6] He focused on Riesling, which the winery still produces today. The modern industry began in 1967 when David Lett planted varieties of Vitis vinifera including Pinot

Polyculture rules in Willamette Valley. Beyond the vineyards on the slope (foreground) are fields of wheat in the plain (background).

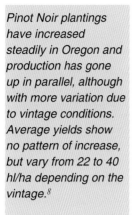

Pinot Noir plantings have increased steadily in Oregon and production has gone up in parallel, although with more variation due to vintage conditions. Average yields show no pattern of increase, but vary from 22 to 40 hl/ha depending on the vintage.[8]

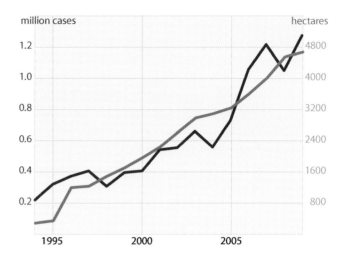

Noir and Chardonnay at the Eyrie Vineyard at Dundee Hills in northern Willamette Valley. (The vineyard was named for a pair of hawks that had an eyrie in a massive old fir tree on the property.) By 1970 there were five wineries and 14 hectares of Vitis vinifera in Willamette.[7]

Pinot Noir was a focus right from the start, following a controversial study by Charles Coury, one of the early growers, who wrote a thesis at UC Davis arguing that climatic similarities with northern France suggested that Oregon should grow Pinot Noir, Chardonnay, and Riesling.[9] Also trained at UC Davis, David Lett believed that it was criminal to grow Pinot Noir in the too-warm climates of California, and was convinced by Coury that soil and climate made it right for Oregon.[10] David Adelsheim, one of the pioneers who followed David Lett in 1971, recalls that much of the impetus for the early growers was an anti-California sentiment coupled with a belief that Burgundy had not got it all right either.[11] (Remember that in the 1970s and 1980s Burgundians were busy over-fertilizing inferior, over-productive clones; it wasn't until the late 1980s that the toxic effects began to wear off.) The idea was not so much to compete with Burgundy as to make a good match of grape variety with climate and soil, with results that would be different but equally valid.

Yet it was hard to shake off California's training. Eyrie's first vintage in 1970 was such a light color that David Lett decided it might not meet the standard for Pinot Noir, and instead he labeled it just as "Spring Wine." It sold (with some difficulty) for a decent price, $2.65 a bottle (by comparison, another, somewhat better known standard, Robert Mondavi's Cabernet Sauvignon Reserve from Napa Valley sold for $4.00 in 1974). But by the following vintage Lett was convinced, and the first Pinot Noir label appeared. In 1979, a 1975 Eyrie Pinot Noir placed third in an international competition in France: already the potential for quality was recognized.

The rapid growth of viticulture in Oregon is striking. The number of wineries has increased from 34 in 1980 to almost 400 today. Vineyard area passed the 500 hectare mark only in 1980, but today measures 7,850 hectares. But as an economic activity, viticulture pales into insignificance compared with the cultivation of seeds and vegetables.[12] Indeed, even in the heart of wine country in Willamette Valley, viticulture does not immediately impress itself on the landscape. Vineyard areas are quite well separated, and between them you encounter other types of agriculture and forested areas. The major activities on the valley floor are ornamental nurseries and general agriculture. Vineyards are located on the hills to the side, but it's rare to get an expanse of continuous vineyards such as you would find in Napa Valley or Russian River, for example.

Pinot Noir is by far the most important grape variety in Oregon today. It is about 60% of all wine grape plantings,[14] mostly concentrated in Willamette Valley.[15] It has been growing steadily since the 1990s, when it was less than 40% of all varieties.[16] Yields have not changed very much, so production has increased more or less in proportion with plantings. It's a measure of the drive to quality that the average yields are roughly comparable with those for premier crus in Burgundy's Côte d'Or.[17] And perhaps not incidentally, when you buy a Pinot Noir from Oregon, it really will be Pinot Noir. Oregon has the tightest labeling rules in the country; varietal labeling means the wine must be at least 90% of the stated variety[18] (for Pinot Noir it will usually be 100%).

There was not a great deal of choice for clones of Pinot Noir at the outset. It was illegal to import material directly from outside the country, so growers were restricted to clones that were commercially available in the United States (except, of course, for those prepared to smuggle suitcase clones across the border). The main supply came through an organization run at the University of California,[19] where the criteria focused on "sanitary selection for disease freedom" and high production, rather than quality.[20]

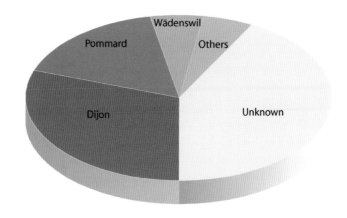

Dijon clones have now overtaken Pommard and Wädenswil in Oregon, but the origins of many Pinot Noir plantings remain unknown.[13]

Essentially two clones were available. The Pommard clone is supposed to have been imported from the Château de Pommard by Harold Olmo at UC Davis in the 1940s.[21] There's some confusion about its origins, because some of the Pommard clones distributed by Charles Coury were smuggled into Oregon from Europe in the 1960s and 1970s, so there may in fact have been some heterogeneity in the Pommard "clone."[22] At all events, by the end of the 1980s, Pommard clones were two thirds of known Pinot Noir plantings in Oregon.[23] The rest of the plantings were the Wädenswil clone, named for the grapevine research station in Switzerland; it is presumed to be equivalent to one of the major clones grown in Switzerland, although no one is sure exactly which one.[24]

These clones have some issues. Pommard tends to produce a somewhat dense wine. Wädenswil, although it is rather productive, gives higher toned fruit, and is often blended with Pommard to add finesse. But the main issue is that they ripen a little late for Oregon, pushing into the period of the autumn rains. The so-called Dijon clones, originating from Domaine Ponsot's vineyard at Clos de la Roche in Burgundy, which became available in Oregon in 1989, offer the advantage of beating the rain by ripening earlier.[25] Most new plantings of Pinot Noir in Oregon now use one or more of six Dijon clones (113, 114, 115, 667, 777, 828). Their small, tight, berries give good fruit concentration. There's some controversy as to whether using a single Dijon clone leads to too much homogeneity of flavor, but they remain the wave of the present.

When the pioneers came to Oregon, there was no phylloxera, so the vines

Vines on their own roots in the Eola Hills of Willamette Valley now need to be replanted because of damage from phylloxera, visible where vines are missing in each row.

The original Pinot Noir vines from 1967 are still growing on their own roots in the Eyrie vineyard.

were planted on their own roots. But in 1989 the first phylloxera infection appeared. Within a decade, many of the original vineyards were dying and had to be uprooted. Some of the original vineyards still survive, but everyone acknowledges that it's only a matter of time before they succumb. Almost all plantings since 1990 have been on rootstocks. There is at least the compensation that rootstocks can be chosen to encourage low yields and early ripening.

The vine population remains relatively youthful. Partly this is because plantings have expanded so greatly in recent years, but also because the clock was reset after 1990 when original vines, going back to the 1970s or 1980s, had to be replaced. So it's hard to judge the true style and potential of the region, since this may change as the vines generally become older (especially since the only old remaining old vines are Pommard or Wädenswil and there are as yet no old vines of the Dijon clones).

Oregon viticulture remains relatively small scale, although some outside investors have moved in, notably Calpers, the giant California pension fund,

All extremes of spacing are found in Willamette Valley. The Eyrie Vineyard was planted in 1967 with very wide spacing between the vines (left). Drouhin planted their vineyard in 1988 with a narrow Burgundian spacing (facing right).

which now owns vineyards through a joint venture with Premier Pacific Vineyards from Napa. This purely financial endeavor is intended to produce a good rate of return by owning land, and by growing and selling grapes rather than by making wine.[26] Premier Pacific now has around 400 ha in Willamette Valley, much of it in large expanses of vineyard that change the local landscape.[27] The scale has certainly changed; when the Sokol-Blosser winery opened in 1978, the local press exclaimed at the large scale of the operation—4,500 cases per year![28]

The pioneers tended to be individualists, often iconoclastic and skeptical, but they created a collegiate atmosphere, which persists today. There is the usual division here between producers and growers, but it does not seem to have created the conflicts of interest and tension that you find elsewhere. Roughly half the wine is made from estate-grown grapes, the other half from purchased grapes.[29] Somewhat like Burgundy, you may see the same vineyard names appear on wines from multiple producers. This reflects ownership of many vineyards by growers who farm but do not make wine, or sometimes who make wine from only part of the vineyard. Sometimes the different parts of a vineyard will be farmed differently for each producer. Around ten producers make Pinot Noir from the well-known Shea Vineyard, for example, so in Burgundian manner there is the chance to experience different winemakers' interpretations of the same terroir. Sometimes there are long-term contracts with growers, sometimes the contract runs out, and the producer can no longer offer that wine. At the other extreme, where blended wines are concerned, often enough winemakers will trade lots from their various vineyards in order to get more complexity in the blend. Some producers pride

themselves on using only estate-grown grapes, but others use a mix of estate-grown and purchased grapes. At St. Innocent winery, Mark Vlossak prefers to buy grapes from top growers and sites. "It gives you more choices and control over quality," he says, rather then being stuck with the production of a specific vineyard (Y page 262).[30]

Notwithstanding the arguments that led to the trek to plant Pinot Noir in Willamette Valley, soils and climate are different from Burgundy. The Côte d'Or is largely limestone based; Willamette Valley alternates between volcanic and sedimentary terrains. Total rainfall isn't terribly different; but Burgundy gets a more or less steady stream (as anyone who has visited the Côte d'Or in the summer can testify), whereas Oregon has something close to drought conditions from June until the autumn rains arrive in September. But many producers now practice dry farming. "We don't irrigate any more, in fact we need reverse irrigation to take out water, that is, a cover crop," says David Adelsheim.[31] Overall summer temperatures are not very different, and the difference between Willamette and Burgundy in any one year is much less than the difference between vintages in either.

One of the main differences is that soils are more fertile in Willamette Valley. Not only are they intrinsically more fertile, but the old orchards where many vineyards were planted had been heavily fertilized. This means that the very dense planting typical of European vineyards, where the soils have much lower fertility, may not be appropriate. In fact, the early vineyards were all planted at a rather wide spacing, although this more reflected the fact that this was required by the only tractors that were available. Vines were often trained on the high trellis known pejoratively as "California sprawl." The first vineyard to be planted at a narrow, European spacing was when Domaine Drouhin arrived from Burgundy. Today there is a variety of spacings, with most new plantings settling somewhere between the two extremes. But there is no general consensus on the effect of spacing. The main factor anyway in determining quality is the yield, which translates to roughly one grape cluster per shoot.

Domaine Drouhin is a special case. When Drouhin—a major negociant and grower in Beaune, well known for their wide range of both red and white Burgundy—came to Oregon in 1987, it was taken as a validation of the whole concept of producing Pinot Noir in Willamette Valley. They purchased 40 hectares in the Dundee Hills (and subsequently purchased another 60 hectares); today about 35 hectares are planted to vines, mostly Pinot Noir. This makes Drouhin a major player, although Operations Manager Arron Bell says that it's a measure of the changing scale of production in Oregon that Drouhin was considered to be a large operation when it started, but now it's at the lower end of the medium scale wineries.[32] At the time, Drouhin's winery—unassuming from the outside but going several stories deep into the hillside—was the first purpose-built winery in Oregon. Special tractors were imported from France that could straddle the closely spaced rows. All this occasioned a certain rueful consideration among existing growers, but today DDO, as it is popularly known (Domaine Drouhin Oregon), is one of the defining influences in the valley.

The differences between Maison Drouhin in Beaune and DDO in Willamette capture the cultural differences between Burgundy and Oregon. Total vineyard areas are similar on the Côte d'Or and at Dundee Hills. But in Burgundy the vineyards are divided into 28 different appellations (and several of those consist of multiple plots), each producing a different wine. Average production is a few hundred cases each. The top wines are identified by individual vineyard sites, a series of ten grand crus. In Willamette, there are just three cuvées of Pinot Noir and a Chardonnay. Most of the production goes into the 10,000 case production of Dundee Hills Pinot Noir (Y page 256). The top Pinot cuvées come from barrel selections; Cuvée Laurène is about 2,000-2,500 cases; and only the exclusive Cuvée Louise at just a couple of hundred cases is of Burgundian proportions. It would be an oversimplification to say that Burgundy is all about differences between terroirs while Oregon is about blends, but there's an element of truth in it.

It is rare, indeed it may be unique, for the same winemaker to make wine in the same way in both Burgundy and the New World. But Véronique Drouhin oversees the winemaking at Domaine Drouhin in Beaune, and then flies to Oregon to make the wine at DDO. So here is an opportunity to see whether there is an intrinsic difference between Europe and the New World. Viticulture and vinification are similar. To get the same ripeness in Oregon as in Burgundy they need to pick relatively a little later, which gives an extra half per cent alcohol to the wine. There is complete destemming in Willamette and some use of whole clusters in Beaune. Otherwise fermentation and maturation are much the same, and the features Véronique wants to see in the wine are the same. "The idea is not to copy Burgundy but to produce an elegant Pinot Noir,"[33] she says of winemaking at DDO—but the same striving for elegance could just as well describe production in Beaune.

Comparing wines from the two domains side by side is complicated by vintage differences, but one interesting insight came from a vertical tasting that included the 1993 vintages of Cuvée Laurène (where the barrel selection represents up to about a quarter of production), and the Beaune premier crus Clos des Mouches and Grèves (ⵣ pages 104 and 256). Vintage conditions were relatively similar in Beaune and Willamette, so this is a fair comparison.[34] The wines are aging very much in parallel, each showing its typical characteristics. Clos des Mouches shows its typical finesse with a touch of minerality and developing notes of sous bois; Grèves, a little sturdier, is lagging behind. Cuvée Laurène has slightly more obvious fruits, but development closely matches Clos des Mouches, with minerality and a delicious note of sous bois. Both seem set for the next decade, an evident demonstration that Pinot Noir from Oregon has the potential to age well.

Winemaking styles vary as much in Willamette as anywhere else. Mark Vlossak of St. Innocent sees grape growing as the key to style. "If you want to make a wine with 15% alcohol and intense fruit concentration, you will grow your grapes very differently from if you want to make a wine with low alcohol and more nuanced fruit flavors," he says. There's general agreement on criteria for harvesting, although the actual decision on when grapes are ripe varies somewhat. There's wide variation whether grapes are destemmed (giving more obvious fruits) or whole clusters are used (giving more tannic structure), and many producers have an open mind, varying the treatment according to the vintage (typically destemming in cool 2007 but using some whole clusters in hot 2008). There's the same debate here whether to ferment at lower temperatures (preserving volatile aromas and fruit) or at higher temperatures (obtaining more extraction), although they tend perhaps to be slightly higher here than in Burgundy, usually between 30° C and 33 °C.

How natural are the wines? The low-tech methods of chaptalization (adding sugar at the start of fermentation when the grapes aren't ripe enough), saignée (bleeding off some juice at the start of fermentation to concentrate the remaining must when rain is a problem, such as in 2007), and watering-back (adding water, typically acidulated, to reduce the sugar level in a hot vintage such as 2006) all have been used by most winemakers at one time or another. But the high-tech methods such as reverse osmosis, spinning cone, or other sophisticated techniques for adjusting alcohol, have made less impact here as a result of the relatively small scale of operations. A few of the larger producers have recently invested in reverse osmosis machines, not a surprising development in a climate where rainfall around harvest is common.

So what does all this mean for the style of Pinot Noir from Willamette? A first impression is almost always of higher alcohol. Growers say they pick grapes when they reach physiological ripeness, which most often means when they taste right, and when the pips have turned brown and separate easily from the pulp, but this typically happens at sugar levels that translate to 13.5% alcohol or more. Alcohol levels everywhere have been pushed up by a transition from harvesting according to the sugar/acid balance to assessing phenolic ripeness. Russ Raney of Evesham Vineyards recollects that levels were around 13% when he started production in the early 1980s, but now are more often up at 14% (Υ page 259).[35] Although growers say their criteria for harvesting are pretty much the same as in Burgundy, it is usually rare to find Burgundy with alcohol this high (the 2009 vintage may be an exception). Lack of water, and the fact that ripening often depends on heat late in the season, may be one reason why phenolic ripeness occurs at higher sugar levels in Oregon. John d'Anna of Cristom Vineyards sees it as a consequence of modern viticulture. "We have become so efficient as farmers, we have done everything to make this photosynthetic machine work at a maximum, we now need to throttle back the canopy management," he says (Υ page 255).[36] (An ironic counterpoint to Charles Coury's original thesis that Oregon was ideal for Pinot Noir as opposed to a warm climate where grapes would accumulate too much sugar before ripening.)[37]

Fruits are more forward in the typical New World style, although not so brash as most Pinot Noir in California or New Zealand. The issue of whether Willamette has a characteristic style was brought to a head by the debate as to whether sub AVAs should be introduced to reflect regional differences. Some believe the terroir is paramount; others that the winemaker is more important. Ken Wright, of the winery that bears his name, is a big believer in the value of the individual appellations. When he talks about the crucial importance of the "parent material," he is not referring to the grapevine, but to the underlying structure of the land. He believes firmly that extraction of minerals from the subsoils drives wine aromas and flavors. "Young vines have no character until they become old enough for the roots to reach down into the distinctive subsoils," he says.[38] He was involved in a movement to establish the AVAs in 1995, but at that time it gained little support. Five years later, opinion had changed and there was universal agreement to proceed. Most winemakers seem satisfied with the system, even if they are skeptical about the exact basis for differences between the AVAs. John d'Anna of Cristom says, "It's the hand not the land," that makes the wine, and argues that winemaking style is far more determinative than lo-cale.[39] Yet he agrees that others can see consistent stylistic differences between the appellations.

The usual description of sub regional character is that the wines of Eola-Amity Hills and McMinnville, where cooling from the van Duzer corridor is the dominant climatic effect, show more black fruits, with good tannic struc-ture. Ribbon Ridge is described in similar terms, but as having finer structure. Yamhill-Carlton is said to have rich, black fruits, with lower acidity. Dundee Hills and Chehalem Mountains are described as having red fruits. The most interesting aspect of these descriptions is their lack of correlation with the soil structures, which are more volcanic in Eola-Amity Hills and Dundee Hills, more sedimentary in McMinnville, Yamhill-Carlton, and Ribbon Ridge, and a wide mixture, including half loess, in Chehalem Mountains.

I don't entirely accept the conventional view myself. There is clearly higher acidity in the wines from Eola-Amity Hills, and very likely this is a direct effect of the cooling breezes. To my mind, this often gives the wines a lighter, more Burgundian impression, and I see as much red fruit as black. Comparing Eola-Amity Hills or Dundee Hills with Yamhill-Carlton or Rib-bon Ridge, the volcanic soils give a greater sense of tension to the wines, with Dundee Hills coming over as lean but smoother than Eola-Amity Hills. I see more roundness in the fruits from the sedimentary soils of Ribbon Ridge, and more variability in Yamhill-Carlton. It's hard to get a bead on the varied soils of Chehalem, where the wines vary from quite elegant to more rustic.

It's fair to say that I see more consistency among the various wines of any single producer than between the wines of any AVA, although within each producer's wines, the same relative differences show between terroirs. Ken Wright likes wines that display primary fruit, and intends his wines to be enjoyable immediately (Ⴒ page 261). The wines show soft, rich fruits, taut from vineyards on volcanic soil, more rounded from those on sedimentary soil. Archery Summit also has a tradition for going for rich fruits, and a reputation for using lots of new oak (Ⴒ page 251). But the style is changing here as elsewhere. "The stylistic aim is that elusive state of being which is concentration without mass. Of course, each site should express itself. In early years lots of oak was used but today winemaking is more about the fruit and the site and the balance," says winemaker Anna Matzinger.[40]

"Oregon doesn't follow the New World model of bigger is better, those who were in that style have backed off from it. Oregon should emphasize elegance and complexity, not extraction," says David Adelsheim, who makes wines completely dispelling the early notion that Oregon wines don't age (Ⴒ page 250).[41] Tasted recently, his 1993 and 1988 were still going strong; it might be difficult to distinguish them from Burgundies of similar vintages in a blind tasting. Several of the top Willamette producers believe in finesse rather than power, in spite of market pressure. "Elegance doesn't sell in America," says Brick House's distributor, but owner Doug Tunnell has been reducing new oak and turning to a lighter, fresher style in recent years (Υ page 252). "*If* there is a model it would be Burgundy," he says, "but the circumstances are different."[42] The lightest hand with oak may be Jason Lett at Eyrie, where there's very little new oak, and the Reserve wines actually have less than the estate bottling (Υ page 260). "I wish people would reject over-oaking as a flaw like they regard Brett as a flaw," Jason told me.[43]

Oregon Pinot's offer a range of styles from quasi-Burgundian to overt New World, influenced by vintage as well as by winemaker. Growing seasons in Oregon range from cool vintages where ripening is a real problem to warm vintages where it can be difficult to avoid excessive alcohol levels. In vintages such as 2010 and 1999, prolonged cool weather left producers holding their breath to see whether the vintage would be rescued by an Indian summer stretching into October. In vintages such as 1998 or 2006, a hot growing season pushed up sugar levels to a point at which many wine-makers felt uncomfortable with the high alcohol levels. Recent vintages demonstrate a range of extremes, from a rather lush 2006, to a distinctly restrained cool-climate vintage in 2007, and to a somewhat opulent vintage in 2008. But growers reckon that in the past decade there has been a transition from having a minority of good vintages to having a majority (interestingly, you might say the same about Burgundy).

The 2007 vintage got a bad press, especially from wine writers in California, who wrote it off as too cool even before the grapes had been harvested. (The comments may say more about California than about Oregon.) This has left winemakers somewhat defensive about the vintage, but the fact is that many 2007s now show more classic purity of line than the 2008s, and are developing well in a style of what might be called European restraint. In fact, terroir differences often show more distinctly in the 2007s than in the 2008s, where the rising tide of ripe fruits has lifted many wines to a common state of near-opulence, partially obscuring terroir differences. It won't surprise me if some of the 2007s outlast the 2008s, and in many ways it's a better vintage for understanding the region. Yet, as my tasting notes suggest, the 2008s usually have the advantage in terms of current enjoyment.

Past vintages are not necessarily a good guide to present styles. Over the past decade, winemakers have backed away from "bigger is better" and are using less extraction and less new oak. Even the arch proponents, Beaux Frères and Archery Summit, make lighter wines than they used to. And older vintages can be misleading: while some age beautifully, others seem to go into a state of arrested development in which they get older without aging. Wines from the cool 1993 vintage can be quite lovely at this point, with the original fruits now giving way to savory aromas and flavors to achieve a delicious balance. On the other hand, I have liked very few wines from the warmer 1998 vintage, which tend to my mind to be clumsy and heavy, rarely showing any interesting development. Indeed, my general experience is that the wines of cooler past vintages may age beautifully, although those of the warmer vintages may seem a little rustic. But changes in style mean that current releases from the same winemakers can be quite different from older vintages, tending to be more elegant and restrained today, and often offering promise for interesting future development.

Until the AVA system came in, all wine was labeled simply Willamette Valley, sometimes with an additional description such as Yamhill County. There was little emphasis on single vineyards; most wines were blended and the top cuvées were based on selection rather than location. Ken Wright was the standard bearer for the move towards single vineyards, and reinforced by the system of sub AVAs, place has now become the most important determinant for most producers. Many producers divide their production into an entry level wine, a selected cuvée or cuvées, and then reserve the production from single vineyards for their top wines. Although Oregon lacks cult wines commanding the heights of the marketplace comparable to Napa Valley Cabernets, it has a dedicated following for its top wines. Many of them are sold exclusively through mailing lists, or occasionally at the winery itself; few are in general distribution. Production at the top is often very small, with no possibility of expansion. The vineyardists have definitely won the argument over the blenders.

One identifiable feature uniting most Willamette Pinot Noirs is their evident cool climate origins. Some of the acidity may have been added, but the alcohol will probably be natural. There's a bright quality to the fruits, usually stopping short of New World brashness, and far removed from the jammy notes or cooked fruits of Pinot Noir from warmer climates. The wines tend to show attractively in the first few years. As Harry Peterson-Nedry of Chehalem says, "Tightly wound Burgundy wines open up slowly but the wines here are more mid term."[44] Yet they can age (Ƭ page 254). Assessing ageability from the early years is clouded by the youthfulness of the vines, some problems with corks that weren't of the top standard, and sometimes a heavy hand with new oak. It will be another ten or twenty years before the full potential of the region becomes evident. The question is not so much whether the wines age, but whether they become more interesting as they get older.

Vintage variation has been less extreme in Oregon than in Burgundy. Over the past twenty years, Burgundy offered more really outstanding vintages, but also many more really disappointing vintages.[45] However, the relationship may be changing, as global warming seems to have had a greater

effect on Burgundy than on Oregon. One impetus for turning to Oregon for
Pinot Noir production was of course the similarity in the climates, and until
the end of the twentieth century, average season growing temperatures were
fairly comparable; some years Burgundy would be warmer, some years Oregon would be warmer. In the past decade, however, Burgundy has been
warmer in every year but one.

But the real measure is of course to compare the wines. Because climatic
conditions and the overall rating of the vintage rarely coincide, pairwise
comparisons are not very practical, but to form a general assessment of
stylistic changes and ageworthiness, I turned again to Domaine Drouhin,
where Véronique Drouhin has applied the same criteria to making the wines
for the past twenty years. I compared DDO's Pinot Noir from Willamette
with some of Maison Drouhin's village wines from 1988 to 2007 to see what
pattern I could discern (page 258).[46] (The closest parallels in rating vintages, incidentally, were in Burgundy's better years, where for 2002 and 1999,
Robert Parker gave vintages in both locations fairly similar ratings. That is
not to say that the vintages necessarily have similar characters.[47])

Several tastings had already made the point that at the top levels, Oregon
Pinot Noir can age well. But I wondered to what extent this might be true at
the level of comparing the estate wine from Oregon with village wines from
Burgundy, where longevity and complexity are less emphasized in both cases.
The difference between them was consistent: the wines from Oregon give a
richer impression, with fatter fruits on the palate, and more sweetness, sometimes with a tell-tale touch of nuts and vanillin, on the finish. This may be
partly due to higher alcohol, in current vintages running a full percent between a typical 14% from Willamette and 13% from Burgundy.

The difference between the regions is more evident in the younger wines,
but both regions displayed the same general pattern of young Pinot Noir

*Burgundy and
Willamette Valley had
temperatures in the
same general range
until the past decade,
when Burgundy has
become warmer.[48]*

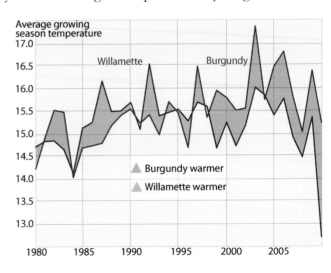

showing significant vintage variation, a clear validation of the growth of Pinot in Oregon. The difference between Burgundy and Willamette is less marked than it might have been a decade ago, although more variation in style is shown between vintages in Burgundy. For current vintages, the more voluptuous character of Oregon makes the wines frankly more enjoyable at this point, although they are just a touch less refined. The young Oregon wines in this tasting did not give the impression of anticipating substantial longevity, but this may be deceptive, as tastings of the older wines showed.

Going back to older vintages, there was more overlap in style; the playoff of development and vintage character becomes more important than the region of origin, although as a rule the Willamette Pinots remain just a touch softer and richer, with a touch of alcohol-derived sweetness, and a slightly nutty impression. The cooler vintages in Oregon overlap in flavor spectrum and style with the warmer vintages in Burgundy. As the wines get older, distinctions between the regions become less obvious. The most striking feature of the tasting was the interest of the oldest Willamette vintages, all the more impressive because the very first vintages were made from purchased fruits, and the following vintages came from very young vines.

Although Oregon winemakers disavow direct comparison with Burgundy, it's to Burgundy they refer more often than to any other region producing Pinot Noir. Wines tasted in the region seem to offer more direct fruit, higher alcohol, and less obvious tannic structure than equivalent Burgundies. But there is wide variation in Willamette as there is in Burgundy, and their stylistic ranges overlap sufficiently (especially allowing for extensive vintage variation in each) that it is not necessarily easy to identify the origins of every wine in a blind tasting. In fact, a tasting to compare two different producers in Burgundy might well demonstrate just as much variation in style. Of all the Pinot-producing regions I visited, I think the range of expression was the widest in Oregon, from wines that could be confused with Burgundy to those in full blown New World style. But however similar or different they are to Burgundy, they speak of Pinot Noir. For my money, the top single vineyard wines reach that delicious turning point, when I like them best, at ten to twelve years of age from good vintages. It is fair to say that at this point they might be considered close in complexity to premier crus from Burgundy.

A quite different expression of Pinot Noir is found over the border to the south, in California. I still remember the first Pinot Noir I had from California. It was the Carneros Creek 1977, which made quite a stir on release. This was nothing at all like Burgundy, but was clearly a wine of unusual quality and interest. My tasting note in 1981 read, "Rather nutty, slightly buttery bouquet matched by taste of nutty Pinot Noir. Marvelous long finish. Very heavy texture, silky unctuous, solid (almost too chunky)." But by 1984 the tannins had become more overt, and I asked "Will it ever mature to a smooth elegant Pinot Noir?" And by 1986, when the wine was less than a decade old, it had lost interest for me, and I noted, "Very heavy and opulent, too much dry tannin on the finish. Not at all coarse, but just too much of a good thing, lacking the subtlety Pinot Noir should have." Indeed, "too much of a good thing" remained the criticism of California Pinot Noir. Has this changed with the focus over the past decade on planting Pinot in cooler sites?

The entire viticultural scene is different in California. Production of Pinot Noir has more than doubled since 2004; but the area of Pinot Noir has increased by only about 50% over the same period.[50] The big difference is that Oregon has gone for quality and kept its yield more or less steady (allowing for vintage fluctuation), but average yields have become much higher in California, now running to an average for the state overall of up to 80 hl/ha—a level at which I defy anyone to make Pinot Noir with typicity.[51]

The key to quality wine production in California is fog. Essentially all fine wines are produced in areas where fog can penetrate from the Pacific, cooling average temperatures in the interior. And for no grape is this more important than Pinot Noir, which is especially susceptible to loss of character at high temperature. So in looking for Pinot typicity in California, we need to focus sharply on the quality areas of Carneros, Russian River Valley, and Santa Barbara, all of which have cooler climates driven by pronounced susceptibility to fog from the ocean.

Pinot Noir has had a chequered history in California. Attempts to grow it for varietal production during the initial burst of enthusiasm for European varieties in the late nineteenth century were largely unsuccessful.[52] In fact, wines labeled as "Burgundy" were as likely to be made from Zinfandel as from Pinot Noir.[53] After the debacle of Prohibition, Pinot Noir was pio-

California produces more Pinot Noir than Oregon.[49]

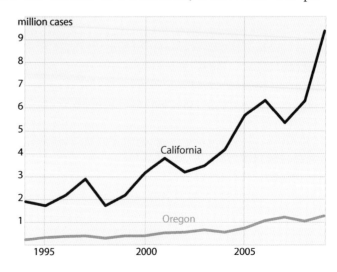

Morning fog rolls into Sonoma Valley. *Photograph courtesy Mark Malpiede.*

neered by Louis Martini in Carneros, but never achieved any penetration comparable to Cabernet Sauvignon, which soon emerged as the quality black variety of choice. Part of the problem was the failure to define appropriate viticultural conditions for Pinot Noir, which was often planted next to Cabernet Sauvignon in sites that were simply too warm for it. And vinification was not adjusted for the variety. Josh Jensen (who founded the Calera Wine Company) comments that "most wineries had a standard red wine method" that was applied indiscriminately.[54]

Attempts to produce quality Pinot Noir started in the 1970s, some of the pivotal moments being in 1973 when Joe Swan released his first Pinot Noir from Russian River, and Davis Bynum produced the first single vineyard Pinot Noir (from the Rochioli vineyard). More idiosyncratic in his choice of location, Josh Jensen planted the first vineyards for Calera Wine on Mount Harlan in 1975. But during the seventies and eighties, many wineries gave up attempts to produce Pinot Noir. Part of the reason was economic: Cabernet Sauvignon could give a much better wine at higher yields, and it was simply too costly to reduce yields of Pinot Noir to a level appropriate for the variety. Confusion also arose because one predominant clone of Pinot Noir was misleadingly called Gamay Beaujolais.[55] All this contributed to a belief that Pinot Noir belonged in Burgundy, not California. Looking back, Rod Berglund of Joseph Swan Vineyards comments that, "The oldest vines in the estate were planted in 1969. Anyone who planted Pinot Noir at that time was a visionary or a lunatic, and to say they were a visionary is revisionist history."[56]

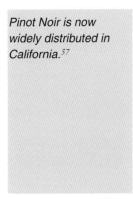

Pinot Noir is now widely distributed in California.[57]

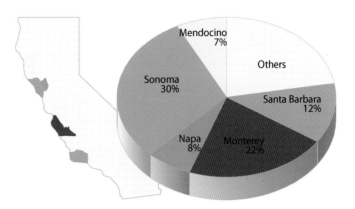

The current renaissance of Pinot started in the nineties with a focus on planting in cooler areas, together with an emphasis on specific clones.[58] When vineyards were planted up to the 1970s, available clones had basically been selected for their virus-free status, with little concern for quality.[59] The impetus for really thinking about the nature of the grapevines came from the clonal selection experiments that Francis Mahoney started in the 1960s at Carneros Creek. "When I started to talking to producers, asking them what was good and what was bad, and then taking cuttings, they thought I was mad. At that time, the common opinion was that the best plant was the one that produced the most fruit," he recollects.[60] Material came from many old line producers, including Chalone, Inglenook, Louis Martini, Hanzell, and Beaulieu. "The original search was looking for the über-clone, we were like Monty Python, we thought we would find the perfect clone," says Francis.[61] The successful plantings were given to the viticultural department of the University of California, Davis, who in due course produced virus-free clones from them.

So clones where quality had been a major criterion in selection became available only in the 1980s. Now popularly known as the heritage clones, these in essence are cultivars of Pinot Noir that have been adapted to growth in California over several decades. Among the heritage clones are the Martini clone (an early selection from the Martini vineyards in Carneros), the Swan clone (from Joe Swan's vineyard in Russian River), and the Chalone clone (rumored to have originated in Vosne Romanée). Other clones include Pommard (with an undefined heritage from France), and the Wädenswil clones from Switzerland. But none of these clones were felt to be completely satisfactory and a major shift occurred when the Dijon clones became available. They certainly made a big difference in Oregon, but there is some concern as to whether they are optimal for California. As Robert Sinskey comments, "Burgundian clones of Pinot Noir were chosen for their early ripening, and in California this doesn't work. Here we want clones that ripen later so that you get full flavor development before 25 Brix. And it's not necessarily the small berried clones that work best, sometimes those with larger berries ripen more slowly and are better."[62]

For this sort of reason, the Dijon clones are more controversial in California than elsewhere. "People in California started planting Dijon clones and throwing everything else away," says Merry Edwards,[63] who inter alia is famous for developing the Rae clone from the old Mount Eden Pinot Noir vineyards. "The Dijon clones were developed for cool climates and are not necessarily the most appropriate for this climate," she adds. Winemaker Bob Cabral of Williams Selyem Winery is not a fan of the Dijon clones either: "They ripen too fast and become photosynthetic machines producing high sugars before the phenolics develop," he says, adding that "Williams Selyem is largely a Dijon clone-free zone."[64]

Certainly the pendulum seems to swing to and fro, and in recent years many producers have backed off from the Dijon clones, and are going back to the old heritage clones. My own tastings of wines from individual clones in Carneros or Russian River suggest that it is fair comment to say that the Dijon clones reinforce the propensity of the region for the fruit-forward style. Certainly I did not find any one of the clones to give a complete wine, although blends can show more complexity. On the other hand, some of the old clones, such as Mariafeld or Wädenswil, give a very superficial impression, developing sugar rather than fruit. All of which to my mind reinforces the importance of diversity in the vineyard.

Although each region producing Pinot Noir in California is distinct, still there is a general commonality of deep color, ripe fruit, high alcohol, and varying degrees of forcefulness. All producers are individualists, but still there are some common approaches. It is usual to destem the grapes. Removing the stems eliminates one source of tannins, especially those that are harsher, and so increases fruitiness. Most producers destem completely; some leave up to a quarter of whole clusters (meaning the grapes remain on their stems) to give a bit of structure to the wine. A cold soak of about five days, when the grapes are essentially left to macerate, is virtually *de rigeur* before fermentation is allowed to start. This puts color into the wine.

Alcohol levels are rarely below 14%. In fact, watering back (meaning that water is added to the must before fermentation) is often needed to keep the level below 15%. The rationale for this is that the final increase in sugar levels in the grapes is not due to photosynthesis, but results from desiccation as water evaporates from the berry. So producers feel it is reasonable to add that water back directly to the must. "In France they chaptalize, in California we add water. Those are the alternatives," says Victor Gallegos of Sea Smoke winery in Santa Barbara.[65] Often the balanced acidity of the wines is due to addition of tartaric acid before fermentation begins. "Acidification is a fact of life in Sonoma Valley," one producer said to me.

It's a lost cause to hark back to the days of wine at 12.5% or even 13% alcohol. Most New World winemakers define moderate alcohol as anything from 13.9 to 14.5%. They may be scathing about alcoholic monsters at 15% or 16% but think nothing of going into the mid fourteens. If you ask producers in California whether they are worried about alcohol levels, they tend to say, yes, it's a concern, and then shrug as though to say, what can you do? 14.5% is the new 13%. "I'm not looking for alcohol, I'm looking for ripeness," says Anne Moller Racke of Donum Estate, "but saying that a wine must have less than 14% alcohol is a bit like telling a chef that he should make a three star meal and it must have less than 1000 calories."[66]

The need to acidify and water back (often combined by adding acidulated water to the must) is increased by the trend to later harvesting, when grapes have higher sugar and lower acidity. But in the past two or three years, producers have begun to back off a bit. "The style of Russian River Pinot has changed. The point at which people are picking has changed. The early 2000s were marked by wines that were bigger and looser with ripe flavors. If we had never gone to the edge of things with ripeness we would never have got back to the pure style we have seen in the past few years," says winemaker Brian Mahoney at DeLoach Vineyards.[67]

Against what might be seen as a barrage of criticism above, it should be stated upfront that some winemakers are struggling valiantly to make natural wines without excessive extraction. Merry Edwards does not believe in watering back. "What's the point of getting the grapes ripe and then adding water? Ugh!" she said to me.[68] "We avoid acidification like the plague," says Ted Lemon of Littorai Vineyards, where if necessary he picks earlier to be sure of good acidity, and limits use of whole clusters if acidity is an issue (whole clusters decrease acidity because the stems have potassium) (Ⴢ page 270). At Au Bon Climat in Santa Barbara, Jim Clendenen picks a week earlier than everyone around him. "We are looking for total balance rather than some balance of brown seeds on which to judge ripeness," he says (Ⴢ page 277). Brix is an important criterion in picking, with a target of 24. "What is the point of going out and farming your vineyards so badly that you get to physiological ripeness only at 15.5% alcohol?" he asks.[69]

The neo-classicists believe that highly extracted wines eliminate terroir. These may not be the only producers to follow this path, but they are certainly the exceptions that prove the rule. Yet none of them necessarily take Burgundy as their reference point. "I've lost all interest in making world class Pinot Noir; that doesn't interest me any more. I want to make the best Pinot I can. I want to make the most Hirsch-like Hirsch. [Hirsch is a top Pinot Noir vineyard in the Sonoma Coast.] We will never achieve the full potential of the New World unless we put the Old World in a box. Slavish references to the Old World are a hindrance, you will never concentrate on what you can produce, which is the essential part," says Ted Lemon.[70] "There was a time back in the 1980s when we had a sense of place, but now the marketing people are running the business, and only wines that are dark and rich enough to get high points will sell," says Francis Mahoney.[71]

Wine styles are far from monolithic. There are characteristic variations between Carneros, Russian River, and Santa Barbara, and as you dig deeper, within the sub-areas of each region. Winemaking varies from exuberant New World to more restrained quasi-European styles. But if we assume that Pinot Noir has a responsibility to reflect place (that is a sizeable "if," but most producers describe it as their aim), how do these combinations of region and style play out?

Pinot Noir has never been able to compete with Cabernet Sauvignon in Napa Valley either for varietal quality or in terms of economics. It has a better chance in Carneros, the region at the base of the valley that in fact joins the Napa and Sonoma Valleys. This is a curious area, rather depressed before viticulture was introduced, not to say a derelict dumping ground for trash. The Louis Martini vineyard in Carneros was planted in 1948 with cuttings supposed to have been taken from vines that had been imported into Inglenook in Napa Valley in the nineteenth century. But viticulture did not make a great impact here until Francis Mahoney planted Pinot Noir at Carneros Creek Winery in 1972. Other vineyards followed through the 1980s, mostly owned by producers from Napa Valley. The terroir is not the most obvious for Pinot Noir, since the soils are mostly clay, typically fairly shallow (about a meter deep), with poor drainage, but this is ameliorated by rather low rainfall. Going south towards San Pablo Bay, clay content increases in the soil and the clay turns from gray to black. The climate is dominated by cool breezes blowing from the expanse of San Pablo Bay; sometimes the "breezes" are strong winds. Today Pinot Noir and Chardonnay form the focus of the 3,500 ha of vineyards in Carneros. Some of the production goes for sparkling wine, but this has been cut back in recent years.

Does wine from Carneros have a distinct character? There's agreement that it can do so, but no consensus on whether the character is emerging more or less clearly with time. Robert Sinskey says that, "Defining character and style for Carneros is a problem because it has become technique driven, which hasn't allowed it to define itself. In the eighties there were more similarities, but as things became Parkerized and Dijon clones become available, everything became homogenized"[72] (⟲ page 266). But Dick Ward of Saintsbury has a different view. "Since the 1950s Carneros has not been well served by many of the wines made from Carneros fruit. If you are looking for the typicity of Pinot Noir, you are really talking about the last 10-15 years. Some people think the problem in the early years was with the clones, but it's more a matter of getting better matches of clones to sites"[73] (Ⓨ page 265).

All that said, if you directly compare Carneros Pinot with Russian River Pinot Noir made by the same producer, you see a consistent difference. Russian River tends to be more immediately generous, the first impression being the sumptuous quality of the fruits; Carneros tends to show its structure more clearly, in the form of more evident tannins. Anne Moller Racke of Donum Estate captures the difference. "There is a Carneros typicity, it is more linear but has more layering [than Russian River] although the technical measurements of progress through the growing season are similar. Russian River has coolness from fog, Carneros from wind, which gives thicker skins and more linear tannins."[74] (And if you go north of Sonoma, to Anderson Valley in Mendocino County, where some producers also have vineyards, you see a generally leaner style to the wines.)

One insight into winemaker influence versus terroir came from my tasting at Donum Estate, where there were two bottlings of the 2008 vintage, one unfiltered and one which underwent a light filtration (Ⓨ page 263). Contrary to my expectations, the filtered wine gave a more elegant impression, with refined tannins emphasizing the precision of the fruits. It seemed more typically Carneros. By contrast the texture of the unfiltered wine seemed a little obtrusive. Ann Moller Racke told me that the next day, the opened bottles showed differently, with the unfiltered wine having more presence.

To the northwest of Carneros, Pinot Noir is grown all over Sonoma, and bottlings range from Sonoma Coast AVA, meaning anywhere in the vast area, to single vineyard names. Because of geological history, there is a great variety of soil types; in fact, they are fond of saying locally that there are more soil types in Sonoma Valley than in the whole of France. The best known area is the Russian River Valley, one of several valleys that come together at the town of Healdsburg.[75] The Russian River used to flow directly south to San Pablo Bay, but volcanic eruptions some millions of years ago caused it to swing west to where it now empties out into the Pacific.

The terrain in Russian River Valley varies from flat expanses near the river to gently rolling hills. Soils vary, alluvial in the flood plain immediately around the river, sandstone, granite, or sandy loam elsewhere. There is more homogeneity to the west of Sebastopol, where soils are based on the so-called Goldridge loam. Just to the south of the Russian River Valley is the Petaluma gap, where a break in the mountains allows cool air to sweep from the Pacific across to San Francisco Bay, providing lots of fog and an important cooling influence. Penetration by coastal fog is the important climatic influence; indeed, there have been attempts to redefine the boundaries of the AVA to confine it to the area covered by the fogs.[76] Resulting from prox-

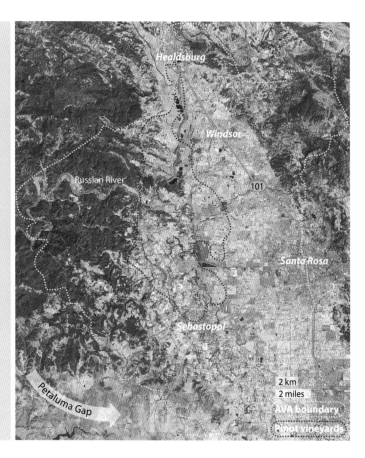

The Russian River AVA extends south of Healdsburg. Most of the Pinot Noir vineyards lie between Healdsburg and Sebastopol.

imity to the ocean, the western side of the AVA is cooler than the eastern. Overall the coolest part of the valley is the sub-AVA of Green Valley at the southern end. Today there are more than 6,000 ha of vineyards in Russian River Valley, with Chardonnay as the lead variety, followed by Pinot Noir; together they are close to three quarters of all plantings.[77] Some top vineyards lie to the west of Russian River in the area known to locals as "True Sonoma Coast," to distinguish it from the broad AVA. It is fair to say these are not delicate wines; the style fairly bursts with fruit.

Russian River was one of the centers for wine production in the nineteenth century, when Zinfandel was the main focus. But by the start of the second half of the twentieth century, fruits trees, especially apples, were far more important. Pinot Noir was first planted in the 1960s after Joe Rochioli asked the University of California, Davis for advice on how best to use the land; they advised planting grapevines. So the famous Rochioli vineyard, whose grapes are now used by several top producers, was planted as an alternative to other crops.[78] There was no intention of making wine, only of selling grapes. The first vintage actually passed through multiple hands until it ended up in Gallo's Hearty Burgundy (in retrospect probably the most dis-

The Middle Reach of Russian River running along Westside Road is a flat flood plain.
Russian River is behind the trees and last flooded these vineyards in 1995.

tinguished grapes ever used in that brand). By the mid 1980s this region became the trendiest spot in the country for Pinot Noir production. In the 1990s, more vineyards were planted and production increased dramatically.

The Rochioli vineyard offers a microcosm of developments in Russian River, with other crops (most often orchards) or cattle grazing land being replaced by vineyards. And more recently there has been greater concentration on Pinot Noir and Chardonnay, and an increasing focus on replanting with Dijon clones when vineyards come up for renewal. Having started as a grower, Rochioli slowly moved into wine production, and today about 40% of the crop is vinified under the Rochioli label, with the rest being sold to a variety of purchasers. But Joe Rochioli retains a tight control on the use of his name, and only a handful of purchasers (for Pinot Noir, most notably Williams Selyem and Gary Farrell; ⟨ page 269) are allowed to identify the source on their labels;[79] others can buy the grapes, but the wines do not meet Joe's standard for using the Rochioli name.

The division between grape growing and wine production is common in Sonoma; probably more grapes are purchased than are estate grown.[80] The top producers buy their grapes on long-term acreage contracts, which means that they take the grapes from the same plot within the vineyard every year.[81] Often the producer has a significant say in viticultural management, extending from pruning and control of yields to choosing the date of harvest. One consequence is that (like Burgundy) there is the chance to see different pro-ducers' expressions of the same vineyard. Following the pioneering example of Rochioli, it's not uncommon for growers to turn their hands to wine production. The 29 hectare Hirsch vineyard in Sonoma Coast, for example, sees Pinot Noir and Chardonnay made by about ten producers, including the eponymous Hirsch Vineyards.[82]

If I were compelled to use just a single word to describe the Pinot Noir of Russian River, it would be "sumptuous." The fruits are almost always for-ward, the impression on the palate is rich, tannins are rarely obvious. But vineyard differences come through the rich style. Russian River may have as many individual vineyard designations for its Pinot Noirs as anywhere on the West Coast. The highly varied soil types make any general grouping rather difficult. Together with variations in exposure to fog and general aspect of the land, not to mention clones and the age of the vines, the individual site acquires increased importance. If you ask winegrowers to disentangle which of these influences are the more important, they shrug and say, "all of the above." But although winegrowers are certainly sensitive to variations in the quality and style of wines that come from different vineyard sources, you rarely hear anyone try to relate that quality or style to the specifics of the soil type as they might in Burgundy. You get the impression that climate is at least a more identifiable factor. Indeed, the most important single factor may be the hours of fog, which determine the daily growing temperature. Take the difference between the Hirsch Vineyard in Sonoma Coast and the Ro-chioli River Block vineyard in Russian River, for example.

The Rochioli vineyard consists of about 50 ha, half planted to Pinot Noir, another quarter to Chardonnay, and the last quarter divided among several varieties. About half of the Pinot Noir is Rochioli's own selection from the West Block (WBk), but the most recent plantings tend to concentrate on the Dijon (D) clones. Size of plot, clones, and dates of planting for Pinot Noir are marked in approximate locations on the map.

Much of Russian River has gently rolling hills. This view looks north towards Mount Helena a few miles away in the background.

The Hirsch vineyard is 13 miles northwest of River Block as the crow flies. Average elevation is around 450 m, and the top part of the vineyard is above the fog line. It is planted with a mix of clones, including Pommard (50-60%), Mount Eden (30-40%), and Swann. Grapes develop thicker skins and therefore more tannins here. It flowers and harvests about one month later each year, and shows more variation with vintage, compared to River Block. On sandier soils in the Russian River flood plain, River Block was planted with a mixture of Dijon clones (115 and 777) and Rochioli's own West Block selection (some in 1989, some in 2000). The major characteristic of the wine is its finesse. A comparison of Williams Selyem's single vineyard wines over two decades showed that the same thread of commonality runs through each vineyard as it shows its character over a series of vintages (ⵣ p. 272). Hirsch is deeper and broader, River Block is tighter and lighter. You might say that Hirsch is more masculine and River Block is more feminine. In each year, River Block is more developed and I perceive a touch more complexity. The reflections of these nuances through vintage are every bit as interesting as a comparison of two premier crus in Burgundy.

Pinot Noir is not usually thought of as a mountain grape, but its need for cool climates can be satisfied by elevation as well as by latitude. The immediate south of San Francisco used to be wine country, but now has been transformed into Silicon Valley. But there are vineyards of Pinot Noir in the mountains nearby. In the Santa Cruz Mountains, microclimates vary to the point at which on successive ridges (within five miles as the crow flies), you can find the famous Ridge Montebello vineyard where Cabernet Sauvignon triumphs, and Fogarty's vineyards of Pinot Noir. An hour or so farther south on Mount Harlan are the vineyards where Josh Jensen founded Calera Wines in 1972 when he found limestone.

Soils in Santa Cruz Mountains are shale or sandstone, generally without much clay. Perhaps because the area is circumscribed, Santa Cruz is one of the few AVAs to be relatively unaffected by politics. Vineyards have to be above the fog line. Here the pattern is the reverse of elsewhere with morning sun and afternoon fog. Thomas Fogarty was the pioneer for Pinot Noir (Υ page 274), but now has been followed by several others. The wines tend to spicy black fruits with good tannic support, and age well for up to two decades.

"Trespassers will be transmogrificated," says the sign at the entrance to Calera Wine Company on Mount Harlan, an indication that Josh Jensen has lost none of his feisty character with age. As an avowed Burgundian, Josh believes that nothing but limestone terroir can make great Pinot Noir. "For me the definition of great wine is that it's extremely complex. The classic great Pinot Noirs are grown on limestone soils—I took as my theoretical start on Pinot Noir that they were great because they were grown on limestone. All of the vineyards here are on limestone," he told me.[83] That simple statement belies a long and dedicated search for limestone terroir in California.

Vineyards in the Santa Cruz mountains are elevated and steep, with views over San Francisco Bay fifty miles to the north.

An old lime kiln gave the clue that this was the terroir for Pinot Noir where Calera was established.

Photograph courtesy of Calera Wine Company.

After spending 1969 and 1970 working in Burgundy, including a spell at Romanée Conti, Josh Jensen returned to the United States with the ambition of growing great Pinot Noir. He looked for limestone terroir all over California, and finally found a marker in the form of an old lime kiln (used to produce lime at a quarry) on Mount Harlan. The name of his company reflects these origins; Calera is the Spanish for lime kiln. At almost 700 m elevation, the vineyards are among the highest (and coolest) in the United States. The cool climate comes not only from the elevation but also from cold breezes and fog direct from the Pacific, only a few miles away. The vineyards are well isolated from all other vineyards, the nearest being the Santa Cruz Mountain AVA fifty miles to the north. Calera's unique quality is recognized in the existence of the Mount Harlan AVA in which it is the only winery.

Spread over more than 250 hectares on the mountain, there are now six separate Pinot Noir vineyards.[84] Selleck, Jensen, and Reed were planted in 1975; Mills, Ryan, and De Villiers were planted between 1984 and 2001. (Mills vineyard is on its own roots; the soil may be sandy enough to have some resistance to phylloxera, and the vineyards are isolated.) Most of the plantings are the Calera selection, which came from 18 original vines at Chalone. (No one will comment any more on the old story that the original source of these vines was cuttings liberated from Romanée Conti. It's often described as the Calera clone, but in fact consists of a selection with some variations.) The wines of each vineyard have their own character; there is also a Mount Harlan cuvée that includes lots declassified from the individual vineyards. The two vineyards that give the most different wines are Selleck and Reed, close together but on opposite sides of a stream with opposed aspects. Selleck faces south and makes Calera's most intense wine; Reed faces north and makes the lightest wine.

In the earliest vintages, from 1978-1981, the aim was to have 12.5% alcohol. Then Josh started picking a little later to get greater ripeness, and the wines went to 13.5%. In the past decade there's been some bracket creep, picking a little riper each year, but Josh says that since 2005 there's been a pull back to earlier picking. Usually each vineyard is harvested in several batches, typically producing more sugar (higher potential alcohol) in the later pickings. The assemblage can give more complexity than a single picking. "If you aspire to make great wines, you often have to take risks, you are living on a knife's edge between picking too early and picking too late," says Jensen.[85] In spite of the cool climate and the limestone soils, usually it's necessary to acidify. Jensen's winemaking may be more Burgundian than the Burgundians: there's no protracted cold soak, most grapes go into the vat as uncrushed whole clusters, fermentation occurs naturally by indigenous yeasts, and continues until the cap falls.

Overall it's just a fraction warmer here than in Burgundy, but the key to character and ageability, Josh says, is the soil. Tasting a horizontal of Calera's single vineyard wines is an exercise comparable to travelling from the Côte de Beaune to the Côte de Nuits, with de Villiers, Mills, and Reed on the lighter side with a red fruit spectrum, Ryan offering a half way house, and Jensen and Selleck showing greater density and structure in a black fruit spectrum (Υ page 275). There is no mistaking the differences. The wines have savory and even herbaceous elements in the Old World style, but the forwardness of the sweet ripe fruits and the high alcohol is New World. Wines from the lighter vineyards seem to lose some of their distinction with age, however, and reach a peak somewhere under a decade. Jensen and Selleck are the wines with real aging potential. I felt Josh had gone a long way towards proving his point about aging on limestone when I tasted the 1990 Jensen vineyard, whose savory notes and delicious tones of sous bois seemed quite Burgundian. Perhaps it ages just a little more quickly than Burgundy; in a blind tasting, had I placed this as Burgundy, I would have thought about the 1985 vintage.

Only a hundred miles north of Los Angeles, almost as far south as grapes are grown in California, Santa Barbara is scarcely the most obvious place to grow Pinot Noir. You would think it was far too hot; after all, it is a hundred miles to the south of Paso Robles, which has become famous for growing warm-climate Rhône varieties. The microclimate is the key here. The valleys where the vineyards are located run west to east, so cooling breezes enter

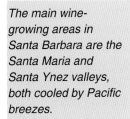

The main wine-growing areas in Santa Barbara are the Santa Maria and Santa Ynez valleys, both cooled by Pacific breezes.

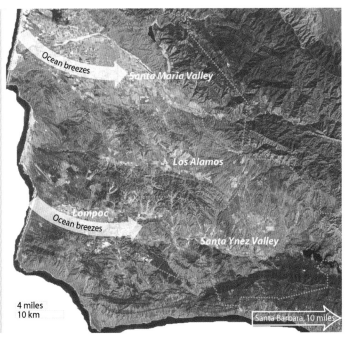

directly from the ocean and are channeled along by the mountains, and there is strong diurnal variation. Vineyards are located at elevations from 70 to 500 m, where the fog levels offset the hot sun. Summer temperatures are actually somewhat cooler than in parts of Russian River Valley.[86]

As elsewhere in California, vineyards in the area started with the establishment of missions in the nineteenth century. Much of the wine was the usual sweet red produced from the Mission grape. But wine production generally shifted farther north, and then Prohibition caused the vineyards to be abandoned. Serious planting and production did not resume until the 1960s. Without any real knowledge of terroir and microclimates, a pot-pourri of grape varieties was planted.[87]

Pinot Noir obtained its first major recognition in the late 1970s in response to the pioneering efforts of Sanford and Benedict, who planted the first Pinot Noir, and Brooks Firestone, who created the first major premium winery. All the same, there was a distinct sense of waiting for Godot, with newspaper articles asking when the Great American Pinot Noir would appear.[88] In any case, as vineyards were planted and wineries established, much of the action came from investments by producers farther north, who actually shipped the grapes out rather than making wine locally.[89] Santa Barbara became recognized as a source for quality grapes, but the focus on Pinot Noir came later.

In fact, Chardonnay led the way into quality wine best suited to the region. Santa Barbara now produces a little more white wine than red. Today three quarters of the white is Chardonnay; more than half of the red is Pinot Noir. The change from twenty years ago is not so much in the whites, but in the development of the reds. Total production of white wine has increased, but the proportions of varieties have remained more or less the same. What is new is the focus on Pinot Noir. At the start of the 1990s, less than a third of plantings were black grapes, and they were split between Pinot Noir and Cabernet Sauvignon. By 2010, Pinot Noir had increased five fold, to become the second most important variety after Chardonnay.[90]

The scale here is different from the vineyards to the north. Santa Barbara has always been agricultural country, and the wine industry originated with farmers growing grapes to replace other crops. The vineyards are usually large. The reason goes back to the old Spanish land grant system that divided up California, and which survived much longer here. Many of the original holdings still exist, and it is rare for a property of less than 100 acres to change hands. In fact, in some areas, the minimum zoning is 100 acres (40 hectares). Reflecting the history in which Santa Barbara started by supplying the northern vineyards with grapes, many of the vineyards continue to be owned by growers rather than producers. But now the grapes are mostly purchased by local producers. At Santa Barbara's well known Bien Nacido vineyard, almost all of the fruit was shipped to the north coast in the 1970s, but today about 80% stays in the region.[91] Producers vary from large owners

Vineyards in the Santa Maria Valley lie on a flat plateau close to the mountain peaks.

of vineyards to boutique operations that purchase grapes in small amounts and make wine in a custom crush facility. But there is a common contempt for the "lifestyle wineries" of Napa Valley—although one or two can now be found in the Santa Barbara area. The wine may be more local, less "international" than, for example, Russian River—but the producers are equally obsessed with their scores from Robert Parker. Driving around, the valleys seem more agricultural than tourist oriented; you see vineyards but few glitzy tasting rooms. Most of the tasting rooms are in one of the two small towns in Santa Maria Valley, Los Olivos and Solvang; the larger towns seem somewhat industrial.

Santa Maria was the first of the valleys to be established for growing grapes and producing wine. It is a broad alluvial fan, and as a generalization, its vineyards tend to be relatively level. You have the feeling of being on a flat plateau with the mountain tops (or perhaps hill tops) around you. Soils are diverse, ranging from sandy to loam or clay. Monterey shale is a common bedrock, and its softness explains the weathered, gently rounded tops of the hills. The first vineyard was planted in 1963 on 40 ha of what had been a cattle ranch; all the grapes from the first harvest, in 1966, were sold to the Christian Brothers Winery of Napa Valley. Today Santa Maria Valley has about 3,000 ha of vineyards. Ownership is somewhat concentrated. The two largest producers, Cambria Estate and Byron Estate, are both owned by giant Kendall-Jackson, and account for about a quarter of the planted area (🍷 page 278). There is no phylloxera in the valley, and the older plantings are on their own roots.

Originally a single land grant covered the Cambria and Byron Estates and the Bien Nacido vineyard, which is one of the best known in Santa Maria Valley. The Miller family, who have been farming in Santa Maria for five generations, and converted Bien Nacido from vegetables to wine grapes in 1973, retain the right to approve use of the vineyard name. Bien Nacido provides high quality grapes for single vineyard bottlings by roughly 15 producers, as well as a program for grapes produced at higher yield for generic Santa Maria Valley bottlings. An insight into the role of the winemaker versus terroir comes from the range of differences in choosing harvest dates, as explained by vineyard manager Chris Hammell. "We'll use for our example an extended period of time in September with foggy mornings clearing by 10 or 11 a.m., a 74 degree high (1 p.m.) and 53 degree low (7 a.m.). Under these conditions Pinot Noir should ripen at about 0.22 Brix per day (depending on crop load) with a correspondent drop in acidity. Let's say that there were ten producers in one block. Stylistically-speaking, we could theoretically begin the first harvest on August 30 with numbers around 22 Brix and 9.0 g/l acidity. The last winery could plausibly pick the same section four weeks later on September 27 at 28 Brix and 5.5 g/l acidity. This would most likely be watered back and slightly acidified. The rest of the group would fall some-where in-between, but most likely be skewed toward the earlier pick... we are seeing a general backing away from excessively ripe Pinot Noir."[92]

The largest single purchaser of grapes from Bien Nacido is Au Bon Cli-mat, which started the trend to local wine production. As Jim Clendenen of ABC (as Au Bon Climat is known to everyone in the trade) recalls, "The Millers started Bien Nacido to sell grapes to large corporations up north, and it was to their credit that they agreed when we approached them to buy grapes in the mid eighties."[93] Jim is one of the great characters of the region, famous for the lunches he cooks at ABC for the staff and visitors. His winery was actually built by the Millers in the Bien Nacido vineyard. Success with Pinot Noir is a recent phenomenon, he feels. "Pinot Noir was planted here in 1972 but I didn't think it was a great place for Pinot Noir until the late eight-ies. The problem was that the grapes were badly farmed and most were sent off to the north. Farming and planting density had to change. Mediocre stuff held back the reputation for a while. Almost everything has been replanted now."

The philosophy at ABC is that top cuvées come from selection rather than single vineyard sites, although there are some fine single vineyard wines (⧉ page 277). Most of the wines come from Santa Maria Valley, with the top selections either from estate-owned vineyards or from vineyards that are farmed specifically for ABC. After Jim said over lunch that he had originally been considering a purchase in Burgundy, but decided that instead of buying one acre in Volnay he could buy a hundred acres here, I asked whether his aim was to emulate Burgundy? "Well, no. We are trying to reflect Burgundy in [the conditions of] California. I'm trying to graft the fruit we get in Cali-fornia, which is very special, onto the historical perspective we need [from Burgundy]," he said. The ABC style is unusually elegant for the region, per-

Vineyards in Santa Rita Hills lie on the lower slopes of the mountains.

haps related to the fact that ABC picks early at lower Brix. "The self delusion says people pick on flavor—but where did you learn to judge flavor? The American palate has developed on Kool-Aid and Jell-O, not on fruit."[94]

Santa Ynez Valley took to wine production more recently. Of its 900 planted ha, almost 700 ha are in the Santa Rita Hills AVA (formally now changed for legal reasons to Sta. Rita Hills), where the vineyards tend to be on the hillside slopes.[95] Because they were planted more recently, Santa Rita Hills vineyards usually have more modern trellising and more recent clones. The vineyards originated in much the same way as in Santa Maria, by converting ranches, but somewhat later. Sea Smoke is a case in point. Originally this was a horse ranch, part of which was sold off to make the Sea Smoke vineyard. Manager Victor Gallegos says that, "If you were someone who was a Burgundy freak—which is the point of reference—Santa Rita Hills looks like a terribly bad idea. It is at the latitude of Tunisia and is a semi desert with less than ten inches of rainfall per year. The big mitigating factor is right out there—basically the ocean channels fog through two corridors into the valley from Point Conception."[96] Heavier clay soils in the southern corridor give slightly weightier wines, he feels. The problem with Santa Rita Hills, he says, is that yields are so low it's difficult to manage in a corporate environment. This, of course, may be part of the quality. The wines at Sea Smoke are definitely on the richer side. They traditionally have had alcohol in the high 14 percents but have now scaled back to 14.5%, which they think is the sweet spot. "Our move towards lower alcohol needs to be tempered by what I call the yummy factor. We are living in a culture in which people have been brought up on sweet foods and expect a certain viscosity and sweetness in the mouthfeel" (🍷 page 279).

I asked a group of small producers who make wines from both valleys whether they thought each had its own character, and if so, whether that was intrinsic to the terroir or reflected the different conditions of planting. "Santa Maria suffers from being seen as second grade because of mistakes when the vineyards were planted, so it is under appreciated relative to Santa Rita," said Paul Lato.[97] But they were in complete agreement that each region is distinct, although they had some difficulty in reaching consensus on just how to describe its character. Because Santa Maria Valley is wider and more open, the wind whips through; Santa Rita Valley has a series of switchback hills that offer more protection. The closest we could get to a consensus was that wines from Santa Rita tend to have more density and overt structure, more black fruits as opposed to red. But they felt that it's the name of the producer that drives the market, and individual regions or vineyards don't have the same allure as Burgundy (albeit with some exceptions).

Santa Rita grapes are more expensive than Santa Maria's. This is a follow-on from the extraordinary effect the movie Sideways had on the region.

Although the lead character is an unsympathetic wine boor—you might think he would be more likely to make viewers become teetotal rather than convert to his preferred tipple of Pinot Noir—there was an immediate general increase in sales of Pinot Noir after the movie came out. The effect on the Santa Barbara region was not entirely healthy: grape prices shot up, especially in Santa Rita Hills, as producers from the north fought to get a supply of Pinot Noir grapes, putting pressure on the smaller producers in the region.

There is a wide variety of Pinot Noir styles in California, but I see some commonalities as well. The entire range is shifted into higher alcohol and extraction. Whereas red Burgundy in recent years has mostly been at 13-13.5% alcohol, with outliers at 12.5% in cool years and at 14% in the ripe year of 2009, the range in California is about a percent higher; most Pinot Noirs are 14-14.5%, but you can find exceptions down at 13.5% or up to 15.5%. Extraction levels run more or less in parallel. Together with the higher extraction often goes a sense of slightly uplifted aromatics, which is my marker for the more extracted style of Californian Pinot (albeit far from an infallible one). In terms of regional differences, the fruits are more opulent in the northern regions, most especially in Russian River. But there are hold-out producers in more restrained styles in every region.

The French have won one battle. The extent to which their view of terroir has been adopted on the West Coast is indicated by the emphasis on single vineyard designations for the top wines in both Oregon and California, and by the frequent references winemakers make to "appellations"—you hardly ever hear AVAs referred to as such, but winemakers will frequently refer to their appellation or sub-appellation wines. Part of the emphasis on individual vineyards comes from the large scale and heterogeneity of the AVAs. As winemaker Ken Foster of Mahoney Vineyards says, "The appellations are not relevant. What is relevant is the exact site. We can get quite different results from two adjacent blocks in the same vineyard, so to look for common features in an appellation is ridiculous."[98]

A consequence of the increased focus on single vineyard wines is the difficulty of finding the top Pinot Noirs of the West Coast. If you took the very best wines of Burgundy available in the marketplace and compared them with the top wines available at retail from Willamette Valley or Russian River Valley, Burgundy would blow away Oregon or California. There would be no competition, because you would be comparing the top appellations such as Romanée Conti or Chambertin with generic AVAs. The top single vineyard wines of Oregon or California are rarely available at the retail level. Often they are produced in small amounts comparable to a Burgundian producer's premier or grand crus. A system of managed scarcity usually sells these top wines exclusively through a mailing list; in some cases there is a waiting list of years to get on the list. While this is a terrific commercial strategy for the winery, insofar as the top wines sell out rapidly and effortlessly at undiscounted prices, the near universality of the model means that unless you are in the magic circle of aficionados, you may never experience the range of single vineyard vines. There is no halo effect to set the generic wines in context. And if you can only taste the generic appellation wines because the best wines are never available in restaurants or wine stores, how can you appreciate their potential quality or sense the nuances of expression between vineyards. Does this hold back recognition of the full potential of the regions?

Producers and Tastings in Willamette Valley

Vintage is more important in Willamette than in many New World regions. The cold summer of 2010 led to a nail biting autumn as producers waited to see whether dry, warm weather would last long enough to get to harvest (it did, although the harvest was one of the latest on record). The previous year, 2009 showed extreme alternations of temperature from week to week, with warmth at the end of the summer but then a cool period extending through the harvest in the autumn. Dry warm conditions led to a generally opulent vintage in 2008, with the wines drinking well immediately. The 2007 was distinctly in the style of restrained cool climate, while the problem in 2006 was struggling with a hot vintage.

Adelsheim Vineyard

David Adelsheim is regarded as one of the movers and shakers who created the Oregon wine industry. He arrived in 1971, but to some extent thinks of himself as a second generation winemaker, because David Lett had already led the way at Eyrie. He concentrated on three varieties, with the main focus on finding south-facing slopes of Jory soil for Pinot Noir. His handsome winery was constructed in 1993 in Newberg, but he extols the virtues of Chehalem Mountains and makes wine from several vineyards there. Total vineyard area is around 75 ha. Under the Willamette Valley label, Adelsheim produces Pinot Noir, Chardonnay, and Pinot Gris. At the top of the Pinot Noirs are several wines from individual vineyards in Chehalem Mountains, and the Elizabeth's Reserve, presently used to describe a selection of the best barrels. His stylistic aim is that the wines should emphasize elegance and complexity, not extraction. His wines age well. "Many Pinots are approachable quite soon, which would make many think they would fall off a cliff in five years, but they don't," he says. Wines were tasted at Adelsheim in September 2010.

Bryan Creek, Chehalem Mountains, 2008
This vineyard of 8 hectares on basalt soil at over 200 m elevation in the Great Landslide area was planted in 1988-1989 on its own roots. It was Adelsheim's first single vineyard bottling. The current vintage shows a youthful nose with faint aromatics of raspberries and strawberries, and some spices of cinnamon and cloves. Elegant red fruits follow on the palate with continuing touches of spice, supported by balanced acidity and refined tannins; overall impression is the purity of line, a good result in a vintage where some succumbed to over-opulence. *** Drink 2012-2018.

Quarter Mile Lane, Chehalem Mountains, 2008
This vineyard was planted in 1974 on its own roots. It has always been part of the Elizabeth's Reserve, but only more recently became available as a single vineyard bottling. Restrained red fruit nose with faintly herbal overtones. Ripe black cherry fruits on the palate, refined but drying tannins on the finish, elegant with clean, pure lines. *** Drink 2011-2020.

Ridgecrest, Chehalem Mountains, 2008
This is one of the warmest sites in Chehalem Mountains, reflected in the generosity of the wine. Faintly spicy, faintly nutty on the nose. Soft opulent fruits on the palate, black cherries with hints of plums, supported by ripe, sturdy tannins. A nice reflection of vintage and vineyard. *** Drink 2011-2017.

Bryan Creek, Chehalem Mountains, 2007
Already some savory notes are joining the red fruits on the nose. A leaner style than the 2008, reflecting the cool conditions of 2007, with some nutty notes and cereal overtones adding to the red fruit palate, but somehow not quite coming to life yet on the finish. ** Drink 2011-2017.

Bryan Creek, Chehalem Mountains, 1999
Aging beautifully in a Burgundian style. Restrained nose, faintly aromatic but not showing much obvious development. Ripe sweet fruits slowly evolve in the glass, slightly earthy and nutty rather than tertiary, lovely balance with acidity and resolving tannins. Soft, earthy strawberries show retronasally, reminiscent of Beaune. There's a faint touch of bitterness showing on the aftertaste, so probably time to drink in the next few years. **** Drink up.

Elizabeth's Reserve, Yamhill County, 1993
The vines for this cuvée come mostly from the Quarter Mile Vineyard. This older vintage is just at the turning point from fruity to savory, with some spice notes and hints of gunflint. Delicious palate just balanced between the original red fruits and developing tertiary flavors, supported by balanced acidity with soft, supple tannins. It's always a delight to catch Pinot Noir at this stage; reaching this point after 17 years is quite impressive, somewhat reminiscent of Burgundy, Côte de Beaune rather than Côte de Nuits. Drink in next few years. **** Drink soon.

Elizabeth's Reserve, Yamhill County, 1988
Lovely savory, tertiary nose. Delicious balance on palate, the savory notes showing here as just a faint tinge to the mature red fruit flavors, and then coming back more intensely on the finish. At a beautiful point of balance, with good supporting acidity and resolved tannins, but good for some years yet. Who says Oregon Pinot doesn't age! **** Drink now-2015.

Archery Summit

Archery Summit was founded in 1992 by Gary Andrus, who became famous for the story that he planted his Renegade Ridge vineyard with grapevine cuttings filched from Romanée Conti. Whether or not this is true (the winery coyly will not comment), the emphasis is definitely on Burgundian clones, with the vineyards now mostly planted with a variety of Dijon clones. There are about 50 ha of vineyards, all on volcanic Jory soils, including the Archery Summit Estate immediately around the vineyard, and other vineyards in the Dundee Hills. Wine is made only from grapes grown in their own vineyards. Archery Summit was known for strong use of new oak, but has backed off somewhat under winemaker Anna Matzinger, with the single vineyard wines having 50-60% new oak today. The general style here is relatively opulent (a bit leaner for Renegade Ridge), with intense fruit on the palate, ripe tannins integrating with the fruits, but not overwhelming. Black cherry fruits tend to be the dominant feature, overlaid by herbs and spices that vary with the vineyard. Wines were tasted at Archery Summit in September 2010.

Archery Summit Estate, Dundee Hills, 2008
Archery Summit's top bottling comes from the home vineyard immediately around the winery. Black cherry fruits on the nose mingle with plums and blueberries, and a faint touch of alcohol. The palate follows the nose, with spicy black cherry and plum fruits, smooth ripe tannins, the fruits more direct and making a richer impression than the 2007. Smoothness is the hallmark here, with a slightly chocolate impression on the long finish. **** Drink 2012-2020.

Archery Summit Estate, Dundee Hills, 2007
This is more intense on the nose than any of the other individual vineyard bottlings from this vintage, showing red and black cherries with a mineral edge. The dense palate shows brooding, spicy black cherry fruits. Some nutty, chocolaty, tannins mark the long finish. Already all the components are integrating beautifully. **** Drink 2013-2023.

Willamette Valley Premier Cuvée, 2007
This is a blend of fruits from all of Archery Summit's vineyards, amounting to 50-60% of production, and is the only wine in general distribution. It shows a restrained nose with faintly piquant red cherry fruits. Smooth red cherry fruits on the palate, a little glyceriny on the finish, supported by ripe tannins, quite supple, but still needing a couple of years. ** Drink 2012-2019.

Renegade Ridge, Dundee Hills, 2007
The wine reflects the basalt soils of the vineyard. There is a herbal spicy nose with faint notes of cereal. Soft red and black cherry fruits have a taut quality on the palate; the tendency to leanness gives precision to the black cherry fruits on the finish, which shows a little heat. *** Drink 2012-2019.

Looney Vineyard, Ribbon Ridge, 2007
Sedimentary soils here lend more roundness to the wine, which comes from an 8 ha leased vineyard (named for its owner). The herbal and spicy nose has more obvious red fruits on the nose than the Renegade Ridge from Dundee Hills. Soft red and black cherries with hints of plums on the palate, but a bit less well defined, with slightly rustic tannins. In short, more power, less elegance: a typical comparison between sedimentary and volcanic soils. ** Drink 2012-2019.

Arcus, Dundee Hills, 2007
Mineral red strawberry fruit nose with herbal and spicy overtones, a little tarry. Nicely rounded fruits show more as black than red cherries with some plums. Ripe, opulent tannins are quite silky, with a long refreshing finish showing good acidity. **** Drink 2012-2019.

Red Hills, Dundee Hills, 2007
Slightly tarry red fruit nose with strawberry and cherry fruits showing some mineral notes; some alcohol is evident. This is very similar to Arcus (the vineyards are close), but perhaps a little denser on the palate, with just an extra touch of glycerin on the long finish of spicy black cherry fruits. **** Drink 2012-2020.

Bethel Heights Vineyard

Bethel Heights was one of the first vineyards in Eola Hills, and dates from 1977, when the first vines were planted on their own roots. Some of them still remain, but phylloxera is forcing replanting. Three quarters of the 28 ha are Pinot Noir. Originally the grapes were sold to other producers, but production of wine started in 1984. Winemaker Ben Casteel says that the stylistic goal is transparency, aiming for food-friendly wines at modest alcohol (12.8-13.3%). The main source of Pinot Noir is the vineyard immediately around the winery. Nearby they have the Justice Vineyard, most of which is used for their own production, but some of which is sold to other producers. Single vineyard wines come from the Justice Vineyard and blocks in the home vineyard, but their top wine is the blended Casteel Reserve. Bethel Heights' wines are among the most delicate and elegant of the valley. Wines were tasted at Bethel Heights in September 2010.

Bethel Heights Estate, Eola-Amity Hills, 2008
The estate wine is a blend from all Bethel Height's' blocks. Restrained faintly red fruit nose. Bright red cherry fruits on the palate supported by fresh acidity, with elegant, light tannins on the finish. Quite Beaune-like. ** Drink now-2015.

Justice Vineyard, Eola-Amity Hills, 2008
There are some hints of black fruits and blueberries as well as red fruits on the nose. The richness of the palate reflects the vintage, with black as well as red cherries, supported by refined tannins and a slightly glyceriny touch to the finish. ** Drink 2012-2017.

Southeast Block, Eola-Amity Hills, 2007
This block was planted with the Pommard clone on its own roots in 1977. The wine spends 12 months in barriques using half new oak. A restrained nose shows only some faint strawberry fruits. Very elegant red cherry fruits on the palate, supported by light tannins with a slight chocolate aftertaste. Thirty per cent whole clusters were used in this vintage. ** Drink 2010-2016.

Casteel Reserve, Eola-Amity Hills, 2007
This comes 70% from the south block and 30% from the Justice vineyard. Restrained slightly tarry nose of light red cherry fruits. Quite sweet ripe fruits with a light, elegant touch on the palate, supported by nice acidity, with some light tannins on a slightly chocolaty finish. ** Drink 2010-2016.

Bethel Heights Estate, Willamette Valley, 1989
Medium garnet color. Characteristically restrained on the nose, with tertiary aromas emerging in the glass, but still showing evidence of ripe fruits, which come through clearly on the palate. There's a lovely balance with tertiary overtones emerging nicely on the finish. The developing layers of flavor are a powerful demonstration of the ability of Oregon Pinots to age. **** Drink now-2015.

Brick House Vineyards

Brick House was founded in 1990 when Doug Tunnell bought 16 ha of hazelnut orchards on Ribbon Ridge. The vineyards are biodynamic. All the soils fall into the Willakenzie series but otherwise are quite heterogeneous (one small area has some volcanic basalt). Doug makes wine only from his own estate, and is focused on clonal selections. The original planting was the Pommard clone, on its own roots, which succumbed to phylloxera and had to be replanted in 2010. This has been used for the Cuvée Tonnelier. Dijon clones were planted in 1994, and since 1998 have been used to produce the Les Dijonnais bottling. Some years there is a separate bottling from Boulder Block. But his top wine is the Evelyn's cuvée, made in tiny quantities from a barrel selection. The style has lightened significantly in recent years. "I used to be more into oak and bigger wines," Doug says. Les Dijonnais usually has a little more presence than Cuvée de Tonnelier, and is the best representation of the house style. Wines were tasted at Brick House in September 2010.

Evelyn's, Ribbon Ridge, 2008
This is a barrel selection from plantings around the winery, a mixture of Pommard and Dijon clones. Only eight barrels were made, two of them were new, so this has 25% new oak. The current vintage shows elegant red fruits of cherries and strawberries with some spice and faintly herbal notes on the nose. Good acidity supports light bright red fruits on the palate, more strawberries than cherries, with spice notes following. Refined tannins are tea-like and a little chocolaty on the finish. *** Drink 2012-2022.

Les Dijonnais, Ribbon Ridge, 2008
Light nose of red and black fruits, slightly austere, faint touch of spicy cloves. Sweet ripe fruits of red cherries and strawberries on the palate, nice clean lines with a little spice and refined tannins on the finish. ** Drink 2011-2017.

Les Dijonnais, Ribbon Ridge, 2005
Slightly spicy red fruit nose shows cherries more than strawberries. Lovely spicy red cherry fruits on the palate, with tea-like tannins elegantly supporting the finish. This is now in perfect balance before it turns to more savory and tertiary aromas and flavors. Very fine and elegant. **** Drink now-2017.

Evelyn's, Willamette Valley, 2002
Restrained nose with some faintly spicy red fruits. Sweet ripe fruits on the palate, more strawberries than cherries, faintly mineral, with nice supporting acidity. Lovely balance with refined tannins on the finish, although a little closed at the moment. ** Drink now-2016.

Cuvée de Tonnelier, Willamette Valley, 2001
First savory notes just beginning to develop on the nose with the red fruits diminishing. Sweet ripe fruits of earthy strawberries on the palate, just a touch of savory flavors creeping in, but intensifying a little in the glass. There's a touch of gunflint on the finish. *** Drink now-2017.

Les Dijonnais, Willamette Valley, 1999
Earthy, slightly piquant red fruit nose with some high toned aromatics. Earthy fruits with mineral overtones on the palate, just a hint of tertiary development, a touch of dryness to the smooth fruits on the palate. A little bitterness on the finish is slowly overtaking the fruits. ** Drink now-2016.

Cuvée de Tonnelier, Willamette Valley, 1998
Still quite a dark ruby color; seems less developed than the 2001. Still showing black cherry fruits on the nose with some tea-like aromas. Palate follows the nose, with ripe sweet black cherry fruit supported by some firm, ripe tannins. The wine has softened with age but has not really developed as much as you would expect. ** Drink now-2016.

Cuvée de Tonnelier, Willamette Valley, 1997
Medium garnet color with broadening rim. Suspicions of spice and savory herbs on the nose. Fruits lightening up with nice tertiary notes and touches of sous bois, showing more on the palate than the nose. This was a tight year, when rain forced early picking, but the wine is holding up well, although it will probably not develop any further. ** Drink now-2013.

Chehalem

Harry Peterson-Nedry started Chehalem in 1990 to market wines made from his Ridge-crest Estate on Ribbon Ridge, which he first planted in 1980 on the site of an old walnut orchard destroyed in the Columbus Day storm. He is surprisingly reserved about the importance of the winemaker, and in a discussion with David Adelsheim agreed that the vintage and the site have more importance (although they could not agree on which was more important). Chehalem presently produces wines that express the character of three vineyards. Two are on Willakenzie soils in Chehalem Mountains: the original Ridgecrest, since extended, at elevations of 150-200 m; and Corral Creek at a lower elevation of 70-150 m. The youngest is the Stoller vineyard on the red Jory soil of Dundee Hills. Harry says that, "The characteristics of Willamette are bright forward fruits and retained acidity, resulting from the protected environment between the two mountain ranges." Wines were tasted in September 2010.

Reserve, Willamette Valley, 2009
Restrained nose of red fruits with some hints of aromatic black fruits. Taut, elegant black cherry fruits on the palate with blueberry overtones, quite opulent soft fruit impression overall. *** Drink 2011-2020.

Ridgecrest Vineyard, Ribbon Ridge, 2009
This comes from the same fruit as the Reserve, but shows more purity. Slightly aromatic black fruits on the nose. More elegant, feminine fruits on the palate, more obvious tannic structure, with purity of fruits shining through. *** Drink 2012-2020.

Ridgecrest Vineyard, Ribbon Ridge, 2008
Red cherry fruit nose leading to nicely balanced palate of sweet ripe red fruits balanced by acidity and ripe tannins. Soft, ripe finish with opulent tannins, still showing a little youthful dryness on the finish. *** Drink 2012-2020.

Stoller Vineyard, Dundee Hills, 2008
Faintly spicy red cherry fruit nose. Ripe red fruits on the palate with ripe tannins showing some dryness on the finish. Overall impression is just a little tighter than the Corral Creek, fruits not quite as obviously sweet, acidity just a touch more obvious, and tannins a fraction drier, but this may have the advantage of greater longevity in the long run. *** Drink 2012-2020.

Corral Creek, Chehalem Mountains, 2008
Slightly spicy red cherry fruit nose. Sweet, ripe red fruits are quite opulent on the palate. Nice balance between fruits and acidity, quite soft tannins on the finish in the style of the vintage. *** Drink 2011-2020.

Ridgecrest Vineyard, Ribbon Ridge, 2007
Restrained nose with faint red fruits. Lean on the palate, reflecting the vintage, with quite bright red cherry fruits supported by balanced acidity. Elegant and refined. ** Drink 2012-2018.

Stoller Vineyard, Dundee Hills, 2007
Slightly austere red fruit nose with hints of spices. Sweet ripe red fruits, strawberries more than cherries. Sturdy ripe tannins. Style intermediate between the leaner Ridgecrest and the fuller Corral Creek. ** Drink 2012-2018.

Corral Creek, Chehalem Mountains, 2007
Piercing nose of savory aromas: lots of character here. Ripe red fruits on the palate, slightly nutty and mineral, herbal spicy undertones. Very nice overall balance, fruits supported by balanced acidity, with slightly rustic tannins on an earthy finish. *** Drink 2012-2018.

3 Vineyard, Willamette Valley, 2007
Tea-like aromas on the nose. Very earthy and tea-like on the palate, with hints of strawberries, and just a faint dry touch on the finish. Evidently a cool climate production (indeed reflecting the vintage). * Drink now-2015.

Willamette Valley Reserve, 2006
Dark hue for Chehalem, a medium ruby to purple color in appearance. Slightly tarry nose with notes of tea. Quite rich, deep fruits on the palate, balanced acidity, good depth, a slightly tannic bite to the finish. *** Drink now-2017.

Willamette Valley Reserve, 2002
Still a deep ruby-garnet color. Some savory tertiary notes beginning to show on the nose. Direct black and cherry fruits are more evident on the palate than the nose, tannins now are nicely integrating. Savory notes intermingle with the fruit notes to give a lovely balance. *** Drink now-2016.

Ribbon Ridge Reserve, 1994
Medium deep garnet color. Tertiary aromas show on the nose with faint notes of gunflint. Just at the cusp with the ripe fruits turning from overtly fruity to savory, with nutty overtones. The fruits are drying out just a little, giving a note of austerity, but still very good. *** Drink now-2013.

Cristom Vineyards

Cristom has a beautiful estate surrounded by vineyards that rise up from 70 m to almost 300 m. Altogether there are 55 hectares, with about half planted, almost all Pinot Noir. Most of the vineyards are around the winery, but some lots are traded with other wineries to improve the complexity of blends. They believe in a mix of clones for complexity, and the vineyards include Pommard, Wädenswil and the Dijon clones, mostly planted in tight spacings. The single vineyard wines are named for six family matriarchs, and include Marjorie, Eileen, and Louise. There is also a blended wine and a reserve selection, which include purchased grapes. Manager John d'Anna believes firmly that the hand of the winemaker is the definitive factor in wine styles. "The trio of factors determining style is the hand, the land, and vintage," he says. The policy here is to use whole clusters (which often entails the need to acidify at the start of fermentation to counter the spike of potassium coming from the stems). This can give a slight austerity in some of the wines. Wines were tasted at Cristom in September 2010.

Mount Jefferson Cuvée, Willamette Valley, 2008
This wine used 30% whole clusters and was matured in barriques for one year, with 30% new oak. Red and black fruits on the nose are accompanied by faintly nutty overtones. The palate follows the nose, quite elegant, with some warm red fruit notes and a refined finish. ** Drink 2011-2015.

Eileen Vineyard, Eola-Amity Hills, 2007
Earthy, nutty, strawberries on the nose, becoming more herbal in the glass. Solid, ripe fruits on the palate, dense and almost glyceriny on the finish. Fruits are quite forward but a little monotonic. Ripe tannins show a youthful bitterness. The high alcohol is associated with a certain lack of elegance. ** Drink 2012-2018.

Sommers Reserve, Willamette Valley, 2007
This wine comes from the same source as the Mount Jefferson Cuvée, but represents a selection. It includes a higher proportion of whole clusters, uses more new oak at 50-60%, and spends longer in barriques (18 months). The nose is quite closed. Earthy strawberries show on the palate, with the characteristic leanness of the vintage, but somehow with a certain flatness to the flavor profile. * Drink 2012-2016.

Marjorie Vineyard, Eola-Amity Hills, 2007
This is Cristom's oldest vineyard. A slightly austere nose with some spices and notes of cereal, but then opening up into nice light, ripe fruits on the palate, which shows notes of earthy strawberries; some light tannins leave a slight bitterness on the finish. ** Drink 2012-2018.

Willamette Valley Reserve, 1999
This wine has since become the Sommers Reserve. Tertiary notes mingle on the nose with red fruits and a touch of spice. Nice balance on the palate between red fruits and savory flavors,

but the fruits are lightening up quite a bit—a reflection of the vintage, which was long and cold, in fact the wine came around only recently—and it's probably going to dry out a bit in the next year or so, although it's very nice now. ** Drink up.

Dobbes Family Estate

Joe Dobbes is one of the holdouts who believes that stylistically you get the most complexity by blending. He produces about one third of his own fruit and buys from 25-30 different vineyards under individual contracts. In addition to his own wines, he makes custom wine for others. After his entry level cuvée, Grand Assemblage, he has three cuvées that are described as "elegant," "opulent," and "ageworthy," with a range of prices. Although he started with blends, he reckoned that in time he would find single vineyards that would stand alone. So in addition to the cuvées, he now has four single vineyard bottlings, all at the same price just above the top cuvée, although not every vineyard gives a standalone wine every year. The cuvées are produced in amounts of 350-1000 cases, and the single vineyards in amounts of 75-300 cases. He says there is now a mindset that single vineyards are best, following the Burgundian model. At first he was skeptical about the legitimacy of the sub AVAs, but slowly became convinced there was merit to the description of Dundee Hills as a separate AVA. He sees McMinn-ville and Eola-Amity Hills as having more black fruit and tannin. But the distinctions are not so clear cut here as in Burgundy, he believes. Wines were tasted at Joe Dobbes in September 2010.

Grand Assemblage, Willamette Valley, 2008
Warm blueberry fruits on the nose. More like black cherries on the palate, supported by bal-anced acidity. Youthful, needs some time; a little monotonic at the moment. Slightly burning on the finish. ** Drink 2013-2018.

Patricia's, Willamette Valley, 2007
This is Dobbes's "opulent" cuvée, mostly coming from the Eola Hills. Some red fruits on the nose as well as black. Smooth quite silky fruits on the palate, good acidity, well rounded with elegant tannins. ** Drink 2011-2016.

Quailhurst Vineyard, Chehalem Mountains, 2007
Slightly minty nose hiding the red fruits. Slightly mineral red cherry fruits on the palate, layers of flavor slowly developing. *** Drink 2012-2016.

Griffin Vineyard, Willamette Valley, 2006
Taut black fruit nose. Sweet ripe black cherry fruits on the palate. Some tight tannins and a little alcoholic burn on the finish. Still too young. ** Drink 2012-2018.

Domaine Drouhin Oregon

Domaine Drouhin could scarcely be a greater contrast with Drouhin's ancient cramped cellars in Beaune. It owes its origins to the enthusiasm of Véronique Drouhin, who worked in Willamette in 1986, and persuaded her father, Robert, to buy the property in 1987. Together with her brother Philippe, she now makes the wines in both Beaune and Willamette. The winery is mostly underground, with several stories of gravity-fed opera-tions. It is surrounded by a sizeable estate with 30 ha of Pinot Noir and 5 ha of Chardonnay planted out of 100 ha. The first plantings in 1987 were of Pommard clone on its own roots. After 1990, Dijon clones were planted on rootstocks—Drouhin were among the first to plant on rootstocks. The first couple of vintages were made from purchased fruit, but estate-grown grapes were used as soon as the vines were ready. Usually there is complete destemming followed by fermentation by natural yeast. (The wine is made in much the same way in Beaune and in Oregon, the only significant differences being that picking needs to be (relatively) a little later in Oregon (and is therefore associated with an extra half per cent of alcohol), and some whole clusters are used in Beaune.) The major part of production is the Willamette Valley bottling, but since 1992 (when the vines at DDO, planted in 1988, came on line) there has also been the Cuvée Laurène, based on a barrel selection. In 1999 they introduced an even more exclusive selection, called Cuvée Louise. You might compare the difference between Cuvée Laurène and the estate bottling to a premier cru versus the village AOC in Burgundy. A vertical of Cuvée Laurène from the present back to the first vintage made the point forcefully that these wines have aging capacity. Wines were tasted at DDO in September 2010 or Maison Drouhin in November 2010.

Willamette Valley & Cuvée Laurène

Willamette Valley, 2008
Some whole clusters were included in this vintage to tame the opulence of the fruits, and this succeeded in maintaining the more restrained style of the house. The wine is presently a medium ruby garnet with some rosy hues. The strawberry fruit nose shows some minerality. Fruits are more rounded and softer than the 2007 vintage, with red cherries and strawberries supported by light, ripe tannins, but still quite restrained on the finish. ** Drink 2011-2017.

Willamette Valley, 2007
Medium density color more garnet than ruby. Fresh red fruit nose. Nice lean fruits on the palate, reflecting the vintage, perhaps just a touch angular, with slightly aromatic overtones, and light tannins. A little heat shows on the finish. * Drink 2012-2018.

Cuvée Laurène, Dundee Hills, 2007
Slightly tarry nose of red cherries and strawberries. Elegant and refined on the palate, slightly lean style (characteristic of the vintage) but richer than the estate bottling. Generally an elegant impression. *** Drink 2010-2016.

Cuvée Laurène, Dundee Hills, 2006
Light nose shows mineral strawberry fruits, becoming earthy in the glass. More opulence and depth to the palate than the estate bottling, with rich, ripe red fruits, more strawberries than cherries, characteristic earthiness of Pinot Noir, a nice finish with ripe sturdy tannins. Generally a mineral impression, would benefit from another year or so to assimilate. *** Drink 2011-2017.

Willamette Valley, 2002
Medium garnet color. Overt fruits are giving way to savory, tertiary aromas with some notes of sous bois. Soft ripe fruits show on the palate, still rich and red, with tertiary notes only just appearing retronasally. Dryness on the finish shows that tannins are still there, but nicely integrated into the wine. This is a generous wine with lots to offer, caught just at the delicious turning point from fruity to savory. *** Drink now-2016.

Willamette Valley, 1999
Still a medium to deep garnet color. Tertiary aromas show immediately on the nose with a touch of anise. Ripe fruits of red cherries and strawberries show on the palate, with some sturdy tannins still drying the finish. Style is characteristically lean, the fruits are perhaps lightening a little now, but this is still vibrant with time to go. *** Drink now-2016.

Cuvée Laurène 1998
Dark color for age, still quite ruby in hue. More of a black fruit nose with some pungent savory notes showing the start of development. Developing black fruit is vibrant on the palate, becoming slightly more aromatic in the glass with a touch of liquorice, undertones approaching sous bois, almost at the turning point. *** Drink now-2015.

Cuvée Laurène 1993
This was a cool vintage with a late harvest. Still quite a deep garnet color. Mineral, savory nose, with lovely notes of sous bois. Developed red fruits on the palate with some smoke, quite deep and still vibrant. Minerality persists nicely on the finish and this seems set for the next decade. Comparison with the 1992 suggests good aging capacity (actually very comparable to the Burgundies of 1993). ***(*) Drink now-2020.

Cuvée Laurène 1992
This was the first vintage of Laurène, from a warm year with an early harvest in August. It shows a medium garnet color. The developed nose shows some perfume of violets followed by

notes of sous bois, which carry over to the palate. There's a faint raisiny hint. Softer than the 1993, less acidity and minerality, with the warmth of the vintage showing, and there seems to be more like five than one year's difference between the wines. *** Drink now-2015.

Willamette Valley versus Côte d'Or Village AOCs

This tasting was held in May 2011 to compare the development of Drouhin's estate wine from Willamette with village wines from Burgundy. No attempt was made at pairwise comparisons, because individual vintages are rarely comparable, but the wines were tasted in groups corresponding to half decades. Differences were more marked in younger than in older wines, but the similarities were more evident than the differences when comparing a wine from a warm Burgundy vintage with a cool vintage within two or three years from Willamette. Difference in alcohol was consistently stated at 1% on the label, typically 13% for Burgundy and 14% for Willamette in current wines, and partly accounts for the richer mouthfeel of the Oregon wines, and their sweeter finish. (Until the mid nineties, Willamette was around 13%, so the difference was less.)

Pommard, 2007
Restrained nose has some herbaceous strawberry fruit aromas turning earthy in the glass. Balance on the palate more in the style of Beaune than Pommard, with light red fruits, a sensation of mineral strawberries, and an average length finish. Rather tight with a medicinal touch on the palate, in the style of the vintage. * Drink now-2014.

Willamette Valley, 2007
Restrained nose of earthy, slightly herbaceous strawberry fruits. Sweet, ripe, quite full on the palate, smooth finish with those earthy strawberries coming back and a touch of herbaceous-ness cutting the finish. ** Drink now-2015.

Pommard, 2006
Slightly earthy strawberry fruit nose. Slightly thin impression on the palate, more an impression of Beaune than Pommard, with light, slightly acid red fruits, leading into a dry finish of average length. * Drink now-2014.

Willamette Valley, 2006
A sturdy red fruit nose with the strawberries overlaid by faintly herbaceous notes. Sweet ripe fruits on the palate give a slightly rustic impression, becoming a little nutty on the finish, with a slightly bitter tannic edge still just evident on the finish. ** Drink now-2015.

Pommard, 2005
Earthy strawberry fruit nose. Sweet, ripe fruits, relatively full on the palate, a slight mineral impression backed up by good acidity, quite dry on the finish. The tannic structure begins to show in the glass. Well structured, relatively elegant for Pommard, still a little tight. ** Drink now-2016.

Willamette Valley, 2005
Fairly fruit forward nose with some notes of strawberries and raspberries. Sweet ripe fruits are quite forward on the palate with some buttery notes coming out on the finish. Full bodied for Oregon Pinot Noir, although cut on the finish by good acidity and a sense of earthiness, turning perhaps just a touch too nutty (and possibly limiting longevity) ** Drink now-2014.

Chambolle Musigny, 2003
Developing red fruits show on the nose with earthy red notes breaking through. Rich and full, quite resembles the Willamette wines on the palate, but there is a touch of over cooked fruits, even a hint of raisins on the finish. This is a very big wine for Chambolle, but that's the nature of the vintage. ** Drink now-2015.

Volnay, 2001
Restrained nose is very faintly spicy with a suggestion of ripe, earthy fruits. Nicely rounded fruits on the palate but good supporting acidity shows on the finish, with a touch of tannic bitterness on the finish. It's just a touch light, even allowing for being only a village wine (but then 2001 was not a distinguished vintage). * Drink now-2013.

Willamette Valley, 2001
Restrained, slightly gamey nose. May be a touch of cork here, as shown by a faint cardboard-like bitterness on the finish, with slightly suppressed fruits. Putting that aside, this is a well balanced wine with quite elegant fruits in a generally feminine style. ** Drink now-2015.

Chambolle Musigny, 1999
Bright garnet color. The nose is developing along the line of nutty and earthy strawberry fruits. Rich, ripe fruits have softened with age, there's almost an impression of the fullness you get with New World fruit, but good acidity and some tannic structure in the background. Overall the impression is just a touch rustic. ** Drink now-2014.

Chambolle Musigny, 1997
Complex nose with array of fruity and spicy aromas, just a very faint hint of savory development. Ripe but elegant on the palate, with that light touch of Chambolle, smooth and well integrated, light tannins on a nice finish. The palate doesn't show as much interest as the nose promises. * Drink now-2015.

Willamette Valley, 1996
Restrained nose shows some bright red fruits. A little thin at first on the palate, showing more like the Cote de Beaune than Cote de Nuits, then some sweetness of the fruits showing through, but beginning now to dry out a little. ** Drink now-2013.

Chambolle Musigny, 1996
An impression of green tea developing on the nose. Developing rich red fruits on the palate with just a touch of savory elements showing. This has now achieved a very good balance, and it is at its peak. It is unusually rich for both the vintage and the appellation. *** Drink now-2014.

Chambolle Musigny, Premier Cru, 1995
Savory notes beginning to develop on the nose. The palate is more developed than the nose, with the fruits drying out just enough to let some tannic bitterness show through, but you can see the original ripeness. What this lacks is the characteristic elegance and refinement of Chambolle; it's holding on rather than developing, which is often typical of this vintage. ** Drink now-2013.

Willamette Valley, 1994
Development shows on the nose as gunflint and mineral red fruit aromas. Elegant on the palate but an almost medicinal acidity just shows on the finish—a bit reminiscent of Burgundy 1996. This is now coming up to its peak. Should hold for three or four years yet, but the bitterness is going to take over as the fruits dry out. ** Drink now-2015.

Willamette Valley, 1993
Medicinal, herbaceous nose, some leathery impressions, just a touch of Brett. Elegant and fine behind the medicinal overlay, fruits quite ripe and still rich, it's really just on the edge with regards to the Brett obscuring the fruits. Relatively undeveloped for the vintage since there isn't much savory development. This is lovely if you like wine with leathery developed notes, but not for those who like more primary fruits. It's a love it or loathe it wine. ** Drink now-2014.

Willamette Valley, 1991
Earthy, nutty, strawberry aromas with a faintly savory impression. Rich ripe fruits with that faint touch of nuts and vanillin that marks Willamette, although now much toned down with age, as acidity begins to overtake the fruits. The risk here is of becoming a little sickly as it ages further. ** Drink now-2013.

Willamette Valley, 1990
Restrained nose with a faintly mineral impression. Full on the palate with some richness and depth, nutty, and notes of vanillin coming through. Then some herbaceous slightly medicinal notes. A slightly rustic impression from the warm tannins. This has developed well although it is unlikely to improve any further. *** Drink now–2014.

Willamette Valley, 1989
Some savory notes on the nose, a touch of gunflint, replacing the initial more nutty and earthy fruits. Sweet ripe fruits on the palate, characteristically full with those nutty, vanillin overtones. Not quite as complex as the 1990, but there is not much in it. ** Drink now–2013.

Nuits St Georges, 1988
Very restrained nose, suppressed fruits. a herbal impression develops in the glass. Nicely balanced fruits, unusually elegant for Nuits St. Georges, drying out a little now to reveal some acidity and a touch of bitterness. * Drink up.

Evesham Wood Vineyard

Evesham Wood is one of Oregon's old line vineyards, started when Russ Raney came to Portland in 1983 searching for the holy grail of Pinot. "Obviously we were in a different climate and soil, but in terms of winemaking we were trying as much as possible to emulate the Burgundian style," he told me. He tends to pick early to emphasize elegance rather than power. The estate vineyard, Le Puits Sec, is on an east-facing slope at 100-140 m elevation. The estate's top wine is a selection of the best barrels from Le Puits Sec, called Cuvée J. Other wines include a Reserve and an entry-level wine, both including purchased fruit from vineyards in the immediate vicinity as well as from Evesham's own vineyard, which is organic. Evesham Wood was sold recently to Erin Nuccio, who has been making the Haden Fig wines, but Russ Raney continues to consult and no changes are planned. Wines were tasted at Evesham in September 2010.

Willamette Valley, 2009
This entry level wine is blended from three sites. It shows a light strawberry nose, following on to soft red fruits on the palate, more strawberries than red cherries, with light soft tannins in the finish, which is just a touch short. * Drink 2011-2014.

Illahe Vineyard, Willamette Valley, 2008
This vineyard is just outside the Eola Hills which is why the wine carries the Willamette Valley appellation. It was planted with Pommard vines in 2000. The wine shows spicy black and red fruits on the nose. The palate has beautifully rounded black fruits in the style of the Côte de Nuits, with a little spice, supple tannins, and balanced acidity. It's in a lovely balance already and should continue to show well. **** Drink 2012-2020.

Le Puits Sec, Eola-Amity Hills, 2008
This wine comes from the home vineyard, extending in front of the winery, and planted in 1986. Nice spicy black cherry fruits on the nose with some red fruits. Smooth and spicy on the palate, notes of cloves, opulent but refined tannins, all leading to an elegant impression. This should have good longevity. *** Drink 2011-2022.

Cuvée J, Eola-Amity Hills, 2008
Evesham Wood's top bottling represents about 250 cases out of the 800 produced from the whole Le Puits Sec vineyard. There is a restrained nose with faint black cherry fruits. The restraint carries over to the palate, which shows a good sense of structure, with black fruits a bit more intense than Le Puits Sec itself, showing as black cherries with hints of blackcurrants and plums, verging on the exotic. There are tighter tannins on the finish and the wine should age very well. **** Drink 2012-2020.

Le Puits Sec, Willamette Valley, 1998
This is an exceptional 98 that has developed really well. The nose is quite tertiary, with savory, pungent sous bois and gunflint. As often true in Oregon, it is less developed on the palate, but the flavor spectrum is generally savory. There's just a slight tertiary touch to the finish, with a nice kick of sweetness at the end. Fine tannins are still present. Vibrant and with life yet to go. *** Drink now-2016.

Eyrie Vineyards

Eyrie vineyards is run on a very personal scale. When I arrived at the winery—still in its original location in downtown McMinnville in a converted turkey processing plant—Jason Lett was running the bottling line and checking samples for dissolved carbon dioxide. I helped to run the equipment for a short break while he oiled the apparatus. Only after this was dealt with was there time for a discussion and tasting. Since Eyrie was a major driving force for Pinot Noir in Oregon, it's ironic that the majority of estate production is now Pinot Gris, but the estate Pinot Noir is a blend from all four of Eyrie's vineyards in Dundee Hills. The Reserve comes only from the original vineyard, and so is effectively a single vineyard wine, but Jason Lett says that, "The marketers have taken over terroir—the word is employed so cynically I can't use it any more." (1990 was the first year that Reserve meant the wine came exclusively from the oldest vines in the Eyrie vineyard.) The objective of letting the wine express place is accomplished by minimal use of new oak. Jason also produces wine under the Black Cap label. Eyrie wines are universally admired in the region for their longevity, with people saying that the famous 1975 is still drinking well. Wines were tasted at Eyrie in September 2010.

Dundee Hills, 2008
Red cherry fruits with some black notes and faint tea-like aromas. Nicely rounded red cherry fruits on the palate with black overtones and good supporting acidity. Some light tannins dry the finish. Quite fine. The expression of vintage is wonderfully clear when comparing Eyrie's 2007 and 2008. ** Drink 2012-2018.

Daphne, Dundee Hills, 2008
The nose shows red cherry fruits with hints of strawberries and some tea-like aromas. The palate has well rounded fruits supported by balanced acidity, with those tobacco and tea-like notes coming back retronasally. There are refined tannins on the finish. This shows a similar aroma and flavor spectrum to the estate wine, but with a little more intensity, and slightly more savory notes. *** Drink 2012-2019.

Dundee Hills, 2007
Attractive nose of tea-like aromas overlaying red fruits. Light, elegant strawberry fruits on the palate with tea and tobacco showing on the finish. You sense immediately that this will age to an elegant softness. *** Drink 2010-2016.

Dundee Hills Reserve, 2007
Mineral nose with some savory notes, a suspicion of development, following through to savory fruits on the palate. Developing nicely, if a little quickly. *** Drink 2010-2020.

Dundee Hills Reserve, 2005
Slightly savory notes on the nose together with some tea-like aromas. A suspicion of tertiary aromas comes through as the fruits seem to lighten up. ** Drink now-2014.

Willamette Valley, 1988
Savory developed nose, with underlying notes of sous bois and some slight mineral overtones. A little less obviously developed on the palate than the nose, with ripe fruits in the red spectrum still showing through with some mineral savory overtones. Still vibrant, although the fruit density is lightening a little, with some tea-like tannins on the finish *** Drink now-2015.

Ken Wright Cellars

Ken Wright is a firm believer in terroir, and one of the moving forces behind the introduction of single vineyard wines. He was also one of the first to sell his wines en primeur to a mailing list, an accident which happened when people tasting barrel samples demanded to be allowed to buy the wine. (Their names started the mailing list!) He has vineyards on both types of soil, sedimentary in Yamhill-Carton and volcanic in Eola-Amity Hills. He has ten individual vineyard bottlings. His viticulture is proactive. "Organic viticulture is a list of chemicals you cannot spray, but that does not necessarily produce compelling results," he told me. Vineyard soils are regularly inspected, microbial activity is measured, the results are used to direct the addition of manures and composts to deliver nutrition, and microorganisms are sprayed as necessary to improve the life of the soil. His individual wines are as good a way as any to see the intrinsic differences between sedimentary and volcanic terroirs. He is a believer in expression of primary fruits and says, "What attracted me to this region was the wonderful attractive mid palate, lush and sweet. Burgundy tends to higher acidity, more savory, less generous initially." Wines were tasted at Ken Wright in September 2010 or earlier in the year.

Abbott Claim Vineyard, Yamhill-Carlton, 2008
The Abbott Claim vineyard was planted in 2001 with one third each of the Pommard clone, clone 777, and clone 115, on sedimentary soils. There are earthy strawberry fruits on the nose. Rich, round, but precise, elegant red cherry fruits with hints of black fruits show on the palate with a long but tight finish on which some earthy strawberries return. *** Drink 2012-2020.

Savoya Vineyard, Yamhill-Carlton, 2008
This vineyard was planted in 1999 with a mixture of clones: Pommard, Wädenswil, 777, 115, 667, on sedimentary soils. Slightly austere strawberry fruits on the nose. A touch softer on the

palate than the Abbott Claim, showing rich, ripe fruits, with opulent tannins on a slightly glyceriny finish. *** Drink 2012-2019.

Canary Hill Vineyard, Eola-Amity Hills, 2008
Planted in 1983 with two thirds Pommard clone and one third 777 on volcanic soil. Slightly darker color compared with the wines from sedimentary soils, a dusky ruby hue. Red and black cherry fruits show on the nose. Tight precise red cherry fruits frame the palate, with more linearity and precision than the wines from the sedimentary soils of Yamhill. Quite restrained at the present and needs some time to open out. *** Drink 2013-2020.

Carter Vineyard, Eola-Amity Hills, 2008
This vineyard was planted in 1983 mostly with Dijon clones (40% of 777 and 40% of 667), and 10% each of Pommard and Wädenswil. The soils are volcanic. The nose shows the typical restraint of volcanic soils with tight red and black cherry fruits. The tautness continues on to the palate, where precise cherry fruits are supported by tight tannins on the finish. This still needs some time. ** Drink 2013-2020.

Guadalupe Vineyard, Yamhill Carlton, 2008
This vineyard represents the point at which the red Jory soils of Dundee Hills change to the Willakenzie sedimentary soils of Yamhill-Carlton. Soft fruits on the nose, well rounded on the palate, good fruit density, some earthy strawberries coming though, long finish. *** Drink now-2017.

Nysa Vineyard, Dundee Hills, 2008
Light on the nose with restrained aromas showing hints of raspberries. Light Pinot fruits, more mineral than earthy, supported by good acidity. Almost a little sharp on the finish. ** Drink now-2016.

Shea Vineyard, Yamhill-Carlton, 2008
Restrained nose, faint mineral red fruits. Acidity a bit lower than other vineyard bottlings, but still generally mineral on palate, but with some earthy notes and strawberry notes coming through to the finish. ** Drink now-2016.

Elton Vineyard, Yamhill-Carlton, 2004
Medium to deep ruby color doesn't show much sign of development. Still a little tarry on a rather restrained nose with an impression more of black fruits than red; tobacco notes emerge slowly in the glass. Rich black cherry fruits on the palate are balanced by firm tannins, with just a touch of bitterness showing through a tobacco-tinged finish. It's just a little spirity on the finish; the alcohol tastes higher than the stated 13.5%. This is developing very slowly, with the fruit spectrum still a little monotonic, intense, rich, and black, but I would have expected a little more development of flavor variety over six years. ** Drink 2012-2018.

St. Innocent Winery

St. Innocent Winery was founded in 1988 and named for Mark Vlossak's father, who was born on All Innocents Day. Mark holds that wine should be produced to go with food. " 'More is better' is completely flawed as a paradigm for making wine," he says. His wines are largely made from purchased fruits, which he thinks gives better control and quality, and only some of the estate-grown grapes are used. Growers agree on specifics of viticulture, including time of picking, so the grapes are essentially grown to Mark's specifications. There are seven single vineyard wines (changing occasionally when contracts run out with growers). There is also a blended wine called the Village Cuvée. A supple style is encouraged by complete destemming. Wines were tasted at St. Innocent in September 2010.

Villages Cuvée, Willamette Valley, 2008
This wine carries the Willamette Valley appellation because it comes from a vineyard just to the south of the Eola-Amity Hills. Light strawberry fruits on palate; not a lot of flavor variety. A little heat shows on the finish. * Drink 2011-2014.

Justice Vineyard, Eola-Amity Hills, 2008
This 9 ha vineyard was planted in 2001 at high density (5,000 vines/ha) with the 777 Dijon clone. It has a mix of sedimentary and volcanic soils. It is farmed biodynamically. 80% of the production goes to Bethel Heights, the rest to St. Innocent. The St. Innocent version has a restrained nose of red and black cherry fruits. There's an elegant red cherry fruit spectrum on the palate with a nice ripeness supported by soft, supple tannins. *** Drink 2012-2017.

Freedom Hill, Willamette Valley, 2008
Freedom Hills is on sedimentary soil, which comes out in the rounded quality of the fruits. It's a touch darker ruby than most of St. Innocent's wines. The black cherry fruit nose has a faint perfume of violets. Ripe fruits have a sweet kick to the finish of black, slightly perfumed cherries with spicy support from tight, refined tannins. **** Drink 2011-2020.

Momtazi Vineyard, McMinnville, 2008
This vineyard is at high elevation, and the block used for this wine is at 200-250 m. It has shallow rocky soil on top of a ridge. Its exposure increases diurnal variation, with warm days but rather cold nights. This has a more intense nose than other wines from St. Innocent, with aromatic black fruits. Purity of fruits shows through the palate, with precisely delineated black cherries, supported by refined tannins on the finish. The elegant, almost feminine, style could easily come from Chambolle Musigny. **** Drink 2011-2020.

Temperance Hill, Eola-Amity Hills, 2008
The thin volcanic soils of this vineyard, and its exposure to cool breezes, are reflected in the taut quality of the wine. The nose shows stern red cherry and strawberry fruits, some hints of black cherries, ripe but tight, with clean lines, elegant and very fine with a taut finish. *** Drink 2011-2010.

White Rose, Dundee Hills, 2008
This is an east-facing vineyard at high altitude, planted with 30-year old vines. Tarry nose hides the red fruits. Sweet ripe black cherry fruits dominate the palate, with notes of tobacco and some tight tannins on the finish. A touch of heat. *** Drink 2012-2017.

Justice Vineyard, Eola-Amity Hills, 2007
Restrained but fruity nose with more strawberries than cherries. Nicely ripe fruits with a restrained edge on the palate, a touch of spice. Restrained tannins and balanced acidity support the finish. ** Drink 2012-2017.

Shea Vineyard, Willamette Valley, 1998
Very restrained on the nose, just some faint black fruits, which follow through to the palate. The wine has softened but has not yet reached a stage of tertiary development. This is more extracted and powerful than recent vintages (not uncommon when you compare 1998 with the last few years). There is still a touch of bitterness on the finish. ** Drink now-2016.

Producers and Tastings in Carneros

Vintages in northern California have certainly seen strong variation in recent years. The 2010 vintage was as difficult here as it was in Oregon. It was unseasonably cool and damp until a record heat spike at the end of August was followed by another heat wave in late September. Harvest was a month later than usual. The 2009 vintage was cooler, but more even in temperature than usual, and the rains that spoiled the harvest for late-picked varieties in October were not a problem for Pinot Noir. The 2008 season was difficult throughout, from problems with frost at the start to uneven ripening at the end. A hot September divided those who picked early to preserve acidity from those who sat it out. Crops were small. 2007 was a golden year, with a prolonged growing season that allowed winemakers freedom to pick exactly when they chose. Most producers are enthusiastic about the richness of their Pinot Noirs. Overall 2006 was a leaner vintage with uneven conditions, including heat spikes during the growing season.

Donum

The Donum Estate was created in 2001. Previously it had been part of the Buena Vista Carneros vineyards, but when the Moller Racke family sold Buena Vista to Allied Domecq, 80 ha of the 400 ha of vineyards were split off to form the Donum Estate. These include 28 ha in the old Tula Vista Ranch in Carneros, 8 ha of the well known Ferguson Block a mile way, and another 4.5 ha of the Nugent Ranch in Russian River.

There are 56 ha altogether, almost all planted with Pinot Noir; there is just a little Chardonnay. The vineyards were mostly planted in the late 1980s and 1990s at a time when there was more emphasis on rootstocks than clones. Plantings include a clone obtained from Roederer Estate in Anderson Valley, but it seems to be distinct from the clones that Roederer uses for sparkling wine production, as it has small berries with thick skins that produce dark wines. This is now known as the Donum clone. Some vineyards were grafted over to Dijon clones in 2001 and 2004. The headquarters for vineyard operations are on the Carneros ranch, but wine is made at a custom crush facility in Russian River. There are two labels: Donum Estate itself and also Robert Stemmler, which mostly represent different vineyard blocks, but with some barrel selection. When Donum started, they made only one wine, but then decided to move to single vineyard designations. Presently there are 6 different Pinots under the Donum label and 3 under Stemmler, with a total production around 8,000 cases. "I have been thinking about stylistic aims because we get blame because the wines are so intense. They are vineyard-driven more than by winemaking techniques. I do like wines with concentration, but I do not want to lose delicacy," says Anne Moller Racke. Wines were tasted at Donum in January 2011.

Los Carneros, 2008 (Robert Stemmler Winery)
Restrained nose. Slightly spicy red fruit palate supported by balanced acidity, tannins still showing on the finish, not as generous as some vintages. ** Drink 2013-2021.

Los Carneros, 2008
There are two lots of the Donum 2008, one unfiltered, and one which went through a light crossflow filtration just before bottling. Color and the restrained red fruit nose with faint hints of spices are the same in both.
  The unfiltered wine offers red and black cherry fruits, generous on the finish with a faintly nutty, spicy touch, with refined tannins but a slightly gritty underlying structure.
  On the palate of the filtered wine, the fruits seem a little finer, and the tannins are a little more refined, giving an impression of greater precision to the elegant black cherry fruits. *** Drink 2013-2021.

Los Carneros, Thomas, 2008
This wine comes from block 23 in Ferguson. It is matured in one year oak. The spicy red fruit nose leads into a palate where good acidity supports linear red fruits. Good intensity here with the tannins still needing a little time, although this does not have quite the concentration of 2007. *** Drink 2013-2019.

Los Carneros, West Block, 2008
Spicy red fruit nose. There's no mistaking the intensity here: sweet ripe fruits of red and black cherries on the palate, generous but fresh with crisp tannins with some spices on the finish. *** Drink 2013-2021.

Russian River Valley, 2007 (Robert Stemmler Winery)
Restrained nose. Deep, generous, ripe cherry fruits, more black than red, with a faint aromaticity on the nose. A bit superficial but generous and pleasing, a touch of glycerin bringing fat to the finish, already drinking well. ** Drink now-2017.

Los Carneros, 2007
Spicy nose of red and black fruits. Nicely varied flavor spectrum on the palate, spicy black cherry fruits, refined tannins now resolving, but is it a bit short on the mid palate? ** Drink now-2015.

Los Carneros, Ferguson Block, 2007 (Robert Stemmler Winery)
Matured in 40% new oak and 60% one-year, this latest release has a dusky purple color. The spicy red fruit nose is followed by sweet ripe fruits on the palate with some intensity, spice showing also on the palate with quite taut fruits. ** Drink 2012-2019.

Russian River Valley, 2007
Slightly spicy red fruit nose. Generous ripe fruits on the palate, more black cherries than red, supported by balanced acidity, good persistence on the finish. Very approachable and immediately drinkable, quite long and generous in the mouth. *** Drink now-2017.

Los Carneros, 2006
Restrained nose about to turn from fruity to savory but not quite there yet. Slightly spicy red and black cherry fruits, still a spicy fruit edge to the palate, supported by supple generous tannins. Overall impression is refined and elegant with the first savory notes just becoming detectable in the glass. *** Drink now-2019.

Los Carneros, 2005
Two bottles gave slightly different impressions of development. The first was more developed, with slightly perfumed notes mingling with some savory aromas on the nose. Caught in fla-grante just at the delicious turning point from fruity from savory. Perfect point of balance, with red fruits that are more cherries than strawberries, supported by balanced acidity, and the resolving tannins allowing the fruit/savory balance to show clearly through. Another bottle was a more youthful color, with more restraint on the nose, and with fruity rather than savory notes predominating. **** Drink now-2017.

Los Carneros, 2004
Restrained nose, just the first barely detectable savory overtones mingling with the spicy notes. Nice generosity of fruits, a faint spiciness on the finish, some chocolate notes developing in the glass. *** Drink now-2017.

Los Carneros, 2003
This estate wine came from the West Block (which was bottled separately as a single vineyard in some later years). Pungent savory notes on the nose show a touch of gunflint. Good acidity supports red fruits which are more strawberries than cherries, with a strong savory edge, although less evident on the palate than on the nose. Slowly the fruits intensify in the glass. The tannins are resolving nicely. *** Drink now-2016.

Los Carneros, 2002
Developed garnet color. Very developed nose, savory and pungent. Less developed on the palate, the fruits have turned from primary to savory but still have lots of intensity, the red fruits coming back in savory form on the finish. *** Drink now-2015.

Saintsbury

Saintsbury was established in 1981 when Dick Ward and David Graves, who met at oenology classes at UC Davis, decided on Carneros for their vineyard because of its history with Pinot Noir. They have always purchased most of their fruit, although they grow a higher percentage of Pinot Noir than other varieties. Their own vineyards are the home ranch, the RMS vineyard just down the road, and the Brown Ranch, which comprise 12 ha of the total 21 ha from which they source grapes. They have control of the viticulture at vineyards where they buy grapes. In 1983 it became apparent that individual vineyards varied differently in each vintage so they split production into regular production and the "Garnet" value bottlings intended for early drinking. The distinction was based on selection. In 1990 they started to make a Reserve Pinot Noir, then they moved to single vineyard bottlings in 2004. Grapes are destemmed, there is cold soak for a few days, followed by a mix of natural and inoculated fermentation. Blends use 15-25% new oak; the single vineyard wines use 30-40% new oak. All of the appellation blends are under 14% alcohol; the single vineyards are under 14.5%. Single vineyard wines are about 10% of total production, which is around 45,000 cases. A vertical tasting gave a very good sense of aging potential. The wines reach a turning point with sous bois showing within a decade, but then they continue to develop beauti-fully and slowly for another decade. Wines were tasted at Saintsbury in January 2011.

Los Carneros, 2009
Brilliant ruby color. Bright red fruit nose with almost peppery spices. Sweet ripe fruits showing as red cherries and raspberries, light tannins, not a lot of stuffing. ** Drink 2012-2017.

Los Carneros, Toyon Farm, 2009
The soils in this vineyard are unusual for Los Carneros, with about 20% volcanic and the rest sedimentary. The wine is a bright purple color, with a black fruit nose of cherries and some

hints of blackberries. Fairly taut on the palate, with delicate tannins making a quite refined impression. Just a touch of chocolate on the finish, which is slightly hot. ** Drink 2013-2018.

Los Carneros, Stanly Vineyard, 2009
This vineyard lies on the typical rolling hills of Los Carneros, with a clay and loam soil, and is Saintsbury's closest vineyard to the sea. It is a medium purple color, with a faintly spicy nose, more black than red fruits, and some faintly savory notes. Nice balance here, with a touch of glyceriny opulence fattening the finish against good acidity and black cherry fruits. A touch of chocolate develops in the glass. In this vintage, this wine has more grip on the palate than the Lees Vineyard, although that is not usually the case. *** Drink 2013-2019.

Los Carneros, Lees Vineyard, 2009
This vineyard has the classic clay and loam soils of Los Carneros but is relatively flat. Just a faint touch of allspice shows on a black cherry nose. The spice is more evident on the palate, which is quite fat, showing a glyceriny opulence. A touch of sweetness on the ripe fruits is balanced by supple tannins. Just a touch richer, with more evident fat than the Stanly. *** Drink 2013-2019.

Anderson Valley, Cerise Vineyard, 2009
This wine comes from a relatively cool spot, with the vineyard at around 300 m elevation, fairly steep, with sandstone-derived soils (in Anderson Valley to the north of Russian River). There are spicy black cherry fruits on the nose, leading into a leaner palate where the spice is more evident, and the tannic support underneath the fruits is quite tight. *** Drink 2013-2019.

Los Carneros, Brown Ranch, 2009
There are 10 separate blocks in the Brown vineyard, and each is vinified separately; a selection is made before the final bottling, which includes only the best blocks. Reflecting the greater concentration of the fruit, some whole clusters are used in this wine. Chocolate notes add to the black cherry fruits on the nose. A touch of mocha carries over to the dense black fruits on the palate, which are supported by supple tannins. This is the most intense of Saintsbury's single vineyard wines. ***(*) Drink 2013-2021.

Los Carneros, Reserve, 2000
Medium garnet color but still with some rosy hues. Restrained nose, a little perfume, a touch of sous bois, which remains subtle although more evident on the palate. Generally an elegant impression, with the developed red fruits remaining lively and vibrant, and the sous bois coming back on the finish. *** Drink now-2016.

Los Carneros, 1995
Medium garnet color shows some age. Restrained nose with some savory touches just showing. Ripe sweet fruits still evident on palate, leading into a touch of spice, with sous bois just barely perceptible. A subtle, elegant wine, with the savory perfectly balancing the fruity. *** Drink now-2017.

Los Carneros, Reserve, 1991
Savory nose with a touch of gunflint. Still shows sweet ripe fruits, a touch of sous bois, good acidity, well rounded palate with just a faint leathery touch on the finish (some Brett developed in the bottle in this vintage). *** Drink now-2014.

Los Carneros, 1989
Developed garnet color with quite developed savory nose shows some age. There's still a touch of spice left on the nose. This is at the turning point, with those delicious notes of sous bois dominating the palate. Lovely balance with the fruits still lively, the palate still vibrant, tannins resolved, and spicy matching savory influences. **** Drink now-2015.

Robert Sinskey Vineyards

The modern winery is located on the Silverado Trail in Napa Valley, but the vineyards are in Carneros, where Sinskey has four Pinot Noir vineyards (there is also a vineyard in Sonoma). About half of all production is Pinot Noir, making Sinskey a Pinot Noir specialist in the area. Wines are made only from estate fruit. Until 2001 Sinskey made a Carneros Pinot Noir and a reserve bottling, but felt that "Reserve" had little meaning since the wines were not produced in a rich oaky style, so the change was made to single vineyard bottlings. There is complete destemming for all wines, cap irrigation during fermentation rather than pigeage to give better control of extraction, and maturation in

30% new oak. The wines are intended to drink well from soon after the vintage, and Sinskey says that he sees about ten years as the natural life span for most vintages. Wines were tasted at the winery in January 2010 and again in January 2011.

Los Carneros, 2008
This is Sinskey's entry level Pinot Noir, made in a more forward style intended for drinking sooner. Smooth light fruits show on a spectrum of cherries and strawberries. The style is quite fruit forward, with less sense of underlying structure than the single vineyard wines. Yet stylistically it follows Sinskey's general aims of wines that reflect Pinot Noir without over extraction. * Drink now-2017.

Los Carneros, Vandal Vineyard, 2007
The Vandal vineyard, 4 ha planted on the hillside of northern Carneros close to the town of Napa and under Mount Veeder, is one of the first to pick of Sinskey's Pinot Noir vineyards. "Its characteristic note is the bright fruit with a cranberry essence," says Robert Sinskey. In this vintage, it was certainly the leanest of Sinskey's single vineyard wines, although in the past year it has lost some of its initial austerity. The tight, red cherry fruit nose leads into a palate with crisp acidity and light tannins supporting bright red fruits, somewhat in the style of Beaune. ** Drink 2013-2019.

Los Carneros, Three Amigos Vineyard, 2007
The three Amigos vineyard is close to the San Pablo Bay, just by the Napa marina. Demonstrating the coastal influence, it is usually the last of Sinskey's vineyards to be harvested. In the past year, the wine has put on weight and some initial earthy notes have given way to more obvious fruits. Red cherry fruits on the nose are more rounded and less acid than those of the Vandal vineyard. Smooth on the palate with some black as well as red cherries. Supple tannins show on a smooth finish. *** Drink 2012-2019.

Los Carneros, Capa Vineyard, 2007
This is a small vineyard of only 2 ha, close to Vandal, but with a west-facing exposure that gets sun all day, making it Sinskey's warmest location. Dijon clones are prominent, and it is usually the first plot to harvest. It is the most "Californian" in style of Sinskey's Pinot Noirs. The black fruit nose offers cherries and plums. The palate is smooth, ripe and full, with supple tannins showcasing a superficial fatness. ** Drink 2011-2017.

Los Carneros, Four Vineyards, 2007
This is a blend from each of Sinskey's individual Pinot Noir vineyards (in roughly equal proportions). The stylistic target here is a balance showing some elegance. The nose is more restrained than the single vineyard wines, showing cherry fruits that carry though to the palate, more black than red, with a smooth finish with well integrated tannins. More elegant, but perhaps less personality, than the single vineyard wines. ** Drink now-2015.

Producers and Tastings in Russian River

Kosta Browne

Kosta Browne began when Dan Kosta and Michael Browne, who were in the restaurant business, started by buying grapes and a barrel and made some wine. From one barrel (about 25 cases) they moved to 250 cases and then to 2,500 cases. They raised capital in 2001 and became professional. All their grapes are purchased. Kosta Browne is located in an old facility that used to be a center for handling apples in Sonoma. Other producers often refer to Kosta Browne wines as "big." They are felt to be high in alcohol and extract and to represent the forceful Californian style. But I can't say they entirely appear that way to me, although my tasting at Kosta Browne focused on barrel samples from different clones, oak, or means of vinification, rather than finished wines. Forceful to some extent, perhaps, but with balanced smooth palates emphasizing the fruits. Alcohol usually pushes close to 15%, which may be a problem in matching foods, and the supple tannins are subsumed by the fruits. These may well be wines to consume relatively early rather than to age. Tasting the current vintage in February 2011 confirmed the impression from the extensive barrel tastings that the style here is for precision in the wines although they are at the richer end of the spectrum.

Sonoma Coast, Gap's Crown, 2008
This vineyard is relatively cool, near Petaluma but just out of the Russian River Valley appellation. Restrained nose gives faint impression of red cherries with hints of raspberries. Red cherry fruits with a slight sense of darker fruits follow on the palate. *** Drink 2013-2018.

Russian River Valley, Keefer, 2008
Quite a sassy nose with bright red fruits of cherries and raspberries, and a suggestion of good acidity. Elegant balance on the palate, with precise red fruits and just a touch of chocolate on the finish giving an impression of chocolate-coated cherries. ***(*) Drink 2012-2018.

Santa Lucia Highlands (Monterey County), Gary's Vineyard, 2008
Slightly tarry red fruit nose hiding the red cherry fruits, which are more prominent on the palate. Balanced acidity and again a sense of those chocolate coated cherries. *** Drink 2012-2018.

Merry Edwards

Merry Edwards is regarded as one of the pioneer winemakers in California. Her interest in Pinot Noir dates from her first winemaking position in 1974 at Mount Eden Vineyards in the Santa Cruz Mountains. From the plantings there she developed the Rae clone (now known as UCD 37), which is a major part of her own estate. As a Chardonnay specialist, she was the founding winemaker at Matanzas Creek in 1977. Her own winery was founded in 1997. Wines come from six estate vineyards and also from two vineyards under long-term acreage contracts allowing her to control viticulture. "We feel that farming is the only way to come to great Pinot and that is what we have based everything on," she says. In addition to the single vineyard wines, there is a Russian River bottling consisting of declassified lots. The Sonoma Coast bottling, which was made from purchased fruit, is being discontinued. The newest development is a Sauvignon Blanc, barrel fermented in the style of Fumé Blanc. Vinification for Pinot Noir follows the usual lines, although there's a little more use of new oak than average, running to around 55-60% in the regional blends and to 75-80% in the single vineyard designations. Describing her wines, she says, "I probably have two stylistic aims. I like the fruit to come through, I view this as the personality of the wine. And I like to see the texture come through." Wines were tasted in December 2010 or at Merry Edwards in February 2011.

Sonoma Coast, 2008
Restrained black fruit nose shows cherries and plums with faint aromatic overtones. The same black fruits follow on the medium density palate, leaving quite a soft impression, with a touch of chocolate on the finish. ** Drink 2012-2019.

Russian River Valley, 2008
Fruit-driven nose of black cherries, not quite aromatic. Intensity is the word for the palate of dark cherry fruits with an edge of bright tannins. Is it too intense for Pinot Noir, does the intensity hide the delicacy and variety of flavors? Will it ameliorate in time? More powerful than 2006 or 2007 and correspondingly less successful, in my view. ** Drink 2012-2017.

Russian River Valley, Meredith Estate, 2008
Slightly spirity impression to the nose hides the fruits. On the palate there are soft black fruits of cherries and plums, their ripeness giving a sweet kick to the finish, with tannins adding a soft, almost furry, impression. Balanced acidity supports the medium density fruits. The flavor profile seems a touch less lifted than the other single vineyard wines. *** Drink 2012-2019.

Russian River Valley, Coopersmith, 2008
Restrained nose with faintly aromatic black cherries. There is a little more immediate generosity to the fruits here compared with Meredith Estate, with a good impression of black cherries and plums. The fruits give a slightly more precise and elegant impression than Klopp Ranch or Olivet Lane. A faintly piquant impression lingers on the finish. *** Drink 2012-2021.

Russian River Valley, Klopp Ranch, 2008
Very restrained nose slowly opening out to reveal some fine black fruit aromatics. Some generosity on the palate of black cherries and plums, but more obvious structure here than with the other single vineyard wines. Some black aromatics develop on the finish, which is cut by a slight tannic rasp. A couple of years are required for the tannins to integrate fully to allow the fruits to show their full potential. ***(*) Drink 2013-2021.

Russian River Valley, Olivet Lane, 2008
A slightly tarry rasp to the nose promises some structure. Nicely balanced black fruits on the palate, really more plums than cherries, with some generosity to the fruits. A subtle aromaticity shows on the finish. Tannic presence is indicated by the dryness of the finish, which is ameliorated by a slight chocolate coating. Perhaps the slightly lower alcohol here contributes to the sense of a harmonious balance. The most complete of the single vineyard wines. **** Drink 2013-2021.

Sonoma Coast, 2007
Nutty, earthy, strawberry fruits burst with ripeness on the nose. The richness of the vintage shows immediately in the ripe fruits of the palate. Acidity is lower than the leaner 2006—will this age as long? The dense rich style epitomizes Sonoma. *** Drink now-2015.

Russian River Valley, 2007
Earthy strawberries show a touch of minerality, quite intense on the nose with some tarry notes. Dense red fruits give a somewhat earthy Burgundian impression. Although the alcohol is high, it is well integrated. Fruits are full but not jammy. Some mineral and tarry notes show on the finish and faintly buttery notes develop in the glass, becoming slightly nutty. Ripe tannins are subsumed by the fruits. An excellent result for an appellation wine. *** Drink now-2018.

Sonoma Coast, 2006
Nutty, earthy, strawberry fruits on the nose are very Pinot-ish. The relatively lean year is indicated by freshness on the nose and a very slight medicinal edge to the finish; but even in a lean year, the fruits are quite rich. Strawberry fruits on the palate are balanced by the acidity, and the long nutty finish then comes as a surprise. Those accustomed to Burgundy may prefer this to the richer 2007; those accustomed to California will prefer the 2007. *** Drink now-2016.

Gary Farrell

Gary Farrell became involved in winemaking in the Russian River Valley in the 1970s and began to make his own wine in 1982. The model was based on purchasing fruit from top vineyard sites, including Rochioli and the adjacent Allen vineyard. A winery was built in 2000 in a beautiful location overlooking Westside Road with a spectacular view of the area. It was sold to Allied Domecq in 2004 and now is in the hands of Beam Wine Estates. Gary Farrell left in 2009 to start another winery. Currently the winery produces 4,000 cases of Russian River Valley selection, 1,000 cases from Carneros fruit from sister company Buena Vista, and 2,400 cases of single vineyard Pinot Noirs. Typically Pinot Noir is about 60% of production and Chardonnay about 30%. Winemaker Susan Reed says that they want the wines to be fruit driven so they pick a little earlier than most in order to get lower alcohol. They want people to be able to tell the wines are Gary Farrell. There is complete destemming, 5-7 days cold soak, and fermentation until pressing off at 1 degree Brix; all the press wine usually goes into the Russian River Valley bottling. This gets 30% new oak, and the single vineyard wines get 40%. Of the Russian River wines in this tasting, Hallberg is a bigger, darker wine, with black, richer fruits (partly reflecting the Dijon clones), whereas Rochioli and Allen vineyards are all about finesse, leaner with higher acidity and more purity of line. Wines were tasted at Gary Farrell in February 2011.

Russian River Valley, Rochioli Vineyard, 2008
This roller coaster year alternated between wet and dry spells, with frost and wind playing a role as well as heat spikes. Some high toned aromatics of black cherries show on the nose. The fine grained palate has elegant tannins giving finesse to the finish. This can already be enjoyed. *** Drink-2017.

Russian River Valley, Hallberg Vineyard, 2008
High toned aromatic perfume expressed by black cherry fruits, a touch nutty and almost jammy on the nose. Balanced acidity supports supple black fruits of plums and cherries on the palate. Smooth tannins are well integrated. The distinctive character of this vineyard shows in the touch of glycerin opulence on the finish. *** Drink now-2019.

Russian River Valley, Starr Ridge, 2008
This vineyard is planted mostly with Dijon clone 115, together with a little 777 and Pommard. A perfumed nose has underlying black fruits. Smooth black fruits on the palate are as much plums as cherries, with a touch of spice on the finish. Finesse and elegance show here in Farrell's usual style, sitting between the richness of Hallberg and the lean finesse of Rochioli. *** Drink now-2018.

Santa Maria Valley (Santa Barbara), Bien Nacido Vineyard, 2008
More red than black cherries on the nose. Good acidity supports bright red fruits on the palate with hints of raspberries and a touch of spice. You get a sense here of a garden of red berries with faintly spicy overtones. *** Drink now-2017.

Russian River Valley, Rochioli Vineyard, 2007
This year had a ripe, consistent growing season, giving rich wines that were universally praised. There's a slightly herbal, tarragon-driven note to the nose. Acidity is just a little more noticeable than 2006, with spicy black cherry fruits driving the palate. Tannins are resolving. Fine and elegant with a taut impression to the finish. *** Drink now-2016.

Russian River Valley, Hallberg Vineyard, 2007
Medium to deep garnet color with the first garnet hues showing. Black cherry fruit nose has faint notes of spice and cereal. Good acidity here, fresh and lively on the palate of black cherry fruits with firm supporting tannins. *** Drink now-2018.

Russian River Valley, Hallberg Vineyard, 2006
The vineyard has Goldridge clay and loam. Some herbal notes of tarragon show on the nose. Rich and ripe black fruits of cherries and plums, with some aromatic perfumes dominate the palate. Quite fat on the finish with a superficial richness from a touch of glycerin, supported by balanced acidity and supple tannins. *** Drink now-2016.

Russian River Valley, Rochioli Vineyard, 2006
The cool, wet vintage gave a large crop; a lot of fruit had to be dropped to keep yields down. A slightly herbal nose offers hints of tarragon. More spicy than herbal on the palate, focused black cherries show good precision of fruits; refined elegant tannins are taut on the finish, where there is a touch of heat. *** Drink now-2019.

Russian River Valley, Allen Vineyard, 2005
This vineyard is planted principally with the old Pommard clones. The wine reflects the cool growing season of the year. The medium garnet appearance has a broadening orange rim. Fruity, nutty, cereal notes on the nose, then some savory herbal notes with a touch of olives. Red fruits on the palate have savory and herbal tones, the ripeness is a little muted. Harmonious and well integrated elegant style but à point already, so drink in next few years. ***(*) Drink now-2015.

Russian River Valley, Hallberg Vineyard, 2005
This is the coolest site of Farrell's vineyards in Russian River, down in the Green Valley where there used to be an apple orchard. Restrained nose with the first savory notes just poking through. Rich and ripe on the palate with black cherry and plum fruits, supple tannins, a sense of finesse matched by a touch of glycerin giving an impression of opulence. A very nice silky texture with faintly nutty overtones on the finish. ***(*) Drink now-2017.

Littorai

Ted Lemon began Littorai in 1993 with just 300 cases of production. "When we started I did not have any interest in what I think of as the American flamboyant school of wine," he says, so the target was to sell to restaurants where a more elegant style might be better received. This now accounts for roughly two thirds of sales, the rest going to a mailing list. About 40% of production comes from estate vineyards, owned or on long term lease, the rest from purchased fruit. The estate vineyards stretch from the winery at the western edge of Russian River Valley to the Anderson Valley. Ted is an enthusiast for biodynamic viticulture. "We rejected organic viticulture because it substituted organic for synthetic but retained the basic idea of western agronomy," he says, adding that this is not so true of organic viticulture today. Littorai started to go biodynamic in 1998. Consisting of 12 hectares of farmland with about 10% planted to a Pinot Noir vineyard, the home estate will ultimately become completely self sufficient; all it lacks at the moment is a cow. Winemaking is as natural as possible, a major target being to avoid acidification. New oak is usually around 30% except for the two blended Pinots that are about 10%. The wines have an unusual elegance for the region, and were tasted at Littorai in February 2011.

Anderson Valley (Mendocino County), Les Larmes, 2007
More austerity on the nose than on the Sonoma Coast wine, but alleviated by faintly buttery strawberry fruits. A little more weight to the fruits on the palate here, with a touch of phenolics joining the buttery notes on the finish. There's an impression of more sweetness but less flavor variety in the fruits. ** Drink now-2016.

Sonoma Coast, 2007
There are no specifically designated sources for this wine, which includes some declassified lots from the single vineyard wines and also the production from young vines and press wine. The fragrant nose shows some delicate strawberries. The palate follows with light, elegant, earthy-mineral strawberry fruits, and a faint buttery uplift on the aftertaste. The overall delicate impression is retained through the finish, which shows some light tannins and a little heat. Drink now-2017.

Anderson Valley (Mendocino County), Cerise Vineyard, 2007
This vineyard is at mid slope of the northern hills near Boonville, quite exposed and rocky, with low vigor soils, and is farmed on a planting contract. Restrained nose of strawberry fruits is more mineral than earthy. Balanced acidity supports fruits which show more as red cherries on the palate, with some taut tannins, and a faint phenolic edge. This needs another year for the tannins to soften, but already displays nice aroma and flavor variety. ** Drink 2012-2020.

Anderson Valley (Mendocino County), Savoy Vineyard, 2007
This is the only vineyard on the valley floor in the Littorai portfolio. Just outside Philo, the vines are 15 years old, and the goal is to move to dry farming. As can be seen from the moderate alcohol, it is often picked around 22.5 Brix and Ted Lemon can't remember when it last hit 24 Brix. A restrained nose with faintly tarry notes leads into a palate of red strawberry fruits with faint buttery notes on the finish. Tannins are soft enough already to start drinking. ** Drink now-2019.

Anderson Valley (Mendocino County), Roman Vineyard, 2007
This estate property is at the cooler end of Anderson Valley (known as the deep end), where the vineyard is at about 300 m elevation. Recognizing the cool climate, the fruits are completely destemmed. The nose shows earthy strawberries with a mineral edge. The sweetness of the fruits can be seen on the finish, but generally there is a leaner impression, with a more obvious sense of structure coming from the light, fine tannins that are evident on the finish, which all the same shows a touch of heat. ** Drink now-2018.

Russian River Valley, Mays Canyon, 2007
Planted in 1998, the vineyard is at 150 m elevation on the side of the coastal hills and has gravelly loam soils. The wine is a medium ruby color with some garnet hues. Very restrained nose shows a touch of red fruit perfume. Immediately you see more rounded red fruits than in the bottlings from Anderson Valley. There is a very nice balance with just a hint of earthiness to the strawberry fruits, supported by fine, restrained tannins on the finish. Can drink now but better to wait a year. *** Drink 2012-2021.

Sonoma Coast, Hirsch Vineyard, 2007
This vineyard has 7-8 year old vines planted at elevations around 500 m Slightly mineral red fruits show more as strawberries than cherries. Fruits are nicely rounded on the palate but show some austerity from fine tannins and acidity. There is a faint touch of heat on the finish. With more obvious structure than most, the tight fruits are coiled like a spring waiting to unfold; this needs a little more time for the tannins to soften. *** Drink 2013-2022.

Sonoma Coast, B. A. Theriot Vineyard, 2007
At about 300 m elevation, the vineyard is on a south-facing slope to the west of Occidental. The soils are transitional, with elements of Goldridge clay and some red rocks. Usually it ripens later

than the Hirsch or Canyon May vineyards. A restrained red fruit nose shows more cherries than strawberries. Taut elegant fruits on the palate show a relatively lean style of expression, with refined tannic backbone. *** Drink 2013-2022.

Sonoma Coast, Haven Vineyard, 2007
The vineyard is to the west of Occidental, planted in 2001 on a south-facing slope at about 400 m elevation, with a diversity of soils ranging from marine sandstone to shale. The color of the wine is just a touch deeper than the Theriot vineyard. Restrained nose shows a touch of ripe red fruits, with hints of spices, nuts, and cereal. There's a touch of black as well as red cherries on the palate; supple, elegant tannins bring a note of opulence to the finish. The overall impression is most elegant, with a precision of fruits that reminds me of Volnay, yet rich enough to enjoy already. ***(*) Drink now-2023.

Sonoma Coast, Hirsch Vineyard, 2002
The year gave an almost perfect growing season with even ripening and good yields. Two bottles showed slightly different paces of development. Both offered an immediate impression of sturdy, ripe fruits in the style of Hirsch, but on one the restrained nose gave a sense of rich, ripe fruits; on the other, savory hints developed on the nose to mingle with ripe strawberry fruits. One bottle displayed red and black cherry fruits with a slight loss of concentration on mid palate; for the other some savory notes were beginning to emerge. Both give the impression of having reached a point at which they should be consumed over the immediate future. *** Drink now-2016.

Anderson Valley (Mendocino County), One Acre Vineyard, 2001
This vineyard is at an elevation of 500 m near Boonville. Wine was made from this vineyard between 1993 and 2005, when it was replanted. Some development shows in the medium density garnet color. Some savory notes on the nose stop just short of reaching sous bois and mingle with rich, red fruits. Ripeness of the fruits is the first impression on the palate, less developed than Savoy, showing a mix of savory and fruity elements. Fine tannins are resolving. A long finish completes the impression of ripeness. **** Drink now-2017.

Anderson Valley (Mendocino County), Savoy Vineyard, 2001
This was a much riper vintage than 2002 with more flamboyant wines. The savory nose offers a compression of developed red fruits and sous bois. The palate is at a delicious turning point; developing more quickly, the wine feels quite a bit older than the 2002. Sous bois shows on the palate with a generous, savory, ripe red fruit backbone. *** Drink now-2016.

Williams Selyem

Williams Selyem is one of the standard bearers for Russian River Valley, and one of the few original pioneers still to remain independent. Started by Ed Selyem and Burt Williams, who had been amateur winemakers, the first vintage was made in a two-car garage in 1981; the original name of Hacienda del Rio was changed to Williams Selyem in 1984. Burt Williams made the vintages through 1997, when the winery was sold to John and Kathe Dyson, after which Bob Cabral took over as winemaker. Production functioned out of what was virtually a trailer park until 2010, when a splendid new winery was built at the top of the hill. Pinot Noir is about 85% of production. Wines range from the Central Coast, Sonoma County, and Russian River Valley appellation bottlings to an impressive series of single vineyard wines from top sites, including the 30 ha of estate vineyards. Winemaking is straightforward, with 20-25% use of whole clusters, five day cold soak, and addition of Williams Selyem's own strain of yeast to start fermentation. "It's very cookbook winemaking" says Bob Cabral. "Whether I'm making a $30 or $100 Pinot, the only real variable will be the proportion of new oak, from 40-80%." Appellation wines get bottled in August and the single vineyards after Christmas. There is no fining or filtration. One legacy of Williams' winemaking is the use of low sulfur levels (10-15 ppm), as Burt was allergic to sulfur. More than 90% of the single vineyard production sells to the mailing list, so the wines can be hard to find. Notes come from a comparative tasting of two decades of Rochioli versus Hirsch Vineyard at Williams Selyem in February 2011.

Russian River Valley, Rochioli River Block, 2008
Medium to deep dusky purple color. Fruity nose shows black cherries and plums with faint aromatic overtones. Taut fruits of black cherries on the palate are reminiscent of the Côte de Nuits, with a lovely precision of fruits, and some faintly aromatic overtones. Ripeness shows clearly on the palate but there is a fine sense of tension. Very youthful and needs a couple more years to start. **** Drink 2013-2023.

Sonoma Coast, Hirsch Vineyard, 2008
Medium ruby color with some garnet hues. Faint spice notes on a nose of red and black fruits. Full black fruits on the palate are supported by balanced acidity and supple tannins, with some spice notes coming through to the finish. Very youthful, scarcely developed at all, but the balance of fruit to tannin is so smooth that already the wine is approachable. *** Drink-2021.

Russian River Valley, Rochioli River Block, 2006
Medium ruby color not showing much garnet yet. A little spirity on the nose, becoming more phenolic and Port-like in the glass. Rich and full on the palate but a raisined note shows on the back palate. The alcohol seems to be pushing the tannins on the finish. Very rich although not as obviously so as the 2007, with a less harmonious balance, becoming a little hot on the finish. ** Drink now-2018.

Russian River Valley, Bucher Vineyard, 2006
Medium ruby color. Very restrained on the nose, with a slightly acrid touch to the red fruits. Good acidity on the palate seems a natural reflection of a cool year. Quite lean with fruits of sour red cherries supported by taut, fine tannins. Slowly the fruits broaden out in the glass and the usual forward fruitiness of Russian River reappears. *** Drink 2012-2018.

Russian River Valley, Rochioli River Block, 2005
Medium to deep ruby-garnet color. Faintly aromatic red fruit nose. Lovely smooth palate shows mélange of red fruits supported by balanced acidity. Delicious layers of flavors with some spice notes. Ripe and intense, some spicy/savory contrasts with a barely perceptible note of sous bois. A fine life ahead. **** Drink now-2022.

Sonoma Coast, Hirsch Vineyard, 2005
Medium ruby color with a translucent rim. Muted nose with a touch of red cherry and redcurrant aromatics. Palate shows more as black cherries and plums, with a sweet, ripe kick counterpoising some herbal and spicy notes on the finish. The first faint savory notes add to the delicious balance of fruit to acidity. **** Drink-2021.

Russian River Valley, Rochioli River Block, 2001
Medium to deep garnet color. Slightly nutty, spicy nose of red fruits. Balanced acidity on the red fruit palate, a touch of cinnamon and nutmeg spices, some very faint savory notes just beginning to emerge, a kick of ripeness showing on a finish with some delicious spice notes. **** Drink now-2020.

Sonoma Coast, Hirsch Vineyard, 2001
Medium ruby-garnet. Restrained nose with a touch of red fruit aromatics. A spicy herbal touch leads into the palate of red cherry and strawberry fruits, with balanced acidity and firm tannins, with a slightly nutty, spicy touch to the finish. **** Drink now-2021.

Russian River Valley, River Block, 1997
This vertical tasting led to some discussion as to where between 2001 and 1997 was the perfect turning point from fruity to savory, but the range seems to be around 10-12 years. The 1997 has now acquired a medium garnet color and is rather restrained on the nose. The nicely balanced palate shows a perfect counterpoise of slowly developing red fruits against acidity and fine tannins, with a delicious ripe touch kicking in on the finish. **** Drink now-2018.

Sonoma Coast, Hirsch Vineyard, 1997
Medium to deep garnet color. Slightly herbal nose with a touch of tarragon. Delicious balance of sweet ripe fruits against balanced acidity. A touch of bitterness on the finish dissipates in the glass against a relieving touch of piquancy. *** Drink now-2016.

Russian River Valley, River Block, 1994
The garnet color with some mahogany hues shows a respectable age. There is a delicious mélange of spicy and savory aromas on the nose. Crisp acidity shows on the palate with a touch of savory notes, but there are still some spices of cinnamon and nutmeg in the background. The fruits are no longer forceful, but there is a subtle interplay with savory development. The acidity is a touch piquant on the finish, and the wine gets marked down a point because acidity has become just a touch pressing with age. *** Drink now-2016.

Sonoma Coast, Hirsch Vineyard, 1994
Medium to deep garnet color, more youthful in appearance than River Block. Nose is quite muted. Balanced acidity supports ripe fruits, but less developed than River Block. Faintly nutty on the finish, fruity rather than savory, some ripe tannins still evident. *** Drink now-2017.

Producers and Tastings in Santa Cruz & Mount Harlan

Thomas Fogarty

The eponymous Thomas Fogarty (a surgeon at Stanford) owned this land before he decided to make wine. The vineyards were planted in 1978 and Michael Martella came as the winemaker in 1981. The location has spectacular views all the way out to San Francisco Bay, at a sufficient elevation that you see the blimp cruising along below. Except for one vineyard that is being replanted, all are still the original plantings. The vines came from the David Bruce vineyard or the Martini selection, and have since been supplemented with some Dijon and Swan clones. Originally the best selections went into a Reserve bottling, but Fogarty moved to single vineyard bottling in 2002. Around the winery all the vineyards are planted to Pinot Noir or Chardonnay; there are some Bordeaux varieties at another vineyard 20 minutes farther south. The major Pinot Noir vineyards are Windy Hill (right beside the winery) which is presently being replanted, and Rapley Trail. The 2 ha of the Rapley Trail vineyard are the only areas with clay in the soil (heavier at the top, thinner below); the rest is loam and sand. The Rapley Trail vineyard has now been subdivided into blocks, with the inventive names of M for the middle and B for the bottom; it is picked from bottom to top over a one month period. Wines were tasted at Thomas Fogarty in February 2011.

Santa Cruz Mountains, 2009
1,300 cases of this wine represent the entire estate production for 2009. A faintly aromatic red cherry fruit nose follows through to spicy red cherries on the palate. There's more sense of structure than usual because this wine contains declassified lots that otherwise would have been bottled as single vineyard designates. Spicy tea-like tannins give a touch of dryness to the finish. ** Drink 2013-2019.

Santa Cruz Mountains, Windy Hill, 2008
This wine was not made in 2009, there may be a little from 2010, but after that there will be a pause because the vineyard is being replanted. Slightly tarry bright red cherry fruit nose. Elegant red cherry fruits continue on the palate, with a touch of buttery ripeness, and some phenolics on the spicy finish with a touch of heat. Silky texture shows fine tannins with balanced acidity. Everything is well integrated and the underlying structure is barely perceptible. *** Drink 2013-2021.

Santa Cruz Mountains, Rapley Trail, 2008
Faintly spicy herbal aromatics show on a red cherry fruit nose. Immediate generosity of ripe fruits shows on the palate, a touch of black as well as red cherries, nice balancing acidity. Attractive tea-like tannins on the finish give a more obvious sense of structure. This should age well. *** Drink 2013-2023.

Santa Cruz Mountains, Rapley Trail Block M, 2008
An aromatic nose offers some herbs and spices. Good structure is immediately evident on the palate, with red and black cherry fruits and hints of plums and blackcurrants. There are the faintest buttery overtones as well as some phenolic notes on the finish. Firm tannins need another year to soften. You would never call this lean, but the style is lighter than the richer B block. ***(*) Drink 2013-2023.

Santa Cruz Mountains, Rapley Trail Block B, 2008
Just a touch darker in color than the M block. More overt herbs and spices, but the same spectrum of aromatic black fruits on the nose, with faintly nutty overtones intensifying in the glass. Red and black cherry fruits with some plums are a little more intense and better rounded on the palate, with more of a black fruit impression. Fine tannins but not ready yet, with another

year or so needed to soften. B block is the first part of Rapley Trail to harvest and this shows in the slightly riper fruit impression. ***(*) Drink 2013-2023.

Santa Cruz Mountains, Rapley Trail, 2003
This very hot vintage, with peak temperatures over 100 degrees, shows in the wine, with a heavier feeling than you get from Rapley in other vintages. Still a medium ruby color with little apparent development. Some high toned black cherry aromatics on the nose. Soft on the palate (grapes were destemmed completely in this vintage), with ripe black fruits supported by supple, ripe tannins, but a glacial pace of flavor development on the palate. Unclear whether this is going anywhere interesting. *** Drink now-2020.

Santa Cruz Mountains, Reserve, 1995
Probably all of this wine actually came from Rapley Trail, before it became a designated single vineyard. Still a medium to deep garnet color. Developed tertiary notes on the nose, but the overall impression is a little tired. The palate still shows some ripe fruits but is drying out a bit, allowing some bitterness to show on the finish. The winemakers say that this vintage usually shows much more overt ripeness, and my note may underrate the wine because I suspect there may have been a sub-threshold case of cork here, showing as some cardboard touches on the nose, and reducing fruit concentration on the palate. So potentially a star or more better. Indeed, this was confirmed by the much better performance of a subsequent bottle (⊤ page 388) ** Drink now-2011.

Santa Cruz Mountains, Estate 1991
This wine represented the entire production of the estate in 1991. Age shows in the medium garnet color with some mahogany hues. Developed savory nose with notes of sous bois strengthening in the glass. Crisp to balanced acidity showcases the savory red fruits, with those mushroomy notes of sous bois coming back on the finish. Still nicely ripe and sweet with a delicious piquancy on the finish. **** Drink now-2105.

Calera

Calera is sui generis. There is no other vineyard within fifty miles, there probably isn't any other vineyard in California at such a high elevation, and certainly there is none with limestone soils. The six vineyards of Pinot Noir total 36 ha; there are another 7 ha of Chardonnay and Viognier. Estate fruit is used for the single vineyards and Mount Harlan cuvée; purchased fruit is the basis of the Central Coast bottling. The winery (much lower down the mountain than the vineyards themselves) was converted from an old rock-crushing facility. Before a recent makeover, it was famous as one of the ugliest wineries around. It now houses a multi-storey gravity-fed winemaking facility (with a tasting room at one end for fans who make the pilgrimage up the mountain). Winemaking follows conventional Burgundian principles; the single vineyard wines spend 16 months in oak, 30% of which is new for most vineyards in most vintages. Vineyard differences were the most distinct in the current vintage. In older vintages, south-facing Mills consistently gave rounder wine than north-facing Reed, except for 2002, which seems to be the vintage in which both wines showed best, identifying the peak age as just under ten years. A certain lack of differentiation in flavor between them may reflect the high use of whole clusters for these lighter wines. Wines were tasted in May 2011.

Mount Harlan, de Villiers, 2007
Black fruits on the nose lead into savory overtones. Nice balance on the palate in a lighter red fruit style, some hints of vanillin, a touch of tar, slightly nutty on the finish. Tannins are still tight; a touch of heat on the finish gives a New World impression, This can be drunk now but will be better in another year as the tannins resolve further to reveal soft fruits, but there is a risk the high alcohol (14.9%) will become obtrusive. ** Drink 2012-2018.

Mount Harlan, Mills, 2007
Some nutty notes of vanillin and an impression of black fruits on the nose, showing as cherries and blackcurrants with slightly tarry overtones. Smooth black cherry fruits bring an impression of ripeness to the palate, but there's a slight lack of presence on the mid palate. The overall impression is of a relatively light style, but all in good balance for medium term aging. ** Drink now-2017.

Mount Harlan, Reed, 2007
Most developed color of the vintage, lighter with more garnet. A mix of red fruit and savory notes shows on the nose. More of an impression of red fruits here, showing as cherries with hints of strawberries, some fine tannins supporting the finish with a very faint medicinal impression, but nicely in balance with the fruits. This is more of a Côte de Beaune than Côte de Nuits style, perhaps the lightest single vineyard wine of the vintage. ** Drink now-2018.

Mount Harlan, Ryan, 2007
Some tarry notes give a slightly stern impression to the nose of black cherries and blackcurrants. More intensity to the palate here than the preceding vineyard wines, dominated by the same black fruits as the nose, with a good tannic backbone. There's a sweet, ripe dense impression resembling the lighter villages of the Côte de Nuits, altogether very fine. *** Drink now-2021.

Mount Harlan, Jensen, 2007
Intense nose with tarry notes and some hints of apples, hiding the underlying red fruits. There are smooth, ripe, dense black fruits; firm but fine tannins are nicely integrated with the fruits. Really needs another year although this can be drunk now. There is still a youthful touch of vanillin on the finish. This is a wine built from dense fruits, the most intense and structured single vineyard wine of the vintage, that will age for many years as the tannins gradually resolve. *** Drink 2012-2023.

Mount Harlan, Selleck, 2007
Restrained nose is quite closed although showing some hints of red fruits. The smoothest and most complete single vineyard wine of the vintage. Black cherry fruits dominate the palate with a kick of sweetness on the finish. Tannins are firm and supple, but less obvious than Jensen. Still a touch of youthful nuts and vanillin on the finish. *** Drink now-2019.

Mount Harlan, Mills 2005
Notes of black tea and tobacco on the nose, overlaying some faint hints of savory red fruits. Sweet ripe fruits on the palate present as a mix of red and black cherries, then showing herbaceous overtones on the finish. ** Drink now-2017.

Mount Harlan, Reed 2005
A faintly mentholated note with a slightly herbaceous impression of tomato leaf and pyrazines. Sweet ripe red fruit palate shows more strawberries than cherries, but the aftertaste is tea-like and herbaceous, becoming almost medicinal. * Drink now-2016.

Mount Harlan, Mills 2004
Developed nose with herbaceous overtones and some notes of stewed tea. Red cherry fruits have tea-like overtones. The medium density fruits have a slightly bitter lingering taste on the finish. ** Drink now-2016.

Mount Harlan, Reed 2004
Mentholated, eucalyptus-like notes with a herbaceous impression of pyrazines on the nose. Fruits make a sweet ripe, red impression on the palate, but then the herbaceous impression lingers to give the finish a medicinal impression. * Drink now-2016.

Mount Harlan, Mills 2003
Nose more youthful than you would expect from this vintage, still showing some tarry aromas, giving over to some tea-like aromas. Sweet ripe fruits tending towards red cherries and strawberries are well rounded, but with the tannins bringing a fairly stern touch to the finish. It's touch and go as to whether the residual kick of sweetness from the fruits or the bitterness from the tannins is going to dominate the finish. ** Drink now-2016.

Mount Harlan, Reed 2003
First savory intimations are showing on the nose, followed by some faint tea-like and tobacco notes. Herbaceous notes suggestive of pyrazines come out on the palate, with savory red fruits following and bringing a counterpoise of sweetness. Given the ripeness of the fruits you could not exactly call the wine angular, but the generosity is certainly cut by the finish. ** Drink now-2016.

Mount Harlan, Mills 2002
Rather closed on the nose with a faint cereal and savory impression. Nice texture to the palate here with well rounded strawberry fruits showing a tendency to earthiness. Tannins are firm but not obtrusive. But the wine has not really started yet to develop complexity or flavor variety. Will it survive rather than develop? ** Drink now-2018.

Mount Harlan, Reed 2002
Savory touch on the nose with faint underlying red fruits. The best balanced Reed so far, with the nicely rounded savory strawberry fruits balancing against the fine tea-like tannins on the finish. There's the beginning of a savory impression, and the wine promises to become steadily more savory over the next few years. *** Drink now-2018.

Mount Harlan, Mills 2001
Some cereal and nuts on the nose, cereal aromas intensifying in the glass. Sweet ripe fruits tending to strawberries on the palate lead into a dense finish coated by chocolaty tannins, which are still quite dry on the finish. Superficially this is showing appropriate development with age, but there's a certain lack of complexity which casts doubt on future aging potential. ** Drink now-2015.

Mount Harlan, Reed 2001
Closed on the nose with some savory touches and a very faint touch of gunflint. Palate shows developing savory red fruits, with a suggestion of angularity on the finish, but overall a good balance where the fruits are cut by the tannic support (still a bit dry on the finish). ** Drink now-2015.

Mount Harlan, Mills 2000
Closed nose with some cereal and savory notes. The savory notes carry through to the palate, where there are developing red fruits, with furry tannins on the finish. Still a distinct touch of dryness to the finish. This is now a nicely balanced wine, but the continuing level of tannins makes you wonder whether it will continue to age interestingly or will lose the fruit concentration before the tannins. ** Drink now-2017.

Mount Harlan, Reed 2000
Closed on the nose with some faint savory hints. This is the freshest wine of the early 2000s; fruits are developing and savory, but there's a medicinal touch on the finish, which intensifies in the glass and begins to take over the wine. * Drink now-2016.

Mount Harlan, Reed 1997
Lightening garnet color but still with some ruby hues. Savory nose with hints of sous bois. Savory development on the red fruits has taken over the palate, but still with a faintly herbaceous touch to the finish. *** Drink now-2015.

Mount Harlan, Jensen 1997
Medium garnet color. Savory nose with some herbaceous undertones. A beautiful complete wine, savory notes with just some hints of sous bois, the ripe sweet fruits show through, still some tannic dryness showing on the finish. *** Drink now-2015.

Mount Harlan, Jensen 1996
Medium garnet color. Savory notes to the nose with a touch of gunflint, a very faint herbaceous impression underneath. There's a touch of astringency on the palate, showing as an angular dryness on the finish. The fruits still are ripe and sweet on the palate at first impression, until you come to the finish. ** Drink now-2014.

Mount Harlan, Jensen, 1990
Appearance still quite a bright garnet with ruby hues. The nose is quite developed, very savory with some notes of gunflint, leading into a savory palate, with deep layers of flavor. The fruits broaden in the glass and put on weight, gaining some richness, and the savory notes recede, suggesting that there is still life ahead, although inevitably the fruits are beginning to dry out on the finish. A very fine result clearly demonstrating ability to age on a Burgundian scale. (February 2011) **** Drink now-2016.

Producers and Tastings in Santa Barbara

Au Bon Climat

Jim Clendenen founded ABC in 1982. Grapes mostly came from the Bien Nacido vineyard where the winery was constructed. In 1998 he purchased a 40 ha vineyard, now called Le Bon Climat, directly across the valley from Bien Nacido. Grapes also come from the Sanford & Benedict vineyard in Santa Rita Hills, as well as some other sources.

With a broad enquiring interest in wine, Jim produces not only Pinot Noir and Chardonnay, but a variety of other wines, ranging from Viognier to Petit Verdot. Winemaking here does not follow the usual New World fashion. They started out in 1982 by using whole clusters, but the wines were green, so they backed off and now use up to a third whole clusters only when there is some lignification in the stems. After harvesting grapes, they aerate for a couple of days until fermentation starts, inoculate, and punch down daily. Top wines are matured in 80% new oak. Wines (mostly from ABC but also including one under the Clendenen Family Vineyards label which was started in 2000 for some special small production runs from estate vineyards) were tasted over lunch at Au Bon Climat in February 2011.

Santa Barbara, 2009 (Au Bon Climat)
Light red cherry fruit nose. Sweet ripe fruits show more as mineral strawberries than cherries on the palate, quite light and elegant, with a faint touch of glycerin adding fat to the finish. The overall impression is elegant. In fact, the high quality of this wine creates a problem for ABC, according to Jim Clendenen, because it provides a disincentive for people to move up to the higher level wines.

Santa Maria Valley, La Bauge au Dessus, 2007 (Au Bon Climat)
Medium ruby color. Slightly perfumed black cherry nose. Firm support for black cherry fruits on the palate. Very nice concentration here with no over-extraction. Some tea-like tannins need another year to soften. Its silky texture makes this the finest in terms of structure among the ABC Pinots. ***(*) Drink 2012-2018.

Santa Ynez Valley, Sanford & Benedict, 2007 (Au Bon Climat)
Medium ruby color with garnet hues. Slightly tarry, slightly perfumed black cherry fruit nose. Firm, taut tannins support the black cherry fruits on the palate, counterpoised by a faint touch of glycerin on the finish. Very fine and reminiscent of the Côte de Nuits with its long, smooth, finish. Tannins should fully integrate in the next year or so, but can be enjoyed now as the most opulent of ABC's Pinots. *** Drink now-2017.

Santa Maria Valley, Le Bon Climat, 2007 (Clendenen Family Vineyards)
Medium to deep ruby color suggests more extraction than the ABC Pinots. Rather stern at the moment with slightly tarry, dark fruit nose. Dense, sweet, ripe fruits on the palate, tannins not too immediately obvious, but there is a strong drying effect on the finish, which is lifted by a touch of acidity. *** Drink 2014-2021.

Santa Maria Valley, Knox Alexander, 2008 (Au Bon Climat)
Translucent ruby color. Restrained nose follows through to palate, with light red fruits, a nice balance but less concentrated than 2007. Overall impression shows mineral red cherries with touch of strawberries. ** Drink 2013-2017.

California, Isabelle, 2008 (Au Bon Climat)
The quality of this cuvée entirely belies the broad California designation. Medium garnet color. Slightly tarry nose with some tea-like notes. Medium density red cherry fruits, with some tarry tannins on the finish giving a more evident sense of structure than the Alexander Knox cuvée. Fruits are sweet and ripe; the overall impression is elegant rather than powerful. *** Drink 2013-2018.

Byron

Byron Winery has been on a roller coaster. The winery is in the middle of the Nielson vineyard, which was the heart of the original plantings in Santa Maria Valley in 1964 (under the name of Tepusquet Vineyards). Some of the vineyards were sold off to Ken Brown, who started Byron. Surrounding the winery are 170 ha of contiguous vineyards. In 1991 Mondavi bought Byron and built a new winery. When Constellation took over Mondavi, they sold Byron off to Pegasus Estate, who went bankrupt within six months, spent a year in bankruptcy, and then were purchased by Kendall Jackson, who own next-door Cambria Estate. Today there are 25,000 cases of estate bottling, which account for almost all production except for some single vineyard wines made from purchased fruit. Pinot Noir is 60% of production (up from its minimum of 20%). There are five single vineyard wines; Nielson comes from the home ranch, the others are from purchased fruit. The Monument bottling is a barrel selection from the Nielson vineyard. Wines were tasted at Byron in February 2011.

Santa Barbara County, 2009
The grapes are sourced from both Santa Maria and Los Alamos valleys, hence the broad description. A black cherry and plum fruit nose offers some aromatic overtones. Slightly flat flavor profile on the palate, very soft, supple tannins, but not much structure or length on the finish. Quaffable. * Drink now-2014.

Santa Maria Valley, 2009
This is Byron's flagship wine, with a production of about 10,000 cases. Piquant black fruit aromatics show on the nose. Distinctly more aromatic on the palate than Byron's other Pinots, black plums showing as much as cherries. The piquant aromatics become fairly forceful on the finish. ** Drink now-2016.

Santa Maria Valley, Nielson Vineyard, 2009
350 cases of this selection from Nielson were bottled this year (the rest is declassified into the Santa Maria Valley bottling). Restrained nose but with characteristic black plums and cherries in the background. An immediately approachable style with soft, supple tannins and the structure pretty much hidden. ** Drink now-2019.

Santa Maria Valley, Monument, 2007
Only about a hundred cases of this selection from Nielson were made. It spends 15-16 months in oak, with about 30% new. Slightly tarry nose of black cherries and faintly aromatic plums. Somewhat dumb on the palate at the moment, with fruits following the nose, supported by smooth, supple tannins. This needs time to develop some complexity of flavor variety, although the tannins are soft enough to allow it to be enjoyed already. *** Drink now-2021.

Santa Maria Valley, Nielson Vineyard, 2004
The warm vintage produced wines that are aging relatively fast. 1,000 cases were produced from this vineyard. Attractive nose of earthy, nutty, strawberries. Smooth palate showing ripe fruits with good flavor variety. Softening nicely with age and most attractive except for some alcohol showing on the finish. In fact, the soft, earthy, nutty flavor spectrum could almost be European except for that note of alcohol. ** Drink now-2015.

Sea Smoke

Originally this was a 240 ha horse ranch in Santa Rita Hills. 140 ha were sold off to make the Sea Smoke vineyard, of which 40 ha were planted with Pinot Noir in 23 blocks in 1999. A little Chardonnay was added recently. There are various types of clay on the ranch, 10 clones, and multiple rootstocks. About half the total area is a relatively flat bench, which is easiest to work; this is biodynamic. The rest is farmed by sustainable methods, as the slopes would be more difficult to convert to biodynamics. Every clone and block combination is kept separate in barrel. Sea Smoke's three Pinot Noirs are based on barrel selections. Botella, which is about 5% of production, is the equivalent of a declassified wine (but some people prefer its lighter touch). Southing is the main production, and the most representative of what Santa Rita Hills is all about, says manager Victor Gallegos. Ten, which is a barrel selection of 25% of production, is the most expensive. "It's essentially a high testosterone version of Pinot Noir," says Victor, adding that the aficionados for this wine tend to have a background in cult Cabernets. It's usually 100% new oak (but in 2008 was only 75%). Wines were tasted at Sea Smoke in February 2011.

Santa Rita Hills, Botella, 2008
Only a small percentage of production, this bottling is effectively declassified from the principal Southing production. A slightly aromatic black fruit nose has some tarry notes. Medium density fruits of red cherries with hints of raspberries show on the palate, with some bitter touches from the tannins, which are quite fine. Acidity and fruit seem a little disjointed at this stage. There is some heat on the finish. ** Drink 2014-2019.

Santa Rita Hills, Southing, 2008
About two thirds of production, this is Sea Smoke's principal wine. The restrained nose offers an expectation of black fruits. The palate shows darker fruits and more intensity than the Botella, with full black cherry fruits, a slight piquancy with faintly malic notes lifting the fruits, and some heat on the finish. ** Drink 2014-2019.

Santa Rita Hills, Ten, 2008
About a quarter of production, Ten is Sea Smoke's top cuvée, based on a barrel selection. There's intensity on the nose with some tarry notes. Rich, deep, dark fruits of blackcurrants and blackberries as well as cherries dominate the palate; there is intense concentration with hints of chocolate on the finish. Fruits are more powerful, but less aromatic than Southing. ***(*) Drink 2014-2019.

Santa Rita Hills, Southing, 2007
Slightly savory nose has some herbal notes. Sweet ripe fruits on the palate take the form of red cherries with hints of raspberries and black cherries. There is good acidity, with a slightly bitter edge from the tannins which are big and drying. Some savory notes are just beginning to show on the palate. Needs some time. *** Drink 2014-2021.

Santa Rita Hills, Southing, 2006
Savory notes on the nose are more noticeable than in 2007, with a suspicion of gunflint. Fruits are softening already, giving a sense of earthy strawberries. Tannins are a gentle impression in the background, but there is good structural support for the evidently ripe, sweet fruits. ***(*) Drink now-2020.

Santa Rita Hills, Southing, 2005
Seems more youthful than the 2006. More fruit on the nose of mineral strawberries and only the faintest hint of savory development. Sweet, ripe, red fruit palate of red cherries and strawberries; fruits are soft but there is more evident structural support than 2006. A very nicely balanced wine, although there is a touch of heat on the finish. *** Drink now-2020.

Santa Rita Hills, Southing, 2004
The feature of this vintage was several days of hundred degree heat at the start of September, and you can smell the heat in the wine. The wine is at a turning point from fruity to savory, with sweet ripe fruits balanced by notes of sous bois. Tannins are still quite firm, but a slight bitterness develops in the glass. As often results from very hot conditions, this vintage is developing more rapidly than usual. *** Drink now-2017.

Santa Rita Hills, Southing, 2003
Uneven flowering was the main problem in this vintage, the result being that grapes did not reach their usual uniform degree of ripeness at harvest. They regard this vintage as a little herbaceous at Sea Smoke, but that comment could only be made in the context of the usual extreme ripeness. The restrained nose has a faintly herbaceous undertone if you look for it. Fruits on the palate are more restrained than usual, with less overt generosity, and some tannins are obvious on the finish, in somewhat of a break with the usual style of soft ripe fruits. ** Drink now-2017.

Santa Rita Hills, Southing, 2002
Very restrained on the nose. Sweet ripe fruits with a slightly jammy impression show on the palate. Glycerin gives a fat impression to the finish. Perhaps there is more underlying structure than is evident, but the overall impression here is somewhat superficial. ** Drink now-2016.

Santa Rita Hills, Southing, 2001
Still deep in color, but mature in hue, garnet with a broadening rim. Ripe fruits show on the nose with a faint savory impression. Nice balance on the palate, coming up to the turning point, with fruits now mingling with the first savory aromas. Good structure still shows, but tannins are resolving. Lovely now, although the fruits may soon start to dry out. *** Drink now-2016.

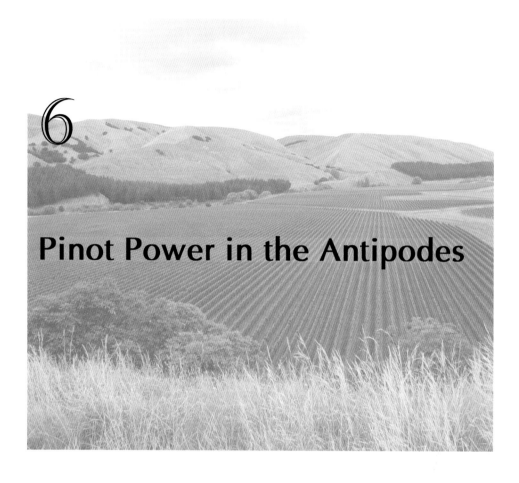

6

Pinot Power in the Antipodes

AUSTRALIA AND NEW ZEALAND HAVE BROUGHT a whole new style to wine. Red or white, the wines are dominated by bright, exuberant fruits. The hallmark is intensity of flavor. Sauvignon Blanc can be piercing in its citrus flavors, often with additional notes of passion fruit. Shiraz (Australian for Syrah) can be dense to the point of opacity, with deep, aromatic aromas and flavors. These varieties aren't necessarily reticent in Europe, but the southern hemisphere versions bring a new intensity to bear. How does this approach play for Pinot Noir, a variety known in its European habitat for its reserve and delicacy?

The development of the Antipodean style, so far as we can generalize, is a recent phenomenon. Wine production dates from early colonial times, but the style focused on sweet, fortified wines. This continued to be the model until the second half of the twentieth century. Varieties had to be robust and high yielding. In New Zealand, the industry was all but destroyed by a powerful Prohibitionist movement during the first half of the twentieth century. "A considerable quantity of the wine made in New Zealand would be classified as unfit for human consumption in other wine-producing countries," said a government report in 1946.[1] Over the next three decades, wine was made as much from sugar and water as from grapes. One sarcastic view of the industry was that growers "were forced to sell the grapes in order to get the money to buy the sugar to make the wine."[2] Wine production remained primitive into the 1970s. There were only about 350 ha of vineyards, and the most widely grown grape was Albany Surprise (a variety of Vitis labrusca). There were less than 100 ha of Vitis vinifera, and none of any quality variety. Plantings were concentrated almost exclusively in the warmer areas of Auckland and Hawkes's Bay. But things have certainly come a long way since then.

The modern industry dates from the 1980s, although its roots were established when viticulture spread south in the 1970s. It was not until the mid 1980s that plantings of Vitis vinifera achieved a majority in the country as a whole, and only in the 1990s that quality varieties became dominant. The focus has been largely on white wine, which still accounts for 85% of production.[3]

No grape has a long history of production in the Antipodes, but Pinot Noir is the newest of the newcomers. Attempts with reds were sporadic in New Zealand.[5] Hawke's Bay attracted some attention for Cabernet Sauvignon in the mid eighties, and Gimblett Gravels followed in the mid nineties. But for New Zealand as a whole, Pinot Noir slowly became the red of choice. The first commercial Pinot Noir was produced by Nobilo in Auckland in 1973.[6] A Pinot Noir from Canterbury won a gold medal in 1982.[7] A group of four wineries was established in Martinborough in the early eighties as a result of a viticultural bulletin of the late seventies highlighting its similarities with Burgundy.[8] The first vines in Marlborough had been planted in 1973; a

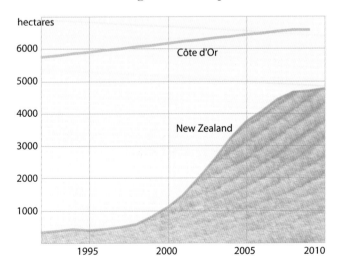

Plantings of Pinot Noir in New Zealand have increased sharply and are catching up to Burgundy's Côte d'Or.[4]

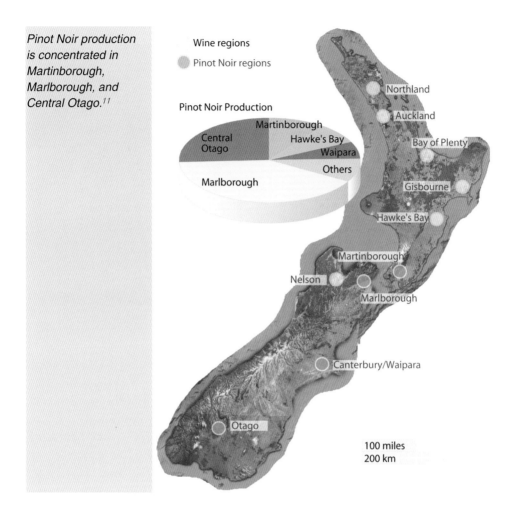

Pinot Noir production is concentrated in Martinborough, Marlborough, and Central Otago.[11]

decade later, Marlborough's reputation for white wine was firmly established with the release of Cloudy Bay's 1985 Sauvignon Blanc. Pinot Noir followed at the end of the eighties. Central Otago is the most recently developed region. Originally it was thought to be too cold; the Department of Agriculture said in 1958 that the "economics of grape growing" were "not very favorable."[9] The first commercial wines were not released from Central Otago until 1987.[10]

Red wines really became important only in the first decade of the twenty first century, when Pinot Noir was the most rapidly increasing variety. It is now the second most important variety in New Zealand, just ahead of Chardonnay. As the engine that pulls the industry in its train, Marlborough has always had the most plantings of Pinot Noir, but today the styles are defined more by Martinborough and Central Otago. Only a decade ago, plantings were almost insignificant outside Marlborough, but today Otago is in clear second place.[12] In Marlborough, Pinot Noir remains over shadowed by

White mulch under the vines is sometimes used to reflect light up to the bottom of the bunch. This helps to level light exposure between the top and bottom, increases phenolics relative to sugar accumulation, and produces more even ripening.

Sauvignon Blanc, but in Martinborough and Otago it is the major variety.[13] Marlborough has it on the numbers, but Martinborough and Central Otago have it on commitment.[14]

New Zealand is altogether a newcomer. The landmass is the most recent on the planet, with the mountainous spine created only some tens of millions of years ago, by a clash between the Pacific and Australian tectonic plates. As a result, the soils are much younger (and therefore tend to be more fertile) than those of other wine-producing regions. And New Zealand is a cooler climate than the latitudes of its grape growing regions would predict. Distant from any major landmass, and with most vineyards within a few miles of the coast, the cooling effects of the ocean are the predominant climatic influence, so summer temperatures do not usually rise above the moderate. Diurnal variation is extreme: it can be really cold during nights even in the summer. But sunshine hours are high. Marlborough is always one of the sunniest spots in New Zealand, and Central Otago gets increased sunshine hours from its southern location.[15]

All of the regions producing Pinot Noir are cool climates. (The Pinot Noir from the warmer climates of Gisbourne and Hawke's Bay mostly goes into sparkling wine.) Because Pinot Noir buds early, frost is a problem everywhere; wind machines to break up the air layers are common. Martinborough and Marlborough are not very different in overall temperatures from Burgundy. Central Otago is cooler, and the vineyards are at higher elevations; the climate is less moderate, as close as you can get to Continental in New Zealand, compared to the more maritime pattern of Martinborough or Marlborough. But the cool climate is compensated by New Zealand's unusual luminosity. The increased level of ultraviolet, resulting from a hole in the ozone layer, increases tannin production in the skins of berries (tannins are a protective reaction against ultraviolet burning). This speeds up phenolic development relative to the accumulation of sugars, and should help to keep alcohol levels down.

Alcohol levels are not nearly such a sensitive issue in New Zealand as in Oregon and California. "Everybody would like to make wine with slightly lower alcohol; we get 14% and would prefer 13.5%, but we are in a pretty cool climate, greenness is not acceptable, and in order to lose that we have to get the grapes properly ripe. Increasing vine age will probably help to lower alcohol a little bit," says winemaker Nick Blampied-Lane of Cloudy Bay.[16] All the same, it is a bit puzzling why alcohol levels in New Zealand Pinots should generally run 13.5-14.0%, roughly half a percent higher than Burgundy, given the comparable temperatures but greater light in New Zealand.

In spite of New Zealand's generally wet reputation, the east coast can be quite dry, and irrigation is often needed. Indeed, some wine-producing regions have less than the 700 mm annual rainfall required by the grapevine. Total annual rainfall in Martinborough and Marlborough is not terribly different from Burgundy, although the summers tend to be dry compared to a more even annual distribution in Burgundy.[17] Central Otago is somewhat drier. The dry summers mean there is little disease pressure, usually not much more than occasional powdery mildew. The main issue with pests comes from birds, which universally love to eat the crop.

All of the vines in New Zealand are young, and assessing Pinot Noir is complicated by the fact that the clones available for the initial plantings were somewhat restricted. The youthfulness of the vines is exacerbated by the fact that some replanting of the oldest vines has now been forced by the arrival

Netting is necessary to protect the crop against birds in New Zealand and Australia.

of phylloxera; this is a more serious issue in Martinborough and Central Otago, where many vines were planted on their own roots, than in Marlborough, where almost all are grafted.[18] (One reason why many vineyards were planted on their own roots is financial; the cost of grafting is about five times more, which can be a significant factor for small producers. And during the nineties, the supply of rootstocks was inadequate, so keeping vines on their own roots was sometimes the only alternative to postponing planting.)

Early plantings of Pinot Noir in New Zealand focused on two clones; Bachtobel, whose light color and weight make it more suitable for sparkling wine production; and AM10/5, a Swiss selection from Wädenswil, with relatively large berries and a tendency to herbaceousness when not fully ripe. But "clone" may be a complete misnomer for 10/5, which is divided into "upright" and "floppy" types. The upright form is predominant in Martinborough and Marlborough, and the floppy form is predominant in Central Otago. These almost certainly have completely different origins. Supposedly the Swiss clone held in Wädenswil is not upright, which would make the upright form the imposter. Its upright growth, and the habit of grape bunches sitting upright until they turn down at véraison, suggest that this form of 10/5 is almost certainly a Pinot Droit (much disdained in Burgundy for its high yield and low flavor, and generally pulled out after the 1980s). The floppy form is presumably a variant of Pinot Fin. The muddle between them makes it difficult to get a bead on intrinsic quality, but it's probably fair to say that producers still growing the upright form do so because the vines are now well established, and they feel that quality would not be improved by replacement with a younger, albeit higher quality, planting.

The Abel cultivar, based on cuttings confiscated by customs agent Malcolm Abel, is New Zealand's own clone. Although this was claimed to originate from Romanée Conti, it's notable that no one has ever come forward to document the Burgundian origins of what is now one of the most widely planted clones in New Zealand. It formed the basis for Ata Rangi's first vineyard in Martinborough, and still is almost half of their plantings. Since the early 1990s, the Dijon clones have been available, leading to the customary rush to plant the usual suspects. Because they flower early, the Dijon clones tend to be more susceptible to frost, but they are generally suitable for the growing season in New Zealand. The Pommard 5 clone from California is also quite widely grown.

Yields for Pinot Noir are low everywhere in New Zealand, typically in the range of 25-30 hl/ha in Martinborough and Central Otago, and somewhat higher on average at over 35 hl/ha in Marlborough.[19] This is significantly lower than Burgundy, where the limit for Grand Crus is 35-37 hl/ha, and premier crus and village wines can crop up to 40 hl/ha.

Dropping crop by cutting off surplus bunches is a common method of yield control in New Zealand, as can be seen from the density of fruit on the ground.

Winemaking decisions vary among producers in New Zealand as they do everywhere, but if there is a common pattern, it is to emphasize destemming followed by several days of cold soak. The need to acidify varies, but is more common than not in Martinborough and Marlborough, and almost universal in Central Otago. Considering that this is the New World with its reputation for technical wizardry, a surprising number of producers (a majority of those I visited) rely on indigenous yeast for fermentation. Temperatures for fermentation tend to be on the warm side, up to the maximum of 34 °C with a variable amount of pigeage (known locally as plunging), usually in open-topped stainless steel fermenters. (New Zealand's reputation for reductive winemaking under a blanket of inert gas does not apply to Pinot Noir, where winemaking is usually oxidative in style.) Extended post fermentation maceration is the exception rather than the rule. There has been some backing away from new oak, which is rarely more than 25-30% these days; and most barrels are emptied before the next vintage (so they are ready to use again). The general common objective is to get soft tannins that are hidden by the fruit so the wine can be drunk immediately on release.

Some trends in New Zealand are universal. Producers are backing off ultra-ripeness. "There's more of a hands-off policy with Pinot Noir and people are thinking about picking a little earlier," says winemaker Clive Jones of Nautilus.[20] "Part of the reason for the move to earlier picking is to reveal the vineyard," said viticulturalist Dave Shepherd of Escarpment.[21] Picking earlier can only go so far in reducing sugar levels, of course. There's a feeling that as the vines get older they will naturally achieve a better balance of sugar to phenolics, which will help to bring down alcohol a bit. "Young vines get over excited about developing sugar," says Malcolm Rees-Francis of Rockburn.[22]

Marlborough and Martinborough are only about 70 miles apart, at very similar latitudes, but the climates are different because the west-east Wairau Valley at Marlborough is protected by mountains from southern winds, whereas the valley around Martinborough runs north-south and is open to the wind.

Of course, all this is relative within the general context of New Zealand, where the wines generally have a fruit-forward, succulent style, and drink well when young.

Although Martinborough and Marlborough are close in terms of distance, they are miles apart in terms of total climatic influence because of the different orientations of their valleys. They are fond of saying in Martinborough that there is nothing between them and Antarctica. Because the valley runs north-south, it is exposed to cool southern winds, which have a major effect on flowering, commonly affecting fruit set, and consequently reducing yields. In fact, high wind is the main climatic feature (which led one early pioneer of Pinot Noir, Tim Finn, to plant his vineyard at Nelson just across Cook Straight in the South Island).[23] It's so windy that it's impossible to grow grapevines at the head of the valley; vineyards are clustered around the town of Martinborough, about ten miles into the valley. Wind toughens the grapes, increasing production of tannins in the skins, but its main effect is to reduce vegetative growth so the vines are less vigorous. Trees are often planted as windbreaks around the vineyards. In Marlborough, by contrast, the main Wairau Valley runs east-west, and the mountains to the south divert the winds, in fact pushing them towards the North Island. Marlborough's more even climate during the spring allows reliable flowering and good fruit set, increasing the yield. In fact, keeping down the yield is a big concern of premium Pinot Noir producers in Marlborough.

There are significant differences in organization between the regions. Martinborough is by far the smallest area, and most wine is produced by small producers. There are some growers who sell grapes rather than making wine. There are few large players. "Because Martinborough is a lower cropping region, it has not been attractive to the corporate culture," comments Clive Paton of Ata Rangi.[24] Marlborough is organized on a much larger scale, with an average vineyard size several times that of Martinborough, and some large corporations.[25] It also has a much larger proportion of contract growers (who outnumber producers by several fold). Central Otago has more of a split personality: there are some large producers but there are also many very small producers, some working on a part time basis.

Winegrowing was actually established long ago in Martinborough, when the first vineyard was planted in the nineteenth century. In fact, the French wife of an early settler produced Pinot Noir that was exhibited in Paris in 1897.[26] Others followed. But all the vines were pulled out in 1908 after Wairarapa voted for Prohibition. By the second half of the century Martinborough was a declining agricultural community. The modern era started in 1979 when Dr. Derek Milne, a soil scientist and wine enthusiast, was commissioned to write a government report on possibilities for grape growing. His identification of Martinborough as having similar conditions to Bur-

Marie Zelie planted the first vineyard in Martinborough in 1892. This shows a harvest soon after. Photograph kindly provided by Martinborough Vineyard.

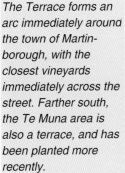

The Terrace forms an arc immediately around the town of Martinborough, with the closest vineyards immediately across the street. Farther south, the Te Muna area is also a terrace, and has been planted more recently.

gundy led immediately to the establishment of four wineries, Ata Rangi, Chifney, Dry River and Martinborough Vineyard, with Milne himself becoming a partner in Martinborough Vineyard. Growth was steady for the first two decades, reaching a total of 300 hectares of vineyards at the turn of century. Since then it has been rapid, almost tripling in the first decade of the twenty first century. Vineyards are small scale operations, only two out of the sixty producing more than 20,000 cases per year. The whole Wairarapa region produces less than one per cent of New Zealand's wine. (Viticulture is still less important overall in Martinborough than sheep farming.)

For the Wairarapa region (of which Martinborough is far and away the best known part[27]), Pinot Noir is almost half of production; it is probably closer to three quarters of production in Martinborough itself.[28] Many Martinborough producers have their hearts in Burgundian varieties, but the market for Chardonnay is so competitive that few have concentrated on it. The most commonly produced white wine is Sauvignon Blanc, which in these difficult economic times is for some the cash cow that keeps the business afloat.[29]

The area of wine production is a river terrace forming an arc around the town of Martinborough. The terrace overlooks the old river bed and the river to the north beyond. The boundaries of the terrace are quite well delineated, with the road more or less providing a dividing point: on one side are the gravel terraces, on the other side are much heavier soils, not suitable for vines. In the 1990s, the producers tried to define the terrace as a legal appellation, but that effort failed, and the legal definition of the Martinborough GI (Geographical Indication) is much broader, including many areas of clay-based soils that are unsuitable for wine production.[30] (In fact, streaks of clay run at intervals though the terrace, but are not usually planted with vines.) "It's an absolute minefield," said Clive Paton when I asked him whether this opened the way for the reputation of Martinborough to be diffused by inappropriate plantings, and should there be a specific GI for The Terrace.[31] "What we have is not ideal but is better than not doing anything," he says. (Ironically the terrace geology is also found just to the north outside the Martinborough GI, where Pinot Noir is produced under the more general Wairarapa label.)

The terrace at Martinborough is built up of layers of gravel and silt. The vineyards are on the top.

When you taste the current vintage in Martinborough, it's easy to form an impression that the character of the region is for sweet ripe fruits, more red than black, with a supple palate and soft tannins receding into the background. The wines aren't brash, the fruits aren't forceful, but there's a certain sense of lushness. This may be reasonable as a general description of the wines in general distribution, but is misleading with regards to the diversity in character of the top wines, especially as they age. Winemaking styles differ here as everywhere else, from the wines of Martinborough Vineyard which show more red fruit character to those of Escarpment (Υ page 324) which are definitely darker and tend towards black fruits. Three of the original four vineyards that established Pinot Noir in Martinborough are still at the forefront, with Martinborough Vineyard (Υ page 325) perhaps the most elegant in current style, Dry River (Υ page 323) showing ageability right back to its first vintages (and having achieved a cult status that sells out the wines within days of release to a privileged mailing list), and Ata Rangi (Υ page 321), the only one left under its original family ownership, making wines that some consider embody the character of the region.

Vintage variation is not something to which consumers of New Zealand wines pay much attention, but has been quite significant lately. "The 2000s have been a difficult decade, the previous decade was more even, so if there is climate change, what's driving it is making conditions more erratic—more like Burgundy used to be!" says Ian Smart of Alana Estate (Υ page 320). My assessment of Martinborough as relatively lush compared to Burgundy may be biased by the fact that the most recent vintage (2009) was exceptionally warm, and the wines are on the rich side. (Although the previous vintage was more classic, those before it were small and concentrated.) But temperature is not the main determinant of vintage variation here, which is due more to wind, frost, and rain. Frost is a big issue in reducing crop size; and by blowing pollen off the vines, the wind not only reduces yield but also can affect quality by causing uneven timing of fruit set, creating variation in berry size within the bunches.

One common feature of Martinborough (and indeed New Zealand in general) is the intention that the wines should be ready to drink on release, which is to say within a couple of years of the vintage. Style is partly being driven by the market. "There is certainly a consumer attitude in New Zealand that once you go past a year or two, why is the wine there," comments winemaker Duncan Forsyth of Mount Edward.[32] Whenever I expressed skepticism as to whether it's really possible to make wines that express their full potential complexity so quickly, producers commonly said that they feel the climate and terroir allow them to make wines with soft and ripe enough tannins that the wines are immediately approachable. I remain somewhat skeptical, however, since for my taste the majority of wines have sufficient tannins that I feel the full flavor spectrum will not be fully appreciated if the bottles are opened immediately, although I will concede that they are not objectionable to drink now. Are producers short changing themselves by pandering to a consumer market that thrives on instant gratification; if only they could hold the wines longer before release, would the reputation of the region rise? Of course, given the general small size and lack of financial resources, that may be too difficult economically.

Regional typicity is not entirely intrinsic to terroir and winemaking desires, but is clearly influenced by external market pressures. The worldwide economic decline has put pressure on grape and wine prices in Martinborough as elsewhere. Some producers have responded by introducing or by increasing production of second labels, essentially wines that are declassified from their estate wine, and designed for instant consumption. These typically run at under half the price of the estate wines, and there's some risk of undercutting the reputation of the region for high-end wines, as well as giving a misleading impression of character. When you remember that most Martinborough Pinot Noirs are in any case drunk within the first two or three years—at the start of 2011, shops and restaurants were largely selling 2009 and 2008 vintages, and even the 2007 vintage was rare—instant consumption becomes so immediate as to threaten typicity.

As a general rule, I feel the first label wines mostly release their full fruit flavors around four or five years after the vintage, and may age well for as long again. (Producers usually express their ambitions for aging in terms of five or so years.) Among the top wines, which vary between reserve selections and single vineyards, there are certainly exceptions that age well for a decade or more, notably from Dry River and Martinborough Vineyard (Ỷ pages 323 and 325). There is a bias towards reserve selections in Martinborough, one reason being that plantings are still young, and in many cases producers feel there has not been sufficient experience to identify significant and consistent differences between blocks, especially given the relatively homogeneous nature of the terrace. (The main variation is in the depth of the soil, with silt varying from 20 to 50 cms on top of the gravel bed.) Some impressive barrel selections are made periodically by Palliser Estate (Ỷ page 326); and Martinborough Vineyard have experimented with Reserve wines. The arch exponent of single vineyards is Larry McKenna at Escarpment, whose three single vineyard wines are quite distinct (Ỷ page 324).

The atmosphere is quite different in Marlborough. New Zealand's largest wine-producing region now accounts for roughly two thirds of all wine produced in New Zealand. The scale is much larger, and most grapes are produced by growers. The majority of mid size and large producers rely on bought-in grapes. Sauvignon Blanc is three quarters of all production. "It's somewhat Sauvignon Blanc versus the rest," says viticulturalist Colin Ross at

Seresin Estate.[33] "We are a region driven by Sauvignon Blanc with a subculture of Pinot Noir" says winemaker Nick Blampied-Lane at Cloudy Bay (Ⲧ page 331).[34] The industrial side is revealed by visiting the commercial estate near Cloudy Bay where most Marlborough wines are bottled by contract bottlers. I do wonder how this relates to the search for quality by minimal intervention during vinification.

Marlborough really consists of two different types of wine-producing regions. The main area is the Wairau Valley, where former sheep-grazing pastures have been almost entirely replaced by stretches of vineyards, making viticulture close to a monoculture; Wairau's 17,000 ha of vineyards account for about three quarters of the total in Marlborough.[35] A wide open plain oriented east-west, the Wairau Valley opens out to the ocean at Cloudy Bay. At the eastern end of the valley, Blenheim is always one of the two or three sunniest places in New Zealand. Visiting Marlborough, it's surprising from a

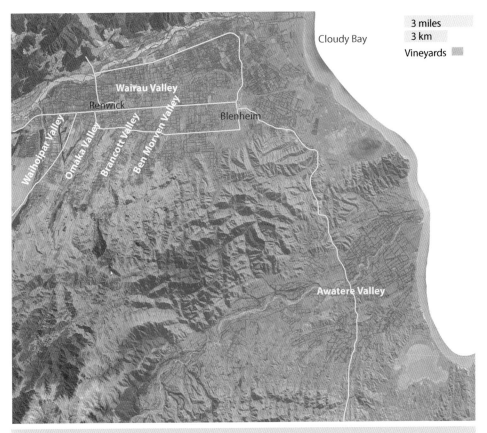

Most Marlborough wineries are located in Wairau Valley. which runs west to east and opens out to the ocean, but much Pinot Noir is planted on the slopes of valleys to the south. Mountains protect them from southern winds. Awatere Valley is farther south.

European context to see so many vineyards on the flat lands in the heart of the valley. Of relatively recent origin, the alluvial soils are relatively rich and fertile (and are mostly used for Sauvignon Blanc, which sprouts like a weed on the fertile valley floor). The other side of the coin, however, is that young soils are free-draining, because they have not accumulated the deposits that would wash off the hills with time. "In France you need to go for the hillsides partly in order to get drainage, but you don't need to do that here," Damien Yvon of Clos Henri explained to me (⟨ page 330).[36]

Protected by mountains from the southern winds, the climate is reliable. The prevailing weather here comes from the north east; rainfall on the north side of the Wairau Valley is double that on the south side. Divided by the highway, to the north are the most free draining soils of the valley, to the south there is more loess that's been deposited by the prevailing wind. Usually they get reliable flowering and good fruit set here. "Marlborough has an advantage with consistency of climate, there is a reason why 65% of the wine industry is based here," says Ivan Sutherland of Dog Point.[37] Yet there is far more diversity in Marlborough than Martinborough.

Spreading from Wairau Valley to the south, like fingers from the palm of a hand, on a northeast to southwest orientation, are the Southern Valleys (Ben Morven, Brancott/Fairhall, Omaka, and Waihopai). Cooler than Wairau Valley, the Southern Valleys have more gravel on the flat; their undulating hills have a greater content of clay. The four Southern Valleys come naturally off the Wairau Valley, but Awatere is a bone shaking half hour drive over Taylors Pass, into a cooler climate with different soil types altogether, dominated by Papa clay. This is the coolest and driest part of Marlborough, but the difference in character is due more to greater wind exposure than to temperature.

The central Wairau Valley is a wide, flat plain. (The white areas are vineyards covered with netting.)

The first vineyard in Marlborough was established at Auntsfield in 1873 on a hillside site in the southern valleys. The grape variety was probably Brown Muscat. Nothing much happened in viticulture until a century later when Montana planted the first vineyard in the Brancott Valley. Since the breakthrough that followed international recognition for Cloudy Bay's 1985 Sauvignon Blanc, growth has been exponential: a decade later there were 2,000 ha of vineyards, and today there are 24,000 ha. Pinot Noir has been a more or less steady 10% of the total planted area,[38] but there's been a change in thinking about where it should be planted and how it should be grown.

"The original production of Pinot Noir was based on the model of over-cropping Sauvignon Blanc," says Mike Eaton of TerraVin. There is now a general recognition that the Wairau Valley floor is not the best place for Pinot Noir; in fact some vineyards have been pulled out. Whereas Martinborough has always concentrated on the high-end, but has been forced by economic circumstances to introduce more entry level wines, Marlborough has gone in the opposite direction, moving away from production of generic Pinot Noir towards production of premium wine. This has led to a tendency to plant Pinot on the clay soils of the Southern Valleys.

Marlborough style is more variable than Martinborough. There remains a fair proportion of entry level wine, well made and pleasant, but without forceful character. The wines from Wairau Valley itself tend to show more superficial, fleshy fruit, with less tannic structure. Premium Pinot from the Southern Valleys tends to cherry-driven fruits, given a rich impression by clay soils. Especially in the Brancott area, the wines have a more obvious sense of gravelly texture. Awatere Valley produces the leanest wines, with a tendency to strawberry fruits showing a mineral or earthy character, and a stronger tannic structure. Although there is a trend towards single vineyard wines, many are blended from multiple sources, not necessarily within the same valley. Sometimes a producer will indicate the origin of a wine from a particular valley, but that's somewhat a matter of personal reference, and so far there isn't enough outside recognition of the difference to make this a selling point (☛ page 328). Single vineyard names function more as brands than as indicators of origin.

Production of Pinot Noir in Marlborough is split between large producers for whom it is a sideline, sometimes managed more or less separately, and smaller producers (usually located in the Southern Valleys) for whom it is more of a focus. "That side of the winery is devoted to the evil commercial side and this side is quite separate for the Pinot," said the winemaker at one large producer, gesturing to two separate facilities. It's really little more than a decade since the start of the movement to treat Pinot Noir differently. "When we planted Pinot Noir in close spacing (1 × 1.5 m), and on a hillside, everyone thought we were mad," says Mike Eaton, recollecting the reaction

The first vineyard in Marlborough was planted as an array of single vines at Auntsfield. As part of the development of Auntsfield Estate, the vineyard is being recreated today. Photograph kindly provided by Auntsfield estate.

to his establishment of TerraVin in 1998 (🍷 page 337).[39] Today the small producers of premium Pinot Noir may outnumber the large producers, although they contribute less to the total volume of production. "There are perhaps twenty serious producers of Pinot Noir," says Nick Blampied-Lane.[40]

It's a universal feeling that the largest impediment to success of Pinot Noir in Marlborough is the reputation for industrial production of Sauvignon Blanc. "As a result, people do not take Marlborough Pinot Noir as seriously as they should. We think Pinot Noir is ideally suited to Marlborough provided it's planted in the right soils, with the right clones," say James Healy and Ivan Sutherland of Dog Point (🍷 page 332).[41] Summarizing the situation, Hätsch Kalberer of Fromm Winery says that, "We want to lift the recognition of Marlborough. The main problem we are facing is the perception that Marlborough should be a wine of convenience, with lifted fruit, and should not be challenging. What creates New Zealand style is due to manipulation, it is more a winemaker-determined style than a terroir-dominated style. We don't want to make Burgundy, we want to make New Zealand wine, we absolutely make New Zealand wine. We follow the school of the Old World and let wine express itself, we have a very similar pedigree with the wines reflecting the terroir. But if you make wine like a grand cru that has real tannins, you will never get high marks."[42]

Certainly no one in New Zealand believes in the maxim that great vintages must be bitterly tannic when young. Tannins are often barely noticeable in the wine upon release. Is this due to winemaking decisions or a natural feature? "The Marlborough fruit profile is very generous, there is always a sweet core, making it very approachable—it's not a conscious attempt to satisfy the market," says winemaker Jeremy McKenzie at Villa Maria (ⴲ page 338). Within the context of winemaking in New Zealand, this may be fair, but I do think that the general consensus on winemaking, especially with regards to extraction, sets a background in which tannins are minimized. They seem to me to be less noticeable in the wines of Marlborough and Central Otago than Martinborough, where the balance of tannins to fruit is tauter.

When you ask producers in Marlborough to define the regional character of Pinot Noir, they tend to be more circumspect than producers asked the same question in Martinborough or Central Otago. This may be because they feel that the character has been defined at a low level by large producers. Mike Eaton argues that, "I'm not a big fan of regionalization, we will have regional strengths [within New Zealand], and that will be more climate dependent, but to try to make a wine each vintage that conforms to some idea of the regional character is for big producers. Wine is the only beverage that has the ability to reflect time and place so why would you want to try to make every vintage consistent?" He believes that the future for Marlborough lies in making distinctive single vineyard wines, but at the moment, there is no incentive to do so: "We are spending what we would spend on producing grand crus but we are not getting grand cru prices."[43]

Another impediment to moving towards single vineyards is the young age of the vines. It takes at least a decade for a vineyard to express itself. But it's becoming an issue for discussion. "Ten years ago everyone was talking about clones, now they are talking about sites. That's natural because when the vines are young the clones show more distinctly, and as they age the site takes over dominance of expression," says Clive Jones of Nautilus Estate.[44] The present situation remains more or less evenly split between producers whose top bottlings are reserve wines and those for whom they are single vineyards. "From a quality view, barrel selection would produce the best wine, but there is more interest in defining single vineyard wines," says Tim Finn of Neudorf, as a general comment.[45]

At the very top level, Marlborough Pinot is fruit-driven (although not as obviously as in Central Otago) and has tannins that are soft enough, or pushed far enough into the background by the fruits, to allow the wine to be drunk on release—although in my opinion it would usually be better to wait another year or so. The wines can be delicious at four to five years of age, although sometimes I find the intensity, coupled with alcohol pushing 14%, can be a little too much to match food. But it has to be admitted that statistically speaking, if you select a wine label at random, you will have a better chance of finding an intriguing wine from Martinborough, where a far greater proportion of producers are devoted exclusively to premium Pinot. I think it is a fair concern that the reputation of Marlborough is brought down by some of the Pinots that are produced in sizeable quantities by larger producers. They are approachable and quaffable but do they represent the true typicity that Marlborough should offer?

Over the mountains to the west and north of Marlborough is the Neudorf vineyard near Nelson. After searching for a location to grow Burgundian varieties, Tim and Judy Finn settled on a site in the Moutere Hills in 1978. Relatively protected from the weather with a maritime climate, the vineyard has clay and gravel soils on north-facing slopes. Neudorf has become famous for its Chardonnay, which is quite Burgundian, but the Pinots are a close second (Ⴁ page 339). "We see our wines as the European cusp of the New Zealand spectrum. This is what the land basically gives us," says Tim Finn.[46] The tendency towards savory rather than jammy fruits comes out clearly after a few years. The style is closest to Martinborough, but perhaps more restrained. Neudorf's pioneering move has been followed by another twenty or more wineries setting up in the hills or on the plain below.

Far to the south, Central Otago is the most geographically and climatically diverse of the Pinot-producing regions. The stereotype of Central Otago is for big wines with lots of upfront red fruits. But my visit to the region—admittedly biased towards the most interesting, cutting edge producers—shows a different picture, with many wines showing a fine edge of elegance, and differences between subregions being revealed where producers have backed away from the full blown style to allow different terroirs to reveal themselves. My tasting notes included mention of elegance and finesse far more frequently than I had expected when I set out for the region (Ⴁ page 340).

Wines of each sub region within Central Otago have their own characteristics, more or less correlated with the heat accumulation during the growing season (although most labels only identify Central Otago as the source). Although there are local soil variations, the differences between the parts of the region are more about climate—heat accumulation, rainfall, and wind exposure—than about the soils. Most producers feel that in any case the vines are too young really to express the soil yet.

The heart of Central Otago is the Cromwell Basin around Lake Dunstan, which accounts for three quarters of production. At the south end of the Basin, in an arc extending out from the town of Cromwell, is Bannockburn, the warmest part of the region. The extremes of Bannockburn are more or less defined by the vineyards of Felton Road Winery. At the eastern edge is

Central Otago has vineyards in several separate areas. Two thirds lie in the Cromwell Basin, to the south of Cromwell or to its north on both sides of Lake Dunstan. Most of the rest are in Gibbston Valley. There is a cluster around Alexandra to the south, and a few at Wanaka to the north. North Otago lies to the east of the map.

the dramatic Cornish Point vineyard, on a promontory surrounded by water, more or less at the foot of Lake Dunstan (which was created when the Clutha River was dammed). At the western edge is the Elms Vineyard, more or less as far as you can go before being blocked by Mount Difficulty. There's a wide variety of soils in Bannockburn, from loess to schist. Bannockburn has the fleshiest, and richest, wines of the region, but with good structure for the top wines, especially from the iconic Felton Road area. At a casual tasting, Bannockburn may seem to have more forward fruits and less structure, but this impression may be biased by the concentration of producers making more entry-level wines for immediate consumption.

Moving up Lake Dunstan, it is a little cooler. Going north provides a contrast between the two sides of the lake. Most vineyards are on the west side of the lake, on slightly inclined land with loess over sand and gravel soils, extending from Lowburn through Parkburn and Pisa. The most recently developed area is Bendigo, on the east side, where the vineyards are on steep slopes based on schist, with about a 150 m rise from the lake to the top of the slope. This side of the lake is warmer, partly because of heat reflected from the rocky soil. Quartz runs through the area, and gold mining in the quartz reef was a major economic activity in the nineteenth century. Wines from the western side are plush and rich; wines from Bendigo on the eastern side have darker fruits supported by the biggest tannic structure of the region. "This vineyard brings tannins very much at the masculine end, our job is to give it a feminine edge," says Rudi Bauer of Quartz Reef, who pioneered wine production at Bendigo (☐ page 351).

Most vineyards along Lake Dunstan are on land sloping up slightly from the western side of the lake and facing east. The vineyards show as large white blocks because they are covered by netting.

To the north of the lake are a handful of wineries around Lake Wanaka, where the climate is significantly cooler. Here there is a tendency to minerality or earthiness in the wines. The farthest sub region to the north, Wanaka resembles Gibbston Valley, located to the west of Cromwell, which is the coolest sub region of all. The growing season in Gibbston starts and ends around three weeks later than in Cromwell, so ripening occurs in a different part of the season. The wines tend to be lighter and more angular, with more of an obvious cool climate impression. This was actually the first part of the region to be planted, with Gibbston Valley Wines along the main road, and Chard Farm (Ⓨ page 344) in a dramatic location high up above the gorge. Both Wanaka and Gibbston give a distinct impression of cool climate in their Pinots. Alexandra Valley, lying to the east, and the farthest from the southern Alps, is hotter and by far the driest part of the region.[47] Gibbston and Alexandra are the farthest apart in terms of climate. Alexandra is hard to get a bead on, because character varies, but aromatics may be more noticeable.

All this is relative, of course, within the context of a style that is generally more fruit-driven than the regions to the north, with a tendency to be if anything even more immediately approachable. But is it too early to assess Central Otago? "People love to say that Central Otago makes fruit-driven wine. Martinborough has savory texture, but its vines were 25 years old when Central Otago was just starting. With sites being defined, and better clones available, and the vines getting older, I don't think we can really view Central

In Gibbston Valley, the vineyards nestle up to the mountains.

Otago like that any more,"[48] says Claire Mulholland, who has come from making wine at Martinborough Vineyard to a new enterprise at Burn Cottage in Central Otago (⏽ page 343). Vineyard management has improved as owners have taken back control from contractual arrangements, and wine-making has become more refined, she says. Winemaker Blair Walters of Felton Road comments that "It's a measure of the quality that people could plant vineyards, manage them under contract, have the wine made for them—and even then sell it successfully."[49]

Although Central Otago is the coolest winemaking climate in New Zealand, acidification is almost universal for Pinot Noir. The reason is curious. The grapes usually come in with a good level of acidity, but by the end of fermentation, pH [inversely related to acidity] has risen to a point that makes winemakers uncomfortable. For incompletely defined reasons, the acid is not stable during fermentation. As a result, most winemakers add some tartaric acid at the start of fermentation, even though it would not necessarily be demanded on the numbers. "We are a cool climate and we have high acid, but a weird thing happens and we have to replace the acid," says Malcolm Rees-Francis of Rockburn (⏽ page 352), who thinks the problem arises from excess potassium and calls the process "potassium fining," a term viewed somewhat ironically by other producers.

The scene in Central Otago is quite different from farther north. There's a much wider range of producer sizes. Only the largest three producers are

The land at Bendigo was a scrub used for pasture (upper) before vineyards were planted on the steep slopes (lower).

above the 25,000 case annual level. There are many small producers, most of whom do not have their own winemaking facilities. Many of them are only part time growers. Called hobbyists slightly pejoratively by the professionals, some of them will become real producers, but others will give up because the operation is not really economic. Contract winemaking is common. "There are few wineries in Central Otago that don't also make wine for someone else," says Pete Bartles of VinPro,[50] the largest contract winemaker in town. Indeed, a large proportion of all Central Otago wine is made at one of two purpose-built contract facilities, VinPro or COWCo, in the industrial area of Cromwell. The winemaking teams at these facilities are highly professional, and respect the varying intentions of their client producers, but all the same, you have to wonder to what extent this results in more commonality of style.

The potential of the region is displayed most clearly by its single vineyard wines. Those that have made the most impression on the outside world come from Felton Road in the Bannockburn area. The wines from Cornish Point and Calvert Vineyard are quite distinct from the Block 3 and Block 5 wines, which come from the oldest parts of the Elms Vineyard (⏀ page 345). Coming up to twenty years of vine age, their potential is now becoming apparent. The extent of vineyard variation is emphasized by the fact that at Mount Difficulty, where single vineyard wines are released only in top years, only once in the past decade have all three single vineyards been released in the same year (⏀ page 349). There is also increasing interest in single vine-

Much wine in Central Otago is made at the VinPro or COWCo facilities in the industrial area of Cromwell.

yard wines from the Bendigo area, which make fewer concessions than usual to the instant approachability of the New Zealand style.

The single vineyard wines remain better known individually than as representatives of sub areas. "I'm strongly of the belief that we need to develop our sub regional identities and I reject the idea that we are too young to do it," says winemaker Chris Keyes at Gibbston Valley Wines,[51] where the single vineyard bottlings come from their vineyards in Bendigo (page 347). Actually, many of the single vineyard wines are really a half way house between single vineyards and reserves: often they are based on a barrel selection from within the single vineyard. I encountered many truly interesting top level wines, whether originating from single vineyards or as reserve selections, but almost all are produced in miniscule amounts. The difference in complexity and longevity between these wines and the general estate wines is often like day and night.

The use of selection in single vineyard wines raises another question. How far is our perception of terroir biased by selection (or declassification)? If you want to express terroir, don't you need to make the wine from the vineyard, the whole vineyard, and nothing but the vineyard? If you have a certain image of what your vineyard should produce, and you select barrels that conform, or deselect barrels that don't come up to expectation, are you turning the vineyard name into a brand where winemaking and selection become more important than terroir? This may make a better wine, but does it truly allow the terroir to express itself in every vintage?

For all the differences between New Zealand's Pinot-producing regions, a certain commonality is evident. Central Otago may be the most fruity in style, and Marlborough may be fleshier than Martinborough, which has the tautest structure, but all this is within a more fruit-forward style than Europe. Fruits are usually the dominant impression in young wines, and it is relatively rare for a wine to require much, if any, aging after release. Pinots today are far distant from the stereotype of heavily-extracted New World wines, yet they show youthful exuberance rather than the austerity one might anticipate from cool climates. It would be a mistake to judge potential quality on the basis of entry-level wines, which unsurprisingly rarely rise above the level of interest appropriate for immediate consumption. Wines at the estate level have levels of extract that would often be envied in Burgundy, yet only sometimes achieve the character that is needed for real interest. It is certainly a different story at the level of single vineyard wines, where not only are there many insights into Pinot typicity through reflections of terroir, but the best become increasingly interesting as they age for a decade or two. One problem outside New Zealand is that the export market is dominated by the estate wines; your chance of finding one of the really interesting single vineyard (or reserve) wines is rather slim. Another impediment to judging potential quality is the youth of the vines (exacerbated by the fact that the oldest vines are from the poorest clones); most vineyards have only just passed the stage where clonal specificity has begun to give way to site specificity. Nor is the extent of vintage variation always appreciated. It is certainly less extreme than in Europe, but is more significant than most consumers realize. Also, climatic conditions in New Zealand's Pinot-producing regions show little consistency within a vintage, and a good vintage in one region may be difficult in another.[52]

A thousand miles or so across the Tasman Sea are Australia's best Pinot Noir-producing regions. Pinot Noir is a very minor part of wine production in Australia, around 5% of all red wine.[53] It's grown in a surprisingly wide range of climates, and just over a quarter comes from the coolest climates, mostly Yarra Valley and Mornington Peninsula, with a smaller contribution from Tasmania.[54] All three areas are quite heavily committed to Burgundian varieties, with Pinot Noir and Chardonnay accounting for two thirds or more of production (although some goes into sparkling wine). Pinot Noir is the most widely planted grape in each region, with 840 ha in Yarra Valley, 430 ha in Mornington Peninsula, and 320 ha in Tasmania (roughly the same total as Central Otago and Martinborough combined).

Wine production in Australia dates from the first plantings made by James Busby in 1824. Following a trip to Europe in 1832, he returned with 678 varieties of grapevines. Busby thought that Clos Vougeot and Chambertin made the best red wines of Burgundy, and he collected his cuttings from

Clos Vougeot. "[I] received from M. L'Ecrivain a small bundle of each of the kinds of vines cultivated in the Clos Vougeot," he wrote after his visit.[55] One of these Pinot Noir cuttings became the origin of the MV6 (mother vine 6) clone. More than a century later, presumably with some adaptation to its new habitats, MV6 remains the predominant Pinot Noir clone in Australia. It has relatively low yields with small berries and bunches, and is usually considered to give a dense, sturdy wine, but with less aromatic fruit flavors than the Dijon clones. As everywhere else, Dijon clones are making some inroads, with some change of style possible since they ripen earlier than MV6. There's some skepticism about their suitability for Yarra Valley, where they are popular for grapes for sparkling wine, but some producers prefer to stick to MV6 for dry wine.

Although each is roughly the same distance from Melbourne, the feeling is quite different between Yarra Valley and Mornington Peninsula. Travelling east from Melbourne to Yarra Valley, the suburbs make an abrupt transition to agricultural countryside. In some areas, vineyards are quite concentrated, giving an impression of local monoculture. Viticulture is relatively large scale in Yarra Valley, where 3,800 ha of vineyards are exploited by 146 wineries. The largest winery, De Bortoli, has around 200 ha of vineyards. Going south to Mornington Peninsula, there is a more varied impression, with fancy residences common near the coast. Viticulture is not the main activity of the Peninsula, which is Melbourne's playground, with horse studs as common as vineyards. The high cost of land, especially in Mornington Peninsula, makes it difficult to produce value-oriented entry-level wines, and is a factor in driving wine production towards premium levels.[56]

On the smaller scale of Mornington Peninsula, the 950 ha of vineyards are divided among 60 wineries. Only a handful of producers have more than 50 ha of vineyards or exceed 25,000 cases of annual production. Some are very

The harvest at St. Hubert's vineyard around 1900, when the winery was well established as the oldest and largest in Yarra Valley.

Photograph kindly provided by Museum Victoria.

small, even on a Burgundian scale. Many of the smaller producers are part-time operations, varying from serious producers who would like to be able to give up their day jobs, to lifestyle operations owned by lawyers or doctors from Melbourne. The "hobbyists" are viewed with some disdain by the more professional, larger scale operations in Yarra. The other side of the coin, however, is that some of the most interesting producers in Mornington are people who have successfully made the transition from a former career to wine producer, and who as the result of the transition tend to have a more skeptical and innovative eye towards winemaking. Yarra Valley certainly has a more commercial feel, which is reflected in the wines, although character is not necessarily a function of size. The largest winery I visited in Yarra made the best wines, and the most overtly "commercial" were made by one of the smallest. The common refrain among the producers with more commercial styles was that the brand should be reliable, that there should be no surprises or challenges for the consumer.

Yarra Valley is relatively cool (depending on which site you examine, Mornington Peninsula to its south may be either cooler or warmer, but the typical harvest is three weeks later, which is perhaps the best indication of relative styles. Tasmania off to the south is certainly significantly cooler). The average growing season temperature in Yarra Valley is roughly in the same range as Russian River Valley in California—warmer than Burgundy or New Zealand (but vineyards can be planted on elevated sites to compensate). Wine production goes back to the first settlers; Yering Station was the first vineyard to be planted, in 1838. By the end of the nineteenth century the top Yarra wineries were good enough to export to Europe. Production collapsed in the twentieth century as the fashion turned to fortified wines, for which the cool climate was not suitable. Dairy farming took over the valley, and grape growing did not resume until the 1960s, paused through the 1970s, and then grew exponentially. At first operations were on a small scale, but larger wineries developed in the 1990s.

Perhaps one should not be too snobbish about hobbyists, since the medical profession was much involved in reestablishing wine production in Yarra Valley. Dr. Bailey Carrodus established Yarra Yering, and his initial vintage in 1973 was the first commercial production in fifty years. Dr. Peter MacMahon followed at Seville Estate, and John Middleton at Mount Mary, in the early 1970s. All of them produced both Bordeaux blends and Pinot Noir. Today Pinot Noir is far more important than Cabernet Sauvignon (but Shiraz is also successful, which gives a measure that Yarra Valley is not on the cool margin.) Some of the original plantings are still producing, although they precede the introduction of the better clones. "In the 1970s you were happy if you just got the right variety from the nursery," says Dylan MacMahon, who is Peter MacMahon's grandson and the present winemaker at Seville Estate.[57]

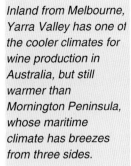
Inland from Melbourne, Yarra Valley has one of the cooler climates for wine production in Australia, but still warmer than Mornington Peninsula, whose maritime climate has breezes from three sides.

"Pinot Noir is the flagship of Yarra," says James Halliday, who pioneered its production at Coldstream Hills in the eighties.[58] But you have to find the right sites. "When the vines are facing south and east, we start to taste the ground. When they are facing west and north, they start to taste Australian," says winemaker Steve Weber at De Bortoli.[59] In addition to orientation, there are some sub regional characteristics, although they are not usually much emphasized here.

The territory is generally divided into two parts: Lower Yarra to the north, and Upper Yarra to the south. In Upper Yarra the elevation is a little higher, and the volcanic soils are red (much like the Jory soils of Willamette Valley in Oregon). Pinot tends to be lighter and brighter here, with a focus towards red cherry fruits. In the wines of Seville Estate from Upper Yarra, I saw a taut structure that reminded me of Pinots from volcanic soils elsewhere (⊤ page 356). The most elevated part of Lower Yarra is the area of Coldstream Hills, where vineyards are on the hillsides, and more clay in the soil is associated with a more savory character. The heart of the valley is around Yarra Glen, where the valley floor has alluvial soils; most plantings are just off the floor on sandy or loam soils. Large vineyards abut one another here. The

Pinot tends to be richer here, ripe and big with evident tannins. But site differences are used more to obtain the producer's preferred style than as a marker for consumers. Some producers think the most complexity is gained by blending all areas.

Climatic differences associated with elevation and rainfall (which declines going south) may be more important than soil differences. "The Australian view is climate over soil. We tend to see soil as a means of anchoring the vine," James Halliday told me, commenting that Lower and Upper Yarra perform differently: in Lower Yarra, cool years are better; in Upper Yarra, warm years are better.[60] The harvest in Upper Yarra is typically a couple of weeks later than in Lower Yarra.

"Pinot Noir does best in cool to moderate vintages, the warmer years push the margins," says winemaker Travis Bush at Sticks Yarra (Ⱦ page 357).[61] There's generally some richness to the style here, but things are changing. Steve Weber comments that, "There's been a real change in my attitude, and generally in the valley in the past ten years. You have to understand the dirt. Emphasis on understanding the characteristics of each bit of land is the new thing of the past decade" (Ⱦ page 354).[62] The ultimate condemnation of Pinot Noir here is "tastes like dry red" meaning it has no varietal typicity. It is still early days in terms of defining sites and styles, but there is growing agreement that Pinot for dry wine does best above the valley floor (this is scarcely a surprise). The recent arrival of phylloxera (carried into Yarra Valley

Agriculture mixes with viticulture in Yarra Valley.

Cool nights followed by warm mornings can create intense mist in Yarra Valley. This view shows hillside vineyards in Coldstream Hills.

on a truck of producer Foster's) may change the situation by forcing people to replant. "With time we're going to get much better mapping variety and clone to the site," says winemaker Willy Lunn at Yering Station (Ⴒ page 359).

If you ask producers in either Yarra Valley or Mornington Peninsula to define the differences between the two regions, they are perfectly clear on the distinction—but everyone defines it differently, from fruit character to tannic structure. Of course, there is wide variation in producer styles, but my own generalization would be that the wines of Yarra Valley tend to be fatter, with more obvious fruit, and those of Mornington Peninsula tend to have brighter fruits with more obvious structure. Driving down from Melbourne to Mornington Peninsula in the middle of harvest, on a hot sunny day with the thermometer at 33°C (90 °F), it was hard to believe that the climate reputed to be the coolest for wine growing in continental Australia was really cool enough for Pinot Noir. A tasting of recent vintages with a group of Mornington producers, however, showed a lighter style than Yarra Valley, although the wines did not necessarily stand out for cool climate origins (Ⴒ page 359).

Mornington Peninsula is cooled by breezes from the large ocean bays on both the west and east, and from the ocean to the south. The interplay of these wind patterns makes for complex microclimates. "The soils play a tiny role compared to what the French would believe," says David Lloyd of Eldridge Estate.[63] It's important to avoid southern exposure, because the cool breezes prevent ripening. The other factor besides wind is elevation, which varies up to 200 m. A study performed by the producers' association showed wide variations within a small geographical area, with a 4-5 °C drop in temperature going from north to south, and 19 days average difference in harvest dates between Moorooduc to the north and Wallis Vineyard to the south.

The boundaries were more or less marked out by the first wineries. Nat White at Main Ridge was the first person to grow vines on the Peninsula in 1975, producing his first vintage in 1980. Main Ridge is now part of the largest cluster of wineries around Red Hill in the southern part of the Peninsula. Identifying a smaller wine-producing area a little to the north, Richard McIntyre bought Moorooduc Estate in 1982. At the time of his first vintage in 1986 there were only half a dozen producers on the Peninsula. "When we started here we were faced with a widely held belief that you were wasting your time planting Pinot Noir outside of the Côte d'Or," says Richard McIntyre (Ⴑ page 361).[64] A quarter century later, it is clear this is far from a waste of time, and Mornington Peninsula now provides various takes on the character of Pinot Noir.

Mornington Peninsula has a maritime climate with the sea never very far away.

Is there any single defining character for Mornington Peninsula? "Most of us are trying to make Pinots that reflect our site. We don't have a specific Mornington Peninsula aim," says Keith Harris of Yabby Lake (Ⓣ page 363).[65] "We are looking for Pinocity," says Kate McIntyre MW, getting assent from a group of producers. "You're not going to get big fruit Pinot from Mornington Peninsula, you've got a more elegant style with ripe fruit flavors and structure," she added.[66] My impression is that the fruits tend to be bright but not too full, usually in the red cherry spectrum, sometimes showing a savory or herbal touch. The peak point for drinking the best wines is around four or five years of age; the 2006s were drinking beautifully at the start of 2011 (Ⓣ page 359). Ageability is an interesting issue. Producers all agree that the wines should be drinkable on release, but in no way do they see this as a defect. "If it's not delicious when it's young, it's unlikely to become delicious with age," says Nat White.[67] Most wines are viewed as lasting for eight or nine years.

Tasmania is the smallest and newest of the Pinot-producing areas in Australia. Throughout the 1980s there were barely more than 100 ha of all varieties; plantings have increased ten fold since then. The cool climate is promising for Pinot Noir, but the late start means it has some catching up to do. The main division is between the north coast, where the best known area is Tamar Valley, which actually accounts for the majority of wine production on the island, and Derwent and Coal Valleys at the south coast. As elsewhere in Australia, climate is considered to be more important than soil; and site differences due to microclimates are viewed as more important than any sub regional character. More Pinot Noir is grown in the north than in the south, but much is used for sparkling wine, so that overall there is more dry Pinot from the south. A bare handful of Tasmania's wineries export out of Australia. Because most vineyards are very small, most production is intrinsically of single vineyard wines, but there are some single block or reserve wines made by the larger producers. This is not a special focus, however. "Tasmania has a terrific reputation for quality Pinot, so we don't need to develop icons or cults," says Dave Milne of Josef Cromy Wines.[68] Indeed, Pinot grapes from Tasmania fetch the highest price in Australia, and a significant part of production is purchased by sparkling wine producers on the mainland.

The cool climate style is reflected in the light color of Tasmanian Pinots—it is evident at a glance that these are not heavily extracted wines—and although natural acidity renders acidification unnecessary, winemaking style here favors soft tannins with a supple finish. A savory edge tends to develop quite rapidly, so that within a year or the wines show an elegant softness cut by savory elements. With rare exceptions, the wines do not give the impression of long aging, but peak around four to five years. There are pronounced fluctuations in weather, and vintage variation is important.

A significant change took place in the early 2000s when most producers switched to screwcaps for their Pinot Noirs in both New Zealand and Australia. The effect on style is more indirect than direct, or to be more precise, it shows more strongly after the first few years. If the wine is to be drunk in the first year or two after release, as most are, the closure makes less difference. But after a decade, the pattern of development is different. It was clear from vertical tastings extending back to the start of the millennium that winemakers in Australia and New Zealand were fully justified in reacting to the terrible quality of the corks by moving to screwcaps. "Winemakers did not use to have a choice, but now they do, so I hold them responsible if they choose a faulty closure," says Tim Finn of Neudorf,[69] summarizing what is perhaps the majority view. Opening several bottles of a wine under cork usually shows serious variation. The problem is not cork taint, but oxidation: the corks failed to seal the bottles properly. Premature oxidation—signs of madeirized or raisiny aromas and flavors in young wine—is common on Pinots bottled under cork from the 2002 vintage or earlier. The collateral damage is that it's hard to appreciate the full potential of the region for producing wines that age. "Ageability is a difficult issue because many of us have gone from cork to screwcap and the aging is slowing down," says Kate McIntyre of Moorooduc Estate.[70]

When there's a chance to make a direct comparison between a wine bottled under cork and the same wine bottled under screwcap, the screwcap version always is brighter and fresh than the version under cork, sometimes appearing as much as two to three years younger, so the switch to screwcaps may well affect aging potential. (My estimates in the tasting notes are based on experience with cork, as there is really no experience with screwcaps for Pinot Noir longer than a decade.) But the freshness of the oldest wines that I sampled under screwcap (around the 2002 vintage) suggests that I could have underestimated aging potential. There are still a few holdouts who believe that slight ingress of oxygen through the cork is necessary for proper aging, and now that they have better quality supplies of corks, it will be interesting to compare the aging of their wines with those under screwcap.

Switching continents now, only the very southern tip of the wine-producing regions of South Africa is really cool enough for Pinot Noir. Although plantings have doubled in the past decade,[71] Pinot Noir remains a very minor variety in South Africa. The bulk of it is still planted in Stellenbosch, Paarl, and Robertson,[72] which are too warm for quality, but there are some producers focusing on cool-climate varieties in the southern district of Walker Bay.

The main wine-growing area of Walker Bay for Pinot Noir is just to the north of Hermanus on the coast (a popular site for whale watching). Recognizing the potential of the area, the best regions have been subdivided into the Hemel-en-Aarde Valley, Upper Valley, and Ridge.[73] (Hemel-en-Aarde means "heaven and earth" in old Dutch.) The valley starts a mile from the coast and extends several miles inland, surrounded by mountains that trap cloud cover, ensuring good moisture. The original vineyards are in the He-mel-en-Aarde Valley itself, many on the north-facing slopes of the mountain range that separates the valley from Hermanus.

They are a bit defensive about the cool climate classification in Walker Bay. It's certainly significantly cooler than the other wine producing regions of South Africa, with about 3 °C lower average temperature than Stellen-bosch, for example. But on the usual scales, this would be a warm climate.[74] They say that this view is too much influenced by the relatively high mini-mum temperatures, and that if you look at just the maximum, it falls (just) into cool climate. The main determinative feature is not the latitude,[75] but winds from the Atlantic, cooled by the cold Benguela current coming up from Antarctica, which create a maritime climate. Vintage variation is signifi-cant, although not as dramatic as in Europe; the main factor is the amount of rain, with perhaps two wet vintages out of five, and outstanding vintages (wet but not too wet) occurring about every four years. Drip irrigation is installed, but is used only in dry vintages.

Among the usual smorgasbord of varieties (35 are grown in the valleys al-together), Pinot Noir and Sauvignon Blanc are the most planted, with Chardonnay following in third place.[76] In the context of South Africa as a whole, production is tiny, with only about 25,000 cases of Pinot Noir—but it's the undisputed quality leader for the variety.[77] The culture of cool climate

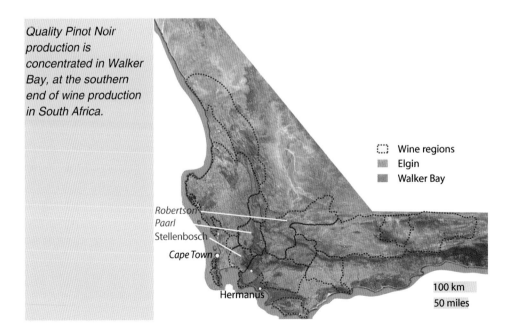

Quality Pinot Noir production is concentrated in Walker Bay, at the southern end of wine production in South Africa.

Wine regions
Elgin
Walker Bay

Robertson
Paarl
Stellenbosch
Cape Town

Hermanus

100 km
50 miles

The Hemel-en-Aarde area is a protected environment.[79]

varieties was pioneered by Tim Hamilton Russell when he established his vineyard in 1975. Next door, Bouchard Finlayson was established in 1989 by Peter Finlayson, who was the winemaker at Hamilton Russell at the time. Hamilton Russell and Bouchard Finlayson are by far the most prominent producers of Pinot Noir in South Africa. They were the only two in the Hemel-en-Aarde area for a while, but now there are more than a dozen.[78]

Soils in Hemel-en-Aarde Valley are based on clay and Bokkeveld shale. "I have adapted our vineyard management to cope with these soils," says Peter Finlayson of Bouchard Finlayson. "Before planting we use a Caterpillar D9 to rip and break these clay shales with addition of 40 tons of lime."[80] Plantings are high density (9,000 vines/ha). The style of the wine is rich: "For some reason unknown to us our particular valley offers wines rich in tannin. This places us in the classic style of Pinot and I may go so far as to say that there are very few places outside of Burgundy which can offer the style which we manage."[81] Peter Finlayson thinks the wines are best drunk relatively young, preferring them between three and five years. The top wine is produced by a barrel selection; there is no emphasis on single vineyard sites. In a fairly sturdy representation of Pinot Noir, the fruits are quite solid, with a spicy overlay when young (Ⓣ page 365). There's a tendency to develop higher toned aromatics in the glass.

Anthony Hamilton Russell sees the terroir as one of the main advantages. "[Our] soils deliver Pinot Noir with an uncanny resemblance to Burgundy.

Stony topsoil on a clay base is common in the Hemel-en-Aarde Valley.

Photograph kindly provided by Anthony Hamilton Russell.

Remember that the Côte d'Or (and particularly the Côte de Nuits) has an extremely high clay content. Many in the New World fixate on the importance of limestone, probably because it is scarce in the New World, and neglect the importance of clay," he says. "Very clay-rich shale-derived soil (with a high iron content in our area) gives rise to a more spicy/savory, structured style of Pinot Noir with a marked minerality and a firmer tannin presence."[82]

Wine styles have changed here over the past two or three decades as every where else. When the first plantings were made at Hamilton Russell, the only clone of Pinot Noir available was the Swiss BK5, which is really more suitable for sparkling wine, but by the time Bouchard Finlayson was established, the Dijon clones were available. Both producers' vineyards are now planted exclusively with Dijon clones. Based on the BK5 clones, the first wines at Hamilton Russell were tight, with a touch of austerity. Greater ripeness was achieved as the Dijon clones came on line. Alcohol has increased steadily, from 12-13% in the 1980s to around 14% today. Anthony Hamilton Russell says his wines can be confused with Burgundy. "I adore good Burgundy and we believe that this expression of Pinot Noir is significantly more interesting and compelling than a lot of the fruit only, fruit forward, soft round easy almost sweet, New World styles."[83] He sees his wines as fairly closed at first, but developing savory secondary characteristics after five to ten years, and lasting well after that. Hamilton Russell produces only a single bottling. He believes that single vineyard sites are too variable, and special cuvées at the top, or second labels at the bottom, tend to undercut the quality of the main wine. Certainly the estate wine develops very slowly, with a vertical back to 2005 showing surprisingly little development across the years. It's a fairly austere representation of Pinot Noir, giving the overall impression of the extract levels of the New World accompanied by the restraint of cool climate Old World (Ⲧ page 366). These are not wines for immediate gratification, but need time.

Soils change from clay and shale in Hemel-en-Aarde Valley to lighter-structured sandstone in the Upper Valley, and then back to clay-rich soil in the Hemel-en-Aarde Ridge (where there is also more diurnal variation due to greater distance from the sea). It is too early to define regional identities, but as a rough rule the wines are more structured in Hemel-en-Aarde Valley, lighter and softer in the Upper Valley, and more New World in character, with brighter fruits, from the Ridge.

Just inland and to the north of Walker Bay, Elgin used to be devoted to apple growing, but more recently has been planted with vineyards. Sauvignon Blanc is the major variety here, with Pinot Noir and Chardonnay tied for second place.[84] Some feel that it is a coming area for Pinot Noir, with elevation compensating for inland location, but so far only one grower, Paul Cluver, has really explored its potential, so the jury is out. Growers in Hemel-en-Aarde feel that Elgin can make good Pinot Noir, but that the style tends to be more typically New World, with lifted red fruits and softer palate, possibly because the soils have higher vigor.

South America has not been very fruitful territory for growing Pinot Noir. Mostly it's too warm, and a tradition of focusing on higher-yielding varieties, and on producing less expensive wines, does not fit very well with the finicky demands of Pinot Noir, which has made little impact in either Chile or Argentina.[85] But there is an exception that proves the rule.

The Patagonian desert may not seem like the most obvious place to grow Pinot Noir (or for that matter any grape variety), but Pinot Noir does tend to be grown in extreme locations—at the northern limits in Europe, at the southern limits in Australasia—and at the southern tip of South America. The Rio Negro valley, a river bed 250 m above sea level, was irrigated in the 1820s to form an oasis in the desert of Patagonia. The climate is really dry, with less than 200 mm of rainfall annually. Phylloxera never arrived here.

The cool climate owes as much to elevation as to the southern location (about 39 °S). Wine production has never been economic in the region, and the majority of old vineyards have been steadily pulled out. Under the impetus of having mistaken an Argentinean Pinot Noir for a Burgundy at a blind tasting, Piero Incisa della Rocchetta, a member of the family that owns Sassicaia, decided there was potential to produce quality Pinot in the area, and looked for a vineyard. The vineyards at what became Bodega Chacra were originally planted with Pinot Noir on its own roots in 1932, but later abandoned. The owners of the original vineyard were on the point of replacing the vines with fruit trees when Piero purchased it in 2004.

Production of Pinot Noir was resumed from the old vines—for the first vintage there was time only to tidy up the vineyard a bit before the harvest (most of which was consumed by the local birds). It took some time to restore the vines and the ground to proper shape—the earth had been compacted over decades by inundation to irrigate the plants. The soil is sand and clay down to a base of pebbles at around a meter. The source of the vines is unknown, but they are ungrafted. Conditions are desert-like, with low humidity, strong luminosity, high winds, and very cold nights.

The vineyard was planted in 1932 and had been abandoned (upper) before Bodega Chacra was founded in 2004, but today has been restored, with mown cover crops and drip irrigation (lower).

Photographs kindly provided by Piero Incisa.

Other old vineyards of Pinot Noir, planted originally in 1955 and 1967, were added in 2006. So the winery may be recent, but production is emphatically from old vines. The old vineyards are planted at a density of about 4,000 vines/ha, but new ones are being planted at 7,000 vines/ha, using a selection massale from the old vines. They were about to plant the first new vineyard with current clones, which had already been ordered from Burgundy, when Piero decided that selection in Burgundy might not necessarily translate well into Patagonia, and it would be better to stay with plants that had adapted, somewhat of a contrast with the worldwide rush to plant Dijon clones everywhere.

The philosophy here is somewhat different from production in Europe. At first, Bodega Chacra followed the European model of trying to limit yields, but then Piero realized that in order to avoid too much concentration and extract, it was necessary to increase yields a little. "Compared to everything we do in Europe, Patagonia is the opposite," he says. Whereas in 2005 there was a green harvest to reduce yields, in 2006 they reversed direction, and started increasing foliage and putting the yields up a bit. From the first vintage of only 1,334 bottles in 2004, now the original vineyard of the oldest vines gives 5,000-8,000 depending on the vintage (corresponding to less than 25 hl/ha).

So what are the stylistic aims here? "I would love to produce wines that are mineral and show typicity—so you can see the place and the identity of the wine through the vintages—not too concentrated or extracted, but showing elegance and finesse," says Piero. "I look for acidity and freshness, the wine should have a balance that drinks well now but has enough acidity to go the distance." [86] The wine certainly shows strong variation with vintage, and if asked to place it geographically in a blind tasting, I would probably think in terms of Europe (Ⅴ page 367).

The transparency of Pinot Noir can show subtleties of terroir as effectively in the New World as in the Old. Whether comparing vineyards in Sonoma or Willamette, within Martinborough, Marlborough, or Central Otago, or between Yarra Valley and Mornington Peninsula, there are always interesting differences to be found relating directly to the site. The most important factors can be a little different; character in the New World tends to relate as much to microclimates as to soil. Two factors stand in the way of a full appreciation of terroir in the New World. For the most part the vines are young, often only just passing the point at which the site begins to show itself over the properties of the clone(s) that have been planted. Development is perhaps a little delayed by the modern habit of planting vineyards in blocks of individual clones. And the style of full frontal fruits isn't best suited to reveal subtlety of terroir; sometimes the character of Pinot Noir is lost in the sheer exuberance of the fruits as there comes a point at which the intensity of fruit (and alcohol) pushes all wines in the direction of homogeneity. Sometimes you feel the wines would be more interesting if the intensity could be toned down a notch. The wines can be delicious when young, but without necessarily really revealing Pinot character. Terroir differences may become clearer as the youthful intensity passes off with age, and it is clear that some New World wines have considerable capacity to age. The time span may be usually be closer to one decade rather than two, but the interesting question is not so much when these wines peak as what complexity they reach at the peak.

Producers and Tastings in Martinborough

The 2000s have been a difficult decade, although the past three vintages (2008-2010) have all been good. 2010 had an average number of degree days (1000), although there were some problems with ripening tannins; 2009 was a warm vintage, well above average with heat spikes producing richer wines; 2008 was a good standard vintage with even temperatures. The vintage was small in 2007 due to millerandage (failure to fertilize the flowers); 2006 gave a relatively even vintage, with small berries leading to good color and extract. Earlier vintages in the decade had the difficulties with flowering and fruit set that are common in the region, often leading to uneven ripening and small berries, with 2005 noted for its tannins.

Alana Estate

Ian Smart bought 25 hectares of land on the Terrace in 1993 with the intention of producing Pinot Noir, and started planting in 1994. Only the old clones were available at this time, but by the next year they were able to plant Dijon clones. Pinot Noir is presently 60% of production; there is also Chardonnay, and economic conditions demand some production of Sauvignon Blanc. All production is from estate grapes, and a second tier Pinot Noir (Lumière) was recently introduced, although the intention is ultimately to return to a single estate wine, possibly with some single block wines as the vines age and differences emerge between parts of the vineyard. (There has been a Reserve Chardonnay produced by barrel selection, but not a Pinot Noir.) "The reference point is obviously Burgundy," says Ian, noting that he feels they really found their own style with the 2001 vintage, and that his stylistic aim is quite different from the stereotype of the New World. Wines were tasted at Alana in March 2011.

Martinborough, Lumière, 2009
Alana's second wine is a distinctly lighter color than the main label, showing a delicate garnet. The light red fruit nose has very faint savory undertones. Sweet ripe fruits make the first impression on the palate, fairly direct in flavor, and with a crowd-pleasing touch of glycerin. A faint touch of earthy strawberries reveals the Pinot Noir origins. This fulfills its aim of providing a wine for more immediate consumption than the estate wine, and it is well made, but less representative of the variety or the appellation. * Drink now-2013.

Martinborough, 2009
Just about to be bottled, the fruity nose shows red cherries with a touch of spice, and some tea-like impressions that follow through to the finish. A slightly glyceriny touch on the palate is accentuated by lower acidity than usual, making the wine immediately approachable on release. ** Drink now-2017.

Martinborough, 2008
At first the nose shows some tea-like impressions and medicinal notes, then clears to show red cherry fruits. Nicely rounded fruits on the palate are followed by an effect of bitter cherries on the finish. The tea-like impression turns slightly mentholated on the finish. This has now come nicely together and is ready to drink. ** Drink now-2017.

Martinborough, 2007
Fruits are more rounded than 2006, the taut tannins are softened by a touch of glycerin, a slight medicinal touch comes through to the finish with a hint of bitter black cherries. Alcohol is well integrated. ** Drink now-2016.

Martinborough, 2006
Slightly tarry red fruit nose. Medium density, bitter red cherry fruits on the palate show a some-what lean style, a little hot on the finish. Tannins are still quite evident and need some time to soften, showing the typical structure of the Alana Pinot. ** Drink now-2017.

Martinborough, Le Coup, 2006
The red and black cherry nose slowly releases some heavy floral aromas. Red fruits are smooth and rounded on the palate, but the wine hasn't yet completely come together, as the acidity sticks out a touch and there is a prickle of bitterness on the finish. There is certainly more extract and concentration than the regular bottling, with a touch of glycerin bringing fat to the finish. Underlying structure is indicated by the emergence of tea-like tannins in the glass. This is a fine effort that needs more time than usual to show its paces. ** Drink now-2017.

Ata Rangi

One of the four founding wineries in Martinborough, Ata Rangi remains under the original ownership of the Paton family. The Abel clone was and is the mainstream of production, 100% until the mid nineties, and about 45% of production today. Clive Paton believes it gives a more tannic structure, compared with the more upfront fruits of the Dijon clones. "We were all green, someone had whispered that Abel was the real thing, but essentially we took a flyer on it," he recollects. "Most people were planting 10/5. Within 5-6 years we knew we were never going to be Burgundy, we knew that we would be Martinborough," he told me. There are two cuvées of Pinot Noir, distin-guished by barrel selection. The second label was originally distinguished as a young vines bottling, but a few years ago it became formalized under the Crimson name. Single vineyard wines are being considered. Clive is confident that the estate wines will age well for 5-10 years—he says that the old Burgundian style of waiting 15 years for the tannins to dissipate never appealed. Wines were tasted at Ata Rangi in March 2011.

Martinborough, Crimson, 2009
This is Ata Rangi's second label. Brilliant ruby color. Red cherry fruit nose with faint hints of spices. Fruits show more as black cherries on palate, not much structural support here, with the wine intended for immediate consumption. While retaining the dark fruit character of the estate wine and to some extent reflecting its style, this naturally has less concentration and it does not show the generosity of the main label. A slight bitterness from the tannins on the finish sug-gests that, even for this second label, waiting a year would be in order. * Drink 2012-2015.

Martinborough, 2009
Medium ruby to purple color. A faintly tarry note on the youthful black fruit nose. Smooth black fruits on the palate, the fleshiness hides the tannins and makes the wine seem a bit obvious at the moment, but should soften in the next year or so. *** Drink 2013-2017.

Martinborough, 2008
I tasted this bottle twice under different circumstances, once in New York in September 2010 and then again at Ata Rangi in March 2011. The differences suggest that the wines taste older after they have been transported to the northern hemisphere. I gave the wine the same rating at each tasting, but a longer lifespan seemed probable from the tasting at Ata Rangi.

   At the winery, some faintly spicy notes show on the black fruit nose. Opulent black plums and cherries show a glycerin and chocolate coating on the finish. A faint touch of bitterness from the youthful tannins should dissipate in the next year, leaving the wine to exhibit its mid-weight fleshiness. This can be drunk already but will be better after another year.

Six months earlier in New York, the wine had an attractive earthy, mineral nose with some notes of tobacco, turning more to earthy strawberries in the glass; some character showing here. Crisp acidity supports the fruits showing more as red than black on the palate; tannins are beginning to dissipate although the palate has not really started to develop. *** Drink 2012-2018.

Martinborough, McCrone, 2008
Across the road from Ata Rangi, the McCrone vineyard was planted more recently, The soils are a bit heavier here, with more clay content, and winemaker Helen Masters says that as a result the wine tends to be a little more aromatic and less structured. There's just a faint whiff of cereal and savory aromas on the nose. Presently the tannins seem more obvious than Ata Rangi itself and need another couple of years to soften. The black fruits are a little sterner, with blackberries showing, and a touch of heat on the finish. ** Drink 2013-2019.

Martinborough, 2003
Restrained red fruit nose has some savory notes just beginning to show. On the palate the wine shows smooth black fruits of cherries and plums, with ripe, supple tannins, and glycerin giving an opulent coating to the spices on the finish. Owner Clive Paton sees this as a typical representation of the winery and appellation for the vintage. ** Drink 2008-2016.

Martinborough, 2002
Some of this vintage was bottled under cork and some under screwcap. The difference at this point is fascinating, with the bottle under cork appearing at least two years more developed than the bottle under screwcap.

Under cork the wine shows a medium density garnet color. The restrained nose is slightly savory. On the palate are sweet ripe fruits of red and black cherries with a mineral edge. The first savory notes are just beginning to show on the palate, making a delicious counterpoise to the fruits.

Under screwcap the wine shows more ruby hues. The restrained nose shows black and red cherry fruits, which follow to the palate with the same mineral edge as the first bottle. The fruits here are not exactly brighter but they are certainly less developed. The wine shows a harmonious balance, but has yet to experience the savory development of the bottle under cork.

At this point I prefer the bottle under cork for its delicious savory to fruit balance, but it is likely that in another two years or so the screwcapped bottle will show better by developing savory aromas to mingle with its primary fruits. *** Drink now-2017.

Craggy Range

Steve Smith MW makes wine for Craggy Range all over New Zealand, ranging from Cabernet Sauvignon at Gimblett Gravels in the north to Pinot Noir at Central Otago in the south. He may be the most peripatetic winemaker in the country. There may be up to 30 different wines each year, including anywhere from two to five Pinot Noirs depending on the vintage. My tasting with him in Martinborough in March 2011 focused on a comparison of current Pinot Noirs from the Calvert vineyard in Central Otago with the Te Muna vineyard on the southern extension of the Martinborough Terrace, followed by some older vintages of Te Muna. Craggy Range in Martinborough and Central Otago have vines of the same age and get the same yields, so this was an unusual opportunity to make a direct comparison of styles from the two regions. "I don't think we are appealing to Burgundy drinkers—we are appealing to a new class of Pinot Noir drinkers who like wine in a slightly plusher style," Steve says as a general comment.

Bannockburn, Central Otago, Calvert Vineyard, 2009
Black fruit nose shows more blackcurrants and plums than cherries. Very lively acidity (all natural) marks the palate of tight red fruits. The overall impression is of a vibrant and lively wine. ** Drink 2012-2017.

Martinborough, Te Muna Vineyard, 2009
More of a red fruit nose with some spicy and savory notes. Soft fruits show more black on the palate than on the nose, with cherries and plums. There's a slightly brooding quality to the fruits, but the overall impression is fine and elegant (compared with the more obvious fruits on the wine from central Otago). ** Drink 2012-2018.

Martinborough, Aroha, 2009
The Aroha bottling comes from two parcels at the Te Muna vineyard, one planted with the Abel clone, and one with Dijon 115 in the most sheltered location at the entrance to the vineyard. Brooding black fruits on the nose, more plums and blackcurrants than cherries. Soft and glyceriny on the palate, the smooth fruits supported by balanced acidity in the characteristic elegant style. There are supple tannins in the background but the wine can be drunk already, with the superficial softness disguising the underlying structure. *** Drink now-2019.

Bannockburn, Central Otago, Calvert Vineyard, 2008
Unlike 2009 where the difference between Central Otago and Martinborough was more evident on the palate than on the nose, in this vintage the palates are more similar but the noses are more distinct. The restrained nose shows some black fruit impressions. This is softer and more rounded than the 09 on the palate, with more of a black fruit impression of cherries and blackcurrants. ** Drink now-2016.

Martinborough, Te Muna Vineyard, 2008
Slightly savory and almost peppery, the black fruit nose turns to cereal and almost nutty notes. Soft black fruits on the palate show less presence than 09, elegant but rather tight at the moment, and not as bright as the Calvert Vineyard from Central Otago. The flavor profile here is a little flatter than other vintages, with the wine a bit closed at the moment. ** Drink now-2016.

Martinborough, Te Muna Vineyard, 2006
Faint savory elements show on a red fruit nose. Soft red fruits of mineral strawberries are developing deliciously with tannins lending gentle support in the background. Good supporting acidity emphasizes a slight savory impression. *** Drink now-2017.

Martinborough, Te Muna Vineyard, 2004
Savory notes are becoming more pronounced as this vintage ages, with a hint of gunflint stopping just short of sous bois. Acidity seems a touch higher than other vintages, reinforcing a savory, herbal impression which has some notes of tarragon. The red fruits are rich and ripe on the palate, and the tannins are softening into the background. Remembering that this wine comes from really young vines (this was only the third vintage) this excellent result promises interesting future development not only of this wine but also of subsequent vintages. ***(*) Drink now-2017.

Dry River

Founder Neil McCallum is still in charge at Dry River, where he planted one of the first vineyards in Martinborough in 1979, although he sold the winery in 2002. The estate has grown to 12 ha organized in three blocks, consisting of the original vineyard, the nearby Craighall Vineyard purchased in 1997 (part of which is also owned by Ata Rangi), and the Arapoff Vineyard purchased in 2002 (now renamed Lovat Vineyard). The first Pinot Noir was produced only in 1989, but Pinot Noir is now three quarters of plantings (the rest is mostly Chardonnay and Gewürztraminer). A great deal of effort here goes into canopy management to ensure that fruit is exposed to sunlight and develops ripe phenolics. Presently there is only one Pinot Noir from Dry River. Neil says that, "We find quite different wine personalities between our blocks (which are all in less than a km of each other) and feel there is a real advantage in blending them from the point of view of balance and complexity. We have one block from the six separate pickings which we could be tempted to have as a single vineyard bottling but we feel that the remainder would not be quite so good. It is possible that one day a block will perform extremely well and be distinctive enough to separate, but at 25 years they are still evolving and we are happy to blend and see advantages in doing so. The Lovat component is elegant, very floral and pretty, Block 5 Craighall is sturdy and provides a good base for a blend, Block 6 Craighall is picked in three separate parcels all of which are distinct and up to two weeks apart. The personality of the latter three varies more than the others according to vintage. The Dry River block tends to have richness and a useful component of florals." His aim from the beginning has been to reflect terroir in producing wines that age, and a tasting of the early vintages demonstrated that he has well achieved his aims. Dry River has stayed with corks as Neil believes that the small amount of oxygen which leaks through them participates in the development of the wine. Wines were tasted at Dry River in March 2011.

Martinborough, 1991
This year gave quite a large crop with the wines often showing a floral character. Medium garnet in appearance. Restrained nose with suggestions of savory elements. Fruits are savory at first impression, but you can still see some sweet ripe flavors. There is a very faint medicinal edge on the finish. Continuously changing in the glass, it's probably wise to finish this vintage up at this point. ** Drink now.

Martinborough, 1990
This was a very difficult vintage with rather atypical growing conditions of cold weather and lots of rain. The wine shows a cloudy garnet appearance (it was not filtered). The nose is quite herbal with some medicinal touches. There is still some sweetness to the fruits but the herbal impression carries over to the palate. The wine remains quite lively although medicinal notes are taking over the finish. *** Drink now.

Martinborough, 1989
Anyone who thinks New Zealand Pinot Noir cannot age should taste this wine. This was the first crop of the vineyard, so came from very young vines, but it is still lively twenty years on. Medium garnet color shows development. Developed nose is savory, with a touch of madeirization that disappears after a while. Sweet ripe red fruits in the strawberry spectrum show on the palate with some herbal notes appearing on the finish, slowly turning to faint suggestions of sous bois in the glass. Considering the youth of the vines and the fact that only clones 10/5 and Pommard 5 were available when the vineyard planted, this is an extraordinary result. A mark that there is still life in the wine is that it seemed more youthful an hour after opening than at the outset. Of course, it is now declining gently, and the present score would no doubt have been significantly higher a few years ago. **** Drink now-2012.

Escarpment Vineyard

Escarpment was established in 1999 in the Te Muna area as a co-venture between winemaker Larry McKenna (formerly of Martinborough Vineyard) and the Kirbys (who also own Yabby Lake in Australia). It has an unusual focus on single vineyard wines, coming from the home vineyard in Te Muna and from three leased vineyards in town (which Larry McKenna originally planted for their owners when he was at Martinborough Vineyard). Production is about 70% Pinot Noir. The Edge is an entry level wine (2,000 cases) which does not depend on oak and uses some contract fruit, there are up to 3,000 cases of the estate wine, and about 300 cases have been produced from each single vineyard since 2006. There are some variations in clay content between the vineyards (Kiwa has a touch more clay and water holding than Pahi), but the major distinction between the three leased vineyards lies between their differing clones and vine ages (and pruning systems). Pahi has 10/5 clones that are 27 years old, and so tends to be more fruit driven. Also 27 years old, Kiwa's plantings come from a variety of clones, with a more savory impression. Te Rehua is 22 years old, planted with a variety of every clone available at the time. "It's a monster, really," says viticulturalist Dave Shepherd. The home vineyard, Kupé, is distinguished by the greater density of vine plantings (6,700 vines/ha). Yields and vinification are the same for all blocks. Escarpment uses Diam corks (treated to eliminate cork taint) because Larry McKenna believes that the very slight permeability of cork to air means that wines matured in oak and intended to age develop more successfully under cork. In 2010 they returned to natural cork for the single vineyard wines. (The whites are about to switch to screwcap.) They believe that the estate wine should last for five years and the single vineyards should age for a decade. Wines were tasted at Escarpment in March 2011.

Martinborough, 2009
This wine is a blend from plots in the home vineyard plus some lots from each of the single vineyards. The nose is fruity and spicy, leading into a palate of dense black fruits, youthfully tarry, with a little heat evident on the finish. ** Drink 2012-2017.

Martinborough, Pahi vineyard, 2009
Spicy nose of black cherry fruits with hints of blackcurrants. Palate follows the nose with a spicy mélange of black fruits. Nice supporting acidity and a light touch to the fruits makes this the most elegant of the single vineyard wines. *** Drink now-2016.

Martinborough, Kiwa vineyard, 2009
A slightly darker color than the Pahi vineyard and a little more intensity to the spice on the nose with some cinnamon coming out and a hint of chocolate. More rounded soft fruits here, with that touch of chocolate coming back on the finish. The softest of the single vineyards, this is already approachable. *** Drink 2012-2017.

Martinborough, Te Rehua vineyard, 2009
New oak shows in the tarry spices of the nose. A touch of piquancy shows on the black fruits of the palate, which are more plums than cherries, the tarry notes of the nose coming through to the finish. This is the densest of the single vineyard wines, and shows a very nice balance, with the fruits ripe and rounded enough to subsume the tannins and make the wine almost ready to drink. *** Drink 2012-2018.

Martinborough, Kupé vineyard, 2009
Muted nose with some brooding spicy black fruits. The blackcurrants and black plum fruits show a touch of piquancy on the palate. The slowest to develop of the single vineyard wines, still very youthful, this needs another year or so for the tannins to fully integrate, although the wine already shows a lively fruit expression. *** Drink 2013-2019.

Martinborough, 2006
Restrained nose shows some tarry notes and aromas of black plums. Fruits are soft and round and almost aromatic on the palate, more black plums than cherries, nicely supported by the balanced acidity. *** Drink now-2015.

Martinborough, Voyager, 2006
This is the former name of the Pahi Vineyard. Appearance shows a dusky ruby color with some garnet hues. The restrained nose shows fruits of red and black cherries, as usual showing the most finesse of the single vineyard wines. Tannins have softened into the background but there is still a fine grained structure. ***(*) Drink now-2016.

Martinborough, Moana, 2006
This is now bottled as the Kiwa Vineyard (the name changed for legal reasons). The savory, herbal nose shows a hint of tarragon with a suspicion of gunflint. This is just a touch more powerful than the Voyager, with a little more presence on the palate, but elegant, fine-grained tannins support the fruits of black plums with hints of blackcurrants. **** Drink now-2016.

Martinborough, Te Rehua, 2006
Restrained but savory and herbal nose. The palate shows a fine balance with the primary fruits of black cherries and blackberries receding into the background and savory elements beginning to emerge. Youthful power is slowly giving way to a more elegant integration. **** Drink now-2017.

Martinborough, Kupé, 2006
Black fruits are just turning savory on the nose. The palate is less savory than the nose, with the black cherry fruits shows a slightly aromatic touch. Less developed than the other single vineyard wines, this is not yet really showing its full potential and may still take a while to develop. *** Drink now-2019.

Martinborough Vineyard

Martinborough Vineyard was one of the four founding vineyards in Martinborough. It has had a series of distinguished winemakers, with some fascinating changes in style over the years. Larry McKenna was the winemaker from 1985 to 1998 (when he moved on to found Escarpment), and his style was more masculine. Claire Mulholland made the wines until 2006 in a lighter style (she is now the founding winemaker at Burn Cottage in Central Otago). Present winemaker Paul Mason describes his style as looking for finesse and texture. The main estate wine is called Martinborough Terrace. Since 2003 there has been a declassified second label called Te Tera. Reserve bottlings were made in the warmer vintages of the 1990s, but the estate has backed off since then to maintain the quality of the estate wine. There is today occasionally a 100 case production of the Marie Zelie Reserve. The 15,000 cases of Pinot Noir are about two thirds of all production. All wines were under screwcap from 2006. Wines were tasted at the Martinborough Vineyard in March 2011.

Martinborough Terrace, 2009
Slightly spicy, savory edge to the strawberry fruits on the nose. A light elegant touch to the palate where spicy red fruits offer suggestions of minerality, but a faintly spirity hot touch to the finish marks this down a point. ** Drink 2012-2017.

Martinborough Terrace, 2006
Spicy nose of strawberry fruits with some savory hints. Adding to the sweet ripe fruits, spiciness develops in the glass, but overall not a great deal of development compared to the 2009; youthful brashness has certainly dissipated, but the slow pace of development seems almost Burgundian. A touch of bitterness shows on the finish. ** Drink now-2016.

Martinborough Terrace, 2005
Savory notes are beginning to show on the nose, with some herbal impressions of tarragon, and a faint suggestion of wood spices making an attractive combination. Acidity is becoming more evident on the palate as the fruits develop and turn from fruity to savory. Touches of gunflint, herbs, and some savory notes come through on the palate. *** Drink now-2017.

Martinborough, Marie Zelie Reserve, 2003
Named for Marie Zelie, a French woman who planted the first vineyard in Martinborough in 1892, only three barrels (737 bottles) were produced of this reserve selection. Savory nose shows some sous bois with a mineral edge to the developing red fruits. The palate is right at the turning point from fruity to savory, with spices balancing herbal notes. Altogether this makes a most elegant, light impression, although the alcohol is just noticeable on the finish. ***(*) Drink now-2017.

Martinborough Terrace, 2002
This was probably the coolest year in the first decade of the twenty-first century, reflected in a leaner wine than usual. Some savory herbal notes on the nose mark its development with age. Following through to the palate, the fruits are a little angular, without the core of sweet ripe fruits that usually marks Martinborough. Still a fine wine, but with an atypical style. **Drink now-2015.

Martinborough Reserve, 1998
This was the last of a series of years that produced a Reserve wine (91, 94, 96, 97, 98). Restrained nose has some faint suggestions of madeirization with a just perceptible touch of raisins showing. From the developed aroma and flavor spectrum you can see that this was a hot year. The fruits are drying out a little and being replaced by savory elements. It is time to drink up. ** Drink now-2014.

Martinborough Reserve, 1996
Age shows in the medium garnet color. Savory nose has hints of minerality and gunflint, generally herbal with a touch of sous bois. Lovely balance of red fruits still showing their ripeness with savory elements ending in sous bois on the palate. There is the faintest raisiny touch just showing with age. As the fruits begin to dry out, the acidity is coming through a bit; the wine is aging well but fruit density is lightening up. Slightly bitter notes of gunflint are just beginning to show on the palate. This is just a touch past its peak, whereas the 2003 is right at the turning point. *** Drink now-2014.

Palliser Estate

Palliser has about 65 ha, half of which is Pinot Noir, and considers itself to be a medium size winery. It was first planted in 1985 and the oldest vines now date from a 1987 planting of the 10/5 clone taken from the St. Helena vineyard at Christchurch. Palliser grows 70% of its own fruit (80% of its Pinot Noir). Originally Palliser made only one Pinot Noir, but as the number of vineyards increased, the estate wine became a selection and the second label was introduced for declassified lots. (It is called Pencarrow after one of the vineyards.) Of the 40,000 case total production, a quarter is Pinot Noir, of which 4,000 cases are the estate wine. Occasionally there is a small bottling of a reserve wine under the name of the Dog series (each named for a dog associated with the winery). Today the estate wines come from Dijon clones. "The house style for Pinot is that I set out to make bigger, rather than more feminine, wines," says winemaker Alan Johnson. The wines were tasted at the Palliser Estate in March 2011.

Martinborough, Pencarrow, 2009
Pencarrow is Palliser Estate's second label, made from a blend of the older clones and the newer Dijon clones. The wine sees just a tiny touch of new oak. The red fruit nose has some spice notes in the background. More of a red fruit than black fruit impression on the palate compared to the estate wine. The structure is lighter and there is less backbone than the estate wine, but this wine achieves a good value that is still representative of the region. ** Drink now-2014.

Martinborough, The Great Marco, 2009
This wine is the fifth in the dog series, representing periodic selections of the best barrels, and named for dogs of the estate. Restrained black fruit nose suggests character, with just a touch of spiciness, and (as always with the dog series) some opulence. The palate does not disappoint: opulent and smooth black fruits have a glycerin coating on the finish showing the typical fleshiness of the Dijon clones. Supple tannins are hidden by the fruits *** Drink 2013-2019.

Martinborough, 2008
Tarry red and black cherry fruit nose, the sweet ripeness of the cherries coming to the fore in the glass. The nose leads into a palate of sweet ripe fruits, showing as black cherries with hints of plums and blackcurrants. Ripe tannins are still evident on the finish, where there is a touch of heat. Altogether a well integrated wine in Palliser's characteristic attractive short term style. Winemaker Alan Johnson considers that the wine is now at the perfect drinking point. *** Drink now-2017.

Martinborough, The Great Walter, 2008
This cuvee was a selection of the best 5-6 barrels, which saw 60% new oak for 15 months. The nose is more restrained than the estate bottling, but its sweet black fruits give a ripe impression of cherries, plums, and blackcurrants. Fruits are relatively soft with just a hint of aromatics, and a touch of opulence to the finish. The tannic structure is revealed by dryness on the finish, but is well integrated and mostly hidden by the opulence of the palate. The ripeness and density of the fruits make this wine already approachable. (A bottle tasted six months earlier in New York was slightly more developed, with spice and tobacco notes showing on nose and palate, and some earthiness developing.) ***(*) Drink 2013-2018.

Martinborough, 2007
Quite undeveloped appearance. But here is a nose with some distinctive character, quite complex, with red and black fruits, wood spices, and tobacco. On the palate the black fruits show more immediate opulence, with the ripe tannins rounded out by some glycerin that fattens the finish. The sweetness of the cherry fruits comes through across the palate. Even allowing for vintage variation, there is a demarcation between the youthful opulence of 2007 and the more savory character of 2006, marking three to four years as the point in time at which the wine begins to turn to a more aged character. *** Drink 2012-2016.

Martinborough, 2006
Faintly earthy strawberries show on the nose with a suggestion of a mineral edge, and just a suspicion of savory development. Fruits are softer and more rounded on the palate than in 2005, showing a very nice balance. Smooth strawberries fruits are a little earthy in a relatively restrained style just a touch lacking in mid palate concentration. Fruits are supported by the underlying structure, but the wine has reached its peak and should be drunk before the fruits begin to dry out. *** Drink now-2013.

Martinborough, 2005
Slightly tarry red fruit nose with some very faint savory hints showing through. Nice balance on the palate of earthy strawberries, although a touch hot on the finish where some phenolic bitterness shows through. Winemaker Alan Johnson thinks this vintage showed better two years ago, although for my palate the savory touch that has developed since then makes the wine more attractive. *** Drink now-2015.

Producers and Tastings in Marlborough

They are very happy about the 2010 vintage in Marlborough, where dry, warm conditions for the six weeks leading to harvest gave a slightly below average crop which is expected to yield big, dark, concentrated wines. The 2009 vintage was a little less ripe and is considered to represent the classic Marlborough style. There was some rain at the end of the season, but after that it was dry until harvest, giving good concentration. 2008 was a difficult year, with rain extending into April and creating problems resulting from humidity; extensive sorting was needed to remove damaged fruit. 2007 was a classic vintage and many producers consider that this was a breakthrough year for Pinot Noir, and that they also made their best Chardonnays. 2006 was the earliest harvest ever, but not due to hot conditions; it resulted from a very early bud break, which shifted the whole season forwards, leading to harvest in February. The wines are considered to be elegant and refined. 2005 had a cool start to summer, which disrupted flowering and gave a low crop. Then conditions were warm right through harvest. The wines are more tannic than usual.

Regional Tasting

A tasting of wines mostly from the 2008 and 2009 vintages showed the regional differences between the various areas of Marlborough. Starting with the Awatere Valley, the wines showed a lean red fruit character, tending to mineral strawberries. There is more sense of structure in the wines from the Southern Valleys, especially Brancott and Omaka Valleys, where red cherries dominate the fruit spectrum. Wines coming from the main Wairau Valley, or blends relying largely on it, tend to show more direct, not to say superficially fleshy, red fruits with less evident tannin. Wines were tasted in Marlborough in March 2011. With regards to estimates of development and aging, however, I should note that some of the same wines seemed more developed when tasted six months earlier in New York, so estimates of aging based on wines tasted at source in New Zealand may need to be advanced by a year for wines that have been transported to Europe or America.

Awatere Valley, Vavasour Wines, 2008
Elegant impression on nose of raspberry and strawberry fruits, with faint tarry notes. Light red fruit palate is slightly aromatic, just a touch of some light tannins; not a big wine, certainly in a more elegant style, but distinct heat showing on the finish. Light style can be drunk now but better to wait a year for the tannins to soften. ** Drink 2012-2016.

Awatere Valley, Foxes Island Wines, 2008
This wine comes from a terrace about 15 km inland with a touch of elevation. The cooler season enhanced the herbal notes on the slightly savory red fruit nose. Light red fruit palate, quite nicely rounded, generally a soft herbal impression. There's a slight touch of heat on finish. ** Drink-2015.

Awatere Valley, Blind River, 2009
Faintly savory nose offers some tea-like herbal impressions and touch of raspberry fruits. Sweet ripe rounded fruits in a lighter style, a faintly floral touch and just a hint of buttery roundness on the finish. Light tannins and supporting structure are already well integrated. ** Drink now-2016.

Brancott Valley, Brancott Estate, 2009
A faintly savory note cuts the strawberries on the red fruit nose. Quite a fleshy red fruit palate shows cherries and strawberries; the firm tannins are there in the background but not at all obtrusive, and there's a nice fruity finish. ** Drink now-2018.

Brancott Valley, Fairhall Downs single vineyard, 2008
Red fruit nose shows raspberries and strawberries with a sense of structure. A nice gravelly texture to the red fruit palate, more cherries and strawberries here, with firm underlying tannins lending structural support. A well structured wine which will show a textured fleshiness as the underlying tannins resolve. *** Drink now-2018.

Omaka Valley Reserve, Saint Clair, 2009
Slightly savory notes show on a red/black cherry fruit nose. Sweet ripe fruits are on the palate of intense black cherries; firm tannins and a touch of dryness show on the finish. Strongly structured, can be drunk now, but will definitely be better in another year. *** Drink now-2018.

Southern Valleys, Marlborough Auntsfield Estate, 2009
This is a single vineyard wine from the most northern of the southern valleys. Classic red fruit nose has more strawberries than raspberries and some youthful tarry overtones. Fruits show as more cherry-like on the palate, with the characteristic sense of texture to the tannic structure that you get with Southern valleys. Although this can (and probably will) be drunk now, it will show its paces much better in another couple of years. *** Drink now-2018.

Southern Valleys, Marlborough, Bouldevines, 2009
Stern nose is more black cherries than red. Superficial fleshiness here of red and black cherry fruits with some faint refined tea-like tannic supporting structure gives an elegant black fruit impression to the finish. *** Drink now-2018.

Southern Valleys, Lawson's Dry Hills, 2008
Restrained nose with savory and herbal hints, some tarry overtones, and underlying red fruits. A sight fleshiness on the palate, strawberry fruits with a slightly earthy edge, gentle tannins just showing on the finish. Can be drunk now but will be softer and more pleasingly earthy in another year. ** Drink now-2017.

Southern Valleys, Gum Emperor, Jackson Estate, 2008
Only ten barrels made. Slightly spicy red and black cherry nose. Fleshy black cherry fruits on the palate, well rounded and integrating with the supple tannins. This richer style shows harmoniously even at this youthful stage and is ready to drink. *** Drink now-2018.

Southern Valleys, Rapaura Springs, 2008
Some faint herbal and savory aromas join the red fruits on the nose. Light red cherry fruits on the palate have a touch of fleshiness. Soft tannins have already receded into the background. A nice effort in a slightly lighter style for the Southern Valleys. ** Drink now-2016.

Southern Valleys, Churton, 2008
Gamey notes on the nose offer a pungent touch of gunflint, becoming more savory in the glass. Palate shows more direct black cherry fruit flavors; the firm tannins should support good future development. The good long term structure of this wine may reflect the unusual location of the vineyards at 200 m elevation, as well as the use of extended post fermentation maceration to increase tannic structure (and no doubt also responsible for greater oxidative exposure leading to development of those gamey notes). *** Drink now-2018.

Regional Blends

Marlborough, Two Rivers Winery, 2009
This wine comes from a mixture of fruit from Awatere and Brancott valleys. A savory nose shows here with herbal overtones. Ripe fruits with a nice depth of red fruit flavors show as mineral-edged strawberries. Soft tannins in the background make this wine ready to drink now, although it will show softer, more earthy character in another year. ** Drink now-2017.

Marlborough, Whitehaven Wine, 2009
A slightly stern red fruit nose. Youthful palate, a touch of bitterness from the tannins cuts the underlying red fruits; just a hint of opulence shows through the tannins on the finish, and promises good development in the next year or so. ** Drink 2012-2018.

Marlborough, Wild South, 2009
Red fruit nose shows raspberries and strawberries with impression of ripeness. There's some fat and opulence on the palate; hints of black and red cherries join the fruits of the nose, with just a touch of bitterness on a medium length finish. ** Drink now-2017.

Marlborough, Mount Riley, 2009
Restrained nose offers hints of mineral strawberries. A red fruit palate is more strawberries than raspberries, rather direct fruits, just a touch of light tannins on the finish. ** Drink now-2016.

Marlborough, Nautilus Estate, 2009
Nautilus were among the first to plant Dijon clones. This wine also has fruit from older plantings of Pommard clone 5. A tarry nose obscures the underlying dark red fruits. Rounded fruits of red and black cherries are on the palate, and you see the fleshiness of the Dijon clones here. Also the wine comes about 70% from the southern valleys where the clay soils increase fleshiness and weight. The cherry fruits turn more to strawberries on the finish. ** Drink now-2017.

Marlborough, Voyage, Astrolabe, 2008
Slightly tarry notes hide the red fruits of the nose. A sort of lean red fruit richness dominates the palate, with a touch of opulence, but cut by some fine tannins giving a sense of underlying structure. This can be drunk now but will certainly benefit from another year or so as it presently shows a touch of toughness and bitterness on the finish. ** Drink 2012-2018.

Marlborough, Nautilus Estate, 2007
Some garnet hues have developed already in the appearance. A slightly savory note has now developed to add to the red fruits on the nose. This has rounded out in the past year or so, the tannins have really receded into the background, and the fleshy opulence of the red and black cherry fruits is dominating the nose. You can see by comparison with the 2008 and 2009 vintages that are currently available that people are missing the full potential by drinking the wine too young. *** Drink now-2017.

The Central Valley Floor

Wairau Valley, Hounds, Allan Scott Wines, 2009
Minty almost gamey notes on the nose have some herbal or mentholated overtones. Sweet ripe black and red cherry fruits are on the palate; those minty overtones come back on the finish. Firm tannins show as dryness on the finish and will soften in the next year. *** Drink now-2018.

Wairau Valley, Grove Mill Wine, 2009
Red fruit nose has savory overtones. There are reserved red fruits on the palate, with some light tannins drying the finish. Fruits are more red cherries than strawberries; a touch of earthiness develops in the glass. ** Drink now-2018.

Wairau Valley, Hunter's Wines, 2009
Slightly mineral to earthy red strawberry fruit nose. Direct red fruits on the palate take the form of cherries and strawberries, tannins already receding into the background. ** Drink now-2016.

Wairau Valley, Lake Chalice Wines, 2009
Slightly tarry overtones to the red fruit nose of raspberries and strawberries. Finely textured red fruit palate is more cherries than strawberries. A faintly nutty overtone is creeping into the finish, and tannins are evident only by a slight dryness on the finish. ** Drink now-2016.

Wairau Valley, Framingham Wine, 2009
Some savory notes tinge the red cherry and raspberry fruit nose. Again there is that direct sweet ripe red fruit character of the Wairau Valley and a faintly nutty note on the finish. Tannins already are resolving. ** Drink now-2017.

Wairau Valley, Staete Landt Vineyards, 2008
Youthful tarry nose with some bright red cherry fruits poking through and some notes of black tea. Red and black cherry fruits dominate the palate, the tannins are quite refined but still evident by dryness on the finish, and they need another year to soften and integrate. A classic effort for Wairau Valley ** Drink now-2017.

Wairau Valley, Legend, Domaine Georges Michel, 2007
Savory-spicy nose with faint medicinal overtones. Delicious red fruits with just suspicions of savory overtones on the balance. Tannins are resolving to reveal the full fruit flavor spectrum. Sweet and ripe but with a lovely underlying texture. *** Drink now-2017.

Clos Henri

When the Bourgeois family of Sancerre (page 176) decided in the nineties that they wanted to make quality Sauvignon Blanc and Pinot Noir overseas, they ended up buying a sheep farm in Marlborough, which they converted to vineyards. Vines were planted in 2000, and the first vintage was 2003. Initially the wines were made in a leased winery, but in 2009 their purpose built winery on the site was completed. Coming from Sancerre, they wanted hills, and about a third of the vineyards lie on slopes. The estate has 110 ha, of which 40 ha are planted, 40% being Pinot Noir. There are three cuvées of Pinot Noir; Petit Clos comes from young vines; Bel Echo comes from Pinot planted on the stony part of the terroir, which is separated by a fault line from the clay-based terroir where the Pinot for the estate wine is grown. The clay soils of the slopes have more silt overlay than those of the flatlands at the bottom. All wines come only from estate grapes. Wines were tasted at Clos Henri in March 2011.

Marlborough, Petit Clos, 2009
This wine is made from the youngest vines. The restrained red fruit nose shows light plums and cherries. Fruits tend to slightly mineral strawberries on the palate, with good supporting acidity, and a very light tannic structure, making this a pleasant wine for immediate consumption. * Drink now-2014.

Marlborough, Bel Echo, 2009
This entry level wine uses only 9% new oak, with the intention of being immediately drinkable. A restrained red fruit nose has very faint savory and cereal notes. The palate makes a smooth, fairly taut impression, in good balance with nicely delineated black cherry fruits; the tannins are really barely noticeable. There's just a suspicion of a sweet aromatic lift to the finish. ** Drink now-2015.

Marlborough, Clos Henri, 2008
This wine sees 25% new oak. Some bottles were sealed under cork, some under screwcap (they were sold in different markets).

   The wine under cork shows a medium ruby-garnet color. Some savory notes with faint animal overtones have already developed on the red fruit nose. The palate shows sweet ripe fruits of red and black cherries, with glycerin adding a touch of opulence to the finish. Overall the style is elegant and shows some finesse, and the touch of opulence—coming from the clay soils—has not diminished the fine delineation of fruit flavors.

   The wine under screwcap has rosier, more youthful hues. The nose veers more towards direct red and black cherry fruits without the savory notes of the version under cork. There's also just a touch more sweetness and ripeness evident on the fruits, and the glyceriny opulence is more obvious, with the fruits a touch uplifted. ** Drink now-2017.

Marlborough, Clos Henri, 2007
This bottle was sealed under cork. It shows a very faint savory touch on the nose. A slightly nutty and spicy touch to the black cherry fruits gives a fine impression of some complexity developing on the palate. There is a touch of opulence from glycerin, cutting the tannic structure, which shows a faint dryness on the finish. Altogether there is more impression of structure here, and the wine seems less ready to drink, than the 2008. ** Drink now-2017.

Cloudy Bay

One of the larger producers in Marlborough, Cloudy Bay today is part of the LVMH empire. Famous for its Sauvignon Blanc since the 1985 vintage, Cloudy Bay has been producing Pinot Noir since 1989 (although it was grown previously for sparkling wine production). Pinot Noir production got into full swing in 1994 with the purchase of the Mustang Vineyard in Brancott Valley. A decade later, Cloudy Bay purchased the Barracks Vineyard in Omaka Valley which today accounts for a major part of the estate wine. Presently Pinot Noir comes from a mix of their own vineyards (85%) and some contract growers, all from the southern valleys of Brancott, Omaka, and Ben Morvan. Pinot Noir is about 10% of all production. There was only a single estate wine until 2007, when there was a separate bottling of the Mustang Vineyard (but selling at the same price as the estate wine; it is priced just slightly higher in 2008). The 200-300 cases of the single vineyard wine are available only at the cellar door. All production was switched to screwcap after 2004. Winemaker Nick Blampied-Lane thinks the wines are ready to drink at 3-4 years of age, and the 2007 is perfect now. Wines were tasted at Cloudy Bay in March 2011.

Marlborough, 2009
Restrained nose with faintly spicy red fruits of strawberries and cherries. Nicely balanced spicy red and black cherry fruits with a touch of light, refined tannins on the finish, in a sweet, ripe, elegant style. Can drink now but best to wait another year. *** Drink 2012-2018.

Marlborough, 2008
Perhaps a faint cereal/savory touch to the red cherry fruit nose. The palate shows elegant black cherry fruits with some notes of mineral strawberries. There's a touch of youthful tarriness from the tannins on the finish, but a fine structure shows just a hint of glycerin giving an edge of opulence. There's some heat on the finish. ** Drink 2012-2017.

Marlborough, Mustang, 2008
The vineyard was planted in the Omaka Valley in 2003 and 2004. The Abel clone is predominant in the mix. Yields are around 35 hl/ha. The restrained nose offers spicy black cherry fruits with an impression of ripeness. A sweet ripe black fruit palate shows plums and cherries, more concentrated than the regular bottling, but also more closed. This wine has really barely started to develop. But the fruit density pushes the supple tannins into the background and allows it to be drunk already. *** Drink now-2019.

Marlborough, 2007
The youthful nose shows some tarry notes on top of the spicy black cherry fruits that intensify in the glass. The palate follows the nose, with Cloudy Bay's characteristic sweet, slightly spicy, black cherry fruits showing a refined, elegant style. A nice kick of sweetness comes from the ripe fruits on the medium length finish. ** Drink now-2016.

Marlborough, Mustang, 2007
Some youthful tarry notes show on the nose, with a touch of cereal and spice, then an almost perfumed fragrance develops in the glass. Sweet ripe fruits of cherries with hints of blackcurrants and spices come out attractively on the finish. Supple, ripe tannins are subsumed by the fruits, and there's just a touch more development than the 2008, bringing an impression of more generosity to the palate. *** Drink now-2018.

Marlborough, 2005
Medium ruby-garnet color. Faintly spicy, cereal notes show on a restrained red fruit nose. Spicy black cherry fruits on the palate offer a barely perceptible development of savory flavors. The tannic structure shows in the dryness of the finish, fine and elegant, with some tea-like tannins emerging. This now seems to be close to its peak. *** Drink now-2014.

Marlborough, 2001
Medium garnet color with browning hues shows development. Slightly madeirized notes on the nose reveal age through the core of sweet ripe fruits. There's more development on the palate with some savory, cereal-like flavors. Fruits are beginning to dry out now, and the residual structure is showing as dryness on the finish. Although a couple of years past its peak, it's still interesting. (I wonder what this would have been like under screwcap?) **(*) Drink now-2012.

Dog Point

James Healy and Ivan Sutherland were the winemaker and viticulturalist at Cloudy Bay until 2003. Ivan Sutherland had been growing grapes at Dog Point, one of the oldest vineyards in Marlborough (converted from sheep grazing in 1979), located at the entrance from Wairau Valley to the Brancott and Omaka valleys, but the grapes had been sold. James and Ivan started making wine on a part time basis in 2002, and the operation became full time in 2004. They make only four wines: Pinot Noir, Chardonnay, and two Sauvignon Blancs (distinguished by differences in oak treatment). Production has now reached about 3,500 cases of Pinot Noir annually. They believe that wine should be enjoyable on release (two years after the vintage), but should be able to age. "We are not trying to make the biggest, boldest, Pinot; it's that soft tannin structure we are looking for," says James Healy. A vertical tasting of Dog Point Pinots from the first vintage to the present showed a refined style whose rich red fruits might be mistaken for Beaune at the premier cru level, except perhaps for the higher viscosity and alcohol. For me this defines a transition from Europe to the New World, because the wines have the unmistakable richness of the New World, but an intense Pinot character reminiscent of Burgundy. Wines were tasted at Dog Point in March 2011.

Marlborough, 2009
Restrained nose has suggestions of red and black cherry fruits. Elegant black cherry fruits are on the palate, where fine grained tannins support the fruits. The silky texture lets the wine be drunk now, but it will certainly be better after another year. There is a touch of heat on the finish. *** Drink 2012-2019.

Marlborough, 2008
Black cherry fruit nose has some faint aromatics. The cherry fruits are riper on the palate than the 2009. Developing more slowly, the wine shows a fatter structure with more viscosity, and is less fine-grained and elegant than 2009. *** Drink now-2017.

Marlborough, 2007
One sniff identifies very sweet ripe fruits with the unmistakable character of Pinot Noir. The wine fairly bursts with fruit in the general aroma and flavor spectrum of Beaune or Pommard. The nose has some tarry tannins, opening out into earthy strawberries with the first savory aromas just beginning to appear. The palate continues with red fruits, compared with the black fruits of younger vintages, showing as full force earthy strawberry fruits, with glycerin bringing an opulence to the finish. I suspect the alcohol is higher than the 13.5% stated on the label. The opulence of the finish and the alcohol level identify this as a New World wine, rather powerful at this stage, but although the wine is certainly fruit forward, it shows bags of character in an intensely Pinot-ish style, ending up supple and fine. *** Drink now-2016.

Marlborough, 2006
Savory red fruit nose shows faint herbal and cereal overtones. The extra year over the 2007 is reflected in increased savory elements, with the red fruit palate showing attractive herbal notes on the finish that strengthen in the glass. Refined tannins support the soft fruits, and a touch of glycerin softens a faint bitterness where the underlying tannic structure shows through to the finish. *** Drink now-2016.

Marlborough, 2003
Restrained red fruit nose with savory hints. Lovely balance on the palate shows red cherry fruits, a faint savory touch, a hint of tarragon, and soft tannins giving good structural support. Altogether a refined, elegant impression with a touch of viscosity fattening the finish. ***(*) Drink now-2015.

Marlborough, 2002
Development shows in the herbal character of the nose with a touch of uplifted aromatics, becoming slightly animal. Sweet ripe red fruits of cherries with notes of strawberries dominate the palate, with tea-like tannins evident on the finish. There is a very fine, harmonious balance with a faint touch of herbaceousness adding complexity to the fruits. **** Drink now-2015.

Fromm Winery

Georg Fromm, who makes Pinot Noir in Graubunden, Switzerland (page 207) is credited with being part of the driving force to quality in Marlborough when he started his winery here. The first vineyard was planted in 1992, and the first vintage (from purchased grapes) followed in 1994. Georg sold the winery in 2006, but he still shares ownership of the Clayvin vineyard, which is the source of one of the single vineyard wines. Continuity has been ensured by winemaker Hätsch Kalberer, who has been there from the start. The estate wine is called La Strada (the original name of the winery) and there are individual wines from Brancott Valley (including production from Clayvin and from sites lower in the valley), from the Clayvin vineyard itself, and from the Fromm vineyard around the winery. The original vineyard was planted on its own roots, and there was a setback when phylloxera forced replanting, but it now produces their top wine. Unusually for Marlborough, everything is under cork here; Hätsch believes this is necessary for proper development of their wines. "Most of our wines have more in common with European wines than with New Zealand styles," he says. Fromm's wines are regarded as being among the most tannic in New Zealand, but the style has been for less extraction since 2006. Wines were tasted at Fromm Winery in March 2011.

Marlborough, La Strada, 2009
Fruity nose shows cherries and strawberries with a touch of earthiness. Quite bright earthy red cherries are on the palate. This offers a light approachable style, bright and fresh, with a faint buttery softness adding to the fruits on the finish. ** Drink now-2014.

Marlborough, Brancott Valley, 2007
Nose of red cherries and strawberries with some faint tarriness behind. There are soft black fruits on the palate, but still some tight tannins in the background. A sense of black cherries develops in the glass, but the palate is still a little closed. This can already be drunk, but will be better in another year. ** Drink now-2017.

Marlborough, Clayvin Vineyard, 2007
Nose of earthy and almost nutty strawberries becomes more floral in the glass. More red and black cherries show a mineral edge on the palate. With better sense of focus and delineation than the Brancott, this is the most elegant of the single vineyard wines, although there's a hard edge of bitter cherries at the moment. Refined tannins give a fine grained structure which should become silky with a year or so of further maturation. *** Drink 2012-2019.

Marlborough, Fromm Vineyard, 2007
Nose here offers red and black cherries with a mineral edge. Soft and elegant on the palate, there are red and black fruits, with tannic support in the background. The flavor profile is relatively closed at this point compared to the other single vineyard wines, but a fine sense of underlying structure suggests this has the greatest potential for aging. ** Drink now-2019.

Marlborough, Fromm Vineyard, 2006
Slightly fleshy strawberry fruits on the nose give way to soft red fruits on the palate, more strawberries than cherries. This makes a great contrast in style with 2005, with much less obvious sense of structure, so this wine should be consumed in mid term rather than long term. This is partly a reflection of vintage, partly a change in style. Also with 2006 the wine began to have a greater proportion of grapes from the Dijon clones, reinforcing the fleshier style. ** Drink now-2016.

Marlborough, Clayvin Vineyard, 2005
Some faintly spicy, nutty notes show on the black fruit nose. Still quite tannic on the palate, with something of the hardness you sometimes see in Gevrey Chambertin, but difficult to see the underlying fruits that will let it emerge from the shell. At the moment this shows surprisingly little development; the fruit flavor spectrum is somewhat monotonic. The typicity of Pinot Noir has been lost somewhere along the way. Winemaker Hätsch Kalberer says this was the last of the massive vintages with those rustic tannins; since then the style has been lighter. * Drink now-2015.

Marlborough, Clayvin Vineyard, 2000
This wine came from young vines, the first crop after replanting when the vineyard was hit by phylloxera. Savory notes show development with a mineral edge stopping just short of gunflint. A delicious balance on the palate with savory elements more evident than they were on the nose, and mingling with the red fruit notes. Fruits are beginning to lighten up a little, and the wine loses a little focus in the glass, so best to drink sooner rather than later. *** Drink now-2014.

Seresin

The first impression you get on visiting Seresin's vineyards is the complete commitment to biodynamics. 103 of the farm's 163 ha are planted with vineyards. The property is self-sustaining, with cows to provide manure, pits for making the CPP preparation, chickens running around, fields of plants for making the biodynamic teas; viticulturalist Colin Ross even leaves the odd row of vines without bird netting as a sop to Cerberus. They try to spray the biodynamic preparations on the lunar cycle, but pruning, picking, etc. are driven by more practical concerns, and indeed, vineyard management is entirely practical. "We crop to purpose," says Colin, which for Pinot Noir means cropping at 8 tons/ha for the MOMA entry level wine, 6 tons/ha for the estate wine, and 3-4 tons/ha for the single vineyard wines (roughly 50 hl/ha, 38 hl/ha, 22 hl/ha). The seven Pinot Noirs are made identically in terms of winemaking, from MOMA (which is Seresin's second label, although this is not directly obvious from the bottle) to the three blended estate wines (Leah, Rachel, and Sun & Moon), and the three single vineyard wines (Home Vineyard, Tatou, and Raupo Creek). With 6,000 cases per year, MOMA is the largest production run of Pinot Noir. Leah is Seresin's entry to Pinot Noir, with about 3,000 cases annual production. Rachel and Sun & Moon rate more highly than the single vineyards on Seresin's scale. Wines were tasted at Seresin in March 2011.

Marlborough, MOMO, 2009
The black cherry fruit nose is slightly tarry. Smooth black cherry fruits follow on the palate with a touch of glycerin counteracting a faint youthful tarry bitterness. The wine is medium weight, but

just a fraction lacking in texture. This will no doubt be consumed immediately on release, but in reality would benefit from a year's aging. * Drink 2012-2015.

Marlborough, Leah, 2009
The black cherry fruit nose shows hints of plums and blackcurrants. There are smooth fruits on the palate, but the wine is a bit lacking in liveliness on the mid palate. Supple tannins are revealed by some dryness on the finish, where there is just a touch of blackcurrant aromatics. This can be drunk now but will be better in another year. ** Drink 2012-2016.

Marlborough, Home Vineyard, 2008
Only 50 cases of this wine were made from the Home Vineyard, which has stony subsoil with a silt topsoil. The dense black fruits on the nose have some suggestions of minerality. On the palate they show as smooth black plum and cherry fruits, with supple tannins already subsumed by the fruits, making this immediately approachable. The softness of the tannins is accompanied by broad fruit flavors. ** Drink now-2017.

Marlborough, Tatou Vineyard, 2008
Only 50 cases (2 barrels) of this wine were made, from Seresin's stoniest vineyard, where two rivers converge. There are some faint aromatics of plums and blackcurrants on the nose with a very faint cereal or savory impression. The wine is smooth on the palate and livelier than the Home Vineyard, with a tighter flavor spectrum and more uplifted flavors, supported by firmer, taut tannins. This needs another year. ** Drink 2012-2018.

Marlborough, Raupo Creek, 2008
This hillside vineyard with very compacted clay soils is definitely the star of Seresin's vineyards, says winemaker Clive Dougall. There's a little more uplift to the nose compared to Tatou, with a black fruit spectrum of plums and blackcurrants. Balanced acidity brings liveliness to the black fruits of the palate, with those faint aromatics showing as cherries and blackcurrants; supple yet taut tannins are evidenced by some dryness on the finish. *** Drink 2012-2018.

Marlborough, Rachel, 2008
There's some intensity to the nose, where a faint animal pungency obscures the black fruits. Sweet ripe fruits on the palate show as black cherries and plums. The sweetness of the fruits hides the supple tannins. This is an elegant style with a refined underlying structure. Because the fruit density hides the tannins, this is presently approachable, but try to wait at least another year. Only 200 cases made. ***(*) Drink 2012-2021.

Marlborough, Sun and Moon, 2008
Only 75 cases were made of Seresin's top Pinot Noir. This was the second vintage. It has a slightly darker and more garnet hue than the Rachel. The nose is restrained but shows some savory hints. Real purity of fruits comes through to the palate, with black cherries supported by taut, precise tannins. Indeed, there is a general impression of precise delineation of fruits. The velvety texture is reminiscent of Chambolle Musigny. The excellent and refined tannic support should ensure some longevity as the fruits continue to develop in their elegant style. **** Drink 2012-2021.

Spy Valley

Spy Valley started as a grower with the purchase of 200 ha on which 160 ha were planted in 1993. They moved into producing wine, built the winery in 2002, and now use all of the production from their own vineyards as well as buying some grapes from other growers. They view themselves as a medium size operation, presently divided into two distinct parts, the commercial side and the premium Pinot Noir. The 6,600-7,000 cases of Pinot Noir are about 10% of production. The transition to screwcap occurred in 2007. There are two major bottlings, the estate wine, and Envoy, a premium line that comes from a selection of 6 barrels from the oldest vines at the Johnson Estate in Waihopai Valley (all 10/5 clones). Winemaker Paul Bourgeois sees two years after the vintage as the perfect time to drink the wines, perhaps marginally later for the Envoy bottlings. Outpost is a new bottling from a vineyard that Spy Valley purchased recently. The estate bottlings seemed a bit on the commercial side, Envoy had more concentration, but I thought Outpost displayed real promise. Wines were tasted at Spy Valley in March 2011.

Marlborough, 2010
Cereal notes turn spicy in the glass; fruits are more red than black on the nose. Immediate red cherry fruits are quite nicely balanced with some light tannins. This is a wine to drink on release and not to cellar. * Drink now-2014.

Marlborough, Envoy, 2010 (barrel sample)
Strongly aromatic nose of red and black cherry fruits, with aromatics carrying through to the palate of cherries and blackcurrant fruits. Very soft on the palate, with supple tannins. You could drink this already, it scarcely needs to wait to be bottled. ** Drink 2012-2014.

Marlborough, Outpost Vineyard, 2010 (barrel sample)
Nose of aromatic black cherries and plums. Quite elegant on the palate with fine, aromatic fruits. The aromaticity of the barrel sample will ameliorate by the time of bottling, leaving an elegant wine with some finesse. *** Drink 2012-2015.

Marlborough, 2009
Red fruit nose shows restrained hints of cherries and strawberries. More generosity on the red fruit palate than on the nose, with a hint of spiciness. The youngest vintages of the regular bottling are the best for current drinking. * Drink now-2014.

Marlborough, Envoy, 2009
Restrained nose with some black plum aromatics. Nicely rounded black cherry fruits on the palate are supported by firm tannins. Already ready to drink, this has a good balance, but does not have the structure for the long term. *** Drink now-2014.

Marlborough, 2008
Rather subdued on the nose with just a hint of red fruits. Medium density red fruit palate shows red cherries with some hints of strawberries. Flavor profile is a little flat on the finish. * Drink now-2013.

Marlborough, Envoy, 2008
Faintly tarry black fruit nose. Slightly fleshy, soft black cherry fruits with a touch of cassis coming out on the palate. Well rounded with a touch of glycerin on the finish. *** Drink now-2014.

Marlborough, Outpost Vineyard, 2008
Aromatic black fruit nose leads into black cherry fruits on the palate and a faint savory note. The sweet ripe black fruits show more generosity than the regular Spy Valley bottling and more elegance than the Envoy. This is a style with some finesse. *** Drink now-2015.

Marlborough, 2007
Some faintly tarry, spicy notes show on the black fruit nose. That sense of spicy tarriness comes through to the palate, which is a little subdued, with a lack of generosity on the mid palate. * Drink now-2013.

Marlborough, Envoy, 2007
Restrained, faintly spicy, black fruit nose. Sweet ripe fruits seem more than a year younger than the 2006; perhaps this reflects the transition from cork to screwcap between these vintages. More red cherries than black, not much development showing. Quite nicely balanced with supple tannins on the finish. ** Drink now-2013.

Marlborough, 2006
Very muted nose. Sweet ripe black cherry fruits show on the palate, turning more to red cherries in the glass, with a hint of aromatics on the finish. Just a touch lacking in generosity on the mid palate, with a hint of bitterness escaping through to the finish. * Drink now-2012.

Marlborough, Envoy, 2006
Muted nose. Some fleshiness to the fruits, a touch of viscosity to the black and red cherries, not much development showing. ** Drink now-2014.

Marlborough, 2005
Restrained black cherry fruit nose has a touch of spiciness, following through on the palate with just a hint of aromatics. Firm tannins recede into the background with a faint touch of heat on the finish. There has not really been very much development here, raising the question of whether the wine will develop interestingly or merely survive. * Drink now-2012.

Marlborough, Envoy, 2005
Some gamey notes show on the black fruit nose, following through to the palate where fruits of viscous black cherries have faint animal overtones, forceful rather than generous. ** Drink now-2014.

TerraVin

Mike Eaton at TerraVin marches to the beat of a different drum. He is regarded as the pioneer for hillside plantings in Marlborough (starting at a time when everyone else was on the valley floor), and further emphasized his individuality by using close plantings (1 × 1.5 m). When they planted the first vineyard in 1998, there was widespread skepticism, but now others have followed. An advocate of single vineyard bottlings, he makes an estate Pinot Noir, the Hillside Reserve, the Eaton family vineyard, and has just added two more vineyards to the portfolio. The Hillside Reserve was originally called Hillside Selection, but the name was changed to Hillside Reserve to avoid legal problems with Shafer's Hillside Select from Napa. The first vintages came from the small vineyard plot immediately in front of the TerraVin winery half way up the Omaka Valley, which was planted in 1999; the vineyard area was broadened for later vintages. There will be a shift in style from the 2010 vintage due to a switch to earlier picking. "I suspect that by the time you taste ripe flavors in the seeds, you should have picked the day before," says Mike, explaining the change. Wines were tasted at TerraVin in March 2011.

Marlborough, 2009
Light black cherry fruits show on the nose. Elegant fruits show some finesse on the palate, black cherries following the nose with some hints of plums. Light refined tannins need at least another year to soften. There is a touch of heat on the finish, but otherwise the refined style might be compared with Volnay. ** Drink 2012-2017.

Marlborough, Hillside Reserve, 2009
(Not yet released.) Slightly aromatic raspberry and red cherry fruits contribute to an attractive nose. Sweet ripe fruits show more as cherries on the palate, with some taut, slightly tarry, tannins on the finish. A distinct dryness shows more depth of tannic support than is immediately evident. This needs at least another year. *** Drink 2013-2020.

Marlborough, Eaton Family Vineyard, 2009
Spicy red fruit nose has touches of cinnamon and cereal. Fruits are presently tight on the palate with a mineral edge, but fine grained tannins give an elegant impression, with a nice sweet kick of ripeness to the finish. The light elegance makes this approachable now but it will be better after another year. *** Drink 2012-2021.

Marlborough, Hillside Reserve, 2008
Youthful, slightly tarry, black cherry fruit nose. Elegant fruits on the palate are supported by taut tannins and balanced acidity, with slightly nutty notes showing on the finish. The tannins are soft enough to allow the wine to be drunk now, with the softness giving more of a New World impression than the older vintages. The wine carries its high alcohol well, and should improve for some years. *** Drink now-2018.

Marlborough, Hillside Reserve, 2006
Some developed aromas are just beginning to show on the nose in the form of savory and nutty notes. Sweet ripe red and black cherry fruits are supported by refined tannins that bring a fine-grained texture to the finish. The overall impression is fine and elegant. *** Drink now-2018.

Marlborough, Hillside Reserve, 2004
There are cereal notes on the nose with some nutty notes showing a little development with age. There is a lovely balance on the palate, with the fruits offset by some beautiful faintly leathery notes. (In the interests of full disclosure it should be noted that this is due to a slight contamination with Brett. While this may have made the wine unacceptable to those committed to the New World style of bright pure forward fruits, personally I think it has a delicious complexity.) In any case, the palate tends more to nutty notes than to animal, making a nice counterpoise to the fruits. **** Drink now-2016.

The Delta

Matt Thompson started The Delta specifically to make Pinot Noir. He looked for a vineyard with a consistent clay slope, started planting his 32 ha in 2001, and made his first crop in 2004. He uses about half the grapes for his own production and sells off the rest. There are two cuvées: the estate wine, and the Hatters Hill, which is based on a selection from parts of the vineyard that produce a little more tannin. "Many people say our wines are half way between Europe and the New World," he says, adding that he thinks the best point to start drinking is at 4-5 years. Wines were tasted at The Delta in March 2011.

Marlborough, 2009
Austere nose with strawberry fruits slowly emerging in the glass. Good fresh acidity supports bright red cherry and strawberry fruits. Some finesse shows here, with fine tannins and a touch of sweet ripeness cutting the finish. This wine is intended to be open and forward. and indeed the balance of fruits to tannins allows the wine to be drunk immediately. ** Drink-2016.

Marlborough, 2008
Restrained nose offers red fruit impression. Light, elegant red cherry fruit palate has some slight chocolate overtones. Bright acidity is perhaps a touch too crisp, giving the finish a note of piquancy. * Drink now-2015.

Marlborough, Hatters Hill, 2008
Medium ruby color is a little darker than The Delta itself, and the difference applies to nose and palate as well as the color. A touch of black cherries joins the red cherries on the nose. The palate offers smooth but taut fruit, with a slightly sharp acidity. The elegant fruits and fine tannins give an impression of finesse. The overall silky balance allows the wine to be enjoyed immediately. *** Drink now-2018.

Marlborough, 2007
Sour red cherry fruits show on the nose. Nice balance of acid to fruit, with some softly nutty notes developing with the red cherry fruits of the palate. The characteristic elegant style shows through, soft and smooth on the finish as the supple tannins recede into the background. ** Drink now-2017.

Marlborough, Hatters Hill, 2007
A touch of austerity is on the nose (does that come from the inclusion of some whole clusters?) Sweet ripe fruits on the palate have a touch of piquant acidity offset by some glycerin silkiness. Tannins are supple but there's still an impression of tension in the wine. A faint dryness on the finish speaks to the presence of an underlying tannic structure. *** Drink now-2017.

Marlborough, 2005
Faintly savory and acid notes on the nose. Lovely balance on the palate has red fruits showing just a touch of savory overtones. A hint of dryness on the finish seems to match a lightening of the fruits, which suggests they may be beginning to dry out, but the smooth silky finish ends with a touch of sweet ripeness that carries the palate through. A bit reminiscent of Beaune. *** Drink now-2015.

Marlborough, Hatters Hill, 2005
Mineral red fruits on the nose with a savory, almost animal, note. Rich red fruits are sweet and ripe on the palate, with some notes of darker fruits, and the increase in concentration and structure over The Delta bottling is immediately evident. The finish is long and some nutty overtones develop in the glass. Here there is no sign of the fruits drying out, and there is plenty of life yet. *** Drink now-2016.

Villa Maria

Started in 1961, Villa Maria is the largest individually owned winery in New Zealand. Total production is around 800,000 cases annually. They have vineyards all over the North Island, including 400 ha in Marlborough, and expanded by purchasing the Thornbury winery in Central Otago in 2005. Around 60% of production comes from estate grapes. Aside from the Thornbury Pinot Noir, most of the Pinot Noir comes from Marlborough, where the first vines were planted in 1995. In addition to the estate wine, there is a cellar selection, a reserve, and three single vineyard wines coming from the southern valleys, including the Seddon and Taylors Pass Vineyards which come from the Awatere Valley. Wines were tasted at Villa Maria in March 2011.

Marlborough, Cellar Selection, 2009
The major sources for this wine are the Taylors Pass and other vineyards in the Awatere Valley. Aromatic red fruits tend to raspberries on the nose. Good acidity on the red fruit palate,

with fruits showing as mineral raspberries with some sour red cherries. Light tannins in the background give a slight texture, and the wine is already ready to drink. * Drink now-2015.

Marlborough Reserve, 2008
This wine is usually a composite of the three single vineyard wines, but it is not based on lot classification, rather a blend of the same lots that go into the separate bottlings. Slightly spicy, cereal, black fruit nose. More black cherries here than the red fruits of the Selection bottling, quite a precise elegant style, but still with just a touch of tannic bitterness. ** Drink 2012-2017.

Marlborough, Southern Clays, 2008
This wine comes from a vineyard planted twelve years ago in the Ben Morvan valley at the base of the foothills, with a mixture of Dijon and Abel clones. Characteristic nose of spice and cereal, with a hint of apples. Sweet ripe fruit in the red and black cherry spectrum, good acid support, light refined tannins, overall a silky impression. ** Drink now-2018.

Marlborough, Seddon Vineyard, 2007
Located on the south bank of the Awatere river, this vineyard is one of Villa Maria's earliest ripening sites for Pinot Noir. Youthful appearance of deep ruby color gives an impression of high extraction. Rich and deep black fruits on the nose, more ripe plums than cherries; notes of tea and tobacco show an aromatic touch. Rich fruits in the blackberry spectrum carry the palate over the tannins. The structure offers an impression of black tea and tobacco. This really needs another year. ** Drink 2012-2017.

Marlborough, Taylors Pass Vineyard, 2007
This vineyard is 40 ha of terraces that drop down to the river, with terroir of metamorphic rock and papa clay. This is a warm site for the Awatere Valley (but even so harvests two weeks after the Wairau Valley). Red and black cherry fruit nose. Fuller on the palate than the other single vineyard wines, with nicely rounded red fruits and an impression of blackcurrants, balanced acidity, and some tarry tannic support on the finish. This shows a sturdier style than the Seddon vineyard and is less ready to drink. *** Drink 2013-2019.

Producer and Tasting in Nelson

Neudorf

Tim Finn was the pioneer for wine production in the Nelson region (at the northwest of the south island) when he established Neudorf in 1978. Located in the Moutere Hills a few miles inland, the winery is surrounded by the home vineyard. Neudorf produces five varieties altogether, with Chardonnay and Pinot Noir as the flagship wines. Pinot Noir is just under a quarter of total production. There are three Pinot Noir Labels. Tom's Block is a mid-level wine, made from the younger vines. Moutere comes from the older vines. (Winemaking is the same for both). In some years there is a Home Vineyard bottling, made exclusively from older vines of the Pommard 5 clone. Tim Finn says that the wines can be drunk between 1 and 4 years of age, but should last another four. When I asked whether the style was being driven by consumer demand for early drinking wines, he said this was true of Tom's Block, but not of the Moutere. Neudorf switched to screwcaps in 2002. Wines were tasted at Neudorf in March 2011.

Nelson, Moutere, 2009
The production of 826 cases of this wine has just been released. The smooth, elegant nose offers black cherries and plums. The sense of elegance carries through to the palate with just a touch of black plum aromatics. Tannins are light and very fine. There is a little heat on the nutty finish. *** Drink 2012-2018.

Nelson, Home Vineyard, 2009
This wine now comes mostly from Dijon clones. Some faint tarry impressions add to the black cherry and blackcurrant fruits of the nose. The increase in concentration over Moutere is evident. The overall impression is very fine, with an excellent balance of fruits to supple tannins. The elegance of the house style is coming clearly through. The supple balance allows this wine to be drunk even now. *** Drink now-2020.

Nelson, Moutere, 2007
Elegant black fruit nose has cherries and plums with spicy notes and hints of tobacco and chocolate. The spicy tobacco notes follow on the palate with the fine black fruits. Light refined tannins give a very fine structure. There is a touch of heat on the finish. *** Drink 2012-2019.

Nelson, Home Vineyard, 2006
Savory herbal notes emphasize the mineral strawberry fruit nose. The red fruit palate is refined, with fine-grained texture and supple tannins, savory elements matching the kick of ripe fruits on the finish. The overall impression here is quite mineral, with a nicely defined edge to the strawberry fruits. ***(*) Drink now-2016.

Nelson, Moutere, 2005
Rather closed on the nose. Sweet ripe fruits of black cherries with hints of plums and blackcurrants are dense and more concentrated than 2007 or 2009, as is characteristic of the vintage. The fruits have not really developed much here, and the flavor profile is a bit flat at the moment. ** Drink now-2015.

Nelson, Home Vineyard, 2005
Less developed color than the 2006, deeper and more ruby in hue. More of a black fruit nose, faintly spicy with perhaps the first savory hints just developing. The characteristic muscular density of the vintage comes through, with the black fruits showing full force on the palate. There is more flavor density and complexity than the Moutere, and this is developing more slowly. *** Drink now-2016.

Nelson, 2003
More of a red fruit nose here, with cherries and strawberries, a touch of spice with savory elements developing in the glass. Sweet ripe fruits have a spicy touch on the palate. There is a kick of sweetness on the finish from the sweet ripe fruits, supported by supple but ripe tannins, with a touch of heat on the finish. A tasty impression as those savory notes begin to come out. *** Drink now-2016.

Nelson, Moutere, 2001
Restrained nose with a mix of faintly jammy notes and savory elements. The fruits may be lightening up a bit. A nice hint of tobacco shows on the palate, but a touch of bitterness creeps into the finish. Time to drink up. ** Drink now-2013.

Producers and Tastings in Central Otago

Vintage variation in Central Otago expresses itself as much in crop size as in quality. The 2010 and 2009 are similar vintages, big and rich in style, the most similar back to back vintages the region has experienced. In 2008, a wet spring preceded a warm summer with more rainfall than usual, then dry but cool for the harvest period. The wines are tauter than those of 2009. Cool weather and frost in the spring of 2007 impinged on flowering and reduced crop size, but it's regarded as a very good, concentrated vintage, sometimes over-ripe. Hot dry weather in 2006 led to a large crop with large berries. The very cool spring in 2005 reduced crop size and many wines are more tannic than usual.

Regional Tasting

Gibbston Valley

Tiwha, 2008
This wine comes from a single vineyard in Gibbston Valley. Restrained black nose with a stern impression of black fruits. Restrained fruits in the black spectrum, a touch of blackcurrants as well as cherries, restrained tannins with just a hint of opulence coming through to the finish. Some heat on the finish. Certainly there is an impression here of a wine built for aging from a cooler climate. The structure is quite fine and this may soften to a more gentle elegance in two or three years, but at the moment it is rather tight. ** Drink 2012-2017.

Bannockburn

Domain Road, 2009
Slightly tarry red fruit nose with some notes of mineral strawberries. Red fruit palate of cherries and strawberries, some nice light tannic support, but the tannins are fairly well in the back-

ground, and the wine can be enjoyed now, although the fruits will show more clearly in another year. There is a touch of heat on the finish. ** Drink now-2015.

Tatty Bogler, 2009
Rather closed on the nose but faint suggestions more of black fruits, perhaps blackcurrants, than red fruits. Black fruit palate shows cherries and plums; some firm tannins in the background are light enough to allow the wine to be drunk immediately, but there is not enough stuffing for much future development. * Drink now-2015.

Jackson Barry, Olssens, 2009
Not very much showing on the nose at this stage, just a faint intimation of red fruits. Soft red fruits on the palate show a tendency to earthy strawberries, but not a great deal of stuffing. This is ready for current, uncomplicated drinking, and should hold for another couple of years. * Drink now-2014.

Jackson Barry, Olssens, 2007
Slightly piquant black fruit nose. Aromatic black cherry and blackcurrant fruits extend to a touch of cassis. Taut tannins give the fruits some support on the palate. Most people will find this ready to drink, but I would wait another year when the tannins will subside to let the fruits really show through. ** Drink 2012-2017.

Untamed Heart, Desert Heart, 2008
This is the second label from Desert Heart. Muted nose shows some soft red fruits. Very soft approachable red fruit, tannins nowhere in sight, this is clearly intended for current drinking, but still it does express that soft opulence of the Bannockburn subregion. * Drink now-2015.

MacKenzie Run, Desert Heart, 2008
The soil here is a mix of schist and free-draining alluvial soils, running down close to the river. There are quite intense black cherry fruits, still a little bright and agressive. There's a touch of aromatic uplift on the palate and a slightly hot finish. ** Drink 2013-2015.

Hawkeshead, 2008
This wine emphasizes its regional identity by stating Bannockburn on the label. Slightly earthy red strawberry fruit nose. Soft red fruits on the palate, with gentle tannins in the background, allow the wine to be drunk immediately. The soft earthiness is attractive now, but there is not much support for any future development, making this a wine for immediate consumption. * Drink now-2014.

Cromwell Basin

Lowburn

Mathilde Reserve, Aurum, 2009
The Mathilde Reserve comes from the Te Wairere vineyard in Cromwell. The nose offers black cherry fruits with hints of wood spices. The fruit spectrum of the palate follows the nose but is quite tight, with the fruits still quite reserved. Fine tannins give a tight texture to the palate. In another year or so, as the tannins soften, the wine should mature to show some elegance and finesse. ** Drink 2012-2017.

Pisa Range

Two Degrees, 2009
This wine takes its name from the two degrees difference between the Pisa Range, where the winery is located, and the Clutha River that runs down Central Otago. This allows frost to roll off the vineyard into the river. There is a touch of blackcurrant aromatics on the black fruit nose, following through to a palate of black cherries and blackcurrants. Soft, supple tannins in the background are hidden by the fruit density, making it possible already to drink the wine, although the fruits will show through more clearly in another year. There is a touch of heat on the finish. ** Drink 2012-2016.

Pisa Range Estate Vineyard, 2008
This wine is made for the Pisa Range vineyard (planted 15 years ago) by Rudi Bauer at Quartz Reef. It shows a slightly aromatic black fruit nose. Stern black fruits on the palate get an aromatic uplift from a touch of blackcurrants. There is some heat on the finish. The tannins are still tight and need some time. ** Drink 2013-2017.

Archangel, 2009
In its second vintage, this wine comes from two terraces at an elevation of 300 m in the region along the lake between Cromwell and Wanaka. The nose gives a fresh impression of red and

black cherry fruits with a touch of strawberries. Bright fruits are showcased by crisp acidity and tight tannins, with a slightly sharp impression and a touch of heat on the finish. The edges should soften in another year to reveal a gentle, red fruit-driven palate. ** Drink 2013-2016.

Bendigo and the northeast

Mondillo, 2009
Rather closed on the nose. Black fruits tend to a superficial opulence on the palate, but supporting tannic structure is hard to discern. The impression here is that the wine is made for immediate consumption, at which it succeeds, but there isn't much potential for aging. * Drink now-2014.

Northburn Station, 2008
Northburn Station is a sheep farm with a vineyard. In the eighth vintage of this wine, only 740 cases were produced. Black fruit nose has a slightly aromatic touch of blackcurrants. Sweet ripe dark fruits dominate the palate in the characteristic style of the Bendigo subregion, with a kick of sweetness from the ripe fruits showing on the finish. Firm but soft tannins are hidden by the fruits, giving an overall impression of richness. ** Drink now-2016.

Maori Point, 2008
The Maori Point vineyard is located to the north of Bendigo on the eastern side of Lake Dunstan. Red fruit nose has some touches of earthy strawberries. The palate tends more to cherries, black as well as red, with medium fruit density, and a slight prickle of acidity. The tannins give a cool climate impression. * Drink now-2015.

Maori Point, 2006
Apparently this wine had such massive tannins it was difficult to drink for the first three years, but now it has come around. It is rather muted on the nose. There are slightly sharp red and black cherries on the palate. Slowly the tannins are coming into balance to show quite elegant red fruits. There's just a touch of sharpness on the finish. ** Drink now-2015.

Wanaka

Rippon Vineyard, 2008
Rippon is considered to be the defining winery in the Lake Wanaka region at the northern tip of Central Otago. Its vintages from the early 1990s are still held in high regard. Restrained red fruit nose hovers between mineral and earthy. Soft red fruits with touches of earthy strawberries show on the palate, acidity is balanced, tannins are firm, perhaps a little rustic. This is just a touch lacking in concentration on the mid palate, but with moderate alcohol giving a more European impression. ** Drink 2012-2016.

Regional Blends

Wild Earth, 2008
This wine is a regional blend from vineyards in the Pisa and Bannockburn areas. A mix of black cherries and strawberries shows on the nose. The palate follows with an impression of fine, precise fruits showing purity of line with mid level concentration. This is far from the stereotype of upfront boisterous fruits, although the ripe core of fruit comes through clearly, accompanied by a touch of heat on the finish. The fine-grained tannins recede into the background and allow the wine to be drunk now. ** Drink now-2016.

Swan, Mud House Wine Company, 2009
The origins of the lots for this wine vary each year. Some piquant gamey notes come through the black fruits on the nose. The palate follows the nose, already quite soft and approachable, with some developing overtones to the black fruits. Not much evidence of underlying structure for future development, but very drinkable at this point. * Drink now-2014.

Amisfield

Amisfield has a large contiguous block of vineyards in Lowburn, partly on a lower terrace coming more or less straight off the western side of Lake Dunstan, leading to an upper terrace that runs right up to the base of the mountains. Soils are loess on the upper terrace and silt on the lower terrace. 78 ha are planted out of a total estate of 480 ha. The first vines were planted in 1999. All fruit is estate-grown. Production splits between Pinot Noir and aromatic white varieties. There are two Pinot Noirs: the estate wine and the Rocky Knoll, which is based on a barrel selection from the Rocky Knoll part of the vineyard. Wines were tasted at Amisfield in March 2011.

Central Otago, 2010 (barrel sample)
This vintage has just been blended and will be bottled in April. It's a purple color with black hues and the intense aromatics of the barrel sample. Deep black fruits on the palate are supported by good acidity, with firm dense tannins drying the finish. This shows some promise and may well be ready to drink by the time it is released in another year. *** Drink 2013-2020.

Central Otago, 2009
This vintage is about to be released. Tarry nose has some hints of chocolate overlaying the black fruits. Sweet ripe fruits show as black plums on the palate, a touch of plummy aromatics, with firm but fine tannins in support. Good structure. *** Drink 2012-2019.

Central Otago, 2008
This is the current release. Still tarry and a bit chocolaty on the nose, overall a rather austere impression, but now a little softer than the 2009. Tannins are quite soft and furry, with a slight chocolate impression showing on the finish. ** Drink now-2017.

Central Otago, 2007
Spicy strawberry nose has some animal notes coming in. The first impression on the palate is the heat of alcohol. There's a lot of extraction here in the rich Central Otago style. The ripe rich strawberry fruits are quite earthy, and the tannins are silky. This has all the right flavor components of Pinot Noir—but too much of them. If everything was a quarter less intense, the balance would be a lovely representation of Pinot Noir. ** Drink 2012-2018.

Central Otago, Rocky Knoll, 2006
This is the current release of Amisfield's top Pinot. The restrained nose initially seems austere and tarry, then shows some aromatics. Black fruits show more as plums and blackcurrants than cherries. The intensity of the fruits is evident, with soft chocolaty, furry tannins coating the finish. Keep the bottle open for a couple of hours and you get some promising hints of future development. The palate becomes lighter with more red cherries than black fruits. The tannins seem lighter and more elegant, but still show some attractive chocolate notes. There is a potential here for an elegant path of development. *** Drink now-2020.

Burn Cottage Vineyard

One of the newest vineyards to be established in Central Otago, and the first set up right from the start on biodynamic principles, the Burn Cottage vineyard is on land converted from sheep farming in 2002. The contiguous hillside site in the foothills of the Pisa Range on the western side of Lake Dunstan is part of a 28 ha biodynamic farm. The 10.25 ha of vines are planted more than 90% to Pinot Noir, with a little Riesling and Grüner Veltliner. Ted Lemon of Littorai wines in Sonoma (a fervent biodynamicist) is a consultant, and the winemaker is Claire Mulholland, who came from Martinborough Vineyard. A small crop was picked in 2008 and bottled under a second label, but 2009 was the inaugural vintage for the estate wine. A more representative volume of production should be reached for the 2010 vintage; and the intention is to work up to 2,000 cases annual production over the next few years. There are hopes that this will lead the way into elegance for Central Otago. The wine was tasted at Burn Cottage in March 2011.

Central Otago, 2009
This inaugural vintage was released a month ago and still shows some intimations of the barrel with appley aromatics leading into black fruit aromatics of cherries. The fine black fruit palate has a tight acidic supporting structure, with the aromatics coming back retronasally. Fine, firm tannins bring some tension to the wine. More like Cote de Nuits than Cote de Beaune with some promise for the future. *** Drink 2013-2018.

Carrick

Established in 1994, for the first few years Carrick sold grapes. The first vintage was 2000, and the winery was built in 2002. Plantings are predominantly Pinot Noir, but Riesling does well on the schist soils (Carrick's soil variety is especially diverse). "The Carrick wines have a core of sweet fruit that is typical of Central Otago but it is hidden by the tannins," says winemaker Jane Docherty. There are three Pinot Noirs: an entry level intended to be for light, easy drinking; the estate wine; and the Excelsior, which is a barrel selection from a single vineyard. Each vineyard block is grown to purpose, with lower yields for the estate and Excelsior than for the entry level. All grapes are estate-grown. Carrick switched to screwcaps in 2002. Wines were tasted at Carrick in March 2011.

Central Otago, 2009
Slightly tarry tannins on a black fruit nose, developing some notes of chocolate and coffee. Sweet ripe fruits on the palate, slightly chunky tannins, balanced acidity, a touch of blackcurrant aromatics. Slightly nutty finish with some heat. ** Drink now-2016.

Central Otago, 2007
Tarry notes on the nose with hints of chocolate and coffee. Sweet fruits on the palate still have some firm, stern tannins in support. The tarry impression from the nose comes through to the tannins on the finish. Balancing acidity has a slight piquancy. Winemaker Jane Docherty says that originally this wine was a fruit bomb, but now it is calming down. ** Drink now-2015.

Central Otago, Excelsior, 2007
The top cuvée Excelsior has been made since 2005 (although not in 2008). It spends 18 months in 50% new oak and then is kept for three years in bottle before release. There's a suspicion of spice and coffee on a rather restrained black fruit nose. There is a characteristic dark fruit spectrum on the palate, showing sweet ripe cherries and plums. Tannins are more supple than in the estate bottling, and there is more sense of structure on the dry finish. The flavor spectrum remains a bit monotonic and needs to develop as the tannins soften further. *** Drink 2013-2019.

Central Otago, 2004
Rather dumb nose. The entire flavor spectrum has calmed down and the tannins have re-solved, so finally you can see the potential of the wine. With age the fruits have turned more to the red spectrum, and there is some flavor variety, backed up by a slightly piquant acidity. Some savory elements are beginning to creep on to the palate. There is a touch of heat on the finish, with some bitterness now showing. ** Drink now-2015.

Central Otago, 2002
Some medicinal notes on the nose are not so directly noticeable on the palate, where the sweet core of fruit still shows. The retention of fruit is impressive, the tannins are still there, and it is possible if this had been bottled under screwcap instead of cork, it might now be at its peak instead of in decline. * Drink now.

Chard Farm Winery

Nestled right into the mountain, accessed only by a narrow unpaved track with a sheer drop of several hundred feet into the gorge below, Chard Farm was originally a fruit orchard until the 11 ha property was purchased in 1986 by Rob Hay, who came from adjacent Gibbston Valley Wines. When it was planted with vines the following year, it became the largest vineyard in Central Otago. The initial plantings included all sorts of varieties, and there are still some Pinot Noir vines growing from that period. Since then Chard Farm has acquired additional vineyards in the Lowburn/Parkburn area on the western side of Lake Dunstan. Chard Farm remains one of the largest producers in the region, presently with about 20,000 cases annually. There is a series of Pinot Noirs, from the entry level River Run, to the Mata-Au estate wine, and the two single vineyard wines that come from the west side of Lake Dunstan, The Tiger (in Lowburn) and The Viper (in Parkburn). Winemaker John Wallace feels that the estate wine drinks well for 3-6 years after the vintage, with subsequent longevity depending on the style of the individual vintage. He sees the single vineyard wines as benefiting from an additional year or so.

Central Otago, River Run, 2009
Light translucent ruby color. Soft red cherry fruit nose. Fine elegant red cherry and strawberry fruits on the palate convey a faint mineral impression and a touch of black fruits, but are a bit lacking in presence. There's a touch of heat on the finish. * Drink now-2015.

Central Otago, Mata-Au, 2009
Slightly perfumed red cherry fruit nose has a touch of black cherries. Light fruit impression on the palate is nicely balanced. There are fine elegant tannins, but a touch of heat, on the finish. Light years away from the stereotype of heavy New World fruit. ** Drink now-2016.

Central Otago, The Tiger, 2009
A single vineyard wine has been made from Tiger Run since 2002. It's rather closed on the nose with a touch of red fruit perfume. More structure is evident on the red fruit palate of strawberries and black cherries than for the regular bottling. The smooth refined finish gives an elegant impression. Already almost ready to drink, there is a touch of tightness on the finish, which should lift in the next year. *** Drink 2012-2018.

Central Otago, The Viper, 2009
The perfumed nose is quite fragrant, leading into some faint herbal savory notes on the red fruit palate. Showing some austerity at the moment, there is more sense here of overt structure, with the fruits a bit closed and tight. The tannins are already quite well integrated and don't as such require more time, but the fruits need to open out. *** Drink 2012-2019.

Central Otago, Finla Mor, 2006
This was the original name for the estate bottling, which is now known as the Mata-Au. Red cherry fruit nose shows a touch of spice. The red fruit palate is softening, with a sense of texture to the mineral red strawberry fruits. The soft texture and structure make this more approachable than either of the single vineyard wines from this vintage, but some dryness on the finish attests to the well integrated tannic structure. ** Drink now-2015.

Central Otago, The Tiger, 2006
More intensity is evident on the nose than the estate wine, with some developed savory, animal notes. Lovely red cherry and strawberry fruits on the palate have not yet developed the savory spectrum suggested by the nose. There is a smooth red cherry impression on the finish. This is the finest and most generous wine of the vintage. *** Drink now-2015.

Central Otago, The Viper, 2006
Medium ruby color with some garnet hues, just a touch darker than the Tiger. Taut palate shows fruits more as black cherries than red, still not really coming out. Tight and reserved, this is the most structured wine of the vintage. ** Drink now-2016.

Central Otago, The Tiger, 2002
Some developed notes show on the nose, more towards mineral and gunflint than really savory. Sweet ripe fruits still show through, softening as the tannins have resolved, with a kick of earthy strawberries defining the finish. The characteristic earthiness of the vineyard comes through clearly, but the fruits are now lightening up, and there isn't the sense of structure that might support further longevity, so time to drink up. ** Drink now-2013.

Felton Road

In twenty years, Felton Road's single vineyard and block wines have acquired iconic status. The first vineyard was planted by Stewart Elms in 1992; the Elms vineyard is now 14.4 ha. The 7.6 ha Cornish Point vineyard was planted in 1999 by Nigel Greening, who purchased Felton Road in 2000. Felton Road also leases the 10.1 ha Calvert Vineyard. Winemaker Blair Walters has been there from the start. All the vineyards have complicated patterns of planting, with multiple clones; Pinot Noir is in the majority. Belief in the value of diversity extends to plans to plant the next vineyard by selection massale. Current production is around 5,000 cases of the estate bottling (which bears the specific name Bannockburn as of 2009), up to a thousand cases of individual single vineyards, and 500-600 cases of the individual blocks. Essentially Blocks 3 and 5 come from barrel selections from blocks at Elms vineyard, the rest of which go into the vineyard bottling with lots from other blocks. Felton Road is certified biodynamic. Wines were tasted at Felton Road in March 2011 or previously in September 2010.

Central Otago, Bannockburn, 2009
Black cherry fruits show on a fairly restrained nose and tight, elegant palate. Light, fine-grained tannins give a good sense of finesse, with some chocolate overtones on the finish. This can already be drunk. Drink now-2016.

Central Otago, Cornish Point Vineyard, 2009
Intriguing nose with some perfumed, herbal, nutty aromas hiding some black fruits. Just in the past six months the fruit, acidity, and alcohol all have integrated into the palate, which now shows a real purity of line, with lean, elegant black cherries dominating. Fine grained tannins bring a silky texture to the finish and should support interesting aging for some years, although the smoothness of the palate makes the wine already drinkable. Here is a sense of finesse that quite sets the lie to the notion of boisterous New World fruit. *** Drink 2013-2018.

Central Otago, Calvert Vineyard, 2009
Warm, slightly nutty, earthy, red fruit nose. Crisp acidity shows on the palate, giving a lean impression to the bright red cherry fruits. Tighter and more refined than the Bannockburn, a far cry from the stereotyped fruit bombs of the new world. But very youthful now, needs time for flavor variety to develop. (September 2010) ** Drink 2012-2018.

Central Otago, Block 3, 2009
Lean nose, with some earthy, mineral strawberries, and just a hint of smokiness (new oak was 40% here, compared with 30% on the individual vineyard bottlings). A nice depth to the well rounded red cherry and strawberry fruits shows immediately on the palate. There's a slightly spirity impression from high alcohol, but otherwise good balance, with the ripe fruits supported by vibrant acidity and opening out nicely in the glass. (September 2010) ** Drink 2014-2019.

Central Otago, 2008
Herbal overtones mark the black fruit nose. Taut black fruits on the palate are accompanied by a touch of tobacco and tea-like impressions on the smooth, supple, finish. This elegant wine carries its high alcohol lightly. Already it is highly drinkable, but a sense of structure that will support aging reminds me of Volnay. *** Drink now-2019.

Central Otago, 2007
Here there is a faint aromatic touch to the black cherry nose. A slightly piquant acidity supports the black fruit palate, with tea-like tannins and tobacco showing on the finish. This is a touch more aromatic and less herbal than the 2008. *** Drink now-2018.

Central Otago, Block 3, 2007
Some smoky notes show on the nose, hiding the red fruits that emerge slowly in the glass. Sweet bright red cherry fruits on the palate are supported by vibrant acidity and some tight tannins. Ripeness of the fruits is evident on the finish. This may well mature to elegance, but needs some time. (September 2010) ** Drink 2012-2010.

Central Otago, Block 3, 2006
Some development showing on a slightly animal nose. Tight red fruits on the palate are supported by crisp acidity, with some earthy strawberry fruits showing more retronasally on the finish than directly. Fruits are a little monolithic at this point, and there's some heat on the finish. (September 2010) ** Drink now-2016.

Central Otago, 2005
Deep garnet color from this low-yielding vintage. Savory animal notes on the nose show some development. The developed notes are also present on the palate, but more subdued by the fruit concentration. Fruits are deeper and denser than more recent vintages. A touch of spice comes through to liven up the fruits in the glass. There's a very nice balance between the weighty fruits and the supporting acidity, with firm tannins that are a touch more rustic than usual. ** Drink now-2015.

Central Otago, 2004
Some developed savory, almost animal, aromas on the nose. Sweet ripe fruits show the density of 2005 but more lightness of touch, and greater elegance. Tannins are very fine. This is a little less developed than 2005, showing a lovely balance with some real elegance. ***(*) Drink now-2016.

Central Otago, Block 3, 2004
Medium garnet color shows some development. Interesting mix on the nose of jammy strawberry fruits with hints of sous bois. Coming up to the turning point, the red fruits are developing their first tertiary aromas, but the palate delivers less complexity than the nose promises. Ripe fruits are supported by a steely minerality on the finish, this should be quite interesting in another year or so. (September 2010) *** Drink now-2016.

Central Otago, 2001
Savory nose with mineral hints and just a suspicion of sous bois. This is at a turning point on the palate, with the savory sous bois notes mingling with red fruits. A delicious point of perfect balance right now, with tannins resolving but still sufficient to give structural support. **** Drink now-2015.

Central Otago, Block 5, 2000
A bit dumb on the nose, with a suspicion of black fruits and some savory touches. Fruits lightening up on the palate with animal notes in the background. Seems less bright than the 2001 and has probably reached its natural life span. (This might well have gone on some years further if screwcap had been available rather than the cork that was used at the time.) *** Drink now-2012.

Central Otago, Block 3, 1998
Leathery hints with a faint touch of Band-Aid suggest some Brett, which is actually quite attractive on the nose, but becomes a touch overt on the palate. The richness of the fruits carries the palate past the Brett into a complex and interesting finish. ***(*) Drink now-2014.

Gibbston Valley Wines

Gibbston Valley was the first commercial winery to be established, in 1981 by Alan Brady (who left in 1997 and now makes wine next door at Mount Edward). The first Pinot was released in 1987. It's now expanded into a winery, a restaurant, and located on the main highway out of Queenstown, it's become a stop for tour buses. It's one of the largest wineries in Central Otago. Having passed through a phase when grapes were purchased, now all wine is made from estate grapes, but there are also vineyards in other parts of Central Otago as well as Gibbston Valley itself. 2.5 ha of vines around the winery are among the oldest in Central Otago. The entry level, estate, and reserve wines are all blended; and there are three single vineyard wines, from plantings in the Bendigo region. China Terrace comes from a vineyard at 300-500 m where the soil has lots of clay; School House is at 350-400 m with more schist and loess. Both are produced in 400 case lots; the smallest single vineyard, Le Maitre has only 75 cases of production. The single vineyard wines are mostly sold at the cellar door. Wines were tasted at Gibbston Valley in March 2011.

Central Otago, 2009
"Of all the wines we make now, this is the one we would consider to define house style," says winemaker Chris Keyes. The grapes come mostly from the vineyards on the lower terraces. The red fruit nose is slightly tarry. The supple red fruit palate offers some slightly buttery strawberry fruits with notes of black cherries. A touch of acidity shows with light tannins on the finish. This is intended to be ready to drink on release, but although it can be enjoyed now, it will be better in a year as the tannins soften further. ** Drink 2012-2016.

Central Otago, China Terrace, 2009
The China Terrace is in Bendigo, which produces the most muscular wines of the region. The vineyard is at 250-300 m elevation, with some clay in the soil, and it ripens relatively late. Its weighty character is reflected in the use of 15% whole clusters at fermentation, followed by 60% new oak during maturation. A black fruit nose with some hints of red cherries offers an austere reserved impression. Dense ripe black cherry and blackcurrant fruits have some aromatic overtones on the palate. Sturdy tannins are pretty much hidden by the fruit concentration, making this almost ready to drink. Winemaker Chris Keyes believes this wine will age well for a decade. *** Drink 2012-2020.

Central Otago, School House, 2009
This wine comes from a vineyard planted with Dijon clones. The red and black cherry fruit nose has some mineral notes, savory overtones, and a fragrant perfume. It is taut and restrained compared to the opulence of China Terrace, with a tighter structure of fine but firm tannins on the finish. *** Drink 2012-2020.

Central Otago Reserve, 2009
Stern black fruit nose. The lushness of the vintage shows as black cherry and plum fruits, which are faintly aromatic on the palate. Tannins are firm but elegant, just a touch of bitterness still showing. Dense black fruits almost hide the tannins, and this may be ready to drink sooner than the tight 2008 vintage. ***(*) Drink 2012-2021.

Central Otago Reserve, 2008
Black fruit nose with faint apple aromatics. This is a lighter, more elegant style than the Reserves of earlier years. Black fruits on the palate are more plums than cherries, and there's a mineral impression with taut tannins. Many would be happy to drink this now given the fruit character, but personally I'd give it a couple of years to let the tannins soften. *** Drink 2013-2020.

Central Otago, Le Mineur d'Orient, 2008
This wine was subsequently renamed as China Terrace (both names referring to the Chinese miners who came to the area in the nineteenth century gold rush). This vintage was matured in 100% new oak. Some perfumed black fruits show on the nose with a hint of a mineral edge. The palate follows with smooth black fruits with a more evident tautness than 2009 and overall a tighter structure. The strong tannic structure shows in the glass. The wine should benefit from some aging. ** Drink 2012-2018.

Central Otago Reserve, 2005
This powerful wine came from a mixture of fruit from Gibbston Valley and Bendigo in a low yielding vintage, and structure was emphasized by using 30-40% whole clusters. The herbal nose has some savory notes, and a fugitive impression of gunflint, followed by a powerful herbal note retronasally on the finish, very dry, aromatic, almost an impression of bell peppers or the leathery tones of Brett. Very fine development is showing here, the structure for longevity is evident, with the black fruits remaining dense. *** Drink now-2016.

Judge Rock Wines

Paul Jacobson planted a 4 ha vineyard around his house in Alexandra in 1998, and the first vintage was 2002. Plantings are mostly Pinot Noir, with a very small amount of St. Laurent. Production is split 60:40 between the Judge Rock bottling and the Venus bottling (which functions as a second label). There is 50-60% new oak in Judge Rock and only 10-15% in Venus (which sometimes does better in tastings because it is more approachable). This is the only difference in winemaking. Wines were tasted at Judge Rock in March 2011.

Central Otago, 2010
Aromatic black fruit nose. Palate follows the nose with light aromatic black cherry fruits. The aromatics make this seem more like a barrel sample than a bottled wine, which is really closer to its status since it will not be released for another two years. It's not the tannins that make the wine seem unready, it's the intense aromatics, but overall style should be light and elegant by the time of release. * Drink 2013-2017.

Central Otago, 2009
Recently bottled but not due to be released for another year. Slightly nutty, over-ripe, stewed notes on the nose. The palate shows direct fruit flavors of black cherries, with scarcely noticeable very light tannins, but flavor variety is a bit lacking at this stage. * Drink 2013-2016.

Central Otago, 2008
This is the current release. Nose shows red fruit aromas with faint strawberries and raspberries, making a somewhat light impression. On the palate the fruits seem darker, quite elegant with a fine structure, and light tannins just showing. Needs another year, when the wine should show some elegance and should be pleasant for short term consumption. ** Drink 2012-2016.

Central Otago, Venus, 2007
Restrained nose shows some floral touches and hints of strawberries and raspberries. The influence of less oak is evident in the smooth black fruits on the palate. There is a just a simple

touch of aromatics on the finish rather than the more structured texture of the Judge Rock. *
Drink now-2013.

Central Otago, 2007
This year gave a smaller crop than usual. Red fruit nose of warm strawberries with some hints
of raspberries. Very nice balance on the palate here, with some fresh black cherry fruits followed by tea-like tannins retronasally on the finish. Fine tannic structure gives refined, elegant
impression of some finesse. This wine may need more time to develop than the later vintages
of 2008 and 2009. *** Drink now-2014.

Central Otago, 2006
First developed notes of the vertical show some savory, slightly pungent, mineral impressions
with gunflint. Sweet fruits with a prickle of acidity show on the palate, with nice texture and
balance, but are the structural underpinnings there for longevity? A touch of bitterness is
creeping on to the finish. ** Drink now-2014.

Central Otago, 2005
This was the last vintage made by William Hill as winemaker, before production was switched to
VinPro. A very small crop was picked late. The nose has more direct red fruits of perfumed
strawberries than 2006, with a touch of violets. There is a sweet, ripe, red fruit palate, showing
a good balance with acidity and smooth tannins, but the fruits are beginning to lighten up now,
and there is less pizzazz than 2006. * Drink now-2013.

Misha's Vineyard

Looking for that rare thing in Central Otago—a frost-free zone—Andy and Misha
Wilkinson established their vineyard on the steep slopes of the former Bendigo Station,
an old gold-mining site that later became a sheep farm. Vineyards rise up steeply for 150
m from the lake front. So far 27 ha have been planted out of the 57 ha total, with two
thirds Pinot Noir. The first plantings were in 2004, and the first commercial vintage was
2008. There was a trial bottling called The Audition in 2007. Now three Pinot Noirs are
produced by barrel selection: the Impromptu entry-level wine, the High Note estate
wine, and the Verismo. Wines were tasted at Misha's in March 2011.

Central Otago, High Note, 2009
This vintage is about to be released. There is an attractive bright red fruit palate, with fine
tannins in the background, making the wine ready to drink. There's a nice balance of fruit to
acidity and tannins, with just a slight tannic rasp on the finish that will soften in the next year. It
is more loose knit in structure than the 2008, which is common when comparing these vintages
from Central Otago. ** Drink now-2015.

Central Otago, High Note, 2008
Closed on the nose, a little more intensity on the palate with notes of strawberries. Tannins are
evident from the dryness of the finish but otherwise are hidden by the fruits. When the tannins
soften in another year, the wine should show an attractive soft, earthy, red fruit spectrum. **
Drink now-2016.

Central Otago, The Audition, 2007
This was the first production from the vineyard, with a trial 100 cases produced from a small
area at the very top of the hill. Restrained nose with hints of red fruits and perhaps a faint
savory background. Sweet red fruits of strawberries and raspberries show on the palate,
supported by balanced acidity and soft tannins. The strawberries become a touch earthy on the
finish. The overall impression is fairly restrained except for a touch of heat on the finish. ** Drink
now-2014.

Mount Difficulty

Founded by a group of families who variously contributed land, expertise, or capital,
Mount Difficulty has grown to become one of the larger producers in Central Otago.
The first vineyard was planted in 1991, but grapes were sold until the first vintage was
bottled in 1998. Pinot Noir and Chardonnay are the mainstay, with Pinot Noir about
85% of plantings. Pinot Noir production extends from the 25,000 annual cases of the

Roaring Meg entry level wine, to the 7-10,000 cases of the estate wine, and the tiny production of 300 cases each of up to three single vineyard wines (rarely all produced in the same vintage). Target Gully was produced in 2009 and 2003, Long Gully in 2009, 2008, 2007, and 2005, and Pipeclay Terrace in 2009, 2007, 2006, 2005, and 2002. The vines for the single vineyards are now around fifteen years old, and they feel at Mount Difficulty that specificity really began to show itself around twelve years of age. The increase in quality going from the estate bottling to the single vineyard wines is striking. Target Gully is the most precise with a tendency to spiciness, Long Gully has a touch more weight but is still quite reserved, and Pipeclay Terrace is the most generous. Wines were tasted at Mount Difficulty in March 2011, except as noted.

Central Otago, Roaring Meg, 2009
This entry level wine has a muted nose. On the palate are soft red strawberry-ish fruits with a sweet jammy finish in the style of a Frühburgunder, soft without much tannin. The wine comes from younger vines with a bias to Dijon clones, from vineyards elsewhere in the Cromwell Basin rather than in Bannockburn. Drink now-2013.

Central Otago, Target Gully, 2009
Attractive slightly spicy red fruit nose with nutty strawberries. Soft red fruit on the palate shows a mineral edge with a finely delineated impression. Fine tannins are only just showing on the palate, a touch of dryness on the finish revealing the underlying structure. This is the most elegant (and ready to drink) of the single vineyard wines. *** Drink 2012-2019.

Central Otago, Long Gully, 2009
More restrained nose with suggestions of spices; strawberry fruits are more mineral than earthy. A touch more opulent than Target Gully with nutty strawberries on the finish. The sweet core of fruits shows clearly. The lushness of the fruits subsumes the tannins, but the finish is quite dry. The impression is of soft opulence, not so precise as Target Gully. *** Drink 2013-2019.

Central Otago, Pipeclay Terrace, 2009
Spicy red fruit nose shows cherries and strawberries. Fruits verge on opulence but are presently restrained by the fine tannins. The fruit density makes this almost approachable, but the tannins are flattening the flavor profile, and this needs time. It should come to life in a couple of years. This is the most structured of the single vineyard wines. *** Drink 2013-2021.

Central Otago, Roaring Meg, 2008
Restrained nose with just a faint hint of herbal spices. Quite sweet soft fruits on the palate supported by balanced acidity. Just a touch of bitterness still showing on the finish, with a faint mineral edge. Very young, needs some time, but should soften in the next few months. (September 2010) * Drink now-2016.

Central Otago, 2008
The estate wine shows a restrained but attractive nose with a faintly mineral edge to red cherry and strawberry fruits. Some depth to the red fruit palate, slightly hard edged tannins showing on the finish, with the mineral edge returning. As always, needed a few months after bottling to soften. (September 2010) ** Drink now-2016.

Mount Edward

Founded in 1997 by Alan Brady after he left Gibbston Valley Wines, Mount Edward focuses on Pinot Noir, Chardonnay, and Riesling. Winemaker Duncan Forsyth became a partner in 2004. Only estate fruit is used. The home vineyard next to the winery is on a striking 30 degree slope; there are now other estate vineyards in Lowburn and Bannockburn. About 2,000 cases are produced of the Earth's End entry level wine, 1,200 cases of the estate wine (which comes from three of the single vineyards), and from 80-150 cases each of the various single vineyard wines. "We are not trying to make big fruity wines, we are looking for more delicacy and reserve," says Duncan Forsyth. Wines were tasted at Mount Edward in March 2011.

Central Otago, Earth's End, 2009
This entry level wine was made from declassified fruit. The restrained nose offers some hints of mineral strawberries. The immediately approachable palate follows the nose, with the overt fruits making this immediately drinkable. The light strawberry fruits have just a hint of supporting tannins, with a ripe kick of sweetness on the finish. ** Drink now-2015.

Central Otago, 2009
Faintly aromatic black fruit nose with blackcurrant and cherry fruits. Lovely aromatic black cherry fruits on the palate, with very clean, pure fruit lines, perhaps just a touch too much blackcurrant showing on the finish for varietal purity. Some hints of black tea and a touch of heat show on the finish. ** Drink 2012-2017.

Central Otago, Susan's Vineyard, 2009
This vineyard was planted 13 years ago in the Gibbston Valley. A red and black cherry fruit nose has some faintly aromatic plums and a touch of cereal. There's a hint of piquancy to the black plum and cherry fruits on the palate, which gives a very fine aromatic impression, still with a touch of bitterness on the finish. This is the most forward, and at this stage the most obviously ripe, of the single vineyards. There's a touch of heat on the finish. *** Drink 2013-2017.

Central Otago, Morrison Vineyard, 2009
This vineyard in Lowburn (between Cromwell and Wanaka) was planted 14 years ago with the 667 and 777 Dijon clones. The black fruit nose has slightly spicy notes. The palate shows a very fine style with purity of expression. A touch of black tea and tobacco cuts the sweet ripe fruits on the finish. This is the most delicate of the single vineyard wines. *** Drink 2012-2018.

Central Otago, Muirkirk Vineyard, 2009
This vineyard was planted 15-16 years ago along Felton Road in Bannockburn. Very restrained nose with some hints of cereal. Elegant, refined black fruits are taut and pure. The most restrained of the single vineyard vines, the tannins are still pretty tight on the finish, and there is the best structure for future aging. *** Drink 2013-2019.

Quartz Reef

Quartz Reef was the first, and remains the defining, winery for the Bendigo region. Rudi Bauer discovered the area when he was the winemaker at Rippon. Bendigo Station was a very large piece of land, used only for sheep farming, until Rudi identified its potential for viticulture. Quartz Reef takes its name from a streak of quartz under the land. Quartz Reef has two vineyards at Bendigo. The 15 ha of Bendigo Estate have fine gravel and quartz soils, planted to Pinot Noir, Pinot Gris, and Chardonnay, on a slope about as steep as you can find. The adjacent (less inclined) vineyard has sandy loam soils and provides grapes for sparkling wine production. (Sparkling wine production was a plan B in case everything went wrong, but was so successful it became part of the regular production.) Quartz Reef is fully biodynamic, with everything except its own cows. The first harvest was 1998. The power of Bendigo certainly comes through the Quartz Reef wines, with dense fruits and powerful tannins that need to be tamed. In addition to the regular bottling, there is the Bendigo Estate, which is based on selecting the best of the 25 fermentations; the source varies each year. Wines were tasted at Quartz Reef in March 2011.

Central Otago, 2008
Black fruit nose with cherries, plums, and blackcurrants has a very faint aromatic edge, a touch more intense than the 2007. Here the sweetness of the fruits on the palate, showing as dense ripe black cherries and blackcurrants, is balanced by a fine acidity. Tannins are refined, and the purity of fruit shines through, with that faint aromatic note coming back on the finish. Allow at least another year for the tannins to soften, and the well delineated fruits should show increasing elegance. *** Drink 2012-2018.

Central Otago, Bendigo Estate, 2008
Slightly spicy black fruit nose. A more concentrated version of the regular Quartz Reef bottling of this vintage, with a slight aromatic note to the black cherry and blackcurrant fruits. Acidity is balanced, tannins are firm but fine, a faint cereal and spice note shows on the long finish. There's lots of life ahead. *** Drink now-2019.

Central Otago, 2007
Slightly spicy black fruit nose with some cereal notes. Core of sweet, ripe, dense fruit comes through, with firm almost rustic tannins on the finish. Passing through a closed stage at the moment, but showing a fruit density that should carry it past the tannins. ** Drink now-2015.

Central Otago, Bendigo Estate, 2007
Muted nose. Sweet, ripe, dense fruits on the palate, a touch more youthful on the finish, which gives a slight impression of heat. Lots of concentration here, with a firm but unobtrusive tannic structure. This seems a rare wine from the region that may be for the long haul. ***(*) Drink now-2022.

Central Otago, Bendigo Estate, 2006
Muted nose shows faint savory and cereal notes. Sweet ripe, dense black fruits show lots of concentration with spices coming out on the finish. Tannins are firm, and spices linger on the finish. The wine seems in its infancy. *** Drink now-2021.

Central Otago, 2005
An intriguing mix of spicy and savory aromas on the nose, even a touch of cinnamon and nutmeg. Sweet ripe fruits, black cherries and spices still showing, less developed on the palate than on the nose, with the fruits just a touch more youthful than the 2006. *** Drink now-2015.

Rockburn Wine

Rockburn's winery is in the unglamorous industrial area of Cromwell, but the two estate vineyards are located in Gibbston Valley and the Parkburn area of Lake Dunstan. It started as Hay's Lake Vineyard in 1991, but the name changed in 2002 as it expanded out of the original small area. Production is about 12,000 cases annually from estate grapes, and as much again from purchased grapes (used for the second label, Devil's Staircase), making Rockburn one of the larger producers today. Pinot Noir is about two thirds of all production. The estate wine is a blend from the two estate vineyards, and in good years there is a reserve made from barrel selections. Wines from 2006 were made by present winemaker Malcolm Rees-Francis; older wines were made by Rudi Bauer of Quartz Reef. Wines were tasted at Rockburn in March 2011.

Central Otago, 2009
This wine is a regional blend. There's a slightly mineral and earthy red fruit nose. Almost crisp acidity leads into a palate in the red fruit spectrum, more strawberries than cherries. More mineral than earthy on the palate with some heat on the finish. Although no doubt this would be regarded as ready to drink in the region, it will show the light fruits more clearly if the rustic tannins are given a few months to soften. * Drink 2012-2016.

Central Otago, 2008
A faint suspicion of spice on the red strawberry and raspberry nose. Smooth ripe fruits on the palate with a hint of piquant acidity, a touch of opulence, but there's a lack of follow through on mid palate. Already ready to drink. ** Drink now-2016.

Central Otago, 2007
Some developed notes on the nose, animal as much as savory, and then a touch of spice. Nice balance on the palate between savory and fruity, with the fruits retaining character but developing, and the tannins resolving. For my palate, this is at the right point to drink, but those who like upfront fruits might consider it a little old. ** Drink now-2014.

Central Otago, Eight Barrels, 2006
This wine is Rockburn's top barrel selection of Pinot Noir. Presently a medium ruby-garnet color, it shows a pungent savory nose with some touches of gunflint. This has more of a Burgundian balance than the regular bottling or the more recent vintages, perhaps reflecting the inclusion of some whole bunches and the use of low levels of new oak, but also significantly the low alcohol level (only 12.5%). There's a nice balance with an acidic edge cut by a touch of opulence. Winemaker Malcolm Rees-Francis sees this wine as a harbinger for the future, even, he says, if it is his children rather than he who get to make wines in this style. *** Drink now-2015.

Central Otago, 2006
Some whole bunches were used this year. Savory notes on the nose take the form of gunflint. Mid weight sweet ripe fruits are maturing on the palate with more of a mineral edge, but less

developed than the 2007 vintage. Crisp acidity accentuates the minerality on the finish, which shows some heat. ** Drink now-2014.

Central Otago, 2005
Medium garnet developed color appears more than a year older than the 2006. Savory pungent nose offers mineral notes and gunflint with some ripe strawberry fruits poking through. Sweet ripe fruits on the palate are less developed than you would expect from the nose, with slightly piquant acidity, and tannins resolving. The wine carries the high alcohol (14.5% on the label) very well. *** Drink now-2013.

Central Otago, 2004
Medium garnet color shows some development, but perhaps a touch rosier and more youthful in appearance than 2005. This is at a very nice stage of development, with a savory/fruity balance showing on both nose and palate. Touches of minerality and gunflint on the nose are followed on the palate by sweet ripe strawberry fruits that cut the savory impression. This is a lovely point at which to enjoy the wine. *** Drink now-2015.

Central Otago, 2003
Some pungent savory notes on the nose have just a faint touch of underlying sweet red fruits of raspberries and strawberries. The palate is less developed than the nose, with the red fruits beginning to dry out a little, although there is still some life. Tannins are resolved; alcohol is not perceptible. Attractive faintly nutty notes develop on the finish, which remains quite sweet and thick. ** Drink now-2014.

Central Otago, 2002
This was the first crop from the young vines. Savory notes of gunflint and minerals on the nose. Sweet ripe red fruits on the palate are less obviously developed than the nose, but at a nice point of balance. Like the 2003, the finish is quite viscous. A touch of bitterness comes through. ** Drink now-2014.

Wooing Tree Vineyard

Located in the heart of Cromwell, Wooing Tree has an 18 ha vineyard on wide, flat land, planted almost exclusively to Pinot Noir. The 7,500 cases annual production may represent the most varied line of wines made from Pinot Noir in the region: a white wine called Blondie, a rosé, a sweet rosé, and then three dry red wines: the Beetle Juice entry level wine is made from fruit declassified from the estate; there is the estate wine itself; and the Sandstone Reserve comes from part of the vineyard that is cropped to a lower yield, so is effectively a single block wine. Wines were tasted at Wooing Tree in March 2011.

Central Otago, Beetle Juice, 2009
Rather restrained on the nose with a slight impression of black cherry fruits. Slightly spicy black fruit nose, very soft with little backbone, clearly intended for current consumption. Simple and direct. * Drink now-2013.

Central Otago, 2009
This vintage will be released in a couple of months. It contained 5-10% whole bunches. Slightly spicy, plummy black fruit nose makes a soft impression. Sweet ripe fruits on the palate reinforce the impression of softness. This is a little weak on the mid palate, with not very much tannic support in the background. ** Drink now-2014.

Central Otago, Sandstorm Reserve, 2008
Red fruit nose of slightly acid strawberries. Tight red fruit palate of strawberries with hints of raspberries shows more elegance than the regular bottling. Smooth fruits on the palate are supported by silky tannins in the background, becoming nutty on the finish. Overall quite an elegant impression, with a soft finish stopping just short of buttery opulence. There is some heat on the finish. ** Drink now-2016.

Central Otago, 2007
Some faint savory elements mix with spices on the black cherry nose. The black cherries follow through to the palate with hints of plums and blackcurrants, and are supported by some faintly tarry tannins. More stuffing is apparent here than in the younger vintages, showcasing light fruits with slightly noticeable acidity. ** Drink now-2014.

Central Otago, Sandstorm Reserve, 2007
This was the first vintage of the reserve wine. The medium ruby color with its garnet hues actually looks darker and less developed than the 2008. The slightly tarry red fruit nose has some hints of black fruits. The ripe fruits on the palate are darker and have more density and structure than the 2008, bringing a sterner impression to the finish. *** Drink now-2017.

Central Otago, 2006
A mix of red and black fruits on the nose with a touch of cereals and spice. The palate doesn't quite live up to the promise of the nose, falling just a bit flat in the middle. * Drink now-2013.

Central Otago, 2005
This was the first vintage at Wooing Tree. Owner Steve Farquharson says this wine started out as a fruit bomb but has now calmed down and become more silky. There's more pizzazz than in the succeeding 2006 vintage. The nose shows slightly spicy black cherry fruits with some overtones of apple. The fruits are a mix of red and black cherries with some silkiness to the texture on the palate, uplifted by the sense of malic acidity. Tannic structure is quite fine. ** Drink now-2016.

Producers and Tastings in Yarra Valley

2010 was a relatively humid season, generally warmer than average, but without botrytis infections that would be problematic for Pinot Noir; winemakers are enthusiastic about Pinot Noir. Vintages 2009-2007 were all warmer than historic averages. A major problem in 2009 was the bush fires, which tainted some vineyards and prevented wine production. There were heat spikes in 2008 all over South Australia, with continuing drought, producing variable results. 2006 was a hot vintage, with the harvest the earliest on record, so could be challenging for Pinot Noir (often compared with 2003). 2005 was a cooler vintage marked by high rainfall (sometimes compared with 2002).

De Bortoli

De Bortoli is one of Australia's largest family-owned producers. The main site for wine production was in the Riverina until the move into premium wine in Yarra Valley, where De Bortoli is now the largest winery. Production is split between a premium wine operation and boutique wines. A total of 200 ha are planted out of a 300 ha estate. The 60 ha of Pinot Noir account for roughly one third of all production. Steve Weber makes wines under several labels, including single vineyard wines from Phi and from Riorret (including some from Mornington Peninsula well as Yarra Valley), in addition to the wines under the winery name of De Bortoli. There's an estate wine, reserve wine, and usually three single vineyard Pinot Noirs. The general policy is that wines should be drinkable on release, and they are held back when this is not the case. Wines were tasted at De Bortoli in March 2011.

Yarra Valley, (De Bortoli) 2010
This wine comes from four estate vineyards. Faintly tarry notes show on a nose of strawberry and raspberry fruits. The palate is a touch flattened at the moment, but promises to offer generous fruits of black cherries as the tannins soften. ** Drink now-2015.

Yarra Valley Reserve, (De Bortoli) 2010
The reserve comes from the older plantings of clones 4 and 5 which were rejected by the local wine board at the time because the berries and bunches were too small! Attractive nose shows some spice and savory elements. Fruits show as red and black cherries on the palate with a touch of glycerinic opulence on the finish. The ripe tannins are hidden under the fruits but show in the dryness of the finish. The good structure offers potential for long aging. *** Drink 2013-2021.

Yarra Valley, The Abbey, (Riorret) 2010
This vineyard in Tarrawarra was planted with the MV6 clone in 1993. The 2010 vintage is about to be released. Black fruit nose has some undertones of raspberries. Sweet ripe fruits on the palate show more red than black, and have some austere underpinnings. Supporting tannins are fine, and the wine is almost ready to drink; within a year or so the tannins will soften to reveal an elegant palate. ** Drink 2012-2020.

Yarra Valley, Emu Vineyard, (Riorret) 2010
This is a south-facing slope at De Bortoli's home vineyard which was planted in 1993. Re-strained nose offers black fruit spices with hints of plums, with some black tea and tobacco notes developing in the glass. Following through to the palate are black plums and cherries, supported by crisp acidity and fine tannins, leading to a smooth finish with just a touch of heat. This is the most structured of the Riorett single vineyard wines. *** Drink 2012-2020.

Yarra Valley, Lusatia Park Vineyard, (Phi) 2010
This wine comes from a vineyard in the Woori Yallock area of the Upper Yarra. The vineyard was planted in 1985. Slightly austere black fruits show on the nose. The palate follows with smooth fruits of plums and cherries supported by supple tannins and crisp acidity giving an elegant finish. This is the most evidently generous of the single vineyard wines. *** Drink 2012-2019.

Mornington Peninsula, Balin Vineyard, (Riorret) 2009
Black fruit nose shows cherries and plums with faintly spicy and tarry overtones. Sweet ripe black fruits dominate the palate; fine tannins dry the finish. The fine structure of this wine needs at least a couple of years for the tannins to soften to allow the elegant fruits to shine through. The single vineyard wines from Mornington tend to show more elegance and structure than those from Yarra. *** Drink 2014-2020.

Mornington Peninsula, Merricks Grove Vineyard, (Riorret) 2008
Strawberry fruit nose with some hints of ripeness and jam cut by some savory aromas. Sweet ripe fruits on the palate are in the red spectrum, with a touch of glycerinic opulence. Tannins are not overt but are present in the background and dry the finish. There is a fine structure. The wine needs at least a couple of years for the tannins to soften, when the elegance of the fruits should become apparent. *** Drink now-2018.

Yarra Valley, The Abbey, (Riorret) 2008
This was the first vintage from this single vineyard. Restrained nose offers faint savory impres-sions. Ripe fruits are quite delicate on the palate, with a mineral edge to the red strawberries. Tannins appear to be resolving already, although the wine shows some dryness on the finish. *** Drink now-2019.

Yarra Valley, Lusatia Park Vineyard, (Phi) 2008
Medium garnet color from this lighter vintage. Some mineral impressions to the strawberry fruit nose. Lovely palate at a delicious point of balance, the sweet ripe fruits cut by mineral rather than savory notes, stopping just short of sous bois. The red fruit notes become progressively earthier in the glass. Delicious now but how long will it last? This could easily come from the vicinity of Beaune. ***(*) Drink now-2015.

Yarra Valley, Lusatia Park Vineyard (Phi) 2005
This was the first vintage at Phi. The developed red fruit nose shows mineral overtones. Sweet ripe fruits are quite developed on the palate, more mineral than savory. The sweet ripeness of the fruits is evident, but the mineral edge is taking over the palate, with a slightly sharp note developing. *** Drink now-2014.

Yarra Valley Reserve, (De Bortoli) 2005
Developed garnet color. Warm strawberry fruit nose with just a touch of oxidation showing at first, but then giving over to a more savory impression. Sweet ripe fruits on the palate are showing their age just a little. Touch of minerality accompanies the tannic dryness on the finish. It's time to drink before the fruits dry out. ** Drink now-2015.

Yarra Valley Reserve, (De Bortoli) 2004
The nose starts off with some notes of cereal, turning savory and intensifying in the glass. Generosity of fruits shows through the palate, lots of depth here, with the richness of the fruits cut by some mineral notes. A very faint touch of oxidation adds complexity. Compared to the Phi, the style of the Reserve is somewhat richer, a touch rustic and less refined. But lots of life left here, and this could easily be a Burgundy from the late nineties. *** Drink now-2016.

Punt Road

The Punt Road vineyards were established in the eighties but the grapes were sold until the transition to becoming a producer occurred in 2000. There was a period of making contract wine, but now the operation is devoted to production from estate grapes. A quarter of the 90 ha are Pinot Noir. There used to be a single Pinot Noir, but from 2010 the estate wine of 2,000 cases has been supplemented by the 100 case Chemin bottling. The estate wine comes from fruit that is almost all destemmed and is matured in one third new oak. There's an interesting trade off for the Chemin bottling, which is made from whole bunches, but in order to avoid excess tannin uses no new oak. (The Chemin range has started off with Pinot and also Syrah and will be extended to other varieties.) The general style of the wines seems on the commercial side. Tasting notes go straight from 2010 to 2008 because there was no 2009 as a result of taint from the bush fires. Wines were tasted at Punt Road in March 2011.

Yarra Valley, 2010
This was bottled only ten days ago so might still be suffering some effects of bottle shock. Bright aromatic fruits of red cherries on the nose, following through to the palate, with smooth, bright red fruits with aromatic overtones, Very young and drinkable but not a lot of flavor variety. * Drink now-2014.

Yarra Valley, Chemin, 2010
This was bottled within the last week so may still have been suffering from some bottle shock. Restrained nose with faintly tarry overtones. Sweet ripe fruits on the palate and light and smooth with herbal overtones. ** Drink now-2015.

Yarra Valley, 2008
Faint but pungent tarry notes on nose. Slightly tarry strawberry fruits on palate, light concentration without a lot of character. Somewhat interdenominational fruits. * Drink now-2013.

Seville Estate

One of the original estates founded by the group of doctors who reestablished wine production in Yarra Valley, Seville still produces wine from the vines planted in 1972. Today Pinot Noir is about a third of production. About 8,000 cases are produced annually of the entry level wine, The Barber, which comes from outsourced grapes. The estate wine is produced in only 500-600 cases annually. The reserve is made only in top vintages, most recently 2003, 2007, 2008, and 2010. It is based on a barrel selection that usually comes principally from the old vines (which are the oldest plantings of Pinot Noir in Yarra Valley). In 2009 all production was declassified into The Barber entry level wine. The style of wines here reflects the restraint of the Upper Yarra, emphasized in recent years. Winemaker Dylan MacMahon says that, "When I started as a winemaker we were making richer, fuller Pinots, quite different to how my grandfather made the wines." They have been picking earlier for the past couple of years to help lighten the style. Wines were tasted at Seville Estate in March 2011.

Yarra Valley, The Barber, 2010
Bright red fruit nose with a high toned aromatic uplift. Light fruits on the palate, not much stuffing evident, a pleasant quaffing wine, but a bit hollow on the mid palate. * Drink now-2013.

Yarra Valley, 2010
(Not yet released.) Restrained red fruit nose shows cherries more than strawberries. An elegant red cherry fruit palate has light supporting tannins, with just a touch of astringency to the finish requiring another year to soften. ** Drink 2012-2016.

Yarra Valley Reserve, 2010
Restrained nose shows mixture of red and black cherries. There's an elegant style on the palate with faintly buttery overtones, and the fruits now showing more as black than red cherries. The difference with the regular estate bottling is not so much in the weight or concentration

as in the greater purity of fruits. "I hate that urban myth that the reserve needs to be twice the weight of the estate," says winemaker Dylan McMahon. ** Drink 2012-2017.

Yarra Valley, 2008
Some perfumed notes lead into savory aromas on the nose. The elegant palate balances red fruits, more cherries than strawberries, with silky tannins. The overall impression is quite delicate, with a fine-grained texture, and the tannins just evident by a dryness on the finish. This could be drunk now but will certainly benefit from another year to show its full delicacy. ** Drink 2012-2016.

Yarra Valley Reserve, 2008
A faintly perfumed nose offers suspicions of chocolate coating on the red cherry fruits. The smooth red fruit palate tends to cherries, with a touch of glycerinic opulence, supported by some light, refined tannins that dry the finish. There's already a nice balance, but the fruits will show more clearly in another year, giving an elegant red fruit spectrum for consumption in the intermediate term. ** Drink 2012-2017.

Yarra Valley Reserve, 2003
The big warm year is reflected in the wine. Mature nose with quite strong savory notes and a pungent whiff of sous bois. Rich, warm, and concentrated on the palate, where savory notes are less evident than on the nose; still enjoyable, but beginning to tire as a touch of bitterness and a faint raisined edge are released on to the palate. Time to drink up. **

Sticks Yarra Valley

Sticks takes its name from the nickname of Rob Dolan, the founder of Sticks Yarra, who started out as the winemaker at Foster's Yarra Ridge Winery. Sticks Yarra's first vintage was 2000, with wines made at Punt Road for the first five years until the winery was constructed. The estate vineyards lie around the winery, and there are also 15 long term contract growers, mostly on the valley floor, with a couple in Upper Yarra. The philosophy is fruit-driven and value for money, but current winemaker Travis Bush has made a change in style to build more texture into the wine (by using more whole berries, lees contact, and better oak). Pinot Noir is about half of production, mostly the estate wine, but also includes the reserve #29. Screwcaps were used for all production from 2004. Wines were tasted at Sticks Yarra in March 2011.

Yarra Valley, 2009
This wine is a blend from vineyards in the Upper Yarra with those on the valley floor. Bright fruits on the nose are more raspberries than strawberries. Soft fruits show more as cherries on the palate, but fall a bit flat on the mid palate. Smoke taint was cleaned up by reverse osmosis, which possibly explains a certain lack of flavor variety. Not much structural support for aging. * Drink now-2015.

Yarra Valley, 2008
Light strawberry fruit nose follows through to the palate, where some light tannins support the fruits, but the general impression is that this light wine is already fully developed and lacks the structure for much further development. * Drink now-2014.

Yarra Valley, (#29), 2006
This was the first vintage for this special cuvée. Light strawberry fruits show on the nose with some faint aromatics. There is more stuffing on the palate than was suggested by the nose, with soft, full fruits, a touch of glycerinic opulence on the finish, quite ripe tannins, but a certain lack of follow through on the finish. * Drink now-2014.

Yarra Valley, 2005
Lightening garnet color. Weak nose of faint strawberry fruits with some faint savory impressions. Sweet ripe red fruits on the palate show more as strawberries than cherries; soft ripe tannins give a nice balance. This is now at its peak although perhaps there will be some savory development over the next couple of years. ** Drink now-2015.

Yarra Valley, 2004
Ripe strawberry fruits, with hints of jam on the nose, mingle with the first savory notes. Fruits are more savory on the palate but holding up quite well, with a superficial touch of glycerin fattening the finish. ** Drink now-2015.

Yarra Valley, 2003
This was the last vintage under cork and shows a darker, more developed color. Some notes of madeirization show on the nose, becoming more raisiny. You can see the rich, ripe fruits underneath, but the wine is spoiled by the oxidation. This might have been a very fine older wine if only screwcaps had been available at the time.

Yarra Valley, 2002
Two bottles showed somewhat differently, reflecting the states of their corks. The first was much like the 2003, somewhat dark in color and a bit madeirized on the palate. The second was a brighter color, more a ruby-garnet. The red fruit nose shows herbal overtones with a faint touch of black tea. Then lovely rich red fruits come though on the palate with a faint counter-poise of savory and herbal notes, drying out just a touch on the finish (with a faint touch of oxidation, but night and day from the first bottle). Time to drink up as the herbal notes turn medicinal in the glass. ** Drink now.

Yarra Valley, 2000
Medium garnet color. Restrained nose with some developed red fruits. Fruits on the palate are surviving rather than developing, still showing some ripe flavors, but drink up before they fade. * Drink now.

Tarrawarra Estate

The first vines were planted here in 1983, including one Pinot Noir vineyard that is still producing. The estate is a striking series of vineyards strung along the Healesville Road, in two blocks interrupted by some unplanted areas; altogether there are 30 ha of vineyards in a 400 ha cattle grazing property. Pinot Noir is just over half of production, and most of the Pinot plantings are MV6. The original vineyard, plus another planted in 1985, provides the basis for the Reserve wine, which is effectively an Old Vines production consisting of the first vineyard block plus a barrel selection from the second. "The commitment is to the Reserve, not to the blocks," however, says winemaker Clare Halloran. The reserve will be held back until it's ready to drink, whereas the mandate for the estate wine is that it should be drinkable as soon as bottled. The general style here is to showcase red fruits with a slightly glycerinic touch to the finish. In cool years this comes off with elegance, in warm years the style can seem a little fruity, almost obscuring varietal typicity. The first vintage exclusively under screwcaps was 2004. Wines were tasted at Tarrawarra in March 2011.

Yarra/Tumbarumba, Australia (Tarrawarra Estate), 2009
Usually Tarrawarra makes wine only from its own estate grapes, but production was interrupted by the bush fires of 2009, which came right up to the vineyards. As a result, this wine was made from a blend of grapes from Yarra Valley and Tumbarumba, over the border in New South Wales. Red fruit nose is quite fresh. Palate shows balance of red fruits between strawberries and cherries with a touch of glycerinic opulence. Softness of the tannins allows this to be drunk immediately. ** Drink now-2016.

Yarra Valley Reserve, 2008
Sterner on the nose than the estate wine with restrained tarry notes on top of the underlying red fruits. More intensity and richness to the fruits on the palate is evident, with a more concentrated and riper finish, but all in the consistently smooth, slightly glycerinic house style. The tannic structure is hidden by the fruit density except for a drying effect on the finish, and this is certainly ready to drink. *** Drink now-2016.

Yarra Valley Reserve, 2006
This wine gives an elegant impression from a warm year in which Cabernet Sauvignon sometimes did better than Pinot Noir. Strawberry and raspberry fruits on the nose are accompanied by a faint herbal touch with savory notes; on the palate there is a restrained and pure expression of fruits with balancing support and firm tannins in the background. *** Drink now-2017.

Yarra Valley, Tin Cows, 2004
This wine comes from a blend of estate grapes together with the Tin Cows vineyard in the Marooondah area. The nose shows a mix of savory and cereal notes with developing red fruits. Sweet ripe red fruits show on the palate, soft and gentle with just a faint herbal touch, and some faintly tarry tannins. Earthy notes develop on the finish. This has now reached its peak. *** Drink now-2014.

Yarra Valley Reserve, 2001
Two bottles illustrated the injustice done to the New World by the poor supply of corks in the early years. Both showed as good results from a cool year that was marred by rain, but in one the fruits were overtaken by medicinal notes and the wine seemed near the end of its life. In the other, the nose showed purer fruits with developing savory elements, continuing into developed sweet ripe fruits on the palate with only a hint of the medicinal notes of the first wine. Apparently the range can be much wider when a larger series of bottles is opened. *** Drink now-2014.

Yering Station

Just across from historic Chateau Yering, there is the striking new modernistic winery of Yering Station, one of the original pioneering wineries of the nineteenth century. All of the old vineyards were pulled out just before the Depression, after which the land was used for sheep farming. Today's oldest vines were planted in 1991. With a total production around 100,000 cases, Yering Station is one of the largest wineries in Yarra Valley. Half the fruit comes from the estate, the rest from leased vineyards or long term contracts. The Mr. Frog entry level Pinot is produced at 10-15,000 cases annually, the estate wine at 8,000 cases, and the Reserve (made only in some vintages, most recently in 2010 and 2006) at 800-1,000 cases. When a single vineyard performs really well, some may be held back to make an individual wine, but this happens only occasionally (the wine places between Estate and Reserve in the hierarchy). Wines were tasted at Yering Station in March 2011.

Yarra Valley, 2009
Just slightly spicy red fruit nose shows more cherries than strawberries. The cherries show as more black than red on the palate, with a soft glycerinic finish where the tannins are not really much in evidence. This is certainly ready to drink on release, for relatively immediate consumption. * Drink now-2013.

Yarra Valley, Mr. Frog, 2008
The entry level wine has a juicy black cherry fruit nose with some blackcurrants. The palate shows soft black cherry fruits with a touch of glycerin, very approachable and ready to drink. * Drink now-2012.

Yarra Valley, 2006
A faintly earthy, slightly crisp, impression to the nose, Earthy and mineral on the palate, showing a lean style with crisp finish, perhaps just a touch short. * Drink now-2016.

Yarra Valley Reserve, 2006
Some character shows on the nose with a mix of red and black fruits mingling with spices and a touch of savory elements. Smooth opulent black fruits on the palate are cut by spices with herbal overtones. This is at its peak now, but the firm underlying structure has ripe tannins that should support a few further years' longevity. ** Drink now-2015.

Yarra Valley Reserve, 2003
A faint touch of madeirization shows on the nose, a typical problem resulting from the poor corks supplied to Australia in the era. The fruits remain firm and solid on the palate, just drying out a touch and losing flavor variety—but I wonder what the wine would have been like if screwcaps had been available at the time. As it is, this remains a lovely older wine, and you can still see the ripe richness of the original fruits, although as they are losing freshness the tannins come through as a little bitter. ** Drink now-2012.

Producers and Tastings In Mornington Peninsula

Regional Tasting

As Mornington Peninsula emerges from a decade of drought, vintage variation has proved quite important. The 2009 vintage tends to show soft red fruits without a lot of tannic support, and is developing rapidly. The atypical vintage of 2008 had a warm start and cool finish, and there is a classic delineation between people who picked early versus late. The best wines have good tannic structure. The cool start to 2007 reduced crop size, and the small berries gave rich wines with more tannins than usual. The 2006 vintage is my favorite for drinking now. The previous top vintage was 2004. Wines were tasted at Port Philip Estate in March 2011.

Mornington Peninsula, Half Acre, Main Ridge Estate, 2009
This is Main Ridge's top single vineyard wine. It was cropped at the low yield of 1.5 tons/acre and then matured in 50% new oak. The nose is restrained. Bright acidity supports light red cherry fruits, quite an elegant impression, but with a touch of heat on the finish. ** Drink now-2016.

Mornington Peninsula, Port Phillip Estate, 2009
Just about to be released. This comes from the home vineyard on red soils. Restrained nose with black cherry fruits; a touch of tobacco develops in the glass. Nicely delineated red fruits show on the palate, but a little lacking in presence on the mid palate. * Drink now-2016.

Mornington Peninsula, Ferrous, Kooyong Wines, 2009
(Not yet released.) This comes from alluvial soils about 8 km to the south of the Port Philip Estate (which owns Kooyong Wines). Richer, deeper, more developed nose than the Port Phillip wine itself, with a slightly more savory impression. Fuller and richer on the palate, with red fruits already showing some touches of development. ** Drink now-2017.

Mornington Peninsula, Eldridge Estate, 2009
Slightly spicy red fruit nose. Smooth red fruit palate with just a touch of glycerin giving a super-ficial opulence, but a little lacking in presence on the mid palate. Very approachable already. ** Drink now-2015.

Mornington Peninsula, L'Ami Sage, Paradigm Hill, 2009
This is a single block within the vineyard. This year used 50% new oak (more than usual). Faintly perfumed red fruit nose with touch of nuts and cereal. Approachable now but the fruit profile is a touch flattened on the mid palate. * Drink now-2016.

Mornington Peninsula, Windmill, Stonier Wines, 2008
This wine comes from a warm north-facing slope. Quite a large proportion of whole bunches have been used in the past (but reduced in this vintage to 40%, because the winemaker feels that whole bunches can obscure the vineyard). Some savory character shows as a touch of minerality and gunflint with touches of black tea and tobacco. Fine elegant red fruits on the palate show distinct delicacy, with balanced acidity and light tannic structure. Overall a very fine impression. This can certainly be drunk now but the dry finish will become softer and gentler in a few months. *** Drink 2012-2018.

Mornington Peninsula, Paringa Estate, 2008
The estate wine comes from three vineyards (one of which also makes a single vineyard wine). There is some variety in the assemblage as some part of the vineyards are north-facing and others south-facing. The wine sees about 50% new oak. There's an attractive spicy red fruit nose with overtones of tobacco. Black cherries and black plums show on the palate with attractive spice notes on the finish and a faint touch of glycerin opulence. *** Drink now-2018.

Mornington Peninsula, Single Vineyard, Paringa Estate, 2008
More intensity to the wood spices and tobacco on the nose with black cherry fruits following. Similarly the black fruits on the palate have more intensity than the estate wine, with a touch more of the glycerin effect on the finish subsuming the ripe tannins. *** Drink now-2020.

Mornington Peninsula, L'Ami Sage, Paradigm Hill, 2006
Red strawberry fruit nose with earthy overtones, just short of becoming savory, quite attractive. Good balance on the palate, just a touch of savory cutting the fruits, which are evidently ripe and sweet. A very fine balance here, somewhat in the style of Beaune, although with more viscosity and alcohol. A lovely ripe impression on this wine which is now right at its peak. *** Drink now-2018.

Mornington Peninsula, Ferrous, Kooyong Wines, 2006
Savory nose with some pungent elements and a touch of gunflint. Some fine development on the palate, with the wine now at an attractive junction of fruit and savory elements; very nicely balanced with almost a touch of sous bois coming out on the finish, and the ripeness of the fruits still evident against a background of resolving tannins. *** Drink now-2016.

Mornington Peninsula, Windmill, Stonier Wines, 2005
This vintage was the old style with 75% whole bunch. Now after five years it is a medium garnet color. An interesting herbal nose veering towards eucalyptus gives a slightly stern impression, but the fruits on the palate are ripe and sweet, tending towards mineral strawberries, with those herbal notes coming back retronasally on the finish. A delicious balance of herbal and fruity notes mingling on the finish. *** Drink now-2016.

Mornington Peninsula, Half Acre, Main Ridge Estate, 2003
A faintly spicy, faintly aromatic red fruit nose. Quite dry on the palate, with red strawberry fruits, now lightening up somewhat, but still with some life, although the fruits would have been more prominent two or three years ago. Still some sweetness showing from the fruits, although the tannins are beginning to take over, so drink soon. ** Drink now-2013.

Mornington Peninsula, Eldridge Estate, 1998
This wine comes almost exclusively from the MV6 clone. Developed nose with some pungent savory notes, but ripeness of fruits still coming through, although the nose now seems a little tired. However, sweet ripe fruits still show on the palate, although clearly lightening up and allowing some herbal notes to show through. The fruits are beginning to dry out but winemaker David Lloyd believes this is partly due to the poor quality of corks available at this time, and that wines bottled today under screwcap will last much better. ** Drink now-2013.

Moorooduc Estate

One of the first estates to have been established on Mornington Peninsula, Moorooduc is still run by Dr. Richard McIntyre, now joined by his daughter Kate McIntyre MW. Moorooduc produces about 6,000 cases annually, almost half of which is Pinot Noir. The original vineyard was only 2 ha, but today grapes come either from the home vineyard or from three other leased vineyards close by. Grapes for the Devil Bend entry level wine are sourced from local growers. In addition to the estate wine, there is a 100-150 case annual production of The Moorooduc, which comes from a one acre block within the estate (with a third of MV6 and two thirds of Dijon clones). This reserve wine has been produced since 1998 (under its present name since 2001), except for the 1999, 2002, and 2005 vintages. The mark of the style here is purity of line, coming clearly through a vertical tasting extending back for more than a decade. Some problems of condition with the oldest wines can be attributed to the poor corks available, and I expect significantly greater longevity for the vintages that have been bottled under screwcap since 2002. Wines were tasted at Moorooduc Estate in March 2011.

Mornington Peninsula, Devil Bend Creek, 2010
This entry level wine is a medium ruby color. The spicy appley nose is a little reminiscent of mulled wine. Still spicy on the palate, but better integrated with the fruits, which tend to black cherries, a bit hot on the finish. Ready to drink and to enjoy in the next year or so. * Drink now-2014.

Mornington Peninsula, The Moorooduc, 2009
Faintly tarry aromatic nose is youthful. Sweet ripe black fruits of cherries with some notes of plums and some aromatics are cleanly delineated on the palate. Purity of line shows through. A classy impression in a restrained style. *** Drink 2012-2019.

Mornington Peninsula, The Moorooduc, 2008
Some cereal and savory notes on the nose. Lively black fruit palate shows purity with well delineated, precise, fruits. The fruits show as cherries with some aromatic notes of blackcurrants. As true generally in the region, the 2008 shows more precise, tighter edges than the more overtly generous 2009. *** Drink now-2019.

Mornington Peninsula, The Moorooduc, 2007
No whole clusters were used in this vintage. The wine has a darker, more garnet hue than the 2008. Spicy black fruit nose leads into pure black cherry fruits on the palate. Fruits and tannins are firmer than the 2008, and the ripe fruits subsume the tannins, which just dry the tobacco-driven finish. *** Drink now-2019.

Mornington Peninsula, Garden Vineyard, 2007
This was an experiment using 100% whole clusters (the grapes were all from the MV6 clone). Color is a dark garnet. Herbal notes on the nose lead to medicinal notes reflecting the whole clusters. This is much sterner on the palate than The Moorooduc, with medicinal notes on the finish hiding the fruits and obscuring the usual purity of line. Perhaps the tannins will resolve, but it is possible they will outlast the fruits. ** Drink now-2017.

Mornington Peninsula, The Moorooduc, 2006
Some savory notes are creeping on to the nose to mingle with fruits that are more red than black. Sweet red fruits show as developing earthy strawberries, with an attractive finish, but lightening up a bit on the palate. The fruits are quite lush, but in this vintage don't show the usual purity and elegance of other vintages, but this is still a very fine wine. *** Drink now-2015.

Mornington Peninsula, 2005
In this year there was no reserve, only the estate wine. Savory nose of roasted meats. Lovely balance to the red fruits on the palate, elegant but with a touch of opulence from glycerin on the finish. Tannic structure is softer and lighter than usual. ** Drink now-2014.

Mornington Peninsula, The Moorooduc, 2004
Savory nose with just a touch of gunflint and sous bois, then slightly nutty and cereal notes. On the palate this is at the turning point, with savory elements approaching sous bois counterbalanced by a touch of sweetness from the ripe fruits. There is still a touch of tannin showing as dryness on the finish. ***(*) Drink now-2015.

Mornington Peninsula, 2002
This was a year of transition, when the estate wine was bottled under both cork and screwcap. As always, the wines show fascinating differences.

Both wines show a medium garnet color. Under cork the developed nose resembles the 2004, with savory notes of sous bois showing through the tertiary red fruits. There is a delicious balance on the palate, with the fruits lightening up, but showing good breadth, with a sweet ripe kick evident on the finish. At this particular point, the wine is on a tightrope as to whether it will become savory or lose its fruit and become bitter.

The wine under screwcap is slightly less developed on the nose, with more fruit aromatics and the savory elements showing as a slight herbal impression. Fruits show as sweeter and riper, with that herbal touch coming back on the finish. The fruits have been retained better under screwcap, but the savory elements are less. It's a tradeoff: there's no bitterness, but there's less complexity at this stage. **** Drink now-2016.

Mornington Peninsula, The Moorooduc, 2001
Savory notes on the nose show as gunflint and sous bois. Sweet ripe fruits are still evident, although there has been some loss of complexity. Tannins have softened but there is a faint touch of bitterness. My impression is that from here on, the wine will survive rather than develop. ** Drink now-2015.

Mornington Peninsula, 1998
Two bottles gave different impressions. The first had a slightly tired impression to the nose with some notes of madeirization (no doubt due to the poor quality of corks available at the time), although the ripeness of the original fruits is still evident. A second bottle had brighter and richer fruits, quite deep and developed, but as with the 2001 giving the impression of survival rather than promising future development. ** Drink now-2014.

Ten Minutes by Tractor

Ten Minutes by Tractor takes its name from the fact that its three vineyards are all literally ten minutes apart by tractor, yet each has a very different character. The vineyards were planted (Judd in 1990, Wallis in 1991, McCutcheon in 1992) on a combination of own roots and rootstocks. Martin Spedding took over in 2003. Ten by Tractor shares a winemaking facility with Moorooduc Estate. Pinot Noir is about 60% of the total 5,000 case production. Only estate grapes are used. There are two levels of wine. 10X is a blend of the three vineyards; each single vineyard wine (only around 200 cases) comes from a barrel selection from that vineyard. There are plans to introduce an intermediate level as an estate selection. There's a light hand here and the wines are the antithesis of the New World stereotype; although the alcohol is higher than you would find in Europe, the general flavor spectrum resembles the Côte de Beaune.

Mornington Peninsula, 2009
This is a blend of the three vineyards at Ten Minutes by Tractor, or 10X as it is known locally. Very faint nose with some red fruit aromatics and a hint of savory development. The red fruit palate is supported by faintly piquant acidity and light but firm tannins. Nice smooth finish. ** Drink now-2017.

Mornington Peninsula, Wallis Vineyard, 2008
This is one of the three home vineyards, the lowest in elevation and about as far south as wine is made on the Peninsula, in a cool, late-picking site. The medium ruby color is lighter than 2007. Muted nose with faintly savory hints and an impression of nutty red strawberry fruits. Sweet red fruits on palate are a touch nutty and earthy, supported by smooth, soft tannins. This is at its peak for fruit expression, and should become quite savory in the next year or so. As always, it is the leanest of the three single vineyard wines. *** Drink now-2017.

Mornington Peninsula, McCutcheon Vineyard, 2008
Quite a fresh impression on a red fruit nose. Compared to Wallis there is a bit more obvious structure and intensity on the palate, with an impression of some tight supporting tannins on the finish. Not quite as much presence on the mid palate as Judd in this vintage. ** Drink now-2018.

Mornington Peninsula, Judd Vineyard, 2008
A faint impression of ripe red strawberries on the nose. This is the richest and best structured of the single vineyard wines with some earthy strawberry fruits on the palate, and a note of medicinal tannins that is almost hidden by the sweet fruits, which come back with a kick of ripeness on the finish. *** Drink now-2019.

Mornington, Wallis Vineyard, 2007
Restrained nose offers herbal and savory impressions of red fruits. Fine and elegant on the palate, with a linearity to the fruits. Some tight but light tannins show on the finish. This is the lightest, and least intense, of the three single vineyard bottlings. ** Drink now-2018.

Mornington Peninsula, McCutcheon Vineyard, 2007
This east-facing vineyard is just across the road from the winery. There's a sharper touch to the nose, which is a fraction medicinal. The palate shows a more obvious sense of structure than Wallis, with light red fruits, again a touch medicinal on the finish, which is smooth and elegant. *** Drink now-2018.

Mornington Peninsula, Judd Vineyard, 2007
This vineyard is more to the west, on the valley floor. A slightly nuttier touch on the nose with a faint hint of the medicinal notes of McCutcheon. The palate offers sweet ripe fruits with a fraction more of a medicinal impression than the nose. Red fruits are poised between cherries and strawberries with just a note of tannic dryness on the finish. This need a little more time than Wallis or McCutcheon. *** Drink 2012-2019.

Mornington Peninsula, McCutcheon Vineyard, 2006
This actually looks younger than the 2007. There's a faintly stern note to the nose. Sweet ripe fruits mark the entry to the palate, with just a hint of strawberry jam; then some light tannins show structural support, but the general impression is from the sweet ripe fruits. Overall, the fine, elegant style carries the ripeness well. *** Drink now-2018.

Yabby Lake Vineyard

Yabby Lake started when the Kirby family planted a vineyard at Red Hill in 1992; then in 1998 the Yabby Lake Vineyard was planted at Moorooduc, which is where the Pinot Noir is grown. They also have vineyards at Heathcote and Strathbogie Ranges farther north in Victoria. The 40 ha vineyard at Yabby Lake is the largest single vineyard on one site in Mornington Peninsula. Just over half of the plantings are Pinot Noir. The entry level wine under the Red Claw name is declassified from the Yabby Lake estate wine. Yabby Lake started producing single block wines in 2008, moving to more reliance on picking on flavor, with less emphasis on sugar and more on acid; the current aim is to pick with natural acidity of at least 7 g/l. The impact of new oak has been reduced, down to 25%. There has also been a move to 500 liter barrels. There are usually about 3,000 cases of the estate wine and 150-200 cases of each individual block. Wines were tasted at Yabby Lake in March 2011.

Mornington Peninsula, Single Vineyard, 2009
(About to be released.) This is the single vineyard wine, as opposed to a wine produced from one of the blocks within the vineyard. Restrained nose with some faint black fruit aromatics and a touch of nuts. Soft gentle black fruits on the palate, with light furry tannins showing on the finish. Immediately drinkable but just enough undertone of structure to support some aging. ** Drink now-2017.

Mornington Peninsula, Block 2, 2009
(Not released yet.) A stern black fruit nose with spice and chocolate overtones. The rich black fruits make a fleshy impression on the palate, with a glycerinic impression followed by choco-late overtones. Tannins are fine but subsumed by the fruits. The wine is just a fraction closed at the moment, and needs some time to open up. *** Drink 2013-2019.

Mornington Peninsula, 2008
Yabby Lake is one of the more northern points and is a warmer site. Because they are an early picker, in the 2008 vintage they picked before the heat spike and so made a more elegant wine. Restrained red fruit nose. Sweet ripe red and black cherry fruits, but flattening out just a touch on the mid palate. ** Drink now-2017.

Mornington Peninsula, Block 2, Yabby Lake, 2008
Medium intensity black fruit nose has spicy overtones. Chocolaty black fruit palate, more black plums and blackcurrants than cherries. Some depth to the fruit here although a touch of heat is evident on the finish, which shows furry tannins. This is already approachable, but as the slight bitterness of the tannins softens, the full fruit complexity will come through. This gives a livelier impression on the palate than the 2009, and is the most elegant of Yabby Lake's Pinots at this stage. ***(*) Drink 2012-2021.

Mornington Peninsula, Block 5, Yabby Lake, 2008
This is the vineyard block immediately in front of the winery, where the soil tends to hold water, and the grapes always ripen a week after the rest of the vineyard. There's more intensity and spice on the nose than Block 2, with notes of chocolate and coffee intensifying in the glass. Dark black fruits show on the palate, with tannic structure more evident than Block 2, still needing a couple of years to lose that youthful bitterness. This is the most tightly structured of the Yabby Lake Pinots. **** Drink 2014-2022.

Mornington Peninsula, 2007
Lean nose with mineral impression. Some faint liquorice. Angular impression on palate, tight acidity, red cherries and strawberry fruits. A slight mineral rasp to the finish. ** Drink now-2019.

Tastings from Tasmania

Wines were tasted in New York in April 2011.

Josef Chromy, 2009
Located at the southern tip of Tamar Ridge in the north of Tasmania, this is a relatively new winery established by Josef Chromy, who was previously involved in several other wineries in Tasmania. There's a restrained, faintly nutty impression to the red fruit nose. The palate already shows a lovely balance in a lighter style, with a touch of savory notes showing on red fruits that give an impression of already starting to develop. The counterpoise of nutty and savory ele-ments with ripe red fruits makes this genuinely ready to drink on release, but there is unlikely to be significant longevity. ** Drink now-2014.

Dalrymple Vineyard, 2008
This wine comes from the Pipers River area in the north, just to the east of Tamar Ridge. The nose offers a strong impression of black tea (not at all the typical New World impression). At first you scarcely notice the alcohol on the palate, although its intensity becomes more notice-able in the glass. Crisp acidity supports quite lean fruits, which emerge slowly in the glass as

red cherries, somewhat in the manner of Beaune, but a Beaune with this linearity would have much lower alcohol. There seems to be a slight discordancy between the level of alcohol and the fruit. The austerity is all Old World but the brightness of the fruits is New World. * Drink 2012-2016.

South, 2008
Pirie's entry level wine shows a very restrained nose. Soft red fruit palate, with a delicious savory/buttery note on the finish. Perhaps a bit lacking in presence on the mid palate, and not a lot of stuffing, but a nice drink for immediate consumption. * Drink now.

42S, 2008
This is the entry level wine from Frogmore Creek. Restrained nose. Soft palate with mix of indeterminate red and black fruits, very soft on the finish without much stuffing, but very creditable for current drinking. * Drink now.

Frogmore Creek, 2007
This wine comes from the Coal River area in the south, just a little north of Hobart. There's a nutty red fruit impression on the nose, with just a faint savory touch. Nice balance on the palate, savory notes just coming through to mingle with the ripe red fruits, supported by balanced acidity and soft tannins. ** Drink now-2014.

Pipers Brook Vineyard, 2007
Established by Andrew Pirie in 1974 in the Tamar Ridge area, Pipers Brook was a pioneering winery that remains at the forefront of wine production in Tasmania. The wines tend to be a touch more acidic and savory than most. Typical savory aromas on the nose overlay the developing red fruits. The bright acidity carries the developing fruits forward with nutty strawberries showing earthy overtones. The light fruit density lets a touch of bitterness and herbaceousness come through to the finish. ** Drink now-2013.

Moorilla, 2006
This wine comes from the south end of Derwent Valley, just to the north of Hobart at the south end of the island. There's a slight savory edge to the red fruit nose. Soft red fruits on the palate are supported by balanced acidity with just a touch of savory flavors developing. There's a slight mineral touch to the finish. ** Drink now-2014.

Pirie, 2006
This wine comes from the Relbia vineyard, in the upper Tamar Ridge, from the new winery that Andrew Pirie established after he sold Pipers Brook. The dark fruit nose gives an impression of black cherries. Soft black fruits show on the medium weight palate with a nutty/savory edge. Soft tannins provide current structural support but are not likely to develop much further. The wine has reached its natural lifespan, with the mid palate becoming just a little flat. * Drink now.

Spring Vale, 2005
This comes from the East Coast. Development shows in the garnet hues of the medium to deep color. You can see the slightly warmer character of the area in the wine, showing as soft, dark cherry fruits with lower acidity, following naturally from the dark fruit nose. The wine is now declining gently in the typical fashion of warm vintage Pinot. * Drink now.

Pipers Brook Vineyard, 2005
Slightly herbal and savory nose shows the aromatics of development. Nice balance on the palate with light fruits showing a savory edge to the earthy strawberries. Lightening up a bit, but there's a delicious savory/acid/fruit balance. The wine is right at its peak now, with bright acidity carrying the savory fruits through the finish. *** Drink now-2013.

Producers and Tastings from South Africa

Bouchard Finlayson

Peter Finlayson was the first winemaker at Hamilton Russell, and then left in 1991 to found Bouchard Finlayson at an adjacent property. (Burgundy negociant Paul Bouchard was involved for the first ten years.) This is a boutique winery, with 19 hectares of vineyards devoted mostly to Pinot Noir, Chardonnay, and Sauvignon Blanc (out of a total property of 125 hectares). More than half is Pinot Noir. There are also some of the varieties from northern Italy (Sangiovese, Nebbiolo, and Barbera.) Before the vineyards came fully on line, grapes were sourced from nearby Elgin, but since 1995 the flagship wine has been described as Galpin Peak Pinot Noir, named for the estate vineyard on the slopes of Mount Galpin that is now the sole source for the grapes. In addition, there is a barrel selection called Tête de Cuvée. The oak regime is about 30% new oak for Galpin Peak and about 80% for the Tête de Cuvée. Wines were tasted in London in May 2011.

Walker Bay, Galpin Peak, 2009
A deep fruity nose shows black fruits of plums and blackcurrants with some spirity overtones. Lots of fruit shows on the palate, with a fairly direct flavor spectrum of red and black cherries; some light but tight tannins are a little on the rustic side. There's a touch of heat on the finish. Another year is needed for the profile to soften and the wine should then offer a fairly sturdy impression of Pinot Noir with medium term aging potential. ** Drink 2012-2017.

Walker Bay, Galpin Peak, Tête de Cuvée, 2009
Spicy black fruit nose of plums and cherries is quite intense, and significantly more complex than the Galpin Peak estate wine. Black fruits on the palate are more intense than the estate wine, and are accompanied by spice notes carrying over from the nose. Bringing a fine sense of structure to the finish, the tannins are more refined than the estate wine. Fruit intensity makes this possible to drink already, but the wine will really show the elegance of its fruits in another couple of years, and then should mature well for a few years. *** Drink 2012-2019.

Walker Bay, Galpin Peak, 2008
Some savory, almost gamey notes hide the red fruits of the nose; the aromas here seem to be much more than a year more developed than the 2009 vintage. The palate is not quite as developed as the nose, with red fruits showing hints of strawberries and nutty, cereal-like overtones. Tannins give a light impression of structure. The wine is ready to drink, but will develop further for the short term. ** Drink now-2015.

Walker Bay, Cape Winemakers Guild, Bouchard Finlayson, 2007
A red fruit nose has some herbal overtones and a suggestion of black tea. The palate shows light red cherry fruits, with some light tannic support, but not a lot of stuffing. This is a well made wine for current consumption, without pretensions to ageworthiness. * Drink now-2014.

Walker Bay, Galpin Peak, 2007
The nose has lost its primary fruits but has not yet quite turned savory; there are some intimations of herbal aromas, and a faint touch of chocolate develops in the glass. Black cherry fruits on the palate are nicely balanced by refined tannins, with a hint of bitter chocolate, and still with a faint touch of bitterness on the finish. The overall impression remains rather sturdy for Pinot Noir. ** Drink now-2017.

Walker Bay, Galpin Peak, Tête de Cuvée, 2007
Quite complex nose is developing slowly. Initially it shows cereal, almost mentholated or medicinal notes, and herbal tea-like aromas; then in the glass these become spicy and savory with suggestions of tarragon and thyme. As usual, the palate shows more intensity and depth than the estate bottling, very much in the black fruit spectrum, savory and dry, with a very nice herbal counterpoise to the fruits. The overall impression is quite refined, almost chocolaty on the aftertaste; certainly the wine is now ready to drink, but it should continue to develop for several years. *** Drink now-2020.

Hamilton Russell

When Tim Hamilton Russell set out to make cool climate varieties in South Africa, he purchased 70 hectares of virgin land in the Hemel-en-Aarde Valley. When the vineyards were planted in 1975, they were the first to be established in the valley, and Hamilton Russell remained the only producer for more than a decade. Several cool climate varieties were grown (eleven at the peak), although it was clear from the outset that Pinot Noir was the star. When Anthony Hamilton Russell took over in 1991, he focused the estate exclusively on Pinot Noir and Chardonnay. Today there are 22 ha of Pinot Noir and 28 ha of Chardonnay, and wines are made only from grapes grown on the estate. Plantings of Pinot Noir come from four Dijon clones (113, 115, 667, 777) spread over eight separate sites. The wine is matured for up to a year in equal proportions of new, one-year, and two-year oak. The estate wine was labeled Walker Bay until 2006, and then Hemel-en-Aarde Valley after the new appellation was approved. The wines in this vertical all seemed tough on opening, but softened and improved after a few hours, perhaps an indication of future development. They were tasted in New York in May 2011.

Hemel-en-Aarde Valley, Pinot Noir, 2009
Strawberry and raspberry fruits on the nose have faintly acrid overtones giving an impression of gun metal. Medium density fruits with a savory edge show on the palate, with crisp acidity; light but tight tannins with a bitter edge are cut by a faint buttery impression. The overall impression is very tight and a little tart, with fruits that aren't yet releasing their flavors. But this should soften in another year or so. * Drink 2014-2019.

Hemel-en-Aarde Valley, Pinot Noir, 2008
A softer impression than 2009, with the strawberry and raspberry fruits accompanied by some overtones of chocolate-coated cherries. A rounder impression follows on the palate, with fruits tending to earthy strawberries, a glyceriny almost buttery edge on the finish, and firm ripe tannins in the background. Just allow another year for the wine to soften and this should be pleasantly rounded in a slightly rustic style. ** Drink 2013-2018.

Hemel-en-Aarde Valley, Pinot Noir, 2007
A slightly tart cherry and strawberry fruit impression on the nose but faintly acrid. Tart on the palate, with the medium density red fruits falling behind the acidity. There's a generally lean impression, with a faint acrid touch on the finish emphasizing its angularity. * Drink 2012–2016.

Walker Bay, Pinot Noir, 2006
Red cherry fruits with some hints of black fruits and a very faint touch of chocolate and coffee on the nose. Slightly stem but more impression of complexity than the younger vintages. Better rounded fruits on the palate than the younger vintages, supported by firm but ripe tannins, although there is still a bitter edge on the finish. Not much development showing here with age. ** Drink now–2016.

Walker Bay, Pinot Noir, 2005
Restrained but slightly acrid red cherry fruit nose. Fruits are quite nicely rounded, with a touch of sweetness on the finish perhaps aided by a higher alcohol level (14% in this vintage), the firm tannins now softening just enough to let the fruit concentration show through, although the flavor spectrum remains somewhat direct. This vintage has the first barely perceptible beginnings of development. ** Drink now–2017.

Producer and Tasting in Patagonia

Bodega Chacra

Chacra produces four wines, the first two named simply for the age of the vineyards. The flagship wine, Treinta Y Dos, comes exclusively from a 2.2 ha plot planted in 1932, and has been made since 2004. Cincuenta Y Cinco comes from a 5 ha vineyard planted in 1955, and has been made since 2005. The entry level wine, Barda, comes from a vineyard planted twenty years ago (and in much larger amounts than either of the first two). In addition to these Pinot Noirs, there are some old Merlot vines in the property, and from 2008 they were used to produce a wine called Mainqué instead of being sold off. There will also soon be a new Pinot Noir from a vineyard planted with a selection massale from the old vines. The vineyards are managed biodynamically, and the wine is made with minimal interference and adjustment (some acidification is necessary in some years). There was complete destemming until 2010, when some stems were retained for the first time. The lead wines are matured in new oak, but Barda sees no new oak at all. Wines were tasted at a vertical of all vintages of the Treinta Y Dos with Piero Incisa in New York in December 2010.

Barda, 2009
Restrained red fruit nose. Light and appealing on the palate, with red cherry and strawberry fruits, showing a faint minerality. No new oak is used here, so the fruits show through directly. Lighter than the Treinta Y Dos, somewhat like the difference between a wine from the Côtes and wine from a village on the Côte d'Or. * Drink now-2016.

Treinta Y Dos, 2009
Restrained nose is not very revealing. Harmonious and supple fruits on the palate show as mineral strawberries. Fine-grained tannins with some tea-like impressions show on the finish. The balance of this wine makes you feel that with this vintage the winery has really got into its stride and achieved the finesse it is striving for. Overall there is a refined impression of silky opulence. *** Drink 2012-2022.

Treinta Y Dos, 2008
Restrained nose shows some faint suggestions of cereal, developing some austere medicinal notes in the glass. Crisp acidity on the palate accompanies fruits that are more red than black, a little austere. There's less fruit density than other vintages, and acidity is still a bit noticeable on the finish. * Drink 2011-2017.

Barda, 2007
Fugitive buttery whiff on the nose, then more tarry and mineral. Mineral red fruits on the palate, a touch of butter, a hint of earthy strawberries, average length finish, with just a touch of dilution. More European than New World in style. (September 2009). Drink now-2012.

Treinta Y Dos, 2007
The cool vintage is reflected in the moderate alcohol of 12.5%, compared with the 13.5% of the previous, warmer year, giving the wine a lighter, more delicate impression. You can see the cool conditions in the tightness of the fruits, which are quite lean on the palate, and show some medicinal notes on the finish. As the tight tannins resolve, the fruits may reveal their delicacy, indeed the wine opens out slowly with time in the glass to reveal a mineral counterpoise to the fruits. In Burgundian terms this is more Côte de Beaune, whereas other vintages seem more under the influence of the Côte de Nuits. ** Drink 2011-2018.

Treinta Y Dos, 2006
Faintly earthy nose shows mineral black fruits. Earthy minerality follows on the palate, where smooth fruits, more rounded than either 2005 or 2007, have a touch of glycerinic opulence. Taut, fine tannins bring a chocolate coating to the finish, with earthy notes persisting. The initial impression of silky minerality softens in the glass to become earthy and nutty. A fine result reflecting a warm vintage, and an interesting contrast with the more delicate style of the much cooler 2007 vintage. *** Drink now-2020.

Treinta Y Dos, 2005
Tea leaves on the nose, more savory, less overtly fruity than the 2004. Softer on the palate than 2004, with a mélange of red and black fruits. Good supporting acidity for fresh red cherries and strawberries, turning earthy in the glass. Quite stern tannins with those tea-like notes coming back on the finish. ** Drink now-2020.

Treinta Y Dos, 2004
Deep color. Black fruit nose with slightly aromatic cherries. Good supporting acidity on the palate, stern fruits, youthful and vibrant, firm tannins mark the finish, still in front of the fruits. The style here is fuller and richer, just short of over-ripe, with lots of weight, more upfront fruit than later vintages, which turn to a more restrained style. In Burgundian terms, more Côte de Nuits than Côte de Beaune. *** Drink now-2022.

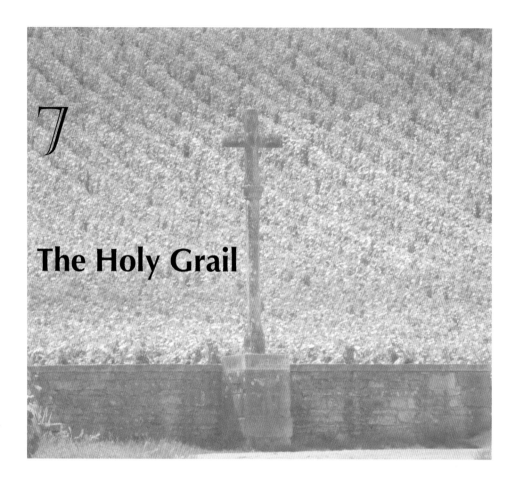

The Holy Grail

THIS IS WHERE I STICK MY HEAD IN THE LION'S DEN. What makes great Pinot Noir? A complex array of aromas and layers of flavors should be difficult to disentangle, the underlying texture should be silky, and as it ages the spectrum of red fruits should become more savory, sometimes finally showing a delicious undertone of sous bois (those savory impressions of the undergrowth.) It goes almost without saying that ability to age, in the form of the development of increasing complexity and variety of aromas and flavors, is a hallmark. Well, yes, but this would serve as a reasonable description for the aging of any great wine. What is distinctive about *Pinot Noir*?

The immediate impression that comes to mind when Pinot Noir is compared with other red wines is its sheer sensuality. The sterner qualities of Cabernet Sauvignon made traditional Bordeaux a more cerebral wine. The transition to a riper style in recent decades may have reduced its austerity, but still Bordeaux, or other wine based on Cabernet Sauvignon, offers power and structure rather than silky elegance. The third of the great black grapes, Syrah, at its best offers a wonderful generosity, but it is forceful rather than subtle. Pinot Noir does not need to be powerful to make its point.

Is Pinot Noir's secret its delicacy? This is not an attribute you would ascribe to many red wines: Nebbiolo as grown in Barolo is the other case that might come to mind. The question of delicacy compared to other varieties brings me to what I think of as a great divide among young Pinot Noirs. In one corner we have European restraint, as typified by traditional Burgundy: wines are rarely intensely colored, alcohol is moderate (albeit less so these days), acidity is often noticeable, and delicate flavors vary from earthy fruits, more often red than black, to savory as the wines age. In the other corner is New World exuberance: wines are more darkly colored, alcohol levels are higher, acidity and tannins are less evident, and the flavor spectrum tends to be overtly fruit-driven: I would not usually call these wines delicate.

And here there is a difference with other varieties. Yes, to some extent this description of the European-New World divide would also fit the difference between Sauvignon Blanc from Sancerre versus the same variety from Marlborough, New Zealand. Or it might describe the difference between Riesling from Germany as opposed to Eden or Clare valleys in Australia. But it would be more difficult to apply to Pinot Noir's rival for the crown among black grapes. There is more similarity of style between Cabernet Sauvignon from the left bank of Bordeaux (even when blended with Merlot) and Cabernet Sauvignon from Napa Valley. But here is the rub. Thirty years ago it was not difficult to tell the difference between Bordeaux with its slightly herbaceous flavors and Napa Valley with its overtly black-fruit spectrum. But as the result of increased ripeness, Bordeaux today has largely lost that traditional herbaceous quality and shows more forward fruits converging on the style of Napa. In fact, you might define two styles of Cabernet, essentially less-ripe and more-ripe, and as winemakers in Bordeaux have increasingly moved towards a riper style, there is more of a universal agreement as to what constitutes Cabernet Sauvignon (the more ripe).

Has there been any comparable shift in the perception of what reflects perfection in Pinot Noir? One difference between Pinot Noir and Cabernet is that there isn't the same dramatic flavor shift with ripeness. As Pinot Noir becomes riper, acidity declines a bit, the wine becomes more alcoholic of course, and the fruits become more evident—but although the flavor spectrum becomes more pronounced, it doesn't really show a comparable shift from herbaceous to fruity. There's more a shift in the intensity of fruits than in their character. Once the grapes become over-ripe, of course, the fruit becomes over-cooked or jammy, as was evident in many wines from the unusually hot 2003 vintage in Burgundy.

The difference between Pinot Noir from the two extremes—let's take these as Beaune on the one hand and Russian River on the other—is in some ways comparable to the difference between left Bank Bordeaux and Napa Valley in the 1970s. But there's a difference in perspective, which is that in the seventies, winemakers in Napa were trying to emulate Bordeaux, a situation that has since reversed as winemakers everywhere have embraced the richer "international style" beloved of some powerful critics. Today, with the increased confidence of the New World, winemakers are doing their own thing, producing a distinctive style of Pinot Noir. This is a real change, since for several centuries Burgundy was regarded as the definitive style for Pinot Noir, a Holy Grail that winemakers everywhere tried, almost entirely without success, to emulate.

Is it all about ripeness? Ripeness in Pinot Noir, to my mind, takes the form of increasing intensity and concentration, up to a point where delicacy is lost. Let me draw a line here. I do not believe that Pinot Noir is a variety that tolerates too much extraction, and especially not too much alcohol. I become concerned about preservation of varietal typicity once alcohol goes into the high thirteen percents, and I'm reluctant to give much leeway to wines over 14% (admittedly with some notable exceptions, and it's true I've been forced to move my limit up). My main reservation is not so much the issue of whether I can detect typicity in Pinot Noir at very high alcohol levels, or even whether I enjoy drinking the wines with dinner (no, I don't), but with whether they will fulfill an essential criterion for great wine: will they age? I believe that, like the Cheshire cat, ultimately nothing will be left but the grin of the alcohol.

This is not to question the legitimacy, as it were, of other styles of Pinot Noir. The fact that Burgundy got there first does not mean we should ignore alternative expressions of Pinot Noir from other locations that might be equally interesting. In fact, we might ask the question: what would have happened if winemaking had started in the New World? Would we regard forward, fruity wines as the definitive style? Would we regard Burgundy as too thin, too acid, and too subject to excessive vintage variation, to make the grade at the very top levels? Abandoning the prejudices of history, we should ask whether Pinot Noirs in these different styles are good, well made wines, whether they are interesting young, and whether they become more interesting with age. Of course, there remains the question of whether the world is ready yet to accept alternative expressions of Pinot Noir, or whether it is still fixated on the Holy Grail. (Not to mention the issue that Burgundy is not static; although the changes towards the international style are less dramatic than in Bordeaux, still there is no doubt that the target has shifted.)

Yet it is difficult to discard the background of cultural inheritance. So I am going to stick to my position that great wine shows interesting variety of aromas and flavors, and that an essential criterion for greatness is that those aromas and flavors change and become more subtle and complex as the wine ages. Subject only to these prejudices and constraints, let's ask how Pinot Noir from different locations fits the bill, and whether the differences of style owe more to terroir and climate or to winemaking decisions. No doubt Burgundy is going to feature at the top of the list of definitive Pinot Noirs (although even here we can ask the eternal question about terroir versus winemaking), but perhaps we will also find vineyards from elsewhere that have found the Holy Grail; and we can ask if there are alternative styles that can be recognized as great expressions of the variety.

Considering the criterion that great wine should age in an interesting way, I'm inclined to the view that the slower the aging process, the better, but I'll accept that a wine from one region that reaches its peak after twenty years is not necessarily better than a wine from another region that peaks at ten years; the issue is how interesting and complex the wine becomes at its peak. Josh Jensen of Calera Wine insists that you can only make ageworthy Pinot Noir on limestone.[1] He supports his case by referring to a book on winemaking in Burgundy, which states forthrightly: "It is known that Pinot demands soils that are more or less calcareous...On granitic soil Pinot gives a common wine without character."[2] When I put this case to Véronique Drouhin, she said with surprise, "Well in that case I shouldn't be making wine in Oregon."[3] She thinks the secret is good acidity. Actually, I think it may be not simply the actual acidity in the wine as such, because all over the New World it's common to add acidity to compensate for an insufficiency at harvest, but some other feature that correlates with natural acidity in the berries at harvest. Of course, you can have too much of a good thing: the 1996 vintage in Burgundy was regarded as giving vin de gardes with good supporting acidity; and fifteen years later it is unclear whether they will ever come round from that punishing, almost medicinal, acidic edge.

Pinot Noir differs from other grape varieties in acknowledging the supremacy of a single appellation and producer. For Cabernet Sauvignon, the other challenger for the title of the world's most important black grape, there are multiple leaders. The traditional source, Bordeaux, splits its leadership among the five First Growths of the left bank. Certainly these have reached unprecedented prices in recent vintages, selling at almost $1000 a bottle en primeur for the 2009 vintage (two years before the wine will even be bottled).[4] And the auction prices for bottles from past great vintages can run into thousands.[5] But they are challenged by cult Cabernet wines from around the world. Napa Valley's Screaming Eagle can sell for hundreds of dollars on current release, and can command thousands for old bottles at auction.[6] If we turn to Syrah, the most expensive wine may well be Penfold's Grange from South Australia, with the first vintages selling for several thousands of dollars.[7] But Guigal's single vineyard Côte Rôtie's or top Hermitage are rivals. Romanée Conti can look them all square in the face, with a price of over $50,000 for a bottle of the great 1945 vintage (the last produced from the ungrafted, pre-phylloxera vines, when yields were so small there were only a couple of barrels).[8] No New World Pinot Noir comes even remotely close.[9] Is this because cult wines of Cabernet or Syrah are so often based on super-extraction, at which the New World can out-compete Bordeaux, but which simply does not play well with the more delicate Pinot Noir?

At all events, Burgundy has the pinnacle all to itself for Pinot Noir. Of course, there is only one Romanée Conti, coming from the 1.8 hectare vineyard in Vosne Romanée that is a monopole of Domaine de la Romanée Conti. Adjacent to Romanée Conti, DRC's other monopole, La Tâche, is second in reputation. During the twentieth century, Romanée Conti and La Tâche pulled well away from Le Chambertin, to which they had previously been closer in price, and for around a hundred years they have been universally acknowledged as Burgundy's best wines. As the sole owner of these monopoles, Domaine de la Romanée Conti was unrivalled as the top producer. In the past two decades, however, DRC has been challenged for leadership by newcomer Domaine Leroy. Of course, *only* DRC produces Romanée Conti and La Tâche, but Leroy produces two other top grand crus of Vosne Romanée, Richebourg and Romanée St. Vivant, as well as Le Chambertin; these can be the most expensive new releases in each Burgundy vintage.

Romanée Conti takes its name from the purchase of La Romanée by the Prince de Conti in 1760. The La Romanée vineyard had previously been owned by the monastery of St. Vivant and was part of the vineyard of Clos de St. Vivant, which dated from 1232. Together with La Tâche, the vineyard was purchased by the de Croonembourg family, who appear to have introduced the name La Romanée. The first reference to Romanée Conti dates from 1794, when the vineyard was sold at auction after it had been seized from the Prince de Conti following the French Revolution.[10] By 1819 it was in the hands of Julien Ouvrard, who had purchased Clos Vougeot the previous year, and also owned some Chambertin. Under Ouvrard's proprietorship, Romanée Conti sold at a marginally higher price than Chambertin or Clos Vougeot.[11]

The modern history of ownership started when Romanée Conti was acquired in 1869 by Jacques-Marie Duvault-Blochet, the largest proprietor on the Côte d'Or. Complicated patterns of inheritance led to the vineyards being partially broken up, but coming into the hands of the de Villaine family in 1912, when the name Domaine de la Romanée Conti was introduced. Under the leadership of Gaudin de Villaine, La Tâche was acquired in 1933. This

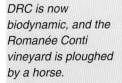

DRC is now biodynamic, and the Romanée Conti vineyard is ploughed by a horse.

was a difficult economic period in Burgundy, and in 1942, Henri Leroy, a negociant from Auxey-Duresses, acquired a half stake in the domain.

Excluding Romanée Conti and La Tâche, the rest of the original Clos de St. Vincent had become the Domaine Marey-Monge. This was leased to DRC in 1966, and then purchased in 1988. DRC's holdings of Romanée Conti, La Tâche, Richebourg, Romanée St Vivant, Grands Echézeaux and Echézeaux today therefore include most of the original Clos.[12] The DRC produces wine *only* from grand crus; in addition to its holdings in Vosne Romanée, the 26 ha of vineyards include a small parcel of Le Montrachet.

If I had to choose a single word to describe winemaking at DRC, it would be subtlety. Everything is designed to produce wines with elegance and finesse. These are never heavily extracted wines, they do not impress with the density of extract, but rather with the silky expression of subtle flavors. Use of new oak has increased steadily since 1945, when the level was quite low, probably around 20%. Experiments showed that quality improved as the proportion of new oak increased, and today it is close to 100%. But it's handled very carefully so as not to overwhelm the wine. "For a few years we have often used barrels (of one year old oak) to rack the new wines after completion of the malolactic, especially in vintages that produced wines with more elegance than power in order to avoid all risk of too much oak," says Aubert de Villaine.[13] The Domaine is well known for its belief in the value of appropriate use of chaptalization, which does not happen in the hot years, and is usually less than 0.5%. "We believe in chaptalization for Burgundy wines, but only on the condition that it is very slight and only to give to the wines the bones that they eventually lack and that will allow them to reach balance and maturity in the bottle... When we chaptalize, we do it at the end of the fermentation, little by little, in order to have a longer fermentation on the skins," says Aubert de Villaine.[14] Stressing the yeast at the end of fermentation adds to the voluptuous mouthfeel. The difference between the very top wines, Romanée Conti and La Tâche, and the next two, Richebourg and Romanée St. Vivant, is less a matter of power and concentration than of subtlety and texture.

After leadership of the Domaine passed to the current generation of each family, represented by Aubert de Villaine and Lalou Bize-Leroy, there was a famous falling out in 1992, and Lalou Bize-Leroy left the domain (although remaining a quarter owner). She had previously purchased the moribund 12 ha estate of Domaine Noëllat in 1988; after renaming it Domaine Leroy, she added other domains and vineyards. Domaine Leroy presently has 22 hectares, including a wide selection of grand and premier crus. (In fact, all of the top grand crus except the monopoles of DRC are represented: Richebourg, Romanée St. Vivant, Chambertin, and Musigny.) Premier crus extend along the Côte d'Or and there are also some village wines. Most of the individual holdings are less than a hectare, comprising 26 different appellations altogether. (In addition, Mme. Bize-Leroy also owns Henri Leroy's original negociant business, Maison Leroy.) Separate from Domaine and Maison Leroy is the much smaller Domaine d'Auvenay, based in Auxey-Duresses, owned by Mme. Bize-Leroy alone, and with more of a focus on white wine.

Domaine Leroy is famous for its punishingly low yields and high prices. Part of the reason is the high concentration of old vines: vineyards are never replanted, but vines are replaced individually as necessary. Most of the vines are around sixty years old. When they need to be replaced, selection massale is used; there are no clones. Training and pruning contribute further to keeping yields low, typically under 16 hl/ha. (In 2010 yields were at a record low, approaching 10 hl/ha.) The domain has been completely biodynamic since 1989 (no mean feat to organize for so many small parcels). There is a fanatical emphasis on quality. Its relative prices are the highest in all Burgundy: its village wines sell at the prices of other growers' premier crus, its premier crus are above most producers' grand crus, and its grand crus set records. Nothing can rival Romanée Conti itself, but older grand crus from Leroy can reach thousands of dollars at auction.[15] DRC and Leroy's prices for current releases place them as a pair of producers simply above all others. For the two grand crus that are produced by both DRC and Leroy, Richebourg and Romanée St. Vivant, the Leroy wines sell at prices even above those of DRC.

Domaine Leroy (left) now challenges Domaine de la Romanée Conti (facing right) for leadership in Burgundy. The unassuming wineries both have their headquarters in the village of Vosne Romanée.

DRC and Leroy share a traditional view of vinification, starting with no destemming, and ending with a long cuvaison.[16] "Jamais, jamais, jamais!" was the response, when I asked Lalou Bize-Leroy if she ever destemmed.[17] She believes destemming damages the grapes and introduces oxidation; and she wants to preserve all the yeasts that may be on the vines in the vineyard. Lalou has a strong belief that wine is made in the vineyard, with the combination of pruning and biodynamic practices giving low yields of exceptionally high quality berries. "We don't 'do' vinification," would perhaps be a simplification, but "we do not have a 'winemaker' in the house," she says firmly. All wines go into new oak. Leroy's wines have the character to stand up to, and indeed, require, new oak, in which they usually mature for 13-14 months.

Direct comparisons are difficult, since Leroy and DRC's ranges of wines overlap only in Richebourg and Romanée St. Vivant. One difference is that while all DRC's holdings are in grand crus, Leroy produces a complete range down to Bourgogne. Indeed, the truly remarkable quality of Leroy's wines may be most evident at the village level, where there is really nothing else comparable: the intensity and purity are overwhelming.

So does style trump terroir for Leroy? Well, yes and no. Leroy's wines are fine, elegant, and concentrated. The style runs through the whole range. Her village Nuits St. Georges, for example, shows a refinement and precise delineation of fruit flavors that is far from the stereotype of the appellation, which usually has much broader flavors. But when you move to her Vosne Romanée, there is the same increase in power that you expect to see when comparing Vosne with Nuits St. Georges. It's somewhat as if the whole spectrum has been shifted towards a more refined level, but you still see the

same relative gradations between terroirs. At every level, the wines show unusual concentration and purity, bringing the traditional definitions of terroir into a new focus.

There are few extraneous factors to influence the display of appellations in Leroy's wines because the vine populations are comparable, yields are similar, and there are no variations in winemaking. A tasting of barrel samples from the 2010 vintage at Domaine Leroy in May 2011 was a revelation about the potential of each appellation. As a range, the wines showed an intensity and concentration that would put most producers to shame, but each appellation showed a purity of expression through which their relative differences were magnified. We were a bit restricted by the fact that some wines had finished their malolactic fermentation and been racked the day before, so could not be tasted, but the Chambolle Musigny was precise and feminine; the Gevrey Chambertin was tighter and harder edged; the Latricières Chambertin added minerality and depth to the tight Gevrey fruits; the Vosne Romanée Genevrières and Brulées had that unmistakable silky combination of power and elegance, cut by a fine minerality; Corton Rénardes was rich, full, and generous; and the Chambertin showed a savory mineral nose leading into intensely structured rich black fruits—"you are virtually eating the grapes," Lalou exclaimed.

Is Leroy the *garagiste* of Burgundy? Once again, yes and no. The garagistes of Bordeaux, especially of the right bank, came to fame for micro production in limited conditions, sometimes literally in garages (from which their name was taken). Their hallmark was the production of intense wines from undistinguished terroirs, by applying forceful methods of viticulture and vinification, including restriction to extremely low yields and methods for high extraction.[18] They are quite controversial in their divergence from the traditional character of Bordeaux. It might be fair to say that Leroy shares with the garagistes the emphasis on very low yields, but without going into the excesses of over-extraction. Do the Leroy wines reflect a potential of the terroir that others have missed or they simply *hors de terroir*? As comparisons show the same *relative* differences between different appellations as those of other producers, but simply at a greater level of purity and intensity, I would argue that Leroy is demonstrating an unappreciated depth to the terroir. Although initially disdained, the methods of the garagistes have spread into mainstream Bordeaux and are partly responsible for a change in its character over recent years. May we hope that others in Burgundy will follow Leroy into achieving similar depth and focus in their wines?

Comparisons may be invidious, but in trying to define the typicity of Pinot Noir, and the influence of the winemaker on style and quality, where else to start but with the two grand crus shared by DRC and Leroy? Richebourg is universally acknowledged to be the best grand cru in Vosne Romanée aside from the monopoles. Often the most generous of all the Vosne Romanée grand crus, it is full, rich, and sumptuous. Romanée St. Vivant is the most delicate, with an exquisite subtlety of flavor, perfumed and silky, often compared with Le Musigny. A side by side tasting of the two grand crus from both producers highlights their differences in representing the two terroirs (Υ page 384).

In almost every pairwise comparison, Romanée St. Vivant takes the award for sheer silky elegance, while the Richebourg often has an extra dimension of concentration. The DRC wines are completely consistent: Romanée St. Vivant is always silky and elegant, Richebourg is always more masculine and intense. The Leroy wines show more variation, with Romanée St Vivant usually distinctly lighter than the Richebourg. Perhaps because Leroy's plots are only about a quarter of the size of DRC's plots, they may be more subject to the vagaries of climatic variation, so there is less ability to compensate for vintage variation.

My relative ratings between appellations and producers changed with the vintage. For the punishingly hot year of 2003, when many wines were so over-extracted that they might be confused with wines from farther south, the best wine for me came from the combination that usually produces the most elegant and polished wine: DRC's Romanée St. Vivant, given just a slight extra push of intensity by the vintage. In the cooler year of 1996, when although touted as vin de gardes, so many wines will never come around from the punishing acidity, my favorite wine was Leroy's Richebourg, where the extra intensity of the producer and appellation overcomes the problematic acidity. The comparison between 2003 and 1996 to my mind once again brings home the point that the relationships between appellations are not immutable, but are susceptible to revision in terms of changing climatic conditions.

DRC's wines are supremely elegant—rarely powerhouses, the hallmark is that silky refinement, intense but never massive. Leroy tends to show more overt concentration, with the structure more evident when young. The two producers' wines were always distinct, but I would not presume consistently to prefer one to the other. Indeed, preferences may change not only with appellation and vintage, but with time, as the wines pass through various stages of development as they mature. (Of course, these wines age so slowly that the fifteen year span of this tasting was far too short to assess them beyond the infant stage.) The quintessence of Pinot is captured in purity of fruits, those seamless layers of aromas and flavors, and increasing complexity as the wines age. As always, there is no single answer to what constitutes typicity, but each producer reflects terroir through the prism of its own style. Although each pushes the boundaries, beyond doubt, each expresses a variation on the Burgundian aesthetic. Other producers obtain fine results with individual grand or premier crus, but none offers a range that impresses like DRC's representation of the grand crus of Vosne Romanée, or that is simply *hors de classe* at each level like Leroy. This is the ultimate rather than the typical.

Intense though they are, none of the wines in the tasting pander to the consumer: at up to fifteen years of age, none was really quite ready to start drinking. All have sufficient tannic structure to reward patience for the consumer who really wants to see their full complexity. This is part of Burgundy's typicity. Without going so far as to argue that wines should not be agreeable when young if they are to age well, I believe it is fair to say that even in top vintages, such as 2009 or 2005 to take the most recent examples, at the level of premier or grand crus there is sufficient tannin when young to demand some delay: the 2009 vintage comes closest to the exception that proves the rule, with some barrel samples tasting quite delicious. Of course, it is a matter for personal preference when the wines reach their peak.

My impression when I started writing this book was that Burgundy, at least at the premier and grand cru level, would usually age well for two decades or more, whereas one would be lucky to get a decade out of New World Pinot Noir. Yet in tastings at producers over the past year, I encountered many fine examples of older wines from regions other than Burgundy, showing far greater longevity than I had expected. So I set out to discover how much truth there might be in my anecdotal impressions and expectations by directly comparing old Pinot Noirs from Burgundy with other regions.

Pinot Noir's pattern of aging can be more abrupt than some other varieties. A Bordeaux often passes its peak quite gradually, and may remain enjoyable while it declines gently for a decade or more. I still find many Bordeaux from 1970, 1966, or 1961 to be quite delicious, although they no longer have their former fruit intensity. Pinot Noir is less predictable: once it is in decline, it may make a transition from delicious to going over the hill within a few months. Burgundies from old vintages, for example, 1959 or 1969, can still be delicious: but the chance of finding one is much less than with Bordeaux of comparable age.

Pinot Noir shows its most delicious side when aging. As Pinot Noir becomes older, the fruity aroma and flavor spectrum turns savory. The turning point at which this happens is for me the perfect moment to catch Pinot Noir. The timescale on which it occurs is somewhat different for different regions. In Europe the extremes seem to be Burgundy, where aging is slowest, and Germany, where it usually happens within less than a decade. When the transition happens earlier in development, the fruity elements tend to be much more in evidence at the turning point than when it happens later, in which case savory elements seem more to replace the primary fruit. This gives the wine a difference balance at its peak moment.

The timing of the turning point is more difficult to assess for New World wines because of the transition from cork to screwcap that occurred at the start of the century. The big question in my mind is whether wines bottled under screwcap will simply follow the same pattern of development as wines under cork, but delayed by a year or so, or whether the pattern will actually be different. Under screwcap, fruits stay more intense and brighter for longer, and I wonder whether there will therefore be more fruit intensity when the savory elements develop, although this may be at a later time than it would have been under cork.

To compare aging from different regions, I organized a tasting. Burgundy 1995 was picked as the pivot point, and producers were asked to suggest their top wine that would show comparable aging and complexity from a similar vintage (similarity of vintage style and aging being more important than exactly matching the year). Most producers felt that a year close to 1995 gave the best match, but the range extended from 1990 to 2002. The idea was that a range of fifteen or twenty years of age would give wines from all regions a chance to show their optimum complexity. We calibrated the tasting by comparing these wines with a range of Burgundies from 1995 and 1990. Altogether there were 32 wines, including the five Burgundies (⍟ page 386).

Producers were selected on the basis that their older wines had impressed me with having aging potential and complexity. However, an unavoidable bias should be admitted at the outset. Three decades ago, it was close to heresy to suppose that top quality Pinot Noir could be grown anywhere outside of Burgundy. It's maybe only in the past decade or just a bit longer that the pioneers have really made the point that interesting expressions of Pinot Noir can actually be obtained elsewhere. The consequence is that in most cases, the vines were still very young everywhere outside Burgundy in 1995. On top of that, the clones available for planting outside France mostly were inferior. And few producers were making single vineyard wines comparable to their top wines today. Some producers whose recent wines impressed me were not included because they do not yet have older wines that would have been appropriate, and of course some old wines are simply no longer available. With those caveats, the wines in this tasting should represent the best efforts of producers making the most interesting Point Noirs around the world. However, I am sure that if this exercise is repeated a decade from now, the range of producers from outside Burgundy will be much broader. Certainly Burgundy starts out with the advantage that its vines are older and better adapted to its terroir (and there is a classification to offer guidance to a hierarchy of quality).

The New World tends to compensate for its lack of experience in defining the best sites by introducing selection. Some of the top wines are reserve selections from barrels, but even those that are presented as single vineyards often result from some selection within the vineyard (the rest of the production going into the regular bottling). Indeed, most of the European wines in the tasting represented specific terroirs, but many of the New World wines resulted from at least a partial selection. This may change as the vineyards become more mature.

The most impressive feature of the tasting was that interesting wines emerged from all regions. At the risk of over-simplifying, the wines tended to develop in one of two directions: some showed a more taut, mineral quality with a tendency to precision showing more black fruit flavors; others tended to a warmer, nutty, earthy quality with a broader impression of red fruits. There was no very precise correlation between these styles and geographical origin, and indeed, not a great deal of obvious connection with terroir. The New World wines on average showed around half a per cent more alcohol than the European wines (among which Burgundy and Sancerre were generally lower than the rest of Europe) but alcohol levels generally did not seem to be a factor.

Pinot is a very polarizing grape; unanimity among the tasters was hard to come by. "Because Burgundy gets under people's skin, producers around the world try to compete," said Jancis Robinson, but "professional tasters differ more about Pinot than any other grape," commented Tim Atkin. There was, however, agreement that the wines generally did not yet compete with top level Burgundy. Michael Schuster summarized the group consensus by saying that, "The point here is that there is nothing here that is above village level in terms of Burgundy." On the other hand, when we came to select the best half dozen wines for retasting at the end, only one Burgundy made the cut——and this was a grand cru from 1990 at that, although everyone agreed that its quality was really closer to premier cru level. As Michael Schuster commented, "There are no Pinots from outside Burgundy that are at the grand cru level, but there are plenty of grand crus in Burgundy that aren't at the grand cru level." It was revealing that none of the village wines or premier crus from 1990 or 1995 Burgundy made the final flight; in terms of the tasting as a whole, their distribution in terms of overall interest was similar to that of other geographical regions.

The Clos de la Roche 1990 was voted the best wine of the tasting—"this is exactly what Burgundy should be," said Jasper Morris—but there was a certain rueful admission afterward that the group as a whole might have succumbed to an attack of Burgundophilia. Calera's Jensen vineyard from 1995 was a clear second. In my ratings, I found wines at the three star level from every geographical group. Europe outside of Burgundy did not perform especially well at this tasting, but the wines from Alto Adige showed elegance and I thought Gantenbein's 1997 Pinot from Graubunden was still interesting, although less refined than his usual style. Meyer-Näkel's Walporzheimer Krauterberg 2000 was the most complete wine from Germany, still vibrant and interesting, although less typically taut than usual. Reflecting its longer experience with Pinot Noir, North America did best from the New World, with a distinct bias towards the older-established producers. There were especially fine efforts from Domaine Drouhin with the Burgundian Laurène 1993, Au Bon Climat with the elegant Sanford & Benedict 1994, and Fogarty's precise Santa Cruz Reserve 1995, although others came close. With its more recent commitment to Pinot Noir, the southern hemisphere had more difficulty, but Felton Road's Block 5 2001 from Central Otago was generally appreciated, and the Coldstream Hills Reserve 1996 displayed a real elegance that cast a new light for me upon Yarra Valley's potential for Pinot Noir.

Two wines at opposite ends of the flavor spectrum were especially polarizing. Fromm Winery's 1996 Clayvin Vineyard from Marlborough seemed to me to be built to last and was only just coming into its own. Some tasters really liked it, but others thought it would never come around. Perhaps this says something about expectations for New Zealand Pinot Noir, but these reactions are not dissimilar to a split in opinion about 1996 Burgundy. Some people feel the acidity will prevent these wines from ever becoming enjoyable; but Jasper Morris takes the view that, "Pinot will forgive (and recover from) an acid imbalance in a way that Bordeaux will not," and he believes the wines are becoming interesting. In contrast with the general perception that most New World Pinots are based on fruit concentration, Jasper Morris felt that some were built around tannin structure rather than fruit. "Overall I prefer [a style of] restraint and minerality, although I get pleasure out of the rich style it's not my preferred style, Pinot is about fruit acid balance. The restrained character showed individually by wines rather than being a characteristic of any one region," he felt.

Perhaps the most overtly "New World" Pinot Noir was the 1995 Rochioli Vineyard from Williams Selyem in Russian River. The general reaction was that the wine showed too much oak, although Alex Hunt commented that, "I have a rather guilty feeling of finding this delicious." Personally I view this wine as a vindication of the notion that Pinot Noir can have alternative typicities, and that although quite different from Burgundy, they can be equally expressive of the grape. It's definitely rather rich, but the overall balance is indeed delicious, and shows all the appropriate complexity for a decade and half of age.

The tasting as a whole demonstrated without any doubt that Pinot Noir from a variety of climates and terroirs can produce interesting results with age. All wines showed typicity; as Michael Schuster commented, "If you tasted these wines blind, it would be difficult to place them as anything other than Pinot." Pinot character dominated the tasting over any geographical differences, and there was more convergence of style than you detect when you compare current vintages. Producer style seemed to be the most important factor in determining aging potential. Pinot character just comes out and takes over the best wines! Stylistic differences that seem obvious among young Pinot Noirs from different origins are much reduced among those wines that have had the capacity to mature for fifteen or more years. There was no evidence from this particular tasting that Burgundy generally has greater longevity than other regions. When I asked whether in view of this tasting, people would now consider alternatives to Burgundy when looking for an older wine for dinner, Jancis Robinson summarized the consensus: "In all the regions we looked at, the wines have become much more subtle." There was agreement that many of these wines would be good food matches.

Where there were problems, many could be put down to the recent establishment of the vineyards. "A lot of these are two half wines where they don't quite meet in the middle, basically because the vines were just a bit too young," was the view expressed by Tim Atkin. Several wines simply seemed to be a little too old—you could still see that the fruits had been ripe and sweet, but had not had the staying power. These tended to come from younger vineyards, and I would expect that the wines being made there today will show more concentration and greater longevity.

Burgundy does not need to look to its laurels just yet—but the challenge is there. Many wines in this tasting would be more than competitive with village wines from Burgundy. Although none would challenge a grand cru from a good vintage, it surely cannot be long before the best single vineyard or reserve wines show complexity and longevity to match good premier crus from Burgundy. Of course, Burgundy itself can be quite variable: the village wine in this tasting was too old, and neither premier cru from 1995 had much interest. When Burgundy is good, it is very, very good, but if you think back to the nineties, there are not many vintages that are completely reliable. Which route will Burgundy follow now? Will it be the increasing emphasis on purity of fruits and refinement shown by a new generation of winemakers? Or will the recent warming climatic trend lead to too much extraction, higher alcohol, and lower acidity, bringing a different set of problems in terms of aging and in fighting off the challenge from other Pinot Noir producers? But come back in twenty, or perhaps even ten, years, and Pinot Noir may join Cabernet Sauvignon, Syrah, Chardonnay, and Sauvignon Blanc in becoming a truly international grape.

Tastings of DRC and Leroy

Right through the tasting, the difference between Romanée St. Vivant and Richebourg for both producers conformed to a feminine/masculine divide, and the wines truly reflected the best that could be obtained from the vintage. Both producers had a great success in the hot year of 2003 that confounded so many, taking advantage of the conditions to produce extra intensity in the wines. The wines of 1999 seemed much more backward than those of 2003, with perhaps the exception of the Leroy Romanée St. Vivant. The 1996s all have noses that are more typical of the vintage than the appellation or producer, with that slightly acidic, medicinal edge. Neither DRC nor Leroy was able completely to defy this vintage, but both were more successful in Richebourg. This was a vintage where sheer density of fruit was the key to overcoming the problematic acidity. There was a surprisingly high level of acidity in the 1995s, echoing 1996. Wines were tasted in May 2011.

Romanée St. Vivant, Domaine de la Romanée Conti, 2003
Perfumed nose, some slightly tarry notes still showing, full of fruit. Smooth, elegant, and refined on the palate, the perfumed edge of the nose just shows on the finish; very long, very smooth, the finish is coated with deep black fruits, with touches of cherries and blackcurrants, and infinitely silky tannins. Through the intensity of this wine, every inch a grand cru, comes that classic femininity and elegance of Romanée St. Vivant. You could drink this wine now because the fruits are so smooth but it would be infanticide; it will deepen and become increasingly elegant for a decade or more. An immensely subtle wine. ***** Drink 2014-2029.

Romanée St. Vivant, Domaine Leroy, 2003
Perfumed with some notes of violets, deep red fruits underneath, but the perfume just rises up out of the glass. Smooth, black fruits, with an elegant aromatic uplift on the palate, more red and black cherries than blackcurrants, more open knit than the DRC of this vintage. A touch of tobacco develops on the finish. The fresh acidity brings a lightness of touch that entirely refutes the stereotype of the vintage. Indeed, this was the lightest wine of the vintage, giving Leroy positions at both ends of the pole, the Romanée St. Vivant the lightest, the Richebourg the weightiest. **** Drink 2013-2020.

Richebourg, Domaine de la Romanée Conti, 2003
A perfumed black cherry fruit nose offers faintly tarry intimations. The Richebourg gives an immediate impression of more muscularity than the Romanée St. Vivant on the palate, very deep black fruits showing blackcurrants as well as black cherries. The tannins are ripe and firm, and although the fruit density is more than a match for them, they make the texture denser to the point at which the sheer quality of the fruits is less obvious to appreciate. This powerful wine needs several years before it really will show the full elegance of the fruits, but already those

complex layers of flavor are beginning emerge, more powerful but less subtle than the Romanée St. Vivant. Right now I prefer DRC's Romanée St. Vivant to the Richebourg, but that may reverse with time. **** Drink 2016-2029.

Richebourg, Domaine Leroy, 2003
The most restrained nose of the 2003 flight, with a very slightly gamey note overlaying the black fruits. Altogether a more restrained impression than either Leroy's Romanée St. Vivant or DRC's Richebourg from this vintage. The most intensely structured wine of the vintage, this simply needs more time to emerge from its shell. The black fruits are deep and dense, with a touch of blackcurrants; the tannins are ripe and rich, but the wine is fairly closed, a brooding monster at this point. The potential here is immense but it's going to be several years before the full complexity really comes out. A true vin de garde, this wine is hard to appreciate fully just yet. ***** Drink 2017-2030.

Romanée St. Vivant, Domaine de la Romanée Conti, 1999
Soft, earthy, red fruit nose. Sweet, ripe fruits show an edge of blackcurrants on black cherries, very deep, quite dense, with firm ripe tannins in support. More density and less elegance here than you usually find in Romanée St. Vivant, the firmness of the tannins and fruits hiding the usual silkiness of the appellation. Very deep flavors are still quite undeveloped. Slowly in the glass the fruits come out more, but in this vintage, at least at this stage, they do not reach the flavor interest and complexity of DRC's Richebourg. **** Drink 2015-2028.

Romanée St. Vivant, Domaine Leroy, 1999
Slightly gamey, savory, red fruit nose is relatively restrained. Very sweet ripe fruits, inclined more to red than to black cherries, bring out the elegance and silkiness of Romanée St. Vivant, although the wine is still very young and undeveloped. Tannins are firm but silky in the background. Slowly a touch of aromatics emerges in the glass, uplifting the fruits, and making the wine almost ready to drink, by contrast with the more massive Richebourg. It's not exactly a case of beauty and the beast, but Leroy's Romanée St. Vivant is all about elegance whereas the Richebourg is all about power. **** Drink 2014-2026.

Richebourg, Domaine de la Romanée Conti, 1999
A faint tobacco note on the nose intensifies in the glass and comes back on the finish. Fruits are sweet and ripe; the difference with the Romanée St Vivant is in just a touch more intensity and deepness, an extra level to the fruits. This is more youthful and more backward, more masculine and less feminine in the classic way. Over the next few years it may pull well ahead of the Romanée St. Vivant as the structure resolves and the greater density of fruits comes out. It's just a bit too brooding to enjoy fully now. **** Drink 2016-2028.

Richebourg, Domaine Leroy, 1999
The most restrained nose of the 1999 vintage, very faintly gamey, with underlying black fruits. Once again the most massive and backward wine of the vintage. The fruits are intense enough to offset the tannins, which are firm and deep, with enough direct presence on the palate to obscure the fruits and make the wine far too young to appreciate at this point. Certainly the structure is well balanced and there is no doubt that the fruits will emerge as the tannins soften, but how long will this take—certainly several years. **** Drink 2016-2028.

Romanée St. Vivant, Domaine de la Romanée Conti, 1996
Slightly tarry nose with a mineral edge. A much tougher impression than usual from Romanée St. Vivant. The acidic edge of the vintage is ruling the palate. Underneath are red fruits and tight tannins, but the usual silky generosity of the appellation is missing. Slowly the red fruits emerge in the glass, but there is a tight acidic edge to the finish that may not soften before the fruits dry out. *** Drink 2013-2020.

Romanée St. Vivant, Domaine Leroy, 1996
An acidic mineral edge on the nose. More generosity to the palate than the nose, with some elegant black fruits, but that metallic, acidic edge of the vintage comes back on the palate. The question as always with this vintage is whether the acid and tannins can resolve in time to let the fruits emerge. *** Drink 2013-2020.

Richebourg, Domaine de la Romanée Conti, 1996
Very restrained nose, just a hint of mineral red fruits. The Richebourg, with its typically deeper fruits, has more successfully overcome the acidic problems of this vintage than the Romanée St. Vivant. Here the fruits, tending to black cherries, slowly emerge in the glass, perhaps not as profound as usual, but still rich and deep, with the acid receding to a supportive backbone. Pushed by the acidity, the tannins dry the finish, but the ripeness and elegance of the fruits comes through. *** Drink 2014-2024.

Richebourg, Domaine Leroy, 1996
Faintly acidic, mineral nose, becoming just a touch tarry in the glass. Sweet ripe fruits, with the powerful density that Leroy always shows in Richebourg, overcome the problematic acidity of the vintage. Certainly there is too much acidity for perfection, there is still an acidic edge pushing the tannins on the finish, and the fruits are just on the edge of emerging. Possibly another few years will do it. ***(*) Drink 2014-2024.

Richebourg, Domaine de la Romanée Conti, 1995
First signs of development to the red fruits on the nose with savory overtones. Firm fruits, less developed on the palate than on the nose, show the typical masculinity of Richebourg. A touch of blackcurrant adds to the black cherry fruits. Firm tannins show on the finish, becoming more tea-like in the glass, and showing a slight acidic edge. The wine gives the impression that it is not ready yet, but should finally emerge in the next year or so. **** Drink 2013-2023.

Richebourg, Domaine Leroy, 1995
Still fairly direct fruits on the nose with an acidic impression, a little reminiscent of 1996. Rich black fruits, blackcurrants mixed with black cherries; a faintly nutty impression on the finish, good acidity emphasizing the strong tannic background. There is more intensity but less elegance than the DRC, but as the tannins resolve further, this may pull further ahead on the sheer density of the fruits. **** Drink 2014-2024.

The Grand Finale Tasting

The objective of this tasting was to compare aging of top wines from different regions by identifying wines with the same apparent maturity as Burgundy 1995 and to determine what complexity they achieved. Producers suggested most of the matches and directly provided most of the wines. Wines were tasted in May 2011 in flights organized geographically, with a panel including Tim Atkin MW, Alex Hunt MW, Jasper Morris MW, Jancis Robinson MW, and Michael Schuster. At the end of the tasting, the best wines were selected and retasted as a separate flight; these were then placed in an approximate order of preference, as mentioned in individual tasting notes. It is not surprising that wines of this age should show bottle variation, but the range of variation seemed to be broadly similar across regions. I have noted examples where another example of the same wine previously gave a different impression. Whether or not a particular bottle showed well in this tasting, these wines are among the most ageworthy Pinot Noirs produced outside of Burgundy, and it is worth trying older vintages.

Northern Europe

Sancerre, La Bourgeoise, Henri Bourgeois, 1996
Developed nose shows ripe fruits with a very faint hint of raisins; the touch of madeirization becomes more noticeable in the glass against a savory background. Good acidity supports fruits that are drying out slightly (but the bottle was not in tip-top condition and a sub threshold case of cork may have reduced the fruits), allowing some residual bitterness to dominate the finish. It is however a very pretty wine in the general style of a light Burgundy. Interestingly not as fine as the 1990 (ᵀ page 176). * Drink now.

Sancerre, Vacheron, 1995
A slightly gamey nose, some people might call it funky, of ripe red fruits. There's a slightly acid mark to the savory red fruits on the palate, with the gamey quality noticeable on the finish. This is due to a touch of Brett, which lends an interesting complexity if you like that flavor spectrum. This is less generous than some other bottles I have had of this vintage. It has just passed its limit of development, and a slight medicinal or herbaceous note is beginning to show on the finish. It isn't holding up as well as the 1990 vintage, which remains delicious at this point (ᵀ page 175). * Drink now.

Alsace, Jubilee, Les Neveux, Hugel, 1990
The savory nose has a faint hint of stewed fruits. This is riper and richer on the palate than the nose would suggest, although the fruits are drying out a bit, and some residual bitterness is

beginning to take over the finish. Overall the impression is a little lean. There may be significant bottle variation in development at this age, because this bottle does not show as well as one tasted six months ago at Hugel (ⲧ page 197). * Drink now.

Alto Adige, Krafuss, Alois Lageder, 1998
Faintly spicy notes on a nose with some warm red fruit notes and a hint of cereal. A nice balance shows on the palate, with good acidity and some residual light tannins supporting the developing fruits, although the fruits haven't really quite made the transition to tertiary development. This appears to be reaching its life span but is still vibrant. This is impressive considering how young the vines were when the wine was made. Interestingly, this bottle shows less obvious development than one tasted at Lageder six months ago; here there is only a faint hint of the sous bois that was noticeable on the earlier bottle, and which showed delicious promise for the development of Lageder's Pinots with age (ⲧ page 203). ** Drink now-2012.

Alto Adige, Barthenau, Josef Hofstätter, 1995
Savory notes on the nose are followed by some perfume, giving an intriguing and complex bouquet. There is less complexity to the palate than the nose; the red fruits show a savory edge, a nice balance with acidity and residual tannins, just a touch of bitterness coming through. Still showing well, just a touch leathery, and a hint of sous bois develops in the glass, but I think the wine has reached the natural limit of its lifespan. More similar to the 1993, which tended to the herbal, than to the delicious 1997, which showed more harmonious aging (ⲧ page 202). This wine just failed to make the taste off of the best half dozen. ** Drink now.

Graubunden, Gantenbein, 1997
Mineral nose with a touch of gunflint and a mix of red and black fruits, with a touch of sous bois developing in the glass. The ripe palate of black fruits tends to cherries, with a mix of sweet fruits and some bitter cherries. This is a very interesting expression of Pinot, pretty much towards the end of its development, but balanced very much in the smooth style of the Côte de Nuits. The general criticism was that this seemed a little four square, but it shows an interesting array of flavors, although the tannins threaten to overtake the fruits. Alex Hunt thought this was the most impressive of the flight with regards to its basic structure, and Jancis Robinson commented, "Pure, quite Burgundian flavors in concentrated style." The wine is not as developed as the 1996, which followed a more savory route, and which is perhaps a better guide to the complexity of Gantenbein's Pinot as it ages (ⲧ page 206). *** Drink now.

Germany

Walporzheimer Krauterberg, Spätburgunder, Ahr, Meyer-Näkel , 2000
The earthy nose of red fruits tending to strawberries is attractive, developing a more mineral edge in the glass that adds complexity. Sweet ripe fruits on the palate are distinctly earthy on the smoky and nutty aftertaste. This is a warm impression of Pinot Noir, turning towards a sweet, ripe, and nutty, flavor spectrum rather than savory. You would think it more likely to come from limestone than slate terroir. There is still some life here for further development. Everyone viewed this as the most complete wine of the German flight; this was the only German wine to make the taste-off of the top half dozen. It has broader flavors than Meyer-Näkel's usual taut precision and shows more interesting development than the 1999 or 2001 vintages (ⲧ page 180). *** Drink now-2015.

*Rheingau, Rudesheimer Berg Schlossberg, Spätlese *** trocken, Auguste Kesseler, 1999*
Mineral and slightly savory on the nose. Fruits are still showing something of their original sweet ripeness although beginning to dry out a little. Some mineral notes show on the finish. The style shows the taut precision of slate. This is just a touch past its peak, but still very drinkable, and it becomes a little finer in the glass. ** Drink now.

*Baden, Ihringer Winklerberg, Spätburgunder *** trocken, Dr. Joachim Heger, 1999*
A little madeirized on the nose so possibly this bottle wasn't in top condition. Madeirization isn't so obvious on the palate, but it's taking the edge off the fruits and making it difficult to appreciate the potential of the wine. A bottle in perfect condition tasted at Heger nine months ago was much fresher, but my general impression is that the Pinots from Baden peak a couple of years before the end of their first decade (ⲧ page 191).

Pfalz, Oekonomierat Rebholz, 1993
The restrained nose gives a faintly mineral impression. Sweet fruits in the red spectrum show a distinctly mineral edge, but give an impression of beginning to dry out. This is a very calm, well

balanced wine, it is an enjoyable drink, but it doesn't achieve the full complexity of which Rebholz is capable. There's a faintly minty, chocolaty overtone to the finish, but overall the wine is surprisingly four square for this producer. Jancis Robinson said that, "Not too sweet, this one wormed its way into my affections for its texture and structure." ** Drink now-2013.

Pfalz, Oekonomierat Rebholz, 1990
Nose of stewed fruits seems a bit cooked. The palate follows with some cooked red and black fruits. The overall impression is that this is the equivalent of 2003 Burgundy, with conditions that were simply too hot for Pinot Noir. The group consensus was that the wine was a bit chunky. As judged by other vintages, however, Rebholz's wines certainly have aging potential: the 1997 is now at its peak, and the 1979 is still remarkably lively (⊤ page 188). * Drink now.

North America

Willamette, Laurène, Drouhin, 1993
A very faint touch of oxidation shows on a mineral nose. Complex palate shows mineral red fruits; a smoky, faintly leathery touch on the finish adds a gamey note to the palate. This is definitely a mature, developed wine, with savory notes beginning to pick up, but very fine. It shows no sign of going into decline and should continue to develop deliciously for a while. This bottle is a touch less overtly savory than one tasted at Drouhin six months ago, but generally shows good consistency (⊤ page 256). For me, this wine provided one of the clearest challenges to Burgundy in the tasting. It placed third equal in the tasting as a whole. ***(*) Drink now-2015.

Willamette, Elizabeth's Reserve, Adelsheim, 1994
Very restrained nose possibly with a very faint touch of oxidation. Sweet ripe fruits still show as red and black cherries on the palate; this is quite dry on the finish, a touch more austere than you usually find in Oregon. The fruits give contradictory impressions: on the one hand they seem to be developing very slowly, on the other there's a touch of residual bitterness on the finish that suggests they could be drying out. There is a very faint touch of stewed fruits on the aftertaste suggestive of warm growing conditions. On balance the wine should be drunk now as it is not obvious there is potential for further development. The 1994 vintage is more highly rated in Oregon than the cooler 1993, but personally I prefer the older, cooler vintage of this wine, which seems to me to show more complete development (⊤ page 250). *** Drink now.

Carneros, Saintsbury Reserve, 1997
A developed nose shows some remnants of black cherry fruits, possibly with a faint touch of oxidation. The palate is more forthcoming than the nose, but the black cherry fruits are quite austere, with some bitterness showing on the finish. This seems to be surviving rather than developing, and I don't see the potential for future development. However, other vintages in the second half of the nineties have shown more interesting development, especially the 1995 which displays more elegance (⊤ page 265). ** Drink now.

Santa Cruz, Reserve, Fogarty, 1995
A restrained but savory nose suggests some development along Burgundian lines. This is confirmed on the palate with savory flavors of developed red fruits, deliciously balanced just short of the turning point. The finish is quite dry with a faintly nutty edge. This is now absolutely at a delicious peak, but should continue to develop and hold for another year or so. The general impression is of the precision of fruits resulting from cooler climate production, with good aging potential for a span of a couple of decades after the vintage (⊤ page 274). ***(*) Drink now-2013.

Mount Harlan, Jensen Vineyard, Calera, 1995
This wine presented a conundrum. Overall it placed second in the tasting, and there was general agreement that it was one of the few wines that could stand up to Burgundy at the premier cru level. However, I have to declare a conflict, which is that personally I found a strange mix of prunes and herbaceousness on the nose, partly following through to the palate. Admittedly the palate showed better than the nose, with an interesting complexity, but for my taste the aromatics were overpowering. I suspect that I am unusually sensitive to this particular aromatic, so my reaction is atypical, but I would advise drinking in short order before the aromatics become too oppressive. Jancis Robinson thought it was, "Sweet and thick and velvety but not quite refreshing enough." I have not found any over-aromatic quality in other Calera wines, most notably the Jensen 1997 and the 1990, which recently showed a perfect stage of development (⊤ page 275). ** Drink now.

Santa Ynez Valley, Sanford & Benedict Vineyard, Au Bon Climat, 1994
A restrained nose conveys a faintly mineral and faintly savory impression. There is delicious development on the palate; the fruits are just beginning to turn savory, but short of the turning point. The palate develops along more earthy lines in the glass. The overall impression tends toward the mineral but there's a lovely balance in which it's very difficult to disentangle the component influences. The restrained and elegant style might be confused with a wine from Beaune, and is very much in the restrained Old World style that continues to characterize the Pinots at ABC (Y page 277). The wine placed in the top half dozen of the tasting. *** Drink now-2016.

Russian River Valley, Rochioli Vineyard, Williams Selyem, 1995
Smoky on the nose, with perfumed overtones. Tight red fruits on the palate are very refined; the style is rather oaky, but within that parameter, tighter and more precise than the somewhat richer style of current vintages. Here you get an impression of layers of flavor, but it has to be said that some tasters with Burgundian backgrounds found the oak to be obtrusive; others thought the wine was simply delicious, although in an overtly richer style than they were accustomed to. The development of this wine is certainly consistent with past experience that Williams Selyem Pinots develop well for two decades (Y page 272). ***(*) Drink now–2016.

New Zealand

Martinborough, Dry River, 2001
Some raisined notes show on the nose of sweet ripe black fruits; although they are less evident on the palate, but there remains a slight impression of over-ripe fruits. There does not seem to have been much development in this vintage, which gives an impression of high extraction without real fruit concentration. Vintages from a decade earlier, however, have aged much better in my experience (Y page 323). ** Drink now-2016.

Martinborough, Ata Rangi, 1998
There's a mineral impression to the nose of developing red fruits, which follow through to the palate. Good acidity supports red fruits on the palate, but with a distinct dryness to the finish, which gives the impression that the fruits are beginning to dry out. Under cork, ten years seems to be the natural lifespan for Ata Rangi, but this may well lengthen under screwcap as the fruits stay fresher for longer (Y page 321) ** Drink now-2014.

Martinborough, Martinborough Vineyard, 1993
Some over-ripe aromas with slightly rotten or stewed notes on the nose, which becomes slightly perfumed. The over-ripe or rotten note carries over to the palate, making the wine seem past its peak. Tastings at Martinborough suggest that a decade is probably around the limit for longevity (Y page 325) * Drink up.

Marlborough, Clayvin Vineyard, La Strada (Fromm Winery), 1996
The restrained nose offers some mineral impressions of red fruits. Elegant fruits with a taut style stop just short of herbaceous on the palate. Development here is very slow, with a touch of minerality coming through to the finish; you get the impression that the development has really scarcely started to go beyond the primary fruits. The wine shows a refined tautness, with lots of life ahead; the style is built to last. The vineyard was replanted soon after this vintage, so it may be a while until there is another chance to taste a developed wine from older vines (Y page 333). *** Drink now-2016.

Marlborough, Cloudy Bay, 2001
Fruits are ripe, just short of over-ripe but in an interesting contrast show some mineral notes on the nose. This is very nice on the palate, however, with a smooth balance in a taut style of precise black fruits. There's the impression of a well made, clean wine, but the flavor spectrum seems a little monotonic; is there a certain lack of the complexity that you might expect to be developing at this age, and will the wine now survive rather than mature? As always with wines from the southern hemisphere bottled under cork, the risk is that poor cork quality has spoiled the wine, but this bottle is reasonably consistent with one tasted six months previously at Cloudy Bay (Y page 331). It may well be that these wines will show brighter and more long lived fruit after bottling under screwcap. **(*) Drink now-2012.

Central Otago, Block 5, Felton Road, 2001
A curious mix of herbaceousness and over-ripe sensations on the nose, which follows through to the palate. Actually, the extremely ripe impressions on the nose are off-putting, but the palate is more interesting, with a nice complexity of fruits, showing as black and red cherries, with some dryness on the finish. Jancis Robinson shared my reservations about this particular

bottle, "Racy and velvety and a bit like beetroot juice, sweet and sour, not that distinguished," but past experience has shown other Felton Road wines to develop more in the savory direction, peaking somewhere around a decade of age (⊤ page 345). The group consensus placed this wine in the top half dozen of the tasting. ** Drink up.

Australia

Yarra Valley, Coldstream Hills, Reserve, 1996
A smoky mineral impression to the nose gives just a hint of savory red fruits. Sweet ripe fruits on the palate are beautifully cut by a smoky mineral note, giving a really delicious balance. The palate has layers of flavors, ranging from savory red fruits to smoke and minerals, with a long finish. The wine is vibrant and shows every sign of going on for years. This is a knockout in terms of demonstrating Yarra Valley's potential for producing elegant Pinot Noir. It placed third equal in the tasting as a whole. ***(*) Drink now–2016.

Yarra Valley, Mount Mary, 1999
A touch of cork makes this difficult to appreciate but the impression underneath is of slightly over-ripe fruits giving a very slightly stewed impression to the palate. Some decline in the fruits allowing bitterness to show on the finish may be due to cork, but the general impression is that even in top condition, this vintage might be a little chunky.

Mornington Peninsula, Moorooduc, 2002
The restrained nose has a mix of mineral notes with hints of over-ripe fruits. Sweet ripe fruits show on the palate, but there's a touch more herbaceousness on the finish than on a bottle tasted a few months ago at the estate. Developing slowly (this was the first vintage under screwcap), there is a risk that the herbaceousness will overtake the fruits. Not surprisingly, this estate wine doesn't have the aging potential of The Moorooduc selection, which was not produced in this vintage (⊤ page 361) ** Drink now-2015.

Burgundy Calibration

Chambolle Musigny, Jacques-Frédéric Mugnier, 1995
A contradictory nose of some stewed fruits and herbaceous overtones. The dry finish, and the slightly stewed notes of the fruits on the palate, suggest that the wine is now past its peak: it may have been elegant at an earlier stage, but now it is too old.

Volnay Taillepieds, Hubert de Montille, 1995
A little nutty on the nose, an impression of warmer fruits than you usually see in Volnay. Elegant on the palate, but the fruits haven't yet really developed quite enough complexity, and there's just a touch of hardness that you get with Montille. The issue here is really the lack of interesting development, which at this stage raises the question of whether it will happen at all. ** Drink now.

Nuits St. Georges, Les St. Georges, Henri Gouges, 1995
The rather restrained nose doesn't give up much. The wine is a little dry on the palate, but shows clean lines to the fruits, although a little lacking in generosity so there's a surprising impression of angularity on the finish. The dry tannins on the finish are outlasting the fruits. * Drink up.

Gevrey Chambertin Cazetiers, Faiveley, 1990
Minerality shows on the nose with a faint leathery touch due to a slight touch of Brett; personally I found it deliciously interesting. It's not necessarily typical, because another bottle showed no sign of Brett, but did display somewhat dumber fruits. This bottle is a fraction dry on the palate, with the fruits developing in a more mineral style than usual for Cazetiers. The dryness of the finish becomes fairly noticeable and it is fair to say that the wine has reached the limits of its development. ** Drink up.

Clos de la Roche, Hubert Lignier, 1990
A developed nose shows warm, nutty, red fruits, followed by a touch of herbaceousness. There is good depth and concentration to the palate; the earthy and mineral fruits are cut by a touch of herbaceous that is more noticeable on the finish than on the nose. All the same, this now gives the impression that it will not mature any further. It's a ripe style which some tasters felt at first could have been confused with the New World, but then developed a distinctive and attractive tea-like note in the glass, adding complexity. This was judged the favorite wine of the tasting, although there was agreement that it was more reflective of premier cru than grand cru level. *** Drink now-2013.

Bibliography

Jean-François Bazin, *Histoire du vin de Bourgogne* (Jean-Paul Gisserot, Plouédern, France, 2002).

Clive Coates, *The Wines of Burgundy* (University of California Press, Berkeley, 2008).

Roger Dion, *Histoire de la Vigne et du Vin en France. Des Origines aux XIX Siècle, 1st edition* (Imprimerie Cevin et cie, Paris, 1959).

Rolande Gadille, *Le Vignoble de la Côte Bourguignone* (Les Belles Lettres, Dijon, 1967).

John Winthrop Haeger, *North American Pinot Noir* (University of California Press, Berkeley, 2004).

Marcel Lachiver, *Vins, Vignes et Vignerons. Histoire de Vignoble Français* (Fayard, Paris, 1988).

J. Lavalle, *Histoire et Statistique de la Vigne et des Grand Vins de la Côte d'Or* (Picard [Phenix Editions, 2000 reprint], Dijon, 1855).

Benjamin Lewin, *Wine Myths and Reality*, Vendange Press, 2010.

Allen D. Meadows, *The Pearl of the Cote. The Great Wines of Vosne Romanée.* (Burghound Books, Winnetka, California, 2010).

Denis Morelot, *Statistique de la Vigne dans de Département de la Côte-d'Or* (Ch. Brugnot, Dijon, 1831).

Jasper Morris, *Inside Burgundy* (Berry Bros, London, 2010).

Camille Rodier, *Le Vin de Bourgogne, 3rd edition* (Damidot / Laffitte reprints, Dijon, 1948).

John Saker, *Pinot Noir. The New Zealand Story* (Random House, Auckland, New Zealand, 2010).

Notes

References cited in the Bibliography are given in the notes by author and short title. Other references are given in full the first time cited in each chapter, and by author and short title with the indication *op. cit.* for subsequent citations in that chapter.

Chapter 1: The Ancient Pinot Family

[1] Vitis species are distributed across North America and Eurasia, so the common ancestor must have preceded separation of the continents.

[2] Ancient seeds and leaf impressions suggest there was only one type of grapevine at this time (Patrick E. McGovern, *Ancient Wine: The Search for the Origins of Viniculture,* Princeton University Press, Princeton, 2003, p. 7).

[3] The driving force for speciation may have been the isolation of separate populations by the ice-fronts (M. G. Mullins, *Biology of the Grapevine,* Cambridge University Press, Cambridge, 1992, p. 23).

[4] The 60 so-called "species" of Vitis are all inter-fertile. (These are the Euvitis.) This means they are not really *species*, but are actually *sub-species*, that is, more or less well-differentiated members of the same species. Because they are inter-fertile, the number is not exact. In addition, there are 3-4 members of the Muscadinia family, which more recently were recognized as separate species from the Euvitis.

[5] This places wine firmly as a discovery of Homo sapiens, since Neanderthal man had died out about 30,000 years ago.

[6] All members of the Vitis family form grapes, but only those of Vitis vinifera are good for making wine. The grapes of other Vitis species have a "foxy" aroma and flavor, varying in strength, but generally unpleasant enough to require the wine to be sweetened or given some other flavoring component to disguise it. The foxy aroma is caused by the presence of the compound methylanthranilate (related to camphor) in the grapes.

[7] McGovern, *Ancient Wine,* op. cit., p. 72.

[8] Technically known as Vitis vinifera silvestris.

[9] A major distinction between the ancestral wild grapevine, Vitis vinifera ssp. silvestris, and the cultivated form, Vitis vinifera ssp. vinifera is that wild grapevines are dioecious, meaning there are separate male and female plants. They must grow in the same vicinity in order for the pollen from male plants to fertilize the female plants, which bear berries. Domesticated grapevines are hermaphrodite, so a single plant is self-fertilizing, and can generate berries. Probably hermaphrodites that occurred by chance were selected for cultivation because they gave berries more reliably.

[10] The idea that there was a single domestication event is sometimes called the Noah hypothesis (McGovern, *Ancient Wine,* op. cit., p. 16). There's some evidence that there may also have been other, independent domestication events (R. Arroyo-Garcia. et al., *Multiple Origins Of Cultivated Grapevine, [Vitis Vinifera L. Ssp. Sativa] Based On Chloroplast DNA Polymorphisms,* Molecular Ecology, 15, 3707-3714, 2006).

[11] The anthocyanin that was measured, malvidin, is produced by grapes and pomegranates. Pomegranates are also grown in the area (and could have been used to make wine), but the discovery of grape remnants points towards winemaking from grapes.

[12] Hans Barnard et al., *Chemical evidence for wine production around 4000 BCE in the Late Chalcolithic Near Eastern highlands* (J. Archaeological Science, 38, 977-984, 2011).

[13] The shape of the seeds of domesticated grapes is different from seeds of wild grapes.

[14] McGovern, *Ancient Wine,* op. cit., p. 85.

[15] Around 320 B.C., the Greek philosopher Theophrastus (Aristotle's successor) published two series of books, *De causis plantarum* (The Causes of Plants) and *De historia plantarum* (The History of Plants). The Causes of Plants addresses many of the current issues in viticulture, including cultivation of the grapevine, pruning methods, and dealing with pests and diseases (Theophrastus, *Enquiry into Plants,* trans. A. F. Horton, Heinemann, London, 1916).

[16] Around 160 B.C., Cato discussed vineyard management and vines in *de Agri Cultura,* giving a good deal of attention to issues such as pruning methods and the use of wine presses. Around 65 C.E. Lucius Columella published a 12-volume series on agriculture, *de Re Rustica,* including three books on viticulture. In one book he discussed the properties of different grape varieties.

[17] Pliny the Elder (70 C.E.). The XIIII book of the history of nature. *Containing the Treatise of Trees bearing fruit.* Chapter VI.

[18] Andrew Dalby, *Empire of pleasures: luxury and indulgence in the Roman world* (Routledge, London, 2000), p. 28.

[19] Jancis Robinson, *The Oxford Companion to Wine* (Oxford University Press, Oxford, 2006), p. 23.

[20] J. André, *Contribution au vocabulaire de la viticulture: les noms de cépages* (Revue des Etudes Latines, tome XXX, 128-156, 1952).

[21] It appears to be more closely related to Vitis vinifera silvestris and to show more diversity in its genetic makeup than most varieties, but the data are still somewhat indirect (Sean Myles et al., *Genetic structure and domestication history of the grape,* Proc. Nat. Acad. Sci., 108, 3530-3535, 2011).

[22] Jancis Robinson, *The Oxford Companion to Wine* (Oxford University Press, Oxford, 1994), p. 649.

[23] Harrison Boyd Ash, *Lucius Junius Moderatus Columella, On Agriculture, with a recension of the text and an English translation,* Harvard University Press, Cambridge, 1941, p. 249.

[24] Roger Dion, *Histoire de la Vigne,* p. 297.

[25] Camille Rodier, *Le vin de Bourgogne,* p. 14.

[26] Marcel Lachiver, *Vins, Vignes et Vignerons,* p. 61.

[27] According to Philippe de Beaumanoir, in *Les coutumes du Beauvaisis,* tome 1, p. 389, published in 1289 (Béatrice Bourély, *Vignes et Vins de L'Abbaye de Citeaux en Bourgogne,* Editions du Tastevin, Nuits St. Georges, 1998, p. 109).

[28] J. Liébault, *La Maison Rustique, VI,* Paris, 582, p. 548.

[29] "Le noirien, appelée dans d'autres pays pinot, pineau-auvernat est le meilleur" [Noirien, elsewhere called Pinot or Pinot-Auvernat, is the best variety] (Denis Morelot, *Statistique de la Vigne,* p. 158).

[30] Roger Dion, *Histoire de la Vigne,* p. 297.

[31] It was known as Auvernat in the Loire and around Paris (Marcel Lachiver, *Vins, Vignes et Vignerons,* p. 83).

[32] John Bowers et al., *Historical Genetics: The Parentage of Chardonnay, Gamay, and Other Wine Grapes of NorthEastern France* (Science, 285, 1562-1565, 1999).

[33] According to a contemporaneous book: Franz Schams, *Ungarns Weinbau in seinem ganzen Umfange, oder vollständige Beschreibung sämmtlicher berühmten Weingebirge des ungarischen Reichs in statistisch-topographisch-naturhistorischer und ökonomischer Hinsicht,* 3 volumes, Wigand, Pest, 1832-1835.

[34] It was ordered to be pulled out in Lorraine in 1598 and in Besançon in 1731 (Pierre Galet, *Cépages et Vignobles de France: L'Ampelographie Française,* Paul Dehan, 1956, p. 146).

[35] Carole Meredith, *Science as a window into wine history,* lecture at the American Academy of Arts and Sciences, 2002.

[36] "Le très mauvais et déloyal plant de gamay, duquel plant vient très grande abondance de vin... lequel vin est de telle nature qu'il est moult nuisible à créature humaine... car il est plein de très grande et horrible amertume....[Il faudra donc] l'extirper, le détruire, le mettre à néant, à peine de soixante sous tournois par ouvrée de vigne."

[37] Philip's edict is the first clear reference to Gamay as a grape as well as to Pinot Noir. "Desloyaul" at the time meant contrary to law or custom, which suggests Gamay may not have been long established. Other records suggest that Gamay was being grown in the area by the late 1360s (Rosalind Kent Berlow, *The "Disloyal" Grape: The Agrarian Crisis of Late Fourteenth Century Burgundy,* Agricultural History, 426-438, 1982).

[38] Claude Arnoux, *Dissertation sur la situation de Bourgogne, sur les vins qu'elle produit* (S. Jallasson, London, 1728); Jean-Alexandre Cavoleau, *Oenologie Française, ou statistique de tous les vignobles et de toutes les boissons vineuses et spiritueuses de la France, suivie de considérations générales sur la culture de la vigne* (Huzard, Paris, 1827).

[39] By the Congress of Ampelography at Chalon-sur-Saône, in order to distinguish it from Pineau de la Loire (a synonym for Chenin Blanc) (Rolande Gadille, *Le Vignoble de la Côte Bourguignone,* p. 158).

[40] André Jullien, *Topographie de tous les vignobles connus* (Huzard, Paris, 1816), pp. 128-129.

[41] Rolande Gadille, *Le Vignoble de la Côte Bourguignone,* p. 192.

[42] Pierre Poupon, *Le Clos Vougeot, in Le Vin de Bourgogne,* ed. Jean-François Bazin, *149.* (Editions Montalba, 1976).

[43] A pièce is 220 liters; an arpent is 0.4 ha, so 1 pièce/arpent is about 5.5 hl/ha.

[44] Jean Godinot, *Manière de cultiver la vigne et de faire le vin en Champagne, et ce qu'on peut imiter dans les autres provinces pour perfectionner les vins* (Chez Barthelemy Multeau, Reims, 1718), p. 6.

[45] Until then, the usual descriptions had been color, taste, consistency, aroma, and strength (Loïc Abric, *Les Grands Vins de Bourgogne de 1750 à 1870. Production, commerce, clientele,* Editions de l'Armançon, Précy-sous-Thil, 2008, p. 395).

[46] Charles Estienne & Jean Liébault, *L'Agriculture, et maison rustique,* 1583, p. 350.

[47] Marcel Lachiver, *Vins, Vignes et Vignerons*, p. 271.

[48] Benoît Musset, *Vignobles de Champagne et vins mousseux (1650-1830) : Histoire d'un mariage de raison* (Fayard, Paris, 2008), p. 127.

[49] Jean Godinot, *Manière de cultiver la vigne et de faire le vin en Champagne, et ce qu'on peut imiter dans les autres provinces pour perfectionner les vins* (Chez Barthelemy Multeau, Reims, 1718), p. 19.

[50] Musset, *Vignobles de Champagne,* op. cit, p. 128.

[51] A list of taxes on wines in 1564 gave the order: Beaune, Graves, Ay, Auxerre (Marcel Lachiver, *Vins, Vignes et Vignerons*, p. 271).

[52] Marcel Lachiver, *Vins, Vignes et Vignerons*, p. 272.

[53] Musset, *Vignobles de Champagne,* op. cit., p. 140.

[54] It's hard to get an exact equivalence for prices because there was a range of 25-50% between the generic wines and the wines that were recognized as coming from specific, superior vineyards, and existing records mostly refer to the more expensive wines. One analysis of average prices between 1660 and 1788 shows wines from Champagne with an average price of 60 livres tournois compared to 45 livres tournois for Bourgogne (Musset, *Vignobles de Champagne,* op. cit, p. 258). However, the figures are probably not directly comparable, and it is likely that the best wines of each region sold for roughly comparable prices (Benoît Musset, Université de Reims, personal communication). It is at all events fair to say that the price ranges for the two regions were extensively overlapping.

[55] Joseph Adrien Le Roi, Antoine Vallot, and Guy Crescent Fagon, *Journal de la santé du roi Louis XIV de l'année 1647 à l'année 1711*, August Durand, Paris, 1862, p. 222.

[56] Bureau Interprofessionnel des Vins de Bourgogne, *Voyage au travers de l'histoire de la Bourgogne*, www.vins-bourgogne.fr.

[57] Abbé Tainturier, *Remarques sur la culture des vignes de Beaune et lieux circonvoisins* (Editions de l'Armançon 2000, Précy-sous-Thil, 1763), p. 137.

[58] Musset, *Vignobles de Champagne,* op. cit, p. 141.

[59] Rolande Gadille, *Le Vignoble de la Côte Bourguignone*, pp. 192, 380.

[60] Emile Turpin, *Les Vignes et Les Vins du Berry* (Bourges, Paris, 1907), p. 325.

[61] Emile Turpin, *Les Vignes et Les Vins du Berry,* op. cit., p. 331.

[62] In 1448 the Seigneurie of Menetou-Salon, including the château and its extensive vineyards, was purchased by a highly successful local merchant, Jacques Coeur. It is claimed that both red and white wine was produced, and may have been provided to the court in Paris. Although the wine appears to have been well regarded, there is no reliable evidence on its nature, let alone which cépages were grown.

[63] Statistics for the area of the Cher, which includes Sancerre and the surrounding appellations, showed 12,000 ha in 1820, 18,000 ha in 1882, and 7,000 ha by 1947 (Paul Mauron, *La Vigne Et Le Vin En Berry Du Cher*, Tardy, Bourges, 1946, p. 11).

[64] But there is no evidence what grape varieties they may have cultivated.

[65] In 1498, red wine was 7 schillings compared to white wine's 6 schillings (L'Alsace, *Les vignerons et leur vins dans l'ancien Rouffach,* September 24, 1966).

[66] Raymond Dumay, *Le Vin d'Alsace* (Edition Montalba, Paris, 1978), p. 80.

[67] Claude Muller, *Les Vins d'Alsace, Histoire d'un vignoble.* (Editions Coprur, Strasbourg, 1999), p. 47.

[68] Claude Muller, *Les Vins d'Alsace,* op. cit., p. 24.

[69] Out of a total 6,238 ha in the Bas-Rhin (stretching from Strasbourg to Colmar) in 1968, among quality varieties there were only 568 ha Gewürztraminer, 394 ha Riesling, 191 ha Pinot Blanc, 124 ha Pinot Gris, and 64 ha Pinot Noir (*Le Vignoble Français d'après le Cadastre Viticole. Evolution de 1958 à 1968*, Ministère de l'Agriculture, Paris, 1971).

[70] Today the local cooperative, the Cave de Cléebourg, makes about five cuvées from some 17 hectares, but all at the cheapest end of the market (€4-10 per bottle).

[71] Total plantings of Pinot Noir are 708 ha and 865 ha in the Bas-Rhin and Haut-Rhin, out of total plantings of 6,941 ha and 9,180 ha respectively (ONIVINS, *Les cépages noirs dans le vignoble* and *Les cépages blanc dans le vignoble,* 2008).

[72] Tom Scott, *Medieval Viticulture in the German-speaking Lands* (German History, 20, 95-115, 2002), pp. 100-101.

[73] Friedrich Bassermann- Jordan, *Die Geschichte des Weinbaus* (Verlags-Anstalt, Frankfurt, 1907), p. 68.

[74] Heinrich Meinhard, *The Wines of Germany* (Stein & Day, New York, 1976).

[75] Ann-Dominique Zufferey-Périsset, *Histoire de la Vigne et du Vin en Valais* (Musée Valaisan de la Vigne et du Vin, Sierre-Salquenen, Switzerland, 2010), p. 522.

[76] Haeger, *North American Pinot Noir,* p. 38.

[77] Pinot Noir was not even mentioned in the statistics of grape varieties grown in California in the nineteenth century.

[78] Haeger, *North American Pinot Noir,* p. 45.

[79] I suspect this may be because it has a mutator gene, that is, a gene whose action increases the rate of mutation at other genes.

[80] Interview at Louis Latour, May 2011.

[81] A current project in Burgundy aims to characterize the genetics of different clones of Pinot Noir and Chardonnay. This involves Le Centre Régional pour l' Innovation et le Transfert de Technologies "Agro-Environnement" de Dijon (CRITT).

[82] In parallel, another organization, la Coordination des Recherches sur Chardonnay et Pinot Noir en Bourgogne (CRECEP), aims to establish a library of 2-3,000 clones of Pinot Noir and Chardonnay.

[83] *Catalogue des variétés et des clones de vigne cultivées en France,* 2nd edition, ENTAV, 2007.

[84] Interview at Felton Road, March 2011.

[85] Interview at Domaine Ponsot, June 2010.

[86] The domain can't produce them any longer since it is not registered as a nursery.

[87] An open letter to U.S. Pinot producers, Burghound newsletter, 2008.

[88] Peay Vineyards newsletter, Spring 2009.

[89] Both clones were imported by Dr. Harold Olmo of the University of California, Davis, who did much to develop Pinot Noir clones for California (FPS grape program newsletter, October 2003).

[90] Photograph taken August 19, 2010 at Rech in the Ahr Valley.

[91] Interview at the ATVB, June 2010.

[92] See Chapter 5.

[93] Jean Michel Menant has one clone under development that gives low yields and has low alcohol, which may be useful to compensate for global warming, but he is concerned that climate warming is proceeding faster than the 20-year cycle for developing new clones. (Interview at ATVB, June 2010.)

[94] L'Association pour la Sauvegarde de la Diversité des Cépages de Bourgogne was created in 2008.

[95] Interview at Maison Louis Latour, May 2011.

[96] Pinot Droit is probably also the origin of the so called "Gamay Beaujolais" grown in California, which in spite of its name is really an upright-growing form of Pinot Noir. It is better liked in California than it was in Burgundy (see Chapter 5).

[97] The cause is unknown. It's claimed by the Institute at Geisenheim that it is a mutation affecting ripening, and that flavor compounds are more or less identical, but the acidity is 2-3 g/l liter less (personal communication from Prof. Dr. Ernst Ruehl, September 2010). However, the Geisenheim Institute has been unable to provide any evidence to substantiate the basis for the change, and I have been unable to find any other supporting evidence.

[98] The genetic map is shared with two other varieties, Pinot Mouré and Pinot fin teinturier (which has colored juice).

[99] The same genetic change is responsible for lack of color in most white strains. The change is not in the genes actually coding for the enzymes that produce anthocyanins, but in regulatory genes that control expression of the anthocyanin genes. There are two (very similar) regulator genes, either of which can turn on anthocyanin synthesis. Both of them are inactivated in white grapevines. The two mutations (a different one in each regulator gene) are identical in 55 different cultivars, including Pinot Blanc (Amanda R. Walker, *White Grapes Arose Through The Mutation Of Two Similar And Adjacent Regulatory Genes,* The Plant Journal, 49, 772-785, 2007).

[100] According to Pierre Gouges, examination at the University of Montpellier showed that the only change in the Blanc strain from the Pinot Noir is in the color of the skin (personal communication, October 2009).

[101] It turns out that this results from a single genetic difference in the pathway for producing giberellic acid, a plant hormone that controls growth. The result is that the cells don't respond to the hormone (Paul K. Boss & Mark R. Thomas, *Association of dwarfism and floral induction with a grape 'green revolution' mutation,* Nature, 416, 847-850, 2002).

[102] A somatic mutation changes the properties of a cell in the plant and affects all its descendants in the plant tissue, but it does not affect the genetics of progeny generated from seeds. So it can be propagated only by cuttings.

[103] S. Hocquigny, *Diversification within grapevine cultivars goes through chimeric states* (Genome 47, 579–589, 2004).

[104] Data sources: Burgundy - ONIVINS 2009; Germany - German Wein Statistik 2009; Yarra Valley - Yarra Valley Wine Growers Association, 2010; Oregon - NASS Oregon Vineyard and Winery Report, 2009; New Zealand winegrowers statistical annual, 2009.

[105] France 27,900 ha (11,650 ha in Champagne and 10,040 ha in Burgundy); United States, 13,880 ha (3,991 ha in Oregon and 9,889 ha in California); Germany 11,371 ha; New Zealand, 4,650 ha; Switzerland 4,659 ha; Australia, 4,208 ha; Italy, 3,287 ha; South America, 2,848 ha (1,433 ha in Argentina and 1,412 ha in Chile). Data sources for plantings of varieties in individual countries are: ONIVINS (Les Principaux Cépages De Cuve / Departements Principaux : Blancs, Noirs); California Department of Food and Agriculture, Sacramento (California Grape Acreage Reports); NASS Oregon Vineyard and Winery Report; Deutscher Wein Statistik (Deutsche Wein Institut); New Zealand winegrowers statistical annual, 2009; Australian Bureau of Statistics (Annual Reports 1329.0); Argentine Instituto Nacional de Vitivinicultura (Registro de Vinedos y Superficie), Catastro Viticola Nacional, Chile; SAWIS (South Africa Wine Industry Information and Systems; Statistics of Wine Grapes). Data from 2007 and 2008.

[106] Production of Pinot Noir, and its proportion of total production in each region, was:

	annual production (million cases)	percent of all production
Burgundy	5.4	32%
Baden	4.5	30%
Oregon	1.3	55%
New Zealand	3.3	14%

Data sources: BIVB 2009, Statistisches Bundesamt, NASS Oregon Vineyard and Winery Report, 2009; New Zealand winegrowers statistical annual, 2009.

[107] Data from annual reports of the BIVB (*Chiffres-clés de la Bourgogne Viticole*), USDA, NASS Oregon Field Office (*Oregon Vineyard and Winery Report*), and New Zealand Winegrowers (*Statistical Annual*). Production for Oregon and New Zealand has been converted from tons to hectoliters.

[108] The Côte d'Or produces about 59% of Burgundy's Pinot Noir; most of the rest comes from the Département immediately to the south, Saône-et-Loire (ONIVINS, Les Principaux Cépages De Cuve, 2009; ONIVINS, 2009).

[109] This is about 15% of all Bordeaux's production (CIVB, Récolte de la Gironde).

[110] More than a third from New Zealand, less than 26,000 cases from Oregon. Data sources: see note 106.

[111] Benjamin Lewin, *What Price Bordeaux?*, Vendange Press, Dover, 2009, p. 33.

[112] Interview at Thomas Fogarty, February 2011.

[113] Anthony Hanson, *Burgundy, 2nd edition* (Faber & Faber, London, 1995), p. 113.

[114] "[Grapes] are taken up in baskets, with interstices wide enough to allow the grapes to pass through, when a portion of the stalks, generally about two thirds, are taken out" (James Busby, *A treatise on the culture of the vine and the art of making wine, compiled from the works of Chaptal and other French writers ; and from the notes of the compiler during a residence in some of the wine provinces of France*, R. Howe, Government Printer, Australia, 1825), p.118.

[115] Camille Rodier, *Le vin de Bourgogne*, p. 90.

[116] Louis Ferré, *Traité d'Oenologie Bourguignonne* (INAO, Paris, 1958), p. 79.

[117] Camille Rodier, *Le vin de Bourgogne*, p. 96.

[118] Louis Ferré, *Traité d'Oenologie Bourguignonne* (INAO, Paris, 1958).

[119] Personal communication from Aubert de Villaine at Domaine de la Romanée Conti, April 2011.

Chapter 2: A Thousand Years of Burgundy

[1] As shown by discoveries of Roman amphorae in the region.

[2] Roger Dion, *Histoire de la Vigne*, p. 120.

[3] Following a detailed discussion of different pitch and resins, Pliny commented that "the pitch most highly esteemed in Italy for preparing vessels for storing wine is that which comes from Bruttium. It is made from the resin that distils from the pitch-tree; that which is used in Spain is held in but little esteem, being the product of the wild pine" (*The Natural History Of Pliny*, Volume 3, edited John Bostock and H. T. Riley, Kessinger Publishing, p. 267).

[4] Roger Dion, *Histoire de la Vigne*, p. 137.

[5] Roger Dion, *Histoire de la Vigne*, p. 147.

[6] Loïc Abric, *Le Vin de Bourgogne aux XIX Siècle* (Editions de l'Armançon, Précy-sous-Thil, 1993), p. 21; Emile Thévenot, *Les Origines du vignoble bourguignon* (Annales de Bourgogne, 23, 253-266, 1951).

[7] CNRS (Délégation Paris Michel-Ange) *Burgundy Wine Has Long History In France: Remains Of Gallo-Roman Vineyard Discovered In Gevrey-Chambertin. ScienceDaily, March 16, 2009.* Retrieved September 9, 2010, from http://www.sciencedaily.com/releases/2009/03/090310084846.htm

[8] A tomb discovered in 1953 at Mont Lassois near Vix had a large number of Iron Age artefacts including a bronze wine jug of Etruscan origin. It's unknown how the objects reached this location. They are now on display at the Musée du Châtillonnais at Châtillon-sur-Seine. Many Roman artefacts have been discovered in the Burgundy region; the wine jug illustrated here was discovered in a dig in Lyon (Tony Silvino, *Lyon. La fouille du Parc Saint-Georges : le mobilier céramique de l'Antiquité tardive,* Revue Archéologique de l'Est, 56, 187-230, 2007).

[9] The speech was given by a well known local orator and is known as either the Discours de Eumenin or the Panégyrique de Constantin.

[10] Roger Dion, *Histoire de la Vigne*, pp. 142-143.

[11] "Quiconque aura planté une vigne dans un champe en friche, sans que nul ne s'y soit opposé, en restera propriétaire" (quoted in Jean-François Bazin, *Histoire du vin de Bourgogne*, p. 11).

[12] Côte d'Or has two meanings. Describing wine production, it most often refers specifically to the narrow strip of land running from Dijon to the south of Beaune. But the term also describes one of the Départements (political and administrative units) of France. Official statistics for wine production for the Côte d'Or refer to the whole Département. Burgundy, in the sense of what can be included in Bourgogne AOC, covers four Départements: Côte d'Or, Saône-et-Loire (including the Côte Chalonnaise), Yonne (including Chablis), and Nièvre (no significant vineyards).

[13] See Chapter 1.

[14] J. Lavalle, *Histoire et Statistique de la Vigne*, p. 12.

[15] Denis Morelot, *Statistique de la Vigne*, p. 153.

[16] Jean-François Bazin, *Histoire du vin de Bourgogne,* pp. 12-13.

[17] Jean-François Bazin, *Histoire du vin de Bourgogne*, p. 14.

[18] Before the twelfth century, *vin français* described wine made in a large region centered on the Ile-de-France (around Paris), but extending widely to Orléans in the west and Burgundy in the east (Marcel Lachiver, *Vins, Vignes et Vignerons*, p. 62).

[19] Initially the wines of Beaune were relatively rare in Paris, because of the high costs of transport. But by 1337, the tax on wine from Beaune was 5 sous compared with 2 sous for Auxerre, suggesting that by then Beaune had acquired the greater reputation. local wines from the Île de France were taxed only at 1/3 sou (Béatrice Bourély, *Vignes et Vins de L'Abbaye de Citeaux, op. cit.*, pp. 92, 109).

[20] Roger Dion, *Histoire de la Vigne*, p 286.

[21] Béatrice Bourély, *Vignes et Vins de L'Abbaye de Citeaux, op. cit.*, p. 108.

[22] Jean-François Bazin, *Histoire du vin de Bourgogne,* p. 17.

[23] Loïc Abric, *Le Vin de Bourgogne,* op. cit., p. 22.

[24] Denis Morelot, *Statistique de la Vigne,* p. 158.

[25] From Claude Arnoux, *Dissertation sur la situation de Bourgogne, sur les vins qu'elle produit* (S. Jallasson, London, 1728).

[26] Reds and whites were equally well regarded. Those of Clos Vougeot sold for the same price in the seventeenth and eighteenth centuries (J. Lavalle, *Histoire et Statistique de la Vigne*, pp. 55, 119, 154).

[27] J. Lavalle, *Histoire et Statistique de la Vigne*, pp. 119, 154.

[28] Gamay was 22,805 ha and Pinot Noir was 3,661 ha in 1828 (Denis Morelot, *Statistique de la Vigne*, p. 134).

[29] J. Lavalle, *Histoire et Statistique de la Vigne*, p. 79.

[30] J. Lavalle, *Histoire et Statistique de la Vigne*, p. 121.

[31] Denis Morelot, *Statistique de la Vigne*, pp. 38-134.

[32] One formula was to improve finesse by including 5% of Chardonnay and 2% of Pinot Gris (Apollinaire Bouchardat, *Etudes sur les produits des cépages de la Bourgogne*, Chamerot, Paris, 1846).

[33] Rolande Gadille, *Le Vignoble de la Côte Bourguignone*, p. 162.

[34] Abbé Tainturier, *Remarques sur la culture des vignes de Beaune et lieux circonvoisins* (Editions de l'Armançon (2000), Précy-sous-Thil, 1763).

[35] Richard Olney, *Romanée Conti* (Rizzoli, New York, 1995), pp. 96-97.

[36] Jean-Jacques Lausseure, *Les grands vins de table*, Paris, 1850.

[37] J. Lavalle, *Histoire et Statistique de la Vigne,* p. 30.

[38] A. Bouchardat, *Etudes sur les produits des cépages de la Bourgogne,* Paris, 1946.

[39] And it went on to add that, "Yields of Pinot are low: 15 to 20 hl/ha in the grand crus; when production is increased, the quality declines" (*Statistique Agricole De La France, Annexe A L' enquête De 1929. Département de la Côte d'Or,* Ministère de l'Agriculture, Paris, 1937, p. 131).

[40] Camille Rodier, *Le Clos de Vougeot, 3rd edition* (Librairie Venot, Dijon, 1949: Laffitte Reprints, Marseille 1980), p. 132.

[41] Interview on the Côte d'Or, June 2008.

[42] Denis Morelot, *Statistique de la Vigne,* p. 164.

[43] Rolande Gadille, *Le Vignoble de la Côte Bourguignone,* p. 162.

[44] Dom Denise, *Les Vignes et Les Vins de Bourgogne* (Terres en Vues, Clemency, 2009), p. 25.

[45] Soils in Europe are generally more calcareous than in North America, restricting the choice of rootstocks, but the most suitable rootstocks for limestone soils would not grow well in the cool northern conditions of Burgundy. The most common rootstock was 3309 Couderc, a cross between Vitis riparia and Vitis rupestris, which has low to moderate vigor. This was 70% of rootstocks until 1934 (Rolande Gadille, *Le Vignoble de la Côte Bourguignone,* p. 173).

[46] As a result of the replanting, there was no Romanée Conti from 1946 to 1951; the first vintage from the young, grafted vines was 1952 (Richard Olney, *Romanée Conti,* Rizzoli, New York, 1995, p. 83).

[47] Rolande Gadille, *Le Vignoble de la Côte Bourguignone,* p. 172.

[48] The overall decline in planted areas was 12%, but it was only 2% in the Côte d'Or (Robert Laurent, *Les vignerons de la "Côte d'Or" au XIXe siècle,* Société Les Belles Lettres, Publications de l'Université de Dijon, Publications de l'Université de Dijon, Paris, 1958, tome I, p. 360).

[49] Hybrid varieties are crosses between Vitis vinifera and other species of Vitis that are resistant to phylloxera. But they usually retain the "foxy" quality that spoils grapes and wine made from the other species. In 1958, there were still more than 1000 ha on the Côte d'Or of the hybrids Plantet, Oberlin, Baco Noir, and Maréchal Foch, not to mention another 1000 ha merely described as "other" (Ministère de l'Agriculture, *Le Vignoble Français d'après le Cadastre Viticole. Evolution de 1958 à 1968,* Ministère de l'Agriculture, Paris, 1971).

[50] Interview at Domaine Ponsot, June 2010.

[51] Mont Luisants was planted in 1911 with Aligoté when William Ponsot replanted the vineyard. Laurent took out the Pinot Blanc and Chardonnay that his father and grandfather had planted in the 60s and 70s. This is legal because Aligoté was actually the variety planted in the vineyards when they were classified as premier cru in 1935 (discussion with Laurent Ponsot, June 2010).

[52] Rolande Gadille, *Le Vignoble de la Côte Bourguignone,* p. 183.

[53] Chaptal believed that "alcohol is the essential characteristic of wine," and that the problem with current wines was their low alcohol levels. His book on wine production recommended addition of sugar to a level of 5-10% of the weight of the must (the recommended dose was 15-20 livres of sugar per muid [456 liters]), and went through several editions (Jean-Antoine Chaptal, *L'Art de Faire le Vin,* Bouchard-Huzard, Paris, 1801, 1807, 1839).

[54] Denis Morelot, *Statistique de la Vigne,* p. 250.

[55] Camille Rodier, *Le vin de Bourgogne,* p. 91.

[56] Harry W. Paul, *Science, Vine, and Wine in Modern France* (Cambridge University Press, Cambridge, 1996), p. 130.

[57] Christopher Fielden, *Is This the Wine You Ordered, Sir?: The Dark Side of the Wine Trade* (Christopher Helm, London, 1989), pp. 67-68.

[58] J. Lavalle, *Histoire et Statistique de la Vigne,* p. 227.

[59] Jean-Alexandre Cavoleau, *Oenologie Française, ou statistique de tous les vignobles et de toutes les boissons vineuses et spiritueuses de la France, suivie de considérations générales sur la culture de la vigne* (Huzard, Paris, 1827).

[60] John Livingstone-Learmonth, *The Wines of the Rhône,* p. 328.

[61] Jean-François Bazin, *Histoire du vin de Bourgogne,* p. 59.

[62] Data from ONIVINS, 2009.

[63] This is not necessarily typical of other appellations, because there is a tradition of growing Aligoté in the Charlemagne part of Corton that goes back at least to the 1930s (Camille Rodier, *Le vin de Bourgogne,* p. 209). Indeed, a judgment in 1930 affirmed the right to produce Corton Charlemagne from Aligoté (Jean-François Bazin, *Histoire du Département de la Côte-d'Or,* Jean-Paul Gisserot, Paris, 2004, p. 56).

[64] Interview with winemaker on the Côte des Nuits, June 2010.

[65] It has a minimum of one third Pinot Noir and a maximum of two thirds Gamay. It can be either red or rosé.

[66] Data sources: Denis Morelot, *Statistique de la Vigne*, p. 134; J. Lavalle, *Histoire et Statistique de la Vigne*, p. 73; Ministère de l'Agriculture, *Le Vignoble Français d'après le Cadastre Viticole. Evolution de 1958 à 1968* (Ministère de l'Agriculture, Paris, 1971); Peyre, *Le Vignoble de Bourgogne. La question des appellations* (Les Etudes Rhodaniennes, 11, 89-97, 1935); Robert Laurent, *Les vignerons de la Côte d'Or au XIXe siècle* (Société Les Belles Lettres, Publications de l'Université de Dijon, Paris, 1958), tome II, p. 128; ONIVINS, *Les cépages noirs en le vignoble*, 2009.

[67] François Legouy, *La renaissance du vignoble des Hautes-Côtes de Beaune et des Hautes-Côtes de Nuits* (Annales de Géographie, 109, 459-472, 2000).

[68] In 1949, the oldest year for which AOC records are available, the 4,895 ha of AOC vineyards were about half of total plantings of just over 9,000 ha. By 2010, AOC vineyards accounted for 9,500 ha out of 9,700 total plantings. (Data for the Departément from Marcel Lachiver, *Vins, Vignes et Vignerons*, pp. 592-603; data since 1980 from CRINAO; data for AOC from *Pierre Galet, Cépages et Vignobles de France*, Tome III, Volume 1, 2nd edition, Lavoisier, Paris, 2004, and BIVB.)

[69] Quoted by Jancis Robinson, *Bust-up in Burgundy*, jancisrobinson.com, July 8, 2009.

[70] If labeled simply Bourgogne, it must have less than 30% Gamay. To be labeled Pinot Noir requires at least 85% of the variety. Basically the change in the law means that a wine labeled Bourgogne can no longer be made principally from Gamay. The appellation Bourgogne Grand Ordinaire will be replaced by Côteaux Bourguignons, which can be used by any red Beaujolais.

[71] This is a common story all over France. The AOC has grown from less than 10% of all vineyards at its inception in 1935 to almost 60% today (Lewin, *Wine Myths and Reality*, p. 391).

[72] Jean-François Bazin, *Histoire du vin de Bourgogne*, p. 33.

[73] The Hospice owns 61 hectares, mostly premier and grand crus.

[74] This photograph comes from Puy-de-Dome, around 1909.

[75] Private buyers are now more than one third, and have increased roughly five percentage points each year since Christies took over in 2005 (personal communication, Emmanuelle Vidal-Delagneau, Christies, November 2010).

[76] At the 2010 auction, Asian buyers overtook the U.S. to become the second most significant purchasers, with 12.5% of total sales (Guy Woodward, *Record prices paid at Hospices de Beaune*, Decanter online, November 22, 2010). The effect was particularly significant at the top level, with 5 of the 10 most expensive lots being sold to private individuals (Christies report, November 2010).

[77] In fact, my research on prices at the Hospices suggests that the average prices have never had more than a passing relationship with quality of the vintage, but turn up and down more in line with the general economy.

[78] Quoted in Guy Woodward, *Record prices paid at Hospices de Beaune*, Decanter online, November 22, 2010.

[79] Allen D. Meadows, *The Pearl of the Cote*, p. 66.

[80] *Statistique Agricole De La France, Annexe A L' enquête De 1929. Département de la Côte d'Or* (Ministère de l'Agriculture, Paris, 1937), p. 144.

[81] Source: *Statistique Agricole De La France, Annexe A L'enquete De 1929. Département de la Côte d'Or* (Ministère de l'Agriculture, Paris, 1937).

[82] Jean-François Bazin, *Histoire du vin de Bourgogne*, p. 29.

[83] This was by no means a unique situation. For example, in the late nineteenth and early twentieth centuries, wines produced in Napa were largely sold to merchants in San Francisco, who sold it under their own names rather than those of the growers (Charles L. Sullivan, *Napa Wine: A History from Mission Days to Present*, Wine Appreciation Guild, San Francisco, 1995, p. 107).

[84] Gilles Laferté, *La Bourgogne et ses vins: image d'origine contrôlée* (Belin, Paris, 2006), p. 22.

[85] Laferté, *La Bourgogne*, op. cit., p. 51.

[86] The negociants stated their position by saying that they "corrected wines that were healthy, but imperfect, by controlling the course of their development. They could not accept the law of 1919 which relied on the origin of a wine instead of its basic quality" (Olivier Jacquet, *Un Siècle de construction du vignoble bourguignon*, Editions Universitaires de Dijon, Dijon, 2009, p. 169).

[87] Quoted in Allen D. Meadows, *The Pearl of the Cote*, p. 33.

[88] Gaston Roupnel, *La crise du Vin*, Dépêche de Toulouse, November 2, 1922.

[89] Anthony Hanson, *Burgundy, 1st edition* (Faber & Faber, London, 1982), p. 132.

[90] Anthony Hanson, *Burgundy, 1st edition*, op. cit., p 130.

[91] Hectares owned and total production by the leading producers in the Côte d'Or.

Producer	Village	Premier	Grand
Louis Jadot	75	75	
Bouchard Père	12	74	12
Louis Latour	48	15	27
Faiveley	37	16.5	10.5
Joseph Drouhin	32	19	4
Domaine de la Vougeraie	20	8	4
Patriarche	10	?	

Information provided by the producers.

[92] Historic data from Rolande Gadille, *Le Vignoble de la Côte Bourguignone*, p. 364.

[93] Conseil Général de Côte d'Or, www.cotedor.fr, August 2010.

[94] The figures are a little biased by the inclusion of people who own vines but do not produce wine professionally. Of today's 5,117 producers, only 3,842 are officially classified as professional (Agreste Bourgogne, *Mémento de la statistique agricole*, 2009).

[95] Interview at Domaine Dujac, June 2010.

[96] The proportion of growers under 40 declined from 35% in 2000 to 22% in 2007, possibly a worrying sign for the region (Agreste Bourgogne, *Mémento de la statistique agricole*, 2009).

[97] Interview in Beaune, June 2010.

[98] Interview in Beaune, June 2010.

[99] Rolande Gadille, *Le Vignoble de la Côte Bourguignone*, p. 194.

[100] J. Lavalle, *Histoire et Statistique de la Vigne*, p. 100.

[101] J. Lavalle, *Histoire et Statistique de la Vigne*, p. 55.

[102] Appellations are given by the names used in 1910; uncertainty in identifying exactly which modern appellations correspond to some of the old categories may be responsible for some of the variation. Prices for the 1600s are taken from J. Lavalle, *Histoire et Statistique de la Vigne*, p. 55. Prices for 1820-1829 are averages for the decade calculated from the original data reported by Loïc Abric, *Le Vin de Bourgogne aux XIX Sièele,* (Editions de l'Armançon, Précy-sous-Thil, 1993), pp. 30-49. The range was from around 160 francs per pièce (228 liters) for Santenay to 400 francs per pièce for Romanée or Chambertin. Prices for 1910-1919 are averages for the decade as seen on the negociant market, ranging from Ff 1894 for Chambertin to Ff 536 for Monthélie (presumably per tonneau or equivalent unit) calculated from the data reported by Gilles Laferté, *La Bourgogne et ses vins: image d'origine contrôlée* (Belin, Paris, 2006), p. 263. Current prices are based on retail prices for the period 2002-2007 as determined by the author's survey of leading merchants in the U.S., U.K, and France. They range from $23 per bottle for Santenay to over $300 average per bottle for Chambertin, and as much as $10,000 for Romanée Conti (2005 vintage).

[103] Land prices in 1791 were:

Vineyard	livres/ouvrée
Les St. Georges	892
Les Chambertins	777
Vignes de Volnay	644
Clos Vougeot	616
Romanée St. Vivant	583
Les Richebourgs	501
Vignes de Pommard	494
Clos de Tart	415
Vignes de Nuits	350
Clos de la Bussière	224

Data from Amédée Vialay, *La Vente des Biens Nationaux pendant la Révolution Française* (Perrin et cie, Paris, 1908), pp. 134-135.

[104] Gilles Laferté, *La Bourgogne et ses vins: image d'origine contrôlée* (Belin, Paris, 2006), p. 23.

[105] One of the first public discussions was in a book published in 1726, which specifically mentioned Champan in Volnay, Comaraine in Pommard, Grèves and Clos du Roi in Beaune, Vougeot and Chambertin in Côte de Nuits (Claude Arnoux, *Dissertation sur la situation de Bourgogne, sur les vins qu'elle produit*, S. Jallasson, London, 1728).

[106] Robert Laurent, *Les vignerons de la Côte d'Or au XIXe siècle* (Société Les Belles Lettres, Publications de l'Université de Dijon, Paris, 1958), tome II, p. 37.

[107] The cadastral plan of 1860 was followed with some modifications reflecting changes in regulations that had been passed between 1920 and 1936 (Gilles Laferté, *La Bourgogne et ses vins: image d'origine contrôlée*, Belin, Paris, 2006, p. 63).

[108] The average for 1810-1875 showed Chambertin just ahead of Romanée: Chambertin 528 Ff, Romanée 523 Ff, Richebourg 481 Ff, Corton 416 Ff, Vosne 387 Ff, Nuits 383 Ff (Abric, *Le Vin de Bourgogne,* op. cit., p. 49).

[109] Benjamin Lewin*, What Price Bordeaux?,* Vendange Press, 2009, p. 154.

[110] Joseph Capus, *L'Evolution de la Législation sur les Appellations d'Origine. Genèse des appellations contrôlées*, INAO, Paris, 1947.

[111] In France as a whole, the AOC has expanded from 14% of production in 1942 to 44% in 2005. In terms of vineyards, AOC has increased from 12% in 1950 to 60% today. In the Côte d'Or, AOC is today close to 100% of all vineyards. Sources: Capus, op. cit; ONIVINS, *Superficie et récolte revendiquées pour la campagne 2005-2006*; Lewin, *Wine Myths and Reality*, p. 392.

[112] Giving an exact number for grand and premier crus is a little tricky because of the use of overlapping names.

[113] Clive Coates, *Côte d'Or: A Celebration of the Great Wines of Burgundy* (University of California Press, Berkeley, 1997), p. 114.

[114] Approximately half of all producers' holdings are in individual family names in the Côte d'Or as a whole (Agreste Bourgogne, *Mémento de la statistique agricole*, 2009).

[115] Clive Coates, *The Wines of Burgundy*, p. 18.

[116] Average production figures for the 2008 harvest according to the BIVB.

[117] Quoted in Jordan Ross, *Balancing Quality & Yield: Impact Of Vine Age, Clone, And Vine Density*, Practical Winery and Vineyard, November, 1999.

[118] Data from Coates, *The Wines of Burgundy*, p. 835, updated from the BIVB.

[119] BIVB.

[120] Between 1990 and 1996, only two years fell outside a range of 38-44 hl/ha (1990 at 50 hl/ha and 2003 at 29.5 hl/ha).

[121] Clive Coates, *The Wines of Burgundy*, pp. 18-19.

[122] Benjamin Lewin, *Wine Myths and Reality*, p. 373.

[123] Data source: INAO.

[124] The number of grapes per bunch has also increased, by about 30%. The trend is similar for Pinot Noir and Chardonnay in all regions of Burgundy (Christine Monamy & Eve Gueydon, *Changement Climatique : Des Évolutions Déjà Perceptibles Sur Le Vignoble Bourguignon,* BIVB, UNESCO poster, March 2007).

[125] Clive Coates, *The Wines of Burgundy*, p. 825.

[126] Roger Dubrion, *Trois Siècles de Vendanges Bourguignon* (Editions Féret, Bordeaux, 2006), p. 63.

[127] Camille Rodier, *Le vin de Bourgogne,* p. 76.

[128] J. Lavalle, *Histoire et Statistique de la Vigne,* p. 190.

[129] J. Lavalle, *Histoire et Statistique de la Vigne,* p. 192.

[130] Each point on the graph shows the average temperature during April-September for the preceding ten year period. Data from the weather stations in Dijon and Merrimac according to the NASA Goddard weather center.

[131] Benjamin Lewin, *Wine Myths and Reality*, p. 84.

[132] Harvest dates became later during the mini-ice age around 1500, and then stayed stable, with the exception of a warmer period in the 17 century, until the past half-century (I. Chuine et al., *Grape Ripening As A Past Climate Indicator,* Nature, 432, 289-290, 2004).

[133] Benjamin Lewin, *Wine Myths and Reality*, p. 30.

[134] In the case of Burgundy, the increase resulting from later harvesting to obtain grapes with higher sugar is partially offset by avoiding the need to chaptalize. Even so, Burgundy is now found at up to 13.5% alcohol whereas the limit used to be more around 12.5%.

[135] The dates correspond to the official *ban des vendanges*, the date when it becomes legal to harvest. The graph has less significance after 2007 because since then the ban de vendange has been abandoned or relaxed; it may simply be declared early enough to allow vignerons free choice. Data from Roger Dubrion, *Trois Siècles de Vendanges Bourguignon* (Editions Féret, Bordeaux, 2006).

[136] Sugar production depends on heat and light, and up to a point of high temperature at which the grapevine shuts down (over 30°C), sugar production is more or less proportional to temperature.

Anthocyanin (color) production, which correlates with phenolic development, is more a function of time, and shows less dependence on temperature. Indeed, whereas sugar continues to increase between 20 °C and 30 °C, anthocyanins decrease.

[137] The corollary is that going back to the old system and determining harvest on the basis of the Brix (sugar level) or the sugar/acid ratio, would yield unripe grapes if a level was set equivalent to 12.5% or 13% alcohol.

[138] Abbé Tainturier, *Remarques sur la culture des vignes de Beaune et lieux circonvoisins* (Editions de l'Armançon (2000), Précy-sous-Thil, 1763).

[139] Dom Denise, *Les Vignes et Les Vins de Bourgogne* (Terres en Vues, Clemency, 2009), p. 35.

[140] Jacky Rigaux, *Ode Aux Grands Vins de Bourgogne* (Editions de l'Armançon, Précy-sous-Thil, 1997), p. 125.

[141] Jacky Rigaux, *Ode aux Grand Vins*, op cit., p. 20.

Chapter 3: The Quintessential Terroir Grape

[1] Interviews with winemakers, June 2010.

[2] Land in the major communes of the Côte d'Or is classified into village, premier cru, and grand cru, as follows (in hectares):

Commune	Vil-	Premier	Grand
Gevrey Chambertin	369	86	87
Morey St Denis	64	42	40
Chambolle Musigny	94	60	26
Vougeot	5	12	51
Vosne Romanée	105	58	75
Nuits St Georges	175	143	-
Aloxe Corton	90	38	160
Beaune	128	322	-
Pommard	212	125	-
Volnay	98	136	-
Meursault	305	132	-
Puligny Montrachet	114	100	33
Chassagne Montrachet	180	159	-
Total	1939	1412	471

[3] Charles Arnoult, representative from Dijon to the constitutional assembly, suggested Côte d'Or in preference to Département de Seine-et-Saône or Haute-Seine (Jean-François Bazin, *Histoire du vin de Bourgogne*, p. 41).

[4] Suggested by Richard Olney, *Romanée Conti* (Rizzoli, New York, 1995), p. 1.

[5] James Wilson, *Terroir* (Wine Appreciation Guild, San Francisco, 1998), p. 111.

[6] Jean-François Bazin, *Histoire du vin de Bourgogne*, p. 24.

[7] Jennifer M. Huggett, *Geology and Wine: a review* (Proc. Geologists' Assoc., 117, 239-247, 2006), p. 243.

[8] *Alexis Lichine's New Encyclopedia of Wines and Spirits* (Knopf, New York, 1977), p. 163.

[9] Quoted by Nick Passmore, *First-class white Burgundy at a second-class price*, Business Week, April 23, 2009.

[10] J. Lavalle, *Histoire et Statistique de la Vigne*, pp. 154-157.

[11] J. Lavalle, *Histoire et Statistique de la Vigne*, pp. 157-159.

[12] J. Lavalle, *Histoire et Statistique de la Vigne*, pp. 150-154.

[13] Interview at Maison Drouhin, June 2010.

[14] André Jullien, *Topographie de tous les vignobles connus* (Huzard, Paris, 1816), p. 110.

[15] J. Lavalle, *Histoire et Statistique de la Vigne*, p. 126.

[16] R. Danguy & Ch. Aubertin, *Les grands vins de Bourgogne* (H. Armand / Laffitte Reprints, Dijon, 1892), p. 304.

[17] White grapevines were increasingly planted over the first half of the twentieth century to reach the present levels by the times the AOC was introduced in 1936 (Camille Rodier, *Le vin de Bourgogne*).

[18] Clive Coates, *The Wines of Burgundy*, p. 181.

[19] Active limestone is defined formally as calcium carbonate extractable with ammonium oxalate. Its presence means that the soil has more exchangeable calcium and increased alkalinity (higher pH).

[20] Interview at Comte Armand, June 2011.

[21] Benjamin Lewin, *Breaking Ranks*, Decanter, July 2010, pp 48-51.

[22] Rolande Gadille, *Le Vignoble de la Côte Bourguignone*, p. 190.

[23] Numbers of premier and grand crus are:

Commune	premier crus	grand crus
Gevrey Chambertin	26	8
Morey St Denis	20	4
Chambolle Musigny	24	2
Vougeot	4	1
Flagey-Echézeaux/Vosne Romanée	14	2
Nuits St Georges	37	0

[24]   Quoted   by   Ola   Bergman   on   *Bergman's   Bourgogne,*   www.bourgogne-info.eu/html/domaine_jacques-frederic_mugnier.html, 2009, accessed August 2010.

[25] Interview at Domaine Mugnier, November 2010.

[26] Jean-François Bazin, *Chambertin* (Jacques Legrand, Paris, 1991), p. 92.

[27] Clive Coates, *The Wines of Burgundy*, p. 150.

[28] Discussion with Jean-Nicholas Méo, October 2010.

[29] Interview at Domaine Méo-Camuzet, May 2011.

[30] Interview at Domaine Arnoux-Lachaux, June 2011.

[31] "Il n'y a point à Vosne de vins communs" (Abbé Courtépée, *Description Générale et Particulière du Duché de Bourgogne*, Chez Frantin, 1775).

[32] But the vineyard was under contract, with the wines made by Bouchard Père until 2005, after which it reverted to Liger-Belair.

[33] La Grande Rue lies between La Tâche and Romanée Conti so there isn't much doubt about the potential quality of the land, although the general feeling is that the Lamarche wines have not been up to grand cru quality.

[34] Benjamin Lewin, *Breaking Ranks*, Decanter, July 2010, pp 48-51.

[35] This was a general practice in the era, so Dr. Morelot presumably meant it was more common in Chambolle Musigny than elsewhere. He commented that some producers were eliminating their white grapes, but said, "They will lose more than they gain." (Denis Morelot, *Statistique de la Vigne*, p. 30.)

[36] Béatrice Bourély, *Vignes et Vins de L'Abbaye de Cîteaux en Bourgogne* (Editions du Tastevin, Nuits St. Georges, 1998), p. 86.

[37] Béatrice Bourély, *Vignes et Vins de L'Abbaye de Cîteaux,* op. cit.

[38] Benoît Chauvin, *Le Clos et le Château de Vougeot* (Editions du Tastevin, Nuits St. Georges, 2008), p. 45.

[39] Béatrice Bourély, Vignes et Vins de L'Abbaye de Cîteaux, op. cit., p. 105.

[40] The holdings of the Church accounted for two thirds of the vineyards and other lands sold off following the Revolution (Jean-François Bazin, *Histoire du vin de Bourgogne*, p. 39).

[41] Jean-François Bazin, *Histoire du Département de la Côte-d'Or* (Jean-Paul Gisserot, Paris, 2004), p. 16.

[42] Béatrice Bourély, *Vignes et Vins de L'Abbaye de Cîteaux,* op. cit., p. 43.

[43] Béatrice Bourély, *Vignes et Vins de L'Abbaye de Cîteaux,* op. cit., p. 43.

[44] 1336 is the date of the last purchase of land that was included in the Clos, and is usually taken as the year when the wall was completed (Benoît Chauvin, *Le Clos et le Château de Vougeot,* op. cit., p. 93).

[45] Benoît Chauvin, *Le Clos et le Château de Vougeot,* op. cit., p. 91.

[46] A plan of 1719 shows the château essentially as it is today (Benoît Chauvin, *Le Clos et le Château de Vougeot,* op. cit., p. 108).

[47] The price was 1,140,600 livres, twice the estimate. The inventory was sold two weeks later for 56,300 livres (Benoît Chauvin, *Le Clos et le Château de Vougeot,* op. cit., p. 125).

[48] Benoît Chauvin, *Le Clos et le Château de Vougeot,* op. cit., p. 127.

[49] Benoît Chauvin, *Le Clos et le Château de Vougeot,* op. cit., p. 135.

[50] Allen D. Meadows, *The Pearl of the Cote*, pp. 5, 134.

[51] André Jullien, *Topographie de tous les vignobles connus* (Huzard, Paris, 1816), p. 129.

[52] The legend has since been transmogrified into saying that the top was reserved for the Pope, the middle for bishops, and the bottom for monks, but does not appear to have any factual basis. In fact, it

is not clear whether the monks actually vinified separate cuvées. There is also a story that a nineteenth century proprietor, Jules Ouvrard, tried making separate cuvées, and that in fact that from the bottom was preferred at a blind tasting (Jean-François Bazin, *Clos Vougeot,* Jacques Legrand, Paris, 1987, p. 80).

[53] Denis Morelot, *Statistique de la Vigne*, p. 25.

[54] "Undoubtedly all the parts are not the same; but if we follow this path, it will not be possible to stop with two divisions, but there should be at least 5 or 6" (quoted in Rolande Gadille, *Le Vignoble de la Côte Bourguignone*, p. 200).

[55] Personal communication.

[56] Allen D. Meadows, *The Pearl of the Cote*, pp. 105-107.

[57] Adapted from James Wilson, Terroir (Wine Appreciation Guild, San Francisco, 1998), p. 110.

[58] Jean-François Bazin, *Histoire du vin de Bourgogne*, pp. 62-63.

[59] Allen D. Meadows, *The Pearl of the Cote*, p. 96.

[60] The individual climats appear on the label, as in Corton-Bressandes or Corton-Clos du Roi. The total 160 ha of Corton also include a substantial area of 72 ha that can produce the white Corton Charlemagne.

[61] The concept of typicité dates from the nineteenth century. In mid nineteenth century, Lavalle classified the Côte d'Or into four quality levels, but the emphasis was more on defining quality than nuances of expression. One early reference, discussing a tasting of the wines of the Loire, said, "The jury respected the typicité of the wines, in censuring wines that were too oaky (resembling Bordeaux) or rosés that were too colored (recalling Provence) or reds that were too aromatic" (Genèses, vol. 54, Cahlmann-Levy, 1901).

[62] Jean-François Bazin, *Chambertin* (Jacques Legrand, Paris, 1991), p. 50.

[63] Benjamin Lewin, *Breaking Ranks*, Decanter, July 2010, pp 48-51.

[64] Chambertin (including Clos de Bèze) was rated Tête de Cuvée; Clos St. Jacques was rated first out of 10 Première Cuvées (J. Lavalle, *Histoire et Statistique de la Vigne*, p. 93).

[65] Jean-François Bazin, *Chambertin,* op. cit., p. 88.

[66] Armand Rousseau, 2.2 ha; Fourrier, 0.89 ha, Louis Jadot, 1.0 ha, Bruno Clair, 1.0 ha, Sylvie Esmonin, 1.6 ha.

[67] Jean-François Bazin, *Chambertin, op. cit.,* pp. 72, 86.

[68] Which explains Latricières Chambertin, Charmes Chambertin, Griotte Chambertin, Chapelle Chambertin, and Mazis Chambertin, but stretches a point for Mazoyères Chambertin and Ruchottes Chambertin.

[69] Jean-François Bazin, *Chambertin,* op. cit., p.. 95.

[70] Jean-François Bazin, *Chambertin,* op. cit., p.. 89.

[71] Interview at Domaine Rousseau, June 2011.

[72] Quoted in Jean-François Bazin, *Chambertin* (Jacques Legrand, Paris, 1991), p. 95.

[73] Interview at Domaine Damoy, May 2011.

[74] Interview at Domaine Damoy, May 2011.

[75] Roland Masse has been in charge of winemaking for the Hospices since 1999. He is converting the vineyards to organic viticulture. His policy for vinification is to destalk 75% of the grapes (depending on cuvée and vintage), to give four or five days cold soak before fermentation begins, then fermentation lasts 10-12 days at a maximum temperature of 32 °C, and there are usually two or three days maceration after fermentation (personal communication, December 2010).

[76] There are three different suppliers of oak coming from various French forests. Toasting levels are always moderate (personal communication from Rolande Masse, Régisseur, Hospices de Beaune, December 2010).

[77] Interviews with producers at their domains in November 2011.

[78] Emails from Dominique Laurent, February 2011.

[79] Interview with Jérôme Flous, November 2010.

[80] Areas in Burgundy are:

Area	Hectares
Côte d'Or	5,288
Hautes Côtes de Beaune & Nuits	4,402
Côte Chalonnaise	4,430
Mâconnais	6,920
Chablis	4,845

Data from BIVB, *Chiffres-clés de la Bourgogne Viticole*, 2008.

Chapter 4: Cool Northern Limits

[1] Data from ONIVINS, *Les cépages noirs en le vignoble*, 2009, and CICV, 2009.

[2] Historic temperatures give the average monthly temperature during the growing season for the twentieth century prior to 1990 (sources: GHCN version 1; NIWA, New Zealand). 21st century temperatures give the average for the first decade of the century (data sources: NASA GISS; NIWA, New Zealand; Universität zu Köln meterology). Data are taken from the weather station nearest to the vineyard locations.

[3] Each data point shows the average monthly temperature during the growing season (April through September) for the previous ten years for each region, taken from the weather stations at Dijon, Strasbourg, and Bourges (Data source: NASA GISS).

[4] Paul Mauron, *La Vigne Et Le Vin En Berry Du Cher* (Tardy, Bourges, 1946), p. 17.

[5] A comparison between 1958 and 1968 shows changes in plantings in the Départément of the Cher (in which Sancerre is the principal AOC) as follows:

	1958	*1968*	*(AOC) 2008*
Pinot Noir	103	178	888
Gamay	890	784	117
Sauvignon Blanc	928	959	2,914
All grapes	5,081	4,172	3,800

Data sources: 1958-1968, Ministère de l'Agriculture, *Le Vignoble Français d'après le Cadastre Viticole. Evolution de 1958 à 1968* (Ministère de l'Agriculture, Paris, 1971); 2008 figures are for AOC only from ONIVINS, *Les cepages noirs dans le vignoble* and *Les cepages blancs dans le vignoble.*

[6] Discussion at Domaine Lucien Crochet, June 2010.

[7] Discussion at Domaine Henri Bourgeois, June 2010.

[8] Discussion at Domaine Nicolas & Pascal Reverdy, June 2010.

[9] Discussion at Domaine Lucien Crochet, June 2010.

[10] Discussion at Domaine Vincent Pinard, June 2010.

[11] Heinrich Meinhard, *The Wines of Germany* (Stein & Day, New York, 1976).

[12] Quoted in Heinrich Meinhard, *The Wines of Germany,* op. cit..

[13] There are 10,700 hectares in Burgundy. Allowing for the fact that probably around a quarter of the German plantings are used for rosé or Sekt, total production of dry red wine in Germany is probably not much below that of Burgundy.

[14] Interview at Weingut Jean Stodden, August 2010.

[15] Data from the annual reports of Deutscher Wein Statistik, Deutscher Wein Institut. Per cent figures in the table show the proportion represented by Pinot Noir (Spätburgunder) in each region.

[16] Deutscher Wein Statistik, 2009.

[17] Interview at Oekonomierat Rebholz, August 2010.

[18] I wondered whether this might be due to a tendency to chaptalize at the end of fermentation (which stresses the yeasts and encourages formation of glycerin) but a survey of German winemakers in October 2010 showed a split between those who chaptalize at the beginning and those who add the sugar at the end. Most winemakers destem completely before fermentation, which reduces extraction of tannins and lets fruit show more overtly, and this may be a contributory factor.

[19] Interview at Philip Kuhn, August 2010.

[20] Topographic map from Google Earth.

[21] Interview at Weingut Jean Stodden, August 2010.

[22] The latitude of Ahrweiler is 50° 33'.

[23] Heinrich Meinhard, *The Wines of Germany*, op. cit., p. 244.

[24] He described Assmanshausen in the Rheingau as certainly the best, followed by Walporzheim from the Ahr (George Saintsbury, *Notes on a Cellar Book,* MacMillan, London, 3rd edition, 1931, p. 86).

[25] Ahr Winzer has 600 members, who farm 160 ha out of the 580 in the whole valley. Mayschoss Altenahr has 320 members who farm another 121 ha.

[26] Interview at Weingut Meyer-Näkel, August 2010.

[27] 359 ha in the Mosel, out of a total of 8,981 ha, compared with 342 in the Ahr out of a total of 552 ha (Deutscher Wein Institut Statistics, 2008.)

[28] Interview at Oekonomierat Rebholz, August 2010.

[29] Interview with Fritz Becker, August 2010.

[30] Exports from Burgundy to Germany fell from 7.3 million bottles in 2005 to 5.2 million bottles in 2009 (BIVB annual reports, 2006-2010).

[31] Interview at Weingut Joachim Heger, August 2010.

[32] A mere 24 ha in 1958 and 65 ha in 1968 of Pinot Noir in the Bas-Rhin, and 77 ha and 201 ha, respectively, in the Haut-Rhin (Ministère de l'Agriculture, *Le Vignoble Français d'après le Cadastre Viticole. Evolution de 1958 à 1968*, Ministère de l'Agriculture, Paris, 1971).

[33] Topographic background from Google Earth.

[34] Personal communication, August 2010.

[35] Production is 22% Crémant d'Alsace, 74% AOC Alsace, 4% Grand Cru d'Alsace (CIVA, 2008).

[36] Vineyards in the AOC have increased steadily, partly due to new plantings, partly due to incorporation of existing vineyards that were not previously included:

	Pinot Noir		*Alsace AOC*
1969	2.1%	198 ha	9,441 ha
1982	5.9%	711 ha	12,052 ha
1996	8.5%	1,220 ha	14,355 ha
2002	9.1%	1,368 ha	14,956 ha
2008	9.7%	1,509 ha	15,535 ha

[37] In 2009 there were 1,521 ha of Pinot Noir, giving a total production of 105,490 hl. This comprised 38,693 hl of Crémant d'Alsace (including 4,936 hl of Blanc de Noir), and 66,797 hl of Alsace AOC (including 55,917 hl of rosé and 10,880 hl of rouge). (Data from CIVA, October 2010).

[38] The level is increased to 75 hl/ha for rosé. The label requirements are that the wine can be labeled as "rouge" only below 60 hl/ha, but up to 75 hl/ha it can be labeled as Pinot Noir, which effectively means rosé (CIVA, 2010).

[39] Riesling, Pinot Gris, Gewürztraminer, and Muscat.

[40] Personal communication, August 2010.

[41] Interview with Etienne Hugel, October 2010.

[42] Personal communication, March 2010.

[43] Interview with Véronique Muré, October 2010.

[44] Interview with Catherine Faller, October 2010.

[45] Interview with André Ostertag, October 2010.

[46] Interview with Jean-Michel Deiss, October 2010.

[47] Alto Adige became part of the Hapsburg empire in the fourteenth century. It was ceded to Italy after the first world war.

[48] South Tyrolean Apple PGI, 2010.

[49] 5,122 ha in 2006 (Chamber of Commerce, Bolzano).

[50] About 86% of the total area of Alto Adige is above 1000 m and therefore unusable for agriculture. It is difficult for producers who want to expand their holdings, because there is little land for sale, and prices are disproportionate, at €600,000-800,000/ha vastly out of kilter with the price of wine. The shortage of land means that prices are essentially the same, whether the use is for housing, orchards, or vineyards. So producers who want to make more than is possible from their own vineyards must buy grapes. This is usually done by individual contracts, generally long-standing.

[51] Interview with Alois Lageder, October 2010.

[52] Schiava is 31% and Lagrein is another 7.7% of total production. However, Schiava has declined from 2,420 ha in 1996 to 1,450 ha in 2006 (Bolzano Chamber of Commerce, 2006).

[53] Pinot Nero is the most important of the international varieties, at 5.2% of production. Merlot is 4.2% and Cabernet Sauvignon is 2.8% (Bolzano Chamber of Commerce, 2006).

[54] In the past decade, average growing season temperature (April-September) was 19.7 °C in Bolzano compared with 16.0 °C in Dijon. Of course, Bolzano is a hot spot, protected by mountains on all sides, and the vineyards are somewhat cooler. Data from Wetterdienst, Servizio Meteorologico (Bolzano) and Dijon weather station (Nasa Goddard Center).

[55] Pinot Noir was 248 ha in 1006 and was 348 ha in 2006 (Bolzano Chamber of Commerce, 2006).

[56] Some sub areas are defined, but have little impact in the market. They are Lago di Caldaro (includes some areas in Trentino), Alto Adige Valle Isarco, Alto Adige Santa Maddalena (just north of Bolzano), Alto Adige Terlano (white wines from the Terlano area), Alto Adige Meranese (Schiava from the Merano area), Alto Adige Valle Venosta (in Valle d'Aosta), Valdadige and Alto Adige Colli di Bolzano.

[57] Interview with Martin Foradori Hofstätter, October 2010.

[58] The law specifies that if an estate ("hof") is stated on the label, all the grapes must come from that estate. This led to political controversy when the cooperatives removed "hof" from some of their more successful wines in order to expand production, effectively changing the former estate wines into brands.

[59] Interview with Alois Lageder, October 2010.

[60] Interview at Manincor, October 2010.

[61] Tasting of 2007 and 2008 vintages at the Bolzano Chamber of Commerce, October 2010.

[62] Pinot Noir is a total of 4,402 ha out of Switzerland's total of 14,820 ha. The Valais has 1,702 ha (Office Fédéral de l'Agriculture OFAG: L'année viticole, 2009).

[63] Office Fédéral de l'Agriculture OFAG: L'année viticole, 2009, pp 12-15.

[64] Graubunden Wein, 2009 (Postfach, 7302 Landquart).

[65] Interview with Thomas Studach, October 2010.

[66] Interview at Gantenbein, October 2010.

[67] Interview with Georg Fromm, October 2010.

[68] The Valais is the largest wine-producing region in Switzerland, with 5,092 ha out of a total of the country's 14,800 ha (Encyclopédie statistique de la Suisse, Administration fédérale, Confederation Suisse, 2009).

[69] The average elevation is higher than the Côte d'Or. Sion, at the center of the wine growing region in the Valais, is around 500 m elevation, whereas the mid-slope of the Côte d'Or is around 250 m.

[70] Pinot Noir (54%) and Gamay (23%) account for three quarters of the black grapes in the Valais. The most important others, in decreasing order of importance (none more than 0.5%) are Syrah, Humagne Rouge, Cornalin, Diolinoir, Merlot, and Gamaret (Ann-Dominique Zufferey-Périsset, *Histoire de la Vigne et du Vin en Valais*, Musée Valaisan de la Vigne et du Vin, Sierre-Salquenen, Switzerland, 2010, p. 545).

[71] Ann-Dominique Zufferey-Périsset, *Histoire de la Vigne et du Vin en Valais* (Musée Valaisan de la Vigne et du Vin, Sierre-Salquenen, Switzerland, 2010), p. 24.

[72] Ann-Dominique Zufferey-Périsset, *Histoire de la Vigne et du Vin en Valais,* op. cit., p. 19.

[73] Ann-Dominique Zufferey-Périsset, *Histoire de la Vigne et du Vin en Valais,* op. cit., p. 84.

[74] Ann-Dominique Zufferey-Périsset, *Histoire de la Vigne et du Vin en Valais,* op. cit., p. 522.

[75] Ann-Dominique Zufferey-Périsset, *Histoire de la Vigne et du Vin en Valais,* op. cit., p. 320.

[76] Ann-Dominique Zufferey-Périsset, *Histoire de la Vigne et du Vin en Valais,* op. cit., p. 448.

[77] Production of Dôle is up to 2.2 million cases per year, compared with around 500,000 cases of Bourgogne Passetoutgrains. The Valais' other major production is the white Chasselas, known locally as Fendant, around 1.1 million cases per year (Chambre Valaisanne d'agriculture, Rapport 2009).

[78] Legally it must contain at least 85% Pinot Noir and Gamay; the rest can come from other local varieties.

[79] The period in the cuve when the juice is in contact with the skin, including any maceration before fermentation, fermentation itself, and any post-fermentation maceration.

[80] There are no statistics on rosé per se, because official figures divide dry, still wines into red and rosé versus white.

[81] The best rosés are made by direct pressing, essentially using white winemaking methods with red grapes. To make the best rosé, grapes are harvested a little earlier than they would be for making a red wine, with less sugar and more acid. The grapes are pressed immediately, and the juice is kept in contact with the skins in the press for only a short time. This produces a delicate wine, with the freshness of a light white wine, but with just that very faint touch of additional structure, a barely perceptible taint of austerity, coming from skin extraction. A more common method for making rosé is saignée (literally: bleeding) where the grapes are harvested with red wine in mind, but the very first juice is run off to make a lightly colored wine; this decreases the ratio of liquid to skins, and therefore increases color and extraction in the remaining (red) wine. Since the real purpose of saignée is to increase the quality of the red wine, the rosé is more incidental and quality not usually as good.

[82] Regulations for Crémant require that at least 30% must be Pinot Noir, Pinot Gris, or Chardonnay; usually the major component is Aligoté.

[83] Crémant has increased from 4% to 8% of all production. White has increased from 56% to 59%. Red and rosé (which are not distinguished in official statistics) have declined from 39% to 33% (based on production figures from BIVB for the period 1990-2008).

[84] Driving up the autoroute from Beaune to Dijon, you pass the factory-like buildings of Louis Boillot, a major producer of Crémant now owned by Jean-Claude Boiset, which is comparable in size to a Champagne house.

[85] Benoît Musset, *Vignobles de Champagne et vins mousseux (1650-1830) : Histoire d'un mariage de raison* (Fayard, Paris, 2008), p. 255.

[86] Marcel Lachiver, *Vins, Vignes et Vignerons*, p. 272.

[87] Evolution of plantings over fifty years

	Pinot Noir		Pinot Meunier		Chardonnay		Total
1958	3,348	(30%)	5,116	(46%)	2,655	(24%)	11,119
1968	4,773	(29%)	7,431	(46%)	4,075	(25%)	16,279
1988	10,103	(35%)	10,969	(38%)	7,505	(26%)	28,577
2010	13,049	(38%)	11,016	(32%)	9,850	(29%)	33,915

Data from Ministère de l'Agriculture, *Le Vignoble Français d'après le Cadastre Viticole. Evolution de 1958 à 1968* (Ministère de l'Agriculture, Paris, 1971), CIVC, 2010.

[88] Grape varieties in individual areas are:

	Hectares	Pinot Noir	Pinot Meunier	Chardonnay
Montagne de Reims	8,352	3,199	2,794	2,359
Vallée de la Marne	11,989	2,761	7,385	1,843
Côte des Blancs	5,626	450	541	4,635
Côte des Bar	7,948	6,639	296	1,013
Total	33,915	13,049	11,016	9,850

Data source: CIVC, Epernay, 2010.

[89] Technically a Blanc de Noirs may include either or both of Pinot Noir or Pinot Meunier, but in fact virtually all Blanc de Noirs comes exclusively from Pinot Noir.

[90] There are no official statistics, but a survey conducted by the author of one hundred representative Champagne houses in July 2010 demonstrated that only a third produced Blanc de Noirs, and in most cases production was rather small, usually less than 5,000 cases. Virtually all came from the Montagne de Reims. A rather unreliable extrapolation would suggest less than 10% of Champagne's Pinot Noir is used for Blanc de Noirs, corresponding to no more than 4% of total production.

[91] A subsidiary advantage of Pinot Meunier is that if it does get caught by frost, it gives a second crop at about half the yield of the first crop. Pinot Noir may give a much smaller second crop; Chardonnay does not.

[92] Interview with Benoit Tarlant, October 2010.

[93] Interview at Krug, October 2010.

[94] Personal communication, July 2010.

[95] Interview with Stephen Skelton, August 2010.

[96] *The Graduate*, 1967.

[97] A polytunnel (for example, 120 ft long, 14 ft wide, and 9 ft high) raises internal temperature by 3-5 °C in winter, essentially the equivalent of moving the vineyard 500 miles to the south. The problem is that on hot summer days, the temperature increase can be great enough to cause the vines to shut down.

[98] This amounted to roughly 55 ha of vineyards (Tim Unwin, *Saxon and Early Normal Viticulture in England*, J. Wine Research, 1, 61-76, 1990). For a list of vineyards, see Richard C. Selley, *The Winelands of Britain: Past, present & prospective, 2nd edition* (Petravin, London, 2008), p. 24.

[99] The Dissolution of the Monasteries in 1536 is often cited as being the event that destroyed wine production in England, but in fact by then most of the monasteries were no longer making wine, presumably due to economic circumstances.

[100] Annual census of Department of Food and Rural Affairs.

[101] Wine is divided into red/rosé or white in official statistics.

[102] There were 85 ha of the three varieties in total in 2004, and 540 ha in 2009, out of a total vineyard area of 1,350 ha (Stephen Skelton, *UK vineyards guide 2010*, SP Skelton, London, 2009). This means that quality grapes have now overtaken the plantings of hybrid grapes (in which Seyval Blanc and Bacchus used to be the most widely planted.)

[103] Interview with Stephen Skelton, August 2010.

[104] A view expressed in August 2010.

[105] Projections for temperature increase out to 2080 have been used to suggest that by then the north of England might grow Pinot Noir and Chardonnay, while the south might grow Merlot (Selley, *The Winelands of Britain,* op cit., p. 97).

[106] The chalk subsoil of the South Downs, for example, is not unlike the underlying structure in Champagne.

[107] Martin Hickman, *Top Champagne House May Buy English Vineyards*, The Independent, November 17, 2007.

[108] Acidity levels in the grapes at harvest have been falling steadily for twenty years.

[109] Lewin, *Wine Myths and Reality*, p. 505.

[110] The wine merchant Ducasse, who sold the wine to Sieur d'Arques was purchasing wine for €58 /hl compared with the price of Pinot Noir at €97/hl. The difference on 110,000 hl (1.3 million cases) would be several million euros per year. It was stated in court that overall the illicit profits amounted to €7 million, with Ducasse taking €3.7 million and Sieur d'Arques making €1.3 million (Rory Mulholland and Suzanne Mustacich, *French plonk scam spreads to world's top wine group*, AFP News, February 18, 2010).

Chapter 5: The North America Migration

[1] Susan Sokol Blosser, *At Home in the Vineyard* (University of California Press, Berkeley, 2006), p.8.

[2] Interview with David Lett at Eyrie Vineyards, September 2010.

[3] Interview with Ben Casteel at Bethel Heights, September 2010.

[4] Average ph of 5.6.

[5] Average pH of 5.9.

[6] Paul Pintarich, *The Boys Up North* (The Wyatt Group, Portland, 1997), pp. 15-18.

[7] Susan Sokol Blosser, *At Home in the Vineyard* (University of California Press, Berkeley, 2006), p. 221.

[8] Data from the annual Oregon Vineyard and Winery Reports from USDA, NASS, Oregon Field Office. Production has been converted from tons to hectoliters.

[9] Paul Pintarich, *The Boys Up North* (The Wyatt Group, Portland, 1997), p. 20.

[10] Interview with Jason Lett at Eyrie Vineyard, September 2010.

[11] Interview with David Adelsheim at Adelsheim Vineyard, September 2010.

[12] USDA, NASS, Oregon Agriculture & Fisheries Statistics, 2008-2009.

[13] Oregon Vineyard and Winery Report 2009 (USDA, NASS, Oregon Field Office).

[14] Pinot Noir is 4,665 hectares out of a total of 7,850 hectares (USDA NASS, Oregon Vineyard and Winery Report, 2009).

[15] In Willamette Valley, there are 3,290 ha of Pinot Noir out of a total of 5,583 ha of vineyards (USDA NASS, Oregon Vineyard and Winery Report, 2009).

[16] In 1994, Pinot Noir was 1,037 ha out of a total of 2,672 ha, so in 15 years, Pinot Noir has increased 4.5 times, while total plantings have increased 3 times (Annual Oregon Vineyard and Winery Reports from USDA, NASS, Oregon Field Office).

[17] An average yield below 2.25 tons/acre is roughly equivalent to 33 hl/ha; premier and grand crus in Burgundy range from 35-40 hl/ha.

[18] There is an exception for Cabernet Sauvignon.

[19] This has now transmogrified into the Foundation Plant Services, which offers approved versions of many clones that are certified virus-free. The current list includes:

Clone type	Original ID	FPS#
Pommard	04 → 05, 06	91
Wädenswil	1A 2A 3A	30
Mariafeld	Clevner Mariafeld (Wädens-vil)	23
Geisenheim	27	105
Pinot Droit	Gamay Beaujolais	18

Jackson	9 16 29	106
Martini	58 → 13, 15 clone "V"	66
Mahoney (Carneros creek)	Swan A Chalone P Martini 54	97 90, 96 75
Rae (Mt. Eden)		37
Roederer	386	32
Dijon	113 114 115 375 459 667 777	44 46, 47 89 94 38 72, 93 71

Data source: Susan Nelson-Kluk, *History of Pinot Noir at FPS*, FPS Grape Program Newsletter, October 2003..

[20] John Winthrop Haeger, *North American Pinot Noir*, p. 132.

[21] John Winthrop Haeger, *North American Pinot Noir*, p. 139.

[22] Jason Lett, *Mothers and Clones*, Oregon Wine Magazine, 2004.

[23] Today there are two defined Pommard clones (see note 19).

[24] John Winthrop Haeger, *North American Pinot Noir*, p. 140.

[25] See chapter 1.

[26] Vineyard land is said to be increasing in value around 12% per year. Land costs in Willamette Valley are in the range of $40-50,000 per acre, with the costs of planting and developing a vineyard adding about another 50%. There is expected to be a shortage of grapes that will increase grape prices (Global Real Estate Monitor, *Grape Expectations: Institutional investors seek vineyards and wineries*, February 2008).

[27] www.ppvco.com/vineyards.php.

[28] Susan Sokol Blosser, *At Home in the Vineyard* (University of California Press, Berkeley, 2006), p. 49.

[29] Annual Oregon Vineyard and Winery Report from USDA, NASS, Oregon Field Office. 2009.

[30] Interview with Mark Vlossak at St. Innocent, September 2010.

[31] Interview with David Adelsheim, September 2010.

[32] Interview with Arron Bell at Domaine Drouhin, September 2010.

[33] Interview with Véronique Drouhin in Beaune, November 2011.

[34] Growing season temperatures were similar: average from April-September was 15.9 °C in Beaune and 15.7 °C in Willamette, but October was much warmer in Willamette. As picking started on September 15 in Beaune and on September 30 in Willamette, total heat accumulation was probably quite similar.

[35] Interview with Russ Raney at Evesham Vineyards, September 2010.

[36] Interview with John d'Anna at Cristom Vineyards, September 2010.

[37] Susan Sokol Blosser, *At Home in the Vineyard* (University of California Press, Berkeley, 2006), p. 6.

[38] Interview with Ken Wright at Ken Wright Vineyards, September 2010.

[39] Interview with John d'Anna at Cristom Vineyards, September 2010.

[40] Interview with Anna Matzinger at Archery Summit, September 2010.

[41] Interview with David Adelsheim, September 2010.

[42] Interview with Doug Tunnell at Brick House, September 2010.

[43] Interview with Jason Lett at Eyrie Vineyard, September 2010.

[44] Interview with Harry Peterson-Nedry, September 2010.

[45] Robert Parker rated 14 vintages in Willamette between 85 and 90 points for Pinot Noir, with three very good vintages over 90, and three poor vintages below 85 points. But in Burgundy ten vintages were rated below 85, with five at the average of 85-90, and five above 90 points.

[46] The wines were about the same price.

[47] The latest vintage chart in The Wine Advocate has for 2002 Côte de Nuits at 93 points and Willamette at 92 points, for 1999 both are at 92 points. In 1989 ratings were also close, 85 points for Côte de Nuits and 86 points for Willamette.

[48] Temperatures are the average over a growing season from April to October, obtained from the data base at the Goddard weather center.

[49] Annual Grape Crush Reports, California Department of Food and Agriculture; Annual Oregon Vineyard and Winery Reports, USDA, NASS. Production has been calculated from tons of grapes crushed.

[50] Production was 70,000 tons in 2004 and 156,000 tons in 2009. Planted area was 22,645 acres in 2004 and 30,339 acres in 2009 (California Grape Acreage and Crush Reports, 2004 and 2009).

[51] 157,000 tons of Pinot Noir were crushed from a total of 30,339 acres (12,282 ha), corresponding to about 80 hl/ha in 2009. Whereas 36,000 tons were crushed from 9,183 acres (3,717 ha) in 1999, corresponding to about 64 hl/ha. (California Grape Acreage and Crush Reports, 1999 and 2009). Of course, some of this is used for sparkling wine where high yields are not so problematic.

[52] The best known was the vineyard of Pinot Noir planted at Inglenook in Napa Valley, which remained productive until the 1940s. These vines were the basis for the Martini clones planted later in Carneros (John Winthrop Haeger, North American Pinot Noir, pp. 39-40).

[53] There were a few "Burgundies" made from Pinot Noir, but they were rare compared to those made from Zinfandel (John Winthrop Haeger, North American Pinot Noir, p. 41).

[54] Quoted in John Winthrop Haeger, North American Pinot Noir, p. 49.

[55] Gamay Beaujolais is in fact a form of Pinot Droit. Still grown in California, it is available from the FPS (Foundation Plant Services of University California, Davis) as clone 18. Gamay Beaujolais continued to be used as a name for Pinot Noir varietal wines into the present century (John Winthrop Haeger, North American Pinot Noir, p. 48).

[56] Interview at Joseph Swan, February 2011.

[57] Sonoma, 4,500 ha; Monterey, 2,560 ha; Santa Barbara, 1,427 ha; Napa 1,088 ha; Mendocino, 910 ha (California Grape Acreage Report, 2009).

[58] A comparison between 1976 and 2009 shows the huge advance made by Pinot Noir. In 1976, Pinot Noir production was largely focused on to Napa and Sonoma Valleys. Total production for the state was 14,000 tons, compared with Cabernet Sauvignon's 34,000 tons. (Cabernet included a large amount of production in Central Valley as well as Napa and Sonoma.) Pinot's average price was $300 per ton, compared with Cabernet Sauvignon at $400 per ton. In 2009 Pinot Noir remained about a third of Cabernet Sauvignon in total production level (157,000 tons compared to 443,000 tons), but production was more widely distributed. Its average price was $1,641 per ton compared with Cabernet at $1,078 per ton, firmly stamping Pinot Noir as a grape produced largely at the quality level.

[59] There was a curiously mistaken belief that clonal variation was due to virus infection (John Winthrop Haeger, North American Pinot Noir, pp. 132, 134).

[60] Interview at Mahoney Vineyards in January 2011.

[61] All the plantings were on the same rootstocks, pruned the same way, picked at the same Brix of 23-24 (although of course yields were different depending on the individual cultivar), and wine was made by microvinification.

[62] Interview at Robert Sinskey Vineyards in January 2010.

[63] Interview at Merry Edwards Winery, February 2011.

[64] Interview at Williams Selyem, February 2011.

[65] Interview at Sea Smoke, February 2011.

[66] Interview at Donum Estate, January 2011.

[67] Interview at DeLoach, February 2011.

[68] Interview at Merry Edwards Winery, February 2011.

[69] Interview at Au Bon Climat, February 2011.

[70] Interview at Littorai, February 2011.

[71] Interview at Mahoney Vineyards, January 2011.

[72] Interview at Robert Sinskey Vineyards, January 2011.

[73] Interview at Saintsbury, January 2011.

[74] Interview at Donum Estate, January 2011.

[75] Russian River Valley accounts for about 1,820 ha of the total of 5,110 ha of Pinot Noir in the entire Sonoma area (California Grape Acreage Report, 2009).

[76] John Winthrop Haeger, *North American Pinot Noir*, p. 89.

[77] Chardonnay has 41% of plantings; Pinot Noir has 29% (Russian River Valley Winegrowers, 2011).

[78] John Winthrop Haeger, *North American Pinot Noir*, p. 85.

[79] Longboard produce a single vineyard Cabernet Sauvignon identified as sourced from Rochioli.

[80] I calculate that approximately 60% of the crop is purchased and 40% is retained by estates for their own wine production (based on California Grape Crush report, 2009).

[81] As opposed to a tonnage contract, when the grower supplies an agreed quantity of grapes from anywhere in the vineyard.

[82] Failla, Harrington, Kistler, Kosuge, Lioco, Littorai, Siduri, Whetstone, Williams Selyem.

[83] Interview at Calera, February 2011.

[84] The first 130 ha were purchased in 1975; another parcel of the same size was purchased in 1982 (Marq de Villiers, *The Heartbreak Grape, 2nd edition*, McArthur & Co, Toronto, 2006, p. 75).

[85] Interview at Calera, February 2011.

[86] The Santa Maria weather station has had an average growing season temperature of 16 °C since year 2000, while at Santa Rosa in Russian River Valley the average was 17.7 °C (data from Goddard weather database).

[87] Otis L. Graham et al., *Aged in Oak. The story of the Santa Barbara County Wine Industry* (Santa Barbara County Vintners' Association, Santa Ynez, CA, 1998), p. 21.

[88] Frank Prial, *A winery in the making*, New York Times, July 23, 1978

[89] In 1989 70% of the grapes were shipped out to northern producers, and the proportion was down only to 56% by 1996 (Otis L. Graham et al., *Aged in Oak. The story of the Santa Barbara County Wine Industry*, Santa Barbara County Vintners' Association, Santa Ynez, CA, 1998, p. 49).

[90] In 1991 there were 300 ha of Cabernet Sauvignon and 350 ha of Pinot Noir out of 875 ha of black grapes. In 2009 there were 1,840 ha of Pinot Noir out of 3,300 ha of black grapes. In 1991 there were 2,150 ha of Chardonnay out of 2,830 ha of white grapes; by 2009 there were 2,740 ha of Chardonnay out of 3,840 ha of white grapes (California Grape Acreage Reports.)

[91] Interview with Nicolas Miller at Bien Nacido Vineyard, February 2011.

[92] Interview at Bien Nacido, February 2011.

[93] Interview at ABC, February 2011.

[94] Interview at ABC, February 2011.

[95] There is also another AVA at the eastern end of Santa Ynez Valley, called Happy Canyon of Santa Barbara. And between Santa Maria and Santa Ynez lies the Los Alamos Valley, where there are a few wineries, although it does not yet have AVA status.

[96] Interview at Sea Smoke, February 2011.

[97] Interview with Paul Lato at Central Coast Wine Facility, February 2011.

[98] Interview at Mahoney Vineyards, January 2011.

Chapter 6: Pinot Power in the Antipodes

[1] Part of a submission to the Report of the Royal Commission on Licensing, 1946.

[2] Quoted in Rosemary George, *The Wines of New Zealand* (Faber and Faber, London, 1996), p. 17.

[3] New Zealand Winegrowers Statistic Annual 2009.

[4] Data from New Zealand Winegrowers Statistic Annual reports, ONIVINS (Viniflhor) annual statistics, and BIVB.

[5] In 1975, Cabernet Sauvignon was the most planted black Vitis vinifera, with 179 ha.

[6] John Saker, *Pinot Noir, p. 55.*

[7] St. Helena Pinot Noir made by Danny Schuster.

[8] Initially they shared a winemaking facility.

[9] George M. Taber, *In search of Bacchus. Wanderings in the wonderful world of wine tourism* (Scribner, New York, 2009), p. 132.

[10] Michael Cooper, *Wine Atlas of New Zealand, 2nd Ed.* (Hodder Moa Beckett, Auckland, 2008), p. 370.

[11] As of 2009, there were 1,903 ha in Marlborough, 1,202 ha in Otago, and 460 ha in Martinborough, out of a total of 4,777 ha (New Zealand Winegrowers Statistic Annual 2009).

[12] A comparison of vineyard areas (in hectares) over the decade shows:

	2000	2009
Marlborough	527	1,903
Otago	136	1.202
Martinborough	101	465
Canterbury	54	311
Hawkes	117	377
Nelson	33	183
Total	1,098	4,777

Data from New Zealand Winegrowers Statistical Annuals, 2000 and 2009.

[13] Pinot Noir is 54% of plantings in Wairarapa and 78% of plantings in Otago. It is only 12% in Marlborough (New Zealand Winegrowers Statistic Annual 2008).

[14] Sauvignon Blanc is more profitable. Yields average over 12 tons/ha compared to 5 tons/ha for Pinot Noir, and the return on capital is 10% compared with 2% for Pinot Noir (John Saker, *Pinot Noir*, pp. 22, 37).

[15] Average is 2,400 hours annually in Marlborough, 2250 in Central Otago, and 2,000 in Martinborough (based on averages 1971-2000 from the New Zealand National Climate Database).

[16] Interview at Cloudy Bay, March 2011.

[17] Rainfall is generally 700-800 mm annually in Burgundy, with a relatively even distribution through the year. The original definition of the Martinborough appellation included only those areas where rainfall is less than 800 mm per year. The annual average in Marlborough is 700 mm, but there is a strong variation from more in the north (700 mm) to less in the south (450 mm). Central Otago is pretty dry with less than 500 mm (based on averages 1971-2000 from the New Zealand National Climate Database).

[18] For Pinot Noir 72% are grafted in Central Otago, 83% in Martinborough, and 99% in Marlborough (New Zealand Winegrowers Statistical Annual, 2009).

[19] Averages for 2009 (a good year) were 1.8 tons/acre in Martinborough, 1.5 tons/acre in Central Otago, and 2.4 tons/acre in Marlborough, which translates to the approximate ranges of hl/ha given in the text.

[20] Interview in Marlborough, March 2011.

[21] Interview at Escarpment, March 2011.

[22] Interview at Rockburn, March 2011.

[23] Rosemary George, *The Wines of New Zealand* (Faber and Faber, London, 1996), p. 231.

[24] Interview at Ata Rangi, March 2011.

[25] In 2009 there were 61 wineries and 48 growers dividing up Wairarapa's 859 ha (there are no separate statistics for Martinborough, which however has the bulk of production). There were 130 wineries and 568 growers for Marlborough's 18,401 ha. There were 103 wineries and 77 growers for 1,532 hectares in Central Otago (New Zealand Winegrowers Statistic Annual 2009).

[26] Dave Cull, *A Toast to Martinborough and the Wairarapa* (Longacre Press, Dunedin, New Zealand, 2003), p. 15.

[27] Masterton, Gladstone, and the Kapiti Coast are the other parts of the general region.

[28] Official statistics are not available separately for Martinborough alone.

[29] Sauvignon Blanc is about a third of production (Wines from Martinborough, 2011).

[30] The original group of wineries formed the Martinborough Terrace Appellation Committee which tried to define the Terrace in 1986.

[31] Interview at Ata Rangi, March 2011.

[32] Interview at Mount Edward, March 2011.

[33] Interview at Seresin, March 2011.

[34] Interview at Cloudy Bay, March 2011.

[35] As of January 2011, the 23,964 ha in Marlborough were divided between 17,082 ha in Wairau Valley and 6,882 in the Southern and Awatere Valleys (Wines from Marlborough, March, 2011).

[36] Interview at Clos Henri, March 2011.

[37] Interview at Dog Point, March 2011.

[38] New Zealand Winegrowers Statistical Annual, 2000-2009.

[39] Interview at TerraVin, March 2011.

[40] Interview at Cloudy Bay, March 2011.

[41] Interview at Dog Point, March 2011.

[42] Interview at Fromm, March 2011.

[43] Interview at TerraVin, March 2011.

[44] Interview in Marlborough, March 2011.

[45] Interview at Neudorf, March 2011.

[46] Interview at Neudorf, March 2011.

[47] Average temperature regions over the past thirty years for October-April for the subregions are: Bannockburn, 15.0-16.2 °C; Cromwell, 14.5-14.9 °C; Wanaka, 14.3-14.5°C; Gibbston, 14.0 - 14.3 °C (Central Otago Pinot Noir Limited).

[48] Interview at Burn Cottage, March 2011.

[49] Interview at Felton Road, March 2011.

[50] Interview at VinPro, March 2011.

[51] Interview at Gibbston Valley Wines, March 2011.

[52] While 2008 was one of the best vintages in Martinborough, for example, there were problems with humidity and botrytis in Marlborough.

[53] Plantings are 4,690 ha out of a total of 92,431 ha.; production is the equivalent of 2.5 million cases (including what goes into sparkling wine) out of a total of 50 million cases of red wine (Australian Bureau of Statistics, Wine and Grape Industry Report 1329.0, 2010).

[54] Annual production of Pinot Noir is about 250,000 cases in Yarra Valley, 150,000 cases in Mornington Peninsula, and 75,000 cases in Tasmania (Winefacts, Wine Australia, 2011).

[55] James Busby, *Journal of a Recent Visit to the Principal Vineyards of Spain and France*, Smith, Elder, London, 1834, p. 123.

[56] Land costs around $200-300,000 per hectare make this the most expensive farming land in Australia.

[57] Interview at Seville Estate, March 2011.

[58] Interview at Coldstream Hills, March 2011.

[59] Quoted in Tim Atkins, *Australian Pinot Noir*, Wine & Spirits, 2008.

[60] Interview at Coldstream Hills, March 2011.

[61] Interview at Sticks Yarra, March 2011.

[62] Interview at De Bortoli, March 2011.

[63] Interview with Mornington Peninsula producers, March 2011.

[64] Interview with Mornington Peninsula producers, March 2011.

[65] Interview with Mornington Peninsula producers, March 2011.

[66] Interview with Mornington Peninsula producers, March 2011.

[67] Interview with Mornington Peninsula producers, March 2011.

[68] Interview at Wine Australia, April 2011.

[69] Interview at Neudorf, March 2011.

[70] Interview with Mornington Peninsula producers, March 2011.

[71] There were 430 ha of Pinot Noir in 1999 and 844 ha in 2009, out of a total 101,000 ha, placing it at position 15 in the list of grape varieties (SAWIS *Statistics of Winegrape vines*, 2010).

[72] Breakdown is 32% in Stellenbosch, 23% in Paarl, 19% in Robertson (SAWIS *Statistics of Winegrape vines*, 2010).

[73] South Africa organizes its wine regions into a hierarchy of Regions, which contain Districts, which contain Wards. Originally Walker Bay was a Ward, but in 2004 it was reclassified as a District, and three Wards were created in the Hemel-en-Aarde area in 2009: Hemel-en-Aarde Valley, Upper Hemel-en-Aarde Valley, and Hemel-en-Aarde Ridge (which is actually just out of the valley).

[74] It would fall into zone 2 on the Winkler degree day scale, compared with Burgundy in zone 1.

[75] This is roughly equivalent to Santa Barbara in California in the northern hemisphere.

[76] In 2009 there were 90 ha of Pinot Noir, 90 ha of Sauvignon Blanc, and 65 ha of Chardonnay out of a total of 334 he for the three Hemel-en-Aarde wards (SAWIS, *Total Status of Vines*, November 2009).

[77] Walker Bay produces less than 10% of South Africa's Pinot Noir (361 tons out of 4,052 tons total in 2010 according to the *SAWIS Estimate Grape Production*).

[78] There are 4 producers in Hemel-en-Aarde Valley, 6 in the Upper Valley, and 5 in the Ridge. There are as many again growers who farm grapes but do not produce wine (Data from SAWIS, January 2011).

[79] From Google Earth. Scale is only approximate because this is an aerial projection.

[80] Personal communication, January 2011.

[81] Discussion with Peter Finlayson, January 2011.

[82] Discussion with Anthony Hamilton Russell, January 2011.

[83] Discussion with Anthony Hamilton Russell, January 2011.

[84] In 2009 there were 346 ha of Sauvignon Blanc, 86 ha of Pinot Noir, and 88 ha of Chardonnay, out of a total of 834 ha (SAWIS, *Total Status of Vines*, November 2009).

[85] Plantings in each country are less than 2% of total (Catastro Viticola Naciona, Chile, 2009; Registro De Viñedos Y Superficie, Argentina, 2010.).

[86] Interview with Piero Incisa, December 2010.

Chapter 7: The Holy Grail

[1] Interview at Calera, February 2011.

[2] Louis Ferré, Traité d'Oenologie Bourguignonne, INAO, Paris, 1958, p18.

[3] Discussion in February 2011.

[4] Release price on the Bordeaux market was €550 for Lafite Rothschild, Mouton Rothschild, and Margaux, and €600 for Latour and Haut Brion. This translated into around $900 per bottle to the consumer.

[5] The record is $32,312 for Margaux 1900 (Sothebys, New York, May, 2006), followed by $28,800 for Lafite 1825 (Christies, Los Angeles, October, 2007). Not directly comparable, perhaps, since Bordeaux goes back centuries whereas Napa goes back only decades, but top vintages from the second half of the twentieth century can see bottles reach thousands of dollars.

[6] The 2006 Screaming Eagle Oakville Cabernet Sauvignon release price was $750 to those on the mailing list; the wine was then available on the secondary market at $1000. The record to date at auction is $6,453 are the 1992 vintage, in November 2008.

[7] $6,325 for the first commercial vintage, 1952 (Sothebys, New York, November, 2001), and for $10,575 for the preceding 1951 (Christies, New York, October, 2003).

[8] Acker Merrall auction, New York, April 2008.

[9] The highest priced New World Pinot Noir is Williams Selyem, sometimes reaching a couple of hundred dollars per bottle at auction, the record being $167 per bottle for a mixed lot of several vintages from the Rochioli vineyard (Christies, Los Angeles, June 2002).

[10] Richard Olney, *Romanée Conti*, (Rizzoli, New York) 1995, p. 9.

[11] Richard Olney, *Romanée Conti*, (Rizzoli, New York) 1995, p. 43.

[12] Richard Olney, *Romanée Conti*, (Rizzoli, New York) 1995, p. 58.

[13] Personal communication, April 2011.

[14] Personal communication, April 2011.

[15] Leroy's record is $7,110 for a bottle of 1949 Richebourg (Acker Merrall, New York, October 2006).

[16] DRC's view of tradition used to extend to bottling directly from the barrel—which led to criticism of variation resulting from differences between barrels—but since 1982, each appellation has been assembled for a single bottling.

[17] Interview at Domaine Leroy, May 2011.

[18] Lewin, *What Price Bordeaux?*, Vendange Press, 2009, p. 166.

Index